380 publ. @ $108-50 £4-99

THE LOWER DANUBE RIVER

In the Southeastern European Political and Economic Complex from Antiquity to the Conference of Belgrade of 1948

by Spiridon G. Focas.

Translated from the Romanian
by Rozeta J. Metes

EAST EUROPEAN MONOGRAPHS, BOULDER
DISTRIBUTED BY COLUMBIA UNIVERSITY PRESS, NEW YORK

1987

EAST EUROPEAN MONOGRAPHS, NO. CCXXVII

Copyright © 1987 by Spiridon G. Focas
ISBN 0-88033-123-2
Library of Congress Card Catalog Number 87-80510

Printed in the United States of America

TO MY WIFE ANTIGONE

ACKNOWLEDGEMENTS

This book will hopefully provide a modest contribution to the body of research on the so-called "Danube-Question," from the time of the ancient Greeks until the political and economic settlements in Southeast Europe in the present time. (1948)

In regard to my subject, I have tried to emphasize the struggle for ascendancy among the European Great Powers for a free navigation at the Mouths of the Danube, and the antagonism within the riparians of the Lower Danube River.

This book is the result of twenty-five years (not counting time as a political prisoner in a labor camp in Romania after World War II), of practical knowledge in the field of navigation, as well as an exhaustive reading of the juridic and dimplomatic evolution of the Danube topic. Needless to say, I stand on the shoulders of the extremely competent writers who have documented Danube problems. To all of them I owe thanks.

Special thanks are due to Professor Stephen Fischer-Galati, editor of the East European Monographs, to Rozeta J. Metes, for the taxing work of translating this book. Nor can I forget the typesetters and proofreaders, for their conscientious work.

Let me also express deep appreciation to John C. Campbell, former member of the Council on Foreign Relations, who recognized early on the need for a book on this subject and urged me to pursue the research in the United States.

I am profoundly indebted to my wife Antigone, who was an active participant in this project from its very inception. Her patience and her enthusiasm gave me the encouragement I needed when the task of completing it seemed overwhelming

Spiridon G. F ocas

FOREWORD

This unique and exceptionally detailed and thorough study of the history and politics of the Danube, albeit with emphasis on the lower part of the river, represents the lifetime intelligence of the problems and issues of Europe's most important river by someone whose knowledge and judgments are based on first hand experience as much as on mastery of everything written on the subject.

No stone has been left unturned by the author and, as a result, this study is as much a work on the history of the riparain states of Southeastern Europe and their relationships to the Great Powers — particualarly in the nineteenth and twentieth centuries — as one of the economic history of those states in matters related to Danubian problems.

In the dual position of an historian of Eastern Europe and editor of the *East European Monographs* I obviously recommend this masterful work to historians, diplomatic and economic, and to all concerned with international affairs. As editor only, I would like to exonerate the author for the absence of several Romanian diacritic marks which, for technical reasons, could not be incorporated in the printed text. These omissions, however, should not detract from the value of Spiridon Focas' contribution to scholarship.

Stephen Fischer-Galati

Table of Contents

Foreword		v
General Introduction		1
Reasons for Limiting Research to Lower Danube River		5

PART ONE

Forerunners of Lower Danube River Navigation and Their Successors

	Introduction	11
Chapter I	The Greek Penetration of the Lower Danube through the Black Sea	15
Chapter II	The First Successors of Greeks and Romans	37

PART TWO

From the First Attempts of Internationalization of Navigation on the Lower Danube River to the Peace Treaty of Adrianople (1699-1829)

	Introduction	55
Chapter I	The Austrian and Russian Attempts	59
Chapter II	Enactment of the Principles of Internationalization of Navigation on Navigable Rivers by the Congress and Act of Vienna of 1815	77

PART THREE

From the Peace Treaty of Adrianople to the Peace Treaty of Paris (1829-1856)
The Mouths of the Danube River under Russians

	Introduction	99
Chapter I	The Treaty of Adrianople (1829)	101
Chapter II	The Obstacles to Navigation and the English - Russian Conflict	111
Chapter III	The Quarantine as an Obstacle	131
Chapter IV	England's Reaction	141
Chapter V	General Considerations on Quarantine as an Obstacle to Navigation	153

PART FOUR

The Collateral Effects of Obstacles at the Sulina Mouth

Chapter I	Sulina "A Little California"	179

Chapter II	Initiatives for a New Outlet to the Black Sea and a Project for the Improvement of Navigation at the Sulina Mouth	191
Chapter III	Other Effects of the Obstacles	201

PART FIVE
Internationalization of the Danube River Navigation and its Immediate Results

	Introduction	227
Chapter I	The Peace Conferences of Vienna and Paris	231
Chapter II	The Conference of the Danube Riparian Commission and the 1857 Act of Navigation	253
Chapter III	The Paris Conference of 1858	265
Chapter IV	Consolidation of the European Commission of the Danube (E.C.D.)	293
Chapter V	The Paris Conference of 1866	299

PART SIX
Early Modifications of the Treaty of 1856

	Introduction	319
Chapter I	The Conference and Treaty of London of 1871	321
Chapter II	Neutralization of the Lower Danube	333
Chapter III	The Congress and the Peace Treaty of Berlin, 1878	339
Chapter IV	The Effects of the Treaty of Berlin	363
Chapter V	The Conference and Treaty of London of 1883	385

PART SEVEN
First World War and Post War Period

	Introduction	425
Chapter I	From the Beginning of the War to the Treaty of Versailles	427
Chapter II	From the Capitulation of the Central European Powers to the Peace Treaty of Versailles	435

PART EIGHT
Between the Two World Wars

Chapter I	The Conference for the Establishment of a Convention of the Definitive Statute on the Danube River (Paris 1920-1921)	453
Chapter II	The Problem of the Cabotage Navigation	473
Chapter III	Other Regulations	487

Chapter IV	Closing of the Conference	493
Chapter V	The Litigation Between Romania and the European Commission of the Danube Regarding the Jurisdiction Between Galatz and Braila	495
Chapter VI	The Sinaia Arrangement of 1938 and its Immediate Consequences	515
Chapter VII	Situation Prior to War Against Soviet Russia	533
Chapter VIII	German and Russian Attempts to Modify of the International Regime of Navigation	539

PART NINE
After the Second World War

	Introduction	567
Chapter I	The Situation on the Lower Danube After the Beginning of the War Against the Soviet Russia (22 June 1941)	569
Chapter II	Conditions of Navigation Prior to and After the Armistice Agreements with Some Ex-Enemy Danubian States	573
Chapter III	Negotiations Regarding the New Regime of Navigation and its Inclusion in the Peace Treaties with some Ex-Enemy Danubian States	585
Chapter IV	The 1948 Belgrade Conference	595
Chapter V	The Validity Problem of the Danube Convention of 1921	603
Chapter VI	Vishinsky's Comparison of the 1948 Convention with that of the Convention of 1921	613
Chapter VII	The U.S.A. Project Regarding the New Convention	617
Chapter VIII	The New Convention of Belgrade and its Main Clauses	621
Chapter IX	Caducity or Validity of the New Convention?	627
	General Conclusion	629

PART TEN
The Traffic of the Maritime Danube

	Introduction	641
Chapter I	From Antiquity to the First World War	643
Chapter II	Between the Two World Wars	651
	Bibliography	659
	Index	683
	Illustrations and maps	699

GENERAL INTRODUCTION

Particular attention given to the antique epoch is based on the consideration that the first commercial navigation of the Lower Danube was created through the exploitation of the Black Sea by the ancient Greeks.

Due to the forerunners — Greeks, Romans and Byzantines — the Lower Danube and later the entire river had been regarded as an important means of commercial communication. In addition, the mouths of the Danube have since become a political factor.

It might be of interest to know that in the course of developing this study in addition to the pertinent research, treaties, conventions, arrangements and regulations with respect to the Lower Danube problems have been analyzed and commented upon.*

Correspondence between the European capitals, relating to the work of the main Danubian Conferences, has been likewise analyzed, within the limits of publication of that material.

In connection with archeological matters, liberal use has been made of quotations of scientifically qualified professionals. In the same vein,

---

*Although there are only three countries along the Lower Danube between the Iron Gates and the Black Sea — Bulgaria, Romania and, today, Soviet Russia — still, Yugoslavia and Czechoslovakia were added for the following reasons: the first, because it was one belonging to the bloc of small Danubian states defending their rights against the Great Powers; the second, because of its association with that same bloc.

Aside from the English, French and German titles of sources used, those in other languages have been translated into English in the Bibliography.

The footnotes contain only the names of the authors, the titles and pages of the documentation used; the Bibliography contains the name of the publishers, the locality and date of publication.

rather than paraphrasing important and competent statements, quotations have been preferred.

In addition to his research and analysis of the documentary sources, the author was able to use the knowledge obtained in his capacity as former Secretary of the "Special Autonomous Administration of the Maritime Danube," (Maritime Danube Board), the Romanian Administration which, in 1938, had taken over part of the attributes and duties of the former European Commission of the Danube.

The author's practical knowledge concerning the subject of this study can be attributed to the fact that he was born and grew up in the ambiance of the Lower Danube region. Furthermore some family members (Greeks) were active in the field of navigation. The reason that more attention was given to Romanian and less to the other two riparian countries of the Lower Danube — Bulgaria and Yugoslavia — is due to many factors.

Within the political conflicts, to say nothing of the wars between some Great Powers of the time for the control of the Lower Danube and its mouths, the Romanian Principalities, and after Romania, have always been in the center of the controversy. This is due to the "de facto" and since 1878 "de jure," Romania possesses the longest and the most important banks of the Lower Danube and the main key to all conflicts that is the mouths of the Danube.

If the Danube River is the "lungs" of Central Europe, as it is said, then the mouths of the Danube and the ports of Brăila and Galatz are the "heart" of navigation. From these Romanian ports, which are at the upper limit of maritime navigation on the Danube, the economic life of the entire river is connected to the outside world.

An obstacle to the author's research was the fact that most Bulgarian and Yugoslavian literature is written in the national languages.

The fact that the author's cultural background is Romanian, has contributed to the research of the rich Romanian studies and documentations concerning the problems of the Lower Danube River.

As for the present and the future maritime traffic level of the Danube, the author remains skeptical for the following reasons: the diminishing, or even the absence of English and French commercial interests in the Danube region, compared with their levels in the past; the depths of the water at the Sulina Mouth (23 to 24 feet) and reduced width of the Maritime Danube section, both inadequate for access by the newer maritime vessels having greater tonnage and dimensions than those of the past.

The traffic is and will be limited to vessels having a maximum capacity of 8000 tons, which will serve cabotage navigation between

GENERAL INTRODUCTION

the Black Sea and the Mediterranean. However, the fluvial traffic between Center Europe and the Lower Danube regime will be increased.

The author believes that the principle "the Danube belongs to the riparian states," is inapplicable to the present century. In opinion of N. Iorga, a great Romanian historian, was that "the waters of the Danube River must belong to those who use them, not to those who master them."

What is needed is the creation of a European Body, composed of representatives of all the riparian states, as well as the interested non-riparian states, to wit an international forum which will guarantee the complete freedom of navigation, without political and nationalistic interference.

In the final part of the study, the sea vessels traffic of the Maritime Danube before the first World War as well as between the two World Wars, has been researched and analyzed.

The commercial and traffic activities are reported successively to the related political events, and with the development of international navigation. Owing to the fact of current political regimes and ideologies in some countries riparian to the Lower Danube, the statistical data available for the periods after 1944-1945 do not reflect the actual situation.

The principal obstacle to the establishment of a navigation regime which could satisfy both European interests and those of the small countries along the Lower Danube, lies in the lack of important English and French future economic interests, and of any United States political interests in the Danubian regions.

Apart from the Russian interest in political expansion across the Lower Danube, from the Balkans to the Straits, the conflicts between the commercial interests of certain Great Powers, would have never occurred, had the Danube River been flowing from the East to the West of Europe.

The progess of evolution of the problems of the Lower Danube and its mouths, from Antiquity to the present time, created the periodical cycle of the "Danubian Continuity".

While there will undoubtedly arise a diversity of opinions, the author firmly believes that the "file of the Danube Question," is and will continue to remain open.

REASONS FOR LIMITING RESEARCH TO LOWER DANUBE

Geographically, hydrologically, conventionally, and also historically, the Danube River is divided into three large sectors, namely: the Upper, the Middle and the Lower Danube; the sector including the Maritime Danube, a navigation subdivision which consists of the river's mouths, flowing into the Black Sea.

Our research covers only the Lower Danube and its mouths, and the period from recorded antiquity up to the year 1948, a limitation based on the following considerations:

- According to recorded evidence and as determined by political, strategic and economic interests, the multiple successions of political forces aimed at — and at times succeeded in — assuming control expressly of the Lower Danube River, owing to its major importance;

- Control of the Lower Danube section would determinedly reflect upon political and economic conditions in Southeastern Europe;

- It was the Lower Danube section which affected any political and strategical balance. This balance was discontinued in 1948 when Soviet Russia, according to the provisions of the Belgrade Conference, became the sole Great Power to effectively control the mouths of the Danube River.

The general tendency has almost constantly been to extend the Danubian political and economic prominence to the entire length of the navigable course of the river. In reality, the actual importance of these problems has been, and will continue to be, concentrated upon the Sulina mouth in the Lower Danube sector, the only maritime navigable access into the Danube River.

There have been learned opinions which emphasized the political and economic importance of the Lower Danube and in particular its outlets. We mention some of them:

"If you hold the outlets of the Danube River" — Karl Marx pointed out — "you hold the Danube and with it the highway to Asia."[1]

"Le centre de gravité du monde" — said Talleyrand — "n'est ni sur l'Elbe, ni sur l'Adige, il est là bas aux frontières de l'Europe, sur le Danube."[2]

"The Lower Danube River" — wrote Urquhart —, "may be considered a continuation of the Straits of Bosphorus and Dardanelles."[3]

"La navigation du haut Danube" — declared Buol, Austria's Minister of Foreign Affairs, — "n'a soulevé aucun conflit entre les intéressés."[4]

On the Memorandum of Decembere 28, 1854 sent to Russia by Austria, France and England concerning the closing of the Crimean War, the freedom of navigation on the Danube was mentioned for the Lower Sector of the river only, but not for the other two sectors possessed by Austria.

Politically and strategically, only the Lower Danube and its outlets have been, from antiquity on, the crossroads of various political forces: from north to south, the barbarians; from south to north, the Macedonians, Byzantines, Romans, then again the Byzantines and after the Turcs. From central Europe, the Austrians and Germans.

In the 19th century, following the Treaty of Adrianople of 1829, when Russia had annexed the mouths of the Danube, England, France and then Austria appeared; the first two, in order to block the Russian expansion towards the Bosphorus and the Dardanelles, as well as to protect their own interests; while the third, in order to assure her continued access to the Black Sea, in view of the expansion of her steam-powered fleet of ships.

After 1829, navigation through the Sulina Mouth was included in the sphere of European politics, because of the physical and other obstacles maintained by the Russians, and the introduction of the regime of quarantine. The situation became critical for English vessels, and a sort of "cold war" broke out between England and Russia.

In this matter, the opinion of the writer differs from these of other researchers who, oblivious of certain physical situations existing in that period, accuse the Russians of deliberate sabotage. Actually sabotage did exist, but the Russians attributed the navigational difficulties to the hydrographic specifics of the Sulina Mouth (existing to this day) caused by a natural phenomenon.

The difficult navigational situation at the Sulina Mouth was remedied only after the Crimean War when, through the 1856 Peace Treaty of Paris, an international regime was introduced by the establishment of European Commission to carry out the initial operations for navigational improvement. By means of the European Commission of the Danube, composed of representatives of all the Great Powers, including Russia, the balance of power at the mouths of the Danube River was stabilized and, at the same time, Russian expansion was checked. The establishment of this European authority due to pressure from England and France was meant to maintain the international regime in conformity with the principles established in 1856. However, this respective regime suffered successive modifications by the 1871 Treaty of London, the 1878 Berlin Treaty, and the 1883 London Treaty due to pressure from Russia and Austro-Hungary, as well as to the changing political order in Southeast Europe. The modifications took place on the basis of concessions and of "bargaining," England and France being intent on maintaining the balance of power by salving the existence of the European Commission on the Danube.

The political balance was again threatened, this time by Austro-Hungary and Germany, during World War I and by Germany in association with Soviet Russia, before World War II, by the elimination of England and France from the Commission.

After World War II, and due to weakening of the Western Powers, the political balance on the Danube, Lower Danube, and its mouths was eliminated by Soviet Russia, which, in accordance with the provisions of the 1948 Belgrade Convention, established the navigation regime under its direct control.

NOTES

1. Karl Marx, "People's Paper," December 17, 1856, quoted by Dona Torr in "Marxism Nationality and War," Part Two: "National Wars, 1848-71," London, 1941, p.40.
2. "L'Empereur Napoleon III et les Principautés Roumaines," Paris, 1858, p. 35.
3. David Urquhart, "The Mystery of the Danube, showing how through secret diplomacy that River has been closed," London, 1851, p. 108.
4. Peace Conference of Paris, 1856, Protocol No. 5, March 6.

PART ONE

FORERUNNERS OF LOWER DANUBE RIVER

NAVIGATION AND THEIR SUCCESSORS

Introduction

The history of commercial navigation on the Black Sea has its basis far back in antiquity, its early pages telling of the presence there of Greek navigators and merchants, a fact uncontested to this day.

Were not the Greeks the first to populate the western coast of the Black Sea and the valley of the Lower Danube? According to the results of archaeological and historical research, the answer is in the affirmative. In no reconstituted map of the period preceding the presence of Greeks in the Black Sea is there mention of any permanent human settlement on the western coast, although tribal settlements in the interior of that same region are indicated. The first indications of coastal settlements are those of the Greek colonies, as shown on the maps of the 600-300 B.C. period.[1]

The Greek colonization along the Black Sea coast can be considered similar to that of the Pilgrims along the unpopulated shores of what is now the United States of America. If the symbol of the first settlement of the Pilgrim Fathers is the "Mayflower," that of the Greeks in the Black Sea and its shores is the legendary "Argo" and its Argonauts.

Just as American history cannot be conceived without taking into consideration the presence on its soil of the early explorers, of Columbus and of the "Mayflower" immigrants, so also navigation on the Black Sea and the Lower Danube cannot be conceived without reference to early Greek navigators. Commerce and navigation on the Black Sea and the Lower Danube had to have a beginning, an alpha, a starting point, set by the Greeks. They were also the "rerum nervus" setting off the process of developing the rich virgin natural resources of the southern sector of the Danube Delta.

From an economic point of view, the ancient epoch of the Lower Danube cannot be considered separate from that of Scythia Minor (present-day Dobruja) in the areas in which Greek colonies were active. Through this interdependence, Scythia Minor was witness to the creation, the development, and the succession of historical events from the antiquity of the hinterland of the Lower Danube. Regarding the geographic position of Scythia Minor, a Romanian archaeologist noted "... for the Eurasian peoples, Scythia Minor represented a road; for the men of the sea, a quay for their goods; and for the Southerner and the Oriental, the illusion of a frontier."[2] In the light of this definition the activity and the development of the Greek colonies on the western shore of the Black Sea can be evaluated.

The fact that Scythia Minor was the preferred route for the barbarian invasions, until the two stages of the Byzantine retreated[3], can also be attributed to the attraction of the Greek colonies, whose development was at a high level in all domains, their economic status being reflected also in the regions in the Lower Danube valley.

The Greek colonists, with their minimal technical, hydrographic and climatic knowledge obtained through continual experience, created the first maritime and river ports, the sites of which were in accord with the physical conditions of navigation and with the economic potentials of the regions behind them. The combining of these two requirements was so perfect that the present-day ports and wharves along the Lower Danube and the Black Sea, located on the ancient Greek settlements, correspond with the strictest technical norms of today, leaving no need for constructing others in other locations.

Between the Greek colonies on the maritime coast of Scythia Minor and the wharves and ports on the Lower Danube there existed a strong economic interdependence. The former fulfilled the functions of economic basis, centers of initiative and administration; the latter, those of substations, collecting the products of the adjacent regions, from which they were transported on the river to the colonies. The colonies, in turn, carried out the maritime commercial exchanges with the regions along the Aegean and Mediterranean coasts.

The economic interdependence between the colonies and the Lower Danube was gradually diminished by subsequent political events. Although it was continued under Roman and, later, Byzantine domination its potential was substantially reduced under the barbarian invasion which intervened.

The Romans were not actually successors to the Greeks in the colonies along the maritime coast of Scythia Minor and those of the Lower Danube, inasmuch as they continued to maintain them under

INTRODUCTION

the former system. Furthermore, as will be seen later, the activities of the Greeks were protected by the Romans. Those who replaced the Greeks were the Byzantines.

The interdependence between the economic centers of the former Greek, then Byzantine colonies, and the Lower Danube ended much later, at the same time as the Ottoman domination which, by including Dobruja (ancient Scythia Minor) within the framework of the Empire, had displaced it from the Lower Danube area.

Before going into researching the activities of the economic concerns of the maritime colonies and of the Lower Danube settlements, it is necessary to present, in general lines, the process of Greek penetration into the Black Sea and the causes for it, will show the conditions and circumstances under which the pioneers discovered and turned to good account the natural economic potential of the virgin regions of the Black Sea and the Lower Danube.

This movement of the Greeks into the Lower Danube can be rated as an epic event on the same level as that of the discoverers of new paths of maritime communication, in the XLV and XV centuries, or that of the first colonies in North America.

Chapter 1

THE GREEK PENETRATION OF THE LOWER DANUBE RIVER THROUGH THE BLACK SEA

Controversy over the date of the penetration into the Black Sea.

The beginning of commercial navigation on the Lower Danube is directly tied to the process of penetration into the Black Sea. The exact date of the Greek penetration is still an unclarified problem. Contradictory points of view, premises based upon presumptions, interpretations and deductions are, even today, the sole rays of light on the problem. Did the penetration take place before or after the VII century B.C.? The clarification of this controversial problem depends on knowledge of the existence of vessels capable of crossing into the Black Sea despite the natural obstacles existing in the Strait of Bosphorus, the winds and the water currents.[4]

Leaving to archaeologists and historians the scientific deciphering of the problem, some practical possibilities of navigation through the Bosphorus in antiquity can still be pointed out by their analogy with practices in the Lower Danube, as well as those on other navigable waters. In this way, one can reach the conclusion that there was no interdependence between means of communication and the obstacles that made the passage into the Black Sea difficult. The opposite conclusion is held by some researchers.

Among the controversies concerning the problem is also the dispute that arose over the point of view expressed by Rhys Carpenter,[5] that entrance into the Black Sea was not possible before the VII century B.C. due to the non-existence of adequate vessels. This point of view was challenged by A.J. Graham[6] and Benjamin W. Labaree.[7]

Carpenter believes that, prior to the appearance of pentekonter (Pentikontoros) and trireme vessels, crossing the Bosphorus was not possible before 680 B.C.[8] except "on the rowing of an ancient vessel of a speed of more than four knots."[9]

Although Carpenter and Labaree had access to the same documentary sources,[10] concerning the status of winds in the Bosphorus, their interpretations differ. While Carpenter maintains the permanence of the winds from spring to autumn as navigational obstacles, Labaree indicates certain periods of calm, or of favorable winds which made possible passage into the Black Sea.

Referring to archaeological documents, Graham demonstrates that neither the force of the winds, nor that of the water currents constituted obstacles to passing through the Bosphorus. In support of his thesis, he points out the practices followed by navigators of that time, as described by Dionysius Byzantius in one of his studies.[11]

According to Dionysius' description, the Greek navigators did succeed in crossing into the Black Sea at times, even during periods of strong east-west winds and water currents. "Thus", states Dionysius, "mostly they (namely the sailors) tie ropes to the ships and tow them from the shore with force, against the current as it pushes against it with great opposing force."[12]

Although Dionysius' description refers to practices probably current during the II century A.D., Graham extends them back to the earlier period inasmuch as "sailing merchant ships did not alter greatly throughout antiquity and Dionysius' remarks on the navigation of the strait will have been true for the earlier period."[13]

Graham's opinion concerning the towing operation is also supported by the methods of navigation used by the Egyptians who, lacking favorable winds, practiced towing along the Nile. Furthermore, much later, the famous song of the Volga boatmen was composed in the rhythm of the slow movements of the men towing.

Along the entire course of the Danube, on natural canals of the delta and in the fluvial sections where the river banks are accessible to man, towing small crafts and even sailing ships of small tonnage is customary, even today. The decisive proof of the practicality of towing along the Danube, as well as along principal European rivers, is demonstrated by the insertion of the method of carrying out the practice, as well as that of using the river banks involved, in all the treaties and conventions drawn up, especially since the establishment of the principles of internationalization of navigation, by the Act of Vienna, in 1815.[14] Keeping in mind that in antiquity the shores of the

THE GREEK PENETRATION

Bosphorus were uninhabited, or only sparsely so, the towing operation could not have constituted a problem.

Among other practices of navigation against the water current or the wind speed, there is also that still in use on streams and rivers. No vessel, even one of small tonnage motor driven, can navigate upriver through the center of the watercourse, where the force of the current is strongest. It is always preferable to navigate as closely as possible to the shore, where the force of the water and the wind speed are more reduced.

There is also another technique that can be mentioned, one used in sports crafts on running water or the sea. This is the technique of navigating against the current and wind by advancing in zigzag fashion. This technique is disputed by some who claim it could not have been practiced in antiquity because the sailing vessels of that time could be propulsed only by winds from behind.[15] It seems unlikely, though, that navigation in the distant past between Africa and India could have depended only on the Monsoon, or that coastal navigation was practiced only in accordance with the direction of the winds.

If the forward speed of a vessel through the Bosphorus is estimated by Carpenter at four knots per hour[16] (four nautical miles), then the entrance into the advance up the Danube River by the Greeks would have been, if not impossible, extremely difficult.[17] The speed of the winds along the Danube, especially during the winter, varies while that of the river current ranges between 4 and 6 miles per hour.[18]

Furthermore, if certain information from Greek antiquity were taken into consideration, it could be concluded that maritime navigation, hence also through the Bosphorus to the Black Sea, could be carried on only during the more favorable seasons, and be suspended during the winter, the season of strong winds.

In "Theogony"[19] and "Works and Days,"[20] the poet Hesiod writes about navigation and the life of sailors during his time (VII century B.C.). He suggests spring and summer as the most favorable seasons for navigation, recommending that sailors plan the termination of their voyage to coincide with the beginning of the autumn rains.[21] He goes on to say that navigation can be resumed "when the first leaves appear on the fig trees, that is, in the spring when the sea is no longer dangerous."[22]

Schliemann believed that crossing the Bosphorus was possible even in Trojan times, hence much before the VII century, and that Troy was supplied with amber, ceramic vases, horses, etc. also from Danubian and Thracian regions.[23]

Following recent on site research carried out between 1950 and 1960, at Histria and other archaeological sites in the former Scythia Minor, Romanian archaeologists are maintaining scientific prudence concerning the chronology of the establishment of certain colonies, a chronology which could lead to identification of the date when the Greeks first entered the Black Sea. Prudence is also practiced with respect to the dates of the establishment of several ports of lesser importance in that same Scythia, mentioned by a Roman writer in the first century B.C.[24]

As for navigational difficulties through the Bosphorus, it must be noted that, for many archaeologists, they did not constitute an impediment in their research of Greek life in the hinterland of the Black Sea. Nor are they mentioned in the history of Byzantine navigation which, as is well known, had a rich tradition. But, navigational conditions on the Black Sea did create problems which had an echo in Greek mythology and thinking, as well as later in the psychology of the sea-faring world of today. Since these conditions are an integral part of the history of the pioneers of navigation on the Black Sea and the Lower Danube, it can be useful to describe them, even briefly.

Along the same lines is the opinion of Theophrastus who, in "Characters" (the paragraph of the Talkative), writes that it is pleasant to travel on the seas after the great festival of Dionysius, that is in the months of March and April, but not during the winter when navigation is halted.

The obstacle of winter appears also in popular Greek literature of the more modern period. The suspension of navigation is mentioned as coinciding with the yellowing of the leaves; the real springtime comes at once with autumn when the hearts of the families of sailors open to welcome their homebound. The obstacle of winter being evident, obviously navigation through the Bosphorus was interrupted.

Although the passage through the Bosphorus to the Black Sea was so great a problem for navigation in antiquity, absolutely nothing is mentioned concerning the passage from the Aegean Sea into the Sea of Marmara, through the other straits, the Dardanelles, known in antiquity as the Hellespont.

The obstacle of the swiftness of the currents in the Dardanelles is revealed in a work referring to the disembarking attempts made by French and English troops in the Southern Balkans, during World War I.[25] The book is not a scientific study but a military work, nevertheless, the hardships faced indirect the basic problem. The authors also refer to quotations from historical studies. Mention is made that submarines passing from the Aegean into the Sea of Marmara met

THE GREEK PENETRATION 19

difficulties "due to the strong currents." From a sceintific work, it is quoted that "...the bridge of boats constructed by Xerxes in 448 B.C., to carry the Persian armies across, was swept away by the current."

Even though the degree of the current's power is not indicated, its intensity can be deduced from the difficulty had by a submarine of the twentieth century to advance against it. The fact that navigational difficulties through the Dardanelles are not mentioned anywhere in antiquity signifies that for the Greek navigators passing through the Hellespont presented no problem.

Navigation conditions on the Black Sea.

The efforts and risks involved in the pioneering of navigation on the Black Sea can be deduced from this cursory presentation of the subject. Regardless of the exact date of the Greeks' penetration into the Black Sea and of the difficulties they experienced, their success in dominating navigation there for centuries is an established fact. Transforming the Black Sea into a "Greek Lake," they developed its usefulness by connecting its economic basin with that of the Mediterranean. That action affected also the economy of the Lower Danube.

Concerning navigation on the Black Sea, the Romanian archaeologist D.M. Pippidi expresses this opinion: "...in the present stage of archaeological exploration of the Greek settlements in the Pontus, there are few chances that the gaps in our knowledge can be filled by research concerning conditions of Black Sea navigation during the first half of the first century B.C.[26] On the other hand, the presence of the Milesians in the territory of the present day Sinoe Lagoon[27] is reported as certain for the second half of the seventh century B.C.[28]

The expedition of the Argonauts, with its fantastic and miraculous aspects embroidered on the base of the legendary motif of the "Golden Fleece," presents a heroic nautical performance upon a dangerous sea, as in the Black Sea. The Greeks imagined the Black Sea to be an ocean and navigation on it was considered quite risky and completely different from that on the seas familiar to them. Thus, they name it the "Axeinos Pontos"[29] meaning the hostile sea, a name that led to only one conclusion: difficult and dangerous conditions of navigation. "Euxeinos Pontos,"[30] the antonym of the first designation, had the meaning of hospitable sea, favorable to navigation.

The adoption of the name "Euxeinos Pontos" is explained as a deliberate concealment of the difficult sailing conditions on the Black Sea, for the purpose of eliminating fear. The term also expressed a euphemistic sense of abundance, riches, or bringer of good fortune. Thus, through the influence of the legends and of the euphemism, the term "Axeinos Pontos" became "Euxeinos Pontos," encouraging navigation on the dangerous sea through which could be reached the Thracian and Pontic regions named by Theophrastus the "Sitophorii," that is, the granaries.[31]

Also created with the intent of encouraging maritime navigation was the legend of "Eumenides,"[32] the gracious goddesses, substituted for the three Furies, the vengeful ghosts of the slain, or vague embodiments of the avenging powers of nature.

In time, the term "Axeinos" was resumed because of the frequent shipwrecks and the somber aspect of the sea, in contrast to the clarity and the blueness of the Mediterranean waters, especially of the Aegean Sea. The gloomy color of the Black Sea is due to the underwater flora, accentuated in the winter by the reflection of the cloud-darkened sky. Because of these natural characteristics, popular imagination and superstition accorded the Black Sea a connotation of mourning, misfortune and an expression for curses.[33]

Contrary to Horace's belief that "the greedy sea is death to sailors,"[34] the Greeks saw in "Thalassa" (sea) life, independence, liberty, and a path to riches. The philosopher Anacharsis classified men into three categories: the living, the dead, and those on the seas. "Thalassa" was a factor helping the development of the ancient Greek civilization as well as means for its propagation. It represented the same value as did the most fertile agricultural lands. Just as the legends and the folklore of some people tell of the natural riches and beauty of their regions (forests, mountains, granaries, etc.) the legends and folklore of the ancient Hellenes and the Greeks of today bear the imprint of aspects of their life in the mountains and their adventures on the seas. Through the medium of the sea it was possible to develop the overseas economic empire of ancient Hellas and to this day the "floating empire" of modern Greece, sails the seas as the fourth larges commercial fleet in the world.

It is difficult to understand the attribution of heroism to the attempts at sailing perilous seas, as Hellenic legend presents them. The Argonauts' adventure on a hostile sea become a legend because the much sought-after "Golden Fleece" was itself of an imaginary nature, disguising, one might say, the existence of an economic policy. Could the expedition of the Argonauts have been legendary, or an activity

THE GREEK PENETRATION 21

officially organized with the intent to explore new regions of supply and development? Reality seems to lean toward the latter consideration. The sailors of the "Argo" were neither adventurers nor legendary heroes. It has been definitely proven that the expedition was organized under the leadership of a crew of well-versed navigators led by Jason.[35] It has also been proven that the fruitful results of the first expedition led to its being followed by others.

With respect to the "Golden Fleece," there exist different versions.[36] The legend was but the metaphorical expression of an unusual "fleece" having a special sheen, leaving the impression that it was golden. Just as in the case of the "Euxeinos Pontos," it was a habit of the Hellenes to use figures of speech in order to give new meaning to words by virtue of an understood comparison. The "Golden Grain Fields," for example, in Homer's vocabulary, meant the abundance of grain.

Archaeologists have not been able to establish the exact routes of the Greek penetration into the Black Sea. However, the first such incursions must have been indicated by the human instinct of orientation and self-preservation.

Because of the structure and the dimensions of the vessels of that time and especially because of the unknown stretch of space lying ahead of them, it is logical to conclude that the sailors did not hazard heading directly into the open sea. They must have followed the course of the water close to the shores, to the right and left of the exit from the Bosphorus, seeking the possibilities of advancing with the greatest caution. They probably first explored the south-east coast of the Black Sea and the south-north coast, that of present day Dobruja in Romania.

Looking at the problem deductively the navigators chose the safest shelter for their vessels offering minimal strategic protection, as well as the possibility of existing on local sources. The actual designations given some of the first settlements bears out the idea of precautions, as well as the fulfillment of the above mentioned conditions.

Half way up on the west coast of the Black Sea (the Left Shore) there is an extremity, a promotory under which the north-south winds lose some of their speed. In their coastal advance under strong winds, the ancient Greek navigators must have found shelter at this cape, which they named "Kaliacra" (Kali=good, acra=extremity, in other words, a good extremity, good shelter). Today it is the small port of Kaliacra. The sens of the name could be analogous to that of the Cape of Good Hope, or the Cape of Storms, where Vasco da Gama's vessel was sheltered. Likewise, the name of "Tomis" the present day port of *Constanta,* in front of which there is an entrance, a small gulf, a "tomos" (a cut, incision, a sort of bowl). Another explanation of the name "tomos" is that it is of mythological origin.[37]

The two exits routed out of the Bosphorus into the Black Sea had different designations. The Pontus on the left (Ta aristera tou Pontou) referred to the south-north coast of the sea, while "Euonimos Pontos" meant the right side of the sea, the southeast coast.[38]

The religious beliefs of the Greeks were a powerful influence on the ventures on the seas. Actually, even later, they were the principal factor in maintaining the ethnicity of the Greek people, especially during the four centuries of subjugation to the Ottoman Empire, when religion and unity around the cross were a strong impetus toward liberty and independence.

In antiquity, Poseidon and the nymphs of the ocean protected and guided the sailors. In addition, the Greek sailors created Achillés Pontarchos (Pont, Pontus being the name given to the Black Sea; archos meaning leader), to whom they erected a sanctuary on the tiny Island of the Serpents, just in front of the Sulina Mouth.[39] (Leuké, or Achilleis in antiquity).

In the Christian era, Poseidon was replaced by St. Nicholas as general protector.[40] To this day does not exist a Greek vessel that does not contain an icon of St. Nicolas, at times alongside that of the Virgin Mary.

The Greek Colonies of the Left Euxeinos Pontos.

The penetration and settlement of the Greeks in the entire Black Sea basin, including that of the Lower Danube, were also part of the Greek "diaspora,"[41] known in ancient Greece also as the "mégas apoikismós"[42] (great dispersion). Aside from economic and political causes, the diaspora was determined by the system of slavery and by the overpopulation. According to Hesiod, the principal cause of Greek immigration to other regions, by sea, was the fact that the earth was not fertile and the agricultural terrains were not productive.

Sometimes, the immigrations and the new sites for those who had to abandon their native regions were determined and officially organized by certain of the port-states. Often, those who intended to immigrate consulted the Oracle at Delphi, which among its other attributes was also a sort of information center concerning conditions existing in prospective immigration areas.

It is presumed that, initially, the establishment of the settlements was also due to the purpose of expanding the economic spheres of the small port states on the east coast of Asia Minor. In this case, it cannot be a question of forced immigration, but rather one of economic expansion for supplying and distributing the products of these port states.

It could well be that, after a preliminary adjustment to the new regions or immigration sites, among the first activities undertaken by the immigrants would have been exchanges of goods brought on their vessels with those of the local population from the interior coastlands. This would be the explanation of the term "Emporium" (Emporion)[43] given to the first settlements of the Greek dispersion.[44]

The Greek colonization process along the Black Sea coasts could be compared with that of what is now the United States of America, where the Vikings did not find commercial settlements, which only later were established by the Pilgrims. The Black Sea coasts were gradually transformed by the Greeks into "quays for their goods."[45] As has been mentioned, the first settlements along these coasts identified by archaeologists, were those of the Carians, also known as the Thalassokratores (Masters of the sea),[46] during the Milesian epoch. Because of the strong imprint left by the Milesians on the colonization process, the "Euxeinos Pontos" was also known as the "Milesian Limni" (Milesian Lake).[47]

Through the gradual enlargement of the geographic areas and their economic and political development, the first nuclei of emporiums given the name of "Apoikiae"[48] a word derived from the notion of colonization, of colonies,[49] and which later, because of being endowed with certain defensive military means, were named "fortress colonies."

Archaeologists and historians have established the fact that the first emporium which later became a colony was Histria, founded by Milesians in about 650 B.C., on the rocky hill of a small island in the lagoon known today as Sinoe, south of the St. George branch of the Danube. Tomis followed, also founded by the Milesians, situated in the immediate vicinity of the present day port of Constanta. South of Tomis were Dionyssopolis (the small port now called Balcic) and Kallatis (now Mangalia), established about 500 B.C. These four colonies, together with Odessus (modern Bulgarian port of Varna), known in antiquity as the colonies on the left shore of the sea, made up the "Pentapolis Confederation" with its center at Tomis.[50] The latter colony was also referred to as the "Metropolis on the left of the sea";[51] or the "brillant one first to the left of the sea."[52]

The colonists settled in permanently, bringing their families and, in time, forming a deeply-rooted neo-Hellenic population whose principal activities were navigation and trade. The importance and the variety of those activities were a result too of the special attention accorded to navigation by the operation, in Tomis, of a house or corporation of the shipowners of Tomis.[53]

The extent of the Greek's trade activity, transited through the colonies, reached interior regions far from the coast of the Left Pontus, as archaeologists have deduced from the diversity of foreign coins discovered in former Dacia and in other areas of Romania.[54]

The absence of any policy of territorial conquest, or of political domination, gave the Greeks the possibility of peaceful coexistence with the indigenous populations of the interior maritime coast and, later, even with some of the barbarian invaders. Hence, from this point of view, the commercial and maritime world could be qualified as "mercenary" to commerce, under all the dominations that succeeded one another in Scythia Minor. Under the Romans, this world was the component element of Rome's economic system, its activity being developed even far from the up-river areas, in the Geto-Dacian regions.[55]

The political regimes of the colonies could be compared to some degree with those of the city of Hong Kong, in China, or of Goa, in India. The juridic-administrative organizations being self-governing, the colonies were just like independent states under the spiritual "suzerainty" of the states of origin, in Hellas. Since no proof has been found, to date, of any dictatorial regime, it means that the administrations were democratic. Their policy being that of the colony, any conflict between the colony and the surrounding population was avoided. The Romanian archaeologist, Pârvan, noted "... a normal cohabitation between the Hellenes and the native Getts," stating "... the structure of their civilization was not only superimposed, but actually juxtaposed."[56]

Aside from the commercial ties between the colonists and the indigenous peoples, there existed also those of a cultural and religious nature, the Hellenic culture imposing itself strongly. The Scythians borrowed customs, crafts, religious ritual, and way of life from the Hellenes.

The bonds between the colonists and their homeland were indissoluble. As for the economic ties, it can be said that they constituted an integral part of the economy of the states of origin, especially of that of Athens. The origin of European civilization, as Hellas has come to be termed, did not include only philosophical and artistic production or experiments with political systems. Hellas was also the cradle of economic creativity. Along with the cultural "antennas broadcasting" from the Acropolis, there were also those whose economic "transmissions" were being received by the colonies.

The importance accorded to economics in Hellenic life is demonstrated by its being included in the preoccupations even of philosophers.[57] Xenophon, as well as Aristotle, considered agriculture to be "the Mother of all occupations and the source of all nutrition." Describing the activity at the port of Piraeus, Demosthenes pointed out the influence of the port tax on the cereal trade.[58]

It must be noted that, in spite of the spiritual and economic interdependence between the colonists and their countries of origin, the latter never undertook any military action in defense of the former, no matter how often they were threatened with invasions. However, whether for political considerations or for measures of protection of the supply system of continental Hellas, and of the port-states in Asia Minor, the countries of origin resorted to military action in order to maintain freedom of navigation through the Dardanelles and the Bosphorus, actions from which the Black Sea colonies also benefited indirectly.

Whenever the port state of Byzantium was in conflict with any other state, free navigation between these two straits was either made difficult or blocked. Transportation of goods and grain from the Left Pontus was at the discretion of Byzantium. The fact that the supply of provisions to Athens depended upon cereal from the Euxeinos Pontos region as well as on the good will of the fortress of Byzantium determined Athens to conquer the State in 409 B.C. thus assuring freedom of navigation through the Straits.[59]

For the same reason, to assure the supply of cereal from the Left Pontos, Athens entered in conflict with Philip II of Macedonia who blocked navigation through the Hellespont (Dardanelles of today), thus getting hold of the Hellenes most significant line of grain transportation.[60]

It is believed that one of the reasons for Demosthenes' hostile attitude towards Philip II was the Macedonian's threat to normal functioning of grain transportation coming from the Euxeinos Pontos.[61] Only after the Roman conquest of Byzantium in 196 B.C. did the Straits become free to commercial transport.

The Hellenic colonies in the entire basin of the "Euxein Pontos" also followed the evolution of the great empires of antiquity. Their political, social, and economic structure was included in the ones of the successive dominations that followed: Roman, Byzantine- Roman,

Byzantine, and Ottoman. Aside from a very small number, the colonies of the Left Pontos and the emporia in the Lower Danube lost their old designations, new names being given them by new authorities.[62]

The Hellenic organizational structure of commerce also underwent transformation though the different successive dominations. The predominant character of Greek commerce, however, was maintained under the Romans, as well as under the Byzantine Greeks. The numerical diminuation of Greeks, through not of their commercial positions, took place under Turkish domination (400 years), continuing even after 1878, when Dobruja was restored to Romania.

Iorga had this to say of the existence and the disappearance of the Hellenic colonies: "... for a long period of time, Ionian and Dorian colonies were here (Dobruja); the remains of their ancient peoples were preserved with all the interruptions and new influences, which can easily be imagined, throughout the Middle ages."[63]

Concerning the role of the barbarian invasions in the interruption of Danube navigation, under the Greeks as well as under the Romans, Iorga had a totally different point of view. In one of his studies, he rejected the belief that the Danube was for a time a "dead river." According to him "... the Danube has always been alive, from beginning to end, and the theory of a dead Danube is just as false as the theory that the barbarian invasions came all at once and destroyed all."[64] He also stressed, "... It is not true that the entire Roman inheritance was wiped out by the barbarians," or that they were "greedy people."[65] He was of the belief that they became integrated, in time, with the order and civilization introduced by the Romans in the Danube River Valley and that, in Pannonia, Atilla, "... Whose symbol of destruction should be discarded with the rubbish, and introduced civilization and drew to him subjects of the Roman Empire..."[66] Iorga maintained that the Danube was never "barbarian," showing that in the period of ever changing dominations, during the early centuries of the Middle Ages, there existed a "Danube of the Empire" (Byzantine Empire).[67]

The belief held by Iorga, that the barbarian dynamism was diluted by the laws enthroned by the Roman civilization, is also found in a work by an American jurist who maintained "... the barbarians themselves... gradually changing their habits from those of warlike and predatory tribes to those of peaceful and industrious citizens...," and, as an example, pointed out the origin of the Merovingian dynasty of French kings.[68]

Today, the Greek, Roman, and Byzantine settlements in Ancient Scythia Minor are archaeological sites which, for the past eighty years, have been in continual research by Romanian archaeologists. It can well be that, because of the many discoveries made each year, the archaeology of the former Hellenic colonies may equal in importance that of ancient Hellas. In Constanta (Tomis), dwellings are being demolished in the process of creating archaeological sites, and the stone walls built earlier by peasants are being examined closely in search of fragments of statues, temple ornaments, gravestones, and partial inscriptions, to complete those already discovered. The antiquity of the Left Pontus still holds many unknowns.

The Penetration on the Lower Danube.

"The Danube as far as the Siret was a Greek water..."[69]
(Pârvan)
"The Greeks carried out navigation on the Danube"
"This was the contact between us and the Greeks."[70]
(Iorga)

As mentioned earlier, the Greeks' penetration of the interior regions of the west coast of the Left Pontus was a normal development, inasmuch as their relations with the native population were peaceful. "The good relations with the Getic Kings," according to Pârvan, "contributed much to the intensification of merchants' penetrating into the Danube River valley and in general in Dacia."[71]

The only easier means of access to the interior regions was the Danube (Istros). In this respect, it must be taken into consideration that the delta region was inhospitable toward any penetration by land, in the Lower Danube valley. Archaeologists have not discovered sufficient material to describe this penetration in full detail, especially of the conditions under which it was developed. It is assumed that the first attempts took place long after the establishment of the colonies and their organization and consolidation on the maritime coast; the penetration of the interior would have required preliminary explorations.

Furthermore, aside from exploration, navigation on the river presented completely different conditions from those on the sea, especially since there were no navigable rivers in the native regions of the Greeks. The adaptation to hydrographic and climateric conditions (speed of the water current, the winds, and especially the freezing and thawing of the river) required of the navigators time for preparation and knowledge of technique specific to navigation on the Danube. This supposition can be absolved of any speculation if we just refer to the demands for professional preparation in any branch of activity. Even today, a professional warrant for the simple trade of sailor on the Danube is issued on the basis of technical examination and only after a period of apprenticeship on the river. In the vocabulary of Greek sailors there exists the appelation "Moutzos," which means apprentice on board ship. It can be deduced, then, that in the antiquity of Danube navigation, the Greeks were "... the only ones who knew how to adapt themselves to the anthropogeographic rules of the Danube basin."[72]

Unlike the present day principal entrance into the Danube, by means of the Sulina Mouth, the Hellenic initial penetration took place through the Peuce mouth and branch, the present-day St. George mouth, being the one closest to the Histria colony as well as to the Bosphorus. According to archaeological proof, this entrance into the river had, as its initial purpose, fishing activity, after which commercial activity was to follow.[73] In Pârvan's opinion, at first only Histria explored and exploited the regions in the interior of the Lower Danube, the participation of the other colonies developing much later on.[74]

In general, there seems to have been two phases of penetration. During the first, Histrians ventured into the delta interior, then gradually proceeded up to the present-day port of Galatz, the sector of the river termed by Pârvan "The Greek water."[75] In the second phase, they advanced up to the Iron Gates and up the tributaries to the left of the Lower Danube: the Ialomita, the Arges, and the Olt, as they are known today.

Fishing in the Greek maritime colonies, and later in those of the regions of the Lower Danube, became a tradition of the Greeks on the basis of which they could, later, under the Romans, demand the confirmation of their ancestral rights,[76] in this matter with respect to exemption from taxation at the mouth of the St. George branch.[77]

The preponderence of the fishing occupation can be deduced also from the multitude of shells, fishbones, hooks, weights for fishing nets, etc., found under the ruins of Histria. Also, on some of the coins discovered were the contours, in relief, of a dolphin, the symbol adopted as the official emblem.[78]

From the numerous inscriptions found by Romanian archaeologists it was concluded that the Histrians had a sort of monopoly on the regions around the St. George branch, including the many lakes around it,[79] a deduction upheld by the abundance of natural resources in the respective area. Even today, the greatest production of fish and caviar in Romania comes from this region, further enhanced by the production of horned cattle, pomiculture, viticulture, and hunting. The economic importance of Histria was also due to its geographic location by the mouth of the Ulmet, believed to have been an old branch of the Danube.[80]

As Pârvan noted, "... the very existence of the Histrians seemed to have depended upon the fishing in the Danube,"[81] and as Iorga stated, "... it is clear that the place occupied today by Romanian and Lipoveni[82] fishermen was once occupied by the ancient Hellenes."[83]

In contrast to the politically and socially organized maritime colonies, the Greek settlements along the course of the Lower Danube were simple market places, emporia, which could be compared somewhat to small ports known as wharves.[84] Some have remained to this day at that dimension, while others developed later into large ports or fishing centers.

Two principal aspects are evident from the location of these emporia. First, most of them were established on the left bank of the river, in the sector between the present day ports of Galatz and Turnu Severin (by the Iron Gates). The explanation lies in the fact that behind these sites lay the area richest in cereals, known today as the Bārāgan, the granary of Romania. The other aspect is the configuration of the river banks. The choice of the left bank was not accidental. Aside from the economic factor mentioned above, there was that of the natural conditions of the river. The right bank of the respective area, along with its hilly configuration unfavorable for port settlements, has no rich agricultural regions nearby. The left bank, however, is flat, almost at the river level. In addition, fish culture is abundant in the over nineteen lakes and ponds, all of them either beside the river course or at but a short distance from it.[85]

The reasons for the establishment of the Greek wharves and warehouses in the upper course of the Lower Danube are very apparent if one takes into consideration that, today, about 70% of the agricultural production and 40% of the fresh water fish culture comes from the regions behind the left bank of the Lower Danube.

Even the warehouses located on the river bank of the present-day Dobruja had their justification. Along with their activity as collection centers for the products of the eastern regions of the river, it can be presumed that they also carried out their modern functions, that is, the partial transfer of commodities towards the Black Sea ports during the period when the river was frozen.

In the river area between Braila and the Iron Gates, there were the following warehouses: Corsicon (Hârsova today), collection center for cereals from the Naparis River valley (present-day Ialomita); further upriver were Axiopolis (by the Island now known as Hinog), Demnizicos (now Zimnicea), Turis (Turnu Severin), Karavi (Corabia port), Maglavitis, (present-day Maglavit warehouse), Kalafatis (Calafat port), Hersepolis (Vârciorova). On the Kilia Branch of the Danube River were Hili, or Helia (the Kilia port of today) and Licostomo (mouth of the wolf), the present-day fishing port of Vâlcov. Of note is the similarity between the Greek and the Roman names of these ports and their present-day names.[86]

The Greek penetration raises some aspects insufficiently explained to date, when examined in the light of later development of traffic on the maritime navigation sector of the Danube (Brãila - Sulina). They can be answered to some extent by deductions based upon known situations of later dates, as well as by the results of studies, to date, of the geophysics and the hydrography of the river.

In principle, these aspects cover all the river's exits to the sea, whether large or small. Since in antiquity they were known under the generic term of "the mouths of the River Istros," it would appear that access to the Danube was possible through more openings than the three in use today. The confusion arises when archaeology indicates a single access route on it, that of the St. George branch, without mention of any other mouth.

Strabo indicated the St. George mouth as the most considerable, "... l'embouchure sacrée qu'on rencontre la première à gauche en entrant dans le Pont Euxine..."[87] And actually, this mouth is the first that a vessel coming from the Bosphorus meets if it is navigating at a short distance from the coast.

Hecataeus of Miletus (546 - 472 B.C.) mentioned two mouths; Herodotus (484-423 B.C.) recorded five branches with their respective mouths,[88] while Strabo claimed there were seven.[89] They were not wrong about the plurality of mouths and branches; the waters of the main branch, Kilia, divide into seven or eight sub-branches flowing into the sea and those of the St. George branch divide into two.

Although the small displacement of the vessels in antiquity permitted access through mouths of reduced depths, navigation through them seems to have been non-existent due to the marsh regions exposed to flooding, hence inappropiate for human settlement. Even today, circulation in the port of Vâlcov, known also as the "Venice of the Delta," situated at the mouth of the principal branch of the Kilia, is conducted through small canals. Construction of more solid

THE GREEK PENETRATION 31

buildings, in what is now the port of Sulina, was possible only after long processes of drainage, carried out after 1856 by the European commission of the Danube. This might be the explanation for the founding of Histria on a hill and not down hear the St. George mouth, through whose branch navigation to the interior of the Danube was carried on.

Through the mouth of the St. George branch, then known as the Peuce Mouth,[90] passage to the river was carried out through the existing natural canal, Dunavătz, which begins at the St. George branch and empties into Lake Razelm, near Sinoe, where Histria was located. From Lake Razelm the passage to the sea is through a natural canal, now known as Portita. It could well be that in antiquity, as is done today, a temporary closing of the canal made possible the gathering of the fish returning to the sea from their spawning grounds. The annual production there, nowadays, is about one thousand tons.[91]

Because of this chain of connection, Histria fulfilled two functions: that of a maritime port and that of a fluvial one. Its connection with the Black Sea was made through the Sinoe Lagoon and Lake Razelm, while through the natural canal Dunăvetz and the lake complex of Lake Razelm and smaller lakes,[92] the Histrians were able to communicate with the entire delta region south of St. George branch and then head upriver. Along this route, going upriver until the actual river was reached, the water currents were much reduced.

The supposition of a shorter connection between the sea and the St. George branch through the Lake Razelm-Dunăvetz route gains actual merit when we refer to the fact that, much later in 1829 when, because of difficulties provoked by the Russians at Sulina, Austria projected a new exit to the sea by this very route, today used by small motorcraft for fish transport.

Although the Greeks reached far upriver to the Iron Gates, in this matter also archaeology does not bring us much information on the settlements of the Galatz and Brăila ports. Despite the fact that in recent archaeological diggings at Brăilita, a suburb of Brăila, traces of millenary activity were found (1955), but no antique Greek toponymy has been identified as yet.[93] In 1965, amphorae and Greek inscriptions, as well as original coins from Aegean islands, were found,[94] but no trace of a commercial settlement.

Only a deduction seems plausible. It, as Pârvan believes, the Danube between the Siret River and the sea was a "Greek water,"[95] it would have been impossible that no commercial centers existed along this river and upriver to the sites of the present-day ports of Galatz and Brăila, both of them situated at the extremity of a region very rich in cereals. The historian C.C. Giurescu believes "... the Brăila area was subject to Greek influence exercised by merchants from the Pontic city-fortresses, and especially Roman influence, this area having been surrounded on all sides by territories conquered and administrated by Rome.[96]

From Pârvan's conclusions there is only the logical assumption of the existence of Hellenic settlements in the Brăila port site, without the possibility of identifying its ancient name. "That which is very certain," states Pârvan, "is the fact that in the year 500 B.C. Histrian fishermen and merchants were well acquainted with the Geto-Scythian land through which they traversed this part of the river unhindered...,"[97] the area in which the Brăila of today is located.

In the region between the Central Carpathian Mountains and the left bank of the Lower Danube River, the Greeks established commercial sub-centers, beside the existing native settlements, for collecting and distributing products; sub-centers such as those at Mostistea, Coconi, and Sultana (present-day names), having communications with the wharves along the river bank. By means of the communication line known as the "Geto-Hellenic road going through Mostistea and the Buzău pass in the Carpathians, Greek merchants maintained commercial ties also with Dacia."[98]

It has not been possible to ascertain precisely the navigation of Greek vessels upriver from Turnu Severin towards the Middle and Upper Danube, navigation there being rendered difficult by natural obstacles, underwater rocks, existing in the part of the river between the Cataracts and the Iron Gates. In antiquity, the Greek sailors of the Lower Danube named them the "Kataracts," meaning the stones of the Istros River," a passage they compared with the Strait of Sicily.

Traces of any Greek navigation on the Prut and the Siret rivers has not been confirmed archaeologically with any certainty, even though mention has been made of their ancient toponymy.[99] Materials found in the northern regions of these two rivers can be considered proof of the presence of merchants, but not of any navigation, even though it could have been undertaken on the Prut alone for a distance of about 180 miles.[100]

No conclusions could be drawn, from archaeological research, concerning either commercial practice or the methods of Greek navigation on the Lower Danube, just as there are none with respect to the types of vessels used. Judging from methods of navigation used in more familiar epochs, one can be deduced that the vessels plying this sector were the same as those of the sea, having respectively a capacity of 50 to 100 tons and a draught of three to five feet. Vessels of like

THE GREEK PENETRATION 33

capacity, sailing under Turkish and Greek flags, were seen along that same sector of the river up to 1900. In other words, maritime vessels fulfilled also the role of river craft.

There are no sufficient archaeological indications of the existence of any Greek naval shipyards on the Lower Danube. Their presence could be deduced, however, from the fact that the Greeks were well versed in creating other technical projects, as for example aqueducts, drainage systems, building construction, monuments, objects of art, of all of which there does exist archaeological proof. The existence of a naval industry can also be deduced from the fact that special lumber for the construction of vessels was being exported from the forests of Niculitel and Babadag, in Dobruja and a naval industry would be using local raw materials. The existence of the tradition such an industry in the ports of Tulcea, Brăila, Calafat, Turnu-Severin, and Giurgiu, a tradition continued by Greeks and Turks up to the First World War, would also uphold the deduction.

With the succession of political events and changes from the ancient times of the Danube regions, it is difficult to establish in documented and detailed manner the evolution of the Greek presence in Lower Danube navigation. All is credited to the research, the conclusions, and the judgments of archaeologists. What is certain, is that the "inventory" of Greek activity, taken over by the Byzantines, was substantial and the continuation of its exploitation for some time was carried out by the same Greek element, successively, under all political dominations.

The high degree in which navigation and commercial activity on the Black Sea and the Lower Danube was held in antiquity can be also confirmed from the wealth of literature by ancient authors, used today as source material.[101]

The Graeco - Roman Epoch.

During the entire Roman period, the activity of the Greeks in the Scythia Minor and Lower Danube not only did not cease, but reached an even greater development within the framework of the Roman economic system and protection. It has been said that while the essential aim of the Roman installations in Scythia were of a military order, the preoccupations of the Greeks were exclusively commercial.[102] In exchange for the protection offered by the Romans, the Greeks assured the latter of a normal development of the Scythian economy. In addition, the regions in which the Greeks were active could have been considered buffer zones, the administration of which was to the benefit of the Greeks as well as that of the Romans.

Interruptions in normal commercial life were caused by barbarian invasions especially at the Danube mouth, where mobile Roman military posts patrolled in order to maintain security.[103] The Greek commercial fleet of the colonies found itself under the protection of the "praefectus orae maritimae,"[104] which had among its attributes the eradication of piracy. Adding to this the Roman garrisons of the Danubian Limes chain, it is obvious that Greek commerce and navigation operated under favorable conditions.

The protection accorded by Rome to commerce and navigation in the Black Sea and the Lower Danube was part of Rome's economic policy, applied throughout its empire under the auspices of the "Pax Romana" and the principle of the right to use paths of communication considered to be common property, accessible to all citizens of the empire.

The gratitude of the Greeks towards the Roman administration is shown in an inscription, found in the ruins of Histria, in which Emperor Caracalla was termed "ruler of the earth and of the sea."[105]

Archaeologists and historians attest to the fact that the Romans, too, were occupied with navigation and commerce on the Lower Danube. The question arises as to whether the respective merchants and sailors were Romans, or Greek subjects of the Roman Empire. Under the political jurisdiction of Rome, it can be assumed that Roman commerce would have been carried out in great measure by those already in that field of activity in the colonies. It can also be supposed that, aside from commanders of troops and higher officials of the fiscal and administrative control, a fairly small number of Romans made up the armies of the outskirts of the empire. Recruiting of soldiers was generally made from the major ranks of the local population. There were some great Roman merchants based in Rome or other large cities, but it can be assumed that managers and their subordinate ranks were from the colonies along the Black Sea shores and the settlements along the Lower Danube. The status and experience of the Greeks in the economy of the respective regions were factors which the Romans could not ignore. In fact, all those who found themselves under Roman rule considered themselves Romans and many of the rulers and generals of the empire were of other origins. Within the Roman Empire of the East, established by Constantine the Great, the Greeks of Byzantium called themselves "Romioi", citizens of Rome.

THE GREEK PENETRATION

On Trajan's Column in Rome on which are carved scenes representing war against the Dacians, one can see anchored alongside the Roman bridge at Turnu-Severin boats, from which soldiers are unloading sacks, probably containing food. From these scenes one could not conclude the presumed existence of commercial traffic.

The cultural factor, on the other hand, was a real force with deep roots. This can explain conclusions drawn by archaeologists and historians. Instead of the Greek population being assimilated and included in the life of the native population or that of the Romans, it was noted that the institutions of the city of Tomis "... always remained purely Greek,"[106] and "instead of the Gettization of the Greeks, there occurred a gradual Hellenization of the local Getae."[107]

"In fact," noted Iorga, "a complete Romanization could not be reached in these parts in such a short time and with the Hellenic roots so deep and strong."[108] Pârvan also stressed that, on the basis of the evidence in Histria and Apollonia, the Greek way of life was very strong between the seventh and fourth centuries B.C.[109]

From the writings of Ovid, exiled to Tomis, it was concluded that the Greek language had priority, being spoken even by the Getae.[110] Although the intellectual medium was Greek, the commercial one was Graeco-Roman. Some Romanian archaeologists have concluded, in this respect, that the Romans "could not have found more dependable allies than in these centers of Hellenic civilization, interested to the highest degree in the order they brought to a world so wracked with wars.[111]

While the temporary passage of the armies of Darius and of Alexander the Great left destructive traces on the activities of the Greeks in the colonies and on the Lower Danube, the constructive imprints of the prolonged and peaceful Roman dominations are visible to this day; new conclusions of this fruitful Graeco-Roman collaboration have been drawn from the results of recent research carried out by Romanian archaeologists.

Chapter 11

THE FIRST SUCCESSORS OF THE GREEKS AND THE ROMANS

The Byzantines and Italians (Venetians and Genoese).

The presence of the Byzantines in the economics of the former Greek and Lower Danube colonies must be considered also from the point of view of the importance of the Bosphorus and the Dardanelles Straits. Without freedom of passage between the Black Sea and the Mediterranean through these straits, the Danube River would lose its importance as a natural line of communication of European and even world importance. In carrying out this function, the Straits are, as has been shown, a continuation of the course of the Danube. As often as this interdependence was interrupted, navigation along the entire course of the river, and especially that of the Maritime Danube, was practically destroyed. Under such circumstances, navigation was limited to the circulation of local exchanges between the regions adjacent to the Black Sea and those along the river banks, a traffic not corresponding to the economic dynamics of the Danube basin. The activities of the Byzantines in the Black Sea and the Lower Danube and jurisdiction over both straits advantaged as they were by the possession can be evaluated from this point of view.

The city and port of Byzantium, later named Constantinople, became the center for collecting and storing the economic production of the Black Sea and Lower Danube regions, as well as having the function of commercial transit between three continents: Europe, Asia, and Africa. Two nicknames given to their capital by the Byzantines point out the importance of this communication center; from the name "Vasilevoussa" (the Capital of Kings), is understood the political importance, while through Nymphy tou Bosphorou (Bride of the Bosphorus) is made clear its naval and commercial importance.[112]

The presence and activity of the Byzantines were the most efficient of those succeeding the Greeks and Romans on the Lower Danube. The Greek influence was marked here, its effect still evident today in the religion, economy, and social life of the Balkan peoples, even going so far as Russia.

After the gradual decline of Rome influence, the continuity of the activities of the Greek colonies was taken over, step by step, by the Byzantines. Reorganized after repeated barbarian destruction, the colonies were included in the Byzantine economic sphere, the latter being the beneficiary of the foundations laid by the Greeks and Romans. It is almost impossible to follow and to outline the exact basis of the process of demographic superposition between the Greeks of the colonies and those of the new Byzantine state.

After the crystallization of so many waves of people coming one after another through Dobruja and the Lower Danube, the Byzantine flag replaced the Greek and Roman ones on the Black Sea. "The maritime mastery of which," noted Iorga, "belonged to the Byzantines up to the fourteenth century,"[113] and the Byzantine military fleet protected commercial traffic from the attacks of pirates and barbarians.

Constantine the Great, the founder of the new capital Constantinople reorganized, both politically and economically, the newly conquered regions in Dobruja and those north of the Lower Danube, Constantius restored the port of Tyras, at the mouth of the Dniester, and of Tomis, changing their names; the former became Asprocastro (White Fortress) and the second, Constantiana, today known as Constanta.

The economic life of the regions of the Lower Danube and the Dobrujean maritime littoral followed along the same lines of development and prosperity as the entire new empire, being, as it was, under the protection of the former Roman Limes, reorganized and provided with other garrisons.

The status of the new empire in the respective regions was disrupted for almost three centuries following the Slavic, the Avaric, and especially the Bulgarian invasions, the latter actually forming a state in the region south of the Danube and part of the Dobruja. During the entire period of the Bulgarian state, Dobruja was considered disappeared from history.[114]

In the meantime, by the succession of intervening political events and the Byzantine-Roman fusion, thrones passed into Byzantine hands, creating a monarchy of Greek character, the Byzantine Empire, but Hellenic in essence.

THE GREEK PENETRATION 39

After the elimination of the Latin Empire - "the short-lived and parasitical empire"[115] — created by the Westerners of the Fourth Crusade, commerce and navigation on the Danube again resumed their normal course. Byzantine commerce and navigation on the Lower Danube were carried out through the former Greek warehouses and ports, some of the old names being retained, others changed.

Data concerning the ports of Brăila and Galatz are very few and far between for the Byzantine era, also. In the Chronicle of Kiev (also known as the Chronicle of Nestor) it is mentioned, in general terms, that in the market place, but not the port, of Brăila "all the riches were gathered."[116] A German fallen prisoner to the Turks during the battle of Nicopole (1396) related "... in Brăila was the stopping place for vessels and galleons bringing goods from pagan lands,"[117] that is, from far-off regions occupied by the Turks.

The commercial ties of the centers in ancient Scythia Minor went beyond the regions bordering on the river, extending deep into the interior; coins bearing the emblem of the Byzantine Empire have been found there.[118] The commerce, of fresh and salted fish from the river and its delta carried on by the Byzantines, left in the Romanian language the word "Pârparul" (the old Romanian tax), derived from the Byzantine "hyperpyron," a gold coin with which the tax was paid for the loading of fish at the collection centers along the Danube.[119]

As time passed, the Byzantines did not succeed in maintaining their economic preponderence in the Black Sea and the Lower Danube; parallel with their domestic and foreign difficulties, they faced the competition of the Genoese and the Venetians. The Italians following their development of commercial relations with the Middle East Arabs, turned their attention to the economic sphere of the Byzantine Empire of the Black Sea.

The Italian economic penetration was sustained also by political pressure which met weak resistance from an empire racked with struggles for monarchic succession and influence, too, by the disputes between Venice and Genoa for supremacy. In order to ease the economic situation in which the empire found itself at one moment and to satisfy the Venetians, Emperor Alexis Comnen offered them a commercial alliance with results contrary to expectations.

In the hope of maintaining their prestige, the Byzantines also accorded privileges to Genoa, rival of Venice, aiming thus to weaken the latter. In the end, the results of the Byzantine dual policy were unfavorable to its originators. Supported politically, directly or indirectly, by their states and financially by their state banks, the Venetians and the Genoese penetrated the Black Sea and the Lower

Danube. There they established themselves, creating commercial centers; notably among them the famous center at Caffa in the Crimea, and Kilia on the Danube, their activity on the river extending into the interior regions of the littoral.

In the Italo-Byzantine commercial complex, the Danubian port of Kilia was later named by the Turks as "the key and the gate to the Moldavian and Hungarian lands."[120] The port at the mouth of the Dniester, Asprocastro, its Byzantine name changed by the Italians to Moncastro, was considered "the key and gate to all the Polish and Russian lands and to the great ocean." Both ports were also the terminal points of the "Moldavia Road," which began in Lemberg, Poland and of the "Brasov Road," the tie to Transylvania and Central Europe. Working alongside the Byzantines in the other Danube ports and warehouses, the Venetians all but monopolized the Kilia trade, while the Genoese did the same at the Giurgiu port; the initial name of the latter is believed to have been San Giorgio, the patron Saint of Genoa.

Meanwhile, new political transformations and economic factors appeared in the Lower Danube valley. At the beginning of the fourteenth century, the two Romanian provinces of Moldavia and the Romanian Land (Wallachia) came into being, and the Hungarians and Poles turned their attention to the river navigation. Hungarian interests in this navigation had begun to take shape at the beginning of the thirteenth century, when the treaty with Poland provided that in case the Prince of Moldavia would not be allied with them against the Turks, both signatories could divide Moldavia between themselves, each having the right to assure its commercial rights on land and on the water. Also, the Poles would have the right to take the port of Cetatea Albă, the Hungarians the Kilia Branch and mouth, as well as the port of the same name.[121]

The Venetian and Genoese colonies in the Southern Ukraine were in the end abolished by the Mongols and Tartares, their survival also threatened by the Turkish advance into the Straits region and subsequent occupation of Constantinople.

Nevertheless, the Byzantine activity in the Lower Danube and on the Black Sea continued and progressed before, as well as after, the fall of Constantinople and of their empire. Two factors in particular came to their aid; namely, Christianity and the Turks' lack of preparation and training in matters of trade and navigation.

From their establishment and even after their occupation by the Turks, the two Romanian Principalities had become spiritual tributaries of the former Byzantine Empire, due to the Patriarchate of

Constantinople, considered to be the Holy See of the Christian Orthodox religion.

The initial lack of any native commercial world, on the one hand, and the Byzantine religious and intellectual prestige, on the other, not only made easier the Byzantine activity in the young Principalities, but also opened up new fields for exploitation. A recommendation from the Patriarch of Constantinople in favor of some Byzantine merchant or navigator was not only a command, but also gave a Romanian prince the opportunity to prove his devotion to the head of the Church. "The Emperor on the shores of the Bosphorus," wrote one Romanian chronicler, "was the earthly representative of the Romanian prince and the defender of their common faith." Through Orthodoxy, the Romanian belonged to the same spiritual empire. After the fall of Byzantium, the Romanian princes became the trustees of all Orthodoxy and the former imperial economic monopoly was replaced by the spiritual unity. The spiritual unity and dependence was also due to the absence of any political conflicts between the Principalities and the Byzantine Empire.

The strength of the Byzantine prestige was obvious even after the fall of Constantinople, when part of the intellectual and upper aristocratic classes of the occupied capital took refuge in the two Romanian Principalities, Christian and friendly nations. The many intermarriages between refugee and upper class (landed) Romanian families was so common that it gave occasion for the great Romanian historian, Nicolae Iorga, to affirm "there is not in the two Romanian lands a single aristocratic family in which there is not a little Greek blood."[122] The continued influence and presence of the Byzantine concept, according to Iorga, was transmitted to the people of Southest Europe — among them the Romanians — by the fact that the Patriarch symbolized the spiritual continuity of the Byzantine Empire. "Byzantium," he states, "did not die in the fifteenth century."[123]

Even long before the Phanariot reign over the Romanian Principalities (1711-1821), when the two Romanian peoples had the right to elect their leaders under the suzerainty of the Sultan, four Greek princes were chosen as leaders from the ranks of the Greeks or the refugees. The preponderance of Byzantine influence in commerce and navigation was so great that it inspired one Romanian sociologist to state that the Greeks were the Romanians' teachers in commerce.[124]

Native Romanian presence in the actual commercial navigation was practically non-existent, being limited to a very reduced traffic of strictly local trading. With very rare exception, Romanians were not involved in any large scale domestic or foreign commercial activity.

The explanation lies as much in the patriarchal structure of the social life as in the feudal economic system of the Romanian Principalities. The basis of the national activity of the people was agriculture and other natural resources, their commercialization was principally in the hands of foreigners. According to Iorga the Romanian presence was non-existent, especially in the maritime branch.[125] One economist has maintained that Romanian merchants did participate at times in the maritime trade, directly or indirectly.[126] There is a difference, however, between participating in the trade and carrying out the actual maritime navigation. There are historic records of signing of commercial treaties entered into by the Romanian Principalities with Poland and Hungary, but their clauses referred to customs matters or means of transport on the water, not matters of actual navigation. Only after the nineteenth century did more favorable circumstances and conditions intervene for a progressive participation of the Romanians in the domestic as well as in the foreign trade.

Just like the Greeks and Romans in antiquity, the Byzantines contributed to the development of commerce and navigation on the Black Sea and the Lower Danube regions, the mark of their presence persisting under the Ottoman regime, continued successively by new elements from the Greek islands and the continent, up to the time of the first World War.

Similarly, the former presence of the Genoese and Venetians was resumed, by the United Kingdom of Italy, in Lower Danube ports after 1829, having a substantial share in the development of the commercial and navigational activity.

The Turks.

Besides the fact that the Ottoman epoch was the longest (from the beginning of the fifteenth century to 1878), it also represented the last domination over Dobruja and the last foreign suzerainty over the Lower Danube valley regions. From circa 1450 to 1699, when the Treaty of Karlowitz was signed, the entire sector of the Lower Danube and, for almost a century, also the central sector from Budapest downstream, came under the direct control of the Ottoman Empire. During this period, the Lower Danube did not enter into any of Europe's concerns. Only after 1699 did it begin to be figured in Austrian and Russian policy and afterwards in European.

THE GREEK PENETRATION

The frequent Russo-Turk and Austro-Turk wars breaking out after 1699, directly and indirectly influenced the normal progress of navigation on the Lower Danube. The stand taken by the Sublime Porte with respect to the armed conflicts was to maintain its own political domination; the economic importance of the Lower Danube not being considered a determining factor, that being understood to come under the political jurisdiction of the Sultan. The Turks' lack of interest in the economic matters of the Danube was flagrant, not only during their difficult political periods, but even during the favorable ones, such as the period after the Crimean War when, with the help of England and France, they regained the Danube Delta which had been annexed by Russia in 1829. In regions that had been under their direct sovereignty — Hungary and the entire Balkans — they were the beneficiaries of the respective national economies.

Actually, one cannot speak of any policy of direct control or of any general plan for exploiting the national economies of the Ottoman Empire. The principal preocupations of the Turks were the wars and territorial conquests; the economic exploitation was left in the care of the foreigners and the vanquished, the latter being used also in the administration behind the battle fronts.

Byzantine participation in the administration of the Ottoman Empire, as well as in that of the Christian people, is regarded by some historians as a factual continuation of the political-administrative structure of the former empire.[127] According to Iorga, "Byzantium could not disappear completely in the catastrophe of the Empire, broken up, then destroyed by the Ottoman Turks... It contained a complete Roman organization, the patrimony of which it was especially proud, of Orthodoxy, and of these traditions of Greek civilization which corresponded with its inclinations."[128]

After the defeat of Constantinople and of the rest of the Byzantine Empire and after the crystallization of the political situation, the Turks permitted the return of many of the members of the former wealthy Greek families. Settling in the Phanar sector, where the Patriarchate was located, they became known as the Phanariots. These newcomers, being intellectuals and well versed in foreign languages, were placed by the Turks in administrative government positions, replacing the Jews and Armenians.[129]

In a short time the Phanariots became the economic elements auxiliary to the great military potential of the Ottoman Empire. According to Young, "le Phanar à ses débuts fut comme le prolongement de l'Empire grec sous la souveraineté turque. C'était à tous égards un imperium in imperio..." and "le grec est donc la monnaie de billon de la vie courante."[130]

The Phanariots were in charge of the exploitation of the most important commercial sectors of the empire, their enterprises being a sort of monopoly accorded by the Turks.

Among the Byzantine Empire fields of activity taken over by the Turks was that of commercial navigation. The powerful military capacity of the Turks on land was not equalled by their ability at sea, either in matters of war or of commerce. Ch. de Peyssonel, former Consul of France at Smyrna, on the occasion of a Black Sea voyage humorously described the voyage of a Turkish vessel which instead of reaching Odessa, anchored by mistake before the Danube Delta.[131] As for navigation on the Danube, Turkish vessels were refused insurance because of the numerous shipwrecks due to "insufficient understanding of nautical science."[132]

In 1596, the crews of the military and commercial fleets that were sailing under the flag of the Crescent Moon included over 80,000 Greeks, recruiting being obligatory. After the termination of their term of conscription, the Greeks could continue working on their own commercial vessels.

There are no precise statistics as to the number of Greek commercial vessels sailing on the Black Sea and the Lower Danube under the Turkish flag. The fact that the Russians made use of them in order to weaken the Turkish naval potential would indicate that the number was considerable. Through the Treaty of Kütschuk — Kainardji, in 1774, the Russians obtained from the Turks the right to have the Greek-owned vessels hoist the Russian flag, their navigation being free and independent of Ottoman jurisdiction.

Within the framework of the administration of the commercial marine department, the Phanariots also had the function of "fleet dragoman," a post equivalent today to that of minister-adjunct or secretary-general of a ministry. Bearing in mind, on the one hand the role and influence of the Phanariots in the political, administrative, and economic apparatus of the Ottoman Empire, and on the other hand the professional background in commerce and navigation, it is easy to conclude that the Greek element on the Lower Danube also was predominant in the commercial and marine economy. To this must be added the fact that for more than a century (1711-1821) the Phanariot governing of the Romanian Principalities favored the Greek merchants and shipowners. "Turkish goods," wrote Iorga, "were better known than Turkish merchants, Greek merchants taking care of transportation and passage through customs of Levantine commodities"[133] and

THE GREEK PENETRATION

it was the Greeks who "became the principal agents for commercial ties between the East and West, consequently all the commercial activity of the Ottoman Empire was found in their hands."[134] The Greek Revolution of 1821, against the Turks, caused the temporary interruption of Greek participation in the economic circuit of the Ottoman Empire. After 1829, their participation in the commerce and navigation on the Lower Danube was more advantageous, due to the privileged status of the Romanian Principalities, obtained when the Treaty of Adrianople abolished the Turkish monopoly over their foreign commerce.

In conclusion, it can be maintained that, in matters of navigation and trade on the Lower Danube, the Turkish epoch was a continuation of the Greek-Byzantine period. This presentation of the Turkish epoch is relatively brief, inasmuch as it can be followed in the coming pages of this work up to 1878, after which the authority of the Sublime Porte over the Lower Danube and its mouths was to come to an end.

Notes

Chapter 1

1. Among other sources, that of Gilbert Martin, "Russian History Atlas," (1972), Map No. 12.
2. Radu Vulpe, "The Dobruja Through the Centuries, its Historical Evolution and Geopolitical aspects," (1939), p. 50.
3. Idem, ibid. pp. 30 and 31.
4. The water current is produced by the draining of excess water from the Black Sea through the Strait of Bosphorus, its speed accelerated also by the north-south and the east-west winds.
5. Rhys Carpenter, "The Greek Penetration of the Black Sea"; in "American Journal of Archaeology" (A.J.A.), L ii, (1948).
6. A.J. Graham, "The Date of the Greek Penetration of the Black Sea"; in "Bull. Inst. Class., Studies of the University of London," V. (1958).
7. B.W. Labaree, "How the Greeks Sailed into the Black Sea"; in "American Journal of Archaeology," LXI, (1957).
8. Rhys Carpenter, p. 9.
9. Idem, Ibid., p. 1.
10. "The Black Sea Pilot," London, published by the Hydrographic Department of the British Admiralty, (1942).
11. Dionysius Byzantius, "Anaplus Bospori," ed. R. Guengerich; quoted by Graham, pp. 30, 40.
12. Byzantius, p. 31.
13. A.J. Graham, p. 30.
14. Towing by rope, in French, halage.
15. H.W. Van Loon: "Ships and How They Sailed the Seven Seas," translated into Greek under title: "Istoria tis naftilias" (1960), p. 53.
16. Carpenter, p. 1.
17. "Geografia văii Dunării Românesti", pp. 654, 659.
18. Grig. Antipa, "Dunărea si problemele ei stiintifice, economice si politice." pp. 45-60.
19. Hesiod, "Theogony"; quoted by K.N. Antonopoulou, in "Istoria tou Emporikou Naftikou," (in Greek), 1963. p. 34.
20. Idem, "Works and Days," quoted by K.N. Antonopoulou, p. 34.

21. From the commentary of K.N. Antonopoulou, p. 35, on Hesiod's original text: "In Hesiod's epoch, the VII century B.C., earlier and much later, the favorable periods for navigation were considered to be spring and summer. Navigation was interrupted throughout the autumn and winter."
22. Quoted by G.S. Gheorgakopoulou "To Ellinikon naftikon dia mesou ton eonon" (1933), p. 28 (in Greek).
23. H. Schliemann, "Ilios" (1881), p. 240; J.B. Bury, "History of Greece," (1931); quoted by Will Durant, "The Story of Civilization: Life in Greece," (1939), p. 36.
24. D.M. Pippidi si D. Berciu, "Din istoria Dobrogei: Getii si Grecii la Dunărea de Jos din cele mai vechi timpuri până la cucerirea romană," Vol. I, pp. 148-149; D.M. Pippidi, "I Greci nel Basso Danubio," p. 37.
25. Peter Shankland and Anthony Hunter, "Dardanelles Patrol," (1964), p. 26.
26. D.M. Pippidi, "Greci nel...," p. 37.
27. Situated to the north of Tomis, former Greek port, today Constanta.
28. D.M. Pippidi and D. Berciu, "Din istoria Dobrogei: Getii si Grecii...," p. 151.
29. "Axeinos" - (Axenos) is synonym to "Aphiloxenos," both words having the sense of inhospitable. By "Pontos" is indicated the sea between Asia and Europe, also meaning sea in general. One of the origins of the word "Axeinos" is attributed to the Iranian language "Akhshaena," meaning gloomy, black, in the sense of inhospitable. (See Georges Brătianu: "La Mer Noire, des origines à la conquête ottomane," pp 43-44). The Turko-Tatar vocabulary contains the word "Kara-Deniz," meaning black sea, retaining the sense of "Akhshaena." In the Russian Language the term is "Tcherno — Mare" (Black sea). Beginning sometime during the Middle Ages, the Greek maritime world adopted the term "Mavri Thalassa," also denoting the idea of black sea.
30. "Euxeinos," hospitable, kind to strangers, synonym to "Kaloxenos" or "Philoxenos," friendly. Legend has it that the Black Sea became hospitable when Hercules wiped out the pirates from the Black Sea; "Etymologicum Magnum," T. Gaisfort ed., (1848), p. 394; and Liddel — Scott, "A Greek-English Lexicon" (1925-1940), S.V. "Euxeinos."
31. Săuciuc-Săveanu, "Cultura cerealelor in Grecia Antică si politica cerealistă a Atenienilor" (1925), p. 74.
32. "Etymologicum Magnum," p. 894.
33. In Greek maritime circles of Romania, there circulated such curses as "May the Black Sea swallow you," or "May you wear the black of the Black Sea," etc.
34. Horace, "Odes," I, p. 28.
35. K.N. Antonopoulou, pp. 26, 96. The expedition of Jason and his friends, Hercules, Theseus, etc., who sailed towards Colchis, near the Caucasus where they stole the Golden Fleece.
36. A.E. Evans, "The Palace of Minos," Vol. III (1921), p. 227.

37. Legend has it that following a dispute between two Greek sailors the murdered one was cut to pieces, which were cast upon the shore by the wind and the waves, the mouths being called "Tomoi," meaning pieces.
38. D.M. Pippidi and D. Berciu, "Din istoria Dobrogei...," Vol. I, p. 157 (note 1)
39. Radu Vulpe, "The Dobruja Through...," p. 9.
40. K.N. Antonopoulou, p. 32.
41. "Diaspora," a word of Greek origin; dia: through, + speirein to sow, to scatter seed upon or over, to disperse.
42. "Megas apoikismos," in the sens of a great diaspora, or large scale colonization.
43. "Emporium" (Emporion), means trade, belonging to commerce; a place of trade, market place, a city or town with extensive commerce.
44. Stoian Iorgu, "Tomitana," contributii epigrafice la istoria cetătii Tomis, (1962) p. 17 (title derived from Tomis)
45. R. Vulpe, "The Dobruja...," p. 50.
46. Idem, ibid., p. 8 - Thalassocrates (sic)
47. K.N. Antonopoulou, p. 44.
48. Stoian Iorgu, "Tomitana," p. 17.
49. "Apoikiae," colonies means the settlements of groups of people emigrated from their native land.
50. Radu Vulpe and Ion Barnea, "Din istoria Dobrogei": Romanii la Dunărea de Jos, Vol. II, (1968), p. 66.
51. Idem, ibid., p. 149.
52. Iorgu Stoian, "Tomitana," p. 50.
53. J.P. Waltzig, "Etudes historiques sur les corporations professionnelles chez les Romains, depuis les origines jusqu'à la chute de l'empire d'Occident," Louvain, 1895-1900, Vol. III, p. 78; and V. Pârvan, "Die Nationalität der Kaufleute im röemischen Kaiserreiche," (1909), p. 86.
54. A.D. Xenopol, "Istoria Românilor din Dacia Traiană," Vol. I, p. 65.
55. V. Pârvan, "La pénétration hellénique et hellénistique dans la valleé du Danube" (1933), p. 36.
56. Idem, ibid., p. 36.
57. Xenophon, "Oecon." XV, 2 and XVI; quoted by Săuciuc-Săveanu in "Cultura cerealelor...," p. 14.
58. Demosthenes, XXXV, 28; quoted by Săuciuc-Săveanu in "Cultura...," p. 112.
59. Merle, "Die Geschichte der Städte Byzantion und Kalcedon von ihrer Gründung bis zum Eingreifen der Römer," in "Die Verhältnisse des Ostens," Kiel, 1916, p. 9; in Săuciuc-Săveanu. "Cultura...," p. 81.
60. Săuciuc-Săveanu, p. 141.
61. Demosthenes, XVIII, para. 90, in Săuciuc-Săveanu, "Cultura...," p. 139.

62. For example, the name of the colony of Tomis, retained by the Romans, was changed by the Byzantines to Constantiana and Constantia, becoming Kustendje under the Turks, and Constanta today. The Romanians kept the name of Tomis, given to an administrative district in Dobruja. Histria is today the name of a small fishing village near the site of the ancient colony.
63. N. Iorga, "Populatia Dobrogei la 1850" in "Revista Dobrogea," III, No. 1 (1922).
64. Idem, "Drumurile de comert, Creatoare ale statelor românesti," p. 7.
65. Idem, ibid., p. 7.
66. Idem, ibid., pp. 7, 8.
67. Idem, ibid., p. 8.
68. James Coolidge Carter, "Law: its Origin Growth and Function," p. 92.
69. V. Pârvan, "La pénétration...," p. 42.
70. N. Iorga, "Românii in cadrul vietii economice din Balcani" (1935), p. 35.
71. V. Pârvan, "La pénétration...," p. 23.
72. R. Vulpe, "The Dobruja... p. 50.
73. R. Vulpe and I. Barnea, "Din Istoria Dobrogei..." p. 50.
74. V. Pârvan," La pénétration...," p. 42.
75. Idem, ibid., p. 42.
76. Idem, ibid., p. 42.
77. V. Pârvan, "Histria"; Inscriptii găsite in anii 1916, 1921 si 1922, p. 514.
78. From the decree honoring Aristagoras, I century B.C.; Lacroix, "Les blasons des villes grecques"; in "Etudes d'archéologie classique" I, 1955/56, pp. 91-114; quoted by D.M. Pippidi, in "I Greci...," pp. 51, 190, and Plate II.
79. R. Vulpe and I. Barnea, "Din istoria...," Vol. II pp. 50, 51.
80. V. Pârvan, "Ulmetum," (1923), p. 597.
81. V. Pârvan, "La pénétration...," p. 28.
82. A religious sect of refugees fled from Russian persecution at the time of Peter the Great.
83. N. Iorga "Poporul românesc si marea," (1938), p. 14.
84. Wharf: small river port having a single, simple mooring quay, without technical port facilities. Small quantities of cereal and goods could be loaded from these and fishing vessels anchored.
85. "Geografia văii Dunării românesti," pp. 136-141.
86. Although the Greek name of Licostomo (mouth of the wolf) later became Russian, it still retained somewhat the original sense; Vâlcov is derived from the Russian word for wolf.
87. "Géographie de Strabon," p. 80.
88. "Geografia văii ...," pp. 13, 14.
89. "Géographie de Strabon," p. 50.
90. Pauly-Wissova-Kroll," Reale Enzyklopädie der klassischen Altertumswissenschaft," XIX, coll. 1383-1384; quoted by D.M. Pippidi, "I Greci nel...," p. 234.
91. "Geografia văii...," p. 224.
92. Ibid., p. 631.

93. N. Hartuche and I.T. Dragomir: "Săpăturile arheologice dela Brăilita in 1955"; in Materiale si Cercetări Arheologice, III, p. 147.
94. Idem, "Pagini din istoria veche a orasului si raionului Brăila"; in Ziarul "Inainte," 4 and 20 June, Brăila, (1966).
95. V. Pârvan, "La pénétration...," p. 42.
96. C.C. Giurescu, "Istoricul orasului Brăila," (1968), p. 26.
97. V. Pârvan, "La pénétration...," p. 42.
98. V. Pârvan, "La pénétration...," p. 44.
99. The Prut was known by the name of "the Scythian Gate," or "Pyretus." The Siret was mentioned by Herodotus bearing the name of "Tiaranos"; by Constantine the Porphyrogenite as the "Seretos"; quoted by A.D. Xenopol in "Istoria Romanilor din Dacia Traiana," p. 52.
100. Radu Vulpe and I. Barnea, "Din istoria Dobrogei...," Vol. II, p. 289.
101. Hecataeus of Miletus (546-472 B.C.); Herodotus (484-423 B.C.); Polybius (201-120 B.C.); Strabon (58 B.C.); Pliny the Elder (23-79 A.D.); Ptolemy (90-160 A.D.); Priscus of Panion; Procopius of Caesarea, and other Arab writers; quoted from "Geografia văii...," pp. 13, 14.
102. R. Vulpe, "The Dobruja...," p. 14.
103. Idem, ibid., p. 14.
104. Idem, ibid., p. 14.
105. D.M. Pippidi, "Histria," I, pp. 530-533.
106. S. Lambrino, "Tomis, cité gréco-gète chez Ovide"; in "Ovidiana," Bucuresti (1958) pp. 379-390.
107. R. Vulpe and I. Barnea "Din Istoria...," Vol. II, p. 38.
108. N. Iorga "Istoria comertului român, epoca veche," p. 19.
109. V. Pârvan, "Gânduri despre lumea si viata la Greco-Romani din Pontul Stâng," (1920), p. 42.
110. R. Vulpe and I. Barnea, "Din istoria...," Vol. II. p. 40.
111. Idem., ibid., p. 36.

Chapter 2

112. Laimou Andrea, "To Naftikon tou Ghenous ton Ellinon" (in Greek), Tom. A., (1968) p. 77.
113. N. Iorga, "Populatia Dobrogei la 1850," p. 45.
114. R. Vulpe, "The Dobrujua..." pp. 27, 28.
115. D. Obolensky, "The Byzantine Commonwealth: Eastern Europe" (500-1453), (1971), p. 237.
116. "Cronica lui Nestor," translated from the Russian, commentated by G. Popa-Liseanu in "Izvoarele Istoriei Românilor," Vol. VII, (1935), p. 73; quoted by C.C. Giurescu in "Istoricul orasului Brăila," p. 36.
117. Hans Schiltberger, "Reisebuch," edition Valentin Langmantel, Tübingen, 1885, p. 52; quoted by C.C. Giurescu in "Istoricul Orasului...," p. 48.

118. C.C. Giurescu, p. 34.
119. Idem, Ibid., p. 34.
120. Sultan Baiazid to the Rector of Ragusa, 2 Oct., 1484; quoted by Xenopol in "Istoria Românilor din Dacia," p. 35.
121. G. Brătianu, "La Mer...," pp. 295, 296.
122. N. Iorga, "La révolution francaise et le Sud-Est de l'Europe," (1934) p. 14; N. Iorga, "Roumains et Grecs au cours des siècles," (1921) p. 25.
123. N. Iorga, "Byzance après Byzance: continuation de l'Histoire de la vie byzantine," p. 7.
124. A. Hânciu, "Evreii în Tărâle Românesti," (1923), p. 21.
125. N. Iorga, "Istoria comertului," (1937), p. 74.
126. Geron Netta, "Istoria comertului," (1923), p. 54.
127. N. Iorga, "Byzance après Byzance" (1971). In this work Iorga demonstrates the Byzantine presence in the political, religious, cultural, and economic fields of the Christian people in the Ottoman Empire and the fact that the Patriarchate at Constantinople represented the symbol of the former Byzantine Empire.
128. N. Iorga, "Roumains et Grecs...," p. 11.
129. Nestor Camariano, "Alexandre Mavrocordato, le Grand Dragoman: son activité diplomatique, (1673-1709)," pp. 22, 25.
130. Georges Young, "Constantinople depuis les origines jusqu'à nos jours" pp. 222, 224.
131. Ch. de Peyssonel, "Traité sur le commerce de la Mer Noire," (1787), p. 203.
132. From the report of the Sardinian Consul at Brăila, 5 Febr., 1862; in D. Bodin, "Documente privitoare la legăturile economice dintre Pincipatele Române si Regatul Sardiniei," (1941), p. 238.
133. N. Iorga, "Istoria comertului...," p. 133.
134. Cleobule Tsourkas, "Les Débuts de l'enseignement philosophique et de la libre pensée dans les Balkans: la vie et l'oeuvre de Théophile Corydallée," (1563-1646), (1948), p. 17.

PART TWO

FROM THE FIRST ATTEMPTS OF INTERNATIONALIZATION OF NAVIGATION ON THE LOWER DANUBE TO THE TREATY OF ADRIANOPLE 1699 - 1829

"The Zenith of her Eastern power and prestige."

R.W. Seton - Watson

On the importance of the Treaty of Passarowith (1718) for the Austrian navigation along the Lower Danube.

1699 - 1829

Introduction

Political events succeeding one another in Europe and in Southeastern Europe, between the Treaty of Karlowitz and the Congress of Vienna (1815), introduced the "Danube Question" into the framework of the "Eastern Question." The dynamics of both matters in Southeastern Europe centered about the dispute over the political and economic influence, with tendencies towards inheritance of European territories conquered by the Ottoman Empire almost three centuries before. The only rivals to the respective inheritance were the Austrian and the Russian Empires. Austria took the first step towards the Black Sea and the Balkans through the Lower Danube, then under the jurisdiction of the Ottoman Empire, while Russia, reaching the river banks, cut short Austria's advance towards the projected goal of the two straits through which she would have assured her free passage to the Mediterranean Sea and her political influence over the Balkans.

Initially, and without any exact determination of their geographic goals, these two rivals carried on a parallel policy, at times a common one, between 1699 and 1739, then extended to 1812, supporting one another whenever a breach appeared in the aged and deteriorating walls of the Ottoman Empire domination of Southeastern Europe. Nothing would have disturbed the peaceful coexistence of these two empires if their expansion—Russia's political and Austria's economic—had not become antagonistic. The arrival of the Russians at the Lower Danube, with an inclination towards annexation of the two Romanian Principalities bordering the river, threatened the development of Austrian shipping and expansion towards the Southwest

Balkans. Austria would have permitted the Russians to reach the Straits by any other route except that of the Romanian Principalities and Russia would have admitted Austrian access to the Black Sea or the Aegean by any other route than the Lower Danube sector of the Romanian Principalities and the Central Balkans. The moment one of the rivals reached the limits of the Romanian Principalities and of the Lower Danube, the other one reacted.

The first sign of a weakening of the Austro-Russian common political interests appeared with the occasion of the Russo-Turkish War, between 1737 and 1739, following which the victorious Russians reached the Danube by the temporary occupation of Moldavia. This occupation was followed by that of both Romanian Principalities between 1760 and 1774 when Russia, after the Peace Treaty of Kütschük-Kaïnardji, manifested a policy differing from that of the coalition with Austria in the "Oriental Project" or "Greek Project" of Catherine II.

On the basis of this project, the Romanian Principalities were to be united into a single state, Dacia, and Constantinople was to be the capital of a new empire, successor to the former Byzantium. In this way a new zone would have been created, under Russian control, which would have prevented not only the Austrian expansion towards the Black Sea by means of the Danube, but also that projected towards the Western Balkans. After 1812 when-by annexing Bessarabia Russia became a riparian state of the river, with its frontier on the Kilia Branch, Austria veered towards Turkey. During the long period from 1699 to 1812, Europe had witnessed the rise of Austria and Russia to positions of Great Powers, both directing their military potential against Turkey.

The beginning of the 1699-1812 period brought the first contact of West European diplomacy with the incipient "Eastern Question" when the Sultan appealed to England's mediation in the drawing up of the Peace Treaty of Karlowitz.[1] From this point on, the foreign policies of England and France were involved in the problems of Southeastern Europe.

The Austrian and Russian advances had been carried out in successive stages with respective success, the most important being in the "Danube Question," the gradual elimination of the Ottoman Empire influence over the Lower Danube. A political climate favorable to the later internationalization of river navigation was a result of this action.

The new political order in Europe, as established by the Congress of Vienna in 1815, also contributed indirectly to the weakening and ultimate disintegration of the Russo-Austrian coalition. Although in 1815 the Danube was not within the framework of Austria's European policy, nevertheless, the principles of internationalization of navigation, established by the Congress, later became the basis for Austria's realization of her initial efforts towards obtaining complete freedom of navigation of her flag through the mouths of the Danube River.

Chapter 1

THE AUSTRIAN AND RUSSIAN ATTEMPTS

The Peace Treaty of Karlowitz (1699).

The Karlowitz Peace Treaty,[2] signed January 26, 1699, by a coalition of states named "the Holy Alliance,"[3] with Austria as the victorious principal party of the Ottoman Empire as the vanquished, set the bases for the starting points for the first Austrian and Russian advances towards the Lower Danube. From the provisions of the treaty, the pertinent clauses covering these advances will be considered.

By the annexation of Hungary, Transylvania, Croatia, and Slovenia, Austria inaugurated her navigation on the rivers of the new territories, the Mures (Maros) and the Tisa (Tisza), with right of access to the sector later known as the Middle Danube, (Art. II) On the Sava River, which remained the actual frontier between the warring empires, navigation was in common (Art. V) and reciprocal freedom of trade was established on Austrian and Turkish territories, (Art XIV). Practically, the clause with respect to access to the Danube applied only to the Tisa River, the other river, the Mures, not flowing into the Danube.

The Russians, who had aligned themselves with the coalition by attacking the Turks in 1696, obtained the port of Azof, on the sea of the same name connected with the Black Sea. As to navigation on the Black Sea, so much desired by Peter the Great, it was rejected by the Turks who admitted the transportation of Russian cargo only on Turkish vessels.

The ban on Austrian advance along the course of the Lower Danube and Russian access to the Black Sea was due to difficult situations in which these countries found themselves. Emperor Leopold I of Austria, although victorious, was not powerful enough to continue the struggle to the total defeat of the Turks. He was obliged to transfer part of the troops from the Danube, in order to be able to carry on the war against the French, on the Rhine (1688) and the war of succession in Spain. On the Russian front, Sultan Mustafa II, although defeated, was still fairly strong although incapable of continuing the struggle because of the domestic troubles which led to the 1703 revolution in Constantinople. Peter the Great, in turn, was unable to impose too many conditions on the Turks he himself being preoccupied with the Swedish problem. These circumstances can explain the delays in concluding the treaties until 1699 even though the hostilities had ended in 1698. The Austrians and the Russians were later to resume their attacks against the Turks.

Keeping the military success in the limits of the 1699 treaty, a parenthesis can be made, within the frame of the principal subject, to speculate on the consequences of a decisive Austrian victory against the Turks on the perspectives for future navigation on the Lower Danube. Did Austria's policy of expansion during that respective period foresee her advance along the left bank of the Lower Danube by incorporating the Principality of Wallachia? If one took into account certain documents, of the respective period, from which can be deduced such a policy in the plans of some Austrian official circles, the answer would be in the affirmative.

At the January 11, 1689 session of the Karlowitz Peace Conference, Austrian General Caraffa had proposed the inclusion of Moldavia and Wallachia in the Habsburg Empire, in the Empire's capacity of successor to Hungary, which had had in the past some sort of suzerainty over the two Principalities.[4] In support of his proposal, Caraffa presented the Memorandum of some Romanian boyars who were soliciting Austrian suzerainty.[5] Caraffa's idea was met also in Count Starhemberg's report to Emperor Leopold I, in which was suggested that a peace treaty be signed with Turkey on condition that Wallachia be annexed.[6]

Alexander Mavrocordat, one of the principal members of the Ottoman delegation to the Peace Conference, not only rejected Caraffa's proposal, he upheld along with the Sultan the request of Constantin Brâncoveanu, Prince of Wallachia, for permission to attend the discussions of the Conference, without the right to vote.[7].

Although the Sultan had not approved the request of the Romanian Prince, Mavrocordat's intent was to annihilate Caraffa's proposal on the grounds that the Sultan had no right to cede Wallachian territory inasmuch as he had only the authority of suzerain over it, not that of sovereign. Caraffa's proposal did not get the support of either Leopold I[8] or that of Lord Paget, the mediator.[9]

THE AUSTRIAN AND RUSSIAN ATTEMPTS 61

Had Austria been able to annex, or to obtain only suzerainty over Wallachia in 1699, the Danube question might well have been resolved in a totally different framework than the historical one. The doubling, or the substituting of the Sultan's suzerainty by that of the Emperor at Vienna, as solicited by the Philo-Austrian party in Wallachia, would have resulted in placing the Lower Danube region to the sea under two jurisdictions: the course of the river's left bank would have been under Austrian authority, that of the right under Turkish.

Leaving aside the Romanian national aspect, the eventual Austrian suzerainty over Wallachia would have meant the inclusion of navigation on the Lower Danube in the European circuit a whole century earlier. The idea of Austrian annexation or suzerainty over Wallachia was taken up again, for the last time and unsuccessfully, on the occasion of the signing of the Treaty of Passarowitz, in 1718. The success of Vienna's policy with respect to navigation, according to the 1699 treaty, ended up being only a symbolic access to the Lower Danube, being limited to the mouth of the Tisa tributary.

The Peace Treaty of Passarowitz (1718)

Following the new and victorious war against Turkey (1716-1718), concluded with the Treaty of Passarowitz[10] on July 21, 1718, Austria took several steps toward the South and the East, as well as along the Lower Danube. The importance of this treaty for Austria was described by R.W. Seton-Watson as "the zenith of her Eastern power and prestige."[11]

With the occasion of the signing of this treaty, England and Belgium came in contact, through their mediators,[12] with the "Eastern Question" as well as that of the Danube. Among the important acquisitions[13] Austria gained through this treaty were those referring to navigation and commerce on the Lower Danube.

Article I provided for the access of commercial vessels of Austrian subjects to the Danube, from its tributaries, the Tisa and the Olt, the latter being the new boundary between Austria and Wallachia through the annexation of Oltenia, also known as Little Wallachia. Actually, only the Tisa was navigable for vessels of 50 to 100 tons capacity; the Olt was impracticable because of its rapid, irregular current and its shallow depths.

The clause, initially provided for by the Treaty of Karlowitz (Art XIV), concerning reciprocal freedom of commerce for Turkish and Austrian subjects on the territories of both empires, was extended through the new treaty (Art. XIII), with the addition of Austria's right to name consuls in the principal cities and ports of the Ottoman Empire (Art. XIII), including the Romanian Principalities.

The annexation of the port of Belgrade, considered the gateway entry from the South towards Central Europe and vice-versa, offered Austria great economic as well as strategic advantages. From an economic aspect, Belgrade was the terminal point of small volume navigation traffic from the Sava, the Tisa, the Morava and the Timoc tributaries. Its major importance, however, was to be apparent immediately after 1718.

With the annexation of the Banat and of Little Wallachia, Austria obtained a stretch of about 360 miles[14] along the left bank of the Danube, on which are situated the Cataracts, and the Iron Gates. The fact that freedom of communication, between the upriver sectors and the Lower Danube River, depended on the possessor of the above two river points determined Austria to have them as her objective, aim she finally reached in 1878 and 1883.

The Commercial and Navigation Treaty of Passarowitz (1718).

A week after the signing of the Peace Treaty of 1718 and on the basis of one of its clauses (Art. XIII), the Austrians proceeded with the economic development of the new political positions, as well as of the Territories gained. Towards this end, they imposed on the Turks the Treaty for Commerce and Navigation, signed July 27, 1718, also at Passarowitz,[15] the document on which was based the Austrian economic advance towards the Lower Danube and the Balkans. It could be maintained that this treaty reflected more clearly the Austrian policy for economic expansion and, in some measure, Vienna's political policy.

Through the clauses of Art. I, the contracting parties established reciprocal commercial relations on the sea, land, and on the navigable waters of both Empires. Concerning the freedom of navigation of Austrian vessels on the Lower Danube, the clause was ambiguous. In contrast with the freedom of navigation of the flags of both contracting parties on their maritime waters (Art. VII), on the lower Danube it was limited. Austrian vessels sailing the fluvial sectors of the Empire could go downriver only between the port of Turnu-Severin (in Austria's possession in 1718) and the ports of Widin and Rustchuk (Ruse). In these two ports, Austrian goods were transshipped on Turkish or Greek-owned vessels (caïques), which sailed downriver to the port of Brăila or to the warehouses at Isaktcha and Old Kilia. In these ports, the goods were again transshipped on maritime vessels under the Turkish flag, the Austrian merchants having the latitude of sending shipments towards Constantinople, the Crimea, Trebizond, or other ports on the Black Sea or the Mediterranean. In exchange, the Sublime Porte took obligation to give assistance to Austrian vessels in exceptional situations on the Levantine seas, including Constantinople (Art. VIII).

On the basis of that same treaty was reaffirmed the right of the Austrians to establish consulates to protect their rights in the ports of Widin, Rustchuk (Ruse) and Brăila, respectively in the principal ports where transshipment was carried out.

The limitation of navigation on the Lower Danube and its banning on the Black Sea were not a significant impediment to Austrian commerce. Even if Turkey had given Austria the right to sail on the Black Sea, the latter could have not taken advantage of it because of the small number of river craft which could have sailed on the sea. Also, even her maritime commercial fleet, with this home-port of Fiume, was to large enough to include the Black Sea in its sphere of activity. The Austrian fleet at that time was still in the developmental stage. Furthermore, the great natural obstacles, from the Cataracts and the Iron Gates on, hampered the navigation of vessels of larger tonnage towards the Lower Danube.

Political and commercial considerations were behind the Turk limitations of navigation of Austrian vessels to certain ports and warehouses and denial of their access to the Black Sea. Despite the Sublime Porte's lack of any special interest in commercial matters, the perspective of a possible Austrian rivalry could not be overlooked, even though in 1718 the Turkish and Greek-owned river vessels in the Ottoman Empire dominated the traffic.

The political aspect arose from a special situation brought about by Vienna's foreign aims, as well as by the tendencies and activities of certain political circles in the Romanian Principalities towards replacing the Ottoman suzerainty with an Austrian or Russian one. In order to prevent such a development, the Sublime Porte replaced the Romanian princes, leaders of the two Principalities of Moldavia and Wallachia, with persons that could be trusted, thus establishing the so-called "Phanariot" period, which lasted over a century (1711-1821).

The transhipment of Austrian goods in ports designated by the Turks can also be attributed to the measure of political precaution. All these ports[16] were under direct Turkish control, being under the Sultan's sovereignty. However, transshipment was not permitted in ports along the left bank of the Lower Danube because under

Wallachia's suzerainty would have made it very easy for Austrians and Romanians to come in contact.

Some suppositions can be drawn for the prohibiting of Austrian vessels from access to the Black Sea. From the idea that this sea was considered by the Turks to be actually a sanctuary of the Empire could come the Porte's opposition to any foreign interference in Turkish navigation. Furthermore, from an international juridic point of view, the Sublime Porte was fully justified in as much as, geographically, as well as politically, the Black Sea was actually a "Turkish lake," its entire perimeter being at that time under the sovereignty of the Sultans. Hence, in spite of the increase in Austria's possibilities for commercial activity in the Ottoman Empire, the navigation restrictions on the Black Sea were upheld also in the commercial Treaty of 1718, Article II, stipulating that Austrian goods be transshipped on "... caïques et bâtiments propres à la navigation de la Mer Noire."[17]

Austrian opposition could not be based on her own means, even had a potential naval sufficiency existed. Her vessels being built with flat bottoms were inappropriate for maritime navigation, which required round or vee bottoms to fulfill the function of a keel, as used in sailboating today.[18] In general, flat-bottomed vessels are appropriate for navigation on shallow waters, such as certain sectors of the Upper Danube and in the irregular sections of the Cataracts of the Iron Gates.[19]

In 1718, it was also necessary to keep in mind another situation that might arise. According Austria the right of navigation on the Black Sea would have created a precedent which Russia, already at the sea of Azof, could have exploited. Only in 1774 was the latter able to impose on the Turks the free navigation of Russian vessels on the Black Sea, a precedent to be followed in 1784 also by Austria.

Aside from Turkish political and national considerations, there are no documents on the basis of which an exact explanation can be found the reasons for the Turkish restrictions on the Black Sea. In the opinion of a former Hungarian Minister of Commerce, the restriction was merely a circumstantial pretext, inasmuch as Turkish authorities had previously granted an Austrian river vessel access to the Black Sea.[20]

These restrictions were not unique, however, they had been applied in Europe both before and after 1718. One such example is that of the prohibitive measures applied by England through the Navigation Acts of 1650 and 1651, which enabled Charles II and Cromwell to inaugurate the British colonial system.

On certain rivers of Western Europe transshipment of goods from foreign vessels to those of the privileged cities was current practice, the right of continuing navigation on sections under feudal authority not being granted.[21] France applied the same measure on the Rhine in 1810.

In concluding the subject of the principal clauses of the Treaty of Commerce and Navigation of 1718, a clarification is in order. Complete "freedom of navigation" as it is customarily referred to, was not declared nor obtained, either on the basis of the Treaty of Karlowitz or that of Passarowitz. Reviewing the previously mentioned clauses we find that the Treaty of Karlowitz (Art. I) gave the Austrians right of navigation only between the Mures, and Tisa rivers to the Danube and common navigation with the Turks on the Sava and Timoc rivers. (Art. II). Hence, no mention of navigation on the Danube.

The sole clause of the Passarowitz Treaty mentioning navigation on the Danube was in Article I, referring only to the access of Austrian vessels to a reduced portion of the course of the Middle Danube. The words "hither and thither" have the meaning of "access" or "crossing" on a small sector, not access to greater distances.[22]

In connection with the demarcation of the Turko-Austrian boundaries in 1699 and 1718, the intent of the worlds "hither and thither" was as follows: Austrian vessels going downriver on the Tisa would get to the river's mouth where it flowed into the Danube. Thence the vessels would sail upriver on the Middle Danube, which belonged to the Austrians. Permission for Austrian vessels to navigate on the Tisa was necessary because south of Transylvania the river flowed through the Banat territory, occupied by the Turks. In 1718, when the Banat was ceded to Austria, permission became necessary only for the portion from the mouth of the Tisa on the sector of the Danube under the Turks.

By the annexation of Little Wallachia, the Austrians were able to sail along the left bank of the Danube, as far as the mouth of the Olt River, but no farther on the rest of the Lower Danube. Hence, in 1699 and 1718 the Austrians had obtained only the right of "access to," but not of "navigation on the river," which could be interpreted as applying to the entire course of the Lower Danube.

Only through the 1718 Treaty of Commerce and Navigation can it be said that the Austrians obtained, partially, the right to navigate on the Lower Danube. Even this right was restricted, being limited only to the previously mentioned ports of transshipment. After another seventy-six years (1784) did Austria gain complete freedom of navigation on the Lower Danube, or to put it more accurately, the right to sail downriver from her national sector of the Danube, finally achieving access to the Black Sea.

The important development of commercial ties between Macedonia (especially Salonica), Vienna, Budapest, and even Northern Europe, is revealed as a particularity of the Treaty of Commerce and Navigation of 1718, as well as that of Belgrade, following in 1739.

Reciprocal exchanges were effectuated on the Serbian route, the Semlin, the Belgrade and the Danube ports.

The Peace Treaty of Belgrade (1739).

For almost twenty years at their frontier with Austria, (1718-1737) and for twenty-six years (1711-1737) at the Russian one, the Turks were undisturbed. The calm was equally due to all three former belligerents.

Despite their 1718 victory, the Austrians were preoccupied with political problems pending in previously conquered territory (Italy) and, within the empire, with the Hungarian agitations and the problem of the Pragmatic Sanction. The Russians, in turn, had to bring to completion and organize their victories over Charles II of Sweden, the Polish problem, as well as some newer conquests. The Turks, after their 1718 defeat by the Austrians, had to take measures not only to strengthen their military forces in the Balkans, but also to consolidate the new political administrations in the Romanian Principalities.

After their economic and military recovery, the Turks anticipated new and impending initiatives on the part of either St. Petersburg or that of Vienna, initiatives that were not long in appearing.

In view of carrying out a self-appointed mission of eradicating the "pagan" domination in Southeastern Europe, replacing it with a "Christian" and "civilized" one, Empress Catherine I of Russia and Emperor Charles V of Austria concluded an alliance in 1726 which was the forerunner of almost two centuries of "Austrian—Russian parallel action"[23] in inheriting the European territories of the Ottoman Empire. Aside from the revenge which would have reestablished Russia's prestige, fallen low after the disastrous war with the Turks in 1711, the Russians aimed at advancing towards the Southern Ukraine, which was under the Turks. The Austrians were confident that the strength of their military forces would permit them to go beyond the territorial conquests and the economic positions they had gained in 1718 through the Treaty of Passarowitz. The Russians, ready for revenge, presented new demands to the Turks, namely: cession of the Crimea and Kuban, freedom of navigation through the Straits and the independence of the Romanian Principalities under Russian protectorate.[24]

The Austrians demanded the extention of their domination over Bosnia, Servia, and Wallachia.[25] Austria's mediation, in an attempt "to smooth over the disputes between Russians and Turks having been vain,"[26] in 1736 and the Russians attacked the Turks in the Southern Ukraine, occupying also the two Romanian Principalities, as did Austria in 1737. While the Russians obtained partial gains, the Austrians — through the Peace Treaty of Belgrade,[27] concluded on September 18, 1739 in favor of the Turks — ceded the territorial acquisitions won in 1718 through the Treaty of Passarowitz. The Turkish victory over Austria prompted Montesquieu to state that "the fall of the Ottoman Empire was premature."[28] Austria restored to Turkey Belgrade (Art. I), Little Wallachia (Art. IV) and with it the two key points between the Austrian Danube and the Lower Danube, namely the Cataracts and the Iron Gates as well as the fluvial sector between the Olt and the Tisa rivers.

The nonabrogation of certain clauses of the 1718 Treaty of Commerce and Navigation made it possible for Austria to continue partial navigation on the Lower Danube, as far as the ports of Widin and Rustchuck, and to have the right to transshipment in the ports of Brăila, Isaktcha, and Old Kilia, to and from the Black Sea. Navigation on the Sava River remained in common between the Austrians and the Turks (Art. VII). Commerce of the subjects of both signatories remained mutually free on their territories, Austrian merchants enjoying the same privileges as the French, English, and Dutch (Art. XI). Article XII accorded Austrian subjects the right "to go along the Danube and through the States of the Grand Seigneur (the Sultan) to trade in Persia...," without specifying, however, the right also to navigate on the Black Sea.

Aside from the efficient economic and social organization implanted upon Little Wallachia during the twenty years of occupation, continued Austrian presence in this province could have been of value to river traffic on the Lower Danube, had it been possible at that time to overcome the natural obstacles of the Cataracts and the Iron Gates and, of course, had the Turks permitted free navigation along the respective sector.

The Turkish-Austrian War of 1737-1739, as were the two previous wars, was concluded by Western European mediation, this time represented only by France, whose ambassador to Constantinople, the Marquis of Villeneuve, guaranteed the carrying out of the Peace Treaty of Belgrade.[29]

In conclusion, the war ended by the Treaty of Belgrade in 1739 did not substantially hamper Austria's economic expansion in either the Southern Balkan peninsula nor along the Lower Danube. Without obtaining complete freedom of navigation on the Lower Danube, Austria was able to retain some rights in that matter, along with those respecting her rights to commerce on land with the Ottoman Empire, accorded her by the 1718 Treaty for Commerce and Navigation.

The Peace Treaty of Kütschük-Kainardji.

The quiet on the Russo-Turkish War arena was disturbed in 1768 by the Russians, who took advantage of the difficult situation in which the Ottoman Empire found itself, due to the discontinuity in her authority. Also, existing conditions in Europe concurred in Russia's favor. After the death of Charles VI, Maria Theresa and, later, Joseph II, were faced with the war of succession (1756 - 1763) and with the trend towards expansion of Prussia, which had developed into a great power under Frederick II, French political influence was not strongly concentrated in Southeast Europe and England, satisfied with her commercial relations with Russia in the Baltic Sea, favored any initiatives which could strengthen Turkish dependence upon England.

Under these favorable international conditions and with the propaganda of revolt among the Christian peoples of the Balkans under the Turkish yoke, the geographic area of Southeast Europe remained open to Catherine II's initiative to continue Peter the Great's chief aim of gaining freedom of navigation on the Black Sea and passage to the Mediterranean.

Without any declaration of war, in the summer of 1768 the Russian armies attacked Turkish positions in the Southwest Ukraine and, reoccupied the two Romanian Principalities, crossing the Danube as far as Southern Bulgaria. After five years of hostilities, the Turks petitioned on July 6, 1773 for an armistice, followed by the Peace Treaty of Kütschük-Kainardji[30] of July 21, 1774.[31] The date for signing the treaty was set by Catherine II in memory of Peter the Great, who had signed the humiliating Treaty of Husi (Moldavia) on July 21, 1711, after losing the war with the Turks.

With this treaty, Catherine II concluded the penultimate chapter of the plan, the realization of which Peter had not lived to see, that is, control over the maritime coast of the Ukraine and domination over the Black Sea. From this treaty certain clauses referring to commerce and navigation on the lines of communication and in the territories under the control of the Ottoman Empire will be discussed further.

Through the clauses of Article XI, Russia and Turkey established reciprocally their freedom of navigation on the waters of communication in their empires, as well as of commercial activity in their ports "...even as far as to sail on the Danube River."

Two comments can be made concerning this clause. The correct names of the two important straits — Bosphorus and Dardanelles — were replaced by the Russians with "canals and passages" linking the Black Sea and the "White Sea"[32] as though there existed other water connections between the two seas. It is possible that the intent behind these substitutions was the apparent concealment of a situation displeasing to the English and French, who considered the two Straits as barriers to the Mediterranean.

A second observation can be made concerning Russian penetration into the Mediterranean economic area of the Ottoman Empire and that of English and French interests. In matters of commerce and navigation, Turkey was obliged to accord Russian citizens "all the advantages and privileges enjoyed by the nations more liked by the Sublime Porte and which she favors the most in commercial privileges, such as the French and the English." Furthermore, Turkey had to guarantee the commercial relations which Russia was to have initiated later with Tripoli, Tunis, and Algiers (Art. XII).

Aside from free passage into the ports of the Ottoman Empire, Russia also obtained for her commercial vessels" all assistance as is given the most friendly of nations" (Art. XI). To protect the activity of Russian ships and to support the commercial interests of her subjects, Russia also gained the right to establish consulates and vice-consulates" in all places where the Russian Empire shall judge it expedient..." (Art. XI).

A secret clause of the same treaty provided for the right of any Greek vessel, regardless of the citizenship of its owner, to fly the Russian flag, navigating under its protection the entire line of communication on water in the Ottoman Empire, including the Lower Danube.[33] Besides supplanting Ottoman sovereignty by this privilege, Russia injected into the economic territory of the Ottoman Empire a Trojan Horse, thereby gaining a double advantage.

As is known, until Greece became independent, the great majority of Greek shipowners and sailors, with some exceptions, were under the citizenship of the conquerors, that is, the Ottoman Empire. Also well-known is the fact that the hope and faith of the Greeks for their liberation from the Turks lay in the Russians. The Greek element was the most active in the Russian propaganda activities in the Balkans against the Turks.

By flying the Russian flag on Greek vessels, Russia indirectly increased her potential for transport facilities, at the same time getting a measure of control over the Turkish economy, in which Greeks held important positions.

In one study it is noted that, at the beginning of the ninteenth century, the majority of the Greek-owned vessels of the fleet coming from Balkan regions flew the Russian flag, clearly showing the numerical superiority of such vessels over the Russian ones or those of other flags.[34]

The Russian consul to Constantinople reported in 1812 that, of approximately one thousand ships sailing on the Black and the Aegean Seas flying the Russian flag, the majority of them were Greek.[35]

Those same Greek vessels served Russia in her commercial ties with England, rivalling the British flag. Later, when Russia became allied with England, the Greek vessels held an important role in supporting the British blockade, during the Napoleonic War, despite the activities of some Greek shipowners running the blockade and reaping enormous profits.

In 1783, the Russians strengthened the privileges obtained through the clauses of the 1774 treaty by signing the Convention of Commerce and Navigation with the Turks. The latter treaty represented the regulation for clarification of the clauses of Article XI of the 1774 treaty and the contents of its eighty-one articles were tied to the concept of its preamble, that "en prenant pour base le contenu des capitulations accordées aux Français et aux Anglais, qu'on adopterait autant que possible à la nature du commerce de la Russie."

Although Austria, through the treaties of Karlowitz and Passarowitz, had inaugurated the beginning of her economic penetration into the Lower Danube valley, Russia, through the Treaty of 1774 gained political ascendancy on the Black Sea and the Lower Danube. Because of the peasant revolt led by Purgachon[36] in 1773 and the problems raised by the first partition of Poland, Catherine II was prevented from extending her territorial domination to the Danube. Nevertheless, she did gain from the 1774 treaty the protectorate over the Romanian Principalities which bordered the river.

From the contents of the Treaty of 1774, there emerged an important feature of the Russian political tendency: that of obtaining equal treatment with England and France in the Mediterranean and in the Ottoman Empire.

THE AUSTRIAN AND RUSSIAN ATTEMPTS

The Treaty of Kütschück-Kainardji was, hence, a "landmark in the history of the Eastern Question"[37] and "the Road to Byzantium,"[38] that is, Constantinople.

The Peace Treaties of Sistov (1791) and Iasi (1792).

After her great success in 1774, Catherine II actively resumed her plan to break up the Ottoman Empire. The only monarch desirous of going along with her was Joseph II of Austria, with whom she would have shared the results. Among the vast plans of both monarchs were the organization and development of the communication lines of their empires. Catherine, who in 1774 had gained freedom of navigation on the Black Sea and through the two Straits, aimed at conquering the entire north coast of the Black Sea.

Joseph II, in turn, continued the social, economic and even religious reforms brought about by his mother, Maria Theresa. Among other things, these included extending navigation on the Mediterranean towards far-off seas and increasing possibilities of passage into the Black Sea through the Lower Danube.

The port of Trieste, occupied by Austria, was reorganized in 1739 to service that country's naval fleet, then in full development. That same year, twelve commercial vessels had already been scheduled for the route to India, the intent being to establish an Austrian base on the Islands of Nicobar, in the Gulf of Bengal. There, the newly created Austrian East Indian Company was to carry on its activity.[39] However, the failure of the company, as well as that of the Osten Company,[40] determined Austria to direct greater attention towards the Lower Danube and the development of communication lines on land towards the shores of the Adriatic and the Danube.[41] Hence, the possibilities of navigation towards the Lower-Danube — won in 1718 and lost in 1739, — including the ports of Belgrade and Orsova — had to be reincorporated in the Austrian plans for expansion. In order to realize these new aims, the Austro-Russian coalition had again to act against Turkey.

The new Austro-Turkish was was ended by the Treaty of Sistov, August 4, 1791.[42] In exchange for the evacuation of Austrian troops from the Romanian Principalities. Austrian won also the possession of the Danube port of Orsova, a very important site for organization of transports towards ports of transshipment previously set by the Treaty of Passarowitz. The most important acquisition, however, was the confirmation of Austria's rights to navigation on the Black Sea, previously accorded by the Treaty for Commerce and Navigation concluded at Constantinople on February 24, 1784.[43]

The Russians, through the January 9, 1792 Treaty of Iasi, acquired from the Turks the maritime coast of the Ukraine, between the Bug and the Dniester rivers.[44] With the Dniester border, the Russians were now about one hundred miles from Kilia, the northern branch of the Lower Danube, which they were to reach in 1812.

The Peace Treaty of Bucharest (1812). Russia becomes a riparian state of the Lower Danube.

The importance of the Treaty of Bucharest lies in the Russian acquisition of the geographic position of a riparian state to the Lower Danube, through the Kilia Branch.

This new advance was the result of a crucial European political complexity at the beginning of the nineteenth century. The component problems of this complex situation were varied, being created by the confrontation of two main political forces: on the one hand, the continent-wide expansion of Napoleon I's France and, on the other, the European coalition aimed at annihilating it. Parallel with the development of these two principal powers were those of Austria and Russia, localized in Southeast Europe, with the epicenter at the Lower Danube. To reach the Lower Danube, Russia had to invoke some pretext in order to reoccupy the Romanian Principalities. The opportunity arose, within the legality of certain clauses of the latest treaty concluded with Turkey, when the latter violated those clauses without any intention of provoking armed confrontation.

In accord with the provisions of the Kütshück-Kaïnardji Treaty, and of other Conventions, especially that of 1802, Russia acquired the "right of intercession" in appointing or dispossessing the Phanariot Hospodars of the Romanian Principalities.[45] In August 1806, the Sultan, at the request of the French Ambassador Sebastiani, dismissed the Hospodars who had been accused of philo-Russian activities. The reconsideration of this measure being taken up too late, the Russians invaded both Principalities, an act that determined Turkey to declare war on December 24, 1806.

The Turks, trapped between the Russians and the Austrains, abandoned by the English, preoccupied with suppressing the revolts in Serbia and the agitations of the Janissaries, lost the war and concluded a premature peace through the Treaty of Bucharest on May 28, 1812.[46]

The most important clauses with reference to the Lower Danube were those of Articles I and II, through which the new Russo-Turkish border was established. Russia annexed the part of Moldavia between the Prut and the Dniester, named Bessarabia, the southwest extremity of which bordered the Kilia Branch and on whose territory were the ports of Reni, Ismail, Old Kilia, and Vâlcov.

Through the clause in Article IV it was established that navigation "… restera néanmoins commune aux deux parties et les navires marchands de l'une et de l'autre Puissance auront le droit de naviguer sur tout le cours du Danube," including the three branches of the river.

As to the new frontier on the Kilia Branch (Art. I and IV), there are some observations to be made for easier comprehension of the controversies which were to arise later in the juridical regulations of navigation on the three mouths of the Danube. The observations also will clarify the situations arising from the regime of quarantine, introduced by the Russians in 1836 on the Sulina Branch. The subject is that of the "small" and the "large islands" mentioned in connection with the establishment of the new Russo-Turkish frontier (Art. IV).

The "small islands' are directly in the course of the Kilia Branch; the "large islands" (which in fact refers to only one: Letea with its Chatal extension) include the large territory between the Kilia Branch and that of Sulina, bordered on the south and the north by the courses of both branches and, on the west, by the Black Sea.

The "small islands" are sparsely populated and lack any economic value; geographically and in local usage such islands are called "ostrovs" (oases).[47] International standards provide that, in cases in which the territories of different political sovereignties are divided by a water-course lake, etc., their boundaries would be represented by the thalweg[48] of the respective waters, in the center of the direction of the flow in the case of streams and rivers. In the case of the Russo-Turkish border of 1812, the result was that to the left of the thalweg was the part of the waters of the Kilia Branch and the Bessarabian shore, which had been turned over to Russian sovereignty, while to the right were the "small islands," the Turkish shore, and the "large islands." Hence, these islands should have remained under Turkish sovereignty.

The Russians, however, as the victorious party, by exception decided that "les petites îles du Danube, inhabitées avant le commencement des hostilités écherront de fait à l'Empire Russe, entendu qu'elles sont plus près de la rive gauche" (Art. IV). Actually, these islands are closer to the Bessarabian bank, but are beyond the thalweg, in the part belonging to the Turks.

Among the "small islands" are also the seven ostrovs,[49] designated islands by the Russians, formed by the seven sub-branches of the Mouth of the Kilia flowing into the sea. Of these, however, the waters of Stary-Stamboul and Otchakov have a natural negative effect on the Sulina Mouth, the sole navigable route. Hence, any administration entrusted with the maintenance of the Sulina Mouth must take measures at the mouths of those two sub-branches to eliminate those effects. Carrying out such measures would be the function of the possessor of those branches, including the small islands. This dependence created problems each time the sub-branches or "small islands" came under Russian sovereignty. These "small islands," stipulated in Article IV to remain unfortified, could be used with little effort as stepping stones to the "large islands."

The importance of the "small islands" for Russia in 1812 was to be re-evaluated later, in 1940, when Russia reannexed Bessarabia.

After the signing of the Treaty of Bucharest and up to the time of the next one, at Adrianople in 1829, modifications were made in the jurisdictional structure of the Lower Danube. The courses of the waters and the banks of the Sulina and the St. George branches, as far as the Chatal point of Ismail (where the Kilia Branch takes form), remained under Turkish jurisdiction. From the Chatal of Ismail to the confluence of the Pruth River with the Lower Danube, the right bank to the river thalweg remained under Turkish sovereignty, the left bank under Russian. From the mouth of the Prut upriver to the Austrian border, the river remained under Turkish jurisdiction, while the Kilia Branch up to the thalweg of the watercourse remained under that of Russia.

Russia's annexation of Bessarabia, in 1812, raised a question: was it carried out solely because of the Danube factor, or was it the consequence of another consideration of major importance? Undoubtedly, the riparian position represented a political value, but its acquisition do not demand also the possession of all of Bessarabia.

Why do the Russians need Bessarabia? One cannot say that the need for territorial expansion is prompted by over-population. There is a great disproportion between the Russian colossus and Bessarabia; Russia has an area of about 8,600,000 square miles and a population of 250,000,000, while Bessarabia has 13,000 square miles and 2,600,000 inhabitants. The answer lies rather in the strategic needs for Russian expansion towards Southeastern Europe.

Aside from Bessarabia's directly strategic position, she represented for the Russians a buffer zone of protection for her own territory. Independent of which power possessed her and of the origin of her population, Bessarabia was a strategic region whose permanent value is demonstrated by the names successively given to her southern regions, names having meaning of passage through, of communication from and to the Southern Ukraine, in other words between Europe proper and Eurasia.[50]

If one traces on the map of Eastern Europe the paths of the barbarian invasions of the continent, one can see that the first was over the large, open plain of what is now Poland, while the second came from the Ukraine, over the shallow waters of the Dniester, crossing the lowlands of Southern Bessarabia that lie between the wooded regions of her central area and the deep and wide Danube River; continuing then over the smaller rivers, the Prut, Siret, and the Milcov, to stop in the Wallachian Bărăgan, — rich in cereals and in hayfields for the horses. Here the invaders laid in fresh supplies for their surge towards Central Europe, or towards the Balkans by way of several points of the Danube easy to cross. Control of the Delta and of the mouths of the Danube were necessary for control of the commercial traffic. The same routes have served, in the opposite direction, for the Turkish expansion towards the Southern Ukraine.

With the routes of the Turkish and the Russian expansion crossing over the territory of the two Romanian Principalities, it is easy to understand why they were annexed by the Ottoman Empire under its suzerainty and why, later, Russia occupied them repeatedly, or imposed her will upon their political matters. This also explains why those two empires opposed the union of the Principality of Moldavia with that of Wallachia, a union which could put the obstacle of an organized state in their path. Actually, this was the formula adopted by the Great Western Powers in 1856 when, in order to put a halt to Russian expansion, they adopted Napoleon the Third's idea of instituting a "Latin citadel" in the path of Panslavism by means of the Treaty of Paris, signed after the Russian defeat in the Crimea.

The Treaty of Bucharest was one of the principal cornerstones in the "Danube Question". Russian advance to the Danube being listed on the agenda for European policy in Southeast Europe, required the active presence of England and France in problems respecting the Danube. Their aims were, in association with Austria, to eliminate Russia from the Danube, thus assuring freedom of navigation.

The annexation of Bessarabia and the advance to the Danube in 1812 were to be considered by Russia her "historic rights," in support of which she would seek always to be involved in the political matters of Southeastern Europe, as well as those of Central Europe.

Chapter 2

ENACTMENT OF THE PRINCIPLES OF INTERNATIONALIZATION OF NAVIGATION ON NAVIGABLE RIVERS BY THE CONGRESS AND ACT OF VIENNA OF 1815

The Origin of the Principles

The origin of the principles of internationalization of navigation on the navigable rivers lay in the concept of the French Revolution of 1789, taken up on a conservative level by the Paris Peace Conference of 1814, adopted and applied within the framework of the new political and economic order of Europe, as established by the Congress of Vienna in 1815.

In the same way, the initiative of applying these principles in navigation on rivers of Northwestern Europe can be attributed as much to the consequences of the incipient affirmation of the liberal political concept, to the detriment of the feudal one, as well as to the new economic rhythm of the beginning of the nineteenth century.

The decisions taken in 1814 and 1815, with respect to the lines of communication on the waters, can be considered also on under the effects of two political concepts, diametrically opposed, namely: absolutist and feudal. On the one hand, there was the feudal concept of Emperor Joseph II of Austria who "pense avoir la souverainete pleine, entière et indépendante de toutes les parties de l'Escaut..."[51] and, on the other, that of the feudal lords, absolute rulers over the fluvial sectors of their riparian territories.

The philosophy of the original concept of internationalization of navigation was expressed by General Bourdonnaye in a statement made before the French Provisional Executive Council on November 20, 1792. Among other things, he stated "... que le cours des fleuves est la propriété commune et inaliénable de toutes les contrées arrosées par leurs eaux..." and "... une nation ne saurait sans injustice prétendre au droit d'occuper exclusivement le canal d' une rivière et d'empêcher que les peuples voisins qui bordent les rives supérieures, ne jouissent des mêmes avantages..."[52]

Parallel with the economic justifications, it can be concluded that the point of view of the revolutionary French Government was distinctly political, aiming at maintaining its domestic prestige and weakening that of the absolutist regimes of the countries neighbouring France.

Before being set in entirety by collective action, certain principles with respect to internationalization of navigation were provided for in bilateral treaties. In 1795 they were mentioned in the Hague Treaty concluded by France and the Republic of Batavia (the Low Countries) in 1795; again in the 1797 Peace Treaty of Campo Formio, between France and Austria; and, in 1798, in that of Radstadt Congress (1798) between France and Germany, for regulating navigation on the Rhine.[53]

Looking over the clauses of the Regulation for navigation on the Rhine, as set up by the Congress of Radstadt, the partial origin of the principles established can be found in the 1815 Act of Vienna and subsequently in all the Conventions, Regulations and Treaties concerning certain rivers, including the Danube.[54] It must be stressed that the idea, of extending to the Danube the advantages of the navigation Regulations introduced on the Rhine by the Congress of Radstadt, was expressed for the first time in 1798.[55]

In a very short time, however, within the framework of the incipient international navigation order, the first cracks appeared, created this time on the basis of the imperialist spirit, raised high by Napoleon Bonaparte. Thus, in 1810, after the occupation of the entire left bank of the Rhine by the French, freedom of navigation for foreign vessels was suspended, transportation of goods having to be carried out by vessels of the riparian nations.[56] In a way, the feudal system was revived by this measure. It also became evident that, within the framework of the attempts to free navigation from the restrictions existing prior to the French initiative of 1792, as well as in the Congress of 1815, the aim of establishing complete freedom, in the sense desired later in 1856 by England and France, was not sought. Freedom of navigation was understood and established exclusively in favor of the riparian states, not also for the non-riparian ones.

The humanitarian philosophy and the human rights, for use of the navigable rivers, which rang out from the "memorable"[57] declaration of General Bourdonnaye, referred exclusively to the common inalienable property "de toutes les contrées arrosées par leurs eaux" and "les peuples voisins qui abordent les rives supérieures...," but not to other countries or flags, as was understood in 1856 by the internationalization of the Danube. By decision of the Congress of Radstadt, navigation on the Rhine could be permitted to other countries, under the condition of the "consentement" and "aux conditions agréées" of the two riverine countries, France and Germany.[58]

The national claims of each country over the river courses had precedence over any international principle. Here, however, we find exceptions in the under-estimation of the sovereign rights of the smaller riparian states whenever the interests of the big ones so dictated. This was abundantly proven later, on the Lower Danube, by Austrian pressure, from which that of England and France was not absent, either. Yet, the riparian states of the Lower Danube, also later, did not take into consideration the commercial interests of their Upper Danube co-riparian states in the fluvial sectors and, especially, at the mouths of the Danube, whenever the latter states disregarded their sovereignty. Actually, even the creators of the Act of 1815 had understood the primacy of the sovereign rights of the riparian states.

In conclusion, it can be seen that the idea proposed by the French revolutionary concept of 1789, later resulted in the conservative idea of the Treaty of Paris in 1856.

The Peace Treaty of Paris (1814).

Among the multiple European subjects to be dealt with by Napoleon's conquerors was that of navigation on the rivers in the northwest sector of the continent, a problem pending since 1789. Given the urgent need to establish general order in a Europe unbalanced by Napoleon's conquests, the Allies at the Paris Peace Conference of 1814 set only the general framework of the problems, leaving their solution to a congress to take place in a near future. Freedom of navigation being among these problems, the authors[59] of the peace treaty concluded at Paris on May 30, 1814 established, in principle, the following general standards in Article V and in secret Article III.[60]

Article V. "La navigation sur le Rhin du point où il devient navigable jusqu'à la mer et réciproquement, sera libre, de telle sorte qu'elle ne puisse être interdite à personne; et l'on s'occupera, au futur

Congrès, des principes, d'apres lesquels on pourra régler les droits à lever par les Etats riverains, de la manière la plus égale et la plus favorable au commerce de toutes les nations.''

"Il sera examiné et décidé de même, dans le futur Congrès, de quelle manière, pour faciliter les communications entre les peuples et les rendre toujours moins étrangers les uns aux autres, la disposition ci-dessus pourra être également étendue à tous les autres fleuves qui, dans leur cours navigable, séparent ou traversent différents Etats.''

The separate and secret clauses of Article III provided that ''... la liberté de navigation sur l'Escaut sera établie sur le même principe qui a réglé la navigation du Rhin dans l'article 5 du présent Traité.''

The texts of the above two articles contain some basic decisions which later gave rise to many controversies, interpretations, and even heated discussions in all the debates concerning the successive regulations of navigations which followed after the 1815 establishment of the international principle of navigation.

The confusion concerning the expression of facilities between nations, as well as the possibility of extending the Rhine navigation system to all the navigable rivers, is apparent in the text of paragraph 2 of Article V. In reality, as will be seen later, the authors of this text understood the people and rivers of Northwestern Europe, not also those in the rest of the continent. From this text, however, it came out as a general principle which, by later extension and interpretation, was applied to all rivers separating or crossing several countries, as was the case with the Danube.

The preliminary work of the Congress of Vienna.

From the way in which the Conference of 1814 developed, as well as the preliminary work of the Congress of Vienna for the establishment of the principles of internationalization of navigation, may be pointed out some aspects.

The first is that of the level of relations between the victors and the vanquished. As a rule, at the conclusion of a peace treaty the voice of the vanquished is heard with the understood condition that the dictates of the victor will be accepted. At the 1814 Peace Conference and at the Congress of Vienna, Talleyrand-Périgord, the representative of the defeated France, not only was treated on an equal basis with the other participants, but was also reserved the role of mentor and organizer. His exceptional diplomatic qualities, has long experience, along with the esteem in which he was held by Tsar Alexander I, the Almighty of Europe at that time, must be taken into consideration.

A second point concerns the positions of England, Austria, Prussia and Russia. In setting the conservative and autocratic framework of Europe they adopted some of the concepts of the French Revolution; from these were drawn the principles for internationalization of navigation. The third point is Russia's total lack of interest in taking up the problem of navigation; the fourth is Austria's indifference towards the proposal of the eventual application of the new principles also to the Danube. Finally, note must be made of the fruitful contribution, with respect to navigation, made by Dalberg, the representative of France, the country originating the new principles.

Aside from the non-inclusion of the "Eastern Question" in the agenda of the Paris Conference of 1814 and of the Congress of Vienna of 1815, the neutral positions of Russia and Austria were justified. Russia, which two years previously (1812) had become a riparian state, would have had no interest in participating in the establishment of principles, the application of which could be extended also to the Danube. She did not consider the Danube to be within the political sphere of Western Europe, but in that of the Southeast; in other words, in the zones reserved for her own expansion. Proof of this was shown when — in the war with Turkey which followed (1828-1829) — Russia annexed the mouths of the Danube, an act which could not have succeeded had the principle of internationalization of navigation been applied to the Danube.

The same reasoning was behind the abstention of Austria, which could better serve her navigational interests through bilateral arrangements with Turkey; the latter having jurisdiction over the principal route of the Lower Danube.

In the December 10, 1814 session of the eight Powers participating in the 1814 Conference, Talleyrand proposed the establishment of three commissions, each composed of eight members, charged with the following objectives:[61]

1. "... des moyens d'executer les dispositions de l'article 5 patent du Traité de Paris, 1814 et du second paragraphe de l'article 3 secret du même Traité;

2. "des dispositions relatives à la libre navigation du Rhin et de l'Escaut, et,

3. "à l'application des principes qui seraient établis à cet égard aux autres fleuves qui, dans leurs cours navigables séparent ou traversent différents Etats."

This proposal was opposed by the Russian representative, Nesselrode, who proposed that a single commission, instead of three, be appointed, to be made up exclusively of representatives of countries directly interested in navigation problems.[62]

The Nesselrode proposal being approved, the Committee on International Rivers was established, composed of Lord Clancarty (England), Baron Wessenberg (Austria), Baron de Humboldt (Prussia), and the Duke of Dalberg (France).[63] Hence, instead of twenty-four members of the committee proposed by Talleyrand, the number was reduced to four, among whom the most active were Dalberg and Humboldt, the representatives of the countries most involved in disputes over navigation on the Rhine. The Secretary of the Committee was Counselor Martens, A Russian jurist.[64]

As to Talleyrand's role, the opinion of Ch. Depuis appears to be correct concerning the contribution of the former to the editing of the 1814 Treaty clauses relative to navigation and his influence on the representative of France in the Committee on International Rivers.[65]

Although Talleyrand did not take part personally in the debates of the Committee on International Rivers, he did channel his opinions through the Duke of Dalberg, the political man he had named in the Provisional Government presided over by himself, the Government under which Napoleon was dethroned.[66] Talleyrand's conception concerning the need for juridical settling of navigation on an international level may have been the result of the relationship he drew, immediately after 1815, between the European political situation and the factor of the Danube, the river he placed in "le centre du monde,"[67] a prescience which proved to be just, in the light of the successive political events in Southeast Europe, and which was described by Hajnal to be "a proverbial remark."[68]

Did Talleyrand, in his complicated clairvoyance, perhaps include the "Danube Question" which, after 1856, was to create so much dissension among the Great Powers? Did he have in view, by including the Danube in the debates of the Congress of Vienna as proposed by Dalberg, to create discord among the allies, particularly between Russia and Austria since the latter two considered navigation on the Danube as being in their political sphere, not in that of Western Europe? Did Talleyrand aim, through discussion of the problem of navigation on the Danube, to give occasion for inviting Turkey to the Congress, in her capacity of Suzerain of the lower section of the river, thus raising the pending problems of the Near East, a subject avoided by Russia?

THE PRINCIPLES ON THE NAVIGABLE RIVERS

The answer to these questions risks not being supported by any positive bases. In any case, it is significant that the rejection of Dalberg's proposal to include the Danube in the principles of internationalization of navigation was not accompanied by any remarks at all from the other members of the Committee on International Rivers. Diplomatic silence reign over the Danube!

From the manner in which the Committee on International Rivers was made up, certain contradictions of a procedural order arose. In conformity with Nesselrode's general suggestions and with the decision of the Committee on February 2, 1814, there were also invited to participate in the discussions of navigation problems along with the four members, the representatives of the tributary rivers in Northwest Europe, that is, those of Holland, Bavaria, Baden, Hassen-Darmstadt, and Nassau, countries which were not part of the Peace Conference of 1814.[69]

The work of the Committee on International Rivers was carried out between February 2 and March 24, 1815 in twelve Conferences, the basic discussions being in connection with navigation on the Rhine, the regulation of which in some respects became the model for that of its tributaries and of other navigable routes in the immediate neighbouring regions.

At its twelfth session (March 24) the Committee drew up the texts of ten articles concerning the principles of internationalization of navigation; thirty-two articles concerning navigation on the Rhine; and seven articles with respect to navigation on the Main, Neckar, Moselle and Escaut.[70]

On March 28, 1815, the Committee presented to the Congress of Vienna the final results of its deliberations, included afterwards in the Act of the Congress, of June 9, 1815, in Articles CVIII-CXVII. Thus were set the general principles regarding the internationalization of navigation on navigable rivers which separate or pass through territories under different sovereignties.

Concerning navigation regulations on the Rhine, the Main, the Neckar, the Moselle, the Meuse, and the Scheldt (l'Escaut), mention was made in Article CXVII to the effect that "... les règlements particuliers..." (of these rivers) "tels qu'ils se trouvent joints aux présents actes, auront la même force et valeur que s'ils y avaient été textuellement insérés."

General Analysis of the Preliminary Work.

As has been seen, the Danube was not included either in the work of the Committee on International Rivers nor on the agenda of the Congress of Vienna. In general, the application of the new principles, not being mandatory, was left to the free will and understanding of the riparian states on other rivers. Mention of the Danube appears for the first time, in the framework of the Committee work, in the project presented by Dalberg.[71]

In Article 17 of his project, Dalberg proposed that the regime adopted for the Rhine be applied also to the other large rivers (the Weser, the Elba, the Oder, the Vistula, the Danube, the Po, ect.) allowing for modifications which might be necessary because of specific characteristics of each river or of decisions of the riparian countries.

At the second session of the Committee, on February 8, 1815. Humboldt also referred, in his Mémoire,[72] to the extension of other rivers the navigation order fixed upon for the Rhine, but with the reservation that it be done in the time and the measure which circumstances would permit. Hence, in both proposals, the extension of freedom of navigation on the Danube had the value of being proposed for possible future realization.

Provision was made, in both the Dalberg Project and the Humboldt Mémoire, for the principle of facilitating the communications and the commercial interests of the riparian countries, of bringing them into agreement with those of all nations.

The omission of the Danube in the Committee's final work can be attributed also to the geo-political considerations and the existing conditions under which the members understood the limiting of the application of internationalization of navigation to the rivers of Northwestern Europe. In the first place, the Danube was not in a region where misunderstanding between the many sovereignties over the navigable rivers of Northwest Europe could unlease political situations undesired by the Allies; the latter were engaged in creating a new order for Europe. The political situation of Southeastern Europe not being part of that mission, the lack of any preoccupation with the Danube was normal.

Furthermore, the application of the new navigation regime, presumed to be applied to other rivers hence also the Danube, was conditioned on "... la volonté des puissances copropriétaires des susdits fleuves" of the "... gouvernements contractants" (the Dalberg

Project) or "des puissances à s'engager mutuellement à convenir ... tant entr'elles qu'avec d'autres arrangements sur la liberté de la navigation de celles des rivières de leurs Etats qui leur sont communes avec d'autres..." (Humboldt's Mémoire).

In the sense of these concepts, both Dalberg and Humboldt suggested inviting the countries which were to sign the Act of Vienna to the drawing up of conventions regulating navigation on their rivers common with other countries, rivers not in the considerations of the Committee on International Rivers.

In 1815, however, of the countries bordering the Danube, only Austria and Russia were signatories to the Act of Vienna, Turkey not having been invited to the Congress. Hence, the only countries which could have been interested in navigation on the Danube were Russia, which had become a riparian state in 1812, and Austria, full sovereign over the Middle Danube and over part of the Upper Danube, but both Powers avoided discussion of the application of the new regulations also to the Danube.[73]

Inviting Turkey to the Congress could have extended the debates to the Eastern Question. The political reason for Turkey's absence can also be attributed to Russian policy especially that of Tsar Alexander I having been transformed into a sort of religious mysticism. Later, in the Declaration of War against the Turks in 1828, Russia stated, "... no Convention of guarantee, no political combination connected the fate of the Ottoman Empire with the healing protection reposed in civilized and Christian Europe."[74] Hence, Turkey was not invited, not being a "civilized and Christian country" on Russia's level.

Possibly foreseeing what was to be established in 1815, Austria — before signing the Peace Treaty of Paris (May 30, 1814) — concluded a Treaty of Navigation, on April 14, 1814, with Bavaria, which bordered the Upper Danube, and in March 1815, obtained from the Turks a firman extending her right of navigation along the Lower Danube to the sea.[75]

Dalberg's idea with respect to concluding navigation conventions between riparian states had already been adopted in the 1812 Treaty of Bucharest when Russia, as a Danube riparian state, drew up with Turkey the navigation regulation on the Kilia Branch and on a partial sector of the Lower Danube. The same idea also came out of the Treaty of Adrianople in 1829, providing for the two countries bordering the Lower Danube, Russia and Turkey, to regulate in common accord the procedure for the navigation of their vessels. Also within the framework of bilateral conventions, this time between two of the signatories of the Act of Vienna, was the 1840 St. Petersburg Convention of Navigation, drawn up also between riparian states, respectively Austria at the Middle and Upper Danube, and Russia at the Kilia and Sulina branches and mouths.

Even in the absence of political events and the effects of the Crimean War, following which navigation on the Danube was internationalized, the principles of 1815 would have been applied, either on the basis of existing conventions and treaties, or through new regulations between those same riparian states (Turkey, Russia, and Austria), if no territorial changes had occurred. In such a case, however, the non-riparian states: England, France, and Italy, included after 1856, would have been excluded.

England's aim, of assuring free access for her commercial vessels also on rivers not bordering her territory, was apparent even during the deliberations of the Committee on International Rivers. At the Committee's second session (February 8, 1815), England's representative, Clancarty, proposed the modification on the texts of Articles I and II of the Dalberg Project. Instead of "la navigation sera entièrement libre et ne pourra être interdite à personne...,"[76] he proposed the text "... la navigation du Rhin sera entièrement libre au commerce et à la navigation de toutes les nations..."[77] In the end, probably as a compromise, the text of Article CIX of the Act of 1815 included the phrase "... la navigation sera entièrement libre et ne pourra, sous le rapport du commerce, être interdite à personne..." without stating "toutes les nations" requested by England's representative. The phrase "sous le rapport du commerce" must be emphasized; it was later to come in opposition to the generic "sous le rapport de navigation" in the sense of being to the advantage of the navigation of all riparian or non-riparian nations, but not of their commerce.

The international navigation principles of the Act of Vienna.

In résumé, the principles of internationalization of navigation issuing from Articles CVIII to CXVII of the 1815 Act of Vienna,[78] termed by Hajnal "the Code of Laws,"[79] are the following:

Art. CVIII. The Regulation of free navigation between states bordering the same rivers, which cross or separate their territories, in accordance with the principles established by this Act;

Art. CIX. Internationalization of rivers on their navigable courses. Granting of equal commercial rights to all nations, excluding their vessels, navigation in fact being limited to vessels of the bordering states;

Art. CX. Standardization of maintenance and administrative taxes on the rivers and their mouths;

Art. CXI. Facilitation of commerce by standardizing and avoiding excessive taxation, of navigation, any modification being in the domain of the riparian states in common;

Art. CXII. Establishing by statutes the tax collecting sites.

Art. CXIII. Assignment of the maintenance of navigation as the charge of each riparian state for its own fluvial sector, with the exception of the sectors in common, which come under that of the central administration;

Art. CXIV. Prohibition of any port tax excepting navigation ones.

Art. CXV. Exclusion of the customs tax system from that of navigation taxes, the former not being permitted to be an obstacle to navigation.

Art. CXVI. Establishment of a common regulation for navigation by including the terms of the preceding articles.

Art. CXVII. Corroboration of the regulations previously carried out on the Rhine, Neckar, Main, Moselle, Meuse and the Scheldt (l'Escaut) rivers with those of Articles CVIII and CXVI.

The subsequent application and interpretation of the principles outlines in Articles CVIII to CXVI on the Danube River can be followed in all the conferences and conventions to be presented hereafter; deviations from the principles and flexibilities to which they may be subjected will not be overlooked.

Difficulties in applying the principles of the Act of 1815

Even during the period in which the Committee on International Rivers was working on the project, there arose difficulties in harmonizing the former navigation regime of the Northwest European navigable rivers with the new principles to be introduced. The most important objections were made by the small states and duchies defending their old feudal systems.

Only because of the unity in the viewpoints of the titular members of the Committee was final endorsement of the new principles possible. The six months term, set by the clause in Article CVIII of the Act, during which time the riparian states which fulfilled the conditions of the respective article were to proceed with the application of the new standards of navigation, was much exceeded.[80] For exemple, on the Rhine, the most important communication route in the Committee's attention, standardization of navigation took place in 1831, only to be revised later in 1868.[81]

The incident provoked by Holland with respect to an expression of interpretative character, seemed to be based more on underlying chicanery and excessive demonstration of political sovereignty rather than on a desire to protect the rights due her with respect to traffic on the Rhine.[82] The Government of Holland argued that through the phrase "jusqu'à son embouchure," in the text of Article CIX, was excluded the international regime of navigation "into the sea." In other words, freedom of navigation was interpreted by the Dutch to be up to the mouth of the Rhine, not through the mouth into the sea. From her point of view, Holland expected to continue applying the old regime of taxation of traffic passing through the mouth of the Rhine, a measure which was contrary to the principles of the Act of 1815 and detrimental, especially to Prussia's commercial interests.

Neither Dalberg, who in his Project stipulated navigation on the rivers "... jusqu'à leurs embouchures...,"[83] nor Humboldt, in his Mémoire where he uses the expression "jusqu'à la mer"[84] had understood that freedom of navigation on international communication routes, whether upriver or downriver, be limited to their mouths, without access to the sea. To accept the point of view of Holland would have meant creating two juridical systems, one on the river courses and another at their mouths; a policy which would have been in flagrant opposition to the rationale and the necessity of internationalization of navigation. Holland's position aroused strong protests. The question was debated also in the framework of the Conference of Verona on 1822 at which England's representative considered Holland's opposition actually a means of returning to the former system, hence, "... against the commerce of the world..." and "of the spirit and letter of the Act of Vienna..."[85]

In 1826 Metternich evaluated the sovereign authority of the King of Holland over the mouth of the Rhine to be subordinate to the provisions of that same Act for Internationalization of Navigation.[86]

Also in 1826, the French newspaper, "Journal des Débâts," carried rather unpleasant remarks concerning the King of Holland, reminding him, among other things, "qu'il ne doit son trône qu'à la générosité des monarques alliés qui ont proclamé dans le même traité la liberté de la navigation des fleuves et la souveraineté de la Maison d'Orange."[87] Holland's case was partially resolved in 1831,[88] hence, sixteen years after the appearance of the Act of 1815, and finally only in 1868.[89]

To avoid future repetitions of the Holland incident, the text of Article 15 of the 1856 Treaty of Paris carried the formula by which the principles of the 1815 Act "... seront également appliqués au Danube et à ses embouchures." In the 1921 Definitive Statute of the Danube is the statement "... la navigation du Danube est libre... entre Ulm et la Mer Noire."

If the 1815 Congress of Vienna is considred a landmark in the history of Europe, its decisions in the matter of international navigation can be evaluated to the same degree. The philosophy of Roman Law, with respect to national navigation on the expanse of the Roman Empire, was transposed in 1815 on an international regime.

Notes

Chapter 1

1. Along with Lord Paget, Belgian Ambassador Jacob Colyer also took part in the mediation; see Fred Israel, "Major Peace Treaties of Modern History, 1648-1967," Vol. II, (1967), p. 870.
2. F. Israel, "Major Peace Treaties...," Vol, II, pp. 869-882; Naradounghian, "Recueil d'Actes internationaux de l'Empire Ottoman" (1300-1902), Vol. I, 1897, No. 16, p. 182.
3. Austria and Venice on the Balkan fronts, Poland and Russia on the Eastern; not to be confused with the 1815 Holy Alliance.
4. "Colectia de documente Hurmuzachi," Vol. V, partea I. p. 194.
5. R.W. Seton-Watson, "A History of the Roumanians: From Roman Times to the Completion of Unity," (1963), p. 121.
6. "Colectia... Hurmuzachi," p. 232.
7. Ibid., Vol. I, pp. 232-234.
8. R.W. Seton - Watson, "A History ...," p. 121.
9. "Colectia ... Hurmuzachi," p. 194.
10. F. Israel, "Major Peace..." Vol. II, pp. 883-895; Noradounghian, "Recueil...," Vol. I, (1897), No. 19, p. 28.
11. R.W. Seton-Watson, "A History...," p. 136.
12. Robert Sutton, England; Jacob Colyer, Belgium; F. Israel, p. 885.
13. All Banat, with its principal city Timisoara; the Port of Belgrade and Northern Serbia; some districts of Northwestern Bosnia; Oltenia (Little Wallachia), belonging to Wallachia.
14. 140 Km. between the mouth of the Tisa (Tisza) River and the port of Bazias, and 478 Km., between Bazias and the mouth of the Olt River, the port of Turnu-Măgurele, a total of 622 Km., or about 360 miles.
15. Traité de Commerce et de Navigation avec l'Autriche conclu à Passarowitz le 27 Juillet 1718; Noradounghian, "Recueil d'Actes Internationaux de l'Empire Ottomane, (1680-1784)"; Great Britain, Foreign Office State Papers (Austria and Turkey), Vol. 100, p. 721.
16. Widin and Rustchuk were on Bulgarian territory; Old Kilia and Isaktcha on Dobrogean territory, the province being included in the Ottoman Empire; and Brăila, even though belonging to Wallachia, was included under the sovereignty of the Sultan.

17. From Art. II of the Treaty for Commerce and Navigation, signed between Turkey and Austria, July 1718,: "Comme il a été convenu que les bâtiments imperiaux du Danube n'entreront point dans la Mer Noire, ils se rendront par le dit fleuve à Ibrail, à Isaktche, à Kilia et autres Echelles, oú il se trouve des caïques et des bâtiments propres à la navigation de la Mer Noire; ils y débarqueront leurs marchandises, les chargeront sur les dits bâtiments qu'ils fréteront pour cet objet, et ils auront la liberté pleine et entière de les transporter à Constantinople et Crimée..."

18. A longitudinal timber, or series of timbers, or in a metal vessel a combination of plates extending along the center of the bottom of a vessel. It often projects below the bottom. The function of a keel is to keep the sailing ship, or a sport sailboat, in the desired direction, avoiding the lateral veering caused by strong winds against the sails.

19. Only after 1878, after technical improvements had been made at the Iron Gates, was it possible for vessels with round or vee bottoms to also sail there.

20. Details in Gyulay Ludwig, "Die Donau, Ungar und die anderen Donaustaaten," in "Die Donau, ihre wirtschaftliche und kulturelle Mission in Mittel und Osteuropa," (1932), p. 13.

21. Ed. Engelhardt, "Du régime conventionnel des fleuves internationaux," (1879), pp. 20-22.

22. From Art. I of the Passarowitz Treaty of Peace: "Let it be permissible for the freight ships of the German subjects of the same (Majesty) to navigate from Transylvania in the Danube, hither and thither."

23. R.W. Seton-Watson, "A History...," p. 138.

24. Idem, ibid., p. 139.

25. Idem, ibid., p. 139.

26. See Preamble to Treaty of Belgrade of 1739.

27. Peace Treaty of Belgrade September 18, 1739; Israel "Major Peace..." Vol. II, pp. 897-912.

28. Quoted in "The History of Nations." Turkey, Vol. XIV, (1928), p. 299.

29. Preamble of Peace Treaty of Belgrade of 1739.

30. Turkish name of a Bulgarian village south-east of the Danubian port of Silistra.

31. Fr. Israel, Vol. II, pp. 913-929.

32. The Aegean Sea.

33. Laimou Andrea. "To naftikon tou...," Vol. I, p. 97.

34. G.L. Ars, "O russkoj sisteme pokrovitel'stava i o nekotorih ee social'no-ekonomiceskih i politiceskih posledstvijah dlja naselenija balkankonec XVIII-nacalo XIXVV." Translation by Gheorghia Ioanidou-Bitsiadou, review in "Balkaniki Bibliografia," Tom V-1976, published by the Institute for Balkan Studies, Thessaloniki, 1979, pp. 329-342.

35. In 1812, among the 3895 Russian and foreign vessels in all the ports of Southern Russia, 817 were Greek and only 609 were Russian. See the above source.

36. Hugh Seton-Watson, "The Russian Empire, 1801-1917." (1967), p. 36.
37. R.W. Seton-Watson, "A History of ...." p. 148.
38. Inscription Potemkin had set above the portal under which Catherine II and Joseph II of Austria passed, to the occasion of their meeting at Mogilev (a small town in southwest Russia) to discuss their division of the European territories under Ottoman Empire domination; R.R. Palmer, "A History of the Modern World," (1963), p. 317; and Paul P. Bernard, "Joseph II," (1968) p. 82.
39. Paul Bernard, "Joseph II," p. 124.
40. Idem, Ibid., p. 124.
41. Geoffrey Drage, "Austria-Hungary," (1909), pp. 99, 392.
42. R.T. Martens, Vol. V (1791-1795), p. 244.
43. Idem, ed. II, Vol. III, p. 720.
44. Idem, Vol. V, p. 291.
45. The 1779 Convention of Ainali-Kavac, the Convention of 1802; See L. Hertslet, "Treaties... between Turkey and Foreign Powers (1535-1855), p. 762.
46. F. Israel, "Major Peace Treaties...," Vol. II; Martens, N.R.T., Vol. III, p. 397; Great Britain, Foreign Office State Papers, Vol. XIII, p. 908.
47. A similar term to ostrov is "oasis," but not in the sense of a fertile or green spot in an arid region, rather that of a bank or raised ground surrounded by water.
48. Thalweg, the line that follows the lowest part of a valley; in a watercourse, the boundary line between two banks under different territorial sovereignty.
49. Among them: Tatarul, Babina, Cemov, etc; see "Geografia văii...," p. 665.
50. The region of Southern Bassarabia, bounded by the Dniester, the Danube, and the Black Sea, was known to the Hellenes as the "Ogglos" (triangle) by the Romans the "Angulus," and by the Ural-Altaics as "Budzak" (Bugeac of present day). The meaning of these terms was that of a passageway; see Nistor Ion, "Bizantinii în luptă...," p. 712, (20).
51. Excerpt of demands of Joseph II transmitted by the Government in Brussels to the United Provinces; quoted by H. Hajnal in "The Danube, its Historical, Political and Economic Importance," (1920), p. 24.
52. From the declarations of General Bourdonnaye recorded in the November 20, 1792, Decree of the "Conseil executif provisoire de France"; quoted by H. Hajnal in "The Danube...," p. 26, and Ed. Engelhardt, "Histoire du droit...," p. 51.
53. Ed. Engelhardt, "Histoire du droit...," pp. 51, 52.
54. Idem, ibid., pp. 50-53.
55. "Congrès de Radstadt," 1798, extrait de la note des Ministres Français à la députation de l'Empire du 14 Floréal de l'an V1 in "La Question du Danube," M.A.E., p. 2.
56. Ed. Engelhardt, "Histoire du droit...," p. 62.

57. Expression used by Ed. Engelhardt, "Histoire du droit...," p. 51.
58. From the clauses of the Treaty of Radstadt; quoted by Ed. Engelhardt in "Histoire du droit...," p. 52.
59. England, Austria, France, Portugal, Prussia, Russia, Spain, Sweden.
60. Hertsler, "Map of Europe by Treaty," Vol. I, 1875, p. 8.; "La Question du Danube," M.A.E., p. 5.; D. Sturdza, "Recueil...," p. 1.
61. Extrait du V-ième Protocole de la séance du 10 décembre 1814 des Plénipotentiaires des huit Puissances, signataires du Traité de Paris; in "La Question du Danube," M.A.E., pp. 5, 6.
62. Vl-ième Protocole de la séance du 14 décembre 1814, des Plénipotentiaires des huit Puissances..."; in "La Question du Danube," M.A.E., p. 6.
63. Ibid., p. 6.
64. "Committee on International Rivers," Vienna, 2 February 1815 in "La Question du Danube," M.A.E., p. 6.
65. Ch. Depuis, "Le Ministère de Talleyrand en 1814," Vol. I., p. 374; quoted by H. Hajnal in "Le Droit...," p. 14, note 2.
66. H. Nicolson, "The Congress of Vienna," (1965), p. 86.
67. Quoted previously.
68. H. Hajnal, "The Danube, its...," p. 3.
69. "Procès Verbal de la première Conférence de la Commission relative à la libre navigation des rivières" (Committee on International Rivers); in "La Question du Danube," M.A.E., p. 7.
70. Sessions of February 2, 8, 20, 23, 24, 28, and 3, 14, 16, 20, 22 and 24 March 1815.
71. The Dalberg Project: "Projet d'articles pour le règlement de ce qui concerne la navigation des grands fleuves traversant plusieurs territoires," Annexe 1, au Procès-Verbal de la première Conférence de la Commission relative à la libre navigation des rivières"; in "La Question du Danube," M.A.E., p. 7.
72. Mémoire Humboldt: "Mémoire préparatoire sur le travail de la Commission de navigation, présenté par M. Humboldt" Annexe 1, au Procès-Verbal de la deuxième Conférence de la Commission pour la libre navigation des rivières, séance du 8 Février 1815, (Vienna); in "La Question du Danube," M.A.E., p. 12.
73. Vl-ième Protocole de la séance du 14 Décembre 1814, des Plénipotentiaires des huit Puissances signataires du Traité de Paris (1814); "La Question du Danube," M.A.E., p. 6.
74. From Russia's Declaration of War on Turkey in 1828; in Hertslet, "The Map of Europe by Treaty," Vol. II, p. 777.
75. H. Hajnal, "The Danube...," p. 53, note 2.
76. Dalberg Project.
77. Procès-Verbal de la deuxième Conférence de la Commission pour la libre navigation des rivières, séance du 8 Février 1815; "La Question du Danube," M.A.E., p. 10.

78. Hertslet, "Map of Europe...," Vol. II, (1815), pp. 269-271; D. Sturdza, "Recueil...," pp. 2-4; "La Question du Danube" M.A.E., p. 113. Also termed the "Treaty of Vienna, of 1815." The act was signed by England, Austria, France, Portugal, Prussia, Russia, Sweden and Spain.

79. H. Hajnal, "The Danube...," p. 46.

80. The Elba, in 1821, the Ems, 1843; the Escaut, 1839, 1842, 1863; the Prut, 1866, 1871, 1895, etc.; H. Hajnal, "The Danube...," p. 53; D. Sturdza, "Recueil...," pp. 561, 575, 596, 760, 768.

81. Details in H. Hajnal, "The Danube...," pp. 52 and 53; J.P. Chamberlain, "The Regime of the International Rivers, Danube and Rhine," pp. 201-264.

82. H. Hajnal, "The Danube...," p. 49.

83. Dalberg Project (Art. 17), quoted previously.

84. Humboldt Mémoire (Art. 1) quoted previously.

85. Procès-Verbal de la Conférence de Verona, du 27 Novembre 1822; quoted by Hajnal in "The Danube...," p. 50.

86. Metternich's statement in regard to the Holland Government's note of February 14, 1826 "... la liberté de la navigation du Rhin jusque dans la mer est une condition expresse de l'existence du royaume des Pays-Bas et que le droit international européen veut que S.M. le Roi subordonne sa souveraineté aux conditions établies par les traités"; quoted from H. Hajnal, "The Danube...," p. 51.

87. "Journal des Débâts," May 22, 1826; quoted by H. Hajnal, in "The Danube...," p. 51.

88. Treaty of Mayence; see Hertslet, Vol. III, p. 848.

89. H. Hajnal, "The Danube...," p. 52.

PART THREE

FROM THE PEACE TREATY OF ADRIANOPLE TO THE PEACE TREATY OF PARIS
1829 - 1856

1829 - 1856

— The Mouths of the Danube River Under the Russians —

> "La bouche de Solina sera la pierre d'achoppement, si d'autres questions politiques ne hâteront pas un dénouement à cet égard."
> Bartolomeo Geymet.[1]

Introduction.

The Austrian and Russian attempts initiated in 1699 to free navigation, on the Lower Danube River and at the river mouths, from the domination of the Ottoman Empire ended, temporarily, in favor of the latter.

The annexation of the Danube mouths, on the basis of the Treaty of Adrianople, did not abolish the former Ottoman domination, simply replaced it. Russia did not introduce complete freedom of navigation, but allowed some carefully controlled and limited freedom to trickle through.

Because of the new annexations resulting from the Treaty of Adrianople (signed by Russia and Turkey after the 1828-1829 war), navigation through the Sulina Branch and Mouth, the only navigable route to the Black Sea, passed under Russian control and administration. Although not officially banned or interrupted, navigation ran up against great difficulties because of the many problems created as much by natural obstacles and the quarantine, as by Russian administration; problems the partial resolution of which depended upon the Russians.

The difficulties affected the interests of two Great Powers: Austria's economic expansion, in continuing development along the Lower Danube route intensified by the introduction of steam navigation, and England's great need for cereals because of her industrial development. The key to the success of both these interests lay in navigational facility through the Sulina Mouth.

On a political, economic, and strategic-military plan, the Treaty of Adrianople had four effects. The first brought Russia closer to Constantinople and strengthened her protectorate over the two Romanian Principalities, Moldavia and Wallachia, territorial bridges to the Balkans. The second effect was the weakening of the Sultan's influence by according administrative and economic autonomy to the Romanian Principalities and Serbia, his vassal states. The third effectively aroused Europe's attention to the consequences of Russian expansion; and the fourth publicized the importance of the Lower Danube and its mouths emptying into the Black Sea. The effects of the Treaty of 1829 were positive, in part, for the vassal states, but somewhat negative for English and Austrian commercial interests.

Because of Turkey's absence from the Congress of Vienna in 1815, the new political arrangements established in Europe by that Congress could not avoid the 1828-1829 war. For that matter, England's apathy and Austria's expectations were responsible for the Treaty of Adrianople.

The warning of the Sardinian Consul of Galatz was proven correct by the onset of an Anglo-Russian diplomatic conflict caused by the navigational obstacles created by the Russian administration, a conflict termed by Prof. R.R.N. Florescu "...the cold war..."[2] which lighted the wick of the bomb that exploded into the "hot war" in Crimea, a war among the causes of which was also that of navigation from the Sulina Mouth and Branch.

Chapter 1

THE 1829 TREATY OF ADRIANOPLE

"La bouche de Solina est la seule qui soit navigable; la Russie s'y établit son empire à droite et à gauche." (sic)
     Bartolomeo Geymet[3]

"As the apathy of the Duke of Wellington had made possible the Treaty of Adrianople, so did the indifference of Palmerston result in an even more serious blow to British prestige in Turkey."
     R.R.N. Florescu[4]

Clauses referring to Navigation.

 Articles III and VII of the Treaty of Adrianople stipulated the most important points concerning navigation on the Lower Danube, particularly at the Sulina Mouth.[5]

 Article III provided for the new Russo-Turkish boundary in the Danube Delta region.[6] The line of the new frontier started from the junction of the Prut and the Danube rivers, following the course of the latter to the point where the St. George Branch formed, thence in continuation along the thalweg of that branch to the Black Sea.

 Inside the demarcation line were included the two large islands formed by the watercourses of the Kilia, the Sulina, and the St. George, the three branches flowing into the Black Sea: Letea Island, with its Chatal extension, lying between the Kilia and Sulina branches and the Black Sea, and the St. George Island, between the Sulina and St. George branches and the Black Sea. These islands, together with the respective river branches form the Danube Delta.

 The right bank of the St. George Branch remained in Turkish possession, without the right of habitation for a distance of two hours from the bank, excepting for quarantine post installations. Military restrictions on the two islands were also applicable to the Russians.

Turkish and Russian commercial vessels were accorded free navigation along the entire course of the Lower Danube, the Turkish ones having the right to sail on the Russian-annexed Kilia and Sulina branches. Commercial vessels of both signatories had freedom of navigation on the St. George Branch. Access of war vessels to the Kilia and Sulina branches was restricted exclusively to those bearing Russian flags, Russia thus extending her presence on the Danube up to its confluence with the Prut, hence up to the border between Bessarabia and Moldavia.

Thus, through the clauses of Article III, Russia added to her 1812 annexation of Bessarabia and the Kilia Branch the rest of the Danube Delta, including the Black Sea coast from the mouth of the Dniester River to the river course of the St. George Branch.

The clauses of Article VII confirmed and stipulated the norms established by previous treaties for carrying out navigation and commerce, the citizens of both signatories having reciprocal rights on their navigable waters.

In an indirect allusion to past difficulties made by the Turks, it was stipulated that "Russian subjects, vessels and merchandise shall be protected from any violence or chicanery..." In addition, taking for example the privileges accorded England and France by capitulation regime, the Russians obtained from the Turks also the right for her citizens and commercial vessels "to remain under the jurisdiction and police of the Russian Minister and Consuls only and Russian vessels shall never be submitted to any visit whatsoever on board by the Ottoman authorities, neither on the open sea, nor at any of the ports under the domination of the Sublime Porte" (Art. VII).

On the basis of the same article, passage of the Bosphorus and the Dardanelles was declared free and open to Russian vessels carrying merchant flags. Passage was declared free and open also to "all merchant vessels of the powers that were on a status of peace with the Ottoman Empire, under the same conditions as for the Russian flag."

Also with the intent of preventing the same difficulties previously made in the past by the Turks, Russia assumed the right to secure for itself the guarantees of full freedom of commerce and navigation on the Black Sea (Art. VII). Furthermore, in case the Sublime Porte were to disregard claims made by the Russian Minister concerning violations of the stipulations, it had to acknowledge to the Imperial Court of Russia, in advance, the latter's right to consider such violation as an act of hostility and to take immediate reprisals towards the

Ottoman Empire. This clause created for Russia's advantage, a permanent motive for invoking navigation disturbances of vessels on the Black Sea, at the same time preventing the Turks from exercising their rights in their own Straits.

The Treaty of Adrianople affected the political jurisdiction over navigation along the entire course of the river. Upriver from the Turko-Austrian border, navigation continued under Austrian jurisdiction. The Turko-Austrian border and the Pruth River mouth remained under Ottoman jurisdiction. From the mouth of the Pruth River down to the sea, jurisdiction was divided between the Turks and the Russians as follows: between the Pruth and the Ismail Chatal point, where the Kilia Branch forms, jurisdiction belonged to Turkey and Russia, in a 50% proportion respectively, the line of demarcation being the low point of the river bed; the same jurisdiction held for the part from the Ismail Chatal point to the bifurcation of the water course into the Sulina and the St. George branches. The Kilia and the Sulina branches passed under Russian jurisdiction, the St. George under Russo-Turkish.

Until 1829, Russian navigation rights, on the Lower Danube in the Ottoman Empire sphere, came from the treaties of Kütschük-Kainardji (1774) and Bucharest (1812); the Austrian rights from the Sened of 1784,[7] both drawn up with the Turks. After 1829, however, no article of the Treaty of Adrianople stipulated freedom of navigation for foreign vessels on the Russian and Turkish sectors, nor was there understood "a complete freedom of navigation on the mainstream and outlets of the Danube" for other countries, as some claim. Navigation through the Sulina Mouth was at the discretion of the Russians, wherein lies a paradox.

Although in the 1829 Treaty freedom of navigation on the Lower Danube was not stipulated for all flags, it had been provided for in the Separate Treaty between Russia and the Porte, relating to the Principalities of Moldavia and Wallachia,, as well as in the Organic Regulations for those same Principalities.

Through certain provisions of Article VII, one of the secret clauses of the Treaty of Kutschuk-Kainardji was confirmed and extended. Thus, along with the rights of Russian nationals and Russian vessels to commerce and navigation on the entire Ottoman Empire territory, "Russian subjects" and "vessels under the Russian flag" were also stipulated. The latter two stipulations would have been justified had they been applied to any foreigner who benefited from being a Russian subject or being under the protection of the Russian flag, but in reality the beneficiaries were exclusively Greeks who, even before their 1821 revolution, were active in Russia's political and commercial interests.

The contradiction between the texts of Articles III and VII produced an item of juridic significance. By obliging the Turks (Art. VII) to allow freedom of navigation through the Straits to the flags of all nations, Russia indirectly facilitated the application of the regime of international navigation between the Black Sea and the Mediterranean, that is, through a communication route that was under the political sovereignty of the Ottoman Empire.

Another clause whose provisions were tied in with Danube navigation was that of Article V. The Romanian Principalities and Serbia, stipulated to continue under the suzerainty of the Sultan, the former also under the protectorate of the Tsar, were granted "a national and independent administration and full freedom to pursue commerce." As a result of this clause, the foreign trade of the Principalities, now free from Turkish monopoly, was carried out mainly on the Lower Danube.

There were a number of aspects to the importance the autonomy granted the three Principalities had for the Russians. For one, it demonstrated and justified the "concern" of a great Christian Power towards its coreligionaries under the Turkish yoke. This was the political platform under which the Imperial Russian expansion developed, to the detriment of the Ottoman Empire. Besides its importance as a Slav region in the Balkans, the Serbian Principality represented also a pinion on which to maneuver in evaluating Russo-Austrian relations, especially in view of the Viennese expansion toward the Aegean Sea, through the Western Balkan peninsula. The closest regions of direct contact with the Turks were Moldavia and Wallachia. Until 1829, four wars had been fought on and through their territories for the purpose of eliminating Turkey from the Balkans.[8]

The problems of the Romanian Principalities had become more acute, even since 1826 when, by dint of the Convention of Akkerman,[9] the Russians, along with their involvement in naming and dismissing native princes, assumed the role of organizers of their administrations under the pretext of improving the status of the people. Also, through the same Convention, Russia obliged the Turks to return some territories to Serbia. The fact that the Turks did not respect the Akkerman Convention, in toto, determined the Russians to attack them and then later, to strengthen and supplement the Convention by the provisions of the Treaty of Adrianople.

The incrimination concerning the non-respecting of the Convention is apparent, too, in Article VI of the Treaty of Adrianople, which states, "...as the circumstance that happened since the Akkerman Convention did not allow the Sublime Porte to deal immediately with the execution of claims of the separate act regarding Serbia and annexed to Article V of said Covenant..."

The Romanian Principalities were then drawn up into a similar organization, in which direct Russian control over internal problems was to be added to the administrative autonomy. On the basis of Article V, of the Peace Treaty of Adrianople, a Separate Treaty signed by Russia and Turkey without articles, covering the organization of the Principalities of Moldavia and Wallachia was signed, also on 2/14 September 1829, in the same locality, an act which was an integral part of the first treaty.[10]

The Separate Treaty could be considered an evolvement or a regulation of the Treaty of 1829. Along with two other acts, entitled "Organic Regulations," stipulated to be drawn up in the final paragraph of the Separate Treaty, it was useful for the efficient support of the administrative autonomy of the Romanian Principalities.[11] Local norms for the organization of the entire economic, judiciary, and political administrative structure were stipulated by both acts. From their texts the provisions respecting navigation and commerce will be discussed.

Brăila, restored to Wallachia, had its Turkish military-fortress character changed to that of a commercial port. In a short time, it became the most important in the export of cereals and the principal center of navigation on the Lower Danube, being also the terminal point for seagoing vessels.

The quarantine clause in Article III of the 1829 Treaty was stipulated and extended in both of the two acts mentioned above, with details for local application. Excepting territorial posts, the quarantine was imposed also on navigation along the Romanian fluvial sectors on the left bank of the Lower Danube, that is, from the right of the Bessarabian port of Reni, to the frontier with Austria.[12]

Complete freedom of commerce was established,[13] as was the abolition of internal customs duties.[14] A special clause was devoted to the general navigation regime on the Romanian fluvial sectors. Article CLV of the "Organic Regulations" of Wallachia states that the Romanian ports and warehouses along the Lower Danube are free without exception for all vessels of Powers at peace with the Sublime Porte.

This clause can be considered surprising. The Treaty of 1829 contains absolutely no provision respecting freedom of navigation for flags of nations other than Russia and Turkey. The fact that the "Organic Regulations" was edited by the Russians and the Romanians and its approval took place in St. Petersburg, leaves room for some questioning.

It is possible that, because of an omission in the initial text of Article III of the 1829 treaty, Russia ordered that freedom of navigation for all flags be included in the "Organic Regulations" or it may be that the decisive factor for its inclusion in Article 155 was the fact that the Romanian ports were under the suzerainty of the Ottoman Empire.

Certain clauses of the Separate Treaty would have been more effective for commerce and navigation if the quarantine, which was directly under Russian control, had not interfered with their application.

England's Position.

The new European political balance that had resulted from the Congress of Vienna in 1815 and the Holy Alliance, was disturbed in Southeast Europe by the new Russo-Turkish war of 1828-1829. This situation brought about the reconsideration of the "Danube Question," this time in an acute form within the framework of the "Eastern Question," with effects also in the European arena.

The Treaty of 1829 surprised Austria as well as England. Concerning Austria, the Sardinian Consul at Galatz wrote in one of his reports that Austria "...s'est apperçue trop tard de la clause du Traité d'Adrianople, elle sait que son commerce est en grande partie à la merci de la Russie."[15]

Although England's major preoccupations, during the period of the 1828-1829 Russo Turkish war, were directed to other international problems, the criticisms addressed to her diplomacy in the matter of the Treaty of Adrianople are very unfavorable. Even though the policy of territorial acquisition was in fashion, Russia following the previous policies of Spain, England, France, and later of the United States, London could not ignore Russia's advance to the Straits, from where she could set her sights towards access routes to India.

London's belated reaction to the Treaty of Adrianople was not attributed to the "hypocrisy of perfidious Albion...but to a national distaste for logic and a national preference for dealing with situations after they have been arisen rather than before they arise,"[16] a policy of "seeing and acting" in contrast with the Russian policy of "acting and seeing."

Harold Nicolson, the English diplomat, in his book "Diplomacy" presents, in general, the most unfavorable comments made by trained observers on the subject of English ministers and political figures, adding his own belief that "...the fine tradition of caution which animates the British Foreign Service declines into timidity."[17] As to the Foreign Office and the English Government, he points out: "...they are apt to prefer their optimistic to their pessimistic ambassadors, and to regard those who warn them of coming dangers or disasters as slightly unbalanced neurotic or unsound."[18] Fitting in with these opinions is that of Professor R.R.N. Florescu, who attributed to Wellington the negative effects of the Treaty of Adrianople.[19]

The alarming of London over Russia's advance came from a number of subordinate English sources. Blutte, the Consul at Bucharest, reported to H. Cowley, the British Ambassador to Constantinople, that the Principality (Wallachia)"...is now administered as though forming a constituent part of the Russian dominions."[20]

Urquhart's cardinal line indicated positive signs of alarm. Referring to England's possibility of annihilating the effects of the Treaty of Adrianople, he wrote: "...the position of the Russian was that the cabinet of St. Petersburg readily would have listened to any proposal."[21] As for the attitude of the Great Powers to that same treaty, Lord Lamb, the Ambassador to Vienna, stated that "They could have reproached themselves for their negligence in permitting Russia to install herself at the mouths of the Danube,"[22] after the 1833 Russo-Turkish Treaty of Unkiar-Skelessi.

Lamb generalized, but Urquhart — referring to the navigational difficulties created by Russia at the Sulina Mouth after 1829 — directly attacked the Government at London, saying, "...it was not her (Russia's) sight, but our blindness that was terrible...and of the belief that Russia was sincere."[23]

Urquhart's criticisms were not based on simple deductions or presumptions. He was not a simple tourist in the Balkans and Ottoman Empire regions, but a journalist and writer. He also fulfilled the function of official information agent sent by Palmerston to the Levant and the Balkans in the guise of "merchant."[24] Lord Ponsonby, the Ambassador to St. Petersburg, considered his reports "worthy of the greatest attention even though here and there he may give way to the enthusiasm which he feels."[25]

In his articles and reports, especially in "The Mystery of the Danube," Urquhart exposes London's lack of action, not only in the matter of the Russian quarantine, but also in the latter's monopoly of the entire Danube Delta. As for the supposed Russian renunciation of new territorial acquisitions, he calls the attention of official circles to the erroneous belief in "...Russia's good faith..."[26] This statement was made in connection with the Navigation Convention of 1840, between Austria and Russia.

His reports drew no results, partly because of direct attacks upon certain political figures. Among them, he had described Lord Melbourne's response to the ineffectual discussions in the House of Commons, on the 1838 Navigation Convention between England and Austria, as "a thing unique and worthy of a place in a museum."[27] His lack of trust in Russian policy and in the appeasement policy of English politicians was for Urquhart sufficient basis to say, that in the matter of the quarantine, England's position was to lay "the matter to sleep."[28]

Some contradictions arise in Palmerston's 1836 position with regard to the 1829 Treaty. Concerning the quarantine, his position against its legitimacy, stipulated by that Treaty, is apparent. In 1838, however, pointed out that "...Russia unaware brought by the Treaty of Adrianople an independent European mercantile community to the ports of countries where we had a political interest..." and "...commerce was called into life..."[29] By this remark, he indirectly referred to Article V of the 1829 Treaty, which accorded the Romanian Principalities freedom to export, an advantage which covered also English commerce on the Lower Danube. In this matter, the 1829 Treaty was legitimate, for Palmerston. His 1838 opinion was also contradicted by the difficult situation that prevented the free development of that same commerce. In 1848, parallel with the inconveniences of the quarantine, three English vessels were recorded as having sunk at the Sulina Mouth, the result of obstacles the Russians had not removed.[30] In 1851, Palmerston protested to St. Petersburg against the negative effects of the obstructions to navigation at the Sulina Mouth.[31]

Although the few English merchants in the Danube ports and Bucharest — George Bell, J. Anderson, etc. — as well as the English consuls and vice-consuls in the Romanian Principalities — E.L. Blutte, Vincent Lloyd and J. Cunningham — alerted London in time of Russian plans and procedures and of the effects of the Treaty of Adrianople, the attitude of the government circles remained apathetic. It took the failure of the Bell and Anderson Company, attributed to the huge expenses caused by Russian administration of navigation at the Sulina Mouth, to arouse the press and other London circles to force the government to take more efficient measures.[32]

The Bell Company's appeal to the Under Secretary of State for Foreign Affairs created a sensation in the political world of London, according to a report sent by the French consul,[33] and aroused the commercial circles as well as some political ones. In the end, Palmerston became convinced of the negative effects of Russia's presence at the Lower Danube, tending towards acquiring the European territories occupied by the Turks. He then "...headed the group of anti-Russian cabinet members...and propounded a definitive corrective to prevent the unlimited commercial and political expansion of Russia."[34]

Palmerston began to give his attention to the matter of freedom of navigation for English vessels on the Lower Danube only after he accepted information directly from the vice consuls in the Danube ports, an unusual diplomatic procedure, heretofore the attribute of the Ambassador to Constantinople, under whose orders the subalterns in the Balkans operated.

From the manner in which navigation through the Sulina Mouth developed after the Treaty of Adrianople, England's protests cannot be considered a total failure. It must be remembered that this treaty stipulated the free navigation of vessels of the two signatories, Russia and Turkey, but not that of other flags. In view of this exclusiveness and of the Russian dominance at the Sulina Mouth, one might ask why other flags were, nonetheless, given access. The answer might lie as much in the characteristic Russian diplomacy as in the political circumstances of the period.

Despite political, military, and propagandistic efforts, compensated by new territorial additions, Russian diplomacy in 1829 had not expected the European reaction, especially England's. Russia permitted access of foreign vessels in the hope of reducing or eliminating such traffic through indirect sabotage activity, such as the quarantine, the lack of maintenance of the Sulina Mouth, and the "procrastination"[35] in respecting her promises, as well as by creating and maintaining a social milieu for the navigational crew among the local population, all factors that brought on excessive expenditures. Russia's policy of two steps forward, one step back, did not succeed.

Referring to the end of London's apathy, Professor R.R.N. Florescu wrote, "...the panic of 1829 may be regarded as a major factor in the conversion to an anti-Russian attitude of such diplomats and statesmen as Stratford Canning, Lord Ponsonby, Lord Cowley, Sir Robert Gordon and Lord John Russell.[36] England's reaction, despite her earlier apathy, was much stronger than that of Austria, which had obtained from the Russians some temporary and interrupted advantages in navigation (1840).

In retrospect, the situation created by the Russians through the Treaty of Adrianople and related to the pragmatism of English policy, raises some hypotheses. If Russia had applied complete freedom of navigation at the Danube mouths and along the river course to Brăila, and had not aimed at reaching Constantinople, Europe and especially England would not have become preoccupied with the annexation obtained through the 1829 treaty. The new acquisitions would have been considered a "fait accompli," as had others in the past. Nor would anything have disturbed navigation had the Russians respected later the 1840 Russo-Austrian Convention of Navigation.

Chapter 2

THE OBSTACLES TO NAVIGATION AND THE ENGLISH — RUSSIAN CONFLICT

A Different Point of View.

Two different actions, one the Russian, the other the English, resulted from the development of the Anglo — Russian diplomatic conflict over the navigation difficulties through the Sulina Branch and Mouth. A different point of view, in this matter, is presented here.

The deliberate sabotage activity carried out by the Russian administration could be justified by the lack of adequate means for remedying the navigational problems, the absence of technical capability and the lack of knowledge concerning the local hydrographic character. The protests and measures taken by the English official and commercial circles were far from the origin of the real causes of the situation. While the deliberate inaction of the Russian administration was manifested by negative deeds and results, official English circles acted through rhetoric, changing attitudes and erroneous argument. In the unfolding of the activities of both there appear discrepancies in opinion and deed, ambiguities, juridic and hydrographic incompetence, egocentrism, frustration, dissimulation, all together having as a common base the antagonism between politics and economics.

Leaving aside the stereotypical incriminations attributed to the Russians as the authors of the nonmaintenance of navigation, an attempt will be made here to show the impossibility of undertaking many of the actions to eliminate the natural obstacles at the Sulina Mouth, even had the Russians expressly intended to do so. The lack of information as to the geography and the hydrography of the Sulina Mouth and, in general of the entire sector of the Lower Danube, not only on the part of the Russians but also that of the specialists of Western Europe of that time uphold the above viewpoint.

This was to be borne out by difficulties that confronted later the European Commission for the Danube, a commission organized specifically to deal with those obstacles. Even the very first members of the European Commission for the Danube reported the great technical and hydrographic problems they were up against, and only some of the problems were evident.

"The early years of the Commission, from 1856 to 1861," noted Sir Henry Trotter, one of the English delegates to the European Commission, "formed undoubtedly the most important and critical period of its history, and it was the success then attained that has more than anything else assured it prolonged existence up to the present time..."[37] This observation was made between the years 1894 and 1906, not between 1829 and 1856.

It must be stressed that the technical work of the European Commission was carried out under the supervision of Sir Charles Hartley, a renowned engineer, of European fame.[38] The problem of a new opening to the sea by means of a future canal, tying the Danube in with Constanta, the maritime port of the Black Sea, as an alternative to the Sulina exit,[39] was researched on site in 1858, but without concrete results by Voisin Bey, the well known French engineer who had worked on the construction of the Suez Canal.[40]

The directive given by the Treaty of Paris, in 1856, to the European Commission of the Danube to complete the navigational improvements within two years — an absolute impossibility — can be considered definite proof of the lack of understanding of the problems involved, rather than lack of technical capability. In Trotter's words, "it was somewhat rashly anticipated by the framers of the Treaty that the European Commission would have finished its task within a period of two years."[41]

Ed. Engelhardt, a French delegate to the Commission, expert in navigational matters, characterized the assignment as a courageous order and commented that the organization would without delay be convinced that it was embarking on a "...véritable travail de Sisyphe, et les plus impatients durent se rendre à l'évidence."[42]

An analysis of each of the obstacles, in part, resorting to the hydrotechnical and hydrographical characteristics brought out by official and private research will support this point of view. The condition of the Sulina Branch and Mouth, between 1829 and 1856, must be considered through the prism of the knowledge available at that time, not through that of today's hydrographic and hydrotechnical techniques. This differing point of view is not aimed at emphasizing personal beliefs nor to plead Russia's cause, but rather to show the scientific objectivity which proves that the navigational obstacles concurred with Russia's sabotage activity.

The obstacles which were involved in the Anglo-Russian conflict were: the Sulina bar, the dredging, the pilots, the navigation tolls, and the quarantine. Because of its major importance, the quarantine obstacle will be dealt with in a separate chapter. The collateral effects of all the obstacles will likewise be examined and the points of view and actions of the respective sides in the Anglo-Russian conflict will be taken up with each obstacle, as well as in the general presentation of the problem.

The Sulina Bar.

The navigation difficulties through the Sulina Mouth after 1829 were known in the "Danube Question," under the title of the problem of the Sulina Bar, which was an integral part also of the Anglo-Russian conflict.[43]

Technically, the word "bar" is understood hydrographically to mean the sand bar formed in the sea at the river mouths, making a sort of submarine wall up to a short distance below the surface of the water.[44]

The Sulina Bar creates and maintains a permanence the technical resolution of which depends constantly on the possibility of attenuation, supervision, and even domination of the natural forces which act directly on the Sulina Mouth as well as, indirectly, those acting on the Kilia Mouth, the northern branch of the river. The three principal causes contributing to the obstruction of the Sulina Bar are: the alluvium, detritus as well as wrecks of vessels.

Alluvium carried down by the current and deposited in front of the Sulina Mouth is the major cause. During the 1880-1919 period, for example, 25,420,000 tons of alluvium drained through the Sulina Canal.[45] The detritus carried by the current during flood stages (tree trunks and branches) gets bogged down in the sand banks and, covered with alluvial deposits, becomes an even larger obstacle.

Obstacles of wrecks are rare enough, but were frequent during the period of the Anglo-Russian conflict. Between 1829 and 1855, they were caused by accident or by deliberate sinking of the vessels in order to create work for the local residents. The real accidents were caused mainly by winds. After 1829, sailing ships of medium capacity

(200 to 500 tons) exiting from the river could be surprised by sudden gusts of wind and beached on a sand bar or submerged. Documents of the European Commission show that, in 1855, a strong wind tossed into the bars or sank twenty-four sailing ships and sixty lighters, resulting in three hundred human victims as well.[46] The lighters added to the list were those used in transshipment. Deliberate sinkings and other actions will be discussed further on. To the alluvium carried through the Sulina Branch must be added almost 40,000,000 tons[47] carried annually by the Stary-Stamboul, the southern subbranch of the Kilia, transported and deposited in front of the Sulina Mouth by the underwater current from the north-south direction. The bar, or natural strangulation of a river flowing into a sea that has no ebb and flow tides, as is the Black Sea, is a natural phenomenon which human intelligence can circumvent or reduce, but not eliminate.

To maintain the flow into the sea and penetrate the banks in front of the river mouths, modern techniques have developed the construction of canals with sluice gates, parallel dikes and continuous dredging. In 1856, through the European Commission of the Danube, Europe took over maintenance of the Sulina Mouth, the last two methods were chosen.

The Commission's initial construction of parallel dikes, to extend the course of the Sulina Branch to greater depths in the sea, did not give the desired results so recourse was made to parallel dredging. The natural phenomenon of the Sulina Bar continued to develop after 1829 and, for a time, even after the establishment of the European Commission in 1856.

In time, the English too became convinced of the special characteristics of the Sulina Mouth under the domination of natural forces, and in 1853 Palmerston, despite his earlier protests, in an address to Parliament "drew a vivid picture of Russia's negligence, but admitted at the same time that unfavorable circumstances had also done much to increase the amount of silt which had collected at the mouth of the Danube."[48]

On the basis of studies of the bar problem made by Hartley, the chief engineer of the European Commission of the Danube, the Foreign Office organized an International Technical Conference which met at Paris, in June 1858, attended by representatives of the signatory states of the 1856 Treaty of Paris, the technical consultants being Captain Spratt, an Englishman, and the Prussian engineer Nobiling.[49]

With that occasion, too, the level of technical preparation required by the characteristics of the Sulina Mouth were revealed. According to Lord Malmesbury's opinion, expressed in a letter addressed to the

British Ambassador to Vienna, the resolution of the navigational problem at the Sulina Mouth and the Maritime Danube required the work of "professional men of experience." He expressed his misgivings that "the plenipotentiaries assembled in Congress (the Conference of Paris which was scheduled for 1858) will not possess sufficient knowledge in regard to questions of this sort to enable them to decide authentically what course should be adopted..."[50]

The choice of capable delegates, stressed Hajnal, was so important as to be the object of diplomatic correspondence between cabinets.[51] To compensate for the low technical level of the diplomats, competent personnel were appointed as assistants or even as direct delegates to the Commission, England's first delegate, for example, was John Stokes background had been taken into consideration by Lord Clarendon in appointing him.[52] France selected Ed. Engelhardt; Austria named Becke.[53] It seems that Russia and Turkey did not take into consideration technical background in choosing their delegates. In the instructions given Stokes, among other details in stated, "...the works must be designated before they are executed..."[54] Even this minute technical detail bears out this author's point of view with respect to the impossibility of improving navigation at the Sulina Mouth during the period of Russian administration.[55]

Directly tied to the Sulina Mouth problem was the dredging one, acute after 1829 and still in existence today.

After the completion of the primary technical projects, the European Commission developed a signalling system to direct maritime vessels entering or leaving through the Sulina Mouth, to avoid the inconveniences caused by depth variations. The signalling system was located on a high tower on the western shore of the Port of Sulina In case of fog, an exploding signal warned maritime vessels of their approach to the Sulina Mouth.

When the depths at the bar were low, transshipment of cargo was resorted to, especially for cereals. This operation was known in Danubian usage as "limbare," "alimbare," or simply "limbo."[56] In the European Commission Regulations, it became "allège."[57]

From this summary survey one can appreciate the importance of the technical factor in the problem of the Sulina Bar.

The Dredging.

Official circles in London, as well as their representatives in Danubian ports, accused the Russian administration at Sulina and St.

Petersburg Government of nonmaintenance of the dredging at the Sulina Mouth. The problem must be considered from another point of view. As technical information of a general order, it can be noted that dredging operations are of capital importance in creating and maintaining navigable depths, counteracting the effects of the large volume of alluvia carried by the waters of the Sulina Branch. The branch receives about 17% of the volume of the Lower Danube, with a flow of 3000 m.c./sec., a volume which in the spring attains 22% with a flow of 10,000 m.c./sec.[58]

In pointing out the possibilities of maintaining the navigable depths at the Sulina Mouth, the English diplomatic representatives invoked the efficient methods applied by the Turks, prior to 1829, in other words before the Russian administration. By means of a rake attached to every passing sailing vessel, sailing above a sand bank to the right of the mouth, depths of fourteen to fifteen feet were maintained.

Cunningham, the vice-consul of Galatz, reported to Stratford Canning (1850) the Ambassador to Constantinople, the efficiency of the Turkish method by which a depth of sixteen and a half feet was cleared, stressing that he had "personal knowledge fifteen years ago of English vessels sailing out of the Danube, drawing between fourteen and fifteen feet of water."[59] In another report, this one to Palmerston, he also indicated the technical operations which could remedy the situation at the mouth.[60]

In his turn, Neale, the vice-consul at Varna, on the basis of information from Cunningham and from a former pilot of the Austrian Lloyd Steam Company, reported to Palmerston methods for remedying the Sulina problems, explaining that "a palisade existed which had been constructed by the Turkish authorities, which still further contracted the breadth of the channel and the result was a greater depth of water."[61]

Palmerston, confident in the reports of Neale and Cunningham, sent them on to Buchanan and Bloomfield, successively ambassador to St. Petersburg, as direct documentation for their interventions to the Russian Government in view of improving navigation at Sulina. It must be noted that neither the authors, nor their superiors, were engineers or knowledgeable about the characteristics of the dredging operations, persons whose competence would impress the Russians. Cunningham was a merchant in Galatz, Neale and Lloyd were vice-consuls, the latter at Tulcea and later Brăila, all in their capacity of simple diplomatic representatives. Prime Minister Palmerston and his ambassadors to St. Petersburg, ignorant of the on-site situation, took as gospel all that was reported to them.

Little can be said of Cunningham's technical capacity when he reported to Stratford Canning that the Sulina Bar was made of stone, not of mud, according to information he had received from the captain of a Russian vessel.[62] To Palmerston, he reported "...there is little doubt that a small steamboat of 20 or 30 H.P....would keep the water on the Sulina Bar at 16 or 18 feet depth."[63] Neale's report, also to Palmerston, expressed his belief that use of a steam dredging machine would have been ineffective and that more practical would be "a steam vessel of about 100 H.P. furnished with apparatus for ploughing or raking of the sand..."[64] Hence, Neale evaluated the ploughing operation more efficient than the dredging machine, the mechanical equipment used in Western Europe by the European Commission after 1856.

London's protests and interventions to St. Petersburg were justified as long as her representatives on the Danube evaluated the Sulina problems as minor ones. Cunningham reported, "...to remove the bar, nothing more is required than to stir up the mud, and the current carries it away...without incurring the slightest expense."[65] However, that same year (1850) Cunningham, becoming aware of the real problems and expenses faced, came up with other suggestions. "It is unjust," he wrote to Palmerston, "to expect that Russia should remove obstructions at her own expense when she has no interest in doing so, but on the contrary..."[66] He suggested that the countries interested in navigation name commissioners who in turn would hire contractors who, in the absence of local workers, would be foreigners.[67] This proposal, which could be considered similar to that applied in 1856 by the European Commission, would have been useful had the Russians accepted the presence of foreign technicians at the Sulina Mouth. At the proposal of England's Ambassador to send specialists and a British vice consul to Sulina, Nesselrode "...raised objections to the proposed arrangement on account of the passport and sanitary regulations."[68]

Absolutely all the information provided by England's representatives on the Lower Danube, with respect to dredging and the general status at the Sulina Mouth, was unconfirmed by the work carried out later by the European Commission as well as by competent persons. The work at eliminating the Argani bend of the Sulina Branch, reported by Cunningham to be easy to effectuate,[69] took the European Commission 16 years to accomplish (1886-1902).[70]

Referring indirectly to those representatives, Engelhardt wrote. "Les résidents étrangers des ports de Galatz et de Brăila jugèrent superflus les travaux à Soulina en se persuadant que de simples opérations de dragage répondraient suffisamment aux besoins du commerce danubien."[71]

The engineers of the European Commission who experimented with the Turkish method of dredging found it without a favorable result, which also confirmed the negative results obtained by the Russians when they had tried the system briefly.[72] Engelhardt disputed both the existence of the rake, attributing it to popular tradition,[73] and the construction by the Turks of some sort of dikes, stating that the European Commission engineers found no vestiges of this work;[74] Voisin Bey also mentioned the failure of the rake.[75]

Several observations must be made concerning the reports made by England's representatives and the effectiveness of the Turkish methods. Although Cunningham had been present at the rake dredging, none of his reports mention the season during which it was carried out or the length of time the obtained depths were maintained. Furthermore, neither the efficiency nor the practical possibility of clearing the bar could be carried out by the traction of the rake. For a vessel towing a rake to have sufficient power to advance while clearing a sand bar, a strong east-west wind would be needed, in the direction of the current. Hence, dredging could be carried out only during appropriate seasons with favorable winds, impossible during storms. The Turkish methods could have been successful with smaller sand bars and only on calm days, but not with the large bars in which could be embedded trunks of trees brought down by the current. The inefficiency of the raking method is readily seen when compared with the results of the European Commission's mechanical dredging.

In the first place, because of the winds, the sea waves, and the rate of flow of the river current, the annual average of working days for a 180 H.P mechanical dredge used by the European Commission between 1894 and 1897, was 177 days, with an annual dredge of 583,930 CM of alluviam.[76] The depths reached during this period varied between 19 and 20 feet. Aside from the impossibility of dredging such a quantity of alluviam by the rake method, not even the necessary navigable depth could have been attained.

Any practical results that may have been obtained by use of the rake were due rather to incidental natural force. During the time off the European Commission, it was reported that, in the spring of 1861, extraordinarily high flood waters swept away the bar into deep water and formed a permanent navigable channel of a depth of 17 feet.[77]

Whether because of England's protests or of Austria's — whose 1840 Convention of Navigation with Russia was expiring in 1850 —

THE OBSTACLES TO NAVIGATION 119

Russia's foreign minister, Nesselrode, promised to send to Sulina a dredge used in clearing the roadstead of the Port of Odessa, confirmed also by Cunningham. The promise was very reserved, Nesselrode warning Ambassador Bloomfield not to expect rapid results from the Russian dredge, the reservation leading Bloomfield to report to Palmerston,"...it was not to be wondered at if we feared further procrastination."[78]

The Sardinian consul at Galatz also reported that the Russians intended to respect their obligations toward Austria, in conformity with the clauses of Article V of the 1840 Convention providing for clearing of the sand bar.[79]

From existing documents it seems that the Russian dredge was a phantom one. In April 1850, Bloomfield reported it to be in the Kherson port;[80] in October of the same year he mentioned that General Feodoroff, the military governor of Odessa, would be sending it to Sulina from Odessa.[81] Cunningham, in turn, reported the dredge's arrival at Sulina, from Constantinople.[82] The reports, being based on information received from the Russians, were evaluated by Bloomfield as "dilatory proceedings."[83]

Even Engelhardt did not give credence to Russian intentions;[84] he felt that bringing the dredge to Sulina was staged with the intent to detour the vigilance of foreign diplomats in the Romanian Principalities. In the ranks of the latter there were some who claimed that the personnel of the Russian dredge not only did not clear the bar, they added to the obstruction by throwing in sacks filled with sand.[85]

After several days of work, the Russians stopped the dredging operations,[86] according to Nesselrode, because of an "absence of trained technicians."[87] Reports as to the duration of the dredging operation are contradictory. The Sardinian consul at Galatz reported the stoppage of operations in October 1850;[88] Cunningham indicated that the operations began on April 3, 1851.[89] After three days, the dredge was returned to Sevastopol for repairs.[90]

As for the lack of technicians and of coal, which were the chief obstacles to the use of the Russian dredge, circumstances bore out the Russian point of view with respect to the first, but not the second. The shortage of technical personnel, as pointed out by Nesselrode, did correspond to the real situation. Mechanical dredging had not been used previously at the Sulina Mouth, hence no specialists had been developed in the use of dredges. Furthermore, even with the Russian dredge personnel, efficient results were unattainable because of the difference between the conditions in dredging the roadstead of the port of Odessa, familiar to the Russians, and those at the Sulina Mouth.

While the Odessa roadstead was protected with dikes, that at the Sulina Mouth opened wide to the sea. Nesselrode had warned Ambassador Buchanan that the results of the Russian dredge would be negative and that the waves of the sea would push the alluvium back.[91]

His observation was pertinent. Normally, the alluvium drawn up into the dredge is carried out to the open sea and dumped there. Lacking appropriate sites, the alluvium is deposited on barges then towed far beyond the bar and dumped in the greater depths.

In an open roadstead, obstruction of the mouth by solid matter brought down by the river current, required of a dredger captain and his assistant technical personnel specific knowledge accumulated over long local experience. The attributes of a dredger captain are not limited exclusively to navigating the dredge; they include thorough knowledge of mechanical, hydrotechnical, hydrographic order, etc.[92] Because of these stringent requirements, personnel of mechanical dredges command high salaries.

Under the European Commission this specialization became a tradition. The future dredge captain began his career as a simple dredge seaman. The entire dredging operation, especially in critical moments at the sand bar, depends on the chief dredger and the dredge captain, not on the person responsible for navigating the dredge. During World War II, because of the lack of a chief dredger, Romanian authorities opposed certain exceptional security measures imposed by the Germans to eliminate from a certain position a person of other than Romanian nationality.[93]

The Sardinian consul at Galatz had listed among the causes of the operational difficulties of the Russian dredge, along with the lack of technicians, the lack of "carbone fosile,"[94] This gives rise to some confusion. The Russian dredges having been of British manufacture,[95] used Cardiff coal, not the lignite mentioned by the Consul. In 1900, of the four European Commission dredges, three were of English manufacture,[96] burning Cardiff coal, imported directly from England and deposited at Sulina, under the benefits of the free port regime established in 1870.

Only after World War I did the European Commission begin to replace the Cardiff coal with that imported from the mines of Zuguldak, a Turkish port on the Black Sea, after certain necessary transformations of the dredge boilers. After 1938, the Romanian State, which took over some of the functions of the European Commission, used coal from the Petrosani mines, again after another series of technical modifications necessary for the process of combustion. Undoubtedly, in 1850, the problem of the fuel would have had a solution, had that been the sole impediment to the operation of the Russian dredge.

It is inconceivable that after 1849 no stocks of Cardiff coal existed in Odessa or Constantinople. According to statistics noted by Urquhart, circa 130,000 tons of Cardiff coal were imported at Constantinople between 1843 and 1849.[97]

Another source reveals that in 1847 imports of English iron and coal at Galatz were in greater quantity than before 1845 and that coal had become an object of speculation because of the importance of steam navigation.[98] In the Sardinian consul's list of imports for 1851 at the Galatz port, the quantity of coal of English origin was entered as 8040 tons.[99] In other words, coal for use on the Russian dredge was available if the Russians wished to procure it. Had there been any private or collective European initiatives to carry out the dredging, neither the operation nor the provision of coal would have been problems. The fact that the Cunningham project[100] — to be financed by Anglo-Austrian capital,[101] for amelioration of navigation at the Sulina Mouth — provided for mechanical dredging is proof that procurement of coal and hiring of technicians was possible, but was refused by the Russians.[102] This rejection must be viewed as the avoidance of any permanent foreign presence at Sulina, "the sort of action the Russians were most anxious to avoid," as Prof. Florescu notes.[103]

Concerning the inactivity of the Russian administration with respect to dredging the Sulina Mouth, contradictory opinions have been expressed, among them two by Russians and one Austrian.

E. Tarlé, a Russian historian, attributes it to premeditated Russian policy,[104] while A. Jomini, a former Foreign Minister of Russia, excluded any deliberate Russian official action, accusing private initiative without specifying it.[105] However, aside from the Russian administration at Sulina, there was no private initiative, nor could any have existed. As previously shown, Nesselrode had rejected even the idea of an eventual initiative on the part of the countries interested in navigation, as suggested by Cunningham.

Defense of Russian position came later when Kremer, the Austrian delegate to the European Commission, reported in 1865 that nothing was more "groundless than the complaints against the Russian administration at the Sulina Mouth by those interested in navigation." Kremer emphasized that during the period of that administration work never accomplished before had been realized and that any lack of success was due to insufficient knowledge of the technical aspects of the related problems.[106]

A contradiction and a statement of fact are apparent in this declaration. Among the "groundless complaints of those interested" were those of Austria who, in order to facilitate the navigation of her vessels through Sulina, had signed a convention with Russia in 1840. Kremer did acknowledge the low level of Russian technical knowledge.

Kremer's statement was contradicted by Prokesch-Osten, Austrian representative to the Preliminary Peace Conference of the Crimean War, convened in Vienna in 1855. When Russia's representative, Gorchakov, spoke of his country's efforts to eliminate the obstacles at the Sulina Mouth, Prokesch answered"...les résultats avaient été en désaccord avec ses intentions."[107] Yet, one can make a connection between Kremer's statement and the need to ensure the necessary votes — hence, also Russia's — at the coming 1866 Paris Conference, at which was to be discussed the problem of the Danube River Commission, in which Austria held the leadership role.

L. Boicu, a Romanian historian, is inclined in one of his works toward Tarlé's opinion, quoting from Prince Vorontsov's archives that the navigational difficulties at the Sulina Mouth were in some measure the fault of the regional Tsarist authorities.[108] From the same archives came the statement that "...navigation at Sulina had not gained any sort of improvement from the Russian administration," and that in this matter Nesselrode had expressed his regret that General Feodoroff, Governor of Odessa, had transferred the dredge from Sulina to Odessa, and had implored the latter to cancel the order which compromised Russia's position vis-à-vis England and Austria.[109]

From all the above, one can draw the conclusion that dredging was a major factor after 1829. The formation of alluvia and their elimination presented a serious obstacle at the Sulina Mouth, especially since the sand bars being formed changed shape and position, their dimensions varying according to the force, direction, and duration of the marine currents, the winds, and other natural obstacles.[110] The dredging problem began to be resolved only after 1856, at the same time as the establishment of the European Commission. Gradually, with the reduction of the bar, the average capacity of the vessels passing through rose from 250 tons in 1859 to an average of 1056, in 1897[111] and to 1421 T. in 1902,[112] a growth to which the technical improvements achieved on the Sulina Branch also contributed.

In conclusion, the dredging problem at the Sulina Mouth remained and will remain a constant problem.

The Pilots.

England requested that Russia provide experienced pilots at the Sulina Mouth, where several vessels flying the English flag had been shipwrecked. The English intercessions were out of touch with the actual situation, not taking into consideration the physical conditions of the Sulina Mouth and by equating the technical and intellectual level of the English or other Western European pilots with that of the pilots available at Sulina. The piloting was carried out from the deck of some simple craft which towing the sailing ships, or even from the small lighters used in the transshipment operations. The transshipment operations were not delicate enough to require "well trained pilots at Sulina," as one study mentioned.[113] The lighters, being simple wooden craft (dump barges), with a loading capacity under 2 - 3 tons, needed neither pilots nor "skippers," especially since the distance between the actual Sulina Mouth and the port in 1829 was one to two miles.

Furthermore, even the function of piloting the maritime vessels through the Sulina Mouth and even upriver to Brăila could be fulfilled, prior to the regulations introduced by the European Commission, by any local sailor with real or claimed experience. According to local custom of the time, which had become semiofficial, anyone from the ranks of such sailors could proclaim himself "pilotos," just as any boatman or operator of a caïque could introduce himself as "capetanios."[114] This pomposity of titles gave rise to much ridicule on the part of the Romanian population in the Danubian ports.

The English vice-consul at Brăila and Tulcea, Lloyd, reported "...good pilots were difficult to be procured...," qualifying those available as "...persons totally incompetent offered themselves as pilots."[115] The lack of good pilots was confirmed also by the Sardinian consul at Galatz, who reported that occasionally for vessels entering the Danube for the first time, pilots from Constantinople were hired, on the grounds that real mouth of the Danube at Sulina was difficult to find.[116]

Russian information about pilots was contradictory and evasive. While Nesselrode, as was mentioned in connection with dredging, invoked an absence of trained technicians in which pilots could be included. Séniavine, his subaltern, assured Buchanan that at Sulina there was "a regularly established body of those persons (pilots) for the use of vessels applying for their services."[117] In reality, there was no body of pilots, just a band of pirates. In defense of the pilots,

Séneavine attributed the sinking of the English ship "Sisters" to the captain's negligence.[118]

Undoubtedly, the assistance of trained pilots at the Sulina Mouth was absolutely necessary, especially since the vessels navigated over the entire surface, not through the specific route of the "navigable canal,"[119] deepened by the swiftness of the water currents flowing into the sea, a channel later dredged out and marked into a route known to pilots after 1856.

From 1829 to 1856, the language barrier also created difficulties for piloting and general navigation through the river mouth. The minimal navigation regulations and sanitary instructions, written in Russian, were incomprehensible to the personnel of foreign vessels and the local mariners' vocabulary was mainly Greek and Turkish.[120] In time, after the establishment of the European Commission, there were introduced in the pilots' restricted vocabulary words of Italian and English terminology, already in use in the navigation world on the Mediterranean, eventually also in the Black Sea and Danube vocabulary. Thus, through brief expressions, communication developed between the pilot instructing the foreign captain or helmsman steering the vessel.[121]

As to the honesty and training of pilots after 1829, Stokes' description is a conclusive one. In writing of the thefts committed by transshipment workers on the Sulina Branch, he wrote, "...les pilotes étaient généralement d'accord avec eux et leur procuraient du travail en faisant échouer les navires, alors qu'en gouvernant bien ils auraient pu éviter l'échouement."[122]

The poor conditions were also brought about by the uneven and sinuous course of the Sulina Branch which made piloting more difficult. These were eased later, when the European Commission eliminated the bends in the river and improved the river banks.[123] Considering the conditions and the professional training of the pilots, it was normal that the navigation time of vessels to Galatz or Brăila took entire weeks, as Stokes claimed.[124]

No matter how much the Russians would have wanted to deny the piloting difficulties, they had to admit to "some exceptional causes for complaint with regard to the efficiency of pilots."[125] The Russian administration, even had it attempted to, could not have remedied a situation created by the existing navigational conditions. Later on, by regulation of the transshipment operations and of the piloting, the European Commission succeeded in gradually eliminating the past inconveniences.

The chiefs of the transshipment crews were named "barge skippers" and they received their license to work only on the basis of authenticated certificates attesting to their good character, their technical capacity, and their general navigational knowledge. The European Commission created a "pilot corps" of well-instructed elements, including sandbar pilots and river pilots. The former piloted vessels entering and leaving the river through the Sulina Mouth and the terminal ports of Tulcea, Ismail, Reni, Galatz, and Brăila. Because of their routine, these pilots became polyglots, able to communicate, within the limits of their attributes, with the crews of foreign vessels.

In 1901, the total number of bar and river pilots licensed and listed according to classification was 70, while a higher rank of pilot captains, recruited from the mosaic of nationalities in Sulina, reached 88.[126] The latter commanded higher salaries and larger pensions and, in the majority, were Greeks[127] and other nationalities; one of the Italians among them eventually became an admiral in the Italian War Navy.[128]

The large number of pilots registered in 1901 was in proportion to the needs for piloting small tonnage vessels, their number being much greater than that of the vessels of larger capacity. In time, the number of smaller craft decreased as the same traffic was being carried out by fewer vessels of increased capacity (3,000 to 8,000 tons). Thus, by 1931 the total number of pilots had decreased from the 1901 number of 158 to only 58.[129] Of note is the fact that, by 1930, the number of Romanian pilots had increased 43% over that of foreign ones, especially the Greeks who were reduced to 13% on the total.[130]

In summary, it is evident that, under the previously mentioned conditions existing at Sulina after 1829, the Russian administration could not have established a "Corps of Pilots" at the professional and intellectual level desired by the foreign navigators, especially the English. To this can also be added Russia's incompetence at training pilots to the level of the specific requirements of the Sulina Mouth.

The Navigation Tolls.

Aside from the other obstacles at the Sulina Mouth, navigation tolls were an important factor in the efficiency of the commercial aspect. Tolls were paid either directly by the captains of the vessels, by the importers' brokers, or at times directly to London by the shipowners or the importers. Urquhart, quoting from an English merchant's letter, stated, "...there were fees to be paid to the Russian consul (at Liverpool) amounting to near one hundred English pounds per cargo.[131]

In the 1840 report the Sardinian Consul at Galatz stated that the navigation tolls at the exit through the Sulina Mouth were in proportion to the vessel's displacement. Hence, for a vessel of 10 1/2 ft. displacement, the toll was 8 colones; for one of 13 1/2 ft. it was 52 colones.[132] A Romanian study in 1861 mentions that during the period of Austrian occupation of the Romanian Principalities, a toll of eight ducats was charged at the exit through the Sulina Mouth, regardless of the craft or tonnage; a toll considered enormous and detrimental to navigation.[133]

In the English Parliament's interpellation of Palmerston in 1836, Dudley Stuart characterized the Russian levying of navigation tolls as "laying hands on British shipping, demanding tribute and exacting tolls at the mouth of the Danube,"[134] considering it contrary to the provisions of the Vienna Act of 1815. The counsel of the Law Officers of the Crown, requested by Palmerston concerning the operativity of the Act of 1815 in this matter, was negative, the navigation tolls not being "...counter to the letter of the treaty regulations."[135]

To be noted, however, is the fact that neither did the Treaty of Adrianople provided for any navigational tolls for vessels entering through the Sulina Mouth. Article VIII of the treaty mentions "paying of duty according to tariffs," but this referred to customs duties which were subject to a fixed rate. In the text of the same article, however, it is made clear that the "duty" referred to goods in transit, transported under any flag through the Straits and "on the open sea or any of the ports or roadsteads under the domination of the Sublime Porte..." Hence, the measure imposed by the Russians could be considered arbitrary, unsupported by any legal basic. Yet, in support of that measure, one could invoke the rationale for the taxes provided for in Articles CX and CXI of the Act of 1815 and intended for covering maintenance costs for the navigation carried out there. This was the conclusion reached also by the Law Officers of the Crown. The navigation tolls established by the Russians were presumed to be for the purpose of carrying on the work at the Sulina Mouth, regardless of how it was done or of its technical level of efficiency.

Furthermore, exemption of English vessels in Danubean traffic from taxation, as demanded by London circles, was totally unjustified, considering that tolls existed at all ports, at entrances to tunnels, canals, or rivers. When taxation was among the provisions of the Treaty of Paris, of 1856, no protests were voiced. Article XVI stated "...pour couvrir les frais de ces travaux (maintenance work), aussi que les

THE OBSTACLES TO NAVIGATION 127

établissements ayant pour objet d'assurer et de faciliter la navigation aux bouches du Danube, des droits fixes...pourront être prélevés..."
Hence, taxation of navigation was justified to cover the costs of maintaining it.

Palmerston also was wrong in his opinion that "no toll is justly demanded by the Russian authorities at the mouth of the Danube...,"[136] his justification being that no provision for any such tolls had been made in the Act of 1815. The Act and the provisions of Articles CX and CXI, for navigational tolls, were not applied at that time on the Danube River.

English demands for exemption of navigation or customs tolls, after 1829 could have been valid only for the ports of Brăila and Galatz, which then were under Turkish suzerainty, a benefit of the terms of the capitulation regime; terms which in themselves could be subject to interpretation.

Not taking into consideration the counsel of the Law Officers of the Crown, J. Blackhouse, of the Foreign Office, at the order of Palmerston advised Bell, a merchant in the Romanian Principalities, to refuse to pay any taxes.[137] The order was an arbitrary one from the territorial jurisdiction point of view of those who would have applied it, risking Russian counter measures. Urquhart's comment in this respect was justified; he stated that only the British Government should intervene directly in the matter of taxation, not indirectly through English agents or merchants.[138]

While Palmerston disputed with the Russians over navigational tolls at the Sulina Mouth, Cunningham anticipated them. In the prospectus for the establishment of a private company for carrying out the work of eliminating the sand bar at Sulina, he provided for taxation only of loaded vessels, the evaluation being in proportion to their draught, the total per vessel being estimated at between 1,200 and 3,600 Colonati di Spagna.[139] Even though objections had been raised to the Russian taxation, Cunningham considered the need for such, even if the work or improving the navigation process were to be entrusted to contractors under the auspices of commissioners appointed by the interested countries. "It ought to be bound to certain conditions," he reported, "and a fair tax levied on every vessel which has the benefit of deep water."[140]

Although the matter of the tolls was part of Palmerston's direct and indirect intercessions to the Russian Government, the situation remained unchanged, the payment of tolls continued to be demanded at the Sulina Mouth or at the Russian Embassy in London.[141]

The principle of freedom of navigation, as is logical, is made up of two principal elements: maintenance of favorable navigation conditions and to the economic aspect of shipping. The Russians, however, did not fulfill the respective conditions; on the contrary, their intention in imposing tolls was to create the opposite conditions.

Other factors, too, contributed to the increasing financial burden for traffic through the Sulina Mouth. Operational costs were not restricted to the "tolls" or the "tribute exacting tolls" referred to by Dudley Stuart. Greater expenses were incurred, not only in the taxing by Russian authorities, but by the charges of private concerns at Sulina, Brăila or Galatz. To the costs for transshipment, towing, supplies of food, etc., were added the occasional services of navigation agents, ships chandlers and, at times, of ships captains connected with the agents.

Not only on the Lower Danube, but generally in all ports, supplying provisions of food, naval articles, making needed repairs, completing necessary forms at local official centers (port captains, police, customs, etc.) represented the most remunerative services for shipping agents and ship chandlers. Captains as well as crews of foreign ships, unfamiliar with the language and customs of the local markets, depended on these intermediaries whose charges were discreetly included in the expense accounts of the foreign ship owners or importers.

The expenses of commercial operation of a vessel were and are in great measure calculated on the bill of lading, usually drawn up between the exporter or his agent and the ship's Captain. The exporter's profit or deficit depended on their honesty, and fraud resulting from collusion between agent and captain, sometimes in association with the company's insurance agent.[142]

In a retrospective report made by a Sardinian diplomat about the general navigation situation on the Danube, there is an interesting case concerning the operational expenses of maritime vessels entering the Danube River. Referring to certain facilities in the Sanitation control, he stated that vessels possessing Sanitation Certificates issued at Constantinople were kept in quarantine only four days, inasmuch as disinfection of the cereal was no longer necessary, a measure which reduced the expenses since the supplies of food and other matters could be arranged for by the ship's captain directly, not through intermediaries. However, he also pointed out that, due to the navigation brokers seeking greater profits, the captains had to incur supplementary costs in the quarantine operations. At the complaints of the English Consul, Lord Palmerston ordered the English captains to refuse to

THE OBSTACLES TO NAVIGATION

submit to the procedures of the navigation brokers.[143] It seems that the situation was not remedied, by either the Russian or the Romanian authorities; dissatisfied complaints continued to be registered, even from vessels flying other than English flags.

As for the conduct of the intermediaries, the role of the English consuls in the Danube ports could have been more beneficial, inasmuch as most of their brokers and ships chandlers were Greeks, either bearing English citizenship or in the service of English importers.[144]

The English point of view with regard to the navigation tolls was unsubstantiated.

Chapter 3

THE QUARANTINE AS AN OBSTACLE

Introduction.

The quarantine regime[145] applied by the Russians at the Sulina Mouth and along its branch, as well as that existing on the Lower Danube and in its neighboring regions, was instituted because of the epidemics of cholera and the plague that had occurred earlier, during and after the Russo-Turkish War of 1828-1829.

The quarantine being the most controversial problem for navigation on the Lower Danube from 1829 to 1855, it became necessary to give serious attention to its influence on Danube traffic, especially in the Anglo-Russian conflict.

The quarantine problem developed within the framework of two positions. On the one side was Russia's exploiting the quarantine as an obstacle to navigation; on the other was England's minimizing the importance of the quarantine and even trying to eliminate it.

Admitting, without any doubt, Russian political aims, still one cannot eliminate the legitimacy of establishing the quarantine among the sanitary measures of the Russian armies of occupation in the two Romanian Principalities, as well as in those of the local civilian population from whose ranks thousands of fatal cases had been registered. Neither can one overlook, in the English point of view, the abusive and arbitrary methods used in applying the quarantine regulations, the subordination of humanitarian principles to commercial interests.

Non-application of the quarantine regime in navigation and in the river areas could have created a most disastrous situation, superimposed upon the accumulation of the consequences of centuries of war and foreign occupation, to which the people of the Lower Danube had been subjected.

Based upon documentation and comparison of similar situations in other countries, an attempt will be made to prove that the introduction of the quarantine was a necessary and justified measure. The epidemics of cholera and the plague of the past being practically a permanent factor in the regions of the Lower Danube, the establishment of the quarantine after 1829 had values of sanitary, political, economic, social and humanitarian order.

A brief description of the origin of the epidemics along the Lower Danube and the level of the sanitary methods for combatting them may seem immaterial to the principal subject of this work, but in it can be followed evidence of the conditions under which the quarantine regime worked during the Russian occupation and administration.

The quarantine regime along the mouth and branch of the Sulina will be compared with that in England, with the aim of showing some of the erroneous bases of the Anglo-Russian conflict. In the same way, the need to establish a regime of quarantine and, in general, of sanitary control over vessels, will be shown by their inclusion in legislation respecting navigation.

Only by the application, in the 1829-1855 period, of modern sanitary methods could a quarantine regime have been established which would not have been an obstacle to navigation. In the end, the quarantine did not give the results desired by the Russians in the sabotaging of navigation. Whether due to English pressure or a lessening in the virulence of the epidemics, the regime was gradually eased by 1855.

Origins and Causes of Epidemics in the Danube Regions.

(A brief glance)

The spread of cholera and the plague in Europe was facilitated by the traffic of commercial vessels coming through such regions as well as through southern Russia. With some exceptions in the Nordic countries of Europe, the respective epidemics broke out in all the other countries of the continent.

In Russia, cholera appeared before the onset of the Russo-Turkish War of 1828-1829. In a study entitled "Russia and the Cholera,"[146] the causes and effects of that epidemic are discussed. Over 100,000 fatalities were recorded between 1823 and 1832.[147] During that same war, almost three-fourths of the Russian Armies on the warfronts in

THE QUARANTINE AS AN OBSTACLE 133

Bulgaria were withdrawn because of the epidemics of cholera, plague, spotted fever, malaria fever, and other infectious diseases.[148]

The intensity of the epidemics during the period of that war would have been considerably lessened, in the Romanian Principalities and the regions bordering the Danube, if to the epidemics there had not been added the extra burden of providing food and animals for the Russian Armies of occupation, forced labor and, above all, the indolence and incapacity of the local and Russian authorities. As for the conditions of the population at that time, the comments of Saint Marc Girardin and Karl Marx are enlightening.[149] The former, a journalist and editor of the "Journal des Débâts," wrote, "Never had there occurred a more frightening destruction of lives as during the Russian occupation." As to the forced labor in which starving peasants were made to pull the Russian wagons and cannons, Karl Marx wrote of a Russian general who had declared he "was not interested in knowing how the labor was carried out, by men or by animals, only that the orders were carried out."[150] The Romanian historian Xenopol, identified the respective general as Joltuchin.

Additional information concerning the conditions conducive to epidemics in the Principalities, because of the misery in which the Russian Armies were living, could be considered subjective had they not been confirmed by foreigners as well as by Russians. Admiral Paul Tchitchagof noted in his memoirs not only facts concerning the Russo-Turkish War between 1806-1812, which had contributed to the aggravation of the sanitary conditions in the Principalities, but also pointed out the abusive behavior of General Kutusov.[151] In this connection, R.W. Seton-Watson reported that Kutusov answered Romanian protests against the requisitioning of laborers by saying, "Je ne leur laisserai que les yeux pour pleurer."[152]

The epidemic in the Danubian and Balkan regions continued to be acute even after the 1828-1829 War. It was prevalent during the Crimean War and during the new Russo-Turkish War of 1877-1878.[153]

English commercial circles were impatient over the long duration of the navigation quarantine, but did not take into consideration the fact that it became possible to discover the way in which cholera spread only because of the epidemics current in the middle of the XIXth century.[154] Only in 1875, when Pasteur — followed by Koch and Osler — discovered the development of micro-organisms, was it possible to identify the causes and means of propagation of cholera and the plague. The principal means of transmitting were indicated by William Osler as the three "F's": finger, fly and food.[155]

The symbol of the three "F's" was perfectly demonstrated in the navigation on the Sulina Branch and Mouth. Referring just to the empire of mosquitos and flies of the ponds, marshes and lakes of the river delta, one can get an idea of the conditions favorable for causing and propagating epidemics.

In the past and possibly even today, in some cases, the latrine bucket of the vessel (where such facilities existed) drained directly into the river water, which was at the same time the source of drinking water. Even if the vessels used porous stone filters, foreign matter was strained out, but microorganisms were not.

Living conditions for sailors on the Danube were no different from those of the personnel of seagoing vessels. Because of lack of space, sailors — after continuous labor of almost 24 hours — had to sleep in their working clothes on top of the bundles of goods in the hold. Fresh water was reserved exclusively for drinking purposes, not for bathing or for laundry. The food was meager and unhygienic and the hard tack was at times warm and bacteria-laden. Generally speaking, a vessel was the realm of mold, bedbugs and filth. At times, not too seldom, the body of a sailor, dead of some infectious disease, was cast overboard into the Danube, leaving behind microbes in the food, clothing, dishes, etc. without the fact being recorded in the ship's log or reported to the authorities at the first port entered. In another fashion, goods stolen from a contaminated vessel contributed to the spread of the epidemic.

All the means mentioned above for spreading diseases were valid also along the Sulina Branch where the quarantine was in effect. Here, too, there existed conditions favorable to the spread of epidemics among the workers carrying out the transshipment operations.

There can be no doubt about the low level of sanitation and the backward social and economic status of some of the people in the Lower Danube region on the periphery of the civilized world of Western Europe. An English traveller saw and described their living conditions as "decadent orientalism," evaluating them at a level much more backward than those of other lands. Among other things, he was shocked by the lack of hygiene and cleanliness in the houses and inns of some of the Bulgarian and Romanian cities and towns on the banks of the Lower Danube, especially the difficulty of bathing, because of the lack of water. He mentioned having a "sleepless night in the practical study of the natural history of various species of insects of prey."[156]

Considering that these deficiencies were the result of the social and economic misery of people who for centuries had been under Turkish

THE QUARANTINE AS AN OBSTACLE 135

and Russian exploitation, one can consider them minor ones in relation to conditions in certain free and civilized countries. In England, for example, the effects of lack of cleanliness and hygiene along with the abundance of bugs was found in all social classes, including the Royal Palace. According to T.M. McLaughlin, Alderman Boydell, who became Mayor of London, "had no water piped into his house, but used to walk every morning to the public pump in Ironmonger Lane, solemnly place his huge wig on top of it, and then douse his head under the spout."[157] McLaughlin goes on to say, "in the nineteenth century bugs contributed to the discomfort, at least, of some very exalted adults. One of the more unusual Royal Appointments was Tiffin and Son, bug-destroyers to Her Majesty. The senior partner of the firm gave a fascinating picture of the life of a Victorian bug-catcher: "I was once at work on the Princess Charlotte's own bedstead who said about a bug — Oh, that's what tormented me last night; don't let him escape. The bug-catcher said: I think he looked all the better for having tasted royal blood."[158]

Lack of Sanitary Facilities.

The initiation of a quarantine, its method of control and its duration are directly connected with the level of sanitation measures for combatting the spread of the epidemic. One could ask here whether there existed such measures in the Danube regions which would have contributed to easing and speeding up the control at the quarantine posts along the Sulina Branch and at the mouth, as demanded by the English and by commercial circles in general. The answer lies in the level of medical information and the existence of such measures in the more civilized regions of Europe, not in those of the backward areas.

Not only the Russians, with their social level at that time not too distant from the period in which the doctor's art was considered as witchcraft,[159] but also the English, not yet cognizant of the prophylactic measures and remedies to epidemics, could not have done anything efficacious.

Because of the empirical sanitation measures and the indolence of the control organizations, the length of quarantine was from 15 to 60 days. The rudimentary measures of sanitation controls were not limited to the Lower Danube quarantine, however. They existed in all the European countries, beginning with England.

In his impressions, the previously mentioned English traveller devoted over twenty pages to the disinfection method used by the Russians, who controlled the sanitation services at the customs points in the sanitation cordon upriver from Brăila. His revelations become important also because his informants, aside from Cunningham, were local persons holding key positions in the Romanian administration of the Principalities. Of interest, too, is the way a foreigner could observe and judge the local situation during the quarantine period in the Lower Danube. He related how in other countries the sanitation control differed from the "barbarous formalities" under which it was carried out in some upriver ports along the Lower Danube.

Aside from their value with reference to sanitation control and to navigation upriver from Brăila, it must be noted that his reports did reach the attention of Britain's ambassador at Constantinople, in whose sphere of concern were included the Danubian regions. The traveller must have been in permanent contact with the embassy circles, inasmuch as the title of his book presents him as having been "...twenty years in the East as an English resident."

English protests against the long duration of the quarantine were justified from the point of view of commercial and navigational interests, but not from that of the level of sanitation measures. Added to this were the delays caused by the Russian administration. If in Western Europe, at a much higher level of civilization, there were no measures for combatting epidemics, it is difficult to expect better conditions in the backward social level of the Danubian regions at the periphery of the continent.

The Russian Ukase of 1836 Regarding the Quarantine.

Through the Ukase of Feb.7, 1838, the Russian government set the norms for the application of sanitation controls along the length of the Sulina Branch, a measure which contributed to the worsening of the Anglo-Russian conflict.[160]

Within the framework of the central administration of the Sulina quarantine and under the orders of a director, two supplementary stations were established on both shores of the Sulina Branch namely; one for "pratique" (permission granted to a ship after passing through quarantine), at the extreme end of Leti Island, to which the quarantine had been extended; and the second, for suspicious vessels, on the shore of the St. George island.

THE QUARANTINE AS AN OBSTACLE 137

From the later station, where no sanitary control was made on the cargo, the vessels could be sent in quarantine either to the ports of Odessa or Ismail, preventing them from proceeding on their voyage up the Danube through contrary winds or the strength of the current. It was stated that at these two ports the vessels could receive a supply of provisions or refit, while "passengers or crew who wished to save time, to hold quarantine on the spot" could "proceed to Ismail by land, over the island of Leti."

Rerouting of the passengers or crew of vessels to Ismail, a port on the Kilia Branch, "by land, over the island of Leti", was theoretical but not practicable. Because of the condition of the terrain, crossing the distance of twenty to thirty miles between the Sulina and the Kilia Branches one was almost impossible.

From the geography and hydrography of the Danube Delta, in which is included Leti Island, we find that the area "is covered for the most part by water."[161] From the Delta's total surface of 430,000 hectares (ha.) only 65,000 ha. represent dry land, and this in periods of low water, leaving only 14,000 ha. non-floodable.[162] Even today, the fishermen of these two islands are forced to alternate their passage over dry portions with those over the water, using "lotci."[163]

Sending the vessels to either the quarantine sectors in Odessa or in Ismail, in order to prevent them from proceeding "on their voyage up the Danube through contrary winds or the strength of the current" was a measure which even the most naive person could find to be totally inefficient.

To reach Ismail, the navigator had two choices. First, upriver, along the Sulina Branch, passing the port of Tulcea then to the right of the fork of the river, that is, the Chatal Ismail, to enter the Kilia Branch, thence down river to the port of Ismail. Along this route the vessel sailed up the Danube, contrary to the water current, a route the Ukase considered disadvantageous. On the second route, the vessel had to back track, going out into the Black Sea through the Sulina Mouth and then, from the sea, to enter the Kilia Branch as far as Ismail, sailing upriver on the Danube. The strength of the current of the Kila Branch is greater than that of the Sulina Branch.[164]

Using the idea of "contrary winds" to deter the vessels was a naive and puerile measure. It is common knowledge that, aside from air currents and breezes coming from the Black Sea towards dry land, the Danube Delta is dominated by winds from the north-south direction, the strongest being the "Crivăt," lasting from autumn to spring, a current that is unleashed in N.W. Siberia and ends up in the Balkans. The intensity of this wind current upon the Kilia Branch, to the north, along which the vessels supposedly would have been "prevented through the contrary winds," is greater than that along the Sulina Branch, to the south of the former.

The concentration of the quarantine at Sulina, the entrance of the maritime vessels, would have been the most favorable, but the lack of any sanitation facilities, of insufficient housing and of potable water diminished their efficiency.[165] Only by 1863 did the European Commission of the Danube construct a hospital for the use of the crews of foreign vessels and of the people, besides a lazaret situated on the outskirts of the city, near the sea coast, Furthermore, the lack of any social or public facilities contributed to the inefficiency of Sulina — a situation commented upon also by the English traveller whose notes also have been consulted in this matter.[166]

Under the above-described conditions, Sulina could not be other than a simple administrative center for the Sulina Branch quarantine. Odessa, on the other hand, a port incomparable in dimension and port facilities, presented a maximum of advantages for sanitation control. Still, the efficiency and rapidity of such control being doubtful, sending the vessels from the Danube to Odessa became questionable, along with the long delay it involved in their schedules, and the risks of sailing on the sea.

Establishing the quarantine on the Sulina Branch, as conceived by the Ukase, actually interfered with the transshipment operations of the vessels going downstream, operations caused by the physical obstacles to which were added those of the labor available in case of shipwrecks. The fact that the laborers used in these operations were in contact with possibly contaminated vessels found at the quarantine points fixed by the Ukase, increased the risks of spreading the epidemics.

Between 1856 and 1880, the route of the Sulina Branch was sinuous, because of the three great bends in "M" form and of other smaller ones, adding about forty miles to the length.[167] Only after 1880 did the branch get an almost straight route, after elimination of the bends and the banks of alluvia at the Argani point, giving it a new name: the Sulina Canal.

Up to 1856, it often happened that, because of the winds, a vessel would be thrown on dry land to the right of the bend, where maneuvering by tiller and sails became almost impossible because of the narrow watercourse (200-300 feet)[168]. In such cases, the vessel had to be towed or transshipped. This happened also in the case of vessels grounded by the shallowness of the water, a very frequent occurrence.[169] The towing operations were necessary at times of unfavorable winds; in such cases, a vessel would be towed from the

THE QUARANTINE AS AN OBSTACLE 139

shore, upriver or down, by men or animals, with the use of a towing rope. Recourse to such towing because of a lack of winds was in general use at that time, practiced on all the remaining course of the Danube where the configuration of the shore line permitted. With time, its use was gradually removed by the European Commission through the elimination of the obstacles.

If the natural obstacles of the Sulina Branch route caused great difficulties for navigation between 1856 and 1880, when it was under the maintenance of the European Commission, one can imagine the ones existing after 1829, especially since the Russians did not have at their disposal either the necessary technical equipment or specialists, even had they wanted to eliminate the obstacles.

In connection with the cautionary measures of the Ukase, another possibility of sanitation control could have been more practical and less costly. Instead of Ismail or Odessa, the vessels could have been sent to the ports of Galatz or Brăila where, besides better possibilities for getting supplies than in Ismail, there existed sanitation centers and even hospitals since 1830, empirically endowed though they were, established under the Russian occupation administration.[170]

The inefficacy, though not the inutility, of establishing the quarantine on the Sulina Branch was due also to another consideration which contributed to the lengthy duration to which the vessels were subjected. The contamination of a vessel detained on the Sulina Branch had to be verified by a medical doctor, or at least by a sanitation officer. The permanent presence of such personnel on the Sulina Branch was out of the question because of lack of housing. The closest point from which they could be summoned was the town of Sulina, from where overland travel was impossible due to the physical condition of the river banks; the two or three day journey could be made only by boat, oar or sail-propelled.

Nowhere in the Ukase was any mention made of the procedure to be followed in the case of eventual patients or of contaminated foodstuffs or cargo. What to do with fatalities? No provision at all in the Ukase.

As for Russia's purpose of shielding vessels navigating up the Danube from "the contrary winds or strength of the current," another flagrant contradiction appears. If the difficulties were to be avoided by the Ismail or Odessa routes, one could question the method of procedure prior to the new Ukase regulations. The fact that, before 1836, the vessels followed the water course upriver on their route to the ports of Galatz and Brăila, and even to Ismail, was proof that such navigation up the Danube was possible without the risks predicted by the Ukase. Statistics of Danube traffic in 1831, hence before the issuance of the Ukase in 1836, 97 vessels were recorded in the port of Ismail, twelve of them flying the English flag.[171] To reach Ismail, these vessels sailed upriver on the Sulina Branch, hence "up the Danube," through "contrary winds or currents," not through the Black Sea and from there through the Kilia Branch.

The contradiction became even more obvious between 1852 and 1856, when the epidemics had come to an end, the vessels navigated upriver and down on the normal route, that is, along the Sulina Branch and the fluvial sector to Galatz and Brăila, without encountering the obstacles foreseen in the Ukase.

Hence, from all the arguments so far presented in support of the establishment of the quarantine regime on the Sulina Branch, as well as in justification of the issuance of the Ukase of 1836, a strong contradiction arises from its ambiguity and from the maze of Russian policy.

In 1879, at a meeting of the European Commission, in which the problem of sanitation control was being discussed, the French delegate referred to a statement made by the Russian delegate at the Conference of Vienna in 1855, preliminary to the Peace Treaty of 1856. The French delegate recalled that the Russian representative "avait reconnu la presque impossibilité de combiner la facilité de naviguer par la Soulina avec l'existence d'une quarantaine sur ce bras du fleuve, et consenti, en conséquence, à ne plus y rétablir la ligne de quarantaine qu'elle y avait établie autrefois."[172] The acknowledgement of the Russian delegate can be credited, inasmuch as in 1855 the epidemics came to an end and the quarantine became unnecessary. The acknowledgement was merely circumstantial, what with the atmosphere preliminary to the peace Russia wished to conclude, after losing the Crimean War.

In conclusion, the Ukase of 1836 had been a deliberate measure intended to hinder navigation.

Chapter 4

ENGLAND'S REACTION

Reaction to the Quarantine and Ukase.

England's protests against the quarantine on the Sulina Branch were frequent, but their effects were diminished by their insufficient and erroneous documentation. Only after seven years had passed since the signing of the Treaty of Adrianople and on the occasion of the implementation of the Ukase, did England become aware of the fact that the quarantine also was an obstacle to navigation; an obstacle apparent during the time of Durham as ambassador to St. Petersburg. Concerning the 1836 Ukase, he reported to Palmerston "it is the same as if fortresses had been erected."[173] Palmerston, in his protest to the Russian Government stressed "...the first step of a plan for greatly impeding if not altogether obstructing that commercial intercourse by which the Danube is so well calculated to become the channel...and unnecessary restrictions are imposed upon the freedom of commerce."[174] It is to be noted, however, that Palmerston did not attack the Treaty of Adrianople in toto, only the clause of Art. III in which the quarantine was included. Therefore, the Law Officers of the Crown, whose advice had been sought by Palmerston, could not say it was illegal.

Commenting upon the order of August 8, 1831 of the Russian Government, addressed to the embassy in Constantinople regarding the establishment of the quarantine on the Russian coast of the Caucasus, Urquhart did not lose sight of the effect of a military action. "Now was the time come," he wrote, "for the exercise of the right reserved by His Majesty to judge of the amount of sacrifices to be imposed by the Treaty of Adrianople; if the English Government was silent now, it could never open its mouth."[175]

As to the possibility of easing the quarantine, the information from the previously mentioned English traveller is very interesting. Referring to the attributes of the Sanitary Commission at Constantinople — in which there were participants from a number of states including England — which issued the "clean bill of health" for vessels whose destination was Odessa or other Black Sea ports, he posed the following question: "If Great Britain participates, how does she suffer that they should not be respected?"[176] In continuation, he added, "...if Russia admits the right of British ships to receive a clean bill of health at Constantinople, how can she deny them free practique (sic) in the Danube? Every Government having a member of the Sanitary Commission has an incontestable right to claim free practique in the Danube. We have the right, and yet our ships are subject to quarantine."[177] The application of this procedure did not depend on this commission, whose prerogative had not included the mouths of the Danube, removed in 1829 by Turkish sovereignty. What England's representative could have invoked was equality of treatment for the mouths of the Danube with that of Odessa, both being under Russian sovereignty.

Regarding the same bill of health, there appears a contradiction resulting from a report made by the Sardinian consul at Galatz (Moldavia). He reported that a bill of health issued in Constantinople was valid for vessels entering the ports of Brăila and Galatz, which had a quarantine duration of only four days, not 40 days as for those without the respective bill.[178] An exception was accorded to the "Governo Valaco."[179] Probably the exceptions were due to the fact that the ports were on territory of the Romanian Principalities under Turkish suzerainty. The information seems unlikely inasmuch as the same vessels would have had to pass earlier through the Sulina Mouth, under Russian control, where the aforementioned bill was not valid.

England's stand in the quarantine matter held a discrepancy also. The quarantine on the Sulina Branch was protested, but not that on the remaining sector of the Lower Danube which was under Turkish suzerainty. Also, nor were the three acts issued on the basis of the Treaty of Adrianople, and which contained the stipulations of the quarantine, attacked — that is, the Separate Treaty and the two Organic Regulations previously mentioned.

The explanation lies in the lack of English navigation interest in the sector upriver from Brăila, where seagoing vessels could not navigate. It was not a matter of not knowing about the quarantine in this sector; Cunningham was in contact with all the ports from which came the cereals and other goods in which his commercial enterprises dealt. Other proof of this is the English traveller's report indicating Cunningham as a source of information also concerning the quarantine upriver from Brăila.[180] He had available many details received from the Romanians who observed, without being able to react in public, all the activity of their Russian "protectors." The durations of the quarantine in the interior sector of the river were shorter than those imposed on the fluvial sector under Russian administration, but, in exchange, the sanitary control was much stricter,[181] infractions being penalized in accordance with the Organic Regulations. The ports and wharves in the fluvial sectors of the Romanian Principalities subjected to sanitary control were drawn up into three categories, in accordance with their importance.[182] Although they were under Romanian administrations, the Russian authorities oversaw their applications of the quarantine.[183]

As for the control at the Moldavian-Russian (Bessarabian) border, over both banks of the Prut River, the English traveller reported that the twenty sanitary cordons were useless; Russia's aim, in his opinion, being "to obtain other objects within her neighbor's frontier."[184] His report corresponded with the reality, the Russians having to supervise at that time any possible passage, into Bessarabia, of spies from the Austrian Army which at the time of the Crimean War occupied the Romanian Principalities.

Regarding England's reaction to the Ukase of 1836, the following aspects can be examined: on the one hand, the English ignorance concerning the topography of the regions to which the Ukase was applicable and, on the other, the Russian familiarity with the geographic and hydrographic details of those same regions. The incompetence of the English in their contradiction of certain measures of the Ukase — such as that of crossing the Delta by means of Leti Island, etc. — was caused by the fact that the Danubian regions were unfamiliar to London. Aside from vague information about certain "Ottoman provinces" along the Lower Danube, it seems that not even the geographic site of the mouths of the Danube were known. As Iorga wrote; "Great Britain had little knowledge of the Principalities (including their neighboring Danube Delta) and only a moderate interest in their affairs."[185] At the beginning of the XIXth century only the inauguration of a correspondence transfer point of the "East & Levant Company" brought a small number of Britishers to Bucharest.[186] At the time of the Crimean War, Western Europe was not familiar with either the conditions in that peninsula, nor with the positions of the people to the east of the Black Sea with respect to the war. American historians have written: "It is hardly possible for the present generation (1928) to realize what ignorance prevailed on these matters. But England was destined to learn many things from the Crimean War."[187]

The remark made by Vorontsov, the Russian Governor of Bessarabia, in the sene that "...beaucoup dans la Chambre des Communes n'ont pas une idée très claire sur la position géographique de la delta du Danube,"[188] was not far from reality. From the sketchy map drawn up by the English officers of the H.M. "Medina," under the orders of Captain Spratt,[189] no details were available on the geophysical and hydrographic aspects of the Danube Delta, yet the Russian maps were almost perfect.[190] Hence, the Russians were aware of the circumstances when they included in the Ukase measures difficult to apply, even unrealizable.

A very important error appeared in the English protests, one due to some ambiguous or incomplete phraseology in the Ukase. The phrases "to construct a quarantine...at the extreme end of the island Leti..." and "the other...on the island of Giorgi" were interpreted in the sense of establishing the quarantine regime on the two river islands ("on the island"), but not on their shores adjacent to the water current of the Sulina Branch on which the vessels sailed. The error becomes apparent by the simple fact that the ships navigating on the Sulina Branch were under sanitary control, but the areas behind the shores of those two islands were not. The error is all the more obvious in that the English took its contents as the basis of the English documentation. It also shows up in Urquhart's criticism. He pointed out the natural obstacles in the territories of those two islands, where he placed the quarantine control center, but not those of the navigable route of the Sulina Branch. In showing the futility of the quarantine on this branch, he revealed the improper physical conditions of the territories of the islands, mentioning that "...the marshy islands forming the delta of the Danube are uninhabited and in themselves utterly valueless."[191]

The two large islands, Leti and St. George, are not entirely marshy nor completely uninhabited. Actually, the dry land is minimal, occupying barely 14% of their total surface, with possibility of habitation.[192] The description of the islands as utterly valueless was also improper, their natural resources being public knowledge.[193]

Urquhart's erroneous statements are found also in Palmerston's opinions. The latter said that "the new quarantines...imply an uncalled for interference with the free navigation on the Danube, because there is no population on the islands of the Delta and that as far from being a means a preventing the plague, it would constitute an additional source of infection owing to the coming and going of Russian troops across the uninhabited steppes of Southern Bessarabia, which constitute in themselves the best possible guarantee of protection.''[194]

Palmerston's opinion as to the quarantine's interference with free navigation was perfectly justified. But the tying in of this interference with the uninhabited state of the islands and of Southern Bessarabia was erroneous. It is true that the population of the two islands is not dense, but it did exist before and after 1829. In 1835, hence a year before the expressed opinion of Palmerston, there existed in the delta seventeen villages and between 1880 and 1883, 83 villages were recorded there, which eliminates the idea of an absence of population.[195] Peremptory proof of the presence of a population before the Russian occupation, thus before the time of the statements made by Palmerston and Unquhart, are the turkish names of some villages in existence since the Delta had been under Turkish sovereignty, before 1829.[196] Also populating the Delta were the Lipoveni and Ruthenian fishermen, originally Russian religious dissidents who had fled from Russia during the reign of Peter the Great.[197]

Southern Bessarabia was not a steppe, nor was it uninhabited as Palmerston described it. The contrary is evident from the fact that when, through the 1856 Treaty of Paris, the three regions of Southern Bessarabia were returned to the Principality of Moldavia, provision was made, in Art. 20 and 21, to give "the inhabitants of Southern Bessarabia the same rights as those of Moldavia proper."[198]

Urquhart expressed his erroneous opinion concerning the issuance of the Ukase only in 1836. He attributed the Sanitary Regulations established by the Ukase to a "pretext" enabling the Russians to retain control over the "station commanding the river in war" and the instituting of the quarantine along the length of the Leti and St. George islands "was already matured" through the Treaty of Adrianople.[199] Through this belief he excluded the delayed application of the measures of the Ukase, effectuated only in 1836 although conceived in 1829.

Aside from the fact that the two islands were, and are marshy, as he himself described them, and inadequate for any strategic station, the assurance of a Russian control over them was of no value since they already had mastery over them through their annexation by means of the 1829 treaty. The delay in issuing the Ukase can be attributed to other causes.

The apathy and classic indolence of the Russian administration can be blamed here, regardless of the political regimes. It must be pointed out, in following up this statement, that between February and October of 1829, the military governor of both Romanian Principalities, including the Danube Delta, was General Petre Joltuchin, whose reduced moral level made him incapable of handling the responsibility of an efficient administration. According to an explanation given by Vorontsov, Governor general of Bessarabia, the quarantine station on the Sulina Branch was to have been eliminated in 1829, but that "des retards nous ont forcés d'en construire seulement l'anneé passée."[200]

The panic in the ranks of the Russian Army of occupation because of the ravages of the epidemics in Russia and the Romanian Principalities, immediately after 1829, alarmed the Government at St. Petersburg. Even the Russo-Romanian Mixed Commission at Bucharest, which drew up the Organic Regulations had suspended its work at the beginning of 1831, its Romanian members seeking refuge in the mountains across the frontier in Transylvania, a decision also taken by the English Consul Blutte.[201]

From the writings of Hugh Seton-Watson it appears that even the Russian Government was overtaken by panic because of the human toll taken by cholera in Central and Southern Russia, among its victims being even Marshal Diebitsch and Grand Duke Constantine.[202] Even more, because of the lack of success in stopping the epidemics and the failure of the quarantine, revolts broke out in Russia.[203]

Another rather important reason for delaying the issuance of the Ukase could have been the need to develop the quarantine clause of Article III of the Treaty of 1829 and its transposition into an internal administrative act of regulamentary order. The Ukase could be considered similar to that of the 1829 Separate Treaty and the two Organic Regulations of the Romanian Principalities through which was developed also the quarantine clause of the Treaty of 1829, for its application of the territories of the Principalities. For that matter, the Ukase was not unique in the regulation of the sanitary control. By a previous Ukase (1822) the norms for the application of the quarantine also on the Kilia Branch were set.[204]

The delayed establishment of the quarantine on the Sulina Branch in 1836 could be attributed also to the Russian Government's decision to continue to support the efficient method for combatting the epidemics, used by General Kisselev in the Romanian Principalities, even after his recall in 1834 from the position of Governor General.

Hence, from the actual facts as well as from deductions drawn, Urquhart's statement with respect to "the pretext of sanitary regulations" and the "maturity" of the quarantine before the signing of the Treaty of Adrianople, was weakened. Palmerston's conclusions, too, based upon the erroneous information of the vice consuls in the Danube stations, could be considered lacking in validity.

If consideration is given to the fact that the European Commission of the Danube had provided and had foreseen the instituting of the quarantine on the Sulina Branch, England's reaction was unjustified.

In Article 20 of the 1865 Public Act of the Commission, provision was made that in case an epidemic "envahit une ou plusieurs des provinces riveraines du Danube, des établissements quarantenaires seront institués là où besoin sera, sur la partie du fleuve qui traverse le territoire de la Turquie."[205]

In 1865, "Turkish territory" also included the Sulina Branch. In Article 4 of the 1881 Navigation and Police Regulations of that same Commission, provision was again made for the quarantine, this time defining its area of application, including the Sulina Branch.[206] "En cas d'épidémie et lorsque des mesures de quarantaine sont appliquées à l'embouchure de Soulina, le Capitaine du Port est également chargé d'exercer la police à l'égard des bâtiments qui stationnent en amont du port, en dehors de la limite déterminée par l'article 12 ci-après, pour purger leur quarantaine." Within the limits mentioned in Article 12 are included "le port de Soulina, le bras de Soulina, sur une longueur de trois milles nautiques, en partant de l'ouverture des digues de l'embouchure."[207]

English circles also protested against the conduct of the Russian soldiers posted on the vessels to supervise the carrying out of the sanitary control. The facts were real and the complaints justified from a social point of view. The behavior of Russian soldiers and officers was not sufficiently known to Western Europe. From the moment a military man leaves his home territory, he amplifies his native behavior, disregarding and abusing any consideration of order and discipline towards those underneath his authority. Abuses of the kind on the Sulina Mouth and branch were noted in Russia, too, where "quarantine regulations were carried out brutally by ignorant policement, and caused hardship and annoyance which led to public riots."[208]

In conclusion, the Ukase was an act of Russian domestic administration applied on the territory newly annexed in 1829, i.e. in the Danube Delta. Any foreign position contrary to it became a meddling in Russia's internal problems. The failings of this Act could be blamed only on the methods of carrying out the sanitary control and on the political aims gained from hindering navigation.

Wrong Reference to the 1815 Act of Vienna.

The Law Officers of the Crown, whose counsel had been requested by Palmerston in 1836, examined also the possibility of applying on the Danube the principle of international navigation of the 1815 Act of Vienna. Palmerston was certain that, by invoking this Act signed by the Russians, he could set aside along with other obstacles to navigation, also that of the quarantine. By its ambiguous wording, the counsel was not the expected one, on the simple consideration of the fact that the Danube had not been included in the 1829- 1856 period in the principles of the Act of 1815.

Although Urquhart, too, referred to the same principles, he still challenged Palmerston's point of view, considering that the efficacy of the Act of 1815 was nullified by the Russian confiscation of the vessel "Cracov."[209]

Invoking, after 1836, the principles of the Act of 1815 was contrary to England's past position. As shown previously, England's representatives had not proposed the inclusion of the problem of navigation on the Danube in the Act of 1815, in either the Committee on International Rivers, in the framework of the 1815 Congress of Vienna, or at the Conference of Verona in 1822. Neither had the Russian delegates done so.

In 1815 and 1829, neither the Black Sea nor the Danube had been included in the sphere of England's commercial interests to induce her to have the point of view shown in 1836. Even had the Danube been included in the principles of 1815, England could not have had the support of Turkey, a riparian state on the Lower Danube, in calling for unconditional freedom of navigation for her vessels, inasmuch as Turkey could not be obliged to apply the clauses of an Act to whose signing she had not been convoked.

Although in 1815 England had not intervened in support of calling Turkey to the drawing up of the international principles of navigation, in 1839 Palmerston suggested her adherence to the Act of Vienna. He addressed himself to Lord Beauvale of Vienna, saying, "...the Sultan should become an according party to the Treaty of Vienna...and it might be desirable with reference to other considerations that Turkey should accede to that Treaty and especially because her doing so would bind her in the same way in which Austria and Russia are now bound to the river stipulations of that Treaty."[210]

Faced with the failure of the attempt to apply the clauses of the Act of 1815 to the Lower Danube navigation, Palmerston invoked, in the case of the quarantine and of other obstacles, "the spirit and basis of that Act," which in his opinion had been "thereby violated."[211] It would seem that, through this last resort invocation, Palmerston was finally convinced of the inoperativity of the Act of 1815 on the Danube.

Neither the "spirit" nor the "basis" of the Act of 1815 had been violated, as long as these two senses could be invoked exclusively for navigation on rivers in Northwestern Europe, for which the principles of 1815 had been formulated. The "spirit", or the thinking creating the principles of 1815 had been limited exclusively to regulating navigation on these rivers, not on the Danube. In the Dalberg proposal the Danube was included in the spirit of 1815, but it remained without an echo.

To the preceding considerations can be added the fact that the Act of Vienna could not have been applied on the Lower Danube, including its mouths, because after 1829 the water course was under two opposing jurisdictions. While one sector was under Turkish suzerainty, the other was under sovereignty; the branch and the mouth of the Sulina were under Russian sovereignty, in accordance with the Treaty of Adrianople.

Also evident was the lack of understanding in English circles of the real meaning of the clauses of the Act of 1815, relative to navigation. The Act had not determined the rules for navigation on Western Europe's northwestern rivers, but only the principles for those regulations. The clause of Articles CVIII of the Act, by which "the powers whose states are separated or crossed by the same navigable river engage to regulate by common consent..." was of general character, its specifics to be drawn up through bilateral or multilateral conventions between riparian States. In other words, the essential condition was the accord between the parties involved. The clause in Article CIX which stated: "the navigation of the rivers referred to in the preceding article (CVIII)...shall be free," also was of a general order, to be applied or taken up for consideration later.

Proof that at Vienna were established the principles and not the regulations for international navigation is evident from the text of Article 15 of the 1856 Treaty of Paris, through which, for the first time, navigation on the Danube was internationalized. "The Act of the Congress of Vienna," states Article 15, "having established the principles...the contracting Powers stipulate that..." Hence, it is clear that the concept of "principles" could not be considered valid for Danube navigation in the period for which England claimed such. Only later, when mention of the 1815 Act is made in the Preamble of the 1840 Austro-Russian Convention for Navigation, could its "spirit and basis" be pointed out. In this case however, the two elements were taken into consideration in regulating navigation by two riparian states "by common consent," in accordance with Article CVIII of the Act of 1815, which was not the case with England.

There is also to be considered the inopportunity of extending the principles of 1815 to the Danube navigation as long as their effective application on the rivers directly in the concern of the Congress was delayed.

The English point of view loses its force by its flexibility on the principle of territorial sovereignty, which in the matter of internationalization was a primordial factor, as well as a very controversial one.

According to the clause of Article CIX of the Act of 1815, the geographic area of the internationalization of the river was "from the point where each of them becomes navigable, to its mouth..." In the case of the Danube this would have been from Ulm to its mouths flowing into the sea, in other words, along the entire course of the river, traversing a number of territorial sovereignties. In the case of the English point of view, however, the application of the principles of 1815 was requested for a partial course, namely from the Sulina Mouth to Brăila, on the sector of the river navigable also for the marine vessels, where England had commercial interests.

Although internationalization of navigation does not include the river banks, it still is tied to the sovereignty over them when the texts of Articles CIX- CXV of the Act of 1815 are applied in reference to the navigation police, technical matters of maintenance, customs, towing, etc.

In the Dalberg Project, which constitutes one of the bases of the preparation of the Act of 1815, provision was made for the application of the principle of internationalization between "Puissances copropriétaires des fleuves" and of "souverains copropriétaires."[212] However, Palmerston's protest was not upheld by these conditions. He did not take into consideration Russian sovereignty over the Sulina Mouth and Branch on the basis of the Treaty of Adrianople. He referred instead to the difficulties which could follow in the event of Turkey's obstruction, as sovereign over Dobruja, on the territory on which had been proposed the construction of the Cernavoda-Constanta Canal, after 1829.

In 1839, when Austria intended to work on this canal project, as an alternative to the Sulina exit to the sea, Palmerston's opinion was "...such a canal being a work of art, might be rendered liable to such regulations, restrictions and duties as the Government of the country through which it passes might choose to impose upon it."[213] Hence, Palmerston was taking into consideration the possibility of Turkey's exercising her sovereign rights over the projected canal, but not those of Russia over the mouth and branch of the Sulina.

Even if one accepted the English point of view, it could not have been of use because, either from negligence or other causes, the quarantine regime had not been included in the Act of 1815. It was mentioned, however, in the navigation treaties and conventions drawn up in the period immediately following the year 1815, between the countries of Western Europe, when the epidemics of cholera and the Black Plague existed.[214]

In the concepts of those drawing up the Act of Vienna, the obstacles to navigation were limited and referred exclusively to navigation police (Art. CX), taxation and the abusive levying of such (Art. CXI and CXII), the lack of maintenance of navigable routes (Art. CXIII), etc., but not to the quarantine. Only in 1856, when through the Treaty of Paris the application of international principles of navigation on the Danube was decided, was the quarantine evaluated, among other obstacles, as an impediment to navigation. Inclusion of the quarantine in this treaty was a consequence of the debates in the 1855 Conference of Vienna, preceding that of Paris in 1856.[215]

The weakness of the English viewpoint as to "the spirit and basis" of the Act of Vienna could also be a result of their definition of the idea of principle.[216] A principle, or a "governing law" imprints upon the object or subject to which it is applied an immovable value, excluding it from derogation or interpretation, excepting if its formulators, or those upholding it by majority decision, consider it necessary to modify it, as was the case at the 1856 Conference for Internationalization of Navigation on the Danube.

On the immovability of principles was later supported the opposition of the riparian states of the river to participation by non-riparian states in the administration and control of application of the international regime of navigation on the Danube. Austria invoked it in 1856, Romania in 1921 at the Conference for Establishing the new Statue of the Danube, and Russia, with the other states, at the 1948 Conference of Belgrade. The 1856 derogations were due to the strong political stands of England and France, as a result of which it was possible to get the agreement of the other signatories to the 1856 Treaty of Paris. Earlier, however, after 1829, England had found herself facing Russia alone.

Application of the principles of 1815 in the regulation of navigation on the Danube in 1829 seemed to be of general opinion in England. In the problem of taxation of vessels on their entrance into the Danube, Dudley Stuart also invoked the clauses of the Act of Vienna.[217]

In conclusion, England's reference to the Act of Vienna in the quarantine matter was wrong.

Chapter 5

GENERAL CONSIDERATIONS ON THE QUARANTINE AS AN
OBSTACLE TO NAVIGATION

The Quarantine on the Lower Danube in relation to that of England.

From a comparison of the quarantine on the Lower Danube to that in England can be discerned the rapport between the headquarters of the public sanitary control and those of the commercial interests.

No matter how doubtful the trust in Russian policy, it is difficult to believe that the solving of a local sanitation problem would necessitate its being included in an international treaty such as that of Adrianople, had it not been imposed by a real peril for one or both of the signatories. Along with the latter, the same dangers applied to the people in the Danube regions, especially those of the Romanian Principalities under Russian Protectorate and on whose territories were the Russian armies of occupation. Counter to the English claim, that navigation was being sabotaged under the pretext of the quarantine, were the tens of thousands of fatalities in the Principalities, including that of E.L. Blutte, English Consul to Bucharest.[218]

The gravity of the situation was not unknown to the English, inasmuch as Blutte in a report to the Foreign Office had written,"...the disease left Jassy a ghost city..."[219] and that, in the Danube ports he "estimated that the plague carried off nine people out of every ten struck down by it..."[220]

Nor could the vice-consuls in the Danube ports have neglected reporting the situations in their own centers of residence, in which a "pluie des morts" reigned and men "tombaient comme des mouches dans la rue..."[221] Added to the human loss was the paralysis of the

153

economic life of Wallachia. "This country," stated an Italian newspaper, "could be one of the richest in the world were it not for two great flagellations: war and the plague."[222]

In the Romanian Principalities, including the Danubian region, the entire regime of combatting epidemics had been organized by Kisselev, the Russian Governor, described by the Romanian historian, Xenopol, as "of righteous character, broadminded and liberal, endowed with remarkable activity and power of work,"[223] and by Prof. R.R.N. Florescu as "...yet another forgotten man of history."[224]

Undoubtedly, the means of combatting the epidemics were not the most adequate, yet they did represent official preoccupation. The measures taken by Kisselev demonstrated concern for public health. Considering the nonexistence of efficacious[225] medical measures and especially the apathy and fatalism of the population, Xenopol says of Kisselev, "...anyone else in his place would have become discouraged..."[226] To this was added the burden of local administrators who, in Xenopol's opinion "presented a picture of chaos and were ignorant of the most elementary rules of cleanliness."[227]

Along with sanitary measures to combat the local causes, Kisselev resorted to drastic action not met heretofore in the Romanian Principalities, in Russia, and not even in all of Europe. Regardless of the indirect support the quarantine gave to the Russian aims on the lower Danube, it must be noted that, without the vigorous, prompt and efficient actions of General Kisselev, the epidemics would have had results much more drastic than any previously known in the history of the Romanian Principalities.[228]

The English indifference to the epidemics in the Lower Danube regions would not have been surprising had the conditions not existed in England, as well. Urquhart's viewpoint concerning the quarantine in the Lower Danube was as absurd as that of the Marquis of Londonderry, who declared in the House of Lords that the alarm over the epidemic in the port of Sunderland was false.[229] Associating themselves with Londonderry's stand probably due to political pressure, an assembly of "most of the doctors in Sunderland...solemnly declared that...as to the nature of the disorder which had created so great an excitement in the public mind, the same is not the Indian Cholera, nor of foreign origin."[230]

As for the alarm expressed by newspapers concerning the epidemic cases in Sunderland, the same assembly opined that the report "...is a most wicked and malicious falsehood."[231] Such expressions of opinion did not come from the Russians or the Romanians during the epidemics in the Principalities. Certain English commercial circles were ignorant of, or were not to be informed of, the epidemics in the Danube regions, inasmuch as the quarantine became the gauge for the cereal stock exchange in London.

Prof. Florescu notes the absence of collaboration between Consul Blutte and General Kisselev,[232] a collaboration which would have been useful in combatting the epidemics. concern for the people in the Danube region under epidemic status was completely lacking in London financial circles, just as it was for the people of England. The number of English residents in the Principalities was infinitely small; aside from the consuls and vice-consuls, and two important merchants Bell and Anderson, the commercial interests of English importers were represented in the Danubian ports by local enterprises conducted by local personnel, "English Houses," as they were termed by the Sardinian consuls.[233] From W. East's report it would seem that there were few English merchants in the Romanian Principalities, but East did not specify whether they were all English or Ionian Greeks with passports issued by the British authorities governing the Ionian Islands.[234]

The crews of English vessels on the Malta-Black Sea-Danube route were, in the majority, Greek.[235] Also, in the service of British commerce were the Ionian flag vessels, their crews also were all Greek.[236] As will be seen in the chapter on Sulina "a little California," these Ionian crews were protected by the English vice-consuls in Brăila and Galatz.

The English even criticized the method of organizing the campaign against the epidemics. Although in England, between 1831 and 1850, coordination of measures of combatting epidemics was nonexistent,[237] in the Principalities a commission of control and coordination was functioning, with headquarters established by Kisselev in Bucharest and Iasi.[238]

Nicholas Mavros, the head of that commission in the Principalities, was described by Colquhoun, British Consul to Bucharest, as "England's greatest enemy,"[239] because of the excessive sanitary control imposed on navigation. Urquhart termed him "one of the most dangerous enemies of Britain in the Principalities."[240] Regardless of whether Mavros was "the Russians' man," as Colquhoun rightly reported, still, in his capacity as inspector general of the quarantine,[241] he was the most competent person heading the commission "composed of Greeks familiar with the character of the contagion."[242]

While Mavros met with no resistance or obstructions in carrying out his attributes, Dr. Kell — who in 1831 had alerted the London authorities as to the danger of cholera—"was persuaded not to attend public meetings because of the danger of physical attack from the businessmen and public figures of the town."[243]

Kisselev, "after superhuman efforts, succeeded in wiping out the cholera epidemic"[244] so that, by 1852, it no longer presented any great danger, but in England it reappeared in 1848-1849, claiming 14,000 victims,[245] and again in 1853-1854,[246] causing some to suggest that Parliament should be moved away.[247]

Even in 1848, while Palmerston was reading the reports of the English vice consuls in the Danubian ports concerning the inconveniences of the quarantine, in London there reigned "the Great Stink"[248] — the name brought about by the pollution of the Thames River, the source of infection. Because of the political freedom in England, the people could criticize or ridicule governmental inactivity. On an etching with humorous sketches, representing public reaction, were inscribed different sarcastic inscriptions referring to London's filthy conditions, describing even the sanitary level of the authorities.[249]

Undoubtedly, there existed a great difference between the state administration level and the level of urban public services and the levels of those services in the small Romanian Principalities. Still, there were some discrepancies in the English governmental measures for preventing sources of infection. Bucharest and some of the Lower Danube ports were small in size, and between 1829 and 1856, had a semi-oriental civic aspect. Yet, the drainage systems being constructed for Bucharest were worked out in 1847 and finished in 1875.[250] In London, however, "open sewers flowed through the crowded parishes"[251] and "...at the time of Queen Victoria's accession in 1837 there was no sanitary legislation on the Statute Book."[252] The work on a sewage system for street and housing commerced only in 1875, on the basis of Disraeli's Public Health Act.[253]

In the history of the quarantine, there appear discrepancies between the public health commands and the commercial ones. With respect to the latter, Urquhart noted, "England pursues the profit of speculations and looks no further than trade; to Russia, trade is only an instrument and a means."[254] Prof. David Dallin wrote, in the same vein, of England that "...in her relentless struggle for existence and power, she has had to accept every ally and to buy assistance with her gold whenever this could be done."[255]

To Prof. Dallin's remark "...no principle in foreign policy — this has been the only British principle,"[256] can be added the absence of humanitarian principles in that same policy. If the idea of friendship includes also that of humanitary, then this precept does not correspond with that of Palmerston: "England has no permanent friends, she has only permanent interests."[257]

Under a humanitarian aspect, the Russian sabotage through the means of the quarantine is of minor value in relation to the attitude of the merchants and suppliers in London. In the last analysis, the Russian sabotage prejudiced commercial interests, but the attitude of those against the quarantine was actually a crime against public health, even in England.

Imposing the quarantine, in November 1831, for a period of fifteen years, over all vessels entering the port of Sunderland, where cholera had claimed human lives, "brought down a storm of protest of the merchants, shipowners and inhabitants, who suffer from the restraints imposed upon an infected place, who are loudly complaining of the measures which have been adopted, and strenuously insisting that their town is in a more healthy state than usual."[258]

The example given by McLaughlin in the quoted work became peremptory proof of the disregard towards orders for public health in England. In the 1828-1856 period, in England and in her colonies, there dominated a specific psychology allowing the supremacy of commercial interests and the British flag over all other considerations.

Between the British position, regarding the quarantine as well as in general towards the epidemics in the Romanian Principalities, and the Russo-Romanian actions to safeguard public health commands, two concrete factors appear. When he departed permanently from the Romanian Principalities on April 25, 1834, General Kisselev was seen off by "a multitude of people from all social ranks,"[259] but at the funeral of Consul Blutte, who "had not gained many personal friends...either among natives or the foreign consular corps...there were few mourners beside his wife and son."[260] While "...Blutte left remarkably little to remember him by,"[261] for Kisselev, the Chamber of Deputies in Bucharest proposed the erection of a monument in 1843.[262] Kisselev refused the honor, suggesting instead that the fund of 15,000 ducats allocated to the proposed work be distributed among other public works,[263] among them also the park and avenue on the outskirts of Bucharest, which still bear his name.

The Quarantine as an Element of Navigation Legislations.

The experience of applying the system of quarantine on the waterways of Europe brought about its being regulated, for the first time, by a treaty of international order, the 1829 Treaty of Adrianople. Until that date there had existed only local, regional or national measures. To the reasons mentioned before for its not being included in the earlier Act of 1815, one could add the influence of the commercial and navigational lobbies, protecting their own interests, which could have been disadvantaged by the effects of the quarantine regime.

It could well be that its later inclusion in navigation legislation was determined by the reaction and publicity given to that of the Lower Danube. There are times when negative or positive effects of measures taken in outlying areas of the European continent can be helpful, even to the Western or Central sectors.

Between 1830 and 1840, the Turkish Government, in association with some of the Great Powers, organized a Sanitary Commission at Constantinople, whose duty it was to issue the dispositions for sanitary control in the ports of the Empire, as well as over vessels in their course through the Straits to the Black Sea. Later, following the Convention of Paris of May 27, 1853, drawn up between France, Sardinia and other maritime nations, the Sanitary Commission was transformed from a consultative organ into a permanent international institution intitled: "The Superior Sanitary Council," with its headquarters at Constantinople.[264]

After the establishment of the European Commission of the Danube, in 1856, the Sanitary Control at the Danube was placed under the jurisdiction of the Constantinople Council. Through the latter's Public Act of 1865 (Art. 18, 19, 20) provision was made for the norms of sanitary inspection and of the quarantine. Locating this Council at Constantinople set the importance of the Straits as the epicenter of the epidemic danger in the regions of the Black Sea and the Lower Danube.

Throughout the Turkish sovereignty, the European Commission's sanitary and quarantine inspections at the mouths of the Danube remained under the orders of the Superior Sanitary Council at Constantinople. After 1878, when the mouths of the Danube passed under the sovereignty of independent Romania, conflict of interests arose between the latter and the European Commission.

Negotiations between the two parties resulted in two sanitary codes: one, that of the Romanian Government and the other, that of the European Commission. In October 1879, both codes were combined, a single one being drawn up by which control was transferred to Romania. The decision was actually theoretic and mainly one of principle, inasmuch as until 1881 the sanitary and quarantine inspection actually remained in the competence of the European Commission.[265]

CONSIDERATIONS ON THE QUARANTINE 159

Following the Treaty of 1856, the sanitary control and the quarantine regime were regulated also by the Navigation Act of 1857, drawn up by the Riparian Commission of the Danube. The Act having been rejected in 1858 by the signatories to the 1856 Paris Treaty, its regulations were applied only on the sectors upriver from the Lower Danube.

The quarantine regime of the Public Act of 1865 of the European Commission was much broader than that of the Navigation Act of 1857, its provision being made exclusively for cases of officially declared epidemics in the regions of the Danube, the Orient, or in ports of origin of the vessels (Art. 19 and 20). Vessels entering through the Sulina Mouth had to present certificates of good health issued by the Sanitary Commission and, in cases in which the inspections proved to be negative, they could continue sailing up the river.

The quarantine continued to be a part also of the new Navigation and Police Regulations of 1881, drawn up by the same European Commission on the basis of the clause of Article 55 of the 1878 Treaty of Berlin. The central headquarters for the quarantine was at Sulina, under the authority of the office of the Port Captain, a European Commission organ. In case of epidemics on the Sulina Branch route, the quarantine was to be instituted and controlled by this same service.

On a European level, the Sanitary Convention of Venice was signed on May 18, 1897 by seventeen European countries and Persia. In this Convention, provision was made for the quarantine at Sulina.[266] Because of past experience and in keeping with medical progress, the methods and manner of applying sanitary control, as provided for in the respective Convention, were much more modern and more practical for navigation. In the absence of any epidemics, a general sanitary examination was obligatory at Sulina for any vessel entering the Danube, the duration of the examination limited to within six days. In case a vessel was declared contaminated, or came from an infected region, a duration of ten days was recommended for its control.

On the basis of this convention, any sanitary control was cancelled when no epidemic existed. On the onset of an epidemic in a maritime port, any vessel reaching the Black Sea which had been granted the sanitary permit, at the Sulina, Kilia, or St. George Mouth, was excused from any formalities other than sanitary supervision up to the Iron Gates.

If an epidemic arose above or below the Iron Gates, the sanitary permit obtained at the first uncontaminated port in the Brăila-Iron Gates sector was sufficient to permit free access of the vessel to any port of this sector of the river. Upon declaration of epidemic status on that same sector, maritime vessels as well as fluvial ones could carry out any operations (of loading or unloading cargo and passengers) as long as they did not stop at a contaminated port en route and as they possessed the sanitary permit.

The sanitary control at Sulina was contained also by the 1911 Regulation for Navigation and Police, but after World War I it passed directly under the jurisdiction of the Ministry of Sanitation of the Romanian State, in collaboration with the organs of the European Commission of the Danube.

The transfer of certain attributes of the European Commission of the Danube to the Romanian State, on the basis of the Sinaia Arrangement of August 18, 1938, included in Article 12 also the sanitary attributes (administration, control, quarantine, health taxes) that had been provided for previously in the Public Navigation Act of 1865 and the 1881 Additional Act to the 1865 Public Act.

The new sanitary attributes taken over by the Romanian State were carried out by the General Direction of the Commercial Marine, under the order of which were the offices of the Port Captains, in collaboration with the Ministry of Health. The full and direct authority of the Romanian State over the sanitation duties ended in 1948, when they took a different form, following the Belgrade Convention. By Article 26 of this convention, sanitary control was provided for over the entire Danube sector, to be carried out by the Danubian States, each one being obligated to communicate the regulations it established to the new Danube Commission, in order that the sanitary system be unified. The Convention also provided that, on the Kilia Branch, the sanitary control was to be carried out exclusively by Soviet Russia.

The quarantine system was introduced also on the Prut River, its navigation having acquired an international character because of the frontier between Moldavia and Bessarabia. In the 1866 Convention for Navigation on the Prut, modified in 1895, between Russia and România, as riparian states, and Austria as a partial-riparian state, provision had been made for measures of control and prevention of spreading of plague and cholera epidemics (Articles 20 and 30). Then, with the Regulation for Navigation on the Prut, signed by Russia and România in 1896, the sanitary regime became part of a Separate Regulation composed of twelve articles, among which provision was made for establishing twelve control posts in case of official declaration of any epidemic.

CONSIDERATIONS ON THE QUARANTINE 161

From this summary can be concluded the need for regulation of sanitary control which, in the light of experiences after 1829, became an element of permanent value for Danube navigation.

As a result of the faulty manner in which the quarantine regime had been applied after 1829, certain measures were indicated in the 1893 Sanitary Convention, signed at Dresden, to be applied to Danube-destined vessels coming from a contaminated area.[267] The vessels were to be detained at Sulina for medical examination and disinfecting. In a reference to methods of control, the Convention stated. "Il y a lieu de perfectionner à Soulina l'établissement sanitaire de le pourvoir de l'outillage moderne comme moyens de désinfection et de le compléter de façon à ce qu'on puisse débarquer et isoler les malades provenant d'un navire infecté, ainsi que les autres passagers."

Considering that, even in 1893, there existed the need for improving the sanitary control at Sulina, one can conclude again that the status of the quarantine regime after 1829 was indeed backward.

Notes

Chapter 1

1. D. Bodin, "Documente Sarde," p. 25, quotation from report of the Sardinian Consul at Galatz, May 24, 1838.
2. Radu R.N. Florescu, "The Struggle against Russia in the Romanian Principalities: A Problem in Anglo-Turkish Diplomacy," (1821-1854). Chapter XI, British Policy and the Russian Stranglehold on the Danube, pp., 248-273.
3. From the report of the Sardinian Consul at Galatz; in Bodin "Documente Sarde," p. 24.
4. R.R.N. Florescu, "The Struggle...," p. 254.
5. F. Israel, "Major Peace Treaties...," Vol. II, p. 931.
6. Art. III (in part): "The Prut shall continue to form the border of the two Empires, from the point where this river touches the territory of Moldavia up to its junction with the Danube. From this point, the borderline shall follow the course of the Danube down to where it flows to St. George, so that while it leaves all the islands formed by the various arms of this river in the possession of Russia, the right bank shall remain, as in the past, to the Ottoman Porte. It is agreed, however, that this right bank, from the point where the arm of St. George separates from that of Soulinah (sic) shall remain uninhabited to a distance of two hours from this river and that no settlements of any kind shall be created there and that, likewise, on the islands that shall remain in the possession of the Russian Court, with the exception of quarantines to be established there, no settlements of fortifications shall be permitted to be made there..."
7. Sened, February 24, 1784; see Great Britian, Foreign Office, State Papers, Vol. 100, p. 727.
8. The wars of 1711, 1736, 1774, and 1806-1812.
9. Martens et Cussy, "Recueil manuel et pratique de traites, conventions," Leipzig, 1846, Vol., III, p. 33.
10. Separate Treaty between Russia and the Ports relating to the Principalities of Moldavia and Wallachia, signed at Adrianople, 2/14 September 1829; see F. Israel, "Major Treaties...," Vol. II, pp. 939-942.
11. Regulamentele Organice ale Valachiei si Moldovei, LIV, p. 368; introduced in Moldavia in 1831 and in Wallachia in 1832.
12. Art. 202 and 203 of the "Organic Regulations" for Wallachia.
13. Art. 154, from the "Organic Regulations" for Wallachia.

14. Art. 163 from the "Organic Regulations" for Wallachia.
15. Bodin, "Documente Sarde," p. 25.
16. H. Nicolson, "Diplomacy," 2nd ed., p. 139; comments of Dr. Kantorowicz.
17. Idem, ibid., p. 100.
18. Idem, Ibid., p. 142.
19. R.R.N. Florescu, "The Struggle...," p. 254.
20. Blutte to Cowley, June 12, 1829, F.O. 97/402; quoted by R.R.N. Florescu, "The Struggle...," p. 133.
21. D. Urguhart, "The Mystery of the Danube," p. 100, note.
22. Quoted by H. Hajnal, "Le Droit...," p. 17, note 2.
23. D. Urquhart, "The Mystery...," pp. 16, 25.
24. G.H. Bolsover, "David Urquhart and Eastern Question (1833-1837); A Study in Publicity and Diplomacy"; in "Journal of Modern History," Vol. III, December 1936, No. 4, p. 447.
25. Ponsonby to Palmerston, October 11, 1934, F.O. 78, Turkey, 239 x.
26. D. Urquhart, "The Mystery...," p. 103.
27. Idem, ibid., p. 47.
28. Idem, ibid., p. 32.
29. Palmerston to Ponsonby, August 1838, F.O. 195/168; quoted by R.R.N. Florescu, "The Struggle...," p. 249.
30. Lloyd, British vice-consul in Brăila, to Palmerston, November 14, 1848; F.O. 195/285 in R.R.N. Florescu, "The Struggle...," p. 271.
31. Palmerston to Buchanan, of the British Embassy in St. Petersburg, September 24, 1851, Foreign Office, 78/977, 78, Turkey, 239 x.
32. R.R.N. Florescu, p. 266.
33. Cochelet to Thiers, June 4, 1836; quoted by R.R.N. Florescu, "The Struggle..." p. 266.
34. Vernon John Puryer "England, Russia and the Straits Question," (1844-1856), p. 77.
35. Expression of Bloomfield, England's Ambassador to St. Petersburg.
36. R.R.N. Florescu, "The Struggle...," p. 253.

Chapter 2

37. "Dispatch by Lt. Col. Sir Henry Trotter, reporting upon the operations of the European Commission of the Danube during the years 1894-1906," presented to both Houses of Parliament, August 1907, with reference to "Commercial," No 9 (1907), printed for His Majesty's Stationery Office, London, 1907. p. 3.
38. Ion Vidrascu, "La voie navigable maritime du Danube," p. 38.
39. The forty-mile long canal was to pass through Cernavoda port, from the fluvial sector upriver from Brăila, through Dobruja to Constanta.

40. Voisin Bey, "Notices sur les travaux d'amélioration du Danube et du bras de Soulina en 1857-1891."
41. "Dispatch ...." p. 2.
42. Ed. Engelhardt, "Les embouchures du Danube et la Commission institueé par le Congrès de Paris"; in "Revue de Deux Mondes," XL année, seconde période, Tome 84, p. 101.
43. In French "la barre"; in Romanian "bara"; in English "bar," "shoal"; a bank across a water course, an obstacle, a sand bar, a bank in the front of a river built by sand, alluvial deposits, of a river, or other solid body carried by the water current. By the "bar of Sulina," or "la barre de Soulina" is understood also the navigational problems through the Sulina Mouth, caused by the sand banks in front of the river mouth. In general usage in the Port of Sulina, "bara" also meant the estuary of the Danube in front of the Sulina Mouth.
44. Gr. Antipa, "Dunărea si problemele ei...," pp. 160, 161; Georg R. Credner, whose comparative study of deltas was considered the most complete, classified the mouths of the Danube in the second group, that is mouths with fluvial alluvium deposited in front of them, separated and without estuaries.
45. Ion Vidrascu, "La voie navigable...," p. 21.
46. D. Sturdza, "Recueil...," p. 873.
47. Ion Vidrascu, p. 21
48. Lord Palmerston's speech in Parliament on July 7, 1853; quoted in H. Hajnal, "The Danube...," p. 64, note 1.
49. H. Hajnal, "Le Droit...," p. 65.
50. Lord Malmesbury to the British Ambassador in Vienna, on the occasion of the International Technical Conference in Paris, June 1858; quoted in Hajnal, "The Danube...," p. 161, n. 2; and Hajnal, "Le Droit...," p. 65, n. 1.
51. H. Hajnal, "Le Droit...," p. 59.
52. Idem, Ibid., p. 59.
53. Idem, pp. 59, 60.
54. From the Foreign Office Instructions; quoted by Hajnal, "Le Droit..." p. 60, note 2.
55. See "A Different Point of View."
56. "Limbare," "Alimbare," "Alléger": to lighten, to alleviate, to relieve, act of unloading and reloading of a ship in order to ease its passage through shallow water. "Limbo" is also used, a contraction of "limbare," but has not connection with "limbes" or "limbo" in the religious sense or that understood by Dante. The motion of a ship "in limbo" is suspended while waiting for reloading of the cargo that was unloaded into smaller vessels in order to sail through the shallow water.
57. "Allège," "alléger," operation of lightening, unloading a ship.
58. "Geografia văii...," pp. 180, 635.

59. Cunningham to Canning, Galatz, Sept. 14, 1850, in "Correspondence between Great Britain and Russia Respecting Obstructions to the Navigation of the Sulina Channel of the Danube," in the "State Papers," Vol. 44 (1853-1854), p. 434. Note: Although printed separately, "Correspondence between..." is included in "British Foreign and State Papers', volume numbers and pages as quoted by the New York City Public Library, with call number X.B.F. To be referred to hereafter as "Correspondence between..." and "State Papers."

60. Cunningham to Palmerston, Galatz, Sept. 30, 1850; in "Correspondence between..."; in "State Papers," Vol. 44, pp. 437-443.

61. Neale to Palmerston, Varna, July 14, 1850, "Correspondence between ...," in "State Papers," Vol. 44, p. 430.

62. Cunningham to Stratford Canning, Galatz, Sept. 14, 1850; "Correspondence between...," op. cit., Vol. 44, pp. 434-435.

63. Idem, Ibid., pp. 437-443.

64. Neale to Palmerston, Varna, July 14, 1850; op. cit., p. 430.

65. Cunningham to Palmerston, Galatz, Sept. 30, 1850, op, cit. p. 434.

66. Idem, Ibid., pp. 434-443.

67. Cunningham to Palmerston, Galatz, Sept. 30, 1850, pp. 437-443.

68. Idem, ibid., p. 428.

69. Idem, ibid., pp. 437-443.

70. D. Sturdza, "Recueil ...," pp. 892, 899.

71. E. Engelhardt, "Les embouchures du Danube et la Commission...," p. 101.

72. D. Sturdza, "Recueil...," p. 875.

73. Ed. Engelhardt, "Etudes sur les embouchures du Danube" (1862), p. 90.

74. Idem, Ibid., p. 91.

75. "Annales des Ponts et Chaussées," Vol. I, (1893), p. 24.

76. D. Sturdza, "Recueil...," p. 909. The example refers to the 1894 and 1897 use of the European Commission merchanical dredge, "Delta."

77. "Dispatch ...," p. 4.

78. Bloomfield to Palmerston, St. Petersburg, Oct. 30, 1849; "State Papers, Correspondence between...," Vol. 44 p. 421.

79. From the Sardinian Consul's report, Galatz, 17 October 1850; in D. Bodin, "Documente Sarde," p. 217.

80. Bloomfield to Palmerston, St Petersburg, April 17, 1850, in "State Papers..." Vol. 44, p. 428.

81. Bloomfield to Palmerston, St. Petersburg, Oct. 22, 1850; op. cit., Vol. 44, p. 436.

82. Cunningham to Stratford Canning, Galatz, Sept. 14, 1850, op. cit., p. 434.

83. Bloomfield to Palmerston, St. Petersburg, Oct. 22, 1850, p. 436.

84. Engelhardt wrote over ten studies and articles on Danubian problems.

85. Ed. Engelhardt. "Les embouchures du Danube et la Commission...," p. 101.

86. Report of Sardinian consul, Galatz, October 12, 1850; from D. Bodin, "Documente Sarde," p. 218.
87. Quoted by R.R.N. Florescu, "The Struggle...," p. 272.
88. D. Bodin, "Documente Sarde," p. 217.
89. Cunningham to Palmerston, Galatz, August 28, 1851; "Correspondence between...," "State Papers," Vol. 44, p. 456.
90. Lloyd to Palmerston, Ismail, Sept. 5, 1851, op. cit., Vol. 44, p. 598.
91. Buchanan to Palmerston, St. Petersburg, 1851, op. cit., vol. 44, p. 452.
92. Operation of the gearing of the scoops with regard to the depth and composition of the bottom of the water, the suction dredger; anchorage and advance of the dredger; on the spot repairs or clearing of blocked scoops; the normal work of the hopper dredger; sounding operations, etc.
93. During World War II in which Romania also participated, the Romanian Government at the time was ordered by its ally Germany to dismiss all persons of foreign citizenship working in the Special Autonomous Direction of the Maritime Danube.
94. D. Bodin, "Documente Sarde," p. 218.
95. Ed. Engelhardt, "Les embouchures...," p. 101.
96. B.N. Youghaperian, "L'Annuaire du Danube," (1902-1903), p. 132.
97. D. Urquhart, "The Mystery...," p. 92.
98. D. Bodin, "Documente Sarde," p. 186, Report of July 14, 1847.
99. Idem, Ibid., p. 230, Report of July 24, 1851.
100. Idem, ibid., Report of Jan. 6, 1840 with annex of Cunningham project.
101. Idem, ibid., p. 230.
102. R.R.N. Florescu, "The Struggle...," p. 272.
103. Idem, Ibid., p. 272.
104. E.V. Tarlé, "Răsboiul Crimeei," (Vol. I-II), translated into Romanian from Russian, Vol. I, (1952), p. 42.
105. A. Jomini, "Etude Diplomatique sur la guerre de Crimée (1852-1856)," Vol. II, (1878), p. 43.
106. Kremer Report to Government at Vienna, February 12, 1865; quoted by H. Hajnal in "Le Droit...," p. 21, note 1.
107. Protocol Nr. 4 of March 21, Conference of Vienna, 1855.
108. L. Boicu, "Austria si Principatele Române in vremea răsboiului Crimeei" (1853-1856), p. 41, note 166.
109. Idem, ibid., p. 41, note 166, from "Arhiva Kneaza Vorontsova, Kniga sorokovaia," Moska, 1895, pp. 433, 434, 448.
110. Ed. Engelhardt, "Les embouchures...," p. 102.
111. D. Sturdza, "Recueil...," p. 884. Tonnage estimated from study of the statistical figures on the respective page.
112. Idem, Ibid.
113. R.R.N. Florescu, "Les incidents de Sulina," p. 44.

168 THE LOWER DANUBE RIVER

114. "Pilotos" and "Capetanios," expressions in Greek sailors vocabulary, derived from Italian "Piloto" and "Capitano." The expressions became common among other nationalities in contact with the many Greeks involved in all branches of navigation on the Danube. A boatman, a skipper of a tug or a small craft, was referred to as "Capitanios de barcucia," barcucia being a corruption of "bărcută," the Romanian word for a very small craft; the Greeks having difficulty pronouncing the Romanian letter "ă" and "t."

115. Lloyd to Neale, Sulina, November 14, 1848; "Correspondence between..." in "State Papers," Vol. 44, p. 417.

116. D. Bodin, "Documente Sarde," p. 142; Castillinard's report to his Minister for Foreign Affairs, May 10, 1842.

117. Séniavine to Buchanan, St. Petersburg, Sept. 13, 1849; "Correspondence between..." in "State Papers," vol. 44, p. 420; Seymour to Palmerston, 1851; in "Parliamentary Papers," vol. 102, p. 9.

118. Buchanan to Palmerston, St. Petersburg, Oct. 2, 1849, from Séniavine's statement to Buchanan; "Correspondence between...," in "State Papers," p. 419.

119. "Canal navigable," an artificial watercourse or channel, especially used for the passage of boats. At Sulina, the "canal navigable" could be compared to a ditch of varying lengths, 150 to 200 feet in width, dredged out between two dams, and after 1880. The dams were made of bundles of twigs tied with wire, boulder and blocks of stone thrown on top of them. The canal followed the direction of the river flow into the sea.

120. Lloyd to Neale, Sulina, No. 14, 1848; "Correspondence between...," "State Papers," p. 417.

121. Some examples: "diritto" (forward"); "Sinistra" (to the left); "Distra," (to the right,)" "Molla" or "Mollare," (ease the cables); "Volta," (change direction); "lento" (slow down); "Scalo," (dock or pull to shore), etc.

122. "La Commission Européenne et son...," p. 11.

123. "Report on improvements in the Danube"; Accounts and Papers," Vol. LXX, 1872, pp. 2 and 3.

124. "La Commission Européenne et son...," p. 10.

125. Buchanan to Palmerston, St. Petersburg, Oct. 2, 1849; "Correspondence between...," "State Papers," p. 419.

126. B.N. Youghaperian, "L'Annuaire du Danube," (1902-1903), pp. 199-201.

127. Idem, ibid., Of the general total of 158 pilots and pilot captions, 89 were Greeks. Among the Greek pilots licensed was the author's father, who died during World War I while on a special mission on the Sulina Branch.

128. Among the foreigners was a former Italian Navy Captain, Rizzo, who, on returning to Italy during World War I participated in a submarine foray through a mine field in the port of Fiume, torpedoing a number of Austrian warships. For this feat, he was raised to the rank of admiral.

129. "La Commission Européenne et son...," p. 109.

130. By nationality: 26 Romanians, 10 Greeks, 9 Yugoslavs, 7 Turks, 3 Italians, 1 Englishman, 1 Frenchman, 1 Russian; "La Commission Européenne et son...," p. 109.
131. D. Urquhart, "The Mystery...," p. 33
132. D. Bodin, "Documente Sarde," p. 62; Sardinian Consul's report, Galatz, Jan. 6, 1840.
133. Alex D. Morouzi, "Progrès et Liberté, commerces, finances, agricultures dans les Principautés Unies," Galatz, 1861.
134. Quoted by R.R.N. Florescu, "The Struggle...," p. 266, note 54.
135. Idem, p. 267.
136. Quoted by R.R.N. Florescu, "The Struggle...," p. 266, foot note 55; see also F.O. of 5 May 1836, quoted by Urquhart in "The Mystery...," p. 33.
137. Palmerston to Colquhoun, May 30, 1836, F.O. 78/131; in R.R.N. Florescu, op, cit., p. 266, foot note 55; with respect to Palmerston's order; see Bodin, "Documente Sarde," p. 273.
138. D. Urquhart, "The Mystery...," p. 33.
139. D. Bodin, "Documente Sarde," op, cit., p. 62, annex to report of Sardinian Consul at Galatz, Jan. 6, 1840; also Cunningham to Palmerston, Sept. 30, 1850, "Correspondence between...," in "State Papers," p. 437, 443.
140. Cunningham to Palmerston, Sept. 30, 1850, op. cit.
141. D. Urquhart, op. cit., p. 33.
142. In 1926 or 1927, in Brăila, some 2,000 sheep were loaded on a ship, destined for Alexandria, the bill of lading stating the number of animals loaded on. At Constantinople, all the sheep were unloaded because of an epidemic among them. It being in the summer, the Captain, in connivance with the ship's agent, had all the sheep sheared. After they were disinfected, the sheep were re-embarked and delivered to Alexandria, minus their wool. The skipper lost the subsequent lawsuit on the consideration that the bill of lading had not mentioned whether the sheep were with or without their wool when originally embarked.
143. Bodin "Documente Sarda," pp. 272-273.
144. Their names are included in the report of the Sardinian Consul at Brăila, February 5, 1852; quoted in D. Bodin, "Documente Sarde," p. 254.
145. Quarantine: from the Italian word quaranta (forty). A term originally of forty days, but now of undetermined length, varying according to the circumance of the case; a term during which a vessel arriving from an infected port or having been or being suspected of having a malignant or contagious disease on board, is obliged to forbear all intercourse with the port at which it arrives until all danger of infection has passed. Quarantine regulations in Europe were first established by town officialdom about the middle of the XVth century in Venice and Florence, when anyone entering the city was put under observation for forty days.
146. McGrew and E. Roderick, "Russia and the Cholera," (1823-1832).
147. Hugh Seton-Watson, "The Russian Empire," p. 214.
148. "Russes et Turcs; la Guerre d'Orient," (1877-1878), p. 1063; Anon.

149. Saint Marc Girardin, "Journal des Débâts," Souvenirs de Voyage, Vol. I, p. 225.

150. Karl Marx, "Insemnări despre Români," unpublished manuscript found in a library in Amsterdam; published for the first time in the original text and in Romanian, by the Academia Republicii Populare Române, Bucharest, 1964, p. 69.

151. "Mémoires de l'amiral Paul Tchitchagof."

152. R.W. Seton-Watson, "A History...," p. 163.

153. "Russes et Turcs," p. 1063; Among the victims were several Russian generals; the epidemics were also among the reasons for the Russians halting their advance within ten miles of Constantinople.

154. The Encyclopaedic Dictionary," Vol. II, p. 985.

155. "Stedman's Medical Dictionary," p. 385.

156. "The Danubian Principalities...," Vol. I, p. 254.

157. T.M. McLaughlin, "Dirt, a Social History as Seen Through the Uses and Abuses of Dirt," p. 104.

158. Idem, ibid., p. 127.

159. "The History of Nations: "Russia and Poland," Vol. II, p. 85.

160. "His Imperial Majesty, in consequence of a representation from the Minister of the Interior, made from a report of the Governor-General of New Russia and Bessarabia, and conformably to a decision of the Committee of Ministeries, has been pleased augustly to order, — 1st. To construct a quarantine at the Soulnich mouth of the river Danube, in two divisions; the one for pratique, at the extreme end of the island Leti, to which the quarantine cordon has at present been advanced; and the other, for suspicious vessels, on the Island of Georgi, with this provision, that this second division of the quarantine, not purifying any kind of merchandise, but sending them either to the quarantines of Odessa or Ismail, should serve merely as a port for vessels prevented from proceeding on their voyage up the Danube through contrary winds or the strength of the current; or wishing to receive a supply of provisions or refit. Sometimes, also, it may receive from ships merchants, their clerks, or other passangers, who meeting with delay in their journey by water, should wish to save time, to hold quarantine on the spot, and afterwards proceed to Ismail by land, over the Island of Leti. It may also receive the crews of vessels which have been shipwrecked on those islands. The division for pratique will overlook vessels proceeding from healthy ports; and the second division will overlook vessels which are in quarantine. Both these divisions to be under one director, in order that vessels in pratique should have no communication with those in quarantine. This quarantine, in so far as regards the Customs, must be regulated by the same laws as the present quarantine of Bazertcheck. 2nd. This last port, established by the Ukase of the 26th of October, 1832, and situated at the Kilian Mouth, as it will be found now quite superfluous, is to be evacuated. This will of His Imperial Majesty, has been published in an Ukase of the Senate, dated the 7th of February 1836, published 12.IV.1836, in the St. Petersburgerzeitung"; reproduced by D. Urquhart, "The Mystery..." p. 43.

NOTES   171

161. "Geografia văii Dunării românești," p. 664; and G. Antipa, "Dunărea si problemele ei...," p. 63.
162. 0.40467 hectare = 1 acre.
163. Lotcă, lotci long narrow wooden canoes with pointed prows, capable of advancing through the reed plots, propulsed by sails, oars, or by towing.
164. The speed of the water currents being in relation to their volume, that of the Kilia Branch was 62.5 Cu.M./sec., while that of the Sulina was 17.7 Cu.M./sec. "Geografia văii Danării...," p. 635.
165. Only by 1893 had the European Commission constructed the water works and partial piping of the water; D. Sturdza, "Recueil..." p. 883. Until then, the river water filtered through porous stone basins was distributed by so-called "water carriers." Drainage from toilets and garbage disposal used the same method current in London until the end of the 18th century. The garbage thrown directly into the water and the latrines drained into a sort of shallow cesspools, the contents then emptied into the river or in the pond behind the town of Sulina.
166. Sulina, "a town of wooden houses, has risen into existence at Sulina, which though very necessary for the shipping, can hardly be classed as quarantine establishment alone"; "The Danubian Principalities, the frontier...," Vol. I p. 385. Author's note: Because of the terrain, where the water table was at 5 to 10 feet beneath the surface, construction of brick or stone houses was extremely expensive. The wooden houses were built on stone posts or on logs. The site of the city of Sulina was actually the result of accumulation of alluvia transported by the river. In 1870, the greater part of the city and the port was reclaimed by depositing the alluvia dredged from the navigable trench of the river. The paving of the sidewalks of the six parallel streets was carried out, also after 1870, with volcanic rock, from Sicily, brought over as ballast by vessels entering the river without cargo.
167. D. Sturdza; "Recueil...," p. 892.
168. "Les coudes du fleuve étaient si prononcés que, même dans les meilleures conditions, les navires devaient forcément rencontrer le vent contraire dans un ou plusieurs tournants, d'où de grandes pertes de temps, des encombrements dans les coudes et une confusion générale"; D. Sturdza; "Recueil...," p. 874.
169. "Ainsi, le navire arrivé à un banc, aux Argagnis, par exemple, devait souvent alléger toute sa cargaison ou la décharger sur la berge, pour la reprendre à bord en aval du banc. Il fallait répéter plusieurs fois à la descente cette opération, au cours de laquelle la marchandise courait toutes sortes de risques"; Sturdza, "Recueil...," 874.
170. Established by Russian General Kisselev in the urban plan of the "Organic Regulations." To this day the site of the first quarantine center and its building carries the name of "Quarantine Street."
171. From the report of the Sardinian Consul at Odessa, May 31, 1831; in D. Bodin, "Documente Sarde," p. 11.
172. European Commission, Protocol No. 341 of November 24, 1879; in "La Question du Danube," M.A.E.

173. Durham to Palmerston, May 1836, F.O. 195/129; in R.R.N. Florescu, "The Struggle..." p. 265.
174. Palmerston to Durham, July 31, 1836, F.O. 78/131; in R.R.N. Florescu, "The Struggle..." p. 267.
175. D. Urquhart, "The Mystery...," p. 27.
176. "The Danubian Principalties...," Vol. I, p. 365.
177. Ibid., pp. 365, 366.
178. Report of Sardinian Consul at Brăila, Feb. 5, 1852; D. Bodin, "Documente Sarde," 239.
179. Report of Sardinia Consul at Galatz, Nov. 10, 1852; in D. Bodin, "Documente Sarde," p. 272.
180. "The Danubian Principalities...," Vol., I, p. 400.
181. The case of Alexander Ghika, ruling lord of Moldavia who, on his return from Constantinople on board a vessel, was subjected to a very rigourous examination at Galatz port; D. Diculescu, S. Iancovici, C. Danielopol and N. Popa, "Relatiile Commerciale ale Tărilor Românesti cu Peninsula Balcanică, 1829-1858," p. 15.
182. Details in "Regulamente Organice ale Moldovei si Walachiei," op. cit., pp. 368 ff.
183. "The Danubian Principalities...," Vol. I, p. 272.
184. Ibid, p. 366.
185. N. Iorga, "Les premières relations entre l'Angleterre et les pays Roumains du Danube (1477-1611)"; in Mélanges d'Histoire, p. 565.
186. W.G. East, in "The Union of Moldavia and Wallachia, 1859; An Episode in Diplomatic History." Appendix One, p. 169.
187. "The History of Nations": Russia and Poland, Vol. 15, p. 310.
188. Quoted by R.R.N. Florescu, "The Struggle...," p. 267.
189. J. Stokes, "Notes on the Danube," (1860), p. 166.
190. Map of 1769 of the Romanian Principalities, including the Delta, and subsequent maps of 1796 and 1830; in I. Vidrascu, "La Voie Navigable...," p. 4.
191. D. Urquhart, "The Mystery...," p. 17.
192. From the total surface of the Delta's 430,000 hectars, only 65,000 ha is dry land at low water and, of these, almost 14,000 hectares remain uninundatable at the highest water level; in Gr. Antipa, "Dunărea si problemele...," p. 63.
193. Fishing, cattle raising, vegetation, reeds, hunting, etc.
194. Palmerston to Durham, July 1, 1836, F.O. 78/131; in R.R.N. Florescu, "The Struggle...," p. 267.
195. "Geografia văii...," p. 680.
196. For example, the village of Caraorman, a Turkish name.
197. For details on the populations of the Delta see E. Englehardt, "Etudes sur les embouchures...," pp. 35-40.
198. Along with the respective treaty, see also R.W. Seton-Watson, "A History of...," p. 243.
199. Urquhart, "The Mystery...," pp. 17, 18.

200. Durham to Palmerston, June 1836, F.O. 78/131; quoted by R.R.N. Florescu, "The Struggle...," p. 267, note 57.
201. From the reports of Consul Blutte to the Foreign Office; Florescu, pp. 142-143.
202. Hugh Seton-Watson, "The Russian Empire," p. 213.
203. Idem, ibid., 213.
204. See last line of text of 1836 Ukase.
205. "Acte public relatif à la navigation des embouchures du Danube," le 2 Novembre 1865, Galatz; in Sturdza, "Recueil...," pp. 80-89.
206. "Règlement de navigation et de police applicable à la partie du Danube entre Galatz et les embouchures" 19 Mai, 1881; D. Sturdza, "Recueil..." pp. 136-188.
207. Règlement de 1881; in Sturdza, "Recueil...," p. 139.
208. Hugh Seton-Watson, "The Russian Empire," p. 213.
209. Urguhart, "The Mystery...," p. 103.
210. Palmerston to Lord Beauvale, Nov. 29, 1839; quoted by H. Hajnal, in "The Danube...," pp. 66, 67.
211. Palmerston to Durham, July 1, 1836, F.O. 78/131; quoted by R.R.N. Florescu, "The Struggle...," p. 267.
212. Dalberg Project.
213. Palmerston to Beauvale, Nov. 28, 1839, F.O. No. 151; quoted by H. Hajnal, "The Danube...," p. 66.
214. The 1821 Act for Navigation on the Elbe, between Prussia, Saxony, Hanover, etc.; the 1839 Treaty between Belgium and Holland; the 1842 Treaty of Navigation between Belgium and the Netherlands; D. Sturdza, "Recueil...," pp. 596, 853, 856 and 869.
215. Protocol Nr. 5, of 23 March of the Conference of Vienna of 1855; D. Sturdza, "Recueil...," p. 20.
216. "A source or origin, primordial substance, ultimate basis in cause; a fundamental truth; a primary or basis law, doctrine; a governing law"; Webster's New Collegiate Dictionary.
217. R.R.N. Florescu, "The Struggle...," p. 266.
218. R.R.N. Florescu, "The Struggle...," p. 153.
219. Blutte to Foreign Office, June 27, 1831, F.O. 97/403; quoted by R.R.N. Florescu, op. cit., p. 142.
220. Idem, ibid., p. 143.
221. "Mémoires du Prince Soutzo," pp. 66, 67.
222. "Gazzetta Piemonteza," No. 78, pp. 1, 2; D. Bodin, "Documente Sarde," p. 17.
223. A.D. Xenopol, Vol. IV, p. 108.
224. R.R.N. Florescu, "The Struggle...," p. 144.
225. A.D. Xenopol, Vol, IV, p. 108.
226. Idem, ibid.,
227. Idem, p. 137.

228. For example, after a locust invasion in the Romanian Principalities during the period of the epidemics, Kisselev obtained flour from the reserves of the Russian army of occupation, to combat the famine which created conditions counter to the methods for combatting the epidemics. He ordered the burning of contaminated villages and the housing of their residents in tents. He established medical services, inspected the temporary hospitals and the infected regions at the risk of his own life, etc; Xenopol, Vol. 1V, pp. 108, 109.
229. T. McLaughlin, "Dirt...," p. 143.
230. Idem, ibid., pp. 143, 144.
231. Idem, ibid., p. 144.
232. R.R.H. Florescu, "The Struggle..." p. 152.
233. "Case Englesi" were represented by Cavadia, Carusso, Diamandis (Greeks); Rocco (Italian), and Amburgher (Austrian Jew); D. Bodin, "Documente Sarde," pp. 254, 433.
234. W.G. East, "The Union of Moldavia..." pp. 169-180 (Appendix).
235. In general, Malta was the transfer point of England's import and export goods. Transportation from eastern regions of the Mediterranean and from the Black Sea was carried out in vessels if lesser tonnage. At Malta, the cargo was unloaded and reloaded in vessels appropriate for navigation on the Atlantic Ocean to England. Transshipment was carried out also at Constantinople. An English traveller calculated that more than 50% of the average annual quantity of 416,378 imperial quarters of cereal exported from Brăila toward England in years 1853 and 1854 had their destination marked Constantinople and Malta.
236. D/Bodin "Documente Sarde." The Ionian flag is met in all the statistics regarding movement of sea-vessels in the Danube.
237. T. McLaughlin, "Dirt...," p. 155.
238. "The Danubian Principalities..." Vol. I, p. 367.
239. R.R.N. Florescu, "The Struggle..." p. 158, note 57.
240. Idem, ibid.
241. A.D. Xenopol, Vol. IV, p. 121.
242. Nicholas Soutzo, "Mémoires...," p. 66.
243. T. McLaughlin, "Dirt...," p. 144.
244. A.D. Xenopol, op, cit., Vol. IV, p. 108.
245. T.M. McLaughlinm "Dirt...," p. 148.
246. Idem, ibid., p. 147.
247. Idem, ibid., p. 148.
248. Idem, ibid., p. 148.
249. Engraving in the Gribb Collection, Royal Institute of Chemistry, reproduced by McLaughin on the Cover of his book.
250. "Istoria orasului Bucuresti," 1965, pp. 200, 300-301.
251. "The Wonderful Story of London," p. 246.
252. Ibid., p. 246.
253. T. McLaughlin, "Dirt...," p. 155.
254. D. Urquhart, "The Mystery...," p. 7.

255. D.J. Dallin, "The Big Three: United States of America, Great Britain, Russia," p. 49.
256. Idem, ibid., p. 50.
257. Idem, ibid., p. 49.
258. T. McLaughlin. "Dirt...," p. 143, quoted from the Diary of Charles Greville, Nov. 14, 1831.
259. V. Slăvescu, "Viata si opera economistului Sutzu," p. 27.
260. R.R.N. Florescu, "The Struggle...," p. 153.
261. Idem, ibid., p. 153.
262. A.D. Xenopol, op. cit., p. 133, Vol. IV.
263. Kisselev's letter of June 7, 1843; in "Règne de Bibesco" I, p. 192; in "Buletinul Oficial al Principatului Valahiei," 1843, p. 293.
264. For details, see "Dictionnaire Encyclopedique de sciences médicales," III, Serie 1.
265. For details, see C.I. Băicoianu, "Dunărea vazută prin prizma Tratatului de Pace de la Bucuresti," pp. 39-43.
266. "Convention sanitaire de Venise du 18 Mai 1897. Règlement sanitaire général pour prévenir l'invasion et la propagation de la peste, du 18 Mai 1897, admis par l'Allemagne, l'Autriche-Hongrie, la Belgique, l'Espagne, la France, la Grande-Bretagne, la Grèce, l'Italie, le Luxembourg, le Montenegro, la Turquie, les Pays-Bas, la Perse, le Portugal, la Roumanie, la Russie, la Serbie, et la Suisse; see D. Sturdza, "Recueil..." pp. 813 to 824.
267. "Annexe XI, La Convention sanitaire entre l'Allemagne, l'Autriche, Hongrie, la Belgique, la France, le Luxembourg, le Monténégro, les Pays-Bas, la Russie, et la Suisse, signeé à Dresde le 15 Avril 1893; see D. Strudza, "Recueil...," pp. 809-810.

PART FOUR

THE COLLATERAL EFFECTS OF THE OBSTACLES AT THE SULINA MOUTH

Chapter 1

SULINA, "A LITTLE CALIFORNIA"
"There where the Old Danube loses its waters and its identity in the sea."[1]

The subject might seem irrelevant to the main theme of this work. Regarded, however, in the light of the benefits derived from describing it as "a little California," it becomes an integral part of the history of the development of navigation through the Sulina Mouth and even on the course of the Danube as far as Brăila, during the 1829 to 1856 period and even after. Furthermore, along with the situation created by the natural obstacles existing at the navigable mouth of the river, the social factor of the "little California" contributed equally to the decision for internationalization of navigation, as it did also to the continuance and aggravation of the Anglo-Russian conflict. In researching this subject, documentation from the past and information from mariners' circles in the Danubian ports were made use of, as was the personal knowledge of the author, a native of Sulina.

By terming Sulina "a little California where fortunes were to be made," Cunningham, the English vice-consul in the Danubian port of Galatz, described Sulina's deficiencies which, in his opinion, were the real obstacles to efficient progress of navigation.[2]

Overnight, the small and insignificant fishing port, but very important because of its geographic position at the entrance to the Danube, became famous throughout Europe. Although in commercial circles in London the geographic positions of the mouths of the Danube were unknown, the fame of the "little California" was public knowledge. The price of grain on the London market was set and fluctuated depending on the activity of the people in the navigational complex

179

of this port. Thus, with a population of about one thousand people in 1829, mainly fishermen, Sulina in short order became one of the principal ports of Southeast Europe. To the original population, newcomers were added, especially Greeks, all eager for instant wealth — not by mining the gold of California — but by exploiting to the maximum the difficulties of navigation through the Sulina Mouth. Supplementary sources of income were created by resorting to pirate-like methods. Though not denying the facts, an attempt will be made to show that the conditions attributed subjectively and exclusively to Sulina were, at that time, common also to other ports of intensive commercial traffic, conditions corresponding to the social milieu specific to the evolution of commerce and navigation in the past along the Lower Danube.

The development of Danubian commerce after the Treaty of Adrianopole changed the social profile of Sulina. Unscrupulous methods of exploiting the natural difficulties of navigation contributed to the worsening of the commercial and social life of the new society in Sulina after 1829.

Cunningham was correct in his relating the conduct of the personnel to the kind of assistance provided for vessels passing through the Sulina Mouth, conduct which also had an influence on Danubian trade. Still, certain facts, circumstances and correctives must be taken into consideration, which would nullify the description of Sulina as the prototype of all ills.

At the entrance to the Danube through the Sulina Mouth, foreign navigators did not come in contact with a nationally and politically homogeneous population, but with a heterogeneous one with an entirely different make up. The interloper circles in Sulina were not composed of national groups, but of cosmopolitan ones; with no unity of language, only a Babel of confusing tongues. This characteristic was excellently illustrated by a former Sulina Port Captain, in the short story "Europolis"[3] a title descriptive of the mosaic of nationalities of the Sulina population up to World War I.[4] To this international population was added also the plurality of new customs, habits, attitudes, manners, etc., etc.

Sulina was not London, just as California was not Washington. It was not even Galatz, where Cunningham was active. At Sulina, there were all those from all over Europe, come to profit from Sulina's great possibilities of enrichment for importers of grain at ridiculously low prices after 1829. Constantinople was a large, cosmopolitan city, but there functioned a state authority which maintained discipline and social order. At Sulina, under Russian administration, there existed corrupt official authority, associated with the interlopers who contributed to the disrupting of any organization. At Sulina, according to Vice-Consul Lloyd, "...it is not in the interests of any parties, either the local authorities or the inhabitants of Sulina, that the obstacles of navigation be removed."[5] In analyzing the Sulina situation, there must be taken into consideration many other factors which, added to its comparison with the fame of California, for example, certain customs in the Galatz and Brăila ports which were detrimental to normal exercise of commerce and navigation.

The documentation concerning the conditions at Sulina is accurate, originating as it does from reports of officials within the European Commission of the Danube, as well as from various other researchers and observers, among them one who holds the view that similar conditions existed also in other ports. Concerning the workers at Sulina, Engelhardt wrote: "Ils rançonnaient la navigation européenne et rappelaient par leur âpreté impitoyable l'avidité du géant des bouches de l'Escaut."(sic).[6]

What were the conditions that gave Cunningham the right to call Sulina "a little California?" They were conditions created by workers and pilots who carried out the various operations: towing, transshipment, piloting, landing, dislodging grounded vessels, etc. To these were added thefts of goods from the ships, cheating in connection with providing supplies of food or naval materials, swindling, and the atmosphere of brothels and bars, etc.

Sir John Stokes, researching the period of the first fifteen years of Russian administration at Sulina, observed: "The pilots in league with the rogues...plundered the vessels...ran them aground in order to oblige them to employ lighters, in whose profits they share..., the lightermen robbed the vessels of their grain by the use of false bottoms to their holds."[7]

The conclusion drawn by Engelhardt, the French delegate to the European Commission of the Danube in 1862, as to the navigation methods in use through the Sulina Mouth during the Crimean War period, was even more specific and severe. He described the methods of the lightermen as "vol organisé..." practiced by "hardis pirates."[8] He attributes the origin of windmills in Sulina exclusively for the purpose of grinding the wheat stolen and hidden by lightermen in the false bottoms of the lighters.[9] He justifies this statement by the otherwise impracticability of such mills at "un point désert de la côte, à l'extrémité d'une plaine de roseaux."[10] This was his impression, the windmills coinciding as they did with the thefts of grain, but actually, such windmills continued to function in later periods even today being one of the picturesque aspects of the Danube Delta often portrayed in tourist literature.

Direct sources of the European Commission also pointed out the unscrupulousness of the pilots and the dishonesty of those conducting the transshipments, activities that gave rise to frequent complaints from captains of vessels.[11]

The same situation was found also on the Sulina Branch, caused by the natural obstacles previously mentioned, and where crews of workers were employed at the towing, transshipment, etc., operations.[12] According to Stokes, the crews were composed of "...matelots cosmopolites qui, disait-on, ne valaient guère mieux que des pirates, propriétaires de petits bâtiments propres à servir d'allèges..."[13]

Thefts from the vessels were organized, the loot being transferred during the night, the pilots generally being in partnership. According to Stokes, shipwrecks could have been avoided by proper piloting.[14]

Among the many reasons for which the Danube Delta had been returned to the Ottoman Empire in 1857, Engelhardt includes: "l'arbitraire le disputait au désordre, le despotisme à l'anarchie, le commerce était privé des garanties les plus élémentaires de sécurité..."[15] He pointed out also that the natural obstacles at Sulina "favorisaient les déprédations des aventuriers qui peuplaient Soulina" and that "l'absence d'une police efficace permettait les actes de baraterie les plus éhontés: vols et naufrages étaient à l'ordre du jour et les abus les plus criants restaient souvent impunis..."[16]

Stokes came to that same conclusion when he stated, "...over and above these evils, the navigation suffered from the entire absence of regulations or order, and thus, collisions or accidents, of all kinds, were frequent and, in the utterly lawless state of things which prevailed in 1856, acts of piracy and intentional loss of vessels were not rare occurrences."[17]

Foreign commercial circles, especially the English ones, complained about the lack of control and order to the Russian administration. The latter however, was complacent about being the beneficiary of the local mores, its own directives resulting in vessels being "stopped no less than eight times by as many different commanders."[18]

During the Crimean War, new vagabond elements transformed Sulina into a no-man's-land,[19] in the absence of any authority; "une bande d'écumeurs de mer s'empara de fait de l'entrée du Danube," was Engelhardt's description.[20] Drastic measures were taken by Austria when her armies were in the Romanian Principalities during the Crimean War period. The expedition of a detachment of sixty soldiers to Sulina to protect Austrian navigation interests, "fut un bienfait pour le commerce européen."[21]

After the murder of British Admiral Parker's son, who had arrived in Sulina on a military vessel[22] in the spring of 1854, the Austrian measures were intensified, martial law actually introduced and "la bastonnade fut mise à l'ordre du jour et consciencieusement administrée."[23]

Also in order to bring about order and protection of navigation, General Coronini, commandant of the Austrian Armies in the Principalities, dispatched two fluvial warships to Sulina, under the command of Major Baumrucker.[24] The latter also reported the Turkish contributions to impeding navigation with the hidden intent of delaying exports.[25] It is interesting to note that, in 1855, Baumrucker, too, described Sulina as "a little California."[26] Among the drastic measures taken by the Austrians, was the organization of a special police along the entire sector of the Lower Danube.[27]

This then, was the level of conditions at Sulina, for the elimination of which drastic measures were necessary; conditions facing the European Commission in 1856, in addition to the natural obstacles, and which it had to solve in time.

As to the conditions at Sulina and their spreading along the Lower Danube, there do appear contradictions in the Anglo-Russian conflict. The most numerous complaints against the conditions came from English officials and private sources. The author of the term "a little California," was English and Sir John Stokes, whom described the conditions, was England's chief delegate to the European Commission. From existing documents, it seems that the great majority of the Lower Danube "pirates" were Ionians, Greeks originally from the Ionian islands,[28] British citizens under the protection of the British vice-consulates in the Danube ports.[29]

Some of the Ionians believed themselves to be entitled not only to dominate the Lower Danube, but also to monopolize all navigational proceedings. The British diplomatic representatives in the Danube ports, as well as Cunningham and at times even London circles, felt it their duty to protect their subjects, the Ionians. This protection was the result of their British subject status, as well as of local commercial considerations. According to the capitulation regime accorded by Turkey, British subjects were under the protection and jurisdiction of the British consuls or vice-consuls. Many Ionians and, in general, the Greeks along the Lower Danube were at the service of British interests, which when necessary could get them passports.

Because of the growth of commerce and navigation on the Danube after 1829, the Ionians and the English found themselves in competition with the Italians (Sardinians), whose presence became felt increasingly. The conduct of the Ionians took an acute form with respect to the local Romanian authorities, as at Galatz and Brăila, where regulations were disregarded. The national self-respect of the Romanian population, representing the majority in these two ports, was insulted by the disrespectful attitude of the foreigners under the protection of the capitulations and of the diplomatic representatives. The disciplinary measures imposed by the Romanian authorities at Galatz and Brăila must be viewed with those factors taken into consideration, as must the occasional Russian measures taken in the framework of its protectorate over the Romanian Principalities,[30] measures the English representatives considered an actual violation of the rights of their citizens, including the Ionians.

In justified cases, or in the abusive ones against the disciplinary measures taken at times by the Russians as protectors at Sulina, Galatz and Brăila, protests came even directly from London on behalf of "British protégés," "Ionian subjects," etc.[31]

The Romanian element in Galatz and Brăila had changed from majority to minority, under the pressure of the consuls protecting their subjects. Of the new foreign population inundating navigation in the Lower Danube after 1829, Iorga wrote: "...it was not in friendly relations with the indigenous one. Especially the Cephalonians from the Ionian Isles, British subjects, assaulted people with sand-filled bags and death threats, throwing knives in the ranks of the soldiers and obliging the authorities to complain to the English consuls."[32]

Information about the behavior of the Ionians also came from Sardinian consular sources, credible inasmuch as they were part of diplomatic reports for domestic circulation. They referred to the actions of the Ionians and the Greeks in general as in contrast to the Italian participation in commerce and navigation along the Lower Danube, the latter being considered by the former as "intruders" in their sphere of activity. In this respect, the report of one of the Sardinian consuls was eloquent. He mentioned brawls of "naval combat" type occurring in the competing market of Galatz and the reaction of the Sardinians who "...voulaient mitrailler les Grecs provenant la plupart des îles ioniennes..."[33]

In other reports of the Sardinian Consul, one finds mention and descriptions of the rivalry and the actions of the Ionian Greeks as "rivalry with the Greek and Turkish fleet,"[34] "observations on the Greek navy"; "jealousy of the Turks and Greeks towards our commercial navy";[35] "bad Greeks and Slovenes";[36] "nervous Cephalonians,"[37] etc.

The Sardinian consuls considered the measures taken by the authorities in Galatz and Brăila as useless against the Ionians and the Slovenes, the former being protected by the British vice-consulates and the latter by the Austrian ones.[38] Contrary to the attitudes of English and Austrian representatives in the Danubian ports, the Sardinian ones were perfectly in accord[39] with the measures taken by the authorities, in Galatz and Brăila, against foreign infractors.

In the competitive markets of Galatz and Brăila, Austria also had her people, the Slovenes (Esclavons)[40] under the protection of Austrian Consul Hübner. A quarrel at Galatz, followed by a hand-to-hand fight between Anglo-Ionians and the Esclavons (the latter instigated by Hübner), was prevented from escalating by Cunningham's intervention, tempering his Ionian subjects.[41]

Interference by the consulates occurred also after 1856, when the autonomy of the Romanian Principalities was declared. The British Consul at Bucharest intervened in favor of some Ionians who "...seemed to have a knack of getting into trouble with the authorities, but oftentimes they were punished without any other notice being sent to the British Consul."[42]

In the case of "the little California," as well as in the Lower Danube commerce and navigation, the native element, whose principal activities were agriculture and fishing, is not to be included. The greatest part of the commerce and navigation in the Lower Danube from 1829 to 1856 and following, was carried on by the following categories of foreigners: Greeks, in the fluvial and maritime navigation; Greeks and Jews in the export of cereals; Greeks, Jews and Austrians in the commerce of collecting cereals.

After 1829 and during the first few decades after 1856, the mosaic patterned population of the Lower Danube ports had transformed even the local commercial structure. Foreign languages predominated, Greek becoming the leader in the commercial and navigational vocabulary. The customs, traditions and mores of the Romanians were changed under the influence of the influx of foreigners seeking their fortunes in the "America of the Balkans." As seen from the above, the British subjects — specifically, the Ionians — contributed in great measure to the reputation of "little California."

The collateral effects of the obstacles at the mouth of the river and along the course to Brăila continued for several decades after the European Commission of the Danube took over. In 1878, when through the Treaty of Berlin (Article 53) the functioning of the Commission was placed outside the sovereignty of the territorial state (România), keeping order in navigation ran up against the obstacle of absence of unification of measures of control. In opposition to that clause, România installed a Commissioner on the town's territory who had the function of Port Captain, along with the Captain set by the European Commission, with jurisdiction over the Port of Sulina and navigation. The measure created some jurisdictional conflicts, as a result of which anomalies arose in the application of policing navigation. "An entire army of agents and intermediaries," noted Băicoianu, "profited from this situation and often in connivance with the captains of vessels, continued their affairs without hindrance to the detriment of the insurance companies, the suppliers, local and foreign commercial houses."[43]

The infractions committed on Sulina town territory entered in the jurisdiction of the Romanian commissioner; those committed by marine of fluvial personnel anchored at the port quays were under that of the Port Captain appointed by the European Commission. The office of the latter could take no action, not having police organs, hence the offenders simply took refuge on their ships, where the jurisdiction of the Romanian commissioner ended.

A strange situation, actually to the advantage of the offenders, resulted from the extraterritorial status of the European Commission, a status marked — aside from the juridic framework — by a "frontier line" symbolically represented by a small fence.

The establishments of the European Commission[44] were on an area of about 100 acres, ceded by Turkey.[45] The symbolic frontier between the extraterritorial section and the rest of the town of Sulina and the port section under Romanian sovereignty, was the little green-painted fence, having a gate through which public access was forbidden only during plenary meetings of the European Commission. On the one side of the fence the Romanian flag was raised, on the other that of the European Commission (white, with blue and red stripes and the logo of the Commission).[46]

Often, common-law offenders (Romanian or foreigners) or those breaking navigation regulations, crossed over the fence into the territory of the European Commission, out of the jurisdiction of the Romanian authorities.[47]

It seems that the conditions prevailing in the "little California" did not disappear completely after 1856, nor did the undesirable elements. Gradually and with great effort was the European Commission able to establish norms to paralyze the piracy of the past. The Commission eventually became the sole and decisive factor transforming the social and economic life of Sulina. By the great technical work it undertook at the Sulina Mouth and the Sulina Branch, it absorbed in its activities a great number of the residents, along with the foreign element, in time creating a new and decent social class. To the influence of the European Commission was added the new technical structure of vessels propelled by steam engines. In spite of the gradual reduction of the "little California" atmosphere, Sulina still retained through its cosmopolitan aura, its aspect of a "Europolis," democratic in nuance. Its theoretic distinctions, but not divisions, of social classes could be seen at the famous Stamati Café and the Camberi Bar,[48] the only such large establishments.

The diminishing of Sulina's importance began almost twenty years before the outbreak of World War I. The consulates and vice-consulates were replaced by honorary agents and the large steamship lines and big commercial enterprises moved their headquarters to Galatz or Brăila. Because of the events and consequences of World War I, Sulina soon experienced its death pangs and in a very short time found itself reduced to being a simple passage for larger vessels and a site for reduced technical activity of the European Commission. The number of foreigners in commerce and navigation diminished gradually, the process being developed by the repatriation to the foreigners' countries of origin, by movement to Galatz and Brăila, and by attrition. The demographic heterogeneity of Sulina of yesteryear was successively replaced by the homogeneous Romanian population. The traces of the former mosaic of nationalities can be seen even today on the inscriptions on gravestones in the Sulina cemeteries.[49] Sulina had inscribed her own antiquity and at the same time her chapter in the "Danube Question."

With the social revival of Sulina, it can be stressed that the majority of the foreign newcomers after 1856 were, apart from the older interlopers, Greeks and even Ionians; some of them beginning with decent activities succeeded in becoming important suppliers on the Lower Danube and, later, in becoming owners of large maritime fleets in Greece, with world-wide radii of activity.[50] The roots of their financial potential were on the Lower Danube and in Romania. In strict objectivity, one cannot eliminate the supposition that, among the ranks of those who reached the heights of financial status, there were some heirs of those from the epoch of the "little California."

Returning to Cunningham's observation, one can see some differences between the "little California," the actual California and London. While Sulina's repute was more or less localized in the European commercial world, that of California was world famous, even to the extent of being named "the Barbary Coast." While Sulina's fame inspired no books, one can find many for California. Among the authors for the latter was one Asbury, who with regard to the abject social ambience of the Barbary Coast wrote, "...owing almost entirely to the influx of gold seekers and the horde of gamblers, thieves, harlots, politicians, and other felonious parasites who battered upon them, there arose a unique criminal district that for almost seventy years was the scene of more viciousness and depravity, but which at the same time possessed more glamour than any other area of vice and iniquity of the American continent."[51]

While in Sulina petty thievery of grain from vessels and modest economic revenue from risky occupations were common, in California the prime movers for robberies of great value, arson, premeditated crimes or crimes committed by professional murderers,[52] were liquor, the bordellos[53] and gambling.[54]

In comparison with the free choice of marine professions on the Danube, in San Francisco the abject system of "shanghai-ing"[55] was current and "many mysteries in early San Francisco were never solved because of this practice of shipping the 'corpus delicti' to sea as a live sailor."[56]

While in the Sulina underworld crimes were not recorded, in California assassinations were organized in the sight of the police organization. While thefts and other infractions of law in Sulina were initiated by unlettered and unorganized crew chiefs, in California organizations of criminals, exploiters of bordellos, etc., became the stepping stones to political platforms for holders of important social and administrative positions.

One cannot deny that in Sulina there reigned, as in many ports of European Turkey, that social atmosphere known as "Balkanic." Objectively analyzed, the respective atmosphere was the result of direct and indirect effects of political and economic situations created by the many wars between the Great Powers, waged on the territory of the Balkan peninsula. The living standard of "little California" was the exponent of the social and economic miseries accumulated over the centuries in the Balkans.

Comparing the Sulina situation with that of London, the capital of one of the Great Powers, its territory protected from barbarian invasions and wars, one cannot find much difference. If the author of the phrase "little California" had read the many works dealing with the life of foreign elements in London and in California, he would have hesitated about giving that title to the tiny port of Sulina.[57]

In England, the Sulina state of affairs was well known, but neither the London circles nor Cunningham took into consideration the fact that the same atmosphere was prevalent in all the levantine ports and even in London. Still, for London merchants, Sulina remained "the Hell of the Danube River." Long after the Anglo-Russian conflict on the Danube, the following poster was still on view at the "Mercantile Marine Masters' Association" in London: "Beware of Peter the Greek"[58] the name of a bar on the outskirts of the town.

Frequently as among sailors of all nationalities, in the throes of drunkenness, quarrels arose, which ended in damages for the proprietor as well as for his clients at the mercy of the ever present thieves. This same atmosphere existed also at the "Englitera", a more luxurious bar in the center of town.

That warning, based on some actual happening, was of minor value when compared with major happenings in London. Leaving aside descriptions in "London's Underworld," for example, those referring to "prostitution in London," 'the dependents of prostitution," 'clandestine prostitution," etc., enough chapters remain with respect to "felonies on the River Thames"[59] analogous to the Sulina of the Danube River. Mention is made of the "great number of robberies committed on the Thames by different parties. These depredations differed in value from the little ragged mudlark stealing a piece of rope or a few handfuls of coals from a barge, to the lightermen of the Thames carrying of bales of silk several hundred pounds in value.

While the foreign element and the Danube navigation authorities were considered immoral, in England sailors for the fleet needed for the Crimean front were being recruited even through the mediation of Paddy Goos, owner of a brothel "popular with the Admiralty authorities."[60] Neither before nor after 1829, could Sulina have been equated with London which, though part of the "land of strongly puritan traditions"[61] and surrounded by the social ambience of the Victorian Age, was dominated by the underworld. Whenever Cunningham's personal presence in Sulina was demanded by his commercial interests, he risked neither his life nor his personal belongings; a security which he would not have had either in London or in San Francisco.

No matter under what criteria the circumstances impeding the normal flow of navigation could be considered, it can be stated definitely that their dimensions at Sulina did not reach the heights attained at the Barbary Coast or in London's Underworld. London was the capital of a Great Empire and Sulina only a former tiny fishing village situated on the arena of political and commercial disputes and of conflicts between colossi. The only difference was that through the mouth of the Sulina, the wheat departed and the gold of countries of Western Europe, including England, entered.

Whether it be considered a "little California," or a "Europolis," Sulina cannot be eliminated from the history of the "Danube Question."

Chapter 2

INITIATIVES FOR A NEW OUTLET TO THE BLACK SEA AND A PROJECT FOR THE IMPROVEMENT OF NAVIGATION AT THE SULINA MOUTH

Introduction.

In spite of English claims the condition of navigation at the Sulina Mouth remained critical. Recourse to force would have complicated even more the situation created by the Treaty of Unkiar-Skelessi, through which Russia strengthened her position at the Straits.[62] Austria's plans for development of steam navigation depended directly on the assurance of easy access to the sea. Even as early as 1815 the policy of the Imperial Royal Committee on Commerce had been to work out projects "with the purpose of opening a connection with the Black Sea."[63]

The only solution to being free from Russian interference, with normal communication between the Danube and the Black Sea through Sulina, would have been to find an alternate exit. The first theoretical projects for such a route on water were Austria's but were in the end unrealizable.

The principal hardships in carrying out Austria's initiatives were the lack of adequate technical equipment and insufficient knowledge on the geophysics and hydrography of the newly projected routes to the sea, factors contrary to the theoretical studies and calculations. Attempts to solve these impediments being too many and demanding too much time, Austria found herself obliged to accept a temporary compromise by signing the 1840 Convention of Navigation with Russia, without giving up her projects. An opening to the sea, by means of a new communication route on water, was Vienna's constant preoccupation, not only during the period of the Russian administration at the Sulina Mouth, but also later between 1853 and 1856 as well as at the time of World War I.

The new opening to the sea became an important problem also in the preoccupations of the European Commission of the Danube in 1856, without being solved. It was taken up again after World War I, without results. After World War II, the idea of a new route through the Danube Delta was abandoned and a connection between the Danube and the Black Sea was considered on Dobrujean territory, through the Cernavoda-Midia Canal.

Initiatives.

Resolution of the problem of entering the Black Sea was demanded also by Austrian merchants, who blamed the inertia of the "First Austrian Danube Steam Navigation" (Erste Österreichische Donau-Dampfschiffahrts-Gesellschaft-DDSG) for the fact that their first steam vessels of about a 500 ton capacity could not pass through the Sulina Mouth except by means of the costly operation of transshipment. The merchants' demand was based also on their losing the bi- monthly sailings of the steam vessels loaded at Sulina for passage to Constantinople.[64]

In 1838, the First Austrian Steam Navigation Company decided to construct a canal between Cernavoda and Constanta,[65] a project originally considered by the Austrian War Council,[66] the construction to be financed by bankers, Rothschild and Sina, of Vienna.[67] This was the canal recommended by Tsar Nicholas I in 1839 and which Palmerston had considered less practical in comparison with the river communication.[68]

Among the causes impeding the realization of the project were technical difficulties, insufficient capital and the impracticability of the port of Constanta for docking vessels and for handling cargo. The project also provided for an alternative which could be used until the canal was completed. The cargo unloaded from vessels docking at Cernavoda Port[69] was to be transported to Constanta on a road to be constructed almost parallel to the route of the projected canal. This alternative also was abandoned because of the impracticability of the port of Constanta. It was used briefly from 1840 to 1841 only by a stagecoach service which had to be abandoned because of insufficient commercial activity.[70] Urquhart blames official English circles for the canal not being realized, because of their prejudices in favor of Turkish interests. He did add, however: "England woke from her trance to suggest a counter project: a railway from Silistra to Varna,"[71] an idea later dropped because of the immense investment involved and its commercial inefficiency.

Mention is made also of another Austrian plan, in 1838, to construct a railroad between the Black Sea and the small port of Isaktcha, on the Dobrujan bank of the Danube under Turkish sovereignty; a project that also was abandoned.[72]

Faced with the failure of the Cernavoda-Constanta canal project, Austria turned her attention to the St. George Branch. This time the project was initiated by the Lloyd Austrian Company for Navigation, which was engaged also in maritime routes. A company vessel serving the Galatz to Brăila route was sent in 1850 to study the mouth of the St. George Branch with an engineer on board, together with other persons, Cunningham among them.[73] The results were negative because of the unfavorable hydrographic conditions.[74]

With conditions at the Sulina Mouth continuing under partial Russian administration during the Crimean War, the Austrians persisted in their plans, During their occupation of the Romanian Principalities, they reconsidered the St. George project and conducted hydrographic research on the basis of an 1851- 1852 study-report on navigation at the Danube mouths, made by Mihanovici, at the time director of the Austrian chancellery in Constantinople and later Consul General al Bucharest.[75] The report was addressed to Buol, the Austrian Minister for Foreign Affairs. The general conclusion of the studies and research carried out on the basis of this report was that use of the St. George Branch was possible and was considered more practical for navigation than the Sulina Branch.[76] In the meantime, however, the European Commission for the Danube was established in 1856 and the project was dropped.

The necessity for creating a new outlet to the sea was mentioned also in the Constantinople press. The anonymous English traveller (previously quoted source) related that the "Journal de Constantinople" suggested a new line of communication with the Black Sea, namely:[77] starting at the right bank of the St. George Branch to the right of the beginning of the Dunavăt Canal, then following the course of this canal ending in Lake Razelm, one would reach the natural passage Portita, which formed the tie between that lake and the Black Sea.[78] This idea corresponded with the local geographic situation, but not with the aim in view. As has been shown in the ancient epoch of Danube navigation, the suggested route had been used by the Hellenes as a time between the Histria colony and the Danube River by means of the St. George Branch, but the type and the tonnage of the Hellenes' vessels were much different from those existing at the middle of the nineteenth century. The limited dimensions of the Dunavât Canal (25 to 30 Mtr. width and 1/2 Mtr. depth) with, low, reed covered banks, were inappropriate for towing of vessels. Furthermore, as its name suggests, the Portita (wicket) passage is too narrow to allow passage of vessels from Lake Razelm towards the Black Sea.

After 1856, the Ottoman Government accorded an English company, represented by J. Trevor Marclay, the concession for construction of a a railroad between the Danubian port of Cernavoda and the maritime port of Constanta on the Black Sea.[79] The cost of the work was estimated to be 500,000 Lira,[80] the inauguration to take place on October 4, 1860.[81] In the end, the work was not carried out inasmuch as, in the meantime, the European Commission for the Danube had scheduled improvement of navigation through the Sulina Branch.[82] After 1878, however, the Romanian Government resumed and completed the project, constructing also a bridge across the Danube at Cernavoda.

The idea of a connection between the St. George Branch and the Black Sea on routes other than those mentioned above, is found in theoretic studies made in certain Romanian engineering circles prior to 1900. One of these studies indicated a canal starting from the right bank of the St. George Branch, to the right of the village of Mahmudia, then crossing a series of lakes and ponds and Lake Razelm, to reach the sea through Portita.[83] However, unlike the Austrian project, the construction of this canal would have required a series of extremely expensive technical constructions (locks, dikes, dredging, etc.)

The Austrian and English projects seemed to have been counteracted by the Russian ones. In 1900, the Russians planned an artificial canal between Solomonoff, a sub-branch of the Kilia Branch, under their jurisdiction and Gibrieni Bay at the Black Sea.[84] The dimensions of the canal would have allowed only fluvial vessels to sail between the Kilia Branch and Odessa.[85] Abandoning this project, the Russians considered the construction of another canal, this one through Otchacov and Polounotchnoi, both of them sub-branch of the Kilia Branch.[86] On this canal, only fluvial vessels of small tonnage could have navigated. During World War I, the Russians blocked it up by scuttling tugboats loaded with rocks.[87] After 1918, when the Kilia Branch, together with Bessarabia were restored to Romania, no other projects were initiated, Danubian navigation continuing to be carried out along the Sulina Canal and Mouth.

The Project for the Improvement of Navigation at the Sulina Mouth.

Concomitant with the above mentioned attempts, a project for improving navigation at the Sulina Mouth was drawn up by private initiative. On December 10, 1839, Cunningham made public a prospectus for creating a share-holding company for the purpose of deepening the Sulina bar.[88] The necessary capital was to be subscribed by means of 200 shares at the rate of 100 colons per share, the company's base being Anglo-Austrian.[89] The initial investment cost was estimated at 20,000 Spanish colons,[90] and the estimated annual operational expenses at 13,000 colons, sums expected to be recovered by taxation of loaded vessels only, in accordance with a fixed tariff for their drought.[91] This was a purely commercial undertaking, the prospectus representing also an annual benefit of 7,000 colons. The maximum depth proposed for maintenance at the bar was of 15 feet, the minimum of 14 feet, the company assuming the obligation of paying transshipment costs in cases of nonnavigable depths.[92]

From the prospectus, the company appeared to be of international character, a juridic form which in no way would have been acceptable to Russia. Aside from the English and Austrian citizenships of its originators, its home base would have been at Galatz and Brăila, that is, on Romanian Principality territory under Ottoman suzerainty, and its technical operational management at Sulina, under Russian occupation.

The possibilities for realization of the Cunningham project will be examined in comparison with those of the 1856 one of the European commission of the Danube. His project corresponded with the navigational needs, but the difficulties of implementation were caused by the insufficient technical knowledge of the time along with the existence of physical obstacles. How could navigable depth of 14 to 15 feet, as specified in the prospectus, be obtained with a mechanical dredge of only 40 HP,[93] when the European commission, using four dredges of a total capacity of circa 830 HP[94] managed to get a depth of scarcely 10 to 14 feet in 1861-1876?[95] The 40 HP dredge was also scheduled to get the navigable depth through a 152 foot wide sand bar, which would have been absolutely impossible.[96] With a much more powerful dredge used by the European Commission between May 1 and July 11, 1857, it was impossible to get any appreciable depth through a bar of the same dimension.[97] How could the maintenance of a permanent navigational passage to the mouth of the river have been assured considering that the same passage was the most difficult problem for the European Commission to resolve, and which remained so until after World War I? These are part of the many other problems.

With regard to the operational costs of the Cunningham project, discrepancies appear in his estimates of them. In the prospectus reported by the Sardinian Consul previously mentioned, the annual cost was 13,000 colons, but estimated at 19,554 in a Cunningham report[98] in which the sums were given in "Spanish dollars." (sic).

Leaving aside the monetary parity and only as a general example, the annual cost of the dredging carried out by the European Commission was 253,473 gold francs.[99]

In no reports from the Sardinian Consuls in the Danubian ports was there any indication of the causes for the non-implementation of the project proposed by Cunningham. The only report given was that, by order of Count Sambuy (sic), the Viennese ambassador, Sardinian merchants of Brăila and Galatz were not to participate in the establishment of the dredging company, with no explanation for the reasons.[100]

In conclusion, the Cunningham project for improvement of navigation at the Sulina Mouth remained unfulfilled. It would have been impossible to achieve the expected results. Resolving the problem began only after 1856, when the European Commission was established.

Russia's Position.

Could it have been possible for a technical project at the Sulina and St. George mouths to have been undertaken without Russian consent? In 1850, when the Foreign Secretary of England suggested a conference "of the interested states to discuss ways of financing an extensive project for deepening the bar,"[101] Russia rejected it on the consideration that it was incompatible with her sovereignty at Sulina and was a rank foreign interference in her political sphere. On the other hand, there was the situation created by Article III of the Treaty of Adrianople. In conformity with this article, the left bank of the St. George Branch to the thalweg of the river, belonged to Russia.

On the right bank, still in Turkish possession, in accordance with the same article, there could not be built any structures necessary for the construction since, for a distance of two leagues, the bank had to be uninhabited. If both river banks and the mouth were to be used, either Article III would have had to be modified, or the express agreements of Russia and Turkey would have had to be obtained.

As for the Cunningham project, that presented another aspect. First of all, Russia would not have accepted any interference which would have involved the presence of foreigners in the administration of navigation at the Sulina Mouth. Secondly, the improvement of navigation would have diminished her possibilities for sabotage. To these considerations there can be added her reaction to the criticism of the Russian administration, made in the prospectus of the company proposed to be involved in the improvement process. Without making a direct reference to the Russian administration at Sulina in the prospectus, it was mentioned that the Sulina Mouth had been abandoned lately and that the depths had not been increased "under the Government which occupied the respective mouth." These remarks could not have been overlooked by Russia, especially since the Prospectus was made public.

There are rather contradictory data in information available with regard to Russia's attitude and to the chronology of certain actions concerning the Austrian project for the Danube-Black Sea Canal (Cernavoda - Constanta). Mention was made of a suggestion made to the Austrians by Tsar Nicholas I, with respect to resolving the problem of passage to the sea, by a canal which would connect Cernavoda with Constanta.[102] The Sardinian Consul to Galatz reported in 1838 that "l'Empereur aurait dit qu'en cas de son effectuation, la Russie en serait quitte par avancer de quelques lieues ses frontières dans les Principautés" (sic).[103]

The same information is found also in an 1837 report from Cunningham to Palmerston, saying that the Tsar's suggestion was made "with no real intention of adopting it, simply as a way of detracting from the importance of the Danube."[104]

Russia's opposition to another Austrian project in 1848, also on the Cernavoda - Constanta route, was revealed by Urquhart who attributed its abandonment also "to the efforts made by Russia preventing the execution of the project for opening of the old mouth[105] of the Danube, within the Turkish territory."[106]

The idea of threatening the advance of the Russian frontier into the Romanian Principalities was not valid; the projected route would have been through Dobrujean territory, at that time under Turkish sovereignty, not through the Principalities.

Could the Cernavoda - Constanta Canal have been achieved before 1856?

The problem of the canal will be considered together with the modern 1948 project for the same connection along the Cernavoda-Midia route of about 60 Km. Midia[107] is neither a port nor a human settlement; it is a cape, a headland situated about 30 miles north of Constanta. Choice of it, instead of the Port of Constanta, as a terminal point of the proposed canal was due to two principal considerations. The first was the construction of a modern commercial port in place of Constanta and the second was of strategic military order.

All the projects in the past for the construction of the Cernavoda - Constanta Canal (Austrian, English, etc.) were based on technical and theoretical knowledge and the practices learned from experience with other European canals constructed under more or less identical geological conditions. In the case of this proposed canal, conditions were different. Aside from comparative deductions of a theoretical order, technicians and geologists of the past were not familiar with the structure of the Dobrujan subsoil of the territory on which the canal was projected. Some premises were based on the existence of the hypothetical Carasu Branch of the Danube, vaguely mentioned in antiquity. Without preliminary verification and on-site geological research and without adequate equipment, the construction of the canal was envisioned by the projectors as a simple process of digging along the barely visible traces of the Carasu.

Insufficient knowledge on the part of past initiators concerning the geological conditions of the Cernavoda - Constanta route is evident, too, in the comments made by Urquhart, who was more or less familiar with all the attempts made for creating an opening to the sea. Commenting upon the Austrian project, he mentioned, "the facility of the execution...of the junction of the Ister and Euxine,"[108] basing his deduction on the pre-existence of the Carasu Branch.

What could have been the duration of the construction of any of the projects of the past, if we consider that the new project of 1948 was planned for ten years (1948-1958)? Urquhart attributed the apparent nonexistence of physical difficulties to the fact that along the proposed canal route "there are neither mountains to tunnel, nor rocks to blast, nor sands to build out."[109] In the hypothesis that a canal was to be built on that direct Cernavoda - Constanta route Urquhart's premise would have been more or less correct, but taking into consideration the new route estimated in 1948 as the most efficient, the physical difficulties he referred to would not have been easily eliminated. He noted that, in case of the change of level of the river, "a pair of locks may be requisite, and as water may be scarce, concrete-locks may be necessary."[110] In fact, in the 1948 project, provision was made for a sluice gate at Cernavoda because of the variations between the water levels of the Danube and those of the new canal.

Also greatly underestimated was the financing of the construction of the proposed Cernavoda-Constanta canal. In comparison with the 500,000 Lire mentioned by Urquhart[111] as the Austrian estimate, the planned cost for the same work, in the 1948 project, for a period of six months only (August- December 1948) reached circa six billion lei,[112] a figure checked by the author of this present study.[113]

For the financing of the Austrian canal project, the Sardinian consul indicated the participation of the Rothschild and Sina Banks of Vienna.[114] What could have been the financing possibilities of these banks, as compared with that of the Romanian State in the case of the 1948 project, taking into consideration the fact that the latter involved the free labor of over 100,000 political and civil law prisoners? What technical possibilities for efficient execution of the work would there have been in the past when, in 1948 they worked with primitive means and aging equipment leased from Russia, stock remaining from the latter's construction of canals between 1925 and 1935?[115] What could the Austrian technical cadres have been when even in 1948 the lack of competent specialists was felt?

The greatest obstacle unforeseen by the Austrian planners, and which surprised those of 1948 as well, was the variety of the stratification of the Dobrujan subsoil. Because of the sandy strata identified on some sectors of the route, water would have leaked through. The ease of construction was envisioned by Urquhart on the basis of "...the distance is between thirty and forty miles, and through half of it runs a follow filled with water, and offering to our hands a ready made canal."[116] In the "half of it," however, is the marshy region to the left of the town of Medgidia, where the 1948 technicians ascertained a possible loss of water. After a year of on-site examination (1950-1951) on the part of the five Russian specialists temporarily established at Constanta, the recommendation was made to cement a length of the canal bed, including that mentioned above, an extremely costly construction.

Another error of Urquhart's though not of the Austrians, was in indicating the kinds of transports which could eventually participate in the traffic of the canal. Demonstrating the ease of navigation of large steamers of the Austrian Steam Company, he suggested replacement of the 2,000 ton barges on the Danube by the steamers, inasmuch as "it would be easier to bring the seagoing vessels up than to bring the barges down."[117]

It must be noted that before 1856 seagoing vessels were not large steamers, their cargo capacity being small. As for the river barges, the maximum load capacity of a reduced number did not exceed 1500 tons before 1850, nor does it even today.

Chapter 3

OTHER EFFECTS OF THE OBSTACLES

The 1840 Austrian - Russian Convention of Navigation.

The agitation and concern of the Great Powers over the Russian preponderance at the Straits, following the 1833 Treaty of Unkiar-Iskelessi,[118] determined the Russians to show an apparent change in their foreign policy. With the intent of weakening the Anglo-Franco-Austrian bloc, they signed the 1833 Secret Agreement of Münchengrätz with Vienna, for the purpose of solving the problems that might arise in the event the Ottoman Empire would be dismembered. The 1841 Convention of the Straits[119] followed, which eliminated the exclusive privileges through the Straits in favor of Russia, obtained on the basis of the 1833 treaty.

Inasmuch as the problem of navigation on the Lower Danube could not be resolved, the Austrians decided to side with England. To this end can be evaluated the 1835 Treaty of Navigation, drawn up between Austria and Greece,[120] followed by the renewal of the one between England and Austria.[121] Although futile insofar as practical application was concerned, still the respective treaties were symbols of opposition to the arbitrary Russian administration of navigation at the Sulina Mouth.

In the ensemble of Southeast European and Near East problems, Austria did not shift basically from the policy of England and France. Nevertheless, because of her immense commercial interests, it was necessary for her to act unilaterally towards Russia, which could scarcely wait for a rift in the Anglo-Franco-Austrian bloc. For

England "free access through the Sulina Mouth, becomes a European question," as the "Morning Chronicle" described it in 1835.[122]

To reach her desired aim and in the spirit of the Agreement established at Münchengrätz, the Russians offered the Austrians the possibility of solving the acute problem of her steam navigation. Hence, on July 21, 1840, at St. Petersburg, the Russo-Austrian Convention for navigation was signed, for a ten- year period.[123]

As for England's tacit reaction to the Convention, one can consider her previous position as it was indicated in an article in the "Morning Chronicle," that: "Austria, instead of isolating herself from the interests of Western Europe, as she has hitherto done for too many years, will feel it to be her best interest to cultivate the good will of these States."[124]

The previously mentioned English traveller, familiar with the opinions of English circles in Constantinople, evaluated Austria's unilateral action as being not only prejudicial to England's interests in the Danube, but also "a nullity for Austria, as far as she was concerned, for some of the articles of the Convention either favored or hurt her interests."[125] Bearing in mind Russia's reduced commercial interests through the Sulina Mouth, the result was that only Austria benefited more from the reciprocity clauses of the Convention.[126]

The absence of Russian navigation interests on the Austrian Danube in 1840 became evident later when the Danubian economy registered greater progress than in the past. At the Conference of London, in 1871, Russians refused to participate in the financing of improvements at the Iron Gates, which would have eased the connection between the Lower and the Austrian Danube, for the reason that the work concerned a sector "placé entièrement au dehors du cercle habituel de l'activité commerciale et industrielle de la Russie."[127]

It is difficult to understand Russia's indifference to Austria's economic expansion which could have been an impediment to the former's political expansion. Yet, leaving aside the temporary application of her political interests, Russia did obtain through Austria's signing of the Convention the "de jure" recognition of her occupation and preponderance over the navigable mouth of the river.

The aforementioned English traveller concluded that "the occupation of Sulina by the Russians received the sanction of Austria in a special convention."[128] His opinion was expressed in 1854.[129] Yet, the Sardinian Consul had reached the same conclusion in 1840, immediately after the signing of the Convention. Russia made it known that, only by permission from her, could advantages at the river mouth be obtained. In 1839, at the request of a Netherlands navigation

OTHER EFFECTS OF THE OBSTACLES 203

company, was the "protezione dell Imperatore della Russia"[130] granted.

The Sardinian Consul at Galatz reported in 1840, "If I am not mistaken, Russia through the stipulations of the Convention had as her principal aim the formal and immediate recognition of her dominion over the useable mouth of the Danube."[131] Even more significant is the fact that the same consul stressed that Russia's aim was "to force other nations in time to conclude similar conventions."[132]

Several remarks concerning the Convention are useful here. Undoubtedly, in conformity with the text of the Convention, special treatment was accorded to Austrian vessels at the Sulina Mouth. An important clause, with respect to the beginning of an indirect recognition of navigation on an international order, was that of the Preamble to the Convention, referring to the Principles of the Act of 1815, respectively the clause of Article CVIII concerning the bilateral regulations between the riparian states of a river. The bilateral character of the Russo-Austrian Convention was supplemented with another principle, namely, the extension of free navigation also to nations which had that right on the Black Sea and which were at peace with Russia (Article II). However, the enunciation of the principles of 1815 was theoretical, not a matter of fact. Extension of freedom of navigation became inoperable through the clauses of Article III and IV of the Convention, which provided for facilities and regulations exclusively for Austrian and Russian sailing and steam operated vessels, leaving for interpretation the status of vessels of nations covered by Article II.

Another discrimination came from the provisions of Article VII. While navigation fees were fixed for Austrian vessels, fees for other nations were arbitrary and changeable. Special facilities were provided for with regard to the quarantine, the sanitary control not being permitted to impede navigation (Article III). Austrian steamships were given special treatment, being considered in the sanitary precautions as navigation vessels of the Black Sea and the Straits. (Article VIII). One useful clause was that concerning the obligation taken by Russia to install a lighthouse at the Sulina Mouth. (Article VI).

Contrary to the principles of the Act of 1815, Austrian navigation was limited exclusively to the Sulina Branch (Art. III), not also on that of the Kilia, under Russian domination. Nor was navigation on the St. George Branch included, that being under the common Russo-Turkish jurisdiction, in accordance with Art. III of the Treaty of Adrianople. The non-inclusion of these branches in the Convention also was derived from the obligation Russia assumed to exclusively maintain navigation at the Mouth of the Sulina (Art. V and VI). Nor was any provision made for Austrian vessels to have access to the southern ports of Russian-occupied Bessarabia, such as Ismail and Kilia Veche, commercial ports. An exception was made for Reni, a Bessarabian port located on the common Russo-Turkish sector (Art. III of the Treaty of 1829).

The obligation to maintain navigable depths at Sulina was ambiguous. A conditional situation was created by the fact that the work was to be performed "...toutes les fois qu'ils seront jugés nécéssaires et que la saison et le temps le permettront." (Art. V). It is true that dredging operations are possible only as circumstances permit, but in the generalization of impediments foreseen there could have been included also minor circumstances such as rains, small storms, etc. which would not have been obstacles. If a point was made of the failure of Russian attempts at dredging, then the maintenance of navigable depths at the mouth of the Sulina remained worthy of record.

A peculiarity of jurisdictional order in the Convention lay in its sphere of application. Between the fluvial sectors covered by the Convention — the Austrian and the Russian ones — was interposed the sector of the Lower Danube that was under Ottoman jurisdiction, that is, between the mouth of the Pruth River and the Austrian frontier, a little distance upriver from the Turnu Severin port. In other words, for Russian vessels to be able to sail on Austrian waters and Austrian ones on Russian waters, they had first to pass through the Turkish sector, a right supposedly exercised by virtue of the Russo-Turkish and Turkish-Austrian Conventions and Treaties previously concluded. The Convention's political and circumstantial character finally resulted in the non-respecting of the obligations assumed by Russia, "...d'empêcher un nouvel ensablement de l'embouchure de Soulina" (Art. V.). This proved the truth of the previously mentioned opinions of the Sardinian Consul at Galatz, that Austria's interests were at Russia's discretion.

In 1842, the Sardinian consul at Galatz reported that Russia began to clear the passage at Sulina, but that the work was proceeding slowly because the orders issued were inappropriate for obtaining the necessary results.[133] Thus, since Russia did not respect the obligation of the Convention, by its expiration in 1850, the navigable depth at the Sulina Mouth had decreased to 8 1/4 feet, compared to the 12 feet existing in 1840, at the signing of the Convention.[134] In spite of the extension of the Convention to July 21, 1851, it still did not reach the aim desired by Austria. The latter then determined to resort to the solution of planning a different exit to the sea.

OTHER EFFECTS OF THE OBSTACLES 205

According to H. Hajnal, the Convention's failure was due to the fact that neither one nor the other of the contracting parties had respected it.[135] He stated, "...l'insuffisance des connaissances techniques et l'indolence des Russes amenèrent un état du chenal si désastreux qu'il fût l'objet de plaintes perpétuelles."[136] This situation was well known to Austria, it having become public following the Anglo-Russian conflict revolving on the navigation difficulties at the Sulina Mouth. Austria's fault was attributed by Hajnal to the violations of Article I of the Convention.[137] By extending, in 1846, the privileges accorded to the "Erste österreichische Donau Dampfschiffahrts-Gesellschaft" to 1880, the Russians could not benefit without competition, from the provisions of Article I which allowed them free navigation on the Austrian Danube. While the considerations involved in Russia's fault were factual, those attributed to Austria were relative from two points of view.

First of all, access of Russian vessels to the Austrian Danube was provided for only under the symbolic aspect of reciprocity, since actually it could not be effectuated without difficulties because of the natural obstacles and small depths at the Iron Gates, the point at which Austrian navigation began down river. Even the traffic of Austrian vessels was constrained at this point, necessitating transshipment operations by land. Keeping in mind the fact that Austria, not Russia, inaugurated steamship navigation on the Danube and that the first such vessels to sail on the Lower Danube did so in 1836, one can see why any such Russian vessels were absent from the river in 1840. From a report of the Sardinian Consul at Galatz, it would seem that only in the spring of 1846 was there a Russian passenger and cargo ship put into circulation, and then only between Odessa and Galatz.[138] No disadvantage for Russia would have arisen, even if Austria — which had accorded that privilege to a company under her control — had eventually extended the right of navigation on her waters. Russian vessels, in their reduced numbers, could not have presented any danger of competition to the Austrian company.

The Convention of 1840, then, did not result in any advantage for Austria; her acute steam navigation problem was to be resolved only after 1856.

The Controversy on the Competition between Brăila and Odessa.

Among the purposes followed by the Russians in sabotaging navigation at the Sulina Mouth it is mentioned also that of protecting Odessa against Brăila's competition, the latter port having developed greatly after 1829. The object of the competition was the grain being exported from Brăila, the port located at the northeastern extremity of the most fertile region of the Romanian Principalities known in the past as the "grenary of Europe," and the terminal point of the maritime vessels on the Lower Danube. Looking at this so controverted problem, an attempt will be made to consider it from a different point of view, based on collateral Russian activities.

Referring to the frequent complaints about the Russian manner of maintaining navigation, Stokes stated, "...on commença alors à accuser la Russie, non seulement de ne rien faire pour l'enlèvement des bancs qui obstruaient l'embouchure de Soulina, mais d'y couler même des navires afin d'aggraver encore l'état natural des choses et cela, à l'effet d'empêcher le commerce maritime d'Odessa de souffrir de l'importance croissante de celui du Danube."[139]

Thus, he was reporting not his own personal finding, but was referring to rumors circulating in commercial circles ("...on commença alors à accuser la Russie..."). The European Commission, however, remained reserved, qualifying the rumors and complaints as "des accusations exagérées..."[140]

Nor was any precise confirmation made by Ponsonby, the British Ambassador to St. Petersburg, who in 1837 wrote to Palmerston, "...it is quite apparent that all the grain from the Principalities enters into competition with the grain of Russie."[141] Even here, uncertainty can be deduced from "it is quite apparent." It is also said that "although the Peace of Adrianople was upheld, Russia did nothing more to aid the development of the Principalities."[142]

A Sardinian Consul mentioned that: "En attendant la Russie, n'incline nullement à favoriser le commerce des deux Principautés et par conséquent la navigation du Danube. Elle voit d'un oeil jaloux l'accroissement du commerce qui se fait dans les ports de Galatz et d'Ibrail (Brăila): la Crimée, Odessa surtout, en souffrent" (sic).[143]

On the other hand, Prof. Puryear states: "it is quite clear that the Principalities were not able to expand their production, however, as rapidly as the increases effected by the southern ports of Russia"[144] (including Odessa). In documenting this statement it was shown that in 1853, "an exceptional period in Danubian exports, Great Britain purchased 1,028,000 quarters of grain from Russia's southern ports" in comparison with 200,000 quarters imported by that same country from the Principalities.[145]

There is a paradox in connection with that competition. Vernon Puryear, a well-known researcher of the commercial complex of

OTHER EFFECTS OF THE OBSTACLES 207

Odessa, was of the opinion that: "Russia herself unwittingly laid the basis for the Danubian competition by her requirement in the Peace of Adrianople that the Principalities of Moldavia and Wallachia be given the same "liberty of commerce" which Russia had acquired for her own trade in the Black Sea."[146] It is difficult to believe Russia did not have a preconceived policy and so equally indifferent to imagine that she could "unwittingly" or "unawares" bring economic independence to any ports "where she had a political interest...," as Palmerston wrote in 1838.[147]

Gardner, the English consul at Jassy (Moldavia) also wrote: "...commerce was called into life by Adrianople...its importance became in a few years sufficient to compete with the celebrated port of Odessa."[148]

A subsequent remark in the same vein as those above was that of Count Vorontsov, quoted by Urquhart. In reference to the competition which Brăila and Galatz were carrying on with the Kilia and Ismail ports on the Kilia Branch, Vorontsov said "...the protecting sceptre of Russia has created these formidable rivals of herself...and if the obstacles which have hitherto impeded the navigation of the Danube come to be entirely removed, this much facilitate the vent of Austrian articles of merchandise in the provinces' Principalities and will open up for some of them a way to arrive at the other countries."[149] What can be retained from this statement is the evaluation of Brăila and Galatz as auxiliary points to the development of Austrian commerce, but not as principal centers for cereal export. Vorontsov's statement is contradicted by Puryear, who based his deductions on official Russian statistics. The latter wrote: "...foreign commerce of the Russian ports[150] of the Danube had doubled their trade exchange in the two years which opened the decade."[151]

If the Brăila exports had influenced those of Odessa, a reduction would have occurred at the latter port. But, from Puryear's statements it appears that in 1840 "the commercial movements at Odessa increased rapidly despite the inadequate facilities for transport."[152]

To Odessa's advantages over the Danubian ports can be added also the difference in the cost of the exported cereal. A quarter of wheat from Galatz to England was reported to cost 13 s., while from Odessa it was 8 s.6 d.[153] The difference was normal considering the more favorable position of Odessa over that of the Danubian ports. Aside from the sufficient mooring space available for vessels of greater tonnage, and the other port facilities, the specific expenses inherent to Lower Danube traffic were nonexistent at Odessa, as was also the uncertainty of the possibility of entering the port because of the instability of the sand bar at Sulina.

In opposition to the idea of "unawareness" can be invoked Russian foresight shown in the clause of Article VII of the Treaty of Adrianople, with regard to assuring the future development of Russian trade in the geographic sphere of the Ottoman Empire. Would it have been possible that Russia could not have had that same foresight in her interests also in the case of possible competition from Danubian ports?

From the above there would appear the absence of any certain proof of competition between Brăila and Odessa. The contrary shows up however, in the many possibilities Russia has to hinder such competition. As victors in the War of 1828-1829, Russia could not have been forced by anyone to provide in Article V of the Treaty of Adrianople for freedom of commerce for the Romanian Principalities. Neither the Separate Treaty nor the two Organic Regulations made obligatory the organization in all areas, including the ports, of the Principalities.[154]

By means of the same Treaty of Adrianople, the Russians removed Brăila from the sovereignty of the Ottoman Empire, to restore it to the Romanian Principality of Wallachia, an action symbolized later by a monument raised in honor of the Russian soldiers.[155] The Russians also confirmed and clarified, for the first time, through an international treaty the very controversial problem of the suzerainty, not sovereignty, of the ottoman Empire over the Romanian Principalities.[156] This clarification was repeated and confirmed later also by Article 22 of the Treaty of Paris in 1856.

In addition to being protectors, the Russians were absolute masters over the Principalities by the presence of their troops of occupation, which remained there until 1834. "The Principality," reported Blutte, the British Consul at Bucharest, "is now administered as though forming a constituent part of the Russian dominions."[157]

Even more, in conformity with the Conventions of Balta-Liman, Akkerman and especially with the Treaty of Adrianople concluded with Turkey, the Russians not only reserved their right to enter into domestic matters of the Principalities but also reserved the right to confirm the appointments of the Romanian princes assigned by the Sublime Porte. The Organic Regulations applied to the Principalities "established Russia's preponderance to an almost absolute degree," wrote Xenopol.[158] If the Russians were capable of prohibiting all national manifestations, of closing schools, banning the importation of foreign publications, etc.,[159] they certainly could all the more have prevented any economic development of the Principalities, but this did not occur.

OTHER EFFECTS OF THE OBSTACLES 209

Regardless of the amnesties accorded to political persons detained because of their opinions or activities against Russia or Turkey during the War of 1828- 1829, after hostilities ceased abusive arrests were carried out, as dictated by Russian interests. Among the many examples was that of Ion Câmpineanu, Mayor of Brăila, arrested in spite of the previous eulogic appreciations by Kisselev for the activity he had carried out for the development of the town and port of Brăila.

In certain circumstances, Russia did not have confidence in Romanian authorities, either, as was the case in appointing the quarantine inspector.[160] In short, the Russians imposed and obtained anything that fit into their interests of the moment or of the future. With all the ability displayed on many occasions and in many circumstances by the Romanian leaders, they could not have frustrated, without risks, either the Russian aims or their methods, had the latter intended to prevent the development of Brăila's commerce. The Russians took the most useful measures for the urban, social and economic development of Brăila, and the town plan was drawn up on the order of Kisselev and the instructions of Baron R. Barrocyn, similar to that of Odessa, designed by the Frenchman, Richelieu.[161]

In description of Brăila, from an urban point of view, Romanian historiographers have pointed out the attention given to the connection between the city and the port by means of the many streets, the construction of quarantine barracks in the port, and the creation as early as 1832 of special funds for construction of port quays, to keep up with the growing commercial traffic.[162] The organization of the city was also reported to be such as generally arranged for largely populated centers.[163] The Russian administration as not opposed either to declaring Brăila a free port in 1836, nor to that of Galatz in 1837, after the 1808 example of Odessa, a status which was in support of their commercial development.[164] Between 1831 and 1845, the growth of the import value of the two ports was 815%[165] and that of their exports 1377%.[166]

Also in the Odessa-Brăila matter, Russia's participation must be revealed in the commercial and navigational competition on the Lower Danube, along with the other flags, English, Austrian and especially the Greek and Turkish. In the traffic of the year 1836, in the ports of Galatz and Brăila, 76 vessels flying the Russian flag[167] were included and, in 1846, the "Gagarin" Company of Odessa was formed and started temporary sailing of passengers on the Lower Danube as far as Belgrade,[168] its fleet of towboats, tugboats, and oil tankers increasing in number until 1900.[169] Besides direct participation, there was also the indirect one represented by vessels owned by local Greeks and flying the Russian flag.[170]

The point of view of this present work eliminates the idea of sabotage of Brăila, although in the Russian contribution to the development of the Principalities (including that of Brăila) the clauses inserted by the Russians in the two treaties of 1829 — in the sense of the "well being of the two Principalities," or "whose prosperity has been guaranteed by Russia"[171]—were not particularly honored. These clauses of ethical and propagandistic value can be considered under a different light, be they even presumptive. Russian policy has its coulisses.

In a political light, the administrative autonomy granted by the Russians to the two Principalities had been planned in support of the anti-Turkish activity in the Balkans and the diminuation of the authority of the Porte's suzerainty over them. In the economic light, the results of the freedom of their foreign trade would have substantially weakened the supply lines for Constantinople and, in the end, the consolidation of the new circumstances in the Principalities would have prepared a favorable atmosphere for their annexation, had any appropriate conjuncture arise. Under these aspects could be mentioned the theory of "fattening the turkey." That description was the humorous replay made at a later date by a Russian diplomat to a diplomatic representative of Romania, who doubted Russia's lack of intentions to annex new territories.[172]

The real competition with Odessa took place after Russia's removal from the mouths of the Danube, in 1856, followed by the application of the international regime of navigation. The traffic through Sulina, including that through Brăila, between 1847 and 1881, increased from 6550 vessels of a capacity of 1,109,653 Tons to 23,362 vessels at 4,203,350 Tons.[173]

In conclusion, until further new documentation appears, the matter of competition between Odessa and Brăila remains controversial.

Was the Danube Commerce Prejudiced between 1829 and 1856?

At the basis of the Anglo-Russian conflict was the reduction of the volume and the lucrativeness of the Danube commerce because of navigational hardships. The problem raises many contradictions resulting from existing conditions as well as from statistics, including those from English sources. According to some statistics, the exports of cereal the principal item — instead of dropping, recorded continuous rising, especially those destined for England.

In evaluating numerically the traffic of vessels and commerce in the Lower Danube, one must keep in mind the veracity of the statistics, the conditions and circumstances under which they were obtained, as well as their author's methods of interpretation. In this matter, one Sardinian consul underlined the causes which hindered those drawing up the consular reports from verifying statistical figures.[174]

It may well be that Cunningham's statistics were so varied for the same reasons reported by the Sardinian consul. On September 17, 1850, Cunningham had reported to Stratford Canning, at Constantinople, the number of 110 English vessels going from the Danube between 1837 and 1847, and 706 vessels between 1846 and 1849, all from the Brăila and Galatz traffic.[175] On September 30 of that same year, he indicated in his report to Palmerston that, from the total of 1018 vessels passing from those two ports in 1843 only 7 were English and in 1849 out of a total of 1,144,297 vessels had England as their destination.[176]

Added to the above information is that from Nicholas Soutzo, a Romanian economist, contemporary to the time of the Anglo-Russian conflict. In one of his many studies in which he dealt also with the situation of the transports, he noted the growth of the general traffic of cereal export and of the number of vessels having Galatz and Brăila as their source. From 209,062 Moldavian Kilos in 1837, cereal export rose by 1847 to 1,206,643 Kilos and the number of vessels carrying out the respective export rose from 879 in 1837 to 2,215 in 1847.[177] Hence in a period of ten years, a growth of 477% in the export of cereal and 152% in the traffic of vessels.

The same economist, in analyzing the foreign trade at the port of Galatz, wrote, "...il est de fait constaté que le commerce de notre port avec l'Angleterre a reçu une extension progressive très prononcée." He also stated that imports of English goods through Galatz and Brăila reached the sum of 26,458,890 Turkish piastres in 1848.[178]

In March of 1847 the Sardinian consul in Galatz reported to his government that the cereal warehouses in that port were filled, that navigation on the Danube was free ("é libera ora la navigazione del Danubio"), and that an extraordinary number of vessels were expected ("una straordinaria quantità di bastimenti"), among them 200 English ones already leased.[179] "The import trade of Moldavian Wallachia"— reported another consul in 1851 — "is in continuous progress and that of England is in first place with 1,439,750 francs."[180]

Also in 1851, from the total of 1598 loaded sailing vessels leaving the ports of Galatz and Brăila, the English flag was the third, after the Greek and the Ottoman, while the Austrian flag flew over 328 steamships and 100 sailing vessels.[181]

From the 1838 reports, of Prussian Consul Neigebaur at Jassy, also is evident the growth in the foreign trade of the Romanian Principalities. He also stated, "England floods all the Black Sea and Danube ports with its manufactures..and so Saxonia's greatest competitor has squeezed her way into Wallachia and Moldavia,"[182] indicating the growth in the value of English imports through Galatz and Brăila to 1,004,500 florins in 1843.

From a Puryear's research is confirmed the high level of English trade with Turkey and with its European provinces. "By 1852"—he noted—"one third of the shipping of the Danube was British" and underlined "the fact of the British development of the Danubian Principalities in grain production for competition with Southern Russia."[183]

The discrepancy between the volume of transports and the number and flags of the vessels effectuating it was caused also by the British objections raised in the matter of the reduction of their trade on the Danube. According to English documentation, England's imports from the Danube were in the amount of 563,000 Imperial quarters.[184] That same year, however, the English flag registered 15 vessels entering the Danube.[185] The inequality between the quantity imported and the load capacity of those 15 vessels would lead to the conclusion that other flags participated in the respective transports a situation that would not disadvantage English trade.

Regarding the participation of means of transportation in exports through the Sulina Mouth, deductions will be made from some of Cunningham's statistical data in which are noted destinations of vessels passing through the Brăila and Galatz ports. Of the total number of 6,758 vessels passing through those two ports from 1843 to 1849, almost 49% had Constantinople as their destination, 19% had Trieste and Venice, 23% had Genoa, Marseille and Livorno, and only 9% were destined for England.[186] It is difficult to believe that the English and Ionian flags did not participate in this traffic. Also from a Cunningham report is deduced the growth of cereal exports to England.[187]

The evaluation by the London Exchange of the conditions for carrying out Danubian commerce depended also on the scrupulousness and objectivity of the sources of information about the Lower Danube, factors which influenced Anglo-Russian relations. As has been shown earlier, one of the main sources of information on the Lower Danube was Cunningham. Although in his earlier reports he indicated a higher cost for transports from the Danube due to the difficult navigational conditions through the Sulina Mouth, in 1850 he reconsidered his date on the basis of new information, this time reporting a better situation, showing a deficit for local exporters, but not for foreign importers, respectively the English.[188]

As to the deficits in English trade, the case of the English firm, Bell and Anderson, mentioned earlier had been called to the attention of the British government. From the reports of the Sardinian consuls, it would appear that the deficits were due to other causes than just those of the obstacles at the Sulina Mouth. In an 1848 report, the Sardinian consul at Galatz listed the "incalculable competition, speculation, lifting of the discount by English banks, evidence of conspicuous failures of some commercial cereal houses in London, found to be tied in with merchants in Galatz." Among the merchants in Galatz who failed was also Cunningham, the British vice-consul, with liabilities of 600,000 francs.[189]

It was normal for all these situations to influence prices of exported goods as well as those of transportation. This explains the fact that in 1849 the price of 27 shillings per kilo of wheat exported from the Danube rose to 31 shillings, excluding the transport cost.[190]

Ignoring sources, variation and exactness of statistical figures, it is certain that the increases in exports were progressive in spite of all the navigational obstacles. Added to the causes which at times facilitated the traffic through the Sulina, one must add the favorable effects of certain natural factors, independent of any technical improvement being carried on in navigational conditions. Proof can be seen in the fact that between 1858 and 1859, when the European Commission for the Danube had not yet begun technical operations, the traffic attained the figure of some 2,000 vessels of a total load capacity of 500,000.[191]

The explanation lies in the natural process of increasing the bar by the great force of the water brought about by the spring rains. In exchange, in the fall, the volume was reduced. For that reason, even today, if the depths of the bar cannot be assured from the end of August, all cereal export (which peaks in August) is imperilled and must be left until spring in silos or stored on barges — costly operations which the English firms and exporters in general tried to avoid after 1829. Cunningham referred to such a situation in a report to Palmerston in which he noted: "I have now taken in consideration as to the quantity of grain purchased in Galatz and Ibraila (sic) intended to be shipped to Great Britain before the navigation closes; portion already in warehouse, and portion purchased for early delivery..."[192]

Among the periods when exports of cereal registered decreases or even interruptions during the Anglo-Russian conflict, must be considered also that of the 1848 revolution in the Romanian Principalities. The Sardinian consul at Galatz[193] reported that the headquarters of the Russian Occupation Army temporarily prohibited the export of cereal, a measure taken on the basis of Articles 154 and 174 of the Organic Regulation and communicated to the foreign consulates by Circular No. 102, of 7 October 1848.[194]

The lack of basis for the English arguments concerning the prejudice against and the reduction of their Danubian commerce, because of the obstacles to navigation, shown up also in a later report of Cunningham's requested by Spratt, commander of the English vessel "Medina", which was at Galatz. Although Cunningham's statistics for the year 1852 differed from previous ones, a conclusion still can be drawn.[195]

"As Danubian commerce grows and can continue to grow," Cunningham reported, "it is not necessary to search out its production over a number of years, any year can be taken as a base. I shall take 1852, a year in which trade was good..."

He reported the number of 1668 maritime vessels leaving the ports of Galatz and Brăila in 1852, with loads of 1,832,855 quarters of cereal (1 quarter estimated by him to be equal to 3 hectaliters). Adding the 332 vessels leaving from the ports of Reni and Ismail, on the Kilia Branch, he indicated 2,000 vessels that emerged from the Danube, with a total load of 2,200,000 quarters of cereal. "Comparing this number with that of the vessels which have left the Danube during the last twelve months, it will be seen that it is greater."[196]

Cunningham's remarks on the status of navigation in general, as well as the depths at Sulina, in particular, are interesting and contradictory to his previous information. "The improvement of the Danube," he states in that same report to Spratt, "has as its aim to ease navigation and to reduce the fees imposed on the vessels, hence it would not be convenient to deepen the water yet have the vessels pay the same tax as when the water was low."

Under the aspect of the above mentioned documentation, the confusion, over the exclusiveness of the negative effects of the obstacles at the Sulina Mouth over English trade on the Lower Danube, appears only natural. Still, admitting as factual all the disadvantages claimed by English circles, the question based on the strict natural laws of commerce arises. If Danubian commerce had not been efficient, could it have been continued, especially in view of the fact that its English entrepreneurs belonged to the capitalist economic system? Furthermore, this efficiency was included in "the mercantile or shopkeeper conception of the British."[197] Hence, commercial traffic through the Sulina Mouth was not prejudiced between 1829 and 1856.

Notes

Chapter 1

1. From "Europolis," p. VI, by Eugen Botez, pen name Jean Bart.
2. Lloyd, vice-consul at Brăila, to Neale, British consul at Varna, Bulgaria, March 30, 1850, F.O. 78/977; quoted by R.R.N. Florescu, in "The Struggle...," p. 271, note 70.
3. Eugen Botez, "Europolis."
4. By nationality, in order of number: Greeks, Turks, Romanians, Russians (Lipoveni), Italians, Croats, Serbians, Slovenes, Englishmen, Frenchmen, Poles, Bulgarians, etc.
5. Lloyd to Neale, March 30, 1850, op. cit.
6. Ed. Engelhardt, "Etudes sur les embouchures...," p. 53.
7. Stokes, in "Dispatch by Lieutenent Trotter...," p. 2.
8. Ed. Engelhardt, "Etudes sur les embouchures...," p. 53.
9. Idem, ibid., p. 53.
10. Idem, ibid., p. 53.
11. "La Commission Européene et son...," p. 10.
12. Stokes, Conference at London, April 22, 1890; in "La Commission Européenne et son..." pp. 4 and 10.
13. Idem, p. 11.
14. Idem, ibid.
15. "La Commission Européenne et ...," pp. 9-10.
16. Ibid., p. 10 and Ed. Engelhardt, "Etudes sur les embouchures...," pp. 52-53.
17. Stokes, quoted in "Dispatch...," p. 2.
18. Gardner to Backhouse, August 3, 1836; F.O. 195/136; quoted by T.W. Riker in "The Making of Roumania," p. 15.
19. "Erinnerungen aus der Walachei während der Besetzung durch österreichische Truppen in den Jahren 1854, 1855, 1856"; in "Österreichische Revue," Vol. I, p. 336, Hajnal, "Le Droit..." p. 58, note 1.
20. Ed. Engelhardt, "Etudes sur...," p. 55.
21. Idem, ibid., p. 55.
22. Idem, ibid., p. 54.
23. Idem, ibid., p. 56.
24. Vessels "Gyula" and "Ceres," mentioned by Ion Nistor in "Corespondenta lui Coronini din Principate, Acte si Rapoarte din Iunie 1854, - Martie 1857," p. 777.

25. Ibid., idem, p. 772.
26. Ibid., idem, pp. 781-782.
27. Hajnal, "Le Droit...," pp. 58-59.
28. A group of seven islands west of Greece, in the Ionian Sea, the largest and most important being Kefalonia, Ithaka and Corfu.
29. In 1801, the Ionian Islands were taken from the possession of Venice and placed under the joint protectorate of the Russians and the Turks. In 1807, they passed from that protectorate to French sovereignty and were later captured by the English and were named the Septinsular Republic. In 1863, they were surrendered and incorporated in the new Kingdom of Greece.
30. "The Russian Consul-General has lately been taking on himself more the character of a dictator than that of the representative of a mere protecting power"; Colquhoun to Palmerston, November 24, 1835; F.O., 198/98.
31. "April 2, 1832, protest against Russian harassment of British protégés in Brăila and Galatz; January 27, 1837; protest against the arrest of three (Ionian) subjects, Sayadino, Toula and Zamfir, February 1840; protest against the arrest of Asprea, a British protégé who was rearrested; cases mentioned by R.R.N. Florescu, "The Struggle...," p. 258, note 24.
32. N. Iorga, "Istoria Romậnilor prin călători," Vol. II, p. 176.
33. From the report of the Sardinian Consul at Galatz, 24 May, 1838; Bodin, "Documente Sarde," p. 39.
34. Galatz Sardinian Consul's report of 26 May 1838 and of November 1852; Bodin, "Documente Sarde," pp. 45, 274.
35. Ibid., 45.
36. Ibid., 9 March 1842, p. 86.
37. Ibid., 17 May, 1841, pp. 73-75.
38. Ibid., p. 73.
39. Ibid., 26 May 1838, p. 45.
40. Natives of the province of Slovenia, the northern part of today's Jugoslavia, at that time part of the Austrian Empire.
41. Report of Sardinian Consul, Galatz, 17 May 1841; in Bodin, "Documente Sarde," pp. 73-74.
42. T.W. Riker, "The Making of...," p. 232.
43. Băicoianu, "Le Danube, aperçu historique, économique et politique," p. 125.
44. Administrative buildings, hospital and morgue, signal tower for indicating depths at the mouth, residences of Captain and of foreign superior personnel.
45. In accordance with the clauses of Articles 4 and 5 of "Acte Public Relatif à la Navigation des Embouchures de Sulina," 2 Novembre 1865, Sturdza, "Recueil...," p. 80.
46. Until 1878, when the Danube Delta came under Turkish sovereignty and the European Commission operated under the Turkish Flag. After 1878, on the basis of Article 8 of the Additional Act of 1881, which modified the Additional Act of 1865, the Treaty of Berlin, which accorded the right of extra-territoriality.

NOTES 217

47. At opportune moments succeeding in disappearing by embarking clandestinely on river or maritime vessels.

48. These two spots were an integral part of Sulina's social transformation, having also a picturesque aspect. During summer, after 6 p.m. tens of tables were set in front of these establishments, about ten to twenty feet from the riverbank. In the "Europolis" democracy was evident at these tables in separate groups one could see some of the European Commission personnel and vice-consuls (English, French, Dutch, Austrian, etc.). At the tables, there were members of the official authorities (chief of police, customs officers, the doctor, members of the Port Sanitary Service, and the Port Captain). Another group included the suppliers, merchants, agents of shipping lines, most of them Greeks. On the periphery, to the west, were the tables of captains, mechanics, sailors, small businessmen, etc., multi-racial in aspect. Communication between the table occupants was multi-lingual, with the sonorous predominance of the Greek, Italian and English.

49. Cemeteries according to religion: Christian Orthodox, Catholic, Protestant, Anglican, Jewish, Mahommedan, etc.

50. N.G. Kyriakides, Embiricos, Troianos, Dracoulis, Valianos, Vlassopol, etc.

51. Herbert Asbury, "The Barbary Coast," p. 3.

52. Idem., p. 185.

53. Idem., pp. 3-38, 110, 148, 167, 184, 306-313.

54. Idem., pp. 18-27, 166-168.

55. Originally said of sailors kidnapped for crew duty on ships of the China run.

56. Herbert Asbury, op. cit., p. 211.

57. "London's Underworld," edited by Peter Quennel; "The Barbary Coast" H. Asbury; J.D. Borthwick, "The Gold Hunter"; C.B. Glasscock, "Bandits and the Southern Pacific"; J.W. Buel, "Metropolitan Life Unveiled of the Mysteries and Miseries of America's Great Cities"; Vilas and Martin, "The Barbary Coast of San Francisco"; to mention but a few.

58. Moussou, Basile, "The Danube and the Rumanian Black Sea Ports," London, 1937, p. 25.

59. "London's Underworld," p. 291.

60. Idem., ibid., p. 65.

61. Idem., ibid., pp. 18, 25.

Chapter 2

62. E. Hertslet, "The Map of Europe by Treaty," 1875-1891, Vol. II, p. 995.

63. Quoted by H. Hajnal, in "The Danube...,": p. 122.

64. Report of Sardinian Consul at Galatz, 1 April 1839; in D. Bodin, "Documente Sarde," p. 56.
65. Idem., 24 May 1838; in D. Bodin, op. cit., p. 24.
66. H. Hajnal, "The Danube...," p. 66.
67. Report of the Sardinian Consul at Galatz, 5 November 1838; in D. Bodin, op. cit., p. 49.
68. Palmerston to Lord Beauvale (Vienna), 20 November 1839, F.O. No. 151.
69. Report of Sardinian Consul at Galatz, 1 April 1839; in D. Bodin, op. cit., p. 56.
70. C.I. Băicoianu, "Studii economice, politice si sociale," p. 342.
71. D. Urquhart, "The Mystery...," p. 121.
72. Ion Filitti, "Domniile române sub Regulamentul Organic," (1834-1848), p. 221.
73. Report of Sardinian Consul at Galatz, 17 October 1850; in D. Bodin, "Documente Sarde," p. 221.
74. Idem., 7 Noembrie 1850, p. 219.
75. Biblioteca Academiei Române, "Correspondence of Austrian Consul to Bucharest," report of Mihanovici, 6 July 1855; quoted by L. Boicu, "Austria si Principatele Române în vremea...," p. 417.
76. Ibid, idem., p. 417.
77. "The Danubian Principalities...," Vol I, p. 386.
78. Map of Danube Delta, in "Geografia Văii Dunării românesti," Map. Annex XXII.
79. Report of Sardinian Consul at Galatz, 23 February 1859; in D. Bodin, op. cit., p. 306.
80. Idem., ibid., p. 307.
81. H. Hajnal, "Le Droit...," p. 70, note 1.
82. Communiqué of French Government, published in "Le Moniteur Universel," 6 January 1856; quoted in Hajnal, "Le Droit" note 1, p. 67.
83. Ion Vidrascu, "La Voie Navigable...," p. 41.
84. Idem., ibid., p. 41.
85. Ten Kilometers long, 22 m. wide and 4 meters deep; Vidrascu, op. cit., p. 44.
86. Idem., ibid., p. 44.
87. Idem., ibid., p. 44.
88. Prospectus annexed to the January 6, 1840, report of the Sardinian Consul at Galatz; in D. Bodin, op. cit., pp. 60-62.
89. Idem, ibid., pp. 62, 63.
90. One Spanish Colon was equivalent to 14 2/40 Turkish Piastres; Febr. 5, 1852 report of Sardinian Consul to Sardinian Consul to Brăila; D. Bodin, op. cit. p. 236.
91. The prospectus.
92. D. Bodin, op. cit., pp. 62-63.

NOTES

93. Prospectus of the company proposed by Cunningham, annexed to the report of the Sardinian Consul at Galatz, 6 Jan. 1840; in D. Bodin, "Documente Sarde," pp. 60-63.
94. D. Sturdza, "Recueil...," p. 908.
95. Idem., ibid., p. 882.
96. D. Bodin, op. cit., p. 61.
97. Engelhardt, "Etudes sur...," p. 92.
98. Cunningham to Palmerston, Galatz, Sept. 31, 1850, "Correspondence between...," in British Foreign and State Papers," Vol. 44, pp. 437-443.
99. D. Sturdza, "Recueil...," p. 354. (The total expenditures from 1857 to 1902 was of 11,406,290 gold francs.)
100. Report of Sardinian Consul at Galatz, 12 March 1840; in D. Bodin, op. cit., p. 64.
101. Palmerston to Bloomfield, August 1950, F.O. 78/977; quoted by R.R.N. Florescu, "The Struggle...," p. 272.
102. Palmerston to Lord Beauvale, Vienna, F.O. No 151, 20 Nov. 1839.
103. Report of Sardinian Consul at Galatz, 24 May 1838; in D. Bodin, "Documente Sarde," p. 25.
104. Cunninghm to Palmerston, F.O. 78/30, 9 February 1837.
105. By "old mouth of the Danube," he was referring to the mouth of the Carasu, the hypothetical branch of the Danube, whose waters flowing through Dobruja emptied into the Black Sea, somewhat to the right of the present day port of Constanta.
106. Urquhart, "The Mystery...," pp. 16, 109.
107. Midia, a cape, a rocky headland without vegetation, a supposed human settlement from the Middle Paleolithic Age.
108. Urquhart, "The Mystery...," p. 107.
109. Idem., ibid., p. 109.
110. Idem., ibid., p. 111.
111. Urquhart, "The Mystery...," p. 111.
112. Lacking information as to the equivalent of "Lira" versus "Leu" (Romanian currency), the 1948 estimate of $1 = 2,000$ Lei, hence 500,000 x 2,000 Lei = 1,000,000,000 Lei, not 6 billion. Lei (Romanian currency).
113. Between 1950 and 1951, the author of this study was assigned to identify, by categories of work, the disbursement of 6 billion lei, invested by the Ministry of Finance of România.
114. Report of Sardinian Consul of Galatz, 5 November 1838; Bodin, op. cit., p. 49.
115. Personal experience of the author, a former political prisoner at the construction of the Danube-Black Sea Canal: wheelbarrows, pick axes, and shovels.
116. Urquhart, "The Mystery...," p. 109.
117. Idem., ibid., p. 110.

Chapter 3

118. Martens, N.R.G.T. Vol. XI (1830-1834), p. 655.
119. Idem., ibid., Vol. II, p. 128.
120. H. Hajnal, "The Danube...," pp. 57-62.
121. State Papers, XXVI, p. 677.
122. "The Morning Chronicle," of October 22, 1835; quoted by H. Hajnal in "The Danube...," pp. 55-56.
123. D. Sturdza, "Recueil...," pp. 7-11; Martens, N.R.G.T., Vol. 1, p. 208.
124. "The Morning Chronicle," op. cit.
125. "The Danubian Principalities...," Vol. I, p. 381.
126. Some comparative figures can demonstrate the superiority of Austrian commerce over that of Russia in the traffic of the port of Brăila and in the Lower Danube, in 1845; from the report of the Sardinian Consul at Galatz. March 26, 1846; in D. Bodin, "Documente Sarde," p. 179.

	Imports	Exports
Total value in Piastres out of which:	17,114,491	28,694,423
Austrian Flag	7,750,393	3,339,039
Russian Flag	1,604,596	1,970,227
Other Flags	7,759,502	23,385,157

127. Conference of London, Protocol Nr. 3, 30 March 1871; in Sturdza, "Recueil...," p. 102.
128. "The Danubian Principalities...," Vol. I, p. 378.
129. Ibid., the date of this book's publications.
130. Report of Sardinian Consul at Galatz, 2 May 1843; in D. Bodin "Documente Sarde," p. 91.
131. Report of the Sardinian Consul, Galatz, Nov. 10, 1840; D. Bodin, p. 65.
132. Idem., ibid., p. 66. "...da constrignere col tempo le altre potenze a procedare a consimile convenzione."
133. Report of Sardinian Consul at Galatz, May 10, 1842; Bodin, op. cit. p. 142.
134. Idem., ibid., 17, Oct. 1850; p. 217.
135. H. Hajnal, "Le Droit...," p. 21.
136. Idem., ibid., p. 21.
137. Idem, ibid., p. 21. Art. I. "La navigation sur tout le cours du Danube... sera entièrement libre... elle ne pourra, sous le rapport du commerce, être interdite à personne, soumise à aucune entrave, ni sujette à un péage quelconque..."
138. Report of Sardinian Consul at Galatz, 25 Novembre 1845; Bodin, "Documente Sarde," p. 172.
139. Stokes' declaration in a Conference given at London, April 22, 1890, concerning the Danube and its commerce; in "La Commission Européenne du Danube et son...," p. 5.

NOTES 221

140. "Il n'est pas douteux que ces accusations sont exagérées et que, si l'on peut reprocher à la Russie de la négligence dans l'entretien du chenal à l'embouchure, on ne saurait l'accuser d'avoirt contribué, en coulant des navires, à l'ensablement de l'entrée de Danube"; in "La Commission Européenne du Danube et son...," p. 5, note 1.

141. Ponsonby to Palmerston, February 19, 1837; F.O. 78/300; quoted by R.R.N. Florescu, op. cit., p. 263, foot note 44.

142. V.J. Puryear, "Odessa: Its Rise and International Importance" (1815-1850); in "Pacific Historical Review," Vol. III, 1934, p. 211.

143. Report of Sardinian Consul of Galatz, 24 May, 1838; in D. Bodin, "Documente Sarde," p. 25.

144. V.J. Puryer, "Odessa: Its Rise...," p. 210.

145. Idem., ibid., p. 211.

146. Idem., ibid., p. 204.

147. Palmerston to Ponsonby, August 1838, F.O. 195/168; quoted by R.R.N. Florescu, op. cit., p. 250.

148. Gardner to Ponsonby, Aug. 1851, F.O. 195/198; quoted by R.R.N. Florescu, op. cit., p. 263 note 44.

149. D. Urquhart, "The Mystery...," pp. 15, 16.

150. Ismail and Reni.

151. "Annales du commerce exterieur: Russie, faits commerciaux," 1843-1856, No 1-12, Paris 1857; quoted by V.J. Puryear in "England, Russia and the Straits," p. 95.

152. V.J. Puryear, "England, Russia...," p. 96.

153. Parliamentary Papers (1852-1853), Vol. 102, p. 21.

154. "Various deliveries requested to supply Constantinople and fortresses located on the Danube..." were considered as "vexations," according of administrative autonomy, abolition of forced labor, liberty of navigation for Romanian vessels, etc. Paragraphs 7 and 8 of the Separate Treaty.

155. A monument set in a small park in the outskirts of Brăila. Even today's name of the park is "Monument."

156. Article V of the Treaty of Adrianople.

157. Blutte to Cowley, June 12, 1829; F.O. 97/402; quoted by R.R.N. Florescu, in "The Struggle...," p. 133.

158. Xenopol, Vol. IV, p. 105.

159. Idem., ibid., pp. 120-130.

160. A quarantine inspector in the Romanian Principalities was appointed by the Romanian Government, but was replaced by the Russian-appointed Mavros, a Greek, their trusted man; A.D. Xenopol, Vol. IV, p. 121.

161. C.C. Giurescu, op. cit. pp. 166-167; data collected by the author from documents in the Archives of the Romanian State.

162. Idem., ibid., pp. 166-168.

163. Idem., ibid., 169, 170 from official documents.

164. Idem., ibid., p. 152; Alex D. Moruzi, "Rapport sur les entrepôts de la ville de Galatz," quoted by V. Slăvescu in "Viata si opera economistului A. Moruzi," p. 334; See also Report of Sardinian Consul at Odessa, 2 May 1842; in D. Bodin, "Documente Sarde," p. 118.

165. N. Soutzo, "Notions Statistiques...," in V. Slăvescu, "Viata si opera economistului N. Sutu," p. 334; Imports: 570,000 Francs in 1831 and 5,219,000 Francs, in 1845.

166. V. Slăvescu, "Viata si opera economistului Moruzi," p. 99.

167. Report of Sardinian Consul at Galatz, 25 Mar. 1839; D. Bodin, in "Documente Sarde," p. 50.

168. Idem., 25 November 1846; Idem., ibid., p. 172.

169. B. Youghaperianu, "L'Annuaire du Danube," (1902-1903), pp. 126, 127.

170. Report of Sardinian Consul at Galatz, 6 April 1848; D. Bodin "Documente Sarde," p. 204.

171. See paragraph 7 of the Separate Treaty of 1829.

172. On the eve of the 1877-1878 Russo-Turkish War, during negociations between Russia and the Principalities over military collaboration against Turkey, Stremoncov, the chief of the Asian Department, assured the Romanian representative of "Russia's support" after the downfall of the Ottoman Empire. In response to the Romanians' expression of doubt, Stremoncov continued, "I know what you are thinking. That we are those who fatten the turkey in order to butcher it. I assure you that it is not true. Any increase of territory can only be fatal to the Empire. As to Romania, it has always enjoyed the disinterested good will of Russia"; N. Iorga, "Politica Enternă a Regelui Carol I," p. 135. (Author's note: from the body of the "fattened turkey" Bassarabia was devoured partially and redevoured in different epochs, in 1812, 1878 and 1944, and half of Bucovina in 1945).

173. "La Commission Européenne du Danube et son..."; Statistics of Annex XXXII.

174. Variety in methods of measuring tonnage of vessels; variety in units of capacity used in cereal export; incorrect customs evaluation with respect to quality and value of cargo imported or exported; non-declaration of exact destination of vessels, etc.; from report of Sardinian Consul at Galatz, 4 February 1854; D. Bodin, "Documente Sarde," p. 282.

175. Cunningham to Stratford Canning, Galatz, 17 Sept. 1850; F.O. 78/977.

176. Cunningham to Palmerston, Galatz, Sept. 30, 1850; "Correspondence between...," in "State Papers," p. 584.

177. N. Soutzo, "Notions Statistiques sur la Modavie," pp. 323-419.

178. Idem., ibid., pp. 334-336.

179. Report of Sardinian consul, Galatz, 4 March 1847; D. Bodin, "Documente Sarde," p. 181

180. Ibid., p. 220; Report of 20 March 1851, Torino.

181. Ibid., Galatz March 17, 1852; D. Bodin, "Documente Sarde," p. 267, Annex.

182. H. Hajnal, "The Danube...," p. 153.

183. N.J. Puryear, "England, Russia...," pp. 126, 123.
184. R.R.N. Florescu, "The Struggle...," p. 262, note 44.
185. Idem., ibid.
186. Cunningham to Palmerston, Sept. 30, 1850; "Correspondence between...," "State Papers," Vol. 44, p. 584.
187. Parliamentary Papers (1852-1853), Vol. 102, p. 152.
188. Cunningham to Palmerston, Galatz, Sept. 16, 1850; Hajnal, "The Danube...," pp. 64, 65, footnote 1.
189. Report of Sardinian Consul, Galatz, 26 April 1848; D. Bodin, "Documente Sarde," p. 202.
190. Ibid., 29 Octombrie 1849; D. Bodin, op. cit., p. 212.
191. Stokes, "Notes on the Lower Danube," p. 171.
192. H. Hajnal, "The Danube...," pp. 64, 65, note 1.
193. Report of Sardinian Consul, Galatz, 23 Oct. 1848; D. Bodin, "Documente Sarde," p. 208.
194. Ibid., Annex to Consul's report; Bodin, op, cit., p. 209.
195. Cunningham, vice-consul at Galatz to Spratt, Galatz, 12 Nov. 1857; copy of the original in the Romanian Academy.
196. Idem., ibid.
197. H. Nicolson, "Diplomacy," p. 144.

PART FIVE

THE INTERNATIONALIZATION OF THE DANUBE RIVER NAVIGATION AND ITS IMMEDIATE RESULTS

> The principles of Act of Vienna of 1815 applied to the Danube in 1856 "form a part of the Public Law of Europe."
>
> From Article XV of the 1856 Peace Treaty of Paris.

The Internationalization of the Danube River Navigation and its Immediate Results

Introduction.

The 1856 Treaty of Paris, internationalizing navigation on the Danube, eliminated the negative effects of the Treaty of Adrianople and with them the Anglo-Russian conflict, thus inaugurating a fifty-eight year period of "peace" in navigation, that lasted until World War I. For Lower Danube navigation, the year 1856 represents the finale of the first act towards internationalization, initiated by Austria in 1699. In three-fourths of a century it symbolized the achievement of the French Revolution concept of extending the regime of internationalization, initially established on the Rhine, also to navigation on other rivers.

The same retrospective views bring out certain aspects of similarity between two epochs during which the problem of internationalization of navigation was debated and resolved on a European level. In 1815, the application of navigation principles on rivers common to different countries occurred in the period during which the Allied Powers of Europe, including Russia, put an end to French expansion. France, aside from her trend towards hegemony over the entire continent, had completely upset the political balance of Europe, the most important point in England's foreign policy. In 1856, internationalization of the Danube was an integral part of the Anglo-French policy of eliminating, this time, Russian hegemony over Southeast Europe.

Removing Russia from the mouths of the Danube and installing there, instead, an international body — the European Danube Commission — can justify Geffcken's belief that the river was "the strategic base of the political equilibrium in the East..."[1] It is no less true that the internationalization measure represents the end of the twenty-seven years of forbearance on the part of the British, exasperated by the Russian sabotage of navigation on English vessels on the Lower Danube. What appears to be symptomatic is the repetition in 1856, this time towards Russia, of the indulgent treatment accorded France at the 1814 Peace Conference. At the latter Conference, the Allies had been, as Harold Nicolson put it, "amazingly lenient" towards France, in matters of war reparations and territorial cessions, "a generosity which was not sentimental, but politic."[2]

In 1856, Russia benefited from that generosity initiated in 1814 by Tsar Alexander I, an attitude that in 1815 set the spirit of the Holy Alliance. In January 1855, Franz Joseph declared to Gorchakov: "My name will never be affixed to a condition which would wound the honor and dignity of Tsar Nicholas"[3] and, in 1856, the manoeuvres of Napoleon III had as a direct purpose a reconciliation with Russia. If Franz Joseph was unable to keep his promise, Napoleon III tried to demonstrate his support to Russia.

The spirit of the Congress of Vienna in the 1815 Assembly, described as "the Congress dances,"[4] was repeated during the 1856 Paris peace negotiations where "all the plenipotentiaries felt the atmosphere of bonhomie in which the Congress began its sittings, for, Paris was in a joyous mood and peace was in every heart..." and "...sixteen diplomats matched their wits in the business of liquidating a war to the satisfaction of all."[5]

The Danube Question was debated in 1856 in an atmosphere of discord among the allies on the problem of autonomy and union of the two Romanian Principalities. It took the meeting at Osborne between Emperor Napoleon III and Queen Victoria of England to settle the problem, avoiding "an imminent war between Austria and France,"[6] the consequences of which could have been unfavorable for Danube navigation.

From the moment in which the allies informed the Russians of the peace conditions, including those with respect to the Danube, to the time of their inclusion in the 1856 Paris Peace Treaty, the establishment of the new regime of navigation was examined under three possibilities. The first was the precise respecting of the principles of the Act of 1815; the second was the modification and adaptation of those principles to the political and economic imperatives with respect to the restabilization of the situation at the Lower Danube, as well as to the commercial interests of England, Austria and France. The third aspect was the co-association of Russia in the application of the new regime, in which case she would continue to retain the branch and mouth of the Sulina.

In the end, it was decided to modify some of the principles of the Act of 1815, with the aim of adapting them to the political and economic conditions of the Danube and to eliminate Russia from the river, retaining her only as a member of the European Commission of the Danube, the organization entrusted with the administration and control of the new international regime, along with the other signatories of the 1856 Treaty of Paris. This, too, demonstrated the leniency of the victors towards vanquished Russia.

The need to modify in 1856 some of the 1815 principles in order to attain the internationalization of Danube River navigation can be considered in the light of a statement made by George Kennan, relative to the flexibility of the principles of the Holy Alliance. "These structures"—he noted—"have always served the purpose for which they were designed just so long as the interests of the great powers gave substance and reality to their existence. The moment this situation changed, the moment it became in the interests of one of the other of the great powers to alter the status quo, none of these treaty structures ever stood in the way of such alternation."[7] The Great Powers which in 1856 modified the 1815 principles of navigation were England and France.

As to the durability of the principles applied in 1856, one can mention the reflection of Gentz who, after attending all the conferences of his time, said: "I am left with the impression that nobody is quite right all through."[8] Referring to Gentz's reflection, Nicolson expressed the opinion that "...accuracy of human prediction...or the efficacy of moral principles...are absolute principles and must in the end prevail...but "their functioning is obscure..."[9] This opinion can be applied also in the case of the modifications made later to the regime established in 1856. During the first stage of the existence of the new regime on the Danube (1856-1921) and then in the second stage (1921-1948), factors and influences of a political nature created fissures in the established doctrines of the new principles of 1856.

Immediately after the signing of the 1856 Treaty, the new order of navigation was threatened by war, which could have broken out because of England's obstruction in the case of the minuscule frontier point at Belgrade and that of the Danube affluents. In 1857, when, on the basis of the clauses of the 1856 Treaty, Austria presented the organization of the navigation regime in accordance with the principles of the Act of 1815, the objections of England and France were the result of non-respect of the same principles. In 1878, concomitant with Russia's return as a riparian state, 1815 principles as well as 1856 ones were changed. After World War I, the essence of the 1815 principles — the status of riparian — was subject to caducity, by depriving Austria, Germany and Hungary of a deliberate vote in 1921, at the establishment of the Definitive Statute of the Danube. Setting aside the principles of 1815 was applied by England and France also after World War I, when, by the Versaille Treaty of Peace they included themselves, as non-riparian states, in the navigation commissions of the rivers of Northwestern Europe, originally reserved exclusively to riparian states.

In the 1856-1921 period, the common Anglo-French position, associated in certain cases with that of Austria, was determined by the method of applying and administering the international regime on the Maritime Danube. Between 1921 and 1948, in the absence of Austria, the Anglo-French position was somewhat diminished by the respecting and applying of the rights of the smaller riparian states — Romania, Bulgaria and Serbia — as well as those of the new state of Czechoslovakia. After 1948, the political capability of all of them was replaced by one unilateral and predominant one, that of Soviet Russia.

Keeping the matter of proportion in mind, one could say that the importance of internationalization of navigation on the Danube, for Central and Southeastern Europe, was similar to that of the Suez Canal for European and even North American economic ties to South Asia.

The complete freedom of navigation established on the Danube in 1856, just as that of the Suez Canal, added new and important pages to the evolution of International Public Law. For Russia, the 1856 Treaty left lasting feelings of resentment which, regardless of her political regime, were to command her return, not only to the Danube, but also to the political domination of the entire hinterland of the river, from Vienna to the Black Sea, an aim accomplished in 1948.

Chapter 1

THE PEACE CONFERENCES OF VIENNA AND PARIS

The First Conference of Vienna (1855).

The development of the two Preliminary Conferences to the 1856 Peace Treaty of Paris was relative to the final results of the Crimean War entered into by England, France, the Kingdom of Sardinia and Turkey, with the indirect assistance of Austria. Although uncertainty reigned as to the outcome of this war, Russia's adversaries seemed certain of victory.

The cardinal line of the Allies, both as to the peace to be signed with Russia and with respect to navigation, was expressed by Count Buol, the Austrian Foreign Minister and president of the 1855 Vienna Conference, at the opening of the first session on March 15, 1855.[10] Among other remarks, he stressed that: "Les bases de paix qui ont été jugées...sont désignées" and "la liberté de navigation du Danube sera complétement assurée par des moyens efficaces et sous le contrôle d'une autorité syndicale permanente."[11] With this statement, Russia was faced with a fait accompli.

On October 24, 1853, three months after the Russian Armies had occupied the Romanian Principalities on July 2, 1853, Turkey declared war on Russia. On June 16, 1854, Russia blocked the Sulina Mouth with rocks and wrecked ships.[12] The fact that Russia refused to evacuate the Principalities determined England and France to declare war on her, and Austria to occupy the same Principalities, on the basis of the June 14, 1854 convention with Turkey.[13] On June 16, 1854, French and English warships, posted in front of the Sulina Mouth blocked all traffic[14] and, on September 14, Allied English and French troops disembarked in Crimea. One month before the debarkation, on August 8, 1854, England, Austria and France had sent Russia a Joint Note[15] entitled "The Four Points"[16] making known the conditions under which the war could be ended. Regarding navigation, point 2 provided that "Freedom of navigation on the Danube shall be completely assured by means under the control of a permanent Syndicate authority." Later on, point 2 was further developed. After the Russian rejection, on August 26, 1854,[17] of the August 8 Note, two decisive actions followed in accelerating its solution. Following the debarkation of the Anglo-French troops in the Crimea, a military alliance was formed on December 2 of the same year, between England, Austria and France, joined on March 4, 1855 by the Kingdom of Sardinia.

Military operations in the Crimea developing unfavorably for Russia, her Government agreed, on November 29, 1854 to a discussion,[18] in principle, of the "Four Points." This took place at the Conference of Vienna between March 15 and June 4, 1855. The contents of point 2 was debated thoroughly at the sessions of March 15, 21 and 23. Plenipotentiaries of Austria, England, France, Russia, Sardinia and Turkey took part, the last two participating for the first time in the debates over the Danube Question on the European level.[19]

At the March 21, 1855 session, the text of point 2 was read, having been included in the Memorandum drawn up by Prokesch-Osten, Austria's second Plenipotentiary.[20] The Memorandum contained the motions referring to the new navigation regime proposed to be introduced on the Danube, put forth in the six points which will be termed here the "Six Points."[21]

Although this Act was the basis of the debates, it underwent modification at the next session, March 23, as well as at the final ones of the Conference of 1856. These modifications became the basis of the five Articles, of the 1856 Treaty of Paris, concerning navigation on the Danube.

Before discussion of the textual matter of each of the "Six Points" was opened, Prince Gorchakov, first Russian Plenipotentiary, made some general observations. Under the political aspect, he showed Russia's contributions also to the freedom of navigation for all flags on the Black Sea, in reference to certain clauses of the Treaty of Adrianople. As to navigation on the Lower Danube, which he considered from a strictly commercial point of view, he attributed the difficulties at the Sulina Mouth, during the Russian administration, to the natural obstacles.

Gorchakov's statements did not go unnoticed by the other representatives. Concerning freedom of navigation through the Sulina Mouth, Prokesch-Osten answered that the results obtained at the Sulina Mouth were in disagreement with the "intentions of the St. Petersburg Government." As to the Black Sea sector, Bourqueney, the French Plenipotentiary, stated in the March 23 session that Russia could not claim only for herself the honor of having instituted freedom of navigation, Turkey also merited it and, in any case, such freedom had existed even before the Treaty of Adrianople.[22] The examination of the first three points of the Memorandum produced no opposition.

Taking up discussion of point 4, Gorchakov opposed the term of Syndicate for the new organization, made up of contracting Powers, to put into application the new navigation regime. Considering the title of Syndicate to be political and scientific order, he believed that a different term reflecting the commercial aspect of the new regime would be more appropriate.

Opposed to this belief was that of Bourqueney, who invoked the political factor of the new legislation in view of the fact that the regime was to be put into application under European quaranty. Gorchakov opposed this opinion inasmuch as it infringed upon Russia's right of sovereignty. It must be noted that, at the date of the 1855 Conference of Vienna, no decision had been made concerning the political status of the Danube Delta, which was still under Russian sovereignty. Russia's representatives opposed also the contents of the last paragraph, of point 4 of the "Six Points" which provided for stationing warships at the mouths of the Danube to assure freedom of navigation. Their consideration did have a basis; the presence of such vessels in the Black Sea, respectively, their entrance through the Straits, was made conditional by the Treaty of July 13, 1841.[23] Although the Plenipotentiaries of Austria, England and France had proposed this idea, they had to revise the Treaty of 1841 and draw up a Convention of the Straits,[24] which was signed with Russia at the same date as the 1856 Peace Treaty of Paris, a convention by which Turkey could accord right of passage through the two Straits to light warships of any nation not at war with her.

A clarification of point 4 was also made: instead of the general mention of "un ou deux navires de guerre," the new Convention of the Straits provided that the right to enter the Black Sea, and respectively at the mouths of the Danube, be accorded only to "bâtiments légers," a modification included later in Article 19 of the 1856 Treaty. Discussions over points 5 and 6 were of minor importance, their texts being more or less a continuation of points 1, 2, and 3.

Following the debates of March 23, certain modifications of the Prokesch-Osten Memorandum of March 21 were made, the new text being annexed to Protocol No. 5. The modifications were due to objections in the preceding session, as well as to a slight yielding on Austria's part. Still, even this session did not finish defining the new regime. As to the word "Syndicate," as proposed in the initial point 4 of the Memorandum, it was replaced by "European Commission."

Some modifications of the Memorandum of Prokesch-Osten followed (points 1 and 4), which clarified the temporary measure and then the permanent one for carrying out the technical work of improving navigation and for application of the supervision of the international regime of navigation. Also in accordance with the Memorandum, the European Commission composed of all the contracting Powers was to draw up the bases for a Regulation for River Navigation and Police on the Galatz-Black Sea sector, to establish an instruction guide for a Riparian Commission composed of riparian states, exclusively, and to carry out the first technical constructions at the Sulina Mouth. After the completion of these assignments, it was to be dissolved in common accord with all the contracting Powers, being replaced by the Riparian Commission — a decision later incorporated into Articles 17 and 18 of the Treaty of 1856.

In the debates during the course of the reexamination of the initial text of point 6 of the memorandum can be discerned the intentions of the Allies in case of the failure of the Crimean campaign. In the text Prokesch-Osten proposed neutralization of the Danube Delta and repeal of the quarantine on the Sulina Branch, Russia to maintain her jurisdiction only over her subjects in the respective region. The French and English Plenipotentiaries brought under discussion, for the first time, the problem of the new Turko-Russian frontier in the Danube Delta, considering the Treaty of Adrianople annulled in view of the state of war between Russia and Turkey. Although raising this question was premature at the date of the 1855 Conference, the results of the Crimean War being still unknown, yet it reflected the future plans of the Allies.

Because of Russia's objections, the proposal for neutralization of the Delta was eliminated from the new modified text of point 6. The new Prokesch Memorandum, with these modifications, annexed to and indicated in Protocol Nr.5 as "développement du second point"[25] was the basis of future debates that took place in the framework of the 1856 Conference, In these last debates, taking place with their approaching victory in the Crimea, England and France hardened their points of view unclarified in the two previous sessions, including also

PEACE CONFERENCES OF VIENNA AND PARIS 235

the elimination of certain provisions in the Prokesch Memorandum which tended to give Austria preponderance in the Lower Danube.

From the modifications made on the initial Prokesch-Osten Memorandum, it would seem that the regulation of navigation had been fixed by common accord with all the Conference members. The Allies, however, as well as Russia, were awaiting results from their army commanders in the Crimea.

Had the armed conflict been unable to bring victory to either of the camps engaged, partial adoption of the Danube navigation regime proposed in the Memorandum modified on March 23 could not have been excluded. In other words, a compromise might have been reached. In such a case, Russia would have maintained her political sovereignty at the mouths of the Danube and, together with the Allies, the regime of the 1815 Act would have been applied by means of two commissions. The Fluvial Commission would have been applied for the Lower Danube, from the Iron Gates to Galatz, and the European commission for the Galatz-Sulina sector, including the river mouths. The fall of Sevastopol strengthened the position of England and France, which then could impose their point of view at the final Conference in 1856.

The Second Conference of Vienna (1856).

With the fall of Sevastopol on September 9, 1855 and the capitulation of the Russian armies, the Conference of Vienna on February 1, 1856 drew up the Preliminary Peace Project, in which was included the clause for internationalization of navigation on the Danube, with the following text:[26]

> 'La liberté du Danube et de ses embouchures sera efficacement assurée par des institutions européennes, dans lesquelles les Puissances contractantes seront églement représentées, sauf les positions particulières des riverains, qui seront reglées sur les principes établis par l'Acte du Congrès de Vienne en matière de navigation fluviale." "Chacune des Puissances contractantes aura le droit de faire stationner un ou deux bâtiments de guerre légers aux embouchures du fleuve, destinés à assurer l'exécution des règlements relatifs à la liberté du Danube."

Attention is drawn in the above text, to the expression "sauf les positions particulières des riverains," which, being contrary to that of "dans lesquelles les Puissances contractantes seront également representées," would later cause much discussion, provoked by Austria in support of the exclusive participation of riparian states in the administration of the new regime. The literal interpretation of the latter phrase corresponded with the intentions of England and France.

The Conference and the Peace Treaty of Paris of 1856 Concerning the Internationalization of the Danube River Navigation.

The Peace Conference of Paris was opened on February 5, 1856, presided by the host's representative Walewsky, France's Minister for Foreign Affairs and chief Plenipotentiary. Present were the representatives of Austria, England, Prussia, Russia, Sardinia and Turkey.[27] The questions relating to navigation on the Danube were debated in the sessions of February 28 and March 6, 12, 18 and 27.

In the brief debate on navigation in the February 28 session, the first to speak was Walewsky, who read the Preliminary Peace Project accepted at the Conference of Vienna on February 1, 1856.[28]

The Allies' plan for neutralization on the Black Sea, in order to avoid any Russian attack against Turkey and the Straits, not being public knowledge, Orloff — Russia's chief Plenipotentiary — again raised the problem of the stationing of warships at the mouths of the Danube, his contention being that the Allies' proposal was a clear violation of the neutrality principle and an exception to Russia's sovereign rights. Acknowledging the exception, Walewsky did not consider it to be contrary to the principle of neutrality. In the following sessions, March 6,12,and 18,[29] priority was given to the debates on a major problem having a double aspect: the geographic division of application of the international regime on two sectors of the river and the jurisdictions of the two Commissions, the European and the Riparian, which were to be established. In both cases, the Anglo-French point of view was in opposition to the Austrian. In the Anglo-French point of view, stated by Walewsky, the international regime would have to be applied to the entire course of the river, in accordance with the principles of the Act of 1815.[30]

At the March 27 session, the new international regime for the Danube[31] was approved, the norms established being the result of a compromise between the Anglo-French and the Austrian points of view. Apart from being admitted to the European Commission, Russia did not succeed in imposing any of her points of view.

From the Conference's work, only two of the major problems will be examined: the geographic division of the application of the new regime and the elimination of Russia from the Danube.

The Geographic Division.

The problem of the application of the international regime for navigation, together with other aspects of the "Danube Question," brought on the first dissensions among the Allies, with Russia as a spectator. In working out this problem divergencies, discrepancies, and confusion developed due to last minute changes in the positions of the English and French Plenipotentiaries, to the lack of coordination of their intentions, and even to their inattention.

Initially, in the peace conditions, in which navigation was also included, provision was made that "...la liberté de la navigation du Danube doit être assurée jusque dans la mer." The mention was of a general order, without specifying either the method of application or the geographic division for its application. Clarification of the problem was taken up at the March 21 session of the 1855 Conference of Vienna.[32]

Point 1 of the "Six Points" of the Prokesch-Osten Memorandum proposed that the principles of the Act of Vienna were to be applied "au cours inférieur du Danube, à partir du point *où ce fleuve devient commun* à l'Autriche et à l'Empire Ottoman, jusque dans la mer." This proposal was adopted at the March 21 session as well as at that of March 23, 1855.[33] Bearing in mind that the paternity of the Memorandum was Prokesch-Osten's he implicitly supported Austria's position. However, by reference to the Act of 1815, the new regime should have been applied to the entire course of the river. In order to carry out and to supervise the method of applying the regime, a temporary compromise was reached over the principles of the Act of 1815. Thus, at point 4 provision was made for the establishment of two Commissions, one European and one Riparian, the former to be of temporary duration and the latter permanent. According to the concept of the Memorandum, the latter was to execute and apply the international regime *exclusively on the Lower Danube, but not on the Middle and Upper Danube.* The Riparian Commission was to be composed exclusively of riparian states, in accordance with the Act of 1815.

In the problem of geographic division of the application of the new regime the Austrian point of view was justified. It was based on two resolutions of the 1855 Conference of Vienna (Protocols No.4 and 5) regarding the Prokesch Memorandum. Point 1 of the initial Memorandum (March 21), as well as of the modified one (March 23) upheld the idea of application of the principles of the Act of 1815 on the fluvial sector "...au cours inférieur du Danube."

Two different situations appeared in this matter from the 1856 Treaty Project. The first was the result of the sense of Article 15 of the Treaty, which stated that the principles of 1815 were to be applied "...au Danube et à ses embouchures..." The second was due to the inattention of the Anglo-French group which twice accepted point 1 of the memorandum, which indicated only the Lower Danube sector.

However, Austria's invoking the double acceptance of point 1 of the Memorandum was voided by the clauses of Articles 17 and 18 of the 1856 Treaty Project. This Treaty Project included the transfer of the mandate of the European Commission to the Riparian Commission. No mention was made of their being carried out along different sectors. Oversights also appeared with respect to the participation of non-riparian states in the application and administration of the new regime. Thus, in the text of point 1, definitely approved by the 1856 Conference of Vienna, provision was made that, in European organizations which were to assure the freedom of navigation, "les Puissances contractantes" must participate. Yet, in the texts of Articles 15-19 of the Treaty Project no mention was made in this respect. On this error, or lack of attention, was the Austrian point of view based.

In the March 6 session of the 1856 Conference of Paris, Walewsky presented a Project consisting of six paragraphs, modifying and completing the "Six Points" of the Prokesch-Osten Memorandum.[34]

According to paragraph one of the Project, provision was made that the principles of the Act of Vienna concerning internationalization of navigation, "seront également appliqués au Danube et à ses embouchures...," hence, on the entire course of the river, not only on sectors. Paragraph five made provision for a European Commission, as a supreme body, composed of all the Conference members (riparian and non-riparian), to determine the technical work needed for the improvement of navigation; to draw up the Regulations for Navigation and Police and to outline the general instructions for operation of a permanent Executive Riparian Commission, to be composed exclusively of riparians, with jurisdiction on the entire course of the river, not only on the lower sector as proposed in the Memorandum.

Supporting the jurisdiction of the Executive Commission exclusively on the Lower Danube, Buol invoked the political consideration in the sense of non-existence of any conflict in navigation in upriver sectors.[35] Walewsky replied, invoking the general commercial interests which called for the international regime on the entire course of the Danube.

In the response of Clarendon, England's chief Plenipotentiary, one could see the reason for the Anglo-French change of position towards the Austrian one. In his opinion, accepting the jurisdiction of the Executive Committee only on the Lower Danube would have created for Austria very special advantages on the Middle and Upper Danube, a situation the Conference could not have approved.[36]

The ambiguity and flexibility in the Anglo-French point of view, as well as in the Austrian one, are apparent in the 1856 debates. The principles of the Act of 1815 were invoked, but they were not applied. Austria wanted the new regime applied *only on the Lower Danube,* but the principles of the Act indicated it for *the entire course of the river* (Act of 1815). The Anglo-French group appeared to consider the establishment of the European Commission to be for a limited period, but actually understood it to be for an unlimited time.

Faced with the strong opposition of the Anglo-French group, Austria had to give in, expecting to be satisfied later, with the possible application of Articles 17 and 18 of the 1856 Treaty of Paris, clauses which remained only theoretical, however, as will be seen further at the Paris Conference of 1858.

Austria's yielding was determined by a number of domestic considerations included in the history of her policies in the matter of communication lines on water and on land. On February 11, 1856, at the Government Council at Vienna presided over by Emperor Francis Joseph, at which was discussed the position to be taken by Austria at the 1856 Conference of Paris, two principal viewpoints were brought out.[37]

The first was that of the Emperor. "There must be," he noted on the instructions entitled "Punktationen" which was given to the Austrian delegation, "a clear distinction made between the question of the Soulina and that of the Danube proper. On the former, all the Powers have equal rights, whereas on the latter only the Riparian States have got a say in the matter..."[38] By "the Soulina" he was referring to the European Commission of the Danube, whose jurisdiction and temporary mandate he considered only for the improvement of navigation at the respective mouth, in which the non-riparian Powers also were to participate. By *"Danube proper"* he understood the Lower Danube between the Turko-Austrian frontier as far as *Sulina,* including the mouth of the same name, administered by the Riparian Commission, proposed to be permanent.

The second point, concerning the participation of non-riparian Powers only in the technical works at the Sulina Mouth, was made by Bruck, a Council member, whose opinion was favorable to the riparian States, inasmuch as he believed that the presence of the others to be an actual foreign interference, which "...was always a ticklish and thorny question..."[39]

Buol's position was a very difficult one. On the one hand, he was obliged to follow the "Punktationen" which included, along with the Austrian navigation policy also the monopoly of the "First Austrian Danube Steam Navigation Company" and, on the other hand, he had to resist the Franco-English pressure.

Aside from these imperatives, Buol had to cope with two other situations. The first was that of pressure from Bruck, who — urged on by the press and by certain Viennese economists — considered Austrian preponderance in navigation on the Lower Danube a direct command for Austria's economic expansion in the Romanian Principalities. The second was his own conviction when in writing to the Emperor he stated: "I consider it a moral impossibility to assert that the principles of the Vienna Congress can never be applied to the Danube" and that "...such an assertion would call forth a unanimous cry of displeasure, it might even frustrate the whole work of the Peace Conference and rob us of the fruits of the freedom of the mouths of the Danube."[40]

On March 13, 1856 Austria's delegates reported to the Emperor that "the English representatives have given us clearly to understand that, as the Upper Danube would not be declared free in accordance with the Vienna Act, the Lower Danube would be closed for Austrian ships, and also for the ships of the privileged Danube Navigation Company, as far as the Turkish frontier."[41]

The author of these threats was Clarendon who, addressing himself to Austria's delegation, said: "You want Europe not only to clear the mouths of the Danube, but also to give you the exclusive right of trading there."[42]

Austria's delegation did all in its power to satisfy the Emperor, reporting to him that "...had exhausted all our resources in trying to keep the Upper Danube beyond the pale of the Conference and of the European Commission about to be organized. But our task was a very difficult one, all the members being against us."[43]

Those same Delegates reported "...If it is decreed to appoint a European Commission, then that commission shall be limited both as to time and function, and shall not, in any way, interfere with the Riparian States Commission."[44] and that "...the functions of the European Commission shall not include the working out of the regulations for the river police, nor the drawing up of the instructions of the Riparian States Commission, but shall be limited to removing all obstacles to navigation at the mouths of the Danube."[45]

As to the drawing up of the instructions of the Riparian Commission, the signatory Powers not only carried out these instructions, but at the 1858 Paris Conference rejected the complete 1857 Act of Navigation concluded by the Riparian Commission.

In spite of all its efforts to eliminate application of the navigation regime on the Upper Danube (Austrian sector) the Austrian delegation was doubtful, reporting that to support this claim was baffling to them and that "...it was also in contradiction to point II of the Preamble"[46] (Preliminary Peace Project concluded at Vienna on February 4, 1856). The delegation revealed also the intention of England and France to incorporate Turkey in the European family, a fact which — it was said—"debarred us from carrying out the idea of internationalizing the Turkish Danube."[47]

In the end, Buol wrote the Emperor: "I humbly beg your Majesty to bear in mind that it is better far to grant this freedom of our will and accord, than to wait until we are forced to do so."[48] Thus, in the penultimate session of the Conference of 1856, Buol announced receipt of instructions empowering him to accept internationalization of navigation also on the fluvial sectors upriver from the Lower Danube.[49] This yielding resulted in the application of the new international regime for navigation along the entire course of the river, in conformity with the Anglo-French point of view.

In connection with Clarendon's threat of closing the Lower Danube to Austrian ships, there can be revealed some of the consequences which not only would have made it inoperable, but would have been detrimental even to English commerce.

As has been shown, English and French commercial interests, especially those of the former, were concentrated exclusively on the maritime navigation sector of the Lower Danube, between Sulina and Brăila, but not upriver from the latter port nor further up along the Middle and Upper sectors of the river. Had Austria rejected the application of the principles of the Act of Vienna on these two sectors, any action of isolating or excluding her from the Maritime Danube would have reacted unfavorably on navigation in the latter sector.

Aside from the natural physical-geographic interdependence between all the sectors of the river, seconded by the economic one, there must be taken into consideration also the dependence of the organizational structure of the Lower Danube's purely fluvial navigation whose modernization, already in progress, had need of technical expertise and of the Austrian fleet. Without the naval shipyards and the sources of supply for technical materials from Vienna and Budapest, the barely commenced process of modernizing the ports of the Lower Danube and the maritime ports, serving also the traffic of all foreign vessels entering the Danube, could not have been achieved. From the study of official and private statistics of the fluvial vessels (barges, tugboats and passenger vessels) on the Lower Danube, up to World War I, it is apparent that, numerically, most of them were constructed at Vienna, Linz or Budapest.

The river vessels, aside from their reduced load capacity and their primitive technical structure, were at that time insufficient in number to cope with the cereal export, which was increasing continuously. From this aspect, the maritime vessel traffic had absolute need on the Lower Danube for a powerful and well-organized river fleet, which was none other than the Austrian one.

The First Austrian Danube Steam Company, with its long experience and with a fleet of 101 steam vessels and 359 barges, in 1856 was the strongest fluvial force, with an imposing activity. In the last analysis, Austria could have opposed Clarendon's predicted boycott with her own unabrogated rights of navigation on the Lower Danube and out to the sea, granted to her by the previous treaties with Turkey. England and France would have had to give in to Austrian pressure, faced with the latter's superiority in navigation and, especially considering the total lack of interest of English and French shipping in purely fluvial navigation.

England and France became aware of the importance of the Austrian factor in Danube navigation after 1878 when, due to the extraordinary development of Danubian commerce, Austria was accorded exclusivity in carrying out the technical works of facilitating navigation at the Iron Gates and the Cataracts.

Another remark can be made in connection with the same debates on the geographic divisions of the application of the international regime. Although in 1815 the application of the principles of the Act of Vienna on the Danube was of no interest to Austria, in 1855 and 1856 they had become the main point of her policy for lines of communication.

Exclusion of Russia from the Lower Danube.

Was the exclusion of Russia from the Danube premeditated, or did it occur as a consequence of the Crimean War? Premeditation is maintained to be the factor, its application awaiting the opportune moment to be provided by victory in the Crimean War. Among other considerations, the idea of excluding Russia came also from the annulment of Article III of the Treaty of Adrianople.[50]

During the debates at the 1855 and 1856 Conferences of Vienna and those at the beginning of the 1856 Conference of Paris, there hovered the atmosphere of a cautious attitude, of vacillation and flexibility in the conduct of the Allies, all being dependent upon the results at the Crimean front. It must be noted that the presence of Russians at the mouth of the Danube was maintained de facto, even for a while after the close of the 1856 Conference, then ending de jure.

Before the communication of the "Four Points" to Russia, Prokesch-Osten was not thinking of total exclusion of the Russians from the Danube Delta, but only of their ceding a strip of land considered neutral,[51] in which Austria would have guaranteed freedom of navigation by installing an Austrian military garrison[52] near the exit to the sea. In fact, the neutralization idea also came from the text of point 6 of Prokesch's Memorandum as modified on March 23, 1855.[53]

The surprise of Russia's exclusion from the Danube appeared at the March 6, 1856 session of the Paris Peace Conference. Eliminating all previous solutions through which Russia would have remained at the mouths of the Danube, either under neutralization of the Delta or by the autonomy of the proposed syndicate of Sulina, in which she would have been included, Russel (England) and Walewsky (France) reactivated the solution presented a year before in the March 23, 1855 session.[54]

Under that reactivation, in the Walewsky project of March 6, 1856 of the Conference of Paris, Russia no longer appeared sovereign over the mouths of the Danube. Instead, the Sublime Porte was designated to be in charge of the work of clearing the Sulina Mouth of obstacles in the way of navigation, "d'accord avec l'administration locale dans les Principautés..."[55]

In the end, Russia's exclusion was determined in the clause of Article 20 of the Treaty of Paris, which provided that "...in order more fully to secure the freedom of navigation of the Danube, His Majesty the Emperor of all the Russians consents to the ratification of his frontier in Bessarabia..." The territory ceded was that of the three riparian countries of Southern Bessarabia — Cahul, Ismail and Bolgrad — on the Kilia Branch. This territory was ceded to the Principality of Moldavia, which was under Turkish suzerainty.

This time, also, can be seen the soft treatment accorded to Russia. She was obliged to cede only the territory bordering the Danube, not all of Bessarabia, "...in exchange for the towns, ports and territories in Crimea,[56] occupied by the Allies." (Article 4 of the 1856 Treaty of Peace.)

The Clauses of the 1856 Treaty concerning Navigation on the Danube River.

The international regime of navigation applied on the Danube was stipulated in Articles 15 to 19, inclusive, of the Paris Treaty of Peace,[57] concluded on March 30, 1856 by Austria, England, France, Prussia, the Kingdom of Sardinia, and Turkey — the victorious states in the Crimee — and Russia, the vanquished. The basis for the new regime was the principle of Article CVIII of the 1815 Act of Vienna.[58]

In short, the main principles of these five articles are the following: Establishment of the international regime of navigation on the entire course of the Danube, on the basis of the principles of the 1815 Act of Vienna (Art. 15); establishment of a European Danube Commission, composed of riparian and non-riparian states, for a two-years period, for the purpose of improving navigation at the mouths of the Danube and on the fluvial sector to the point of Isaktcha (Art. 16); after two years, the transfer of the European Commission's duties to a Riparian Commission composed exclusively of delegates from riparian states, along with the Commissioners of the three Danubian Principalities, Turkish vessels (Art. 17 and 18); stationing of light warships at the mouths of the Danube, in view of ensuring the observance of the international navigation regulations. (Art. 19).

A peculiarity of the establishment of the new regime was the limitation of the jurisdiction of the European Commission of the Danube from the Sulina Mouth to Isaktcha[59] a port of no importance, instead of to Brăila, the terminal point of navigation for maritime vessels. In connection with the delimitation, the fact that the Sulina-Isaktcha route ran through Dobrujan territory, under Turkish sovereignty, as distinguished from the upriver part, belonging to the Romanian

Principalities under the Sultan's suzerainty, must also be taken into consideration.

Divergencies, Controversies and Rectifications after the Conclusion of the 1856 Paris Treaty of Peace.

Several months after the signing of the 1856 Paris Treaty of Peace, certain omissions and errors were noted, with respect to establishing the Russo — Turkish border in Southern Bessarabia. In order to rectify them, it was necessary to name a Delimination Commission, composed of representatives of the signatories of the Treaty, to meet at Chisinău (Bessarabia). This Commission concluded two Protocols, a Definite Act and a Special Treaty. The rectifications referred to the omission of fixing the appurtenance of the Island of Serpents to the Danube Delta and that of the Bessarabian frontier to the point of Bolgrad. Divergencies arose, in resolving the problems, on the one hand between the Allies and on the other between Turkey and the Romanian Principalities.

The Danube Delta Case.

Omitting fixing of the appurtenance to the Delta was directly tied to Articles 20 and 21 of the 1856 Peace Treaty, the drawing up of which was incomplete and confused. This was revealed when the Turkish government Circular of August 7, 1856 was sent to the two Romanian Principalities, informing them of the status established by the 1856 Treaty.[60] Also mentioned was the beginning of the organization of some works at the Sulina Mouth, in conformity with the obligations assumed by Turkey at the 1856 Paris Conference.[61]

Turkey's position, as well as that of the Romanian Principalities in the case of the Delta were based upon the text of Article 21 of the 1856 Treaty, in which it was stipulated that "...le territoire cédé par la Russie sera annexé à la Principauté de Moldavie, sous la souveraineté de la Sublime Porte." This was the text whose interpretation created confusion. The Romanian point of view was put forth by General Magheru in a Protest-Memorandum sent to the signatories of the 1856 Treaty.[62] He asked that the territory ceded by Russia to be restored to the Principality of Moldavia. Also, in support of the

Romanian point of view, Magheru invoked the statements of some members of the Preliminary Conferences to the 1856 Treaty, as well as the Romanians' rights of possession "ab antiquo" over the territory ceded by Russia, including the Danube Delta.

In connection with Magheru's point of view, Walewsky's proposal in the March 6 session of the 1856 Conference of Paris must be noted. "La Sublime Porte" — he stated—"prend l'engagement de faire exécuter, d'accord avec l'administration locale dans les Principautés, les travaux... à l'embouchure du Danube."[63] This was interpreted to mean that appurtenance of the Danube Mouths belonged to Turkey and the Romanian Principalities in common.

The Romanian position was indirectly upheld by another fact. The idea of restoring Romanian administration over the Delta was Austria's, expressly indicated by Emperor Francis Joseph to his representatives at the 1856 Conference.[64]

The Turks in turn, had mentioned in their Circular that "the islands of the Danube (the Delta) rightfully came to Turkey. By stipulation the return of Bessarabia to Moldavia, the Powers had no intention of committing an injustice to Turkey, depriving her of what was rightfully hers in order to reunite (that territory) to a province, i.e. Moldavia, which had no right to it."[65]

Referring to the demarcation of the new border of Southern Bessarabia, as fixed by Article 20, Magheru mentioned in his Memorandum the fact that no enumeration and no designation had been made of territories abandoned by the Russians. "What was above the line of demarcation remained to the Russians, and what was below no longer belonged to her."[66] In his opinion, the Delta, which was below the line of demarcation, to the south, belonged to Moldavia.

"The Treaty of 1856" — the Turks claimed — "mentions only the part of Bessarabia ceded by Russia. Article 20 of the Treaty of Paris fixes the new frontier between the Ottoman Empire and Russia from the Bessarabian portion; a part of this province is restored to Turkey and annexed to Moldavia, but the islands of the Lower Danube cannot enter into this category; they are under a special and separate regime. The territory which must be annexed to Moldavia is a portion of Bessarabia which once was part of Russia, by the 1812 Treaty of Bucharest."[67]

The Turks also maintained that "...the Danube islands reverted to the former state on the consideration of the annulment of the Treaty of Adrianople which, breaking their Russian domination, restored the two islands of the Delta to their former possessors."[68] From an international juridic point of view, this position was justified, inasmuch as the "former state" was Turkey and the Treaty of Adrianople was annulled by the effect of the Crimean War.

Apparently, the arguments of both parties were justified. The Romanian argument was based on a wide interpretation of the incomplete and confusing texts of Articles 20 and 21 of the 1856 Treaty, while the Turkish one rested on a situation resulting from the Russian defeat in the Crimean War, but not specified precisely in the 1856 Treaty.

In rectifying the omission concerning the Delta, by the new Treaty of Paris on June 19, 1857, a new confusion arose.[69] In Article 2 of this treaty, it was stated: "Les Puissances contractantes conviennent que les îles comprises entre les différents bras du Danube à son embouchure et formant le delta de ce fleuve, ainsi que l'indique le plan joint au Protocole du 6 Janvier 1857, au lieu d'être annexées à la principauté de Moldavie, comme le stipulait implicitement l'article 21 du Traité de Paris, seront replacées sous la souveraineté immédiate de la Sublime Porte, dont elles ont relevé anciennement (sic)."

Article 21, however, had not stipulated annexation of the Delta to Moldavia, but "le territoire cédé par la Russie sera annexé à la Principauté de Moldavie, sous la souveraineté de la Sublime Porte." The territory ceded was that provided for by Article 20, respectively, that part of Southern Bessarabia up to the left bank of the Kilia Branch, outside actual Delta territory.[70]

The controversies over the lack of clarification in the Treaty of 1856 were due to the Allies, whose principal preoccupation at all the Preliminary Conferences to the Peace Treaty was directed mainly to the exclusion of Russia from the Danube; that is, to dispossess her of any ties with the river, such as the territory mentioned later in Article 20 of the 1856 Treaty. This primordial preoccupation was clearly evident also in the stand taken by Prokesch-Osten — who, even in 1855, declared that "...neutralité et même l'abandon du Delta eussent été indispensables pour assurer la libre action des Commissions."[71] (The European and the Riparian Commissions. With all this, a precise decision over the Delta was omitted in the drawing up of the 1856 Treaty.

It has been shown, in another section, that in the session of March 23 of the 1855 Conference of Vienna, the Allies — in raising the question of delimitation of the border between Russia and Turkey — considered the abrogation of the clause of Article III of the Treaty of Adrianople (1829) because of the effect of hostilities between the two countries (the Crimean War.) Hence, the territory ceded by Turkey to Russia by Article III, i.e., the Danube Delta, returned to Turkey's possession by the annulment of the 1829 Treaty.

Finally, almost a year and a half after the signing of the 1856 Treaty, the Danube Delta, including the entire Dobrogean region of which it was a part, was restored to the Ottoman Empire by the Paris Treaty of June 19, 1857.[72]

The Serpents Island Case.

The Serpents Island has no economic or strategic value. Situated about twenty miles from the Sulina Mouth, the island is formed of a block of stone about twenty to thirty feet above the level of the sea and has an area of about sixty acres. After 1856, the European Commission of the Danube installed a lighthouse for the protection of vessels, and, after 1878 when the island was annexed to Romania together with the Danube Delta a small picket of two or three soldiers was installed, symbolically representing the sovereignty of the possessor. Because of its lack of importance, the island was not provided for either in the clause of Article III of the 1829 Treaty of Adrianople, as a territory ceded to Russia by the Turks, or in the Treaty of Paris, in 1856, as having been retroceded. This error, too, had to be rectified by the signatory Powers of the 1856 Treaty in the Protocol of the Conference of Paris of January 6, 1857.[73]

The Protocol made provision that "...le traité de Paris ayant, comme les traités conclus antérieurement entre la Russie et la Turquie, gardé le silence sur le sort de l'île des Serpents, il convient de considérer cette île comme une dépendance du Delta, et qu'elle doit, en conséquence, en suivre la destination" (Turkey).

The Bolgrad Case.

The omissions in the case of the Delta and of Southern Bessarabia created litigation between the Turks and the Romanians, but the error committed in regard to the frontier point of Bolgrad unleashed incidents and controversies with nuances of armed conflict between England, France and Austria. If the solution of the Bolgrad case satisfied England, it disturbed Napoleon III, who was aiming at exploiting the controversy so as to support his new policy of approaching Russia.

Referring to the new situation, Riker noted: "Bolgrad became an issue on which the Concert of Europe was in danger of falling to pieces."[74] England strengthened her fleet on the Black Sea,[75] while Austria did not withdraw her troops from the Romanian Principalities under the motive that definite setting of the new Russo-Turkish frontier had not been made.[76]

As has been shown, the discord between the Allies, respectively between the Protecting Powers of the romanian Principalities, contributed much to the agitation among them in the problem of their elections and union.[77]

The Bolgrad case was revealed on the occasion of the delimiting of the new frontier in Southern Bessarabia, as decided by Article 20 of the 1856 Treaty of Paris. Among other geographic points of delimitation, the frontier line was indicated as passing also "au sud de Bolgrad," a small Bessarabian town located at the northern extremity of Lake Yalpouk, having a population of about 12,000 composed also of Bulgarian colonists. The reason for the controversy was the nearness of this point to Lake Yalpouk where through several small canals — one could connect with the Kilia Branch of the Danube.

Aside from Russia's representative, who deliberately did not reveal it, no other member of the 1856 Conference realized that the respective point was right at the edge of the lake. Only a year later did the frontier Delimitation Commission,[78] while researching the maps annexed to the 1856 Treaty and furnished by the French War Ministry (and of which Riker said "...they were found to be inaccurate") discover that "one of the branches of the Danube Delta flowed through Lake Yalpouk."[79] Also, that the town of Bolgrad, mentioned in the delimitation of 1856 was not the one at the edge of the lake, but another, north of the lake, which according to the same maps, bore the name of Bolgrad along with its older name of Tabak. This doubling of the name created a confusion which Russia attempted to exploit, demanding that the initial delimitation made by the 1856 Treaty be respected — and by which Bolgrad would have remained at the margin of the lake.

By setting Bolgrad geographically on the shore of Lake Yalpouk, the English feared that, on the basis of the lake's connection with the Kilia Branch, Russia would invoke a position of riparian state and implicitly the right to interfere in the administration of the navigation regime. This explains the fact that the strongest protest came from the English, who objected that the town of Bolgrad mentioned in the 1856 delimitation was not the one at the edge of Lake Yalpouk, but the one north of it at a point further from the lake.

From discussions at the level of the representatives of the Treaty of 1856 signatories, the Bolgrad case went to the Government level at London, where Palmerston was opposed to any ceding in favor of Russia. Even the compromise presented by the Delimitation Commission, which proposed that the lake shore be considered outside the town limits, was rejected.[80] England's opposition put Napoleon III in a difficult situation. He had accepted Orloff's request that Bolgrad should remain under Russians in consideration of the Bulgarian majority of its population.

To exemplify the erroneous and exaggerated Bolgrad incident, a summary geographic description is necessary. Lake Yalpouk is about 20 kms. north of the Kilia Branch, Yalpouk Brook emptying into it. Between the Kilia Branch and Lake Yalpouk is interposed Lake Kongourlui, the connection between them being another brook. The waters of Lake Kongourlui empty into the Kilia Branch, also through a brook.[81]

Because of the shallow depths and narrowness of these brooks, only some fishing crafts drawing a maximum draught of two to three feet could navigate on them, not military or commercial vessels of small tonnage, as the English believed.[82] Walewsky was correct in assuring the English of the impossibility of there existing any communication of commercial vessels to the river through Lake Yalpouk, which "was so shallow that even fisher boats could hardly use it."[83]

Finally, even the Bolgrad case was clarified, also through the 1857 Paris Treaty which had ratified the preceding Protocols.[84] The new frontier line understood by the English was kept, the one south of the village of Tabak, also known as Bolgrad. The unusual character of the new frontier lay also in the setting of the line, beginning at the Black Sea, 2936 meters farther east,[85] instead of 1000 meters, as had been provided for initially in Article 20 of the 1856 Treaty. By this move, the lakes, ponds and tributaries of the main Kilia Branch were included in the territory retroceded by Russia. The move was another bar to any possible means of Russian communication with the Danube.

In the Bolgrad case, some remarks can be made. The English, through their strong stand in eliminating the Russians from the Danube in any form, opposed not only a direct contact with the river, but also any indirect one. The flexibility of that same position was to be shown in 1878, when England would give in the Russian pressure to reannex not only Southern Bessarabia, but also the Kilia Branch. Again, the flagrant English ignorance was revealed concerning the geography of the Danube Delta, that "none of the branches of the

Danube flowed through Lake Yalpouk," as was deduced from the findings of the Delimitation Commission.[86]

Conclusions.

Retrospectively seen, the principles of the new international regime of navigation, established by the 1856 Treaty, presented some curious points. The temporary two-year term of the European Commission of the Danube had to be prolonged by future Danube Conferences, when the Riparian Commission presumed to replace it did not assume the duties. The introduction of the new regime on the entire course of the river was a theoretic one, Austria applied her own norms on her sector of the river, up to 1921.

The bases of the 1815 Act were respected in part, having been altered by the admission of non-riparian states (England, France, the Kingdom of Sardinia and Russia) in the administration and control of the new regime on the basis of some new principles. The immutability of the principles of 1815, as well as of the new ones of 1856, proved to be flexible in the later developments of the new regime.

Convoking the Kingdom of Sardinia to the 1856 Conference was due to its participation in the Crimean War, as well as to the active presence of its flag in Lower Danube navigation. Prussia was invited (later, on March 18) because of her position as a signatory to the 1841 Convention of the Straits, which was subject to revision by the 1856 Conference. By eliminating Russia from the Danube and the Sulina Mouth, all the difficulties created in the past by the Russian administration at the Sulina Mouth and Branch were eliminated.

Through the autonomy of the Romanian Principalities and that of Serbia, guaranteed by the signatories of the 1856 Treaty, the political expansion of Russia, which also affected freedom of navigation, was temporarily barred.

The interposition of the Romanian Principalitie, with the Latin origin of their population was seen by Napoleon III to create a buffer state, a "Latin Citadel" would be an opposition to Russian expansion. It did not prove to be efficient, inasmuch as the guarantee, by the Great Powers, of autonomy of this "Citadel" was not also assured by any protection on the order of the "Roman Limes."

Chapter 2

THE CONFERENCE OF THE DANUBE RIPARIAN COMMISSION AND THE 1857 ACT OF NAVIGATION

Introduction

It has been shown that clauses 17 and 18 of the 1856 Treaty of Paris made provision for the establishment of a Riparian Commission for the entire course of the Danube, to replace the European Commission.

The importance of a general examination of the components and the works of the Commission is in direct relationship to the application of the principles of 1815, as well as with the ensemble of problems of regulating navigation on the Lower Danube, including the Maritime Danube. Also the tendency toward Austria's supremacy over the entire course of the river was revealed from the method of organization and the activity projected for the Commission.

The Commission, composed exclusively of riparian states, would have begun its functions in conformity with the Act of 1815. The fact that it was to have begun functioning two years after the establishment of the European Commission of the Danube would have eliminated the presence of the non-riparian Great Powers from the Mouths of the Danube.

"De facto," the riparians on the Lower Danube, in 1857, were Austria and Turkey. Austria with a small portion at the Iron Gates, and Turkey as a suzerain. The real riparians — the Romanian and Serbian Principalities, being vassals of the Ottoman Empire, participated only in the capacity of an audience, and Bulgaria was still considered a Turkish province.

Of the two riparians, Austria and Turkey, only the former had a decisive say at the Conference for establishing the Riparian Commission, being the one possessing the largest and most powerful river fleet.

The presence of a Riparian Commission at the Mouths of the Danube, without the participation of England and France, would have made conflicts between Austria and Russia easier. On the other hand, Austria's powerful economic position in Central Europe and in the Lower Danube regions would have strengthened even more her political one, a situation that could unbalance the new order in Southeast Europe as established by the 1856 Treaty of Paris. Under this latter consideration can be evaluated the opposition of the Anglo-French group to the proposed Commission, as well as to the Act of Navigation which it was to work out.

In spite of England's and France's rejections, in 1858, of the plan to set the Riparian Commission in operation and to initiate the Act of Navigation, Austria did not give up. She renewed her efforts in 1878 and 1883. In the development of this policy, she was to meet the permanent opposition of the small states of the Lower Danube, that of Romania taking on an aspect of European conflict.

The Opening of the Conference and the Act of Navigation of 1857.

Eight months after the signing of the 1856 Treaty of Paris, the first meeting of the Conference of the Riparian Commission of the Danube was held at Vienna, on November 29, 1856.[87] Delegates present were those[88] of the riparian states indicated in Article 17 of the 1856 Treaty, that is: Austria, Bavaria, Turkey and Württemberg, plus the commissars from the three Danubian Principalities:[89] Serbia, Moldavia and Wallachia.

The inaugural session was opened by Taggenburg, the Austrian Minister of Commerce. The work of later sessions were conducted by the president of the Conference, Blumfeld, and other Austrian Delegates. The work of the conference absorbed the longest period of time in the history of conferences or any other meetings devoted to problems of navigation on the Lower Danube. It began on November 29, 1856 and concluded a corresponding number of protocols.[90]

In conformity with the stipulations of Article 17 or the 1856 Treaty, the Riparian Commission was to fulfill the conditions of points 1 and

THE 1857 ACT OF NAVIGATION 255

2 of the respective article, that is, the working out of the Regulation for Navigation and River Police, for the entire course of the river (point 1) and the removal of impediments which until then hampered the free navigation accorded by the Act of 1815, including the privileges of certain navigation companies (point 2). The Navigation Regulation was drawn up in the Navigation Act of 7th of November 1857, concluded at Vienna.[91]

The proposed Regulation for Police was worked out separately by October 16, 1857, to be definitely completed later.[92]

All the navigational rules could not be included in the Project for the Navigation Act, the new regulations needing to be put in harmony and related with the administrative customs and police conditions existing heretofore on the entire course of the river and, in particular, on the Lower Danube. Also, the specific physical aspect of the Danube was taken into consideration, as well as the experience of having applied the regulations of the Act of 1815 on the rivers in Northwest Europe, which had to be kept in mind.[93]

Navigation standards were debated and researched under the most modern aspects of navigation at that time, even future administrative and disciplinary regulations concerning crews of vessels being studied. Still, there were many unknowns. As to the unknowns on the river, the Committee for Preparation of the Project for Regulation of the Police on the River reported: "Nous sommes surtout privés de tout renseignement officiel sur ce qui subsiste actuellement sur le Danube comme droit établi, ou même comme coutume ou usage."[94]

Even drawing up the Act of Navigation could not have been accomplished between 1856 and 1857 if its bases had not been quite familiar to the Austrians because of their many on-site studies carried on in previous years. This also can explain the predominance of Austrian imprint on the Navigation Act of 1857. Doubtless, the pressures of the Delegates from Bavaria and Württemberg, familiar with the characteristics of their navigable waters, were also of use. No special competence in navigation could have been attributed to the Commissars of the three Danubian Principalities, nor to the Turkish delegates, at the level of the other participants. Although the Navigation Act was not applied, it later became the guide for the European Commission of the Danube elaboration of the Regulation for Navigation on the Lower Danube sector between Brăila and the Iron Gates.

Disagreements and Incidents at the Signing of the Act.

The disagreements, controversies and incidents, at the end of the work of drawing up the Act of Navigation, occurred between the Commissars of the three Danubian Principalities and the Delegates of the other States, of which Austria's was the leader. The cause was the nonrecognition of the rights of the Principalities representatives to sign the Act of Navigation, on the consideration that their countries were not politically independent. (Serbia, Moldavia and Wallachia).

The significance of those incidents for the subject of this work lies in the fact that the antagonism and divergencies between the three small states and Austria were revealed for the first time. Their political and economic effects were felt on navigation on the fluvial sector between the Iron Gates and Brăila, up to the time of World War I. In the case of the Romanian Principalities, the degree of Viennese pressure later (1875) set off the customs war between them and Austria. The incidents also gave rise to psychological resentments. Even leaving aside the Austrian policy of supremacy on the Lower Danube, one cannot overlook the fact that in 1857 not one of the three Principalities could have taken Austria's place in her role of modernizing the navigation complex. The values of this role was lessened by the manner in which it was imposed.

Austria's role on the Danube was important also from the political and economic prestige she enjoyed in the ranks of the Great Powers, as well as those of the three Danubian Principalities. For the latter, Vienna represented the cultural, economic and political center of Southeastern Europe. Although the intellectual level of the Commissars[95] was equal to that of the Delegates because of more favorable conditions in their countries, they were dispossessed of any political power since they were subordinate to the Ottoman Empire.[96]

Nevertheless, as will be seen in continuation, all three Commissars not only dared to oppose, but also to protest against the proceedings initiated by their big and powerful neighbor. The echo of their protests contributed in great part to the rejection of the Act of Navigation, the three Principalities having intervened with the other Great Powers, especially England and France.

At the end of the preparatory work to the Act of Navigation (November 10), heated divergencies appeared over the procedure followed in the signing of the Act. It was decided that all seven of the participants were to sign four original texts of the Act, to be given to the four independent countries: Austria, Bavaria, Turkey and

Württemberg, while only copies were to be sent to Moldavia, Serbia and Wallachia, vassal states, through their suzerain, the Sublime Porte. Surprised by this procedure, the Commissars immediately reacted.

Up to the penultimate day of the Conference, an academic atmosphere had prevailed, one of equality of treatment between participants. On the last day, however, the relations changed and there appeared to be a "conspiracy" against the small countries. Cavour wrote of Austria's manner in the case of the Act of Navigation, that Vienna "...a tenté de détruire par des voies détournées et des agissements en sous-main ce qu'elle n'osait combattre à visage ouvert..."[97] Cavour's opinion could also be deduced from the entire documentation respecting the development of the rapid and surprising events of the last session of the Riparian Commission.[98]

If the "conspiracy" was humiliating, its after effects were proof of the consideration in which the three Danubian Principalities were held, after the establishment of their complete autonomy, within the suzerainty of the Ottoman Empire. Even Blumfeld, Austria's Delegate and president of the Conference, was embarrassed by the situation created for the three Commissars.

This embarrassment was shown also by Buol, the Minister for Foreign Affairs. On the day after the incident of November 10, he disavowed the measure taken by the Commission, declaring that the consent of the Danubian Principalities was an indispensable condition of the Act of Navigation.[99] As an apology, he assured the Commissars that the error would be repaired, an unkept promise.

The manner in which the work of the session of November 7, 1857 developed was in contradiction with Buol's disavowal. The written protests of the Commissars had brought on the actions, on the part of the other members, to frustrate them by confusing the minutes of the respective meeting. In order to reveal the true facts, the Commissars reconstituted and drew up Separate Minutes of the meeting, affirming "sur l'honneur que ces faits se sont passés tels qu'ils sont relatés ici."[100]

In these Minutes it is stated that, after presentation of the rights of signing by the four Delegates, the president made the following declaration: "Il restait libre aux Commissaires des Principautés d'apposer aussi leurs signatures à l'Acte, après que le délégué de la Sublime Porte, à la demande adressée à cet égard par le président, eût déclaré que, d'après ses instructions, il n 'avait pas à s'y opposer."[101]

The Commissars reacted energetically against this statement, also, which in their opinion would have meant that their right to sign was dependent upon the good will of the other members, not on the stipulations of Article 17 of the 1856 Treaty. In reply to this statement, in the Separate Minutes it was made clear that the Commissars "...ne se rappellent pas avoir entendu dans la séance du 7 Novembre ni la demande du président ni la répose de M. Davoud, Délégué de la Sublime Porte."[102]

Finally, an attempt was made to invite the Commissars to the signing of the Act of Navigation. The first to be invited was the Serbian Commissar, F. Christic. He refused to sign, inasmuch as the Commission had declined to consider certain observations made by him, in connection with stipulations of articles 2, 8 and 36 on the matter of closing the delegates.

The next one, N. Rosetti, Wallachia's Commissar, also refused to sign because of the decision of the four Delegates to draw up the Act in only four originals instead of seven for all the participants in the work of drawing up the Act of Navigation.[103]

L. Steege, the Moldavian Commissar, did not want to take a different position, although he did have his government's authorization to sign the Act independent of the actions of the other two Commissars.[104] Still, on receiving other orders, he did sign the four original examples.[105] Immediately afterwards, he was recalled and replaced.[106] For Bulgaria, which was not autonomous, the Turkish Delegate signed.

As to the position of the Moldavian Commissar regarding the signing of the Act, in the Minutes drawn up by the three Commissars there was revealed an act demonstrative of the real attitude of the Austrian Delegate. After repeating the instructions for signing the Act, "il fait le geste de vouloir signer," but "le Président retire l'Acte de la portée de la plume, déclarant que, vu les doutes de MM les délégués, il était obligé de différer la signature du Commissaire Moldave justqu'à ce que le Protocole du 7 Novembre soit arrêté,"[107] after which, "...il propose que cette séance soit considérée comme confidentielle."[108]

In the same Separate Minutes of the Commissars was disclosed a fact which could be proof of the frustrating actions against them. While the heated discussions were being carried on about the signing of the Act, "les délégués se retirent de côté et semblent se consulter quelques moments...le Délégué de Bavière declare ensuite, avec une certaine vivacité, qu'il lui parait indispensable qu'avant la signature des Commissaires des Principautés, les termes du Protocole du 7 Novembre soient unanimement acceptés, et que le sens et l'esprit dans lesquels signaient les Commissaires, soient exactement précisés."[109] Alluding to the exclusivity of the right to sign, the same Delegate declared,

THE 1857 ACT OF NAVIGATION 259

"'...que le même droit ne saurait s'appliquer aux Commissaires comme aux Délégués et qu'il considère l'Acte par lui même, comme complet sans la signature des Commissaires des Principautés.''[110]

The political status of vassality, that is, the Principalities' lack of independence was for Vienna international law support of the rejection of their position of equality with the Delegates of the other Riparian states.

Finally, the Commissars were given the right to sign the Act of Navigation, but they were excluded from the ratification of the Act, a right accorded exclusively to the Delegates of Austria, Bavaria, Turkey and Württemberg.[111] (1 January 1858).

Under the purely juridic aspect of the international political status of their countries, the Commissars' right to sign appears controversial. The question that could be raised would be whether their participation in the work of the Riparian Commission, as provided for in Article 17 of the 1856 Treaty, also empowers them to sign the 1857 Act along with the Delegates of the independent Riparian states. The answer depends on the way in which one understands the position of legitimate representatives in the Commission, by interpretation of the following quote from the text[112] of Article 17, namely: "...auxquels se réuniront les Commissaires des trois Principautés danubiennes, dont la nomination aura été approuvée par la Porte."

The exigency of analyzing the expression "se réuniront" would seem unnecessary were it not that it can clarify the problem. The etymology of this expression indicates a drawing together, of meeting figuratively of grouping, of reconciliation.[113] The interpretation that could be given to the text of Article 17 could be: to the composition of the Commission by four delegates of the independent countries were united, associated with, grouped together, the Commissars of the three Principalities, in view of reconciliation or resolution of certain problems of common interest. The problem of equality of position, based on the level of independence in taking decisions is very interpretative, depending also on the authorizations implicit in the appointment of the representatives, as stated in Article 17 of the 1856 Treaty.

While the other countries were represented by "Delegates," the three Danubian Principalities were represented by "Commissars" whose appointments had to be approved by the Porte. From this distinction, related to the political status of the countries represented, could come the right to make decisions. While the decisions of the Delegates were independent, those of the Commissars could be considered subordinate to the Porte. Nowhere was there mention either of the Commissars' right to sign or of their subordination to the

Turkish Delegate. The subordination of the Commissars to the will of Turkey was only understood, not expressly stated. As shall be shown, the subordination was often disregarded in other circumstances in the Conference.

From the report made by M. Kogălniceanu, a politician and an assiduous defender of Romanian rights on the Lower Danube, it seems that, initially, the Commissars were treated on an equal footing with the Delegates. Later on, he noted, after the Commission met, the Turkish Delegate regarded them as "...only his aides, bound to conform completely with his work and his decisions...they being considered as some vassals."[114]

In the controversy over the signing of the Act of Navigation by the Commissars also, Hajnal indicates Austria as the author of the incident as she wished to ingratiate Turkey as a counterservice for supporting her point of view.[115] However, there can be added to this statement the fact that the gesture of courtesy was not unilateral, inasmuch as Austria and Turkey were equally interested in tempering the spirit of independence of the Romanian and Serbian Principalities, immediately after the 1856 Treaty of Paris had accorded them complete administrative autonomy. It was a common Austrian-Turkish action with the aim of eliminating any confusion of autonomy with independence, sought by these Principalities. Turkey wished only to maintain her authority as suzerain, while Austria wanted the elimination of any difficulties she might encounter from any independent states in navigation on the Lower Danube. She could organize more efficiently her policy of supremacy on a sector of the river under the aegis of a Turkey disinterested in navigation.

Austria's opposition in 1857 was a circumstantial one, for she, herself, in 1855 and later in 1875 had concluded with the Romanian Principalities, during the period of vassality, a number of Conventions of the sort of the Act of Navigation, among them also one for commerce and navigation. Also, the same Principalities had concluded conventions with Russia.[116]

The problem of the political freedom of the Danubian Principalities must be regarded also from the point of view of its classification with International Public Law. In this light, independent states have absolute freedom over their foreign actions, as a consequence of their full capacity in international politics, in contrast with semisovereign, vassal states or those under protectorate. The vassal states enjoy domestic autonomy, have the right of self-government, but in international matters their actions and decisions are taken by the suzerain or protector.

THE 1857 ACT OF NAVIGATION 261

During the vassality of the Romanian and Serbian Principalities, the handling of foreign problems was the attribute of the Sultan, the suzerain. The Principalities had no diplomatic representatives abroad, only agents known as "Capuchehaie," in Constantinople, acting as connections between the Principalities and the Sublime Porte. They were considered to be administrative employes in the service of the Ottoman Empire.[117]

In the matter of the vassality or of the independence of the Romanian Principalities, for example, there appear great contradictions also in the ranks of the Great Powers. In 1856, at the Conference of Paris, Walewsky considered the Romanian Principalities to be on an equal footing with Turkey when he proposed that "la Sublime Porte prend l'engagement de faire exécuter, d'accord avec l'administration locale dans les Principautés, les travaux...pour dégager l'embouchure du Danube..."[118] but a suzerain, such as the Sublime Porte, would not have needed the "accord" of a vassal, as were the Principalities.

At the same conference, however, the representatives of the same Principalities were considered to be "...only in the unofficial capacity of advisors to the Porte on local affairs."[119] In the case of the Riparian Commission, however, the role of the three Commissars was not that of vassals or of simple attaches to the Turkish Delegate. They worked on an equal basis with the other Delegates, including the Turkish one.

A. Müller, the Württemberg Delegate, together with Steege, Commissar of Moldavia, making up the Committee of Studies approved by the Riparian Commission, presented the idea of beginning preliminary research for working out the Police Regulation.[120] The same Committee presented to the Commission "...les premiers trois chapitres du projet d'un règlement de police..."[121]

Here then are several facts and circumstances which produce confusion and contradictions as to the workings of the Riparian Commission and at the signing of the Act of Navigation.

Cancellation by Turkey of the use of the Navigation Act by the Principality of Moldavia.

Although through the Memorandum and the protests[122], addressed in 1859 to the Powers guaranteeing their autonomy, the Romanian Principalities rejected application of the Act of Navigation, still in May 1858 the Moldavian Government had taken preliminary measures in view of its application.

Godel Launay, Austrian Consul at Jassy, informed the Secretary of State of the Provisional Government of Moldavia of the application of the Act of Navigation on the Austrian sector of the Danube (Middle and Upper Danube), a measure recommended to be taken also by Wallachia in her fluvial sector.[123] That same month, the Secretariat of State of Moldavia informed the Consul of the measure taken,[124] annexing also the list of "Preliminary measures concerning the application of the Act of Navigation.[125]

Serbia and Wallachia took no measures. The Danubian sector of Moldavia, on which the Act of Navigation was to be applied, was, in 1857, between the Mouth of the Siret along the actual river course and the Kilia Branch, up to the Black Sea, including the ports of Galatz, Reni, Ismail and New Kilia.

The measure taken by the Provisional Government of Moldavia was contested in April 1859 by its definitive Government,[126] on the consideration that its application by a provisional commission of the country had, in the meantime been suspended by the Sublime Porte, which "a invité le Caimacam Vogoride à suspendre l'exécution de l'Acte en Moldavie."

The information becomes contradictory faced with the conclusions drawn from the texts of the additional articles to the Act of Navigation, presented later by the Riparian Commission as a result of the proposed modifications of certain provisions of the Act, initially requested at the 1858 Conference of Paris. The fact that the Sublime Porte had taken the obligation to communicate to the three Danubian Principalities the text of the additional articles to the Act, implies that she, as Suzerain Power, expected to apply the Act of Navigation also in these Principalities.

The initial order given by N. Vogoride to the Moldavian Commissar, to sign the Act of Navigation, as well as the haste in carrying it out, was not due to any concern over navigation, but to certain important local events, in which the Great Powers were also involved. In the agitation of the Moldavian and Wallachian nationalistic political circles over the union of the two Principalities following the granting of their autonomy, N. Vogoride had to follow the orders of the Porte, which had appointed him to the position of Caimacam.[127] Because both Turkey and Austria were opposed to the union, Vogoride tried to please both parties, hoping eventually to be definitely appointed Prince of Moldavia.[128]

In the end, the 1857 Act of Navigation was not immediately put into application, remaining to be approved or rejected by the other

Great Powers, the decision which was to be taken at the 1858 Conference of Paris.

Chapter 3

THE PARIS CONFERENCE OF 1858

Introduction

At the 1858 Conference of Paris for the organization of the Romanian Principalities, certain Danubian problems were also debated during the sessions of 9, 16 and 19 August. The most important of these were the coming into operation of the riparian Commission of the Danube, the application of the Act of Navigation of 1857, and the extension of the mandate of the European Commission of the Danube.

At this Conference, England and France reconsidered — or, more precisely put — withdrew from their position at the 1856 Conference and Treaty of Paris, seeking to bar Austrian predominance along the entire course of the Danube and, especially, along the Lower Danube and the maritime navigation sector.

The debates were principally on the clauses of Articles 16-18 of the 1856 Treaty, through which the Riparian Commission would have succeeded the European Commission. The divergencies and controversies were due to the lack of clarity and precision in the respective clauses.

Some outstanding results came from the work of the conference on the evolvement of the international regime of navigation, the most important being the categorical affirmation of the Anglo-French policy of rejecting the assumption of operations by the Riparian Commission, in place of the European Commission and the Act of Navigation.

In theory, the concept of succession was upheld and confirmed by the then established rules of the European Commission pertaining to duties, immediately after 1856,. Thus, in Article 2 of the European

Commission's Public Act of 1865, mention was made that the administration of navigation and other matters were the responsibility of that Commission or "l'autorité qui lui succédera en droit." In other Acts mention was made that such and such an attribution "...sera spécialement réservée à la Commission Européenne, ou à l'autorité qui lui succèdera..." That authority was none other than the projected Riparian Commission.

The rejection of the Riparian Commission's and the Navigation Act's coming into operation was a premeditated action aimed at keeping the European Commission. All the more so when Hübner, the Austrian Plenipotentiary, proposed, at the August 16 session of the Conference, that a term of several months be allotted during which an understanding could be reached, the proposal was rejected. By not carrying out Articles 16,17 and 18 of the 1856 Treaty, the principles of the Act of 1815 were also ignored.

The Work of the Conference.

From the works of the 1858 Conference, the bases for navigation will be examined, as recorded in three Protocols.[129]

The Controversy over the Approval of the Riparian Commission and the Incident of the Acknowledgement of the 1857 Act only.

At the August 9 session, Walewsky requested the Austrian and Turkish Plenipotentiaries to present to the Conference the results of the work of the Riparian Commission and of the Act of Navigation it had drawn up in 1857.[130]

The respective Plenipotentiaries, principal members of the Riparian Commission, expressed their opinion that, in conformity with Article 18 of the 1856 Treaty, the respective works did not have to be communicated to the Conference, nor the European Commission of the Danube. The two latter had only to take note of them.[131] The other members of the Conference were of the opinion that taking note of the results implied previous examination of the Act of Navigation in order to take care of any possible observations that might be made. In the opinion of the majority, there was no idea of dissimilarity between taking note of and examining.

Without waiting for clarification of this problem, England's Plenipotentiary opened the debates on the examination of the Act of Navigation, the other members of the Conference going along with him. Austria's Plenipotentiary reserved his definite response, awaiting the approval of his government, but did not take up again the matter of taking note of or of examining.

We shall attempt a detailed analysis of this problem, based on the texts of Articles 17, 18 and 19 of the 1856 Treaty, as well as on the Austrian point of view, stated before and during the Conference.

According to the text of Article 18 of said Treaty, the idea of taking note of, maintained by Hübner, did have a basis. Actually, in this Article, it was determined that after the fulfillment of the duties specified in Article 17 of that Treaty: "Les Puissances signataires réunis en Conférence, informées de ce fait, prononceront, après en avoir pris acte, la dissolution de la Commission Européenne et, dès lors, la Commission Riveraine permanente jouira de mêmes pouvoires que ceux dont la Commission Européenne aura été investie justqu'alors." Hence, clearly, the role of the Conference was merely to take note of the Act of Navigation presented to it.

The text of Article 19, of the same Treaty, seems to contradict that of Article 18. It mentions that the assurance of carrying out the Regulations which were to have been drawn up was to have been "d'un commun accord, d'après les principes ci-dessus énoncés..." The mention was confusing; the component parts of the "commun accord" were not spelled out and the idea of "les principes ci-dessus enoncés" was vague.

Interpretation of Article 19 could be that "l'accord commun," referred to taking note of the Act of Navigation by the members of the Conference and, from the text "d'après les principes ci-dessus enoncès," which included also Article 18, leads again to the idea of taking note of. According to the Austrian point of view, indicated before the opening of the Conference, the "accord commun" was that of the Riparian states, in opposition to that of the Conference, which included the accord of all its members.

A Memorandum of the Vienna government, issued in March 1858, invoked the text of Article 108 of the Act of 1815, which made provision for the rights of riparians to regulate "d'un commun accord tout se qui a rapport à la navigation;,'' of the rivers which traversed or separated a number of countries. According to the Austrians, the Act of 1815 having come from riparian states, the Conference composed also of non-riparians had no right to examine or censor it.[132]

As to the exclusivity of the riparians over the regulation of all that concerned navigation, the dispute over the European Commission's lack of authority over the work of the Riparian Commission is reasserted. The Commission's request for an exchange of Protocols of the works of the two Commissions was rejected by the Riparian Commission on the grounds that the former had no right to interfere in the work of the latter.[133]

In the matter of examining the works of the Riparian Commission, however, the competence of the 1858 Conference was superior to that of the European Commission for the Danube.

As to the rights of the riparian states, a deviation in Austria's position was observed. The exclusivity of the riparians as provided for in the above-mentioned Memorandum, had been eliminated by Prokesch-Osten, Austria's Plenipotentiary at the Danubian Conference at Vienna in 1855. For the European Commission, he proposed that it not be dissolved except by common accord, that is, with all the participants at the Conference, riparian and non-riparian.[134]

It seems that England and France had become aware of the obstruction Austria would make over the examination of the Act of Navigation. Before the Conference they had intervened with the Sublime Porte to abstain from ratifying the Act of Navigation, conditioning its examination.[135]

The procedure of taking note of, or of examining, was directly tied to the replacement of the European Commission by the Riparian one, on the condition that in two years they complete the duties stipulated in Article 16, 17 and 18 of the 1856 Treaty. The European Commission was to carry out the work of ridding the navigation of any obstacles between Isaktcha and the mouths of the Danube (Art. 16). Of the four duties[136] assigned to the Riparian Commission, only two had to be completed by 1858, namely, the elaboration of the Regulations for Navigation and Police and the elimination of impediments of any nature, that prevented the application of the principles of the Act of 1815 on the Danube.

At the date of the 1858 Conference, however, neither of the Commissions had fulfilled all their mandates. The European Commission had been unable to rid navigation of physical obstacles, construction being still in the projection stage. The Riparian Commission had drawn up only the Regulation for Navigation; the one for Police being still in the Preliminary Project stage, yet to be made definite and later applied.[137] As to the impediments, which added up to elimination of privileges, Austria had earlier abolished, on January 29, 1858, those granted to the Austrian Navigation Company (D.D.S.G.)[138]

The mandates assigned to the two Commissions were found in this stage at the 1858 Conference which was to decide upon the replacement of the European Commission by the Riparian one. Aware of these deficiencies, the English and French Plenipotentiaries debated the problems of sanctioning the Riparian Commission and the Act of Navigation in the light of their prior examination.

Austria was aware of the possible obstructions on the part of England and France, because if she had applied the Act of Navigation on the Middle and Upper Danube sectors, Prokesch-Osten would not have been certain it would be extended along the Lower Danube.[139] In spite of Austria's opposition to the examination of the Act of Navigation, an eventual contrary decision of the Conference was not categorically eliminated. "Nous ne douterons pas que les Gouvernements des Etats riverains"—as the analysis of an Austrian report stated—"se prêteront aussi très volontiers à un tel examen et que l'on trouvera facilement la forme convenable pour la prise en considération des réclamations qui devraient être reconnues comme étant fondées en droit."[140]

In the question of taking note of, or of examining the Act of Navigation, a contradictory situation appeared between the official position in London and that of its representatives at the Conference, a fact that encouraged Vienna. The contradiction was caused by the "Opinion of the Law Officers of the Crown," requested by the English Government regarding the attributes of the Commissions instituted by Articles 16 and 17 of the 1856 Treaty. The "opinion" communicated also to the Government at Vienna, which publicized it, declared that the role of the Conference of 1858 was limited exclusively to "recording" the Act of Navigation, but not to "examining" it.[141]

Opposition to the opinion was put forth in a French "Mémoire" published in 1858, which in its anonymity could have reflected the point of view of the French Government against the Act of Navigation, as well as against the Austrian policy.[142]

Regarding the Act of Navigation, the "Mémoire" invoked the clause of Article 17 of the 1856 Treaty, on the basis of which the attributes of the Riparian Commission were limited exclusively to drawing up the Regulations for Navigation and Police, agreement on their execution to be decided upon in conformity with Article 19, by the 1858 Conference, in common accord with all its members.[143] "La conférence," it was stressed, "examinera, révisera, santionnera ou repoussera dans sa sagesse l'Acte de Navigation."[144] The "Mémoire" not mentioning the name of Austria, evaluated the Act of Navigation in the light of "...calculations égoistes d'une Puissance que essaye d'en faire tourner la solution à son profit particulier."[145]

The author of the "Mémoire" was convinced that the objective of the Riparian Commission had been "dirigée par l'Autriche[146]...qui n'a jamais compris et envisagé cette question que d'un point de vue opposé aux intentions des autres cabinets."[147]

It is not improbable that the hostile position against Austria, taken in this "Mémoire," was determined also by the case of the French firm, Magnan, whose concession on the Siret affluent had been annulled at Vienna's intervention. (The case will be examined further). This supposition can be drawn from the following text of the "Mémoire": "Par suite des calcules particuliers des Puissances riveraines...des grandes societés industrielles formées, ou prête a se former, pour l'exploitation de la libre navigation du Danube, se sont arretées et ont restreint ou suspendu leurs opérations."[148]

This, then, is one of the aspects of the French point of view which may have contributed to the negative vote of France's Plenipotentiary on the acceptance of the Act of Navigation and of the Riparian Commission taking up its duties.

In the end, the 1857 Act of Navigation drawn up by the Riparian Commission was examined by the 1858 Conference.

Freedom of Navigation or Commerce only?

England's Plenipotentiary, Cowley, remarked that in the 1857 Act of Navigation there had not been made provision for the text "la navigation sera entièrement libre et ne pourra, sous le rapport du commerce, être interdite à personne,"[149] the clause stipulated in the 1815 Act of Vienna (Article CIX). This had the sense that the riparian states as well as the non-riparian ones were to be beneficiaries of complete freedom of navigation, including that of cabotage.

In support of his point of view, he invoked the Regulation for Navigation on the Rhine, in which the provision was "d'une manière uniforme, pour tous, et aussi favorable que possible au commerce de toutes les nations."[150] Omission of this freedom in the Act of Navigation meant, in his opinion, the creation of a privileged status for the riparian states.[151] From this point of view there arose a problem which even the authors of the 1815 Act had resolved in favore of the riparian states. On this basis, Hübner upheld his point of view in 1858.

In demonstrating the benefiting of freedom of navigation exclusively to riparian states, Hübner recalled the decision which had been made, within the framework of the works of the Committee on International Rivers as to the new principles of navigation presented to the Congress of Vienna in 1815.[152] He declared that at Article 1 of the Dalberg Project, presented at the first session of the Committee, provision was made that "...le Rhin sera, sous le rapport du commerce et de la navigation, considéré comme un fleuve commun entre les divers Etats qui le séparent ou le traversent."[153] The states to which he referred, separated or traversed by a river, were none other than the riparian ones.

In the following session of the same Committee, Clancarty, England's representative, referred to Article V of the Peace Treaty of Paris, May 30, 1814, in which it was provided that navigation on the Rhine "...sera libre, de telle sorte qu'elle ne puisse être interdite à personne." He requested that in editing Article 1 and 2, of the Dalberg Project, there be added an amendment in the sense that "le Rhin sera entièrement libre au commerce et à la navigation de toutes les nations..." and that "...les réglements seront égaux pour tous, et les plus favorables au commerce de toutes le nations."[154]

In continuation, Hübner added that at the March 3, 1815 session that same Committee had rejected the amendment proposed by Clancarty, the other members being advised that the 1814 Conference of Paris had agreed not to accord "...à tout sujet d'Etat non riverain un droit de navigation égal à celui des sujets de Etats riverains, et pour lequel il n'y aurait aucune reciprocité."[155] Hübner maintained that on the basis of that advise "...une liberté absolute de navigation pour les pavillons de toutes les nations" was not understood.[156]

It must be noted that the expression "toutes les nations" was used also by Humboldt, Prussia's representative on the Committee on International Rivers. In his Mémoire, presented at the February 8, 1815 session of that same Committee, he referred to the text of Article V of the Paris Peace Conference of 1814, proposing that "...en principe, la navigation sur les rivières sera libre, et que les droits que les Etats riverains en perçoivent seront réglés de la manière la plus égale et la plus favorable au commerce de toutes les nations."[157] It is doubtful, however, that in this he understood also the commerce of non-riparian nations, since in the same Memorandum he referred to la conciliation of "...l'intérêt du commerce des Etats riverains." In the new editing of the Mémoire, he eliminated the expression "toutes les nations," retaining only that of "sous le rapport du commerce."[158]

In this matter, too, can be seen the oscillation in the Austrian point of view at the 1858 Conference. In the Austro-Turkish project of the Act of Navigation, within the framework of the Riparian Commission

(1857), with respect to cabotage provision was made that "la navigation du Danube...sera libre pour le commerce de toutes les nations, tant pour le transport de marchandises que pour celui des voyageurs."[159] In the definitive text of the Act of Navigation, however, (Articles 1, 4, 5, 8) the expression "de toutes les nations"[160] did not appear in fluvial navigation. In exchange, at Article 5, with respect to cabotage of maritime vessels on the Danube, provision was made for free navigation only "pour les bâtiments de toutes les nations."[161] The result of this was that, while complete liberty was accorded to maritime navigation on the river, freedom for fluvial cabotage did not include "les bâtiments de toutes les nations."

The divergency lay in the right of fluvial vessels reserved to riparians and the right of exclusively commercial activity, that is, the transportation of goods of all nations. Freedom of commerce for all nations was understood to be carried out by vessels of the Riparian States, but not by the vessels of the owners of the goods. In this matter, there were precedents, as for example, the restrictions of England's 1651 Act of Navigation and that imposed on Austria by Turkey, a Riparian Power, by the Treaties of Karlowitz (1699) and Passarowitz (1718).

The difference between the freedom of navigation and that of commerce was created later also by Russia, in 1878, after her return to riparian status on the Danube by means of the Kilia Branch, when she prohibited the transport of goods by foreign vessels in the ports of Reni, Ismail and New Kilia, on that same branch.

The Austrian protest against Russia's measures were based on the freedom of navigation of the mouths of the Danube, [162] yet, in the response of the St. Petersburg Government, only the right of navigation was invoked: respectively, the idea that resulted from the Dalberg and Humboldt projects. The similarity between the Austrian point of view in 1858 and the Russian measures in 1878 cannot be overlooked. In supporting the Act of Navigation, Hübner had also invoked freedom of navigation for cabotage, in 1858, exclusively in favor of riparians, and which corresponded with the russian measures of 1878.

The contradiction came also from the English point of view in 1878, as against that of 1858. Salisbury's support requested by Andrassy, Minister for Foreign Affairs of Austro-Hungary, against the Russian measures was fruitless. According to the advice of Silborne, England's Delegate in the European Commission, in 1878, and that of the Law Officers of the Crown, the Treaty of Paris (1856) had guaranteed the right, not of free trade, but only of free navigation, and it was argued

THE PARIS CONFERENCE OF 1858 273

that this had nothing to do with the coastage trade between the ports belonging to one of the riverain states.[163]

Regarded from a strictly juridical viewpoint and in relation to the new political status created by the 1878 Treaty of Berlin, Russia's measure was abusive under two considerations. The first, in the fact that Austro-Hungary considered itself a riparian state on the entire course of the Danube, as well as a beneficiary of the international regime of navigation also on the Kilia Branch. The second came from Romania's independence, accorded her by the 1878 Treaty of Berlin and her admission into the European Commission. Leaving aside the other two ports on the Kilia Branch (Ismail and New Kilia), through her independence Romania had the right to navigation also on the common Russo-Romanian sector between the mouth of the Pruth River and the beginning of the Kilia Branch, where Reni was situated and where the Russians applied their own navigation measures.

In the end, with the aim of taking into consideration the objections made in the Conference, Austria later presented some modifications in the matter of freedom of commerce in Danube navigation. These modifications will be examined in connection with the Additional Articles to the 1857 Navigation Act.

The Problem of Cabotage Navigation. Standpoints of Austria, England and France.

The clauses of the Act of Navigation pertaining to cabotage constituted the most debated problem of the 1858 Conference, the principal opponent being England's Plenipotentiary.

In the Act of Navigation two distinctions were made. The first referred to cabotage of maritime vessels on the Danube (Article 5) and the second referred to that between ports of the same riparian state and between them and the ports of other riparians (Article 8), the difference between these two cabotages being the limitation in the traffic of maritime vessels.

The proposals made during the work sessions of the Riparian Commission in 1857, and following which Articles 5 and 8 of the proposed Act of Navigation were drawn up, were those of the Committee composed of the Austrian and Turkish Delegates and the Serbian Commissar.[164] Taking the floor in the session of March 30, 1857, the Turkish Delegate explained the difference between purely fluvial cabotage and that of maritime vessels entered upon the Danube.

Among other considerations he expressed the opinion that the restricting of cabotage navigation to riparian states came from their rights of territorial sovereignty and from the principles of the Congress of Vienna of 1815.[165]

Although they had subscribed, together with the other members of the riparian Commission, to the exclusivity of fluvial cabotage in favor of the riparians, the Delegates of Bavaria and Württemberg and the Commissar of Moldavia proposed in 1857 a more liberal navigation regime for cabotage of maritime vessels on the Danube.[166]. This proposal (amendment) was not taken into consideration at the final redacting of Article 5 in the Act of Navigation. The amendment referred exclusively to the tonnage and type of vessels in the maritime traffic sector of the Lower Danube (Sulina-Brăila), as it had existed when the Act of Navigation was drawn up. At that time, about 80% of the tonnage and 94% numerically was performed by vessels of an average capacity of 180-300 tons register.[167] Because of the small tonnage of maritime vessels came from carrying out local transports also, between fluvial ports, or between ports of one and the same riparian state. In other words, maritime vessels at times fulfilled also the functions of the actual fluvial ones. An example follows of the practical way in which that traffic was carried on before, and for some time after, 1858.

After unloading at Brăila, for example, the cargo of a vessel that had come in from the sea, its owner — for efficient use — had to find export material headed for the sea, for the entire capacity of his ship. Not finding enough at Brăila, he picked up small loads to transport them between the river ports. However, according to Article 5 of the Act of Navigation, the vessel coming from the sea could unload in any port situated in the direction of his navigation, without having the right to effectuate local transports between those same ports. At its passage from the Danube, the vessel partially loaded in different ports, but only with cargo destined for export and only in the direction of the sea.

The introduction of the new restrictions in cabotage navigation of maritime vessels, in accordance with the provisions of the Act of Navigation, would have modified and overloaded the entire network of the sort of traffic which, until then, was deployed under complete freedom. Opposition to the above amendment came from the Austrian Delegate, upheld by justified arguments, but contrary to the usage existing on the Lower Danube up to that time.[168] But the principal result of the opposition to it lay in the confusion which would be created between the regulated and the non-regulated navigation of maritime vessels undertaking cabotage. The Austrian Plenipotentiary to the 1858 Conference argued that according maritime vessels of all nations the same rights as those of fluvial vessels would introduce free navigation on larger bases, incompatible with the regime and the regulated order of work provided for by the Act of Navigation.

To the point of view of the Delegate of Bavaria in 1857, in the sense that a liberalization of cabotage navigation would be in support of commercial relations between non-riparian and riparian states, Austria's Delegate responded that this could be made up for by admitting the participation of foreigners with their investment capital in the Danube navigation, as stipulated in Article 9 of the Act of Navigation.[169]

The Plenipotentiaries of England and France were of contrary opinions to those established by the Riparian Commission in 1857, in the matter of cabotage navigation. In the August 18, 1858 session, England's Plenipotentiary Cowley raised the question of cabotage of fluvial vessels and that of maritime ones on the river, as stipulated in Articles 5 and 8, both considered by him too contrary to the clauses of Article CIX of the Act of 1815 and of Articles 15 and 16 of the 1856 Treaty.

It should be noted that, aside from partially presenting the Articles of the Act of 1815, he omitted an important text from point 2 of the Preliminary Peace Project of the 1856 Conference of Vienna, as well as the connection between this text and the European Commission's Regulations for Navigation and the Police.

The text of Article CIX of the 1815 Act invoked by Cowley, on the basis of which "la navigation...sera entièrement libre et ne pourra sous le rapport du commerce être interdite à personne" was subordinate to the phrase, "bien entendu que l'on se conformera aux règlements relatifs à la police de cette navigation, lesquels seront conçu d'une manière uniforme pour tous et ausi favorable que possible au commerce de toutes les nations."[170]

On this subordination depended those who would have drawn up the Regulation for the Police, the application of which was not obligatory in the matter of commercial traffic, but only "...que possible."[171] But, the Regulations being drawn up by the Riparians, meant that in the case of cabotage the Act of Navigation would be applied as invoked by the Austrian Plenipotentiary. By point 2 of the 1856 Preliminary Peace Project, which Cowley did not mention, provision was made that "la liberté du Danube et de ses embouchures sera efficacement assurées par des institutions européennes dans lesquelles les Puissances contractantes seront également représetées sauf les positions particulières des riverains, qui seront réglées sur les principes établis par l'Acte du Congrès de Vienne en matière de navigation fluviale."

This latter text came to the support of the point of view expressed by Hübner at the 1858 conference. "Les positions particulières des riverains" were no other than those written into the 1857 Act of Navigation, which had been drawn up in accord with the principles of 1815, referring exclusively to navigation between riparians. Although this clause had not been included in the 1856 Treaty, Hübner still invoked it as an initial concept of the authors of the Treaty. Interpretation of the text of paragraph 2 of Article 16 of the 1856 Treaty, with respect to covering the expenses of the technical works at the Sulina Mouth by taxing the vessels of "toutes les nations...au pied d'une parfaite églité" could have revealed the justice of Cowley's point of view. Walewsky, France's Plenipotentiary, also subscribed to this point of view.[172]

The interpretation made by the Plenipotentiaries of England and France led to the idea of complete freedom of navigation, including cabotage, of maritime vessels which would pay tolls at the Sulina Mouth, as would also the fluvial one. Both points of view, however, became contradictory in face of the 1858 jurisdiction of the European Commission which collected the navigation tolls. This jurisdiction, applied in 1858 exclusively on the course of the river between Sulina and Isaktcha, meant that the freedom of navigation to which the Plenipotentiaries referred was valid only for the traffic of maritime vessels on this sector, not upriver to Isaktcha. Related to the geographic space of the application of this jurisdiction, Hübner's point of view did have a basis.

The lack of basis for Cowley's and Walewsky's points of view also stemmed from the ambiguity of the text of Article 16 of the Treaty of 1856. Hajnal relates that, from a January 19, 1859 report of a Stuttgart diplomat, it seems that even Walewsky himself had admitted, in the presence of Baron Wachter of Württemberg, that the phrasing of Articles 15 and 16 of the 1856 Treaty was ambiguous.[173]

In the August 116 session of the 1858 Conference, Cowley requested purely and simply the elimination of Articles 5 and 8 of the Act of Navigation, the clauses dealing with the restrictions imposed on cabotage of maritime vessels (Article 5) and of fluvial ones (Article 8).[174] He understood that the Danube, especially its maritime sector, ought to be completely free for traffic of all flags. He was the representative of a Great Power which, in matters of navigation as a means of communication, conceived it to have complete freedom.

Turkey evolved in her attitude, passing from intransigence to compromise, leaving Austria isolated.[175] Had she continued along with Austria, she too would have been isolated by the other Powers, especially by England which was pressing her. Up to that point, it was evident from a circular sent by the Turkish Foreign Ministry to its representatives abroad in January 1858 — hence before the Conference of Paris — that her position was similar to that of Austria.[176]

From the stipulations of Articles 15-18 of the 1856 treaty, the circular mentioned that Austria and Turkey, as riparians, were obligated to apply the Act of 1815 on the Lower Danube and its mouths, while the non-riparian states signatories to the 1856 Treaty were to acknowledge the result of that application and implicitly all the rights derived therewith for the riparian states. In this respect, the circular stressed that "on ne saurait admettre l'une et exclure l'autre."

The rights of the riparian countries in opposition to those of the non-riparian ones, were — in the opinion of the same Foreign Minister — the result of the territorial sovereignty of the former. However, associating Austria with the Lower Danube, where Turkey considered herself the only riparian in 1858, contravened the principle of the Act of 1815 on the simple consideration that Austria did not have the same geographic position in this sector.

As to the limitation of freedom of cabotage to maritime vessels, stipulated in the Act of Navigation, there appears a discrepancy in the position of Austria and Turkey. Of a total of 23,452 maritime vessels (repeated passages) in the traffic through the Sulina Mouth, between 1856 and 1860, the Austrian flag represented 10% and the Turkish 14%.[177] The question arises whether the restrictions imposed on the cabotage of maritime vessels was applied also to the flags of these two nations. If the answer is in the negative, the exception could be considered a privilege which was not allowed by the Principles of the Act of 1815, which had been evoked by both Power in support of the 1857 Act of Navigation.

For riparian countries, cabotage navigation of fluvial vessels was much more important than that of maritime vessels. While the former were closely tied in with their national economies, the latter also answered to foreign commercial interests.

Still, at the 1858 conference, England's Plenipotentiary requested equality of treatment.

As has been shown not all the participants at the 1858 Conference, in particular the English and the French, had any great interest in fluvial cabotage navigation upriver from Brăila and the Iron Gates. France's interests upriver from those two points were limited to a single isolated case in which the vessel "Lyonnais," flying the French flag, could not complete its course between Galatz and Widin because of the exclusivity of cabotage by riparians.[178] Neither did the Italian and Russian interests extend upriver from those two ports. Later, at the 1871 Conference of London, when the problem of financing the Iron Gates arose, the Italian Plenipotentiary did not find it necessary for his country to contribute, inasmuch as the traffic bearing the Italian flag did not go past the port of Brăila.[179] The same applied to Russia.

Related to the possibility of cabotage, upriver of Brăila also, of maritime vessels entered on the Danube and which could have participated in the traffic on the purely fluvial sectors, the status in 1858 was the following:[180]

Greek flag   48% in number   47% in tonnage
Turkish flag   14% in number   11% in tonnage
Austrian flag   10% in number   14% in tonnage

On the three flags, only the last two belonged to riparian states, the Greek one representing a non-riparian country. To the preponderance of the Greek flag must be added a significant number of vessels in the Turkish percentage which were the property of Greeks from regions still under the Ottoman Empire in 1858.

What with the Austrian trend toward supremacy on the Lower Danube, the Greek flag and element remained the only certain auxiliaries of English commerce which would have benefited from fluvial cabotage as well as from the cabotage of maritime vessels.

After 1857, the Greek vessels became the main target of Austrian and Turkish competition on the Danube, an activity carried on also by trickery. In this respect, a Greek newspaper, in Brăila, in 1876 published the information that the Turks had prohibited vessels flying the Greek flag from fluvial cabotage between their ports on the Dobrogean banks,[181] which they did permit to Austrian vessels.[182]

On the other hand, the elimination of vessels bearing non-riparian flags from fluvial as well as from maritime cabotage could have prejudiced and disorganized local traffic, which served also the export of cereal destined for England and which was registering increasingly greater quantities.

Up to the beginning of modernization of fluvial vessels (about 1870), local transports of goods and cereal were carried out by small crafts, known as "caiques," of a capacity varying between 5 to 50 tons. In these were collected smaller amounts of cereal from different warehouses and ports of the Lower and Middle Danube, transporting them to Brăila or Galatz, where they were unloaded into maritime vessels or deposited in warehouses before the river froze up. Their number, together with that of barges, also of small capacity (50 to 100 tons), was sufficient for the demands of the commerce.

The majority of these crafts being under the Greek flag would have meant that the first Great Power to be affected adversely by the prohibiting of cabotage would have been England, whose great interest was in cereal. Romanian, Bulgarian and Serbian vessels (1857) being numerically reduced, the only ones serving the English maritime fleet were the Greek ones. Their status with respect to the Austrian ones was as follows in 1858: (traffic in various ports.)[183]

On the Upper and Middle Danube.	On the Lower Danube.
Austrian Flag 2,851	Greek Flag 251
Greek Flag 1,050	Austrian Flag 94

Other statistics from which a general idea can be formed, as to the effects of the proposed prohibition of fluvial cabotage to flags of non-riparian nations, are those of the years 1894-1895, representing the status of vessels registered in Romanian ports of the Lower Danube.[184]

	Barges		Tugboats	
	Number	Capacity	Number	H.P.
Fleet in general of which:	455	354,217 tons	88	4043
Greek flag	305	254,315	46	2230
Romanian flag	99	48,402	20	847
Other flags	51	51,500	22	966

As to the dependence of fluvial transport of cereal between the ports of collection and those of export, that is, the cabotage between ports of one and the same riparian state, a characteristic case of later date will be related.

Romanian refused to apply, in her fluvial sector, the new Regulation for Navigation drawn up by the Mixed Commission of the Danube established by the Act of Navigation of 1857 under the auspices of Austria, on the basis of the 1878 Treaty of Berlin. Instead, she initiated her own navigation and police standards, among them also the prohibition of fluvial cabotage by flags of non- riparian states. Faced with this measure, the ship owners, whose barges plied the Danube under the Greek flag by virtue of the international regime of navigation, removed their vessels (barges and tugs) to Reni and Ismail, which were under Russian occupation.[185] That move, which numerically represented circa 47% of the barges and 52% of the tugboats of the total Lower Danube fleet, had negative results on the cereal export and caused the Romanian government to reconsider its initial measure.

Suspending the activity of the Greek flag from the fluvial cabotage would have caused an increase in the presence and competition of the Austrian fleet, whose transport potential and technical superiority supported Austria' tendency toward supremacy opposed to the interests of English commerce and that of the countries in Lower Danube. Aside from the Romanian protests, addresses directly against the Act of Navigation and, indirectly, against the Austrians, one cannot excluse the appeal of Greek and English circles on the Danube to the English Government for retaining the old regime of fluvial cabotage for vessels of the non-riparian states.

In the end, the Conference of 1858 did not succeed in resolving the problem of fluvial and maritime cabotage as provided for in the 1857 Act of Navigation. Its unresolved status continued even after some modifications had been made by the Additional Articles to the Act of Navigation. In conformity with the points of view of England and France, it appears that fluvial and maritime cabotage traffic, regardless of the flags carrying it out, is suited to the regime of complete freedom of navigation in accordance with the provisions for internationalization of navigation, on the basis of the Treaty of 1856.

Standpoints of Prussia and the Kingdom of Sardinia.

The Prussian viewpoint was expressed in a long "Mémoire," drawn up before the Conference of 1858, in reference to the 1857 Act of Navigation.[186] The absence of provisions in the Act of Navigation, for cabotage maritime vessels being revealed, the stipulations of Articles 15 and 16 of the 1856 Treaty were invoked, which would have eliminated any restrictions in navigation of all pavilions. "Interdire le cabotage des bâtiments maritimes sur le Danube," the "Mémoire" stressed, "serait, par conséquent, imposer une nouvelle restriction à la navigation, ce qui est inadmissible." It was also stated that on German rivers cabotage of maritime vessels was completely free.

Sardinia's position was revealed in 1859 when Cavour, in the publication of a Note, accused Austria. Concluding the Note, Cavour expressed the opinion that: "Le débat danubien met en question plus qu'un grand intérêt pour le commerce européen; il concerne l'honneur de la dignité de ceux qui ont participé au Congrès de Paris."(1856)[187]

Sardinia's reaction against the Act of Navigation was a legitimate one in view of the important participation of the Italian flag in Lower Danube navigation.

Cabotage and Territorial Sovereignty.

In the Act of Navigation of 1857, cabotage was included among the natural and national rights of the riparian states and the international rights of the non-riparian ones, both remaining to be conciliated with the principles of territorial sovereignty and of the Act of 1815.

In support of reserving cabotage exclusively for riparians, Hübner invoked also the sovereign right of the riparian states.[188] According to the point of view on the Conference members, the invoking by Austria's Plenipotentiary had no justification on the premise that the international regime of navigation resulting from past treaties, including that of 1856, had not eliminated the riparians' sovereignty over the Danube, but had rather diminished in concept.[189]

Here is a contradiction. Hübner's point of view fell because of a precedent set in a case to which Austria had adhered. In the declaration of the new regime for navigation on the Danube, set by the Treaty of 1856 (Article 15), as being part of the Public Law of Europe, the sovereignty of the riparian states on the course itself of the river was suspended, only the banks were exempted. The fact that Austria had signed this treaty, without expressing any reservation, meant the acceptance of its terms. In spite of this, in a later Memorandum of the Austrian government concerning the rights of riparian states, the decision of the 1858 Conference of Paris was considered to be a direct violation of territorial sovereignty, in imposing the international regime of navigation on riparian states such as Bavaria and Württemberg, which had not participated in the 1856 and 1858 Conferences and which had not been asked consequently to adhere to the decisions taken.[190]

The point of view of Hübner might have been valid, had it not been contradicted by a situation in which Austria had been in a similar case in 1815. In the composition of the Committee on International Rivers, Clancarty had taken part representing England and Wessenberg representing Austria, both being the delegates of two nonriparian nations having no right of sovereignty over the Rhine.

One more case, The initial Memorandum presented to the Conference of Vienna in 1855 by Prokesch-Osten, Austria's representative, set the standards of the regime of navigation proposed to be applied on the Lower Danube, "...où ce fleuve devient commun à l'Autriche et à L'empire Ottoman." On the basis of what right had

Austria set the standards of navigation on a sector of the Danube that was under suzerainty to the Ottoman Empire?

Turkey, also, considered her right of suzerainty to be diminished had the 1858 Conference rejected the application of the Act of Navigation, which was to be applied to a fluvial sector under her control. Still, ulterior, she considered her position protected by the stipulation of Article 15 of the 1856 Treaty, placing the Sultan's rights respecting navigation "sous la protection du droit public."[191]

On the basis of that protection, which came from Turkey's being admitted to participation in the advantages of European Public Law, and her inclusion in the family of European nations (Article 7 of the 1856 Treaty), the Sublime Porte consented to cede some of her rights of territorial sovereignty, assuming also the responsibility of keeping order in the sector of the attributes of the European Commission of the Danube, which were in force also on the territory under Turkish jurisdiction.

Situations did occur in which the sovereign rights of the Sultan had to be evaluated in writing. At first, Turkey had refused to sign the Public Act of 1865 because, in Article 16 of the Treaty of 1845, the European Commission had been invested with administrative attributes over Turkey's sovereign rights.[192]

Also within the framework of her sovereign rights, can be considered Turkey's refusal, at the 1866 Conference of Paris, to extend the jurisdiction of the European Commission as far a Brăila, as Cowlcy requested.[193]

By means of the Public Act of 1865, the Sultan reserved the right to name and dismiss the Inspector General and the Captain of the Port of Sulina, both acting within the framework of the European Commission of the Danube. Also, the sentences for infractions of the Regulations for Navigation and Police, of the European Commission, issued by those two superior officers were given in the name of the Sultan. (Article 8). In Article 22 of the Public Act, provision was made, in the name of territorial sovereignty, that the ratification of this Act by the Powers represented in the European Commission "...seront deposées... à la Chancellerie du Divan Imperial à Constantinople."[194]

In order to assure application of the Regulation for Police in case of infractions, the European Commission could appeal to the intervention of the small warships stationed at the mouths of the Danube, in accordance with Article 19 of the 1856 Treaty, or, in the absence of a warship of that same nationality, the Captain of Sulina Port could have recourse to the intervention of Turkish warship stationed at

Sulina, as one representing the authority of the territorial sovereignty.[195] Also, Turkey could send her warships on the Danube at any time, in her capacity of "territorial Power."[196]

The Sublime Porte's concession of sovereignty mentioned in Article 4, 5, and 6 of the Public Act of 1865, occurred at the beginning of the organization of the European Commission of the Danube, whose juridic framework suffered later modifications. In the matter of subordination of rights of sovereignty and of the international navigation standards complaints were registered also in England's position. While the sovereign rights of the Danubian riparian states were being challenged, those of Turkey were accepted. In this connection it must be recalled that Palmerston took into consideration the Sultan's sovereignty in the case of the proposed Cernavoda-Constanta Canal, whose route was to pass through Dobruja, which was under the sovereignty of the Ottoman Empire.

Cowley's opposition to Hübner's point of view, at the 1858 Conference, concerning the sovereign rights of riparian states, had been previously contradicted by London officialdom. In its interpretation of the provisions of Article 16 of the 1856 Treaty, the Foreign Office informed the signatories of this Treaty, on April 23, 1857, that until the taking over of its duties by the proposed Riparian Commission, only the Sultan could order the application of the Regulation drawn up by the European Commission, on the basis of his right of sovereignty over the Danube Delta.[197];

As to this interpretation by the Foreign Office, Wallewsky, in a note to the French Ambassador at Vienna, wrote that only Turkey in her capacity as territorial Power, could transfer to the European Commission the right to carry out its Regulations.[198]

The resolution of the Prosecutor General of England, in the suit filed by the Austrian Navigation Company against the Greek-Oriental Company after the boarding of the vessel "Mars" by a Greek vessel, confirmed Turkey's sovereign rights.[199] This resolution challenged the validity of the European Commission's Regulation of Navigation as one which did not fulfill the requirements of an international agreement and should have had the approval of Turkey, on the basis of "...the competent legislative acts of the proper territorial authority..."[200]

By a "British Order in Council," of April 1866, English subjects in the Ottoman Empire were ordered to respect the Public Act of 1865, on the consideration that the mouths of the river were "under the immediate sovereignty of the Sublime Ottoman Porte."[201]

The presence and the activity of the European Commission of the Danube on the Turkish territory of Sulina and the Delta of the river was due to the tolerance or tacit surrender of the Sultan's sovereignty. Nor can Turkey's moral obligation be overlooked towards the other signatories of the 1856 Treaty, who apportioned to her, not to the Moldavian Principality, the Danube Delta, together with the rest of the territory ceded by Russia in the 1856 Treaty.

With all its symbolic presence, still, Turkey's sovereignty deprived the European Commission of its complete freedom of action and authority as in international body representing Europe, and which by repeated extensions of its existence seemed to prove its function of buffer state, the midst of the multiple and controversial problem concerning the mouths of the Danube. For that reason, England and France held to the transformation of the buffer zone into a buffer state lying between the neighboring antagonistic Great Powers. The obstacle in the realization of that trend was Turkey. As the possessor of the Straits, the gravity point of the "Estern Question," she had to be handled gently. More favorable political circumstances were awaited, arising after 1878, when Turkey had lost her sovereignty over Dobruja including the Danube Delta. Freeing the activity of the European Commission from any subservice to any sovereignty was to be attained in 1878.[202]

In general, the non-riparian states considered the lessening of the principle of territorial sovereignty as rightful collaboration, not subservience, on their part. Yet, it was not possible to establish precisely whether in the principles of internationalization of navigation were included also the banks of the Danube, or only the actual watercourse of the river. In 1814-1815, the question remained interpretative in the works of the Committee on International Rivers. When the litigation between Romania and the European Commission, concerning the responsibilities on the course between Galatz and Brăila, is taken up, it will be seen that the Permanent Court of International Justice, at The Hague, advised in favor of this inclusion.

Faced with England's intransigence, to which were associated also the other members of the 1858 Conference, Turkey's Plenipotentiary modified his original point of view over territorial sovereignty in the matter of cabotage. Stating that the Act of Navigation could have been applied on the basis of the Sultan's sovereign right, still, his nation, taking into consideration the observations made, consented to await a definitive solution, maintaining the present status as resulted from her treaties with the non-riparian countries.[203]

THE PARIS CONFERENCE OF 1858

The Tributaries of the Danube and the Magnan Case.

The question of the tributaries of the Danube, especially of those in its Lower sector, had been raised at the 1858 conference by Cowley, who requested the regulation of their navigation in the Act of Navigation, no provision having been made for it therein.[204] The main tributaries of the Lower Danube brought into discussion were the Siret and Prut, both being adjacent in 1858 to Austrian and Moldavian territories.[205] With all England's lack of interest in these tributaries, still, Cowley's request had four principal motives as a basis.

The first was the Anglo-French policy of barring Austria's trend toward hegemony also in the lateral regime of the Danube transportation network. The second can be attributed to the competition among the commercial circles of London, Vienna, Paris and Berlin to obtain privileges and concessions in the Romanian Principalities. In Moldavia and Wallachia the possibilities for financial investment were favorable for exploitation of their rich natural resources right after 1856, when their administrative autonomy and their freedom to have their own commercial relations abroad were accorded them.

The third cause was France's actions upholding the concession rights of the French company Magnan. The fourth was the extension of the application of the international regime of navigation also on the tributaries.

The problem of the tributaries would not have occasioned debates if, guided by the experience of almost half a century of the international regime worked out in 1815 for the rivers of Northwestern Europe, the authors of the 1856 Treaty had made provision for its resolution.

The beginning of the debates over the tributaries in the Romanian Principalities dates back to May 1856, when Grigore Ghika, ruling Prince of Moldavia, accorded to a Frenchman, André François Honorin Magnan, the concession rights for exploitation of navigation on the Siret and Prut Rivers.[206]

Magnan had requested a 30-year concession in the name of the Mathis and Parrot Company, organized especially for that purpose.[207] The administration and capital of the company were to be French, and the vessels in the traffic of the respective rivers were to fly the Moldavian flag.[208] The presence of the Magnan company in Moldavia is recorded by the Romanian historian, L. Boicu, in his study "French attempts to penetrate the Moldavian Economy."[209]

Magnan's concession for the Siret River was probably inspired by the theoretic and utopian idea of the Romanian economist, Nicholas Soutzo, who in 1850 and 1851 had drawn up a project of navigation, in manuscript.[210] In drawing up his project, Soutzo had taken as example similar works carried out in Western Europe, without taking into consideration the lack of technical and financial possibilities, in his own country, for the work of diverting the course of the Siret River and for adapting its banks for towing, source of technical personnel, etc.

Austria, whose occupation troops in the Principalities were still present, when the concession was granted, protested through Buol, demanding the cancellation of the Magnan concession.[211] Buol's point of view was based on the consideration that the two rivers originating and traversing also through Austria territory (Bucovina), became international and, consequently, any concession or privilege was contrary to the equality of treatment in navigation provided for by the Act of 1815 and the Treaty of 1856.

In his protest, of June 30, 1856, to the signatory Powers of the 1856 Treaty, Buol presented certain arguments, among them:[212] the politico-juridical lack of authority on Prince Ghika's part to accord privileges directly reserved for the Sultan who, in Buol's opinion, and that of others,[213] was the sovereign, not the suzerain of Moldavia; the right of Austrian vessels to sail on the navigable waters of the Ottoman Empire, accorded by the Sened of 1784;[214] the extension of the 1856 Treaty principles of the Act of 1815. These arguments concurred, perhaps, in the initial non-inclusion of the tributaries in the 1857 Act of Navigation drawn up by Austria through the Riparian Commission. The lack of basis for these arguments will be demonstrated.

In conformity with Article 22 of the 1856 Treaty,[215] the Romanian Principalities under suzerainty, but non the sovereignty, of the Sultan, Prince Ghika's authority was legitimate. On the basis of that same Treaty, "the Sublime Porte undertook to grant to the Principalities "an independent and national administration, as also full liberty of national legislature, commerce, and navigation".

The protest of Gödel-Lannoy, Austria's consul at Jassy, regarding Ghika's authority, was rejected as being offensive in form as well as in basis, as it did not take into consideration Moldavia's autonomy.[216] The application of the 1784 Sened, invoked by Buol, failed inasmuch as it would have required revision of this act. If Buol demanded respecting of the Act of 1815, then one of its main principles would have to be taken into consideration, the idea of the navigability of a means of communication on water, as stated in the text of Article CVIII of that Act. In this Article, provision had been made that the international regime of navigation be applied to waters of communication of common interest "du point où chacun d'elles devient navigable jusqu'à son embouchure..."

The same condition was maintained later on through the 1921 Convention for the Definitive Statute of the Danube, which in Article 1 made provision for the application of the international regime on the entire navigable course of the Danube, between the Ulm River and the Black Sea, but not from the Ulm to the sources of the river, the sector inaccessible to normal navigation.[217]

Also with respect to navigability, one could oppose even the components of the projected Riparian Commission made up of the riparian states of the Upper and Middle Danube. It included Austria, Bavaria and Württemberg, but not Baden, through which the river flows from its source to Ulm.

The possibility of navigation on the Siret and Pruth did not correspond entirely to the principle of Article CVIII. The upper course of the Siret, of which Austrians considered themselves to be riparians, flowing through mountainous regions of Bucovina (under Austrian rule in 1858) was outside any possibility of navigation. Navigation could begin at the passage from this region, where the Siret entered the Moldavian zone, but only by using rafts, exclusively for transportation and even that only in periods of high water.

As to the Prut, whose sources in 1858 were in territory also under Austrian rule, the possibility of small transports drawn by launch or towed (50 to 100 tons) was limited to a portion of about 354 miles, of its total length of 500 miles, from its mouth upriver to its source. And even on this portion, navigation could be carried out only in periods of high water, the river course passing through physical obstacles (many bends and sand banks).

Buol was correct in invoking the principle of the Act of 1815, but its validity depended on a larger interpretation. The Dalberg Project of 1815 made provision for the possibility of applying the regime of steam navigation on the Rhine and its tributaries, as well as on all the larger European rivers.[218] These tributaries, however, were all navigable under the aspect of national and international commerce.

During the drawing up of the 1857 Act of Navigation, the Bavarian Delegate raised the problem of the tributaries.[219] On that occasion, an interesting interpretation of Article CVIII of the Act of 1815 was debated. This Article contained the provision that the regime of levying navigation taxes on branches and confluents were to be applied only on their navigable courses separating or traversing different states, therefore, the Article recognized the conditional status of navigation.

In 1857, it was claimed that the meaning of this Article referred to the subordination of its application to the decisions of the riparian states of the navigable tributaries, but not of all tributaries. The Riparian Commission, taking into consideration the proposal of the Bavarian Representative, decided that the problem of the tributaries should be regulated later, by special commissions, as the need arose.[220] In other words, the problem of the tributaries remained unresolved in the framework of the preliminary work to the Act of 1857.

On the other hand, application of the international principle of navigation, demanded by Buol in the case of the Magnan concession, was belated, inasmuch as no provision had been made for tributaries in the 1857 Act of Navigation. Nor had Austria raised this problem at the 1856 Treaty Conference. When the problem was put into discussion, at the 1858 Conference, Austria had provided for the application of the international regime only on certain tributaries, not on all the Danubian affluents in the sense conceived by the English Plenipotentiary.

If other concessions made by the leaders of the Romanian Principalities are taken into consideration, Buol's protest did have a political element. While he was protesting against the Magnan concession, he kept quiet about the privileges accorded by the Moldavian Prince to the Romanians Rosca, Codreanu[221] (in 1852) and Iacovescu, Alexandri, Gr. Sturdza (1855),[222] for exploitation of navigation on the Siret and another on the Olt, both unsuccessful project. Nor did Buol consider the projects of Austrian official technical organs for eventual navigation on the Arges, an affluent of the Lower Danube in Wallachia, as being contrary to the principles he invoked.[223]

Taking on the character of international litigation, the Magnan case was passed for resolution to the Sublime Porte, where it became the object of evaluating the degree of French and Austrian influence.

The French ambassador at Constantinople, Thouvenel, invoked the authority of the signatories of the 1856 Treaty to resolve this case, not that of the Sultan who, as suzerain of Moldavia, had assumed this right for himself. In such a hypothesis, the rapport between these signatories would have been complicated even more, after having been barely calmed down following the Bolgrad case and the state of the new negotiations would have worsened in the problem of reorganizing the Romanian Principalities — the primordial item on the agenda of the 1858 Conference.

On the other hand, taking the autonomy of Moldavia as a legitimate basis for according the concession, inconvenienced the Sublime Porte at a time when its authority was gradually weakening in the Romanian Principalities. Faced with a dilemma, the Sultan yielded to the pressure of England's Ambassador Stratford and Austria's Ambassador Prokesch-Osten and annulled the Magnan concession.[224]

Walewsky, in view of the new situation, requested that all the affluents of the Danube, without exception, be opened to the navigation of all the Powers,[225] a request taken into consideration later by the Additional Articles to the Act of Navigation, but not also applied. The problem of the tributaries was not resolved by the — Conference of 1858; the solution was found only in 1921 by the Convention for the Establishment of the Definitive Statute of the Danube.

The Quarantine.

In order to avoid the difficulties to the period under the Russian administration at the Sulina Mouth, Cowley objected to the new Quarantine — Regulations in Articles 28-30 of the Act of Navigation, which made provision for the detention for sanitary examination of vessels under suspicion of pestilential disease in European Turkey.[226] He was of the opinion that only the recording of an infectious disease by the official authority of the port of origin, on the sanitation certificate of a vessel could justify its being put in quarantine. He proposed modification of the text of Article 30 to except quarantine for vessels not having such notations on their certificates.[227] The quarantine regulations in the Act of Navigation required application of the regime to fluvial as well as to maritime vessels entering the Danube, the sanitary control being carried out by the local authorities.

In Cowley's proposal, only maritime vessels were specified; their sanitary control falling within the jurisdiction of other authorities than those of the Danube. The sanitation certificate eliminated the source of origin of the possible epidemics, to be replaced by a general indication of the ports of origin of the vessels entering the Danube.

The texts of Articles 28-30 of the Act of Navigation had not been drawn up exclusively by Austria. They represented proposals of a Committee of the 1857 Conference of Riparian States, made up of the Bavarian Delegate and the Moldavian Commissar, that is, of two riparian states. The measures of protection conceived by this

Committee on the Lower Danube (the sector of exclusively maritime navigation) were drawn up in opposition to the eventual propagation of epidemics coming from the provinces of Turkey situated "on this side of the Balkans," to the exclusion of other regions.[228]

The later modifications of the quarantine regime, made by Austria in the Additional Articles to the Act of Navigation, were not approved by the Conference of 1858.

Prolongation of the Mandate of the European Commission of the Danube.

The 1858 Conference was to decide also upon the extension of the mandate of the European Commission of the Danube, whose two-year duration, as set by the 1856 Treaty (Articles 16 and 18) was expiring in 1858. Taking note of the fact that the technical work at the Sulina Mouth could not be finished in the time set, the Conference decided to extend the mandate of the Commission "to the complete achievement of the said works."[229]

The Austrian Plenipotentiary expressed his reservations regarding this decision, conditioning the decision to the results of negotiations between his Government and the other Powers.[230] Ultimately, he agreed to the prolongation. His reservations were of a political nature which would have justified his country's refusal to take part in the International Technical Conference to be held in Paris in June 1858.[231] In addition to his reservation, must be noted the Conference's rejection of the Riparian Commission's going into operation.

Additional Articles to the Navigation Act of 1857 Concerning Cabotage, the Tributaries, and Quarantine.

Faced with the objections made to the Navigation Act at the 1858 Conference, the Riparian Commission, i.e. Austria, took the obligation of working out, within a six month period, the necessary modifications that had been communicated to the signatories of the 1856 Treaty, in the context of the Six Additional Articles to the 1857 Navigation Act.[232] The Commissars of the three Lower Danube countries were not invited to work on the modifications, although they had participated in drawing up the Act of Navigation. By paragraph 2 of Article 3, of the Additional Articles, provision was made for Turkey to communicate the contents to them.[233]

The chief modifications were those referring to freedom of navigation for cabotage, the tributaries, and the quarantine.

Freedom of Navigation for Cabotage.

The regulations of cabotage navigation, as provided for in Articles 5 and 8 of the Act of Navigation, were modified in the sense that the Riparian states could have exceptions in cases in which the necessary facilities were not contradictory to the stipulations of the Act of Navigation. This modification, not according the complete freedom requested by Cowley, was not approved by the members of the Conference. The problem was resolved only in 1921, by the Convention for the Definitive Status of the Danube. Until then, the old regime of complete freedom was applied.

Tributaries.

With respect to navigation on the Danube tributaries, Austria yielded in Article 6 of the Additional Articles. It was established that on tributaries which, in their navigable sectors, separated or traversed a number of riparian states, the regime was to be applied in conformity with the provisions of Article CX of the Act of 1815, i.e. by concluding special conventions between the co-possessing governments of the tributaries.

The modification was not satisfactory because the Article was not being applied correctly; its provisions were being extended on the basis of the Dalberg Project, which had not been approved by the Committee on International Rivers. (1815). The modification did not resolve the objections of the 1858 Conference, either, navigation on the tributaries being free only for riparians, not for "toutes les Puissances" as Cowley and Walewsky had requested.

Although the modification was rejected, still a basis for future regulation had been created, by means of conventions between co-possessors of tributaries. Thus, between Austria, Russia and the

Romanian Principalities, the Convention for Navigation on the Prut River was signed in 1866 and renewed in 1895.[234]

For Austria, the value of the Convention was symbolical one, inasmuch as she intended only to show her commercial interests also on one of the navigable tributaries of the Lower Danube. Actually, the capacity of her fluvial vessels surpassed the obligatory maximum of 300 tons, imposed by the Mixed Russo- Romanian-Austrian Commission for Navigation on the Prut, because of its shallow depths.

The Quarantine.

Article 3 of the Additional Articles was the modification of Article 30, with respect to the quarantine regime of the Act of Navigation. Thus, in cases of suspicion of epidemics, in general, the method of sanitary verification of vessels at the first quarantine center at the Mouth of the Danube eliminated the sanitary certificates issued by any port of origin, as had been requested by Cowley.

The new modification corresponded with the existing traffic. It was logical to have the verification of sanitary control of vessels at the entrance to the Danube. Even if at the port of origin there had existed no epidemic at the time the vessel departed, it could have come in contact with epidemic cases en route to the Danube through Constantinople. The modification did not differ much from the Regulations for sanitary control drawn up later by the European Commission itself, by the Public Act of 1865. In this Act, many cases of suspected epidemics in regions in European Turkey were mentioned, as possible sources of contamination, as were the application of sanitary measures on the Danube by local authorities, a system opposed to that drawn up by Cowley in 1858. This modification was not approved by the Conference.

In the end, the 1858 Conference rejected the entering into operation of the Riparian Commission, as well as that of the Act of Navigation, including the Additional Articles to this Act. The only result of the Conference was the extension of the mandate for the European Commission of the Danube.

Chapter 4

CONSOLIDATION OF THE EUROPEAN COMMISSION OF THE DANUBE (E.C.D.)

After the rejection, by the 1858 Conference of Paris, of the Riparian Commission's entering into operation and of the Act of Navigation of 1857, there followed the consolidation of the European Commission for the Danube, after the extension of its mandate.

Although the duties of the Riparian commission, as provided for by Article 17 of the 1856 Treaty, were somehow fulfilled, still it can be maintained that the reason for rejecting the Commission's entering into operation was the interest of England and France in establishing the permanence of the European Commission. For this reason, it had to be invested with administrative and juridical powers to strengthen its international position.

The Public Act of 1865 and its Annexes.

The first measures taken in view of consolidating the European Commission were the definitive application of the initial Regulations for Navigation, the setting of the toll schedule, and the administrative order of navigation on the geographic area of its competence (the Mouths of the Danube - Isaktcha). The initiative of consolidating, however, risked being abandoned, because of an unexpected situation.

Faced with the failure of getting sufficiently navigable depths at the Sulina Mouth, following the dredging and the construction of two dikes of 3,600 and 4,600 feet,[235] between 1858 and 1860, some of the Commission Delegates decided in 1861 to propose the disbanding of the Commission to their governments. The surprise opposition came from Austria. In spite of her insistence at the 1858 Conference that the European Commission be replaced by the Riparian one, Austria's Delegate in the first Commission received instructions from Vienna to oppose the dissolution.

A report of Becke to his Government[236] revealed the reason for the proposal to dissolve the European Commission of the Danube. It was brought about by the boredom of the other Delegates at having to extend their stay in the uncomfortable surroundings of the Port of Galatz, often flooded, where the central offices of the Commission were situated.[237]

Austria concurred in the continuation of the European Commission by taking the initiative for suspending resumption of the debates on the problem of the Riparian Commission's entering into operation. In the June 21, 1861 session of the European Commission, Austria's Delegate stated that the Riparian Commission was not in a condition to replace the European Commission and that the moment had not yet come to invoke the Riparian Commission again.[238]

When the Public Act originally drawn up in 1861 came into function, Turkey opposed it on the grounds that it violated her territorial sovereignty and it extended the Commission's administrative duties over those belonging to the Sublime Porte.

The most important impediment lay in the Public Act's lack of juridical and police power. It had been drawn up by members of the Commission in their capacity of Delegates, but without an expressed mandate on the part of their Governments, hence the Act had to be examined and approved in the form of Conventions concluded by the signatories of the 1856 Treaty. Without this procedure, the Public Act could have no executive power.

Hajnal related the case of the English vessel "Eglantine," whose captain refused to pay the navigation toll specified in the Public Act. The Commission's protest was rejected by the English Government on the grounds that the Public Act was not in accordance with the standards set by international law.[239]

After repeated negotiations with the Turkish government and some compromise on the part of the Commission, its Delegates signed the Public Act[240] in the November 2, 1865 session at Galatz, on the basis of Protocol 149 of October 17, 1862 and on the authorization of their Governments as Plenipotentiaries. The Act had two annexes: the Regulation for Navigation and Police between the Mouths of the Danube and Isaktcha (Annex A) and the Tariff for Navigation Taxes (Annex B).

The Public Act of 1865, with its two annexes, constituted the foundation of the international regime of navigation on the Lower Danube (Sulina-Isaktcha) on the basis of which the European Commission of the Danube took the first steps towards the creation of a normal and disciplined international navigation, in keeping with the new political, technical and commercial conditions. The Act was completed and strengthened in 1881.[241] Proof of the great importance of this Act is the fact that in 1938, when some of the Commission's attributes were transferred to Romania by the "Sinaia Arrangement," the need to repeal some of the very articles on which the legal and international existence of the Commission was based became obvious.

By Article 1 of this Act, the European Commission — or the authority which might succeed it (the Riparian Commission) — was empowered to execute the work of improving navigation as directed by the 1856 Treaty. The technical works was guaranteed by International Law and placed under neutrality status, together with the establishments, the fleet of vessels, and the foreign executive personnel (Art. 2). Its investment with technical powers and for drawing up the Regulations for Navigation and Police were provided by Article 7.

The juridical-administrative powers were provided by Article 8, on the basis of which infractions, transgressions and fines were to be established by the Inspector General of Navigation and the Captain of the Port of Sulina, the sentences to be pronounced in the name of the Sultan. The Public Act passed through a strict examination before being sanctioned by the 1866 Conference of Paris.

The Regulation for Navigation and Police (Annex A).

The Regulation for Navigation and Police, of November 2, 1865 (Annex A) of the Public Act[242] consisting of 102 Articles, made provisions for the standards of administration of navigation by the Commission and of those regarding the method of the technical procedure of the navigation of vessels. The application of the Regulation was fixed exclusively between the mouths of the Danube and Isaktcha, that is, on the sector of the Commission's authority as provided in Article 16 of the 1856 Treaty, the control over navigation being under the authority of the Inspector General of Navigation and of the Captain of the Port of Sulina, both of whom to be appointed by the Sublime Porte (Article 1).

The application of the Regulation was assured also by the presence of the small warships, of the Commission members, stationed at the mouths of the river (Art. 2). The Regulation contained the most modern standards and instructions in existence at that time, thus placing Danubian maritime navigation at the level of that of Western Europe's rivers, with the exception of navigational discipline, which was introduced gradually. The Regulation was applied on all navigable and adjacent sectors, not omitting the operations specific to the traffic at the mouth and branch of the Sulina.

Articles 7 to 11 contained the regulations for navigation police in the maritime area of Sulina, while Articles 12 to 21 contained those for the Sulina Port; Articles 26 and 37 provided regulations for maritime vessels on the Sulina Branch, with respect to towing (Art. 38-39), towline operations (40-46); piloting operations at Sulina and on the course of the river were provided by Articles 69 to 80.

Standards for piloting the maritime vessels sailing on the river between Sulina and Brăila (Articles 75-78) can be considered as exceptions to the Regulation, taking into consideration the limitation of the European Commission's jurisdiction to only the sector down river from Isaktcha. From this point upriver, the navigational jurisdiction was that of the Principalities, Moldavia and Wallachia, that is, the suzerainties of the Sublime Porte. The fact that in the Public Act provision was made excepting the piloting of vessels by European Commission personnel on the sector upriver from Isaktcha, means that the operation was tacitly permitted by the sublime Porte.

The Tariff and the Navigation Rights at the Mouth of the Danube (Annex B)

Taxation of navigation at the Sulina Mouth resulted from the stipulations of Article 16 of the 1856 Treaty, the respective income being directed to the technical work to be carried out by the European Commission.

The Tariff and Navigation Rights at the Mouths of the Danube,[243] as stated in the Public Act, were substituted for the previous, temporary norms of taxation of July 25, 1860 and of March 7, 1863. Tariff was set for vessels of a capacity greater than 30 tons, the payment of the tax to be made at the vessel's exit to the sea (Article 1). The tariffs set for steam vessels, assigned to transport of passengers and which carried out regular schedules, were lower (Art. 2). It was even lower for cases of transshipment (Art. 5); warships were exempted (Art. 8).

The taxation was calculated on the basis of net tonnage and was related to the distance travelled on the river, excepting the steam vessels, which were piloted by their own captains. This exception was later dropped. In cases of contraventions or difficulties in applying the navigation taxes, the Commission could appeal, as in the case of the Police Regulation, to the assistance of the military vessels mentioned previously. The assistance was actually only symbolic, as no practical cases were recorded.

Considerations over the Public Act.

The deplorable state under which navigation was being carried out, in the period of the Russian occupation, because of natural obstacles as well as because of the absence of any administrative police or control organization, was obvious at the presentation of the state of affairs at the Sulina Mouth and Branch.

Through the Public Act and its two Annexes, the European Commission with legislative, executive, and administrative and juridic powers, as resulted from the Public Act and its Annexes, was it possible to create an efficient communication artery out of the maritime Danube. Under this aspect, all criticisms directed towards it are baseless.

Later on, by the additional Act of 1881, the standards of the Public Act were adapted to the new situation created in the Maritime Danube by the 1878 Treaty of Berlin.

Chapter 5

THE CONFERENCE OF PARIS, 1866

The Conference of Paris, of March 28, 1866,[244] was convoked because of the need for urgent decision on the part of the signatories of the 1856 Treaty. The forced abdication of the ruling prince, Alexandru Ion Cuza, had created a situation in the United Principalities of Romania[245] the consequences of which could have endangered political stability in Southeastern Europe.[246]

Some brief debates took place at the Conference, recorded in four Protocols,[247] over some Danubian problems such as the sanctioning of the 1865 Public Act, the extension of the European Commission mandate and the extension of its jurisdiction to Brăila, and the problem of the Riparian Commission taking over its functions. Although at the 1858 Conference of Paris the intention of the signatories of the 1856 Treaty — with the exception of Austria — to postpone the taking over of its functions by the Riparian Commission was evident, by 1866 they showed a change of attitude.

At the first session of the Conference,[248] France's Plenipotentiary insisted on the priority of sanctioning the Public Act of 1865, considered by him to be the special object of the meeting. Russia's Plenipotentiary requested that, before any other question was taken up, two situations be clarified: the prolongation of the mandate of the European Commission and the examination of the 1857 Act of Navigation, with the modifications made in 1859 by the Riparian Commission.[249]

The investment of the European Commission with all the powers to exercise its functions being of prime necessity, discussion on the approval of the Public Act followed, on the basis of the motion made by France's Plenipotentiary. The Act, together with its Annexes A.

299

and B. being approved without much discussion, was thus given international standing.

Resumption of discussion over the Riparian Commission became unnecessary inasmuch as the decision to prolong the existence of the European Commission had already been taken and the 1865 Public Act strengthened the attributes of the latter. Still, some Plenipotentiaries took into consideration the obligation Austria had taken, at the 1858 Conference,[250] to present certain modifications to the 1857 Act of Navigation, and seemed disposed to resume the debates over the Riparian Commission. The term during which the modifications were to be presented not only was uncertain and evasive ("quelques mois"), but Austria's Plenipotentiary tied it to the termination of the European Commission's technical works, which meant a longer duration.[251] Russia's Plenipotentiary, noting an 8 year delay in the presentation of the modifications, requested that the Conference issue a statement on this "prejudicial matter," as he described the problem of the Riparian Commission.[252]

His request was a spur of the moment one and was contradictory inasmuch as the eventual approval of the Act of Navigation would have been directly tied to the Riparian Commission's assumption of its functions, which would be carrying out the provisions of the Act of Navigation. In his opinion, the Riparian Commission could not take over its functions until the European Commission had finished its technical works.[253]

In the March 28 session, Austria's Plenipotentiary — noting the impossibility of taking up the establishment of the Riparian Commission because of the political situation in the United Romanian Principalities — stated his preference to continue the activity of the European Commission until clarification could be made on the direct negotiations with the governments of the Powers which had formulated the modifications in the At of Navigation.[254]

In the opinion of England's Plenipotentiary, the political situation in the United Principalities did not constitute an obstacle to carrying out the 1856 Treaty, with respect to the Riparian Commission's taking over its functions, but if any other impediment existed the according of an extension would be useful.[255] This opinion merely reflected the intention to cary out Articles 17 - 18 of the 1856 Treaty, respecting the replacement of the European Commission by the riparian one. Taking into consideration not only the extension of the European Commission's mandate, but also the extension of her attributes to Brăila, both previously sustained by England, the Plenipotentiary's opinion can be considered a circumstantial one.

THE CONFERENCE OF PARIS   301

The new situation in the Principalities caused Austria to worry that their opposition to the Act of Navigation would be stronger with the election of a foreign prince as sole ruler. In this respect, England's Plenipotentiary assured Austria's that through the influence of Turkey (which had appointed the ruler of the Principalities) any obstruction could be eliminated.[256]

From the discussions over this case there resulted again the postponement — but not abandonment, at least not formally — of the Riparian Committee's assumption of its functions.[257] The necessity of prolonging the mandate of the European Commission was shown first by England's Plenipotentiary. The chief reasons invoked by him were the lack of financial backing and the unfinished state of the technical works specified in the 1856 Treaty. He requested a minimum extension of at least three years and a maximum of five. In the end, an extension was voted for a new term of five years, up to 1871.[258] In spite of the difficulties confronting the European Commission, conducted, in the opinion of Russia's Plenipotentiary, by "capable, experienced men," he still considered "ce terme comme extrêm et en aucun cas être depassé."[259]

As was shown in other sections of this work, the authority of the European Commission was established, in 1856, between the Mouths of the Danube and Isaktcha. Gradually, with the advance of the Commission's work and especially with the increase in tonnage of maritime vessels entering the Danube, maintenance of the navigable course of the river up to Brăila became imperative. For this reason, England's Plenipotentiary requested extension of the Commission's authority from Isaktcha to Brăila.[260] His request was documented also by the physical obstacles met by maritime vessels en route to Brăila as, for example, low depths especially when waters between Galatz and Brăila were at low point, elimination of which required dredging. To this, he added the lack of discipline in strictly fluvial navigation between Isaktcha and Brăila due to the absence of any Police Regulations. In order to remedy the situation, he requested that the existing Regulations of the European Commission be temporarily applied up to Brăila, on the Isaktcha-Brăila sector, until such a time as the Riparian Commission would be taking over authority, which would include in its Act of Navigation also the maritime sector of the river, that is, between Brăila and Sulina.

The English request brings up some observations. The argument of the low water was baseless. If a loaded maritime vessel could pass through the Sulina Mouth, whose depths varied between 14 and 17

3/4 feet,[261] it could all the more easily navigate between Isaktcha and Brăila, where the depths were between 24 and 28 feet.[262]

The only plausible argument was the assurance of access of maritime vessels to Brăila, the terminal point of their navigation. Furthermore, this assurance had been provided by the Prokesch-Osten Memorandum presented in 1855 to the Conference of Vienna.[263]

In general, the extension of the European Commission's authority, requested by the Plenipotentiary of England, was justified, but its realization would have been complicated, requiring modification of Article 16 of the 1856 Treaty, which had established the Commission's authority up to Isaktcha, in addition to the Public Act of 1865. Such a modification would have complicated even more the relations between the Great Powers in the matter of the political stability of the United Romanian Principalities, barely resolved by the 1858 Conference of Paris and, in addition, possibly advancing by five years Russia's 1871 request for modification of the neutrality regime on the Black Sea, as provided by the 1856 Treaty. The vacillations in the opinions of some members of the Conference could be viewed under these considerations.

Although, in the May 2nd session, the Plenipotentiaries of Italy, Prussia and France approved the English request,[264] the first reconsidered in the May 17th session.[265] In no protocol is there mention of Austria's position in the matter of extending the autority as far as Braila.

Also contributing to the rejection of the English request was the opposition of Turkey, who was still sovereign over part of the Braila-Sulina sector, as a matter of general information, England's request was to be approved later, in 1883, at the Conference of London.

In conclusion, the results of the 1866 Conference were: approval of the Public Act of 1865 and prolongation of the mandate of the European Commission of the Danube to a new term of five years, to 1871.

Notes

Chapter 1

1. H. Geffcken, "La Question du Danube", M.A.E., p. 8.

2. Harold Nicolson, "The Congress of Vienna...", p. 100.

3. Gorchakov to Nesselrode, January 3, 1855; in S.M. Gorianov, "Le Bosphore et les Dardanelles"; quoted by V.J. Puryear in "England, Russia and ...", p. 367.

4. The complete description by Prince Charles de Ligne was: "Le Congrès ne marche pas: il danse". (The Congress is not just moving along, it is dancing); see H. Nicolson, "The Congress of Vienna", op. cit., p. 289, Appendix.

5. T.W. Riker, "The Making of Roumania", p. 38.

6. Statement of Malmesbury, January 12, 1859, F.O. 195. 614; quoted by W.G. East in "The Union of Moldavia and Wallachia", p. 163., note 6.

7. George Kennan, "Mémoires", (1925-1950), p. 218.

8. Quoted by H. Nicolson, "The Congress of Vienna", Introduction.

9. H. Nicolson, op cit., Introduction.

10. Protocoloe No. 1 of March 15, 1855; in "La Question du Danube", M.A.E., p. 129. Note: for all the Protocols of the 1855 and 1856 Conferences of Vienna, concerning the Danube, see D. Sturdza, "Recueil...", pp. 12-24; Great Britain, F.O., State Papers, (Vol. XLV) and "La Question du Danube", M.A.E.

11. Protocol Nr. 1, March 15, 1855.

12. C.F. Wurm, "Vier Briefe", p. 37. in "La Question du Danube", M.A.E.

13. Hertslet, Vol. II, 1221; State Papers XLIV, p. 90.

14. State Papers (1854-1855), p. 894.

15. Hertslet, "The Map...", p. 1217.

16. 1. "The protectorate exercised by Russia over Moldovia and Wallachia shall cease, and the privileges accorded by the Sultans to these Principalities and to Serbia shall hence forth be placed under the collective guarantee of the contracting Powers; 2. Freedom of navigation on the Danube shall be completely assured by means under the control of a permanent syndicate authority; 3. The Ottoman Empire shall be attached to the European economy and the renontiation of the European Straits Convention of 1841 in order to be revised in the sense of a limitation of the power of Russia in the Black Sea; 4. Russia shall abandon the principle of covering with its official protectorate the Christian subjects of the Sultan, but the Christian Powers shall lend their mutual assistance to obtain the consecration and observance of the religious rights of the Christian communities". Hertslet, "The Map...", Vol. II. No. 253, p. 1217.

17. State Papers LXIV, p. 22; Martens, N.R.G.T., Vol. XV, p. 600.

18. Hugh Seton Watson, op. cit., p. 327.

19. Count Buol-Schauenstein and Baron Prokesh-Osten (Austria); Baron de Bourqueney (France); Lord John Russell and Count Westmoreland (England); Prince Al. Gorchakov and Titoff (Russia); and Aarif-Effendi (Turkey).

20. Annex to Protocol Nr. 4 of 21 March 1855; in Sturdza "Recueil...", p. 15.

21. Résumé of the "Six Points": 1) Application of the principles of the Act of 1815 on the fluvial sector between the Turko-Austrian border until the sea; 2) elimination of any obstacles to free navigation; 3) setting navigation fees for covering costs of maintenance of navigation; 4) putting under European guarantee the excution of technical work and the supervision of freedom of navigation by a European Syndicate and stationing, at the river mouths, one or two warships of the contracting parties; 5) the Syndicate composed only of riparian states, to be called "La Commission pour la Navigation du Danube Inferieur" (i.e. the Lower Danube to the Black Sea; 6) Neutralization of the Danube Delta and abolishment of the quarantine regime instituted by Russia after 1829; Sturdza, "Recueil...", p. 15-16.

22. Protocol Nr. 5, March 23, 1855.

23. Martens, N.R.G.T., Vol. II, p. 128.

24. D. Sturdza, "Recueil..." p. 35; Martens, N.R.G.T., Vol. XV (1853-1857), p. 770.

25. The Prokesch-Osten Memorandum (développement du second point), annex to Protocol No. 5 and 23 March; D. Sturdza, "Recueil...", p. 21.

26. D. Sturdza, "Recueil...", p. 24.

27. Hertslet, "The Map of ...", Vol. II, p. 1228; Martens, N.R.G.T., Vol. XV, p. 700; for the Protocols concerning navigation on the Danube, D. Sturdza, "Recueil...", pp. 25-31, and "La Question du Danube", M.A.E., pp. 138-143.

28. Protocol Nr. 2, February 28, 1856.

29. Protocols 5, 8, 10, of 6, 12 and 18 March, 1856.

30. Protocol No. 5, March 6, 1856.

31. Protocols Nr. 10, 27 March, 1856.
32. Protocol No. 4, 21 March 1855.
33. Ibid., No. 5, 23 March, 1855.
34. Protocol Nr. 5, of March 6, 1856.
35. Ibid.
36. Ibid., No. 8, 12 March 1856.
37. H. Hajnal, "The Danube...", pp. 71-72.
38. Quoted by H. Hajnal in "The Danube...", p. 72.
39. Idem, ibid.
40. From a Buol report to Emperor Francis Joseph; quoted by H. Hajnal in "The Danube...", p. 77, note.
41. From report of the Austrian delegation, March 13, 1856; quoted by H. Hajnal, in "The Danube...", p. 76, note. The Danube Navigation Company was the First Austrian Danube Stream Navigation Company.
42. Ibid., p. 75, note.
43. Ibid., p. 74, note.
44. Ibid., p. 75, note.
45. Ibid., p. 76, note.
46. Ibid., p. 75, note.
47. Ibid., p. 75, note.
48. From Buol's report; quoted by Hajnal, in "The Danube...", p. 77.
49. Protocol No. 10, 18 March 1856.
50. Protocol No. 5 March 23 of the 1855, Conference of Vienna.
51. Prokesch's statement as revealed by Bismarck on July 25, 1854; in H. Poschingher, "Lettres politiques confidentielles de M. de Bismarck, 1851-1858," troisième édition, p. 220; quoted by L. Boicu in "Austria si Principatele Române", p. 419.
52. Arhiva Istorică Română, Bucharest; see note quoted by L. Boicu, op. cit., p. 425.
53. Modified Prokesch-Osten Memorandum, Protocol No. 5, 23 Mrch 1855, Annex 6.
54. Protocol No. 5 of 23 March 1855.
55. Protocol Nr. 5, of 6 March 1856.
56. Sevastopol, Balaklava, Kamiesch, Eupatoria, Kertch, Jenikale, Kimbur, etc.
57. D. Sturdza, "Recueil ...", pp. 32-34; "La Question du Danube", M.A.E., pp. 143, 144; Hertslet, "Map of ..." Vol. II, p. 1257.
58. Hertslet, "Map of..."; Vol I, pp. 269-271.
59. Isaccea (Isaktcha), small port having the function of warehouse, on the right bank of the Lower Danube, on Dobrujan territory, at a distance of cca 21 Kms the port of Tulcea and about 93 Kms from Sulina.

60. An unpublished circular the partial text of which was reproduced in the "Memorandum on the Danube", sent by General Magheru to the signatories of the 1856 Treaty. The entire text of the Memorandum was copied from the Archieves of the Romanian Academy and published by the author of this work in "Două Memorii cu privire la incălcarea drepturilor României la Gurile Danării".

61. "The Imperial Government made haste, immediately after the ratification of the Treaty of Paris, to put into application all that was need to commence the work, sending to the Sulina Mouth a dredging machine and a steamship, to aid the work of clearing, and to install a lighthouse for the safety of navigation... "Două Memorii...", p. 13.

62. Magheru Memorandum; in "Două Memorii...", op. cit.

63. Protocol Nr. 5, March 6, 1856.

64. From "Arhiva Istorică Centrală a României,"; quoted by L. Boicu, in "Austria si Principatele Române...", p. 423.

65. Sp. Focas, "Două Memorii...", p. 14.

66. The Turkish Circular, quoted from Magheru Memorandum; in "Două Memorii...". p. 10.

67. Turkish Circular.

68. Ibid.

69. "Traité relatif à la délimitation en Bessarabie, de l'île des Serpents et du Delta du Danube", Paris, le 19 Juin, 1857; in "La Question du Danube", M.A.E., p. 146; Hertslet, "The Map...", Vol II, p. 1298; Martens N.R.G.T., Vol. XVI, Part two (1846-1860).

70. Article 20. "In exchange for the towns, ports and territories enumerated in Article IV of the present Treaty, and in order more fully to secure the freedom of the navigation of the Danube, His Majesty the Emperor of all the Russians consents to the rectification of his frontier in Bessarabia".
"The new frontier shall begin from the Black Sea, one Kilometer to the east of the lake Bouma Sola, shall run perpendicularly to the Akkerman Road, shall follow that road to the Val. de Trajan, pass to the south of Bolgrad, ascend the course of the river Yalpuck to the height of Saratsika, terminate at Katamori on the Pruth. Above that point the old frontier between the two Empires shall not undergo any modification".
"Delegates of the Contracting Powers shall fix in its details the line of the new frontier": F. Israel, "Major Peace Treaties". (Treaty of Paris, 1856).

71. Protocol No. 5. March 23 of the Conference of 1855.

72. Previously quoted.

73. Protocole relatif aux limites de la Russie et de la Turquie vers Bolgrad et l'île des Serpents, signé à Paris le 6 Janvier 1857; in "La Question du Danube", M.A.E., pp. 145-146.

74. T.W. Riker, "The Making of Roumania", p. 64.

75. Clarendon to Cowley, Oct. 20, 1856; in State Papers, No. 1275.

76. Quoted by L. Boicu, "Austria si Principatele Române", p. 442.

77. For details in the problems of the Principalities, these important works are recommended: W.G. East, "The Union of Moldavia and Wallachia, 1859"; T.W. Riker, "The Making of Roumania"; R.R.N. Florescu, "The Struggle...", op. cit.
78. Protocol No. 10, of the Bessarabia Delimitation Commission, Austria, England, France, Russia and Turkey, at Chisinău, 7 to 19 January 1857; D.A. Sturdza, Gh. Petrescu, and Colescu Vartic, "Acte si documente relative la istoria renasterii României, Vol. III, Protocol No. XI of the Bessarabia Delimitation Commission, Chisinau, 12/23 January, 1857, in the same source, p. 1087.
79. Ibid., and Walewsky to Malaret, No. 87, August 25, Aff. Etr., Angleterre, Vol. 705, quoted by T.W. Riker in "The Making of...", p. 63.
80. Persigny to Walewsky, No. 186, Sept. 23, 1857; in "Archives du Ministère des Affaires Etrangères" Paris, Diplomatic and consular correspondence and reports, 1856-66, Vol. 706; quoted by T.W. Riker, p. 65.
81. D. Sturdza, "Recueil...", Carte II du Danube entre Brăila et la mer.
82. Clarendon to Wodehouse, No. 340, Sept. 17; F.O. 65/468; quoted by T.W. Riker, op. cit., p. 64.
83. Ottenfels to Buol, Sept. 10, 1856, in Staatsarchiv, Vienna, diplomatic and consular correspondence and reports, 1856-1866, No. 79, A-1; quoted by T.W. Riker, p. 64.
84. Previously quoted.
85. Protocol of the Conf. of Paris, 6 January 1857.
86. Quoted previously.
87. Protocol No. 1, of November 29, 1856; in "La Question du Danube," M.A.E., p. 147.
88. S. de Blumfeld (Austria); S. Dr. Daxenberger (Bavaria); G.A. Dovoud (Turkey); A. Müller (Württemberg).
89. P. Donici and then L. Steege (Moldavia); F. Christic (Servia), and N. Rosetti (Wallachia); in "La Question du Danube," M.A.E., p. 147.
90. For Protocols of the works of the Riparian Commission of the Danube see: "La Question du Danube" M.A.E., pp. 147-295; Norandounghian, "Recueil d'Actes Internationaux de l'Empire Ottomane," Vol. III, p. 100.
91. "Acte de Navigation du Danube," signé à Vienne le 7 November 1857; in D. Sturdza, "Recueil...," pp. 51-66; Martens, N.R.G.T., Vol. XVI, part 2, p. 75.
92. "Projet préliminaire du Règlement de Police pour la Navigation du Danube," du 16 October 1857, élaboré par la Commission Riveraine du Danube; in D. Sturdza, "Recueil...," pp. 37-50.
93. From the statements of Taggenburg, Austria's Minister of Commerce, made at the opening session of the Riparian Commission of the Danube, on November 29, 1856; "La Question du Danube," M.A.E., p. 147, Protocol No. 1.
94. "Repport du Comité chargé de l'élaboration préliminaire du Règlement de Police sur la Navigation du Danube," Annexe au Protocole No. 33 du 16 October 1857; in "La Question du Danube," M.A.E., p. 283.

95. Graduates of Universities of Vienna, Berlin, Paris and London.

96. As distinguished from the other Balkan countries under the direct sovereignty of the Ottoman Empire, the Romanian Principalities, having the suzerainty regime, had the political and economic possibility of keeping in free contact with the culturally developed countries of Central and Western Europe.

97. Count de Cavour's note on the Question of the Danube, published in the "Gazette Piemontaise" of January 12, 1859; in "La Question du Danube," M.A.E., pp. 357-361.

98. Protocol No. 32 of Nov. 7, of the Riparian Commission, supplement to Protocol No. 31 of November 7; Minutes of the session of November 10, 1857 of that same Commission; copy of the Minutes of the session of November 10, 1857, drawn up by the Minutes of the session of November 10, 1857, drawn up by the Commissars of the Danubian Principalities; Memorandum and protests of the three Principalities against the guarantor Powers of the 1857 Treaty of Paris; Count Cavour's note of 1859; Memorandum of Prussia's Government; etc. For all this documentation, see "La Question du Danube," M.A.E., pp. 293-357.

99. From the Memorandum of the Moldavian Government to the guarantor Powers of the Treaty of Paris (1856), with respect to the method of carrying out the Act of Navigtion, January 2, 1856, Jassy.

100. Copy of the Minutes of the session of November 10, 1857, drawn up by the Commissars of the Danubian Pricipalities; in "La Question du Danube," M.A.E., p. 295.

101. Supplement to Protocol 31 of November 7, 1857 drawn up by the Commissars of the Danube Principalities; "La Question du Danube," M.A.E., p. 293.

102. Minutes of the session of 10 November, drawn up by the Commissars of the Danubian Principalities; "La Question de Danube," M.A.E., p. 296.

103. Supplement to Protocol 31, of Nov. 7, 1857; "La Question du Danube," M.A.E., p. 293.

104. Response of Mr. Steege, Minister ad-interim for Foreign Affaires of Moldavia, to the interpellation of Mr. L. Catargi, concerning the Act of Navigation; in "La Question du Danube," M.A.E., p. 353.

105. Ibid., ibid., p. 353.

106. M. Kogălniceanu, Romanian Minister to Paris, to V. Boerescu, July 29, 1880; in "Mihai Kogălniceanu, documente diplomatice," p. 322, note.

107. Minutes of the session of November 10, 1857, drawn up by the Commissars of the Danubian Principalities; in "La Question du Danube," M.A.E., p. 298.

108. Ibid., ibid., p. 298.

109. Ibid., ibid., p. 298.

110. Ibid., ibid., p. 298.

111. From Kogălniceanu's speach on the participation of the Romanian Commissars in the Commission for drawing up the Act of Navigation, November 9, 1857; "Buletinul Sedintei Adunării Ad-hoc al Moldovei," November 11, 1857; quoted in "M. Kogălniceanu, documente diplomatice," p. 70.
112. For simplification: Art. 17, in part: "Une commission sera établie et se composera des délégués de l'Autriche, de la Bavière, de la Sublime Porte et du Württemberg, auxquels se réuniront les Commissaires des trois Principautés danubiennes, dont la nomination aura été approuvée par la Porte.
113. "Réunir, rapprocher, rejoindre ce qui était separé"; figurativ, grouper, réconcilier; "Petit Larousse Illustré," Paris 1910, p. 867.
114. From Kogălniceanu speech in "M. Kogălniceanu, documente...," p. 70.
115. H. Hajnal, "Le Droit...," p. 53.
116. Austro-Moldavian telegraphic Convention of 1855; The Convention between Austria and the Romanian Principalities for the regulation of telegraphic service, May 22, 1865; Postal Convention between the Romanian Principalities and Austro-Hungary, August 8, 1871; The Convention for Commerce and Navigation between Austro-Hungary and the Romanian Principality, June 22, 1875; Postal Convention with Russia, March 1, 1873; Convention for Commerce and Navigation with Russia, March 27, 1876.
117. "The foreign functions of the Romanian states vassals to the Porte, exercized through Capuchehaie, were limited particularly by the obligation to be within the framework of general Ottoman policy"; in "Reprezentantele diplomatice ale Romañiei," Vol. 1 (1859-1917), p. 68.
118. Conference of Paris, Protocol No. 5, March, 1856.
119. W. East, op. cit., p. 38.
120. Riparian Commission, Protocol No. 32, September 28, 1857; in "La Question du Danube," M.A.E., p. 281.
121. Ibid., Protocol No. 33, October 16, 1857; in "La Question du Danube," M.A.E., p. 282.
122. A.) "Mémoire adressée par la Commission Interimaire de Moldavie aux Puissances garantes, concernant l'Acte de navigation pour le Danube," le 2 Janvier 1859.
B.) "Protestation du Gouvernement de Moldavie, adressée aux Puissances garantes, contre l'acte de navigation pour le Danube," Jassy, 17 Avril, 1859, publié à Vienne le 1 Janvier 1858.
C.) Protestation du gouvernement de Valachie, adressée aux Puissances garantes contre l'acte de navigation pour le Danube, publié à Vienne, le ler Janvier de l'année 1858; in "La Question du Danube," M.A.E., pp. 344, 347, 350.
123. Le Consul d'Autriche au Secretariat d'Etat de Moldavie, Jassy, le 5 Mai 1858; "La Question du Danube," M.A.E., p. 299.
124. Le Secretariat d'Etat à l'agence et consulat general d'Autriche a Jassy, Mai 1858; "La Question du Danube," M.A.E., p. 305.
125. "Mesures préliminaires concernant l'application de l'acte de navigation du Danube"; Bulletin Officiel de Moldavie No. 36, de 1858, op. cit., p. 305-310.

126. "Protestation du gouvernement de Moldavie...," du 17 Avril 1859; "La Question du Danube," M.A.E., p. 348, Réponse du M. Steege, Ministre ad-interim des Affaires Etrangères de Moldavie à l'interpellation de M.L. Catargie, concurant l'Acte de Navigation du Danube (séance de 24 Mars 1859), à la Chambre Elective de Moldavie; "La Question du Danube," p. 353.

127. Caimacam (Turkish) deputy for a ruler whenever the throne was vacant; leader of the country until the Sublime Porte named a prince.

128. For details, see W.G. East, op. cit., pp. 96-98.

Chapter 3

129. Protocols No. 14, 18 and 19, respectively of 9, 16, and 19 August, 1858; D. Sturdza "Recueil...," pp. 67-77; "La Question du Danube," M.A.E., pp. 335-342; Martens, N.R.G.T. Vol. XVI, Part 2, p. 50; British and Foreign State Papers, edited by E. Hertslet, Vol. XLVIII (Conference of Paris, 1858).

130. Protocol No. 14, August 9, 1858.

131. Ibid.

132. "Mémoire du Gouvernement Imperiale d'Autriche sur le droit des états riverains du Danube de conclure, de ratifier et de mettre en exécution l'Acte de Navigation du 7 Novembre 1857, Vienne, Mars 1858; "La Question du Danube," op. cit., p. 316.

133. Conference of the Riparian Commission, Protocol Nr. 12, March 2, 1857.

134. Protocol No. 5, March 23, 1855; in D. Sturdza "Recueil...," p. 23, annex.

135. From "Le Ministre des Affaires Etrangères de la Sublime Porte aux représentants de la Turquie à l'étranger," Pera, le 26 Janvier 1858; in "La Question du Danube," op. cit., p. 330.

136. Duties of the Riparian Commission: 1) drawing up the Regulations for Navigation and Police; 2) Removal of impediments of any nature that still prevent the application of the principles of the Act of 1815 on the Danube; 3) ordering and carrying out the work necessary on the entire course of the river; 4) after termination of the European Commission, to supervise the administration of navigation at the mouths of the Danube and the neighbouring parts of the sea.

137. "Projet préliminaire du Règlement de Police pour la navigation du Danube," élaboré par la Commission Riveraine du Danube, instituée conformement à l'article 17 du Traité de Paris de 1856; D. Sturdza, "Recueil...," p. 37.

138. "Décret du Ministère du Commerce de l'Empire d'Autriche pour l'éxecution de l'Acte de Navigation du Danube en Autriche, en date du 29 Janvier 1858"; in "La Question du Danube," M.A.E., p. 299; Hajnal, "Le Droit...," p. 43.

139. January 5, 1859 report of Prokesch-Osten, Austria's Ambassador to Constantinople, sent to Vienna; H. Hajnal, "Le Droit...," p. 56, note 4.

140. "Analyse d'une dépêche autrichienne du 5 Janvier 1858, relativement à la question de la navigation du Danube"; in "La Question du Danube," op. cit., p. 329.

141. "Opinion of the Law Officers of the Crown" mentioned in "Memorandum of the F.O. 23 April, 1857, repeated in the "Mémoire du Gouvernement d'Autriche sur le droit des Etats riverains du Danube..."; H. Hajnal, "Le Droit...," p. 56, note 2; "La Question du Danube," M.A.E., pp. 310-314.

142. "Mémoire sur la liberté du Danube et sur l'Acte de Navigation du 7 Novembre, Paris, 1858.

143. Ibid., p. 17.
144. Ibid., p. 18.
145. Ibid., p. V.
146. Ibid., p. 14.
147. Ibid., p. 10.
148. Ibid., p. VII.
149. Protocol No. 18, August 16, 1858.
150. Ibid.
151. Ibid.
152. Ibid.

153. "Minutes of the Committee on International River," February 2, 1815; in "La Question du Danube," M.A.E., p. 7, annex.

154. Ibid. February 8, 1815; "La Question du Danube," p. 10.

155. Protocol No. 18 of August 16, 1858; in Sturdza, "Recueil...," p. 72.

156. Ibid., ibid.

157. "Minutes of the Committee on International Rivers," February 8, 1815; "Mémoire préparatoire sur le travail de la Commission de Navigation, présenté par M. Humboldt"; in "La Question du Danube," p. 12.

158. "Nouvelle rédaction d'articles présentés par M.le Baron Humboldt, Plénipotentiare de la Prusse; in "La Question du Danube," p. 65.

159. Conference of the Riparian Commission of the Danube, Protocol No. 15, March 30, 1857. Annex B, "Dispositions relatives à la liberté de navigation des bâtiments et de navigateurs"; in "La Question du Danube," p. 200.

160. 1857 Act de Navigation.
161. Ibid.
162. W.N. Medlicott, "The Congress of Berlin and After," p. 356.

163. Silborne to Salisbury, March 6, 1879; quoted by W.N. Mendlicott, op. cit., p. 357, and note 14.
164. Conference of the Riparian Commission, Protocol No. 15 of March 30, 1857, Annex B; "La Question du Danube," op. cit., pp. 198 and 200.
165. Protocol No. 15 of March 30, 1857.
166. Protocol No. 18, April 27, 1857.
167. "Commission Européenne du Danube et son..."; figures extracted from statistics.
168. Protocol No. 18 of April 27, 1857; in "La Question du Danube," p. 218.
169. Ibid.
170. Protocol No. 18 of August 16, 1858.
171. Article CIX of the Act of 1815.
172. Protocol No. 18, of August 16, 1858.
173. Hajnal, "Le Droit...," p. 56, note 5.
174. Protocol No. 18, August 16, 1858.
175. Ibid.
176. Ministère des Affaires Etrangères de la Sublime Porte aux représentants de la Turquie à l'étranger, op. cit.,
177. See statistics for respective years in "La Commission Européenne et son...."
178. "Mémoire sur la liberté...," op. cit., Paris 1858, p. 37.
179. Protocol No. 3 of February 3, of the 1871 Conference of London; D. Sturdza, "Recueil...," p. 102.
180. Adaptation of the European Commission Statistics; in "La Commission Européenne et son oeuvre..."
181. Until 1878, Dobruja was under Ottoman Empire sovereignty.
182. "Hermis," Greek-Romanian newspaper, Brăila, No. 21, April 1876; in Collection of Greek newspapers abroad, Library of Chamber of Deputies, Athens.
183. "Analele Statistice si Economice ale României," Bucuresti, 1867.
184. Youghaperian, "L'Annuaire du Danube entre 1894-1895" (figures extracted and grouped in categories from various record of the respective source).
185. C.I. Băicoianu," Le Danube aperçu historique...," p. XIV.
186. "Mémoire du gouvernement Royal de Prusse sur l'Acte de Navigation du Danube," du 7 Novembre 1857, Berlin, Mars 1858; in "La Question du Danube," M.A.E., 319."
187. "Note du Compte de Cavour sur la Question du Danube," op. cit.
188. Protocol No. 18, August 16, 1858.
189. Ibid.
190. "Mémoire du Gouvernement Impériale de l'Autriche sur les droits des états riverains du Danube de conclure, de ratifier, et de mettre en exécution l'Acte de Navigation du 7 November 1857," op. cit.
191. "Le Ministère des Affaires Etrangères de la Sublime Porte aux représentants de Turquie à l'Etranger," op. cit.
192. Hajnal, "Le Droit...," p. 61.

193. Protocol No. 6 of April 24 of the 1856 Conference.
194. Public Act of 1865.
195. Ibid., Annex B, Articles 18 and 19.
196. Ibid.
197. Hajnal, "Le Droit...," p. 62, note 1.
198. Idem, ibid., pp. 62-63.
199. Idem, ibid., p. 73.
200. Idem, ibid., p. 73 and note 3.
201. "British Order in Council" empowering Her Majesty's Consuls in the Ottoman Dominions to exercise Power and Jurisdiction over British subjects, for enforcing the Provisions of the Public Act of the 2 November 1865, as amended by the Protocol of 28 March 1866 relative to the Navigation of the Mouths of the Danube, April 9, 1866 at the Court, at Windsor; in "La Question du Danube," M.A.E., p. 399.
202. By the Treaty of Berlin, of 1878.
203. Protocol No. 18, August 16, 1858.
204. Protocol No. 18, August 16, 1858.
205. The Siret, almost 270 miles long, has its source in the Carpathian Mountains of Bucovina, a Romanian province under Austrian occupation in 1858. The Siret flows through the territory of Moldavia, emptying into the Danube by the Port of Galatz. The Prut, almost 500 miles long, originates in the Carpathian Mountains in Bucovina and empties into the Danube between the Danube ports of Galatz and Reni. For a distance of 250 miles it forms the frontier between Moldavia and Bessarabia, under Russian occupation. From there, to the point where it flows into the Danube, it runs along the Moldavian shore and that of Southern Bessarabia which had been reannexed to Moldavia by the 1856 Peace Treaty of Paris.
206. L. Boicu, "Incercări franceze de pătrundere în economia Moldovei în epoca răsboiului Crimeei si a Unirii" (1853-1959), p. 304, footnote 296. Also, Bodin: "Documente Sarde," p. 308.
207. Idem, ibid.
208. L. Boicu, "Austria si Principatele Române...," p. 305.
209. L. Boicu, "Incercări franceze...," op. cit.
210. Nicholas Soutzo, "Exposé des procédés à employer pour assurer la navigation du Sereth" (1850-1851), p. 452; in V. Slăvescu, "Viata si opera economistului Nicolae Sutu," p. 453.
211. In the Archives of the Foreign Ministry of the Socialist Republic Romania; quoted by L. Boicu in "Austria si Principatele Române...," p. 305.
212. Ibid., ibid.
213. Clarendon to Cowley No. 725, July 26, F.O. 7/1113; quoted by T.W. Riker, op. cit., p. 66.
214. Great Britain Foreign Office State Papers, Vol. 100, p. 727: "Sened en faveur du commerce autrichien dans l'Empire Ottoman."

215. Article 22. "The Principalities of Wallachia and Moldavia shall continue to enjoy under the suzerainty of the Porte, and under the guaranty of the contracting Powers, the privileges and immunities of which they are in possession."

216. The Archives of the Foreign Ministry of the Socialist Republic Romania; quoted by L. Boicu, in "Austria si Principatele Române...," p. 305.

217. The Danube River in the Baden territory forms its course by the merging of the Brigach and Breg streams, which spring from the Black Forest. From the point where the Danube is formed, to the Ulm, a distance of 260 Kms., the river is inaccessible because of the rocky region and the low water level to any but light crafts and small fishing crafts.

218. See "The Committee on International Rivers."

219. Protocols No. 21, of May 6 and No. 27, of June 8, 1857.

220. Protocol No. 27, of June 8, 1857.

221. Acte si documente relative la istoria..." op. cit., Vol. III, p. 73; quoted by L. Boicu, in "Austria si Principatele...," p. 308.

222. Archives of the Foreign Ministry of the Socialist Republic Romania; quoted by Boicu, op. cit., p. 308.

223. Ibid., idem, p. 309.

224. Fuad to Balsche, August 6, 1856; quoted by T.W. Riker, in "The Making of Roumania," p. 66, and note 6.

225. Protocol No. 18, of August 16, 1858.

226. Protocol No. 18, of August 16, 1858.

227. Ibid.

228. Protocol No. 5, January 7, 1857, Annex A.

229. Protocol No. 19, of August 19, 1858.

230. Ibid.

231. "Rapport de la Commission Technique Internationale convoquée à Paris pour l'éxamen des questions rélatives à l'amélioration des Bouches du Danube," Paris, 1858; quoted by Hajnal, "Le Droit...," pp. 64, 65.

232. "Articles Additionnels à l'Acte de Navigation pour le Danube, du 7 Novembre 1857," signés à Vienne le 1 Mars, 1859; D. Sturdza, "Recueil...," p. 78; "La Question du Danube," M.A.E., p. 342.

233. Réponse de Stéege, Ministre Ad-interim des Affaires Etrangères de Moldavie, à l'interpellation de L. Catargi, concernant l'Acte de Navigation du Danube; "La Question du Danube," M.A.E., p. 353.

234. "Convention relative à la Navigation du Prut, entre l'Autriche, la Russie et la Roumanie," Bucharest, 15 Décembre 1866, modifiée le 18 Février 1895; Sturdza, "Recueil...," p. 760. Austria for the upper course of the Prut, Russia for the left bank of the river, la Roumanie for the entire bank beginning from the Moldavian frontier with Austria and from the Moldavian frontier with Russia, downriver to the Mouth of the Prut, on both banks.

Chapter 4

235. Engelhart, "Etudes sur les Embouchures," p. 93.
236. Hajnal, "Le Droit...," p. 70, "Dans un raport envoyé alors à Vienne, M. de Becke démontra lui même qu'on ne pouvait pas accuser les délégués de vouloir, dans leur propre intérêt, prolonger la durée de la Commission. Il dit qu'invoquant le peu de confort qu'offrait Galatz à cette époque et le danger qu'une longue occupation spéciale faisait courir à leurs intérêts de carrière, tous les délégués avaient demandé leur révocation à leurs gouvernements respectifs."
237. "... la vie à Galatz en 1856 était loin d'offrir aux étrangers qui habitaient la ville les avantages d'un grand port qu'elle offre aujourd'hui. Des maisons en bois, des rues non pavées qui, pendant la mauvaise saison étaient transformées en bourbiers, la ville basse entièrement inondée au moment des crues du Danube et au printemps la plus grande partie de la population atteinte par les fièvres en raison de la proximité des marais"; informations by Stokes, see "La Commission Européenne et son...," p. 12
238. "La Commission Européenne et son...," p. 19.
239. Hajnal, "Le Droit...," p. 74.
240. "Acte Public rélatif à la navigation des embouchures du Danube," signé à Galatz, le 2 Nov. 1865; Sturdza, "Recueil...," pp. 80-89; "La Question du Danube," M.A.E., p. 363. Martens, N.R.G.T., Vol. XVIII, Series I, p. 144.
241. "Additional Act to the Public Act of 1865," on May 2, 1881, and the "Regulation for Navigation and Police," of May 19, 1881.
242. "Règlement de Navigation et de Police applicable au Bas-Danube," (Galatz-bouches du Danube), Nov. 2, 1865 (Annexe A); "La Question du Danube...," op. cit., p. 369; Martens, N.R.G.T., Vol. XVIII, p. 144.
243. "Tarif et Droits de navigation à prélever l'embouchure de Danube," Annexe B.; "La Question du Danube," M.A.E., p. 385.

Chapter 5

244. Conférences tenues à Paris en 1866, relativement aux Principautés danubiennes et à la navigation du Danube; in Sturdza, "Recueil...," p. 90, and "La Question du Danube," M.A.E., p. 393.
245. Name of the Principalities of Moldavia and Wallachia after the 1858 Convention of Paris following their union in 1859 and the subsequent election of a foreign prince, in the person of Carol I of Hohenzollern.
246. For details see T.W. Riker, "The Making of Roumania," pp. 507-537.
247. Protocols No. 3, 6, 7 and 8, respectively, of March 28, April 24, May 2 and 17, 1866 D. Sturdza, "Recueil...," pp. 90-99.
248. Protocol No. 3, March 28, 1866.

249. Ibid.
250. Protocol No. 18 of August 16, 1858.
251. Ibid.
252. Protocol No. 3, March 28, 1866.
253. Ibid.
254. Ibid.
255. Ibid.
256. Ibid.
257. Ibid.
258. Protocol No. 6, April 24, 1866.
259. Protocol No. 3, March 28 and No. 6, April 24, 1866.
260. Protocol No. 3, March 28, 1866.
261. D. Sturdza, "Recueil...," p. 887.
262. "Geografia Văii Dunării românesti," p. 245.
263. Previously quoted in Protocol No. 4, March 21, of the 1855 Conference of Vienna, D. Sturdza, "Recueil...," p. 22.
264. Protocol No. 7, May 2, 1866.
265. Ibid., No. 8, May 17, 1866.

PART SIX

EARLY MODIFICATION OF THE TREATY OF 1856

Early Modification of the Treaty of 1856

Introduction.

The beginning of modifications to the 1856 Treaty of Paris was due to Russia. Taking advantage of the weakened political balance in Europe following France's defeat in the Franco-Prussian War of 1870, Russia denounced certain clauses of that Treaty respecting the limitation of her naval potential on the Black Sea.

Inasmuch as the main objective of the Crimean War had been to block Russia's expansion by reducing that potential and removing her from the Mouths of the Danube, the negative effects of the Treaty of 1856, which set up the new political balance in Europe, can be inferred. Russia's denunciation, supported by Germany, put England and France face to face with a fait accompli.

The first modification in 1871 of the 1856 Treaty was followed by those on 1878, 1883, 1921 and 1948, respectively by the Treaties of Berlin, London, Versailles and the Belgrade Convention of the Danube, each one of them determined by the political and economic interests of the Great Powers.

All these modifications had an influence over the principles of internationalization of navigation on the Danube, established in 1856, which in turn had developed from those of the 1815 Act of Vienna.

Chapter 1

THE CONFERENCE AND THE TREATY OF LONDON (1871)

The initial aim of the Conference of London, held between January 7 and March 13, 1871, was to make a decision concerning the termination on the prolonging of the existence of the European Commission of the Danube, whose five-year mandate set by the 1866 Conference of Paris was to expire in 1871. The decision was also directly tied to the clauses of Articles 16 and 17 of the 1856 Treaty of Paris, on the basis of which the European Commission was to be replaced by the Riparian one.

The Conference was also to make decisions on certain Danubian problems unresolved at the 1866 Conference. On that occasion, the signatory Powers of the 1856 Treaty were to decide upon the unexpected Russian measure denouncing the restrictions on her naval military power on the Black Sea, as established by Articles 11 to 14 of that Treaty. In the Circular of October 31, 1870, issued by Foreign Minister Gorchacov, Russia declared herself free of those restrictions.[1]

According to the principle of the Law of Nations, no modification of any treaty can be made unilaterally; it must have the consent, or friendly understanding of all the treaty's signatories.

From the correspondence between Beust, the Austro-Hungarian Foreign Minister, and Prokesch-Osten, the Internuncio at Constantinople, we learn that some of the 1856 Treaty signatories were going to the London Conference with different positions than those of their previous policies of rejecting or limiting Russia's measures.[2] In the end, the Conference approved the Russian measure.

Because of the situation created by the 1870 Franco-German War, the Conference of 1871 took place in London, instead of Paris, under the chairmanship of Foreign Minister Granville. For the same reason, the weight in the matter of Danubian problems was borne by England, which defended also the interests of France, whose representatives participated in the last sessions of the Conference.

The discussions at the Conference, concerning the Danube, and its maritime subsector, were brief; only two protocols being concluded,[3] with reference to the discussions of some problems.

The Problem of the Riparian Commission associated with that of the obstacles at the Cataracts and the Iron Gates.

As mentioned before, the removal of the natural obstacles from the Iron Gates and the Cataracts was the difficult-to-solve problem in Vienna's preoccupations with easing navigation between the Middle and Upper sectors of the Danube and that of the Lower respectively, towards the Black Sea. Profitting, on the one hand, from the atmosphere of compromise and of compensation of interests between some of the Great Powers, brought on by Russia's arbitrary measures and, on the other hand, by England's desire to prolong the existence of the European Commission, Austro-Hungary formulated the idea of exclusively carrying out the work of improving navigation at those two points so difficult for navigation.

To carry out these works there existed two solutions. The first can be referred to the clauses of Articles 36 and 37 of the proposed 1857 Act of Navigation, drawn up by the Riparian Commission of the Danube, the technical works to be carried out by all the riparian states on their fluvial sectors. The second solution, leaving aside the two Articles, would have been to assign the work to Turkey and Austro-Hungary, two Great Powers considered to be riparian at those two points. The latter solution was finally adopted. The first solution would have implied acknowledging the application of the Act of Navigation also on the Lower Danube. But, along with its rejection by the 1858 Conference of Paris there had intervened a temporary change of mind on the part or Austro-Hungary. In 1871, the latter did not find it convenient to reopen the problem of the Riparian Commission in its initial form.

A new meeting of the Riparian Commission would have met greater resistance from the Romanian and Serbian Principalities, which in the meantime had become autonomous. In the beginning, to

Austro-Hungary's request to be assigned the exclusive work of carrying out the technical works, Serbia protested in writing to the 1871 Conference, as well as to the Turkish Plenipotentiary, and asked that the Romanian Principalities follow her example.[4] According to Hajnal, Serbia's protest was the result of the fear that Turkish warships would sail closer to her territory under the pretext of removing obstacles from the Cataracts and the Iron Gates, thus being in a position to repeat the 1867 bombardment of Belgrade and other neighbouring localities.[5]

Even though the Romanian Principalities also were against the Austro-Hungarian demand still, because of pressure from Vienna, they did not associate themselves with Serbia's protest.[6] Even later on, when Serbia's Foreign Minister, Ristic, went to Vienna to defend his country's rights, the Romanian Principalities abstained again, from any protest, from the same wish not to appear opposed to Vienna's policies of the moment.[7]

Aside from Vienna's powerful political position, the Romanian Principalities were obliged to maintain good relations with her, especially since the Austro-Hungarian Emperor, two years previously in 1869, had shown some friendliness towards the Principalities by stopping at the Port of Vârciorova, the Romanian-Austro-Hungarian frontier, while on a voyage by ship to Constantinople. Disembarking at this port, he reviewed the Romanian military detachment.[8]

In spite of the friendly relations, Austro-Hungary could not hope for a lengthy silence on the part of the Romanian Principalities if the Riparian Commission of the Danube were to begin functioning. Although by reason of their union the Romanian Principalities would have been represented in this Commission by a single vote, they still expected to have two votes: Moldavia's and Wallachia's, in conformity with Article 17 of the 1856 Treaty.[9] In such a situation, the votes in the Commission would be equally divided: Moldavia, Wallachia, Serbia and Bulgaria, as against Austro-Hungary, Bavaria, Württemberg, and Turkey, and any action of Vienna's could have had results unfavorable to her. If the Riparian Commission were to begin functioning, the position of Austro-Hungary would have been diminished also by the interference of the European Commission, the latter being termed by Beust a "ingérence européenne" or "la surveillance enropéenne."[10]

Beust favored assigning the project for the works at the Cataracts and the Iron Gates to the Vienna Government and, together with the other Powers, would not have opposed there being carried out; on the contrary, he would have congratulated Austro-Hungary for their initiative.[11] "He pressed upon Prokesch-Osten the priority of the works to be carried out, either by the two Riparian states (Austro-Hungary and Turkey) or by the Riparian Commission, of which he said, "que nous n'avons pas renoncé.""[12]

Also in support of having Austro-Hungary carry out the project, Beust pressed upon the other participants of the 1871 Conference the importance of the success of the measures, invoking even Vienna's agreement to the extension of the European Commission of the Danube, leaving it to be understood that the Riparian Commission would be reassembled, according to a previous understanding between the Riparian Powers.[13]

At the first session of the debates over the Danubian questions, Apponyi, the Austro-Ungarian Plenipotentiary, made the following proposals:[14]

1.) Establishment of the conditions for the new meeting of the Riparian Commission, established by Article 17 of the 1856 Treaty of Paris, by prior-agreement of the Riparian Powers, and — in case Article 17 were to be modified — by a special Convention between the signatory Powers of the same Treaty;

2.) Concerning the technical and financial conditions required by the works at the Cataracts and the Iron Gates, Austro-Hungary was to establish them together with the other riparians of the same river. To cover the costs, by derogation the clause of Article 15 of the 1856 Treaty, provision was to be made for a reasonable navigation tax between the two points, equally to all flags.

As can be noted from the above proposals, the works were decided to be carried out exclusively by Austro-Hungary and Turkey. The proposal for point 1 meeting no opposition, it was approved by the Conference. Concerning point 2, several remarks were made.

Granville, for England, expressed the opinion that the taxes and conditions for applying them be set in accord with the European Powers, represented by their Delegates, the collection of said taxes to cease after the amortization of the financial investment. The Italian and Russian Plenipotentiaries declared that vessels not sailing through the Cataracts and the Iron Gates should not be subject to taxation. Attention must be called at this point to the Russian Plenipotentiary's statement that Russia was a Power which "ne saurait participer aux frais d'établissement ni aux garanties financières qui pourraient résulter de ces travaux.''[15]

Finally, the Conference approved that the Riparian States, on the part of the Danube where the Cataracts and the Iron Gates were obstacles to navigation (Austro-Hungary and Turkey), should meet and agree on the manner of carrying out the technical projects.[16]

In spite of that decision, the work on the projects was not started immediately because of financial difficulties, Turkey's obstructions, and the beginning of resistance in the Romanian Principalities. Collaboration with Turkey being unsatisfactory, Austro-Hungary drew up the 1875 Convention with her, by which Vienna temporarily took over exclusive execution of the works. The Romanian Principalities, in their capacity of riparian states, contested that Act.[17] As will be shown in the next chapter, it was only by the 1878 Treaty of Berlin that Austro-Hungary obtained the exclusive right to carry out the works. In 1871, the latter had made one step forward towards resolving the navigation situation at the Cataracts and the Iron Gates, a major problem not only for her, but also for the efficient valorization of the entire course of the river. In any case, with all their opposition, the small riparian countries of the Lower Danube could not have had either the technical or the financial possibilities in 1871 to carry out the projected work.

Beust's opinion concerning the financial matter was just. "Les Puissances non-riveraines," he wrote to Prokesch-Osten, "ne consentiront pas facilement à participer à la garantie d'un emprunt pour les ouvrages en amont d'Isaktcha. Les Etats allemands riverains du Danube superieur n'ont pas d'intérêt direct à une entreprise trop eloignée de leur sphère nationale. Les Principautés danubiennes enfin ne disposent probablement pas des resources suffisantes pour vouloir y prendre part. Toutes les Puissances maritimes ne sauraient donc que se féliciter de voir l'Autriche-Hongrie se vouer à une tâche aussi grande."[18]

On the other hand, following the new situation created by Russia, the atmosphere at the time of the Conference was favorable to Austro-Hungary. England, France and Italy, whose commercial interests and the free navigation through the Sulina Mouth were assured by the presence of the European Commission of the Danube, could not overlook the needs of Austro-Hungary, whose fluvial fleet was the most numerous on the river. The English and French initiatives were directed towards supporting Austro-Hungary, especially since the latter offered financial support.

In 1868, the Foreign Office suggested that the works at the Cataracts be assigned to Sir Charles Hartley, the hydrotechnician who had projected and carried out successfully the technical work at the Sulina Mouth.[19] Before 1871, d'Avril had drawn up a project whose execution was proposed to be given to the European Commission, in which he himself was the French Delegate.[20] Because of the Franco-German War, he was unable to pledge France to support his project. The English Government again came in, empowering Col. Stokes, her Delegate in that Commission,[21] to include also the works project for the Iron Gates in his project for the future administration of Danubian navigation.[22] However, Andrassy, the President of the Hungarian Government and later Minister for Foreign Affairs of Austro-Hungary, did not agree to the idea of extending the Commission's influence over a Danubian sector which was to remain under the jurisdiction of the Riparian Commission, in other words: that of Vienna.[23] The Austro-Hungarian Government was apprehensive that an eventual presence of the European Commission of the Danube at the Iron Gates would result in a diminished role for or even the actual elimination of the Riparian Commission, were it to enter into its function; the Commission of which Beust said, "Wir würden die ganze Uferstaatenkommission am liebsten der Zukunft vorhalten."[24]

Among Andrassy's reasons for rejecting Stokes' proposals was also the effect of abolishing the neutrality of the Black Sea, as requested by Russia. He believed that the neutrality of the European Commission of the Danube would be included in this abolishment, hence the new regime of the Black Sea would be extended indirectly to the Iron Gates and the Cataracts, if the European Commission were present in these two areas. His fear was due to an erroneous interpretation or lack of information as to the juridical status of the European Commission of the Danube, established as far back as 1856. By Article II of the 1856 Treaty of Paris, as well as by Article 21 of the Public Act of 1865, the neutrality of the Commission included exclusively the technical works and the establishment of the European's Commission, plus the immunity of its executive personnel.

Carrying out the project at the Iron Gates and at the Cataracts by this Commission would have meant the extension of the Commission's authority from Isaktcha upriver. This could not have been done except by modification of Article 16 of the 1856 Treaty of Paris, an action that would have raised new debates and eventually new differences among its signatories, along with Turkey's opposition. This is one of the explanations for the fact that the participants at the 1871 Conference made only minor modifications to the Austro-Hungarian proposals concerning the works at the Iron Gates and the Cataracts.

The Problem of the Prolongation of the European Commission of the Danube. (E.C.D.)

With respect to maintaining and extending the mandate of the European Commission of the Danube, Austro-Hungary's and Turkey's positions were, for the first time, with those of England and France. That of the first was due to her being compensated by being assigned the work at the Iron Gates and the position of the second was because of the strengthening of the Russian naval contingent in the Black Sea. Austro-Hungary's interventions with Turkey were also important for supporting the continuance, even though the former's future aim was to replace the European Commission with the Riparian Commission. From the exchange of correspondence between Beust and Prokesch-Osten, it is clear that the retention and continuance of the European Commission was the counterbalance to Russia's presence in the Black Sea.[25]

At Constantinople, Prokesch-Osten succeeded in convincing the Grand Vizier that Europe's presence by means of the European Commission at the Mouths of the Danube" ...se présentera comme la meilleure garantie pour remplacer celle qui doit s'en aller par la modification du Traité de Paris," i.e., Russia's denunciation of the restrictions on the Black Sea. He added in his report to Beust, "... que la Porte ne serait plus contraire à la prolongation ou perpétuer la Commission Européenne."[26]

Beust's anxiety was quite apparent. In his opinion, if it had not been possible to convince Russia in January 1871 to agree to extending the mandate of the European Commission of the Danube, as a compensation, it would have been more doubtful in March of 1871, when, in accordance with the 1866 Conference, the suspension of the Commission would ensure.[27] He suggested that the proposal for the prolongation be made by Turkey, in her capacity as territorial Power at the Mouths of the Danube.[28] In the end, the problem was taken up by England's Plenipotentiary, who proposed an extension of twenty-six years, actually preferring one sine die.[29]

The positions of the other Plenipotentiaries with respect to the extension were as follows: Italy subscribed to both terms proposed by the English Plenipotentiary;[30] Germany, though not rejecting the idea of either of the two English alternatives, still noted the objections of other Plenipotentiaries, and proposed a twelve year term;[31] those of Austro-Hungary and Russia also held to twelve years.[32]

The stand of the Turkish Plenipotentiary was equivocal, differing from of the Grand Vizier, as reported by Prokesch-Osten to Beust.[33] Accepting the extension of the mandate in principle, the Turkish Plenipotentiary could not express an opinion of the term involved, not having instructions on that point from his Government. The tergiversation was deliberate. Granville agreed to the idea of those Plenipotentiaries who advocated an extension of twelve years, expressing his hope that, at the following session, it would be possible to obtain the approval of his initial proposal of twenty-six years.[34]

At the following and last session, the points of view appeared somewhat clarified, each Plenipotentiary subordinating his position to the majority decision. The Austro-Hungarian Plenipotentiary stated that he would reconsider his initial proposal of twelve years in order to favor the English proposal, if the other members of the Conference were in accord.[35] The Turkish Plenipotentiary accepted the term of twelve years, although in the end he would have agreed to the English proposal of twenty-six-years. The Russian Plenipotentiary remained with the twelve-years term[36] and Italy's would subscribe to as long a term as possible, but Germany's stopped at twelve years.[37]

As to France's Plenipotentiary, he declared that he would have favored a term even longer than the one proposed by England's Plenipotentiary, but because of will of the majority he subscribed to twelve years. Finally, the mandate of the European Commission of the Danube was extended by twelve years, from April 24, 1871 to April 24, 1883.[38]

Directly tied to the extension of the mandate of the international organization at the Sulina Mouth was also the problem of the neutralization of the Delta and the establishments there. By abrogation of Article II of the 1856 Treaty concerning the neutralization of the Black Sea, the question also arose in 1871 as to the validity of Article 21, of the Public Act of 1865, which had set the neutrality of the establishments of the European Commission of the Danube. In this matter the interested Powers were Turkey and Russia, border states to the Black Sea. It was brought out that Russia, at the 1855 Conference of Vienna, had opposed the neutralization of the Black Sea and the Danube Delta. On the other hand, the decision to establish light warships at the Danube Mouths in order to assure the regulations for freedom of navigation on the Danube would be carried out, was considered by Russia to be contrary to the principle of neutrality.

Turkey, faced with Russia's denouncement of Article II and with the abrogation of the 1856 Convention between herself and Russia, relative to the ratio of the warships of those two Powers on the Black

Sea, found herself directly threatened. The Plenipotentiaries of England and Austro-Hungary came to her rescue. At the March 13th session of the Conference, the latter made two proposals.[39] The first with reference to the neutralization of the establishments of the European Commission of the Danube only, and the immunity of its executive personnel. The second set aside the neutrality of the Danube Delta, thus compensating Turkey — as a territorial Power — with the right to send her warships through the Sulina Mouth and on the Lower Danube.

Russia not objecting, the proposal was inserted in Article 7 of the 1871 Treaty of London. Accepting the presence of Turkish warships on the Lower Danube, Russia could at any time consider the respective sector as lacking the benefit of neutrality, a situation which would be to her convenience in the Russo-Turkish War of 1877-1878. By neutralization of the European Commission of the Danube establishments, Beust counted on counteracting Russia's remilitarization on the Black Sea. "Nous nous flattons," he wrote to Prokesch-Osten, "que le Grand Vizier approuvera notre intention de ne pas passer sous silence l'Article 21 de l'Acte Public de 1865 sur la neutralité des institutions établies aux embouchures du Danube; car c'est la connexité de cette stipulation avec les articles 11 et 19 du Traité de 1856 qui donne aux co-signataires le droit de réclamer — si la neutralisation de la mer noire venait à cesser — de nouvelles garanties pour la neutralité à sauvegarder aux bouches du fleuve."[40]

Resuming the Problem of Extension of the European Commission's Competence as far as Brăila.

At the February 3 meeting, England's Plenipotentiary again brought up his proposal made at the 1866 Conference requesting the extension of the European Commission's jurisdiction up to the port of Brăila.[41]

Although his proposal had been inserted in Article 5 of the Treaty Project[42] which was to be concluded at the Conference, it still had not been accepted by the other participants, due mainly to Turkey's opposition. Tied to this opposition could have been the implication in the text of Protocol 3, by which the real intention of the English proposal was altered by its own author, because of an incorrect phrase with respect to the limitation of the extension of the European Commission's jurisdiction.

In the English proposal of 1866, as well as that of 1871, the extension of the European Commission of the Danube's Jurisdiction was justified, considering the maritime traffic up to Brăila, the port up to which there existed the need to carry out the technical work for improving navigation. While in the 1866 proposal the extension was requested "jusqu'à Brăila," in 1871 the limits of that same jurisdiction were requested "Jusqu'en amont du port de Brăila."[43] Aside from the concentration of cereal exports at Brăila, maritime vessels, with the exception of vessels of small draught, could not navigate upriver from this port. Since Turkey had opposed, in the past, the extension of jurisdiction up to Brăila, it was all the more expected that she — like Austro-Hungary — would not accept the presence of the European Commission upriver of this port. The extension of the European Commission's jurisdiction upriver from the initial one to Isaktcha was interpreted by Turkey as further diminuation of her sovereignty.

In 1855, at Vienna, Turkey had opposed the proposal made in the Prokesch-Osten Memorandum, that the work of improving navigation upriver from Isaktcha to Galatz and Brăila be carred out by the European Commission of the Danube.

Turkey's opposition was due to the fact that the thalweg on the right of the river, between Isaktcha and Brăila (Dobrujan bank), was in 1871 still under her sovereignty. Hajnal stated that Turkey opposed that English proposal because she objected to the United Romanian Principalities participation as riparian states in E.C.D.[44] Such a situation was unlikely inasmuch as in 1871 the Romanian Principalities were not yet independent and the Mouths of the Danube, the center of the technical activity of the E.C.D. was still under Turkish sovereignty.

In this matter, Hajnal had invoked the Convention of December 15, 1866 concerning the Prut River, concluded between Austria, Russia and Romanian Principalities, on the basis of which the latter was a member of the "Commission of the River."[45] He overlooked the fact that this Commission was not like the European Commission, its exact title being the "Mixed Commission of the Prut Tributary of the Lower Danube River." Turkey's position in 1871 was supported by the Austro-Hungarian and the Russian Plenipotentiaries, in exchange for certain concessions. Austro-Hungary needed Turkey's vote in order to obtain the assignment of the works to be done at the Cataracts and the Iron Gates, Russia needed the assurance that Turkey would not oppose the reestablishment of her naval potential on the Black Sea.

Austro-Hungarian opposition to the extension of the European Commission's jurisdiction is also apparent in Beust's statement to Prokesch-Osten that "... nous ne voyons pas de raisons majeures pour étendre en amont d'Isaktcha l'autorité de la Commission Européenne."[46] This contradicted the belief of Prokesch-Osten who, in his Memorandum of 1855 had proposed the extension up to Galatz and Brăila. In 1871, Vienna's Plenipotentiary repeated the same opposition, but due to the fact that the English proposal was connected with an exclusive commercial purpose, he was disposed to accept the extension, conditional to majority approval.[47] Russia's Plenipotentiary opposed the extension in order not to indispose Turkey.[48] France's Plenipotentiary held the same opinion.[49] Faced with this opposition, England's Plenipotentiary withdrew his proposal.

The Clauses of the 1871 Treaty of London Concerning Navigation on the Lower Danube.

On March 13, 1871, the Powers participating in the Conference of London.[50] concluded the Treaty for modification of certain clauses on the 1856 Treaty of Paris.[51]

In Articles 4 to 7, referring to the Danube, the following decisions were made: extension of the European Commission of the Danube mandate to April 24, 1883 (Art. 4); establishment of the eventual functioning of the Riparian Commission in conformity with Article 17 of the 1856 Treaty through a prior agreement among riparian countries (Art. 5); execution of the technical operations for improving navigation at the Iron Gates and the Cataracts by Austria and Turkey, the riparian countries of this sector (Art. 6); neutralization of the operations, the establishments and the vessels of the European Commission of the Danube and the immunity of its administrative and technical foreign personnel; and Turkey's exception to the neutrality regime, she retaining the right, as a territorial Power, for her warships to have access to the Lower Danube (Art. 7).

* * *

In conclusion, from the bargaining and the reciprocal concessions carried on at the 1871 Conference of London, the following results emerged: retention of the international regime of navigation and the possibility of continuing the efficient activity of the European Commission of the Danube; satisfaction for Austro-Hungary, by assigning her to execution of the technical operations at the Cataracts and the Iron Gates; and the immunity of the technical operations of the European Commission of the Danube.

Russia's upsetting of the military balance of the Black Sea had no immediate repercussions on the international regime of navigation on the Maritime Danube.

Chapter 2

NEUTRALIZATION OF THE LOWER DANUBE

Attempts prior to the Russian — Turkish War of 1877-1878.

The first signs of the recurrence of the "Eastern Question" with its repercussions on the "Danube Question," appeared between August 1875 and July 1876, at the time of the revolutions in the Balkans. All the efforts of the signatories of the 1856 Peace Treaty of Paris to eliminate the threats to peace in Southeast Europe were fruitless, Turkey rejecting any measures for easing her treatment of her subjects.

The Russo-Turkish War appeared inevitable, inasmuch as Russia — in opposition to the policy of some signers of the 1856 Treaty to maintain the status quo in the Balkans — "showed no eagerness for any programme of isolated aggression against the Turks."[52]

In such a situation, Romania[53] attempted the neutralization of the Lower Danube, the frontier between her and the Balkans, in order to avoid a conflagration on her territory. From the very beginning, the attempt could not be successful since no previous treaty had provided for neutralization of this sector of the river. Besides maintaining neutralization in case of an eventual Russo-Turkish conflict, the signatories of the 1856 Treaty complacently considered the neutrality of the Lower Danube as one derived from the international regime of navigation. On the other hand, the fact that through Article 7 of the 1871 Treaty of London, Turkey was permitted access for her warships of the Lower Danube, the neutrality was diminished in value.

Romania's attempt was brought on by two critical situations in the case of a Russo-Turkish war which would include the Lower Danube in its conflict. Her state of vassality to Turkey prevented her opposition; siding with Russia, Romania would have risked repeating the past, when her territory was occupied. To get of this impasse, she invoked the regime of autonomy, accorded and guaranteed by the signatories of the 1856 Treaty of Paris, Article 22, strengthened by Article 2 of the 1858 Convention of Paris concluded by those same signatories.

Under the aspect strictly of the Texts of the Articles mentioned above, but not under that of her natural and historic rights, Romania had no authority to undertake any independent action, such as that of neutralization of the Lower Danube, without the consent of Turkey, her suzerain. A legitimate action could have been based on the text of Article 23 of the 1856 Treaty, in which Turkey took the obligation to accord Romania freedom of commerce and navigation, a freedom which would have been hampered if the Lower Danube were included in any operation of war.

On the Lower Danube, a different jurisdictional condition existed. From the Bulgarian-Serbian-Romanian border to the area east of the Romanian port of Giurgiu, the course of the river ran through two jurisdictions: the portion left of the river's course was under the Romanian autonomy regime, under Turkish suzerainty; the portion to the right of the course, the Bulgarian, was under direct sovereignty to Turkey. Under such a distribution, Romania could neutralize only her portion of the course, a measure which would have made impossible the free navigation which was normally carried out along the center line of the water course. (Thalweg).

The situation along the navigational sector for maritime vessels (Brăila-Sulina) was also different. The Sulina Branch, though under the administration of the European Commission, was included in Turkey's sovereignty.

Kogălniceanu, Romania's Foreign Minister, rejected the consideration that both banks of the Lower Danube belonged to one single state (Turkey), maintaining that the neutralization requested by Romania came from their position as a riparian state situated on the left bank.[54] Under the suzerainty regime, however, under which Romania was the juridical status of riparian state depended on Turkey.

The independence of Romania's action in neutralizing the Lower Danube was tied also to her obligations towards Turkey in the event of an outbreak of war.

Article 26 of the 1856 Treaty made provision that "... in union with the Sublime Porte, Wallachia and Moldavia (i.e. Romania) would be called upon to take measures to repel any foreign invasion." This "invasion" was to take place, in the case of the Russo-Turkish War, by Russian and Turkish Armies meeting on the Lower Danube, the sector which could not be neutralized. Thus is explained the fact that the Grand Vizier telegraphed Prince Carol of Romania, two days before the outbreak of the war, asking him, "... let us together with the Imperial Army, take measures to repel the Russian invasion."[55]

In her appeals to the signatories of the 1856 Treaty, to have the neutrality of her territory and of the Lower Danube respected, Romania invoked the precedent with Belgium. In Romania's case, Iorga stated, "... our neutrality was not sanctioned." England declared formally that no Romanian neutrality existed, [56] while France considered Romanian claims to independence, including the neutralization measures, as ill-timed and dangerous.[57]

From the very beginning of the Balkan revolts, Romania maintained a strict neutrality of the Lower Danube. In October 1863, she opposed the stationing of two Austrian war vessels at Turnu Severin, whose crews were violating Romanian territory. At the express request of the Romanian Government that the vessels depart, the Austrian Consul at Bucharest accused Romania of "political disloyalty."[58]

The Romanian Government in March 1876 also opposed the clandestine transport of over 300 Bulgarians, by the Austrian vessel "Radetsky" from the port of Giurgiu to two ports near Serbia.[59]

The expedition of Turkish warships on the Lower Danube to attack Serbia was considered by Romania an actual violation of the neutrality she considered applied.[60]

Following the refusal of the signatories of the 1856 Treaty to recognize the neutrality of Romania and of the Lower Danube, and under pressure from Russia, Romania concluded with Russia the Convention of April 4, 1877 on the basis of which Russian troops could cross the river towards Bulgaria. This Convention could not be considered a voluntary act on Romania's part, but a constrainedly one. "The Russian Army," noted Kogălniceanu, "with the more or less tacit approval of the Great Powers, merely passes through our land. We could not do what Europe does not do."[61]

On April 24, 1877, Russia declared war on Turkey. After Turkish bombardments of the port of Brăila and of other towns along the Romanian shore, Romania acknowledged the state of war and declared her independence on May 10, 1877, and joined her Army to that of Russia.

On May 6, 1877, Austro-Hungary protested to the Russian Government against the hampering of free navigation by military operations, invoking the international regime of navigation, although admitting the absolute neutrality aside from that accorded to the establishments of the European Commission of the Danube.[62] Russia responded that she considered the interruption of navigation as a temporary incident which did not at all prejudice, for the future, the principle of freedom of navigation on the river.[63]

The neutrality of the European Commission was not respected. Russia, by her Ukase of May 12, ordered the departure of the European Commission's Inspector General of Navigation, a Turkish citizen, on the consideration of the "cessation of navigation on the Danube."[64]

The measure was abusive considering the immunity of the Commission personnel as provided for by the 1871 Treaty.

The fact that Russia's action could hamper the traffic of English vessels, as well, determined Buchanan, the Ambassador to Vienna, to ask that the Foreign Office register a protest.[65]

Stokes, England's former Delegate in the European Commission, in his advice in July 1877 stressed that the neutrality provided for in Article 7, of the 1871 Treaty of London, included only the Commission's establishments and personnel, not also the navigable course of the river under Turkish sovereignty, respectively of a state subject to the risks of war with Russia.[66] For that matter, neither did the European Committee meeting at Galatz in November 1877 take any measures in support of freedom of navigation.

England's protest was inconsistent if one considers Buchanan's opinion expressed before Stokes gave his counsel. In a note sent by Buchanan to Andrassy, he acknowledged the exceptional restrictions made by both belligerents recommending that "... those restrictions shall not exceed the limits of absolute necessity, and as soon as the circumstances of the war permit, the belligerent Powers shall come to an understanding with the European Powers to restore the freedom of navigation of the Danube."[67]

Andrassy protested also at the raising of the Turkish flag over the vessels of the European Commission of the Danube, a measure he considered contrary to the neutrality of the Commission's establishment and vessels, in conformity with the Public Act of 1865 and the 1871 Treaty of London, Article 7.

The protest can be considered interpretive, inasmuch as the Commission was not under extraterritoriality, Turkey being sovereign over the Danube Delta. Thus, the April 25, 1877 decision of the Executive Committee of the Commission as to the flying of its own flag,[68] in the aim of neutralization of its vessels, was without basis.

In no Act of the Commission's until that time had there been any provision for raising its own flag and no where was there any indication as to what flag its vessels were to bear. Only after 1878, when, by the Treaty of Berlin, the Commission's independence of any territorial authority was decided (Article 53), was it authorized to fly its own flag.

Under the state of war existing between Russia and Turkey, the legitimacy of the military measures of both belligerents at the Sulina Mouth can be deduced, the former attacking the latter on her own territory and the latter defending territory over which she was sovereign.

In the light of objectivity and of existing documentation, one could not uphold Romania's neutrality before and after the outbreak of the Russo-Turkish War. Concerning the requests addressed by Romania to the Powers guaranteeing her autonomy and to Turkey in support of neutrality, Iorga stated that the requests "... met no good reception. The provocation came from us and, in order to save Brăila and Galatz, we collaborated in the sinking of Turkish warships at a time when we were telling Europe our decision to not get mixed up in any way in the war, or at the most to guarantee the freedom of the Danube."[69].

Under pressure from Russia, Cantacuzino, Romania's Diplomatic Agent to St. Petersburg, recommended that the Romanian Government "close its eyes, if necessary" to the large number of Russians requesting to pass through Romania before the onset of hostilities, many of them without passports.[70]

Aside from Russian pressure on Romania to permit transit of military assistance sent by Russia to Serbia and Bulgaria, there cannot be overlooked also the Romanias' spirit of sympathy and solidarity towards their neighbouring countries' Bulgarian and Serbian struggles for independence, a situation in which they themselves were involved.

The assistance given by Russia and Romania to the Serbian and Bulgarian revolts was regarded by Kogălniceanu as humanitarian and so solidarity with "... the people of the right bank of the Danube, with whom we have so many relationships...," referring also to the horrors taking place in Bulgaria.[71]

According to the report of the Austro-Hungarian Consul at Constantinople, the Bulgarian colony of Brăila was sending money, munitions, etc., to Bulgaria,[72] and in Bucharest a Bulgarian revolutionary committee was active under the leadership of Stambulov.[73]

In conclusion, Romania's attempts to neutralize the Lower Danube had no results, being hindered by the Russo-Turkish strategic war needs as well as by the indifference of the Great Powers.

In R.W. Seton-Watson's opinion, "The Roumanian attitude was very frankly stated in the Circular Note addressed to the Powers: they had "no other aim," it declared, "save to ensure respect for our neutrality. The Great Powers, while invoking the inadequacy of the provisions on this question, and not taking account either the gravity of the situation or of our well grounded perplexity, refused to comply with a demand subsequent events have proved to be only too justified. Their refusal was therefore almost a foregone conclusion, but it completely absolved Roumania, and inevitably drove her straight into the arms of Russia."[74]

His conclusion did not materialize; in 1883 Romania aligned herself with the Triple Alliance (Germany, Austro-Hungary and Italy), a coalition opposed to Russia's tendencies.

Chapter 3

THE CONGRESS AND THE PEACE TREATY OF BERLIN, 1878

Introduction.

Besides establishing the framework of the new politico-geographic order in Southeast Europe, the 1878 Congress of Berlin took certain decisions concerning the Lower Danube. Among the more important were the reappearance of Russia as a riparian state of the river, the extension of the European Commission of the Danube's jurisdiction as far as Galatz, and the inclusion of Romania in that Commission. The 1856 Treaty thus underwent its second modification by these decisions.

The presence of Russia as a border state of the river influenced the status quo of the international regime of navigation, as upheld up to that time, by England and France. France's position being weakened as a result of the 1870 war, the principal roles at the Congress of Berlin were played by England and Germany.

The Austro-Hungarian position was not far removed from that of England. The former succeeded in getting exclusive assignment of the technical works at the Iron Gates and the Cataracts, to the detriment of the rights of the actual riparian states (Romania and Serbia), as well as strengthening her position in the navigation of the Lower Danube, Germany, under apparent neutrality, supported Russia, who — by attempting to change the political structure in the Balkans by the Treaty of San Stefano — aroused the reaction of the other Great Powers, who then censured that treaty by the Congress of Berlin.

If, after the 1877-1878 War, Russia had respected precisely the basis of the 1856 Treaty regarding navigation on the Lower Danube and had taken into consideration Austro-Hungary's and England's interests in the Balkans, the Treaty of San Stefano would not have been censured.

The representatives at San Stefano were not of the caliber of the former Russian Foreign Ministers, who had been of foreign origin[75] and had disciplined the intemperance of the Slavic nature in the negociations. At the signing of this treaty, the diplomats were those of a "... Russie nouvelle, la Russie des Ignatief, des Tchernaïeff, des Fadeïeff, etc. qui avait fait son apparition dans la diplomatie, comme elle venait de la faire dans la stratégie et la tactique militaire." The peace of San Stefano was described as "... une aventure violante... qui secoua Europe de sa torpeur et la Russie dut compter avec elle." This description was in a voluminous, anonymous work that appeared in Paris.[76] Clause 7 of the 1856 Treaty, respecting the territorial integrity of European Turkey, was also violated by the Treaty of San Stefano. The Congress of Berlin, however, instead of pacifying the Balkans, created a situation that in time turned them into the "tinderbox of Europe."

Unlike other gatherings concerning navigation on the Lower Danube, which were characterized by some diplomatic give and take between the participants, it is said that at the Congress of Berlin there was a single dominant voice, that of Bismarck. Emil Ludwig dubbed him "President of Europe"[77] and Somervell assessed his position at the Congress as "his apotheosis."[78] The true evaluation of this "voice" could be that of Bismarck himself. When Gorchacov opposed the partition of Bulgaria, as demanded by England, Disraeli wrote to the Queen: "I shall break up the Congress if England's views are not adopted...."[79] Bismarck's laconic and cynical remark was "Der alte Jude, das ist der Mann.[80]" This evaluation contrasted, however, with Disraeli's concession to reinstate Russia as a riparian to the Danube River, in spite of all the invoking of the initial decision taken in the 1856 Treaty. In other words, if Disraeli's voice had been predominant, Russia could not have become a riparian state again. But, on the agenda for compensations, there were also England's interests which included the Island of Cyprus, a strategic point for the Suez Canal.

It could be said that on the "Danubian Market," relocated at the 1878 Congress of Berlin, a real bargain unfolded under the direction of Bismarck who, in his role of "harmonizing" the interests of all the participants, considered himself "the honest broker." As to the method of carrying out such a function, Bleichroder — the well-known banker in the deficient concession of the Romanian railroads and close

THE PEACE TREATY OF BERLIN, 1878

friend of the Chancellor — stated: "There is no such thing as an honest broker."[81]

With all the defects of the Treaty of San Stefano and of the Congress of Berlin, still some benefits that accrued to the small countries can be pointed out. Serbia and Romania gained independence, the latter entering also into the composition of the European Commission of the Danube, and the Principality of Bulgaria was removed from under the sovereignty of the Ottoman Empire and was placed under its suzerainty. Also, after 1878, Bulgaria, Romania and Serbia, obtained partial satisfaction of their national aspirations in navigation on the Lower Danube. After 1878, their voices also had to be listened to some degree.

The Work of the Congress.

The work of the Congress lasted one month, June 13, to July 13, 1878. The decisions with respect to the Danubian problem and to the participation of the smaller riparian states of the Lower Danube were recorded in three Protocols.[82]

The Problem Concerning the Participation of the Riparians of the Lower Danube (Bulgaria, Romania and Serbia).

The problem of the participation of the riparians of the Lower Danube at the Congress will be analyzed from the aspect of defending their rights in the debates over the decisions to be taken, over navigation in their fluvial sectors.

Although Bulgaria, Romania and Serbia had participated directly in the Russian success in the 1877-1878 war against the Turks, still they were not invited to either the signing of the Treaty of San Stefano or to the Congress of Berlin, mainly because of their lack of political independence.

At San Stefano, independence was considered in a strict interpretation of International Law, while at the Congress of Berlin, it was a subjective and interpretative factor. Consideration of the independence of Romania and Serbia, gained from Russia by the Treaty of San Stefano, was suspended, being dependent upon the decisions of the Congress, which was to make the treaty definite. This situation gave the Great Powers meeting at Berlin the motivation for limiting the rights of those countries to participation on the consultative basis, not on a deliberative one.

Aside from the matter of independence, the limitation of their participation was also aimed at avoiding any eventual obstruction they could create by using their deliberative voters in a way to hinder the possibility of reaching a majority of votes in the decisions the Congress would be taking on the navigation regime on the Lower Danube.

No obstruction was expected from the Bulgaria since she was represented by the Sublime Porte, her sovereign during the time of the Congress deliberations. Aside from what rights Serbia had from her riparian position at a small section of the right bank opposite the Iron Gates and the Cataracts, she had no other rights to protect on the remaining sector of the Lower Danube. Being in the economic and political orbit of Austro-Hungary, Serbia had to rally to the side of Viennese policy. Regarding this, Medlicott noted: "Andrassy advised Ristič in almost threatening language not to oppose Austria's wishes."[83] This is the explanation for the fact that Serbia, under certain circumstances, had to give up solidarity with Romania in navigation matters. The Serbians' position at the Congress was much more favorable than Romanian's. They did not protest against the Treaty of San Stefano, in spite of the incomplete satisfaction of their plaints, and during the Congress, in which they participated with a consultative vote, they showed themselves to be more flexible and modest.

Even before the Congress debates which set her new frontier, Serbia — in exchange for a favorable vote from Vienna — was forced to conclude a Convention with the latter, on July 8, concerning facilitation of transportation on land and on the Danube, including the technical works to be erected by Austro-Hungary at the Iron Gates and the Cataracts.[84]

Also for the protection of those same works, Austro-Hungary had occupied, as early as May 21, 1878 — hence, before the Congress — Adakaleh, the small island to the right of the Iron Gates, on the basis of an agreement with Turkey, which governed it.[85]

The capitals of the Great Powers had been expecting certain difficulties to be raised by Romania, ever since the period of the attempts to neutralize the Lower Danube, at the beginning of the 1877-1878 Russo-Turkish conflict. Romanian opposition to the reannexation of Southern Bassarabia by the Russians, her objections to Vienna's policy of supremacy on the Lower Danube and its exclusivity in carrying out the works at the Iron Gates and the Cataracts, created for Romania a heavy and unpleasant atmosphere among the Great Powers. They were not in agreement of some unilateral actions taken by Romania, which deprived her of the benefit of the guaranty of her political autonomy they had accorded her in 1856 and 1858. The unilateral declaration of her independence in 1877 and her participation on the side of Russia in the war against Turkey, were the main actions held against her. In this respect, Iorga observed "... it was forgotten that the act of independence as well as the tie with Russia and participation in her war, meant exactly the release from that guaranty which also presupposed a trusteeship."[87]

Opinions as to admission to the Congress differed. Salisbury felt that the representatives of a country which asked to keep a region belonging to her (Southern Bessarabia) should be heard. Bismarck opposed, on the consideration that Romania's complaints could disturb the existing entente of the Congress, an opinion also shared by the Plenipotentiaries of Italy, France, Austro-Hungary and Russia.[87]

Of the discussions, at the June 29 session, concerning the admission of the Romanian representatives, Medlicott related that Salisbury "soon woke up from a brief nap, to demand that the Romanians should also be heard."[88]

At the close of the session, Bismarck announced that the Romanian Delegation had been invited to attend on July 1, M. Kogălniceanu, accompanied by Ion Brătianu, read the Romanian Government's Memorandum, the contents of which referred mainly to opposition to the reannexation of Southern Bessarabia and to the allocation to Austro-Hungary of the technical works for the Iron Gates and the Cataracts. Besides her historic and national rights involved, her opposition to the reannexation was considered by Romania also from the aspect of weakening the international regime of navigation. This argument had been especially emphasized in Romania's intercession to Vienna, even before the opening of the Congress. The participation of Romania and Serbia in the Congress, with deliberative vote, would not have been excluded had the former not been opposed to Austro-Hungary's supremacy on the Lower Danube. According to Waddington, Romania being a Danubian state, she entered into the orbit of influence of Austro-Hungary, the great empire and riparian to the river. Objectively appraised and from the point of view of political and economic potential of the parties involved, the opinion was just. Romania's efforts to affirm her position on the Lower Danube were criticized and disparaged by exponents of Vienna. Among them was also Haymerlé, who had a decisive role at the Congress in Danubian problems. Insinuating that Romania intended to establish navigation companies, Haymerlé in 1877 said to the Romanian diplomatic agent at Rome, "qu'un petit état comme la Roumanie doit se tenir dans la réserve et ne pas prendre les devants dans une question épineuse comme celle-ci."[89]

To the cold atmosphere encountered by Romania at the Congress were added two other matters especially exploited by Bismarck. The first was Romania's refusal to compensate the German firm Strousberg; the second was her refusal to accord citizenship en masse and political rights to Jewish refugees from Russia and Poland. In both cases, Romania yielded, in exchange for recognition of her independence, after the signing of the Treaty of Berlin. Medlicott noted that "The Roumanian Government in 1878 found itself in bad odour...[90] and France, England and Austria agreed to continue the process of strangulation until the railway bill was voted,"[91] (for Strousberg firm).

In the end, the Romanian and Serbian representatives were "heard, but not listened to" according to Kogălniceanu.

* * *

Previous mention has been made that the censuring and revision of the Treaty of San Stefano, by the Congress of Berlin, resulted in suspension of its enforcement. In this suspension were included also the according of independence to Romania and Serbia, hence these two countries were still under suzerainty status to Turkey during the period the Congress was in session. Because of this status, the Congress' rejection of the participation of the two countries with deliberative vote, on the consideration that their independence was not confirmed, could, if widely interpreted, fall within the framework of International Law. Official and international recognition of the two countries was to become effective after the end of the Congress' work and after the signing of the Treaty, not during the sessions.

In this matter, even Romania had to respect international order of procedure in a case that developed after World War I. At the request of Poland's representative to Vienna that Poland be recognized officially, the Romanian Minister of Foreign Affairs answered on November 18, 1918 that "the Polish state not being yet recognized, the Romanian Government is not in a position to recognize you as a Charge d'Affaires of the above mentioned state."[92]

Because of her non-participation in the Congress, Romania refused to take into consideration the decisions referring to navigation, the exclusive attribution of the works at the Iron Gates and the Cataracts to Austro-Hungary, and the reannexation of Southern Bessarabia by the Russians.

The procedure employed against the small riparian states in 1878 created precedents which later, under other circumstances, had repercussions on some countries which had denied them deliberative vote. At the 1921 Conference of Paris for the establishment of the Definitive Status of the Danube, Austria, Germany and Hungary, riparian states, were admitted only with consultative vote on the grounds of their ex-enemy status. The same procedure against the same ex-enemy states was applied also at the Danubian Conference at Belgrade of 1948. Besides their status as ex-enemy states, Germany and Austria were not invited on the basis that peace treaties with them had not been concluded after World War II.

The Return of Russia as a Riparian State of the Lower Danube River.
The Standpoints of the other Great Powers.

Russia's return to riparian status on the Lower Danube came by her reannexation of the region of Southern Bessarabia bordering the Kilia Branch, on the basis of the 1878 Treaty of San Stefano.[93]

Reaction against the reannexation came from Disraeli, England's chief delegate to the Congress, expressed at the June 29 session.[94] England's position concerning the reannexation had been made known even before the Congress, in a circular of April 1, 1878. Salisbury, in that circular, vigorously attacked certain stipulations of the Treaty of San Stefano.[95] It is said that the circular, addressed to England's representatives and to the other Great Powers and which was given much publicity, appeared at a moment when an Anglo-Russian war seemed imminent because of Russian intentions to occupy Constantinople. Also, it was noted, as a result of the circular, that Gorchacov: "invita la presse à mettre une sourdine à ses polémiques contre l'Anglettere et rédigea sans tarder, une reponse à la circulaire, empreinté de beaucoup de calme et de modération."[96]

In his written response, to which was attached also a "Pro Mémoire" referring to all the matters brought up by Salisbury, Gorchacov considered the reannexation of Bessarabia as a fact which was merely "... qu' un retour à un ordre des choses modifiées il y avait vingt-deux ans, pour des motifs qui n'ont plus ni raison d'être... depuis que la liberté de la navigation du Danube a été placée sous le contrôle et la garantie d'une Commission internationale...."[97] By this, Gorchacov was referring to the 1856 Treaty of Paris which had removed Russia from the Lower Danube. He justified the reannexation also by the exchange of Dobrujan territory under Turkish domination, on the basis of Article 19 of the San Stefano Treaty. He also let it be understood that because of this exchange the part of Dobruja, including the Mouths of the Danube, were to be retroceded to Romania. Hence, he claimed there was no tie between the reannexation and the freedom of navigation, which would have been carried out under a sovereignty other than that of Russia, i.e. that of Romania.[98]

The exchange of territory between Russia and Turkey could not occur without the consent of the signatories of the 1856 Treaty, who had removed Southern Bessarabia from Russia's sovereignty. In the opinion of these signatories, the exchange was in violation of the 1856 Treaty and had to be sanctioned by them, an action which fell to the Congress of Berlin.

Disraeli's opposition to the reannexation of Southern Bessarabia was based on the violations of the stipulations of Articles 4 and 20, of the 1856 Treaty of Paris. On the basis of those stipulations, the European bloc returned to Russia certain territories which the former had occupied, during the Crimean War, in exchange for Southern Bessarabia, reannexed to the Principality of Moldavia. This had been done with the aim of assuring freedom of navigation on the Danube, a freedom Disraeli did not consider guaranteed by the Treaty of San Stefano.[99]

Shouvalov, Russia's second Plenipotentiary, presented a point of view supplementary to Gorchacov's response to Salisbury's circular. He did not consider the reannexation as contrary to the 1856 Treaty since the Treaty of San Stefano, which had decided it, was only a preliminary convention between Russia and Turkey, not having any obligatory power except between the contracting states. Also, he stated that Russia's intention in attending the Congress was to obtain the sanction of the 1856 signatories,[100] thus leaving the understanding that the definite decision was to be that of the Congress. His argument had been dictated by the new circumstances arisen after the signing of the Treaty of San Stefano. From the April 1, 1879 Salisbury circular, it was revealed that Russia had refused European interference in the Treaty concluded between Russia and Turkey. Hence, Russia's acceptance to attend the Congress of Berlin was brought about by pressure from the London cabinet. Shouvalov stressed that the ceding of Southern Bessarabia, in 1856, was a result of Russia's losing the war, while the reannexation was the result of her winning a different war (1877-1878).[101]

Above all considerations of juridic order which could be interpreted and associated with assuring freedom of navigation, reannexation of Southern Bessarabia was regarded by Shouvalov also in the light of national sentiment. "La question Bessarabie," he declared, "pouvait être envisagée par la Russie comme une question d'ambition et d'intérêt, où comme une question d'honneur."[102] He disclosed the fact that Russia "...ne redemande pas la partie du territoire dont la possession aurait pu constituer une ménace où du moins une ingérence dans la libre navigation du fleuve."[103] In this he was referring to the Dobrujan territory, including the Delta of the river which, according to paragraph "A" of Article 19 of the Treaty of San Stefano, Russia obtained from Turkey after the war and which she intended to cede to Romania in exchange for Southern Bessarabia. Through this exchange, he saw no loss for Romania to whom, in his opinion, Russia was offering "... en retour, à la Roumanie, un territoire plus vaste, conquis au prix de son sang, et qui doit être consideré comme de bonne prise." Gorchacov added, "... qu'il n'y a aucun traité conclus par la Russie avec la Turquie, depuis un siècle, qui ne contienne des stipulations favorables aux Roumains" and expressed his regrets that "... en rendant service à un ami, on le transforme en adversaire."[104]

To this just statement can be added the common spilling of the blood of Romanians and Russians when their armies, under the command of Prince Carol of Romania, put an end to the Russo-Turkish War by destroying Turkish resistence at Plevna (Bulgaria), a fact recorded by foreign correspondents from the battlefronts.[105] A French journalist was an eye witness of this contribution and the Russian General Totleben acknowledged the contribution of the Romanian Army to saving the situation at Plevna.[106] But "dans ses malheurs, un petit pays n'a vis-à-vis des Grands Etats qu'un seul refuge, celui de s'enfermer dans sa dignité,"[107] noted Kogălniceanu.

Gorchacov also showed that Romania had gained its independence "à la suite de la guerre à laquelle elle a pris part," (1878).[108] Even more, he evaluated numerically the increase in Romanian territory due to the exchange of land between Russia and Turkey.[109]

In rejecting the incrimination of having violated the 1856 Treaty, Gorchacov invoked precedents which, by modification and even annulment of this treaty, freed Russia of the obligation taken. He maintained that by the retroceding of the Danube Delta to Ottoman sovereignty in 1857, instead of its being annexed to Moldavia, the stipulations of Articles 4 and 20 of the 1856 Treaty were modified. He also considered the 1856 Treaty rendered expired and inapplicable both by the 1859 Union of the two Principalities, Moldavia and Wallachia, which in 1856 were considered to be separate, and by the election of a foreign prince, actions he considered contrary to that same Treaty.[110]

Both considerations might have been valid had the cases mentioned by him not received the sanction of the signatories of the 1856 Treaty, including that of Russia.[111] They had not been declared unilaterally, as Russia had proceeded in the case of Southern Bessarabia. Gorchacov's point of view that the 1856 Treaty had expired also reflected the statements made by the Tsar and the Russian Premier to the Romanian envoy to St. Petersburg, to the effect that "...il ne reste plus rien du Traité de 1856...et il n'est pas juste que la Russie seulement le respecte à son détriment."[112]

This point of view had a basis, to an extent, if one considered the modification made by the 1871 Conference of London sanctioning of Russia's protests against the clauses referring to the demilitarization of the Black Sea. Although the signatories sanctioned the modification of the 1856 Treaty, that did not imply its annulment.

As to the consequences of the vaccilating positions, in 1878, of the other signers of the 1856 Treaty, Aarif-Pasha, Foreign Minister of Turkey, stated in a note to the Great Powers that, "... in 1871, one point of the Treaty disappeared, now a second was falling; soon nothing would remain of the entire document and the time will come when you will realize what ruin the disappearance of the Treaty of Paris will bring upon the world."[113] His statement was confirmed by the political events which followed.

Leaving aside the propagandistic motive of freeing Christian people from the Turks, the Russo-Turkish War of 1877-1878 could be regarded from another aspect invoked by Russia. Referring to "une question d'honneur" invoked by Shouvalov in the matter of the reannexation — arguments also endorsed by Bismarck — was not just a passing remark nor intended just to get the compassion of the other Great Powers. Aside from Russia's political aims, Tsar Alexander

II sought to revenge the humiliation brought by the Crimean War just at the moment he had taken over the Russian throne on the death of his father, Nicholas I. His victorious position over the Turks in 1878 offered him the opportunity to carry out that revenge. This also explains the insistence of Grand Duke Nicholas that the Treaty of San Stefano be concluded on March 3, the date of birth of Tsar Nicolas I.

Besides, Russia — just as Austro-Hungary — considered herself entitled to acquire territories of European Turkey. In this matter, Bismarck sustained the annexation of Southern Bessarabia, declaring at the February 19, 1878 session of the Reichstag that "... if Russia could not obtain the acquiescence of the other signatories of the 1856 Treaty, she had to be content with the idea of " 'beati possidentes' ";[114] in the case of Bessarabia, Russia should keep what she took.

Although the intention to reannex Southern Bessarabia was public knowledge, still certain official Russian organs pro forma denied existence of any annexation in Russian policy. "Toute augmentation de territoire," stated the chief of the Asian Department of Russia, "ne pourrait qu'être fatale à l'Empire. Aucun Gouvernement n'oserait en assumer la responsabilité. Pour ce qui est la Roumanie, elle a toujours été de la part de Russie l'objet d'une bienveillance désintéressée."[115] The reannexation of Bessarabia contradicted his declaration.

Through the secret Austro-Russian Convention of Budapest, concluded January 15, 1877, Russia assured herself of Vienna's accord in the matter of the reannexation.[116]

Disraeli's protest in the Southern Bessarabian matter was mostly a formality, "a comedy rehearsed in private," as Joseph Chamberlain put it.[117] Gladstone accused the British Government of "selling Bessarabia liberty to Russia."[118] Disraeli consolation to Romania's two representatives at the Congress who had protested against the reannexation, was "... in politics, ingratitude is often the price of the best services."[119]

Of that same protest, R.W. Seton-Watson wrote; "It is impossible to read the Premier's Congress speech — in which he treated the cession of Bessarabia as an interference with the Treaty of 1856 and as affecting an engagement taken towards Europe respecting the freedom of Danubian navigation — without marvelling at his assurance in hoodwinking the British public as to the perfectly concret pledges which he himself had already given to Russia."[120]

In view of the prearrangement between England and Russia, Disraeli's protest was really a "comedy." In the Secret Accord of London and the Memorandum on May 30, 1878, were outlined the specific points on which the Governments of England and of Russia had reached an understanding with respect to the questions raised by the Treaty of San Stefano. By this accord, England also took the obligation not to contest the decision in this respect[121] (the reannexation of Southern Bessarabia).

As to navigation on the Danube, mention is made at point D. of the Annex of the Accord, that "sans toucher à la question territoriale, le Gouvernement britanique se réserve de discuter les questions de navigation du Danube, ce à quoi l'Angleterre a des droits par des traités."

Medlicott wrote that the British delegates in the Congress "were quite indifferent to the rights and wrongs of the Roumanians, but were very much concerned with the possible effects of the settlement of the freedom of the Danube."[122]

If the position of England's representatives towards the Romanians was as Medlicott described it, the freedom of the Danube would have been served much better had those very representatives been defending it against the danger of Russia's presence as a riparian state to the river. If England had taken in 1878 the same strong position she had adopted in the past, the political balance at the Mouths of the Danube would have remained unchanged.

In 1856, in the Bolgrad case,[123] when Russia could barely bathe in Yalpuc Lake, whose waters ran into the Kilia Branch through a miniscule canal, England threatened a resumption of hostilities to remove Russia from the Danube. Yet, in 1878, Disraeli declared that he would not resort to force in the reannexation of Southern Bessarabia, although by that act Russia became a very real riparian state, by the direct contact with the Kilia Branch and the rest of the Danube.[124]

How real could Disraeli's protest have been when Vienna, whose policy in Lower Danube navigation and other matters was associated with that of London, had already concluded on March 18, 1877, with St. Petersburg, the Secret Convention by which, in exchange for her neutrality, Russia offered Austria Bosnia and Herzegovina, and Austro-Hungary agreed to her reannexation of Southern Bessarabia?

The problem of the reannexation of Southern Bessarabia, as well as other clauses in the San Stefano Treaty which hurt England's policy in Southeast Europe, were resolved through compromises and yieldings of positions, in the Secret Memorandum of May 30, 1878. Among other things, Russia renounced the creation of Greater Bulgaria, decided by the Treaty of San Stefano, in exchange for England's promise not to oppose the reannexation of Bessarabia.

THE PEACE TREATY OF BERLIN, 1878

Even before the "censure" of the Treaty of San Stefano, the Foreign Office, on January 29, 1878, raised the problem of the "intangibility" of European treaties, meaning the obligations assumed by the signatories of the 1856 Treaty of Paris.[125] In the case of the Russo-Turkish Armistice and then of the Treaty of San Stefano, the clause of Article 7 of the Treaty of 1856, by which its signatories — including Russia — had guaranteed the territorial integrity and the independence of the Ottoman Empire was ignored.

Furthermore, on April 15, 1856, Austria, England and France had concluded a treaty guaranteeing the independence and territorial integrity of the Ottoman Empire. With respect to the same integrity, in 1855 in the British Parliament, it had been declared that an eventual independence of the Romanian Principalities "would be the first step towards a dismemberment of the Turkish Empire."[126]

Turkey expected the intervention of the Great Powers to fulfill the obligations assumed in Article 7 of the 1856 Treaty, but her request received no answer, being considered as lacking in precise bases for negotiations. Austro-Hungary pointed out that she did not consider herself a guarantor.[127]

Aside from any Romanian national considerations or from the stipulations of Articles 4 and 20 of the 1856 Treaty, the reannexation of Southern Bessarabia also signified the stripping of the Ottoman Empire of its suzerainty over that territory.

In the last analysis, England's position towards the censuring of the Treaty of San Stefano was determined by the change in the political balance of Southeast Europe, brought about by the assault on the integrity of the Ottoman Empire. Disraeli's concept differed. For him, "integrity of the Turkish Empire was a phrase worth preserving in the official programme of the Government, for consistency is universally esteemed a virtue, but the term 'integrity' would need to be defined afresh, and with considerable subtlety. 'Integrity' would come to mean Constantinople, together with such environs as were strategically...."[128]

The occupation of the Island of Cyprus, on the basis of the Anglo-Turkish Convention of June 4, 1878, also attacked the integrity of the Ottoman Empire, but when Disraeli's policy was denounced as being selfish, he accepted the challenge: "Yes," he said, "as selfish as patriotism,"[129].

As for assuring navigation on the Danube, as indicated by Disraeli, Chancellor Bismarck did not see any connection between that and the reannexation of Southern Bessarabia. According to him, the Treaty of 1856 "... eût été plus solide si l'on eût écarté cette question d'amour propre, cette diminution de territoire qui, d'ailleurs, n'affectait en rien la force d'un si grand Empire."[130]

Bismarck's rather sentimental remark in Russia's favor recalls that of Napoleon III, on the occasion of the delimitation of that same frontier at Bolgrad, after the 1856 Conference. Although in both cases that motive was to show an understanding of Russian complaints, the results differed. Napoleon III's intervention in the Bolgrad case was fruitless because of England's strong opposition, while Bismarck's in the Southern Bessarabia case, succeeded; this time, because of London's political oscillations.

In 1856, the disagreement between England, Austria, and France, in the matter of the Romanian Principalities and the Bolgrad case, "... became an issue," as Riker noted, "on which the Concert of Europe was in danger of falling to pieces," in 1878 — in the Bessarabia question — Bismarck stated that "il craint que le Congrès, en se refusant à satisfaire a un sentiment historique de la Russie, n'atténue les chances de durée de son oeuvre."[131]

Bismarck's thinking could be included in the general description made by Turkey's chief Plenipotentiary, Carathéodory, of the Chancellor's behavior at the Congress, with outbursts and lies aimed at concealing the web of an ingeniously combined intrigue.[132]

Bismarck succeeded in dissatisfying all the participants, even the Russians towards whom he had an obligation, in return for their neutrality during the Franco-German War of 1870, in addition to the many family relationships between the Courts of Berlin and St. Petersburg.[133]

The assistance given to the Russians in 1878, on their return to the banks of the Danube, had negative consequences later on, on Germany's political expansion, a factor Bismarck had not foreseen. His ability as an "honest broker" did not escape the attention of the other members of the Congress. His statement to the effect that "l'Allemagne n'est liée par aucun intérêt direct dans les affaires d'Orient..."[134] was contested by Disraeli[135] and by the Turkish Plenipotentiary.[136]

Carathéodory wrote of Bismarck that he "sut asservir le monde civilisé à ses intrigues et à ses dessins."[137] As to his impartiality, the former remarked, "... il n'a qu'une médiocre estime pour le gouvernement ottomane et pour sa politique."[138]

Although Bismarck had stated sometime that his interests in the East were not worth "les os d'un pomeranien," still, when he realized the effects of an eventual European conflagration on the future of

Germany, he intervened with the Russians to renounce certain fruits of the Treaty of San Stefano.[139]

Upon Salisbury's revelation of England's interests in the Lower Danube navigation, Bismarck found the moment to deny the existence of a "fictitious" opinion that considered the Danube as an artery of German commerce in the Near East, affirming that the Empire's vessels upriver from Ratisbon did not descend down river towards the Black Sea.[140] The statistics disproved his statement. The traffic was reduced, but did exist.[141]

Austro-Hungary remained as though neutral in the Anglo-Russian confrontation. In the Protocol of the June 29 session, when the reannexation of Southern Bessarabia was being discussed, there is no record of the Austro-Hungarian Plenipotentiary having taken the floor. "Il est remarquable," it was said, "que les Plénipotentiaires autrichiens, si directement intéressés dans cette question du Danube, n'avaient pas soufflé mot dans cette discussion."[142] The silence was due to the prior arrangements between St. Petersburg and Vienna, as mentioned earlier.

It is difficult to understand that, faced with the precarious situation existing at Sulina, Austro-Hungary paid no attention, in the Secret Convention of Budapest (March 18, 1877) to Russia's approach to the Mouths of the Danube. This reasoning was based on the fact that in July 1877, i.e. almost five months after the signing of the Convention, the Vienna Government was sure that the Danube Delta would be annexed to Romania, not to Russia. After a meeting with Andrassy, on July 8, Bălăceanu, Romania's Diplomatic Agent at Vienna, reported to Bucharest that "...l'Empereur et Comte Andrassy sont disposés à nous faire donner à la prochaine paix une partie de la Dobruja,"[143] In which was included the Danube Delta.

This statement could not have been made had its objective not been included in the Viennese prior arrangement with St. Petersburg. The Mouths of the Danube, in the hands of a small country like Romania, were considered more secure for Austro-Hungarian navigation than in Russian hands.

As to supporting Romania in the case of the Dobrujan question — i.e. as to her presence at the Mouths of the Danube, — the Romanian Diplomatic Agent from Vienna reported to the Government at Bucharest that "... cette attitude constitue un véritable revirement pour la politique étrangère de l'Autriche."[144] As will be shown further, the Vienna Government also proposed that Romania be admitted as a member in the European Commission of the Danube.

Still in the interests of her own navigation, Austro-Hungary supported Romania's position also in the problem of Silistra, a port and strategic point on the Dobruja shore of the Danube, which after 1878 became a disputed object for the Commission for delimiting the new Romanian-Bulgarian frontier in Dobruja. Finally, the Silistra problem was resolved in favor of Romania, following the Russo-Austrian negociations at Vienna.[145]

It could be concluded that the discussions among the Great Powers in the matter of the reannexation of Southern Bessarabia, that is, the return of Russia to the Danube, were in vain. Bismarck proposed, pro forma, and approved by the other delegates, the postponement of the debates on the reannexation problem until the Romanian Delegation was to be heard.[146] Faced with an accomplished fact, however, the debates were futile, the annexation having been decided in beforehand.

According to R.W. Seton-Watson, the reannexation of Southern Bessarabia was purely and simply " ...an invaluable object of barter"[147] in the oscillation of the scale of compensations and compromises between England, Austro-Hungary and Russia, to the detriment of Turkey, Romania and the international regime of navigation.

In spite of their victorious status in the war with Turkey and of Bismarck's support, the Russians displayed some reticence during the Congress and also towards the Romanians, their allies. From the correspondence of Ghika, Romania's special envoy to St. Petersburg, it appears that, even two months before the signing of the Treaty of San Stefano, the Russians intended to compensate Romania for the loss of Southern Bessarabia by ceding to her a part of Dobruja.[148]

Thus is explained the Russian intention is reserving — in the clause of Article 19 of the Treaty of San Stefano — the possibility of exchanging Turkish territory in Dobruja, including the Danube Delta, for the three counties in Southern Bessarabia. Iorga noted that after the publication of the Treaty of San Stefano, Prince Carol of Romania "... found the Russians much more inclined to maintain an attitude which they never should have forsaken" and that "...even a sort of diffidence is apparent in Russian diplomacy in what before had been expressed brutally. The Russians were avoiding military conflict with us; this is certain today, according to documents we have at hand."[149]

The Congress of Berlin, in Article 45 of the Treaty of Berlin, assigned the three riparian regions of Southern Bessarabia, on the Lower Danube to Russia, thus abrogating Articles 4 and 20 of the 1856 Treaty of Paris, already declared unilaterally by Russia in the Treaty of San Stefano. It received the collective consent of

THE PEACE TREATY OF BERLIN, 1878   355

the signatories of the 1856 Treaty of Paris present at the 1878 Congress.

Debates on some Clauses of the Treaty of San Stefano Concerning Navigation on the Lower Danube.

The debates held within the framework of the Congress of Berlin, concerning certain clauses of the Treaty of San Stefano, resulted in advantages for all interested parties.

Aside from the new navigation structure, Austro-Hungary was successful in the matter of the Regulations for Navigation, Police and Supervision between the Iron Gates and Galatz, and getting the exclusive assignment for the works of improving conditions at the Iron Gates and the Cataracts. The European Commission also was given the right to draw up those regulations.

England obtained the extension of the jurisdiction of the European Commission as far as Galatz, completely independent of territorial authority.

Russia, besides gaining her position was a riparian of the Danube, staked her claims by removing the Kilia Branch from the jurisdiction of the European Commission; Romania became a member of the European Commission, while Austro-Hungary, England, and France upheld and extended the existence of the European Commission.

Paragraph 2 of Article 12 of the Treaty of San Stefano provided that "... les droits, obligations et prérogatives de la Commission Internationale du Bas-Danube sont maintenus intacts."[150] So much and no more. In the haste to conclude the Treaty, the text of this paragraph contained some minor errors.[151]

In the July 2 session, Haymerlé, from the Austro-Hungarian delegation, presented the Project for a new editing and development of Article 12, the contents, of which were the following:[152]

1.) Neutralization of the Lower Danube between the Iron Gates and the Black Sea, including the banks of this sector and the two large islands in the Delta and the Island of the Serpents; destruction of the fortresses and the prohibition of large warships on that sector; the maintenance of light warships, of each member state in the European Commission, at the Mouths of the Danube;

2.) Prolongation of the existence of the European Commission of the Danube and extension of its jurisdiction as far as Galatz, independent of any territorial authority; immunity for its personnel; and the inclusion of Romania in the Commission;

3.) Bringing the Regulations for Navigation and Police, down river from the Iron Gates, in harmony with that applied by the European Commission down river from Galatz;

4.) Assigning the works for improving navigation at the Iron Gates and the Cataracts exclusively to Austro-Hungary.

It must be noted that the basis for the Haymerlé Project had been established at a meeting of the Viennese Government in April 25, 1878.[153] Concerning these proposals, Hajnal noted that they "... provoquèrent par le nombre et la variété des sujets qu'ils contenaient, une consternation générale parmi les Plénipotentiaires."[154]

In spite of previous understanding between London and Vienna, over common attitudes to be taken at the Congress, and of the prior knowledge of the Project by the Foreign Office, the first to express consternation was Salisbury. Although in accord with the general principles of the Project, he pointed out that its text constituted an entire legislation, which would be outside the agenda of the Congress, thus suggesting its being discussed in a separate meeting.

Bismarck, associating himself with this observation, added that the task of the Congress being to "accept, reject, or modify" the Articles of the Treaty of San Stefano, the details of the Project were superfluous. In spite of all this, all the points of the Project were taken up in discussion.

In the end, the President and Russia's second representative proposed that the Project be assigned either to a restricted committee or to the Austro-Hungarian delegation to extract its principles.[155]

At the next session, Shouvalov presented a Counter-Project drawn up by Oubril. This also consisted of four points which, basically were nothing other than a partial addition to Article 12 of the Treaty of San Stefano. The Counter-Project, in brief, contained:[156] keeping the principles of the 1815 Act of Vienna on Lower Danube navigation, as applied by the 1856 and 1871 treaties; destruction of fortifications and limiting access of heavy warships up to Galatz; retaining the European Commission of the Danube and putting the Public Act of 1865 in accord with the new circumstances following the war of 1877-1878.

Although Bismarck considered that there was no difference between the Austro-Hungarian Project and the Russian Counter-Project, he opposed them, invoking the multitude of new measures and norms required by the modification and the improvement of the navigation regime. In his opinion, all these had to be submitted to the approval of the Congress. The President proposed the formation of a restricted

THE PEACE TREATY OF BERLIN, 1878 357

Committee made up of Waddington and Saint Vallier (France), to get together with the authors of both projects, and eliminate the differences between the two and to reach a compromise.

Following are reproduced in résumé and in the order of the debates, the examination of the proposals and counter-proposals of the two Projects.

A.) The maintaining and extension of European Commission competence to Galatz in complete independence of the territorial authority and inclusion of Romania in the same Commission.

It was shown that through paragraph 2 of Article 12 of the San Stefano Treaty, provision was made only for the maintenance of the attributes of the European Commission, with no indication of its prolongation. In the Haymerlé Project, provision was made to extend it to 1883, the term fixed by the 1871 Treaty of London, with the possibility of prolongation.

Reaching an accord, the following formula was established which became an integral part of Article 54 of the 1878 Treaty: "Une année avant l'expiration du terme assigné à la durée de la Commission Européenne, les Puissances se mettront d'accord sur les modifications qu'elles jugeraient nécessaires d'y introduire."

Attention is called to the word "les modifications qu'elles jugeraient nécessaires d'y introduire," an equivocal clause which was to be invoked by Russia in 1883, in support of detaching the Kilia Branch from the jurisdiction of the European Commission.

The Committee agreed, and the Congress approved the Haymerlé proposal to extend the jurisdiction of the European Commission to the port of Galatz and to include Romania as a member, since it was now a sovereign state at the Mouths of the Danube as a result of its being ceded the province of Dobruja. Both decisions were included in Article 53 of the 1878 Treaty. The extension of the European Commission's jurisdiction to Galatz was one point in the partial satisfaction of England's demands, although she has asked for extension to Brăila. This she was to obtain in 1883.

The independence accorded to the Commission was a consequence of the elimination of Turkey from the Mouths of the Danube by the loss of the province of Dobruja. It also avoided interference on the part of Romania, newly independent and sovereign over the Danube Delta.

B.) The Problem of Neutralization of the Lower Danube.

Neutralization of the entire sector of the Lower Danube, as provided in point 1 of the Austro-Hungarian Project, was not acceptable to the Russian Delegation. Shouvalov asked, "... quelle en serait l'étendue et dans quel but cette mésure est elle demandée?"[157]

Shouvalov's question is related to the fact that Russia, being a riparian on the Kilia Branch, sought freedom of action on that branch, as well as on the entire sector of the Lower Danube, especially at the river mouths. Application of neutralization on the islands in the Delta, with their shores, would have meant including also the Kilia Branch, which Russia intended to remove from the jurisdiction of the European Commission.

Salisbury reacted to Shouvalov's question declaring that "la Russie étant désormais riveraine du Danube, un élément nouveau se trouve introduit dans les questions qui touchent à la navigation du fleuve..." stressing that "... des dispositions spéciales sont nécessaires au commerce..."[158], that is, a regime of neutrality for facilitation of commercial activity, also in case of war. This statement was in connection with the difficulties experienced by the commercial activities of neutral countries during the Russo-Turkish War of 1877-1878.

As for Austro-Hungary, she displayed a flagrant contradiction of her past position when Andrassy, in 1871, had opposed neutralization of the river. Actually, the past opposition on the part of Austro-Hungary and Russia explains the neutralization in 1871 of only the technical works and establishments of the European Commission of the Danube, and not the fluvial sector under its jurisdiction.

The proposal for neutralization, not being accepted by the Congress, was not provided for in the Treaty of 1878.

C.) The Problem of Harmonizing the Regulation for Navigation and Police between the Iron Gates and Galatz with those of the European Commission Effective Downstream of Galatz.

The Russian representative in the Committee for studying the Austro-Hungarian and the Russian Projects was opposed to bringing the Regulations for Navigation and Police downriver from the Iron Gates into accord with those of the European Commission downriver from Galatz, as proposed by Haymerlé, considering them to be prejudicial for the riparian states. In addition to that was the control the

European Commission would have over the application of future regulations. He proposed, in exchange, bringing the Public Act of 1865 in accordance with the new political situation created after the Russo-Turkish War of 1877-1878, and the collaboration of the countries of the Lower Danube.

Reaching a compromise between the Austro-Hungarian point of view and the Russian one, the Congress decided that the Regulations for Navigation and Police on the Iron Gates — Galatz sector be worked out by the European Commission, with the assistance of the three states riparian to the Lower Danube, Bulgaria, Romania and Serbia. The decision was included in Article 55 of the 1878 Treaty.

D.) The Entrusting of Austro-Hungary with the Removal of Obstacles at the Cataracts and the Iron Gates.

Since the Congress approved point 4 of the Haymerlé Project, with regard to assigning the execution of the technical works for improving navigation at the Iron Gates and the Cataracts it was inserted in Article 57 of the 1878 Treaty of Berlin, which had assigned the work to Austro-Hungary and Turkey. This modification made apparent Russia's deviation from her position of supporting the small riparian states. She supported Austro-Hungary as the exclusive executant, without the participation of Romania and Serbia, riparians to the Iron Gates and the Cataracts.

Vienna's success was the final result of a protracted activity which wrote important chapters in the history of the breaking up of the natural obstacles at these two important navigation points.

Aside from these considerations the mandate given to Austro-Hungary can be evaluated from two aspects. The first aspect were the wishes of England and France to satisfy Vienna's grievances regarding the obstacles at the Iron Gates and Cataracts which strangulated the Austro-Hungary navigation to the Lower Danube River towards Black Sea, especially after the introduction of the steamship. The second aspect, and probably the more important, was that of the technical and financial possibilities necessary for carrying out the works involved, which Romania and Serbia could not afford at that time.

Article 57 also obligated Romania and Serbia to accord all facilities necessary to carry out the work on the two shores beyond the Austro-Hungarian frontier. This decision suspended the sovereignty of these two riparian states over the portion of the river banks from the Iron Gates to the Cataracts.

The strongest opposition to the exclusive assignment to Austro-Hungary to carry out the works came from Romania. Among the reasons for her opposition was the fact that Austro-Hungary was not a riparian at those two points and that Hungary was assigned to administrating them. Later, the opposition also included the discriminatory taxation levied by the Hungarian Administration on traffic through the Iron Gates.

Clauses of the Treaty of Berlin concerning Navigation on the Lower Danube.

The Treaty of Berlin was concluded on July 13, 1878, between the signatory states of the 1856 Treaty of Paris (Austro-Hungary, England, France, Italy, Germany, Russia and Turkey). It included only six Articles referring to the Lower Danube, namely[159] (in resumé):

Article 52. Acknowledgement of freedom of navigation on the Danube as being in the interests of Europe; destruction of all the fortresses and fortifications between the Iron Gates and the Mouths of the Danube; banning of naval vessels downriver from the Iron Gates, with the exception of light warships of the member states of the European Commission stationed at the mouths of the Danube, with right of access as far as Galatz.

Article 53. Jurisdiction of the European Commission up to Galatz, with complete independence of territorial authority; inclusion of Romania as a member of the Commission;

Article 54. Agreement of the signatory Powers on the extension of the mandate of the European Commission and on eventual future modifications.

Article 55. The drawing up by the European Commission, of the Regulations for Navigation and Police and Supervision between the Iron Gates and Galatz, with the assistance of the delegates of the riparian states, and harmonizing them with the Regulations of the European Commission downriver from Galatz.

Article 56. Assignment of maintenance of the lighthouse on Serpents Island to the European Commission.

Article 57. Execution of Austro-Hungary of the technical works at the Iron Gates and the Cataracts and application of the navigation taxes for the financing of the works. Obligation of the two riprian states (Romania and Serbia) to facilitate the execution of the assignments.

Chapter 4

THE EFFECTS OF THE TREATY OF BERLIN

Reorganization of the European Commission of the Danube (E.C.D.)

Reorganization of the European Commission of the Danube was the result of its juridico-administrative structure being put in accord with the new powers bestowed upon the Commission by the Treaty of 1878: the geographic extension of its competence as far as Galatz and its functioning with complete independence of territorial authority.

The reorganization plans were worked out at the E.C.D. headquarters in Galatz, the projects being: the Regulation for setting the work schedules, the Regulation for Navigation and Police between Galatz and the Mouths of the Danube, and special instructions concerning the attributes of the Navigation Inspector and of the Port Captain of Sulina.

The Regulation for setting the work schedule, drawn up on November 10, 1879, included the attributes of the president, the functioning of the regular and the extraordinary sessions of the E.C.D., the establishment of an Executive Committee, the organization of the Accounting Administration, etc.[160]

The Regulations for Navigation and Police was applied on the Maritime Danube, between the Port of Galatz and the mouths of the river. The work of this Act, started in 1879 was terminated in 1881, the Regulation being effective as of May 19, 1881.[161] The Regulation was augmented by that of November 10, 1911.

Instructions concerning the attributes of the Navigation Inspector and those of the Port Captain of Sulina modified the intial instructions of Article 9 of the Public Act of November 2, 1865, the latter having been further developed in the 1881 Additional Act to the Act of 1865. As will be seen, Romania opposed the assigning of the Port Captain by the European Commission.

The legislative basis for the European Commission of the Danube exercise of its powers remained, from the beginning, the Public Act of November 2, 1865, supplemented by the Additional Act of 1881. The redacting of the 1881 Additional Act was a lengthy procedure (November 5, 1878 to May 28, 1881), over twenty protocols and Procèse-Verbaux being drawn up.[162] The causes for the delay were the agitated debates over the projects and counter-projects for the new Act, as well as Russian and Romanian opposition. The signing of the Act was also delayed because of the "diplomatic absences" of the delegates.[163]

In the Public Act of 1865, the clauses of the 1856 Treaty of Paris were developed so as to legitimize the powers of the European Commission; through the Additional Act of 1881, the new decisions in Articles 45, 46, 47, 52 and 56 of the 1878 Treaty were to be applied and tied in with the proposal at point 4 of the Russian counter-proposal to the Austro-Hungarian Project presented to the Congress. In accordance with the counter-proposal presented at the July 4th session of the Congress, it was proposed that the Public Act of 1865 be revised in order to be put in harmony with the actual circumstances, i.e., those resulting from the Articles mentioned earlier from the 1878 Treaty.

The controversial themes debated within the frame work of the European Commission of the Danube, over the Additional Act, were the Commission's independence of territorial authority, the appointment and attributes of the Port Captain of Sulina, the jurisdiction of the E.C.D. over the Kilia Branch, and the pilot tax on that branch.

At the February 25, 1879 session, Haymerlé (Austro-Hungary) presented to the Executive Committee of the E.C.D. an Additional Act Project, the basis of which referred to the Commission's complete independence of territorial authority, in accordance with Article 53 of the 1878 Treaty and the expressed confirmation of its rights and obligations.[164]

Immediately after the reading of the Project, the Russian Delegate reacted against the proposed independence of the E.C.D., stating, "...le project actuel parait vouloir donner à ce mot une extension que rien ne légitime." In his opinion, the independence of the Commission should refer to everything concerning its own internal administration, but not to navigation proper. He refused to participate in the discussion of the Project because it surpassed the limit of the rights assigned to the European Commission by the Treaties of Paris, 1856, and of Berlin, 1878. He believed that the revision of the Public Act of 1856 and the preparation of the Additional Act should be made by the representatives of the signatory states of the Treaties of 1856 and 1878, not by their Delegates in the European Commission. The problem was seen to be in the differentiation between the authority of Plenipotentiary versus that of Delegate. His point of view was well founded inasmuch as the Public Act if 1865, drawn up by the Delegates of the E.C.D., had received executory powers only after it was sanctioned by the 1866 Conference of the Plenipotentiaries of the signatory states of the 1856 Treaty.

The proposals in Articles 4 and 5 of the Austro-Hungarian Project presented to the E.C.D. were the real motives for the Russian Delegate's opposition; the proposals in which it was specified that Russia and Romania were to assist the Commission in the technical works which the latter would be carrying out on the Kilia Branch, the banks of which belonged to the two countries. Here appears, indirectly, Russia's attempt to contest the Commission's jurisdiction over the Kilia Branch.

The Russian Delegate opposed the presence of the E.C.D. on the left bank of the Kilia Branch and the Stary-Stamboul sub-branch, both being under Russia's sovereignty through her annexation of Southern Bessarabia. Yet, he considered the European Commission's jurisdiction over the Romanian bank of the Kilia legitimate, being derived from the clause of Article 53 of the 1878 Treaty, in reference to the E.C.D.'s independence of Romania's territorial authority, but not of Russia's.

Aside from the exclusion of the Commission's independence on the right bank of the Kilia, the Romanian Delegate opposed the appointment of the Port Captain of Sulina by the Commission, on the basis that this function depended upon the territorial authority, an authority which, however, was deleted from the text of Article 53 of the 1878 Treaty.

Following the objections of the Russian Delegate, the debates were postponed. In the interim, the French Delegate addressed a Note to the other Delegates proposing another Project for the Additional Act.[165]

The debates were resumed on May 17, 1879, at which time the French Project was examined. Its ten Articles made provision for the Commission's independence of territorial authority and for the appointment of the Port Captain of Sulina by the E.C.D. Finally, by eliminating Articles 4 and 5 of the Austro-Hungarian Project, the objections of the Russian Delegate were satisfied and resolved by a Conference of Ambassadors at Constantinople.

France's Delegate proposed an amendment to his Project leaving the appointment of the Navigation Inspector and the Port Captain of the Sulina to the territorial state (Romania), not to the European Commission. The Amendment failed to receive the majority of votes.

Since a consensus was not reached the debates were again postponed to the Fall Session of the European Commission, when the French Delegates Project would be taken up again.

The debates were resumed on November 12, 1879. In response to the French Delegate's arguments for putting the Public Act of 1865 in accord with the stipulations of the 1878 Treaty, England's Delegate refered to Russia's new frontier, extending to the Lower Danube, and to the new possessors of the river mouths: Russia to the Kilia Mouth and Romania to the Sulina's and the St. George's Mouths. These circumstances, he felt, involved certain modifications in the competence of the European Commission. He also referred to the necessity of confirming the extension of the E.C.D.'s jurisdiction in carrying out the work on the Kilia Branch and in supplanting the territorial authority at Sulina.

Admitting the English Delegate's point of view, in which the other Delegates concurred, Russia's Delegate repeated his initial observations concerning the drawing up of the Additional Act. He upheld his observations by invoking parts of some debates held within the framework of the Conference of Berlin (Protocol Nr. 12) in which it was stated that the 1865 Public Act "... sera revisé pour être mis en harmonie avec les circonstances actuelles" and "ce travail sera confié à une Commission spéciale, où seront admis des Commissaires de tous les Etats riverains et soumis à l'examen et à la sanction definitive d'une Conférence des représentants des Puissances signataires."

By including all the Riparian states — Bulgaria, Romania and Serbia in the revision of the Public Act concerning the Maritime Danube sector of the river exclusively, the Russian Delegate's observation led to a deliberate complication in the resolution of the problem. Actually, though, the arguments he invoked were limited to the stipulations in point 4 of the Counter-Project, to Haymerlé's Project, presented by the Russian representation at the Congress of Berlin.

In protocol 11, in which Haymerlé's Project was initially recorded, absolutely no mention had been made of the revision of the Act of 1865. Nor had any decision been made, in the debates of July 4, 1878 (Protocol 12) on the Haymerlé Project and the Russian Counter-Project, as to a revision of the Public Act of 1865. Curiously, the revision does not appear in the text of the 1878 Treaty regarding navigation on the Danube. Only in Article 55 is there mention of harmony with respect to the Regulation on the Iron Gates and Galatz sector, to be drawn up by the European Commission with the assistance of the Delegates of the Riparian States of the Lower Danube. Hence, it appears that the idea of revising the 1865 Public Act was that of the Russian Delegate. It was justified; even the president of the E.C.D. in the November 5, 1878 meeting of the Commission, revealed the necessity of adapting the Act of 1865 to the new circumstances resulting from the 1878 Treaty.[166]

The idea was finally adopted also by the Austro-Hungarian Delegate, who stated, in this meeting, that the clauses of the 1878 Treaty imposed a double burden on the E.C.D. The first was that of the revision of the 1865 Act and the introduction into the Additional Act of those improvements indicated by experience. The second was to draw up the Regulation for Navigation, Police and Supervision between the Iron Gates and Galatz, in formulating the proposals which would become necessary because of the changes which had taken place on the Lower Danube, that is, the independence of Romania and Serbia and the autonomy of the Principality of Bulgaria.[167]

To execute the first task, he proposed the establishment of an Executive Committee within the framework of the E.C.D., to prepare a Project-proposal for the Additional Public Act, for the second (the Regulation), he proposed a collaboration with the riparian states mentioned in Article 55 of the Berlin Treaty.

All during the debates of the Autumn Session, Russia's Delegate continued to oppose the revisions proposed by the Austro-Hungarian Delegate, thus keeping the entire Commission under pressure.

The Romanian Delegate, in turn, showed that the appointment of Port Captain had to be made by the territorial authority, since it was a hyphen between the latter and the European Commission, unifying the activity of the judiciary police in the town as well as in the port of Sulina.[168]

The French Delegate, bringing up his Project again, took an ambiguous stand. Not contesting Romania's right to appoint the Port Captain, he still saw the problem from the point of view of the Commission's independence of any territorial state authority. The status of a Port Captain appointed by one authority, then placed under the orders of another one would, in his opinion, be compatible to complications. As an example, he recalled the complicated experience that had existed in the past under Ottoman authority. The Delegtes of England and of Austro-Hungary also revealed past complications resulting from the double authority — Ottoman and European Commission — over the position of Port Captain.

The problem of the Health Service, initially under the jurisdiction of the Sanitation Council of Constantinople, was resolved partially in favor of Romania. By modification of Article 6 of the French Project and at the proposal of the Austro-Hungarian Delegate, the regulation of the Health Service and of the Sanitation taxes were left to be worked out by the European Commission of the Danube, in accord with an International Council, with headquarters at Bucharest; the Project became definite.[169]

The debates over the Additional Act continued during the next two years (1880-1881); the Act was signed only on May 28, 1881.[170] In brief, its contents were: harmonizing the Public Act of 1865 with the stipulations of the 1878 Treaty of Berlin regarding the European Commission's exercise of its functions as far as Galatz, completely independent of any territorial authority (Preamble); continuation of the Commission's rights, attributes and immunity, as provided by the 1865 Public Act and by the 1878 Treaty, in its relations with the riparian states; appointment of the Navigation Inspector and the Port Captain of Sulina by the Commission and the maintenance of navigation taxes and their distribution by the Commission (Articles 3 and 4); E.C.D. upkeep of the Light-house (Article 5); regulation of the Health Service and the quarantine regime (Article 6), putting it under the control of an international council at Bucharest, replacing the Sanitation Council of Constantiople (Article 7); maintaining the neutrality of the Commission's establishments and personnel, the raising of its own flag (Article 8); maintenance of the stipulations of the 1865 Act which had not been modified in the Additional Act, and the subsequent rivision of the Commission's Regulation for Navigation, Police and Tariff (Article 9); ratification of the Additional Act within the interval of a year.

At the signing of the Additional Act, the Russian Delegate expressed a reservation on the application of the text of Articles 5 and 6 on the Kilia Branch, and the Romanian Delegate expressed his concerning the parity of rights of the riparian states on the same branch.[171] These reservations had no practical value; the European Commission continued to exercise its partial jurisdiction also on the Kilia Branch.

The signing of the Additional Act by the Delegate of Austro-Hungary depended on the former Sanitation Council of Constantinople being supplanted by that of Bucharest.[172] In this matter, Austro-Hungary supported the Romanian point of view. As in the case of the Public Act of 1865, certain clauses of the Additional Act were later abrogated, in 1938, by the Sinaia Arrangement.

The Problem of Elaborating the Regulation for Navigation, Police, and Supervision between the Iron Gates and Galatz, in the Debates of the European Commission of the Danube.

Within the framework of the European Commission of the Danube, the long and agitated debates over the drawing up of the Regulations for Navigation, Police and Supervision, started in December 1879 and terminated in June 1882, with thirty-seven protocols drawn up.[173] The leading position during the discussions was held by Austro-Hungary's Delegate. The most controversial and disputed problems involved him and the Delegates of Russia and Romania, seconded by those of Bulgaria and Serbia, Barrère, the Delegate of France, had the role of peacemaker, harmonizing the multiple points of view.

Before going into a description of the debates, some clarification seems necessary in order to avoid confusion, and to explain certain juridic matters.

Initially, Article 55 of the Treaty of 1878 provided that the sector for application of the Regulation was that between the Iron Gates and Galatz. In the meantime, through the Preliminary Works of the European Commission and of the future Conference of London (1883), the sector was established between the Iron Gates and Brăila — up to the point at which maritime navigation also ends. To the initial title of Regulation for Navigation and Police was also added that of Supervision, in order to correspond with the title given in Article 55.

The reason for giving the European Commission the mandate for developing the Regulation could be attributed to keeping the political balance between, on the one hand, Austro-Hungary's leanings towards supremacy on the Lower Danube, to the detriment of the smaller states, and on the other hand to bringing into harmony the positions of Vienna and Russia.

On December 17, 1879, France's Delegate proposed the establishment of a Study Committee to draw up a Draft-Project for the Regulation, to be presented at a Plenary Meeting of the European Commission by March 1881. England's Delegate, with the aim of putting all the riparian states in identical conditions, proposed the establishment of a Study Committee composed exclusively of Delegates from non-riparian states, a proposal which was accepted.[174] This proposal, to some extent ran counter to the clause of Article 55 which had provided for the participation also of riparian states. Assigning the project to a restricted committee made up only of Delegates of the European Commission can be explained by the fact that a reduced number of participants would facilitate the work involved and would avoid the many obstructions that could be raised by the riparian countries.

Delegates of Austro-Hungary, Germany, and Italy were appointed to the Study Committee, which took as a basis for discussion a study drawn up by the German Delegate.[175] Although Austro-Hungary was not riparian on the Lower Danube, her inclusion in the Committee was in accordance with the French and English consideration of her position as a Great Power with major commercial interests on the Lower Danube.

Taking under consideration the German study, one can substitute "Vienna" for "German," inasmuch as there appears a symptomatic similarity between this study and the 1857 Act of Navigation which had been drawn up by Austria in the Riparian Commission, but had been rejected by the 1858 Conference of Paris.

Although the Draft-Project of the Study Committee was presented to the European Commission in time, the basic discussions were delayed. Hajnal gives a reason the veracity of which is borne out by documentation as well as by the correspondence carried on between the Governments of the States interested in the problem of the Regulation. He reached the conclusion that the work on the Regulation, as well as the debate on it, were deliberately postponed by a "dilatory method he considered unusual for the Commission."[176]

In accordance with the Treaty of Berlin, (Article 55), the new Regulation convering the Iron Gates — Galatz sector, was to be drawn up by the European Commission in harmony with the existing Regulation of that same Commission. Also, in accordance with point 3 of the Haymerlé Project presented to the Congress (Protocol No. 11, July 2, 1878) provision was made for supervision of the execution of the new Regulation, to be carried out by a Representative of the Commission. This provision was upheld also by Andrassy, who expressed the opinion that: "La Commission Européenne fournirait plus de garantie qu'une Commission dans laquelle les petits Etats Slaves(sic) seraient représentées,"[177] Chlumetzky, the Austro-Hungarian Minister of Commerce, was of the opposite opinion. He believed that the super-vision over the execution of the new Regulation should be assigned to any "Inspectorate" consisting of all the riparian states, including Russia, Bavaria, and Württemberg, under Austro-Hungarian presidency, inasmuch as "... une position dominante nous appartient sur la section indiquée du Danube"[178] (between the Iron Gates and Galatz). This proposal, in Hajnal's opinion, was due to Andrassy's being removed from the Ministry for Foreign Affairs; an opinion held also by Haymerlé.[179]

Chlumetzky's point of view regarding the Regulation also appeared in a Vienna newspaper article stating, "Überhaupt tritt an Österreich die gebieterische Forderung heran, die durch die Ausführung des Berliner Vertrages gebotene Gelegenheit zur Stärkung unserer Position an der Donau jenseits des Eisernen Tores nicht unbenützt zu lassen."[180]

Having the direct support of Germany, the Vienna Government concentrated all its efforts at London and Paris to create a favorable platform for itself in drawing up the Regulation, an activity that explains the postponements reported by Hajnal. The Romanian Government, in its turn, keeping a close eye on Vienna's maneuvers, appealed to official French circles to counteract the Austrian Acts. "Austrian diplomats," reported M. Kogălniceanu, Romania's representative at Paris, "carried on an extraordinary activity to convince the governments to share the point of view and the interests Austria was called upon to defend at the Lower Danube. England and even France agreed to keep that in mind." He also pointed out the activity of the "venerable old Beust" in Paris and the sending of Wolkenstein to that same capital. The latter, Undersecretary of state, carried on negotiations with Barrère who was entrusted with presenting amendments to the Draft-project of the Regulation.[181]

There were two points of view concerning the procedure for drawing up the Regulation. The first, held by a majority of the Delegates, upheld the idea of a prior examination of the Draft-Project by the European Commission of the Danube, then sending the project to the riparian states for eventual observations. The second, upheld by the Austro-Hungarian Delegate, provided by the Study Committee, which had drawn it up to present it to the riparian states directly, following which it was to be examined by the European Commission. When the Study Committee for drawing up the Draft Project of the Regulation was established, France's Delegate stated that this Act was "... destiné à être communiqué aux divers gouvernements ainsi qu'aux états riverains... et soumis à l'examen des autorités compétents de chaque Pays, et pourrait être utilement mis en discussion dans la prochaine session plénière," meaning the European Commission session. The Delegate of Austro-Hungary adhered to this statement.

From this proposal it is clear that in its first stage the Draft-Project was to be sent to the "divers gouvernements," as well "aux états riverains," then submitted to the E.C.D. for discussion. By "divers gouvernements," the French Delegate understood the governments represented in the European Commission of the Danube and, secondarily, those of the riparian countries of the Lower Danube.

The confusion was caused by the E.C.D.'s deviation from the clause of Article 55 which provided for the drawing up on the Regulation with the aid of the riparian countries. By transferring this task to the Study Committee, the Draft-Project was drawn up without them and the governments of Bulgaria, Romania, and Serbia, were faced with an accomplished fact.

The Delegates of Russia, Romania, England and Fance requested that the first Body to examine the Draft-Project be the European Commission, in the presence of the Representatives of the three riparian states; a request that was approved by the Commission. Turkey's Delegate expressed a reservation, in the sense that Bulgaria's interests be represented through her suzerain, a point of view that had been expressed at the very earliest stage of the work on the Regulation. At the insistence of the Russian Delegate and after the reassurance that the role of the Bulgarian Representative would be limited, the incident was closed.

The Regulation for Navigation, Police and Supervision was drawn up on June 22, 1882, for the sector from the Iron Gates to Galatz, in the presence of the Delegates of the states riparian to the Lower Danube (Bulgaria, Romania and Serbia). The extension of the Regulation to Brăila came in 1883. The Regulation then was to be approved by the 1883 Conference of London.[182] In spite of all the discussions, they were to be continued at the 1883 Conference.

The Mixed Commission of the Lower Danube.

Article 96 of the Regulation for Navigation, Police and Supervision placed the enforcement of the Regulation under the authority of a Commission entitled The Mixed Commission of the Lower Danube River, in which Austro-Hungary, Bulgaria, Romania and Serbia were each represented by one Delegate.

The Commission was presided over by an Austro-Hungarian, its decisions were taken by majority vote, and the president's vote was to be decisive in case of tie.

Resolving the problem of the Mixed Commission had taken place within the debates on the Regulation. The principal opposition in the European Commission came from the Delegates of England, France,

Romania, and Bulgaria, while the chief supporter was the Austro-Hungarian Delegate. Establishment of such a Commission was considered by England's Delegate as not within the competence of the Regulation, not being a necessary consequence of Article 55 of the Berlin Treaty. Such a Commission, in his opinion, could not be valid except through a new agreement among the governments of the interested countries.[183] He would have accepted the Commission under three conditions, namely: complete freedom of navigation on the Iron Gates — Galatz (Brăila) sector; the duration of the Commission to be equal to that of the European Commission; and the third, the right of appeal to the E.C.D., of all members of the Mixed Commission, concerning decisions contrary to the Regulation. The French Delegate considered the Commission as a valuable issuance from the Study Committee, while Romania's Delegate contested its establishment as not having been provided by Article 55 a justifiable contestation.

Acknowledging that the establishment of a Mixed Commission had not been mentioned expressly in Article 55, the Austro-Hungarian Delegate justified it by the fact that the Study Committee had taken into consideration the spirit of the Article, in which the European Commission had included the participation of the riparians in drawing up the Regulation. Through a broad interpretation, the argument might have been valid, had Austro-Hungary fulfilled the condition she revealed; that is, her capacity as a riparian state of the fluvial sector which would have been under the authority of the Mixed Commission. In a supplementary argument, the same Delegate justified his point of view by citing also the Anglo-French proposal of June 7, 1880, in which provision was made that the Special Commission be replaced by a Mixed Commission, the term "Mixed" coming from the fact that its composition was of three riparians — Bulgaria, Romania and Serbia — and one non-riparian, Austro-Hungary.

Romania's point of view led to the Regulation being applied and carried out by a Commission composed entirely of riparians, without Austro-Hungary, and under Europe's supervision; that is, the European Commission for the Danube. In such an organization, claimed the Romanian Delegate, Austrian commercial interests down river from the Iron Gates could be protected by her Delegate in the European Commission. In support of this view, he invoked the principle and spirit which had resulted from the July 2 session of the Congress of Berlin. At that session, Haymerlé had made provision, in point 3 of his Project, that for the Regulation down river from the Iron Gates a Commissioner's delegated by the E.C.D., would oversee the carrying out of the Regulation. But, in the next session, following a meeting of Haymerlé with Oubril, in order to harmonize the Austrian proposal with the Russian one, the solution proposed for point 3 was reserved for future agreement among the Plenipotentiaries.

Setting aside national-political considerations of the small riparian states the problem of the functioning of the Mixed Commission even under Austro-Hungarian presidency could have been evaluated as a servitude granted by Bulgaria, Romania and Serbia. Granville, the Foreign Minister of England, saw it in this light, giving as an example the situation on the Scheldt River (Escaut) where, Holland, after much resistance, acknowledged Belgium's right to navigation.[184]

Aside from the compensatory factor in the relations between the Great Powers, the presence of Austro-Hungary, as a non-riparian, in the territorial sovereignty sphere of the small riparian states was considered by Haan, Vienna's Delegate in the E.C.D., in the light of "... la situation géographique de cette Puissance, de la multiplicité et de la gravité de ses intérêts sur le Bas-Danube...," as well as from that Power's having the assignment of carrying out the work at the Iron Gates. To this, Arendt, Germany's Delegate, added also the consideration "... de haute convenance et de courtoisie," which he felt should have been considered when Austria was accorded the presidency of the Mixed Commission.[185]

The Delegates of England, Italy, and Turkey were in accord with the German point of view; France's Delegate also invoked "la courtoisie" due a Great Power; Russia's objected to the absence of unanimous accord, in not obtaining Romania's and Bulgaria's agreement and in the application of the principle of equal status for the riparian states. In spite of the Russian Government's position as a protector of the small states, along the route of the Lower Danube, against the supremacy of Austro-Hungary, the Russian Delegate did not insist; he himself needed the support of his Austro-Hungarian colleague in the problem of the Kilia Branch which he was to bring up later.

Still in his capacity of Foreign Minister, Granville, addressing himself to England's representatives abroad, wrote "... il aurait semblé difficile de faire une objection quelconque valable à la présence d'Autriche dans la Commission Mixte en se rappelant les importants intérêts commerciaux qu'elle avait en jeu."[186]

The positions of some of the Great Powers, in favor of Vienna's supremacy over Lower Danube navigation, were contrary to their positions in the past. While in 1858 Germany opposed this suppremacy in a Memorandum, in 1880 her Delegate in the European Commission pleaded in Austria's favor. In 1856, Clarendon, England's representative at the Conference of Paris, opposing that same supremacy declared: "... l'Autriche restant seule en possession du Haut Danube et participant à la navigation du Bas Danube, acquérait des avantages particuliers et exclusifs que la Conférence ne saurait consacrer." In 1880, Siborne, England's Delegate to the European Commission, was in accord with those same advantages. The contradiction was evident also in position taken by Italy's Delegate. In 1859, Cavour has written: "L'Autriche qui n'avait aucun droit de souveranité sur le Rhin vient aujurd'hui se plaindre de la violation des droits des Etats riverains," rights which Austria considered in her favor on the basis of the 1857 Navigation Act. The contradictions could be attributed to the changes in the political scene, brought about by compromises and bargaining between the Great Powers at the time of the Congress of Berlin and after.

After two years of debates, when the problem of the Regulation had reached a critical point (May 1882), England and France pushed for its resolution in order to resolve also the prolongation of the existence of the European Commission of the Danube, whose mandate was to expire on April 24, 1883.

Barrère took over the task of speeding up the matter, scheduling its discussion for the May 2, 1882 session. This session was also the most important, being the penultimate one of the E.C.D. debates. At the time of this session, the problem of the Mixed Commission presented three principal aspects: Austro-Hungary's position as the predominant voice, in case of a tie, and its holding the chairmanship; resolution of the English amendment by which the predominant voice of the chairman was tempered with the right of appeal, by the other three members, to the E.C.D. against the Mixed Commission decisions; and last, the German proposal which although it also retained the preponderence of the chairman's vote, limited the right of appeal to questions of principle.

Barrère brought a compromise solution, proposing a new distribution in the make-up of the Mixed Commission. To the four members, Austro-Hungary, Bulgaria, Romania and Serbia, he added a fifth member, elected from the Delegates to the E.C.D., in alphabetical order of the Powers represented in the Commission. Thus, aside from the correlation and the coexistence between the two Commissions, an impartial voice was introduced which could by its vote neutralize any decision of the chairman that any one or two of the other members did not agree with. The proposal also contained other norms which could satisfy the sovereignty claims of Romania, Bulgaria and Serbia.[187]

Austro-Hungary agreed to the proposal; having discussed it previously with Barrère (1881) and Wolkenstein.[188] The Delegates of Germany, Italy, Serbia, England, and Turkey approved it. Because of Bulgaria's and Romania's disapproval, Russia's Delegate objected to the lack of unanimity. He later approved the proposal with the reservation for limiting the existence of the Mixed Commission and for the equality of votes. Bulgaria adhered, but with the reservation that any Delegate from the E.C.D. whose country was already represented in the Mixed Commission be eliminated. Although Romania, in the opinion of her Foreign Minister, could not isolate herself in a matter of European interest, she still opposed the Barrère proposal. She did not sign the Regulation and she opposed the establishment of a Mixed Commission in which Vienna held the predominant position, in view of the lack of unanimous approval of the Members of the E.C.D. and the riparian states.[189] Aside from the presence of Austro-Hungary, whose riparian status Romania contested, Romania objected to the fact that the fifth member could actually be Austro-Hungary's Delegate to the E.C.D. and thus could, along with that country's Delegate in the Mixed Commission, create the problem of holding the majority of the votes. In other words, two Delegates from Vienna, plus one from Serbia (which always sided with the former) would make of the other two minority.

Romania's Delegate again brought up the initial idea regarding a Supervisory Commission whose composition and attributes corresponded with the principles of the 1815 Act and of the Treaties of 1856 and 1878. The application of those principles would conciliate the sovereign rights of the Riparian States with those of European surveillance. In addition, he proposed that two Delegates of the E.C.D. be included in the Mixed Commission instead of the one proposed by Barrère.

The motion to end the debates was objected to by Romania's Delegate, on the grounds that such a decision was up to the respective Governments, not to their Delegates in the E.C.D., but the objection did not receive a majority vote.

Theoretically, the Mixed Commission had come into being on June 2, 1882, by the approval of the Regulation for Navigation, Police and Supervision (Article 96). Although the Regulation was approved in 1883 at the Conference of London, the Mixed Commission did not go into operation, because of Romania's opposition.

Romania's opposition to Austro-Hungarian supremacy over the Lower Danube was brought on by a number of considerations, among them reasons of economic order and national prestige. The economic reasons were the result of the effects of the 1875 Treaty of Commerce and Navigation imposed by Vienna. The day after the signing of that treaty, the first pages of Bucharest newspapers appeared with the black borders of mourning.[190] The reason of national prestige was stated by Kogălniceanu, who considered a direct insult the opinion held by some of the Great Powers that, because of their low level of technical capacity for organizing navigation, the young states through which the Danube flowed were inexperienced and incapable of carrying out the policing of their fluvial sectors.[191]

Russia Against the Jurisdiction of the European Commission on the Kilia Branch.

The Russian Delegate's action against the E.C.D.'s jurisdiction over the Kilia Branch, began, in general, during the debates over the Additional Act of 1881, and became more concrete when certain Articles of the Commission's 1875 Regulation for Navigation and Police were being reactified. Russia's stand was at an advantage because of some gaps and inaccuracies in the existing Regulation.

Because the 1875 Regulation had not provided for a piloting tax, the President of the E.C.D. proposed its inclusion, on December 8, 1879, in Article 87 of the new Regulation for Navigation and Police.[192] The proposal was made in order to avoid incidents between pilots and maritime vessel captains who refused to pay piloting taxes since no provision for such appeared in any existing Regulation. The proposed taxation including also the Kilia Branch, Russia's Delegate was in opposition, taking advantage of the confusion arising from other Articles in the chapter of the Regulation concerning "piloting services at the mouth and on the course of the river." Article 84 stated that pilots were to pilot the vessels in their navigation between Sulina and Brăila, but no mention was made of the Kilia Branch. Furthermore, the pilot stations were located in the ports of Sulina, Tulcea, Galatz and Brăila, but not in any Kilia Branch ports. The basis of the argument put forth by Russia's Delegate was the absence of any E.C.D. concern over Kilia and the lack of any need for a piloting service on that branch, a service that was generally carried out on the usual route of the maritime vessels, Sulina-Brăila.

According to that same Delegate, only local pilots were familiar with the Kilia Branch route, not those of the E.C.D. His point of view was justified inasmuch as the E.C.D. had begun pilot training also for the navigation on the Kilia only on 1879. In his documentation of the inutility of piloting on the Kilia Branch, he mentioned also the fact that the number of vessels coming into Kilia port was insignificant. He then contradicted himself by saying that "it concerned a principal branch... frequented daily by numerous craft." The traffic in the Kilia port may have been insignificant, but that in the port of Ismail, on that same branch, was important, according to statistics.[193]

In maintaining the lack of any need for E.C.D. pilots on the Kilia Branch, the Delegate also cited the special training of the local pilots in navigation on several branches of that same branch. This argument had no foundation. Due to the shallowness of the branches, navigation by maritime vessels was impossible. Only small fishing craft of low tonnage, not needing piloting, could navigate them. Also invoked were the stipulations of Article 87, among the reasons for not including the Kilia Branch in the route of the maritime vessels on the Maritime Danube. This was a valid argument. Actually, in accordance with the article, for vessels departing from the ports of Reni, Ismail or Kilia, piloting was optional in their passage through the port of Tulcea.

Apparently, the Russian Delegate's point of view could be upheld by certain circumstances in the past. He pointed out that initially, in 1856, the E.C.D. had opted for the Sulina Branch as an exit to the sea, not for the Kilia or the St. George Branch. In other words, the Kilia Branch was not useful navigably, in his opinion.

The opinions of the Delegates of England and France were contrary; they invoked the stipulation of Article 16 of the 1856 Treaty, on the basis of which the aims of the E.C.D. were to free the mouths of the Danube of "sands and other obstacles...," thus referring to the three mouths of the river, including the Kilia. The Kilia Mouth, claimed these two Delegates, not only had not been abandoned, but special funds had been allocated[194] for cleaning it up. The examination of the Sulina Bar had ascertained the need for that. Even if no maritime vessels could navigate through the main Kilia Mouth, clearing it — and especially the Stary-Stamboul sub-branch was an absolute necessity for navigation through the Sulina Mouth. Actual navigation on the Kilia Branch was limited to the area between the principal river route and the ports of Ismail and Kilia, the traffic being carried out through the Sulina Mouth.

The contradiction in the Russian Delegate's point of view regarding the futility of piloting on the Kilia, also arose from a different proposal. He suggested the establishment of a pilot service at Tchatal Ismail, the point where the Kilia Branch took form, the point at which vessels entering this branch could take on pilots. Hence, he did acknowledge the need for piloting up the Kilia Branch, even though he had denied it earlier. The Russians, however, realized that Tchatal Ismail was inappropriate for the construction of any such service, since the area was marshy and lacked any conveniences or facilities for construction. He proposed further that piloting taxes on the Kilia be set directly between the pilots and the ships' captains, in spite of the fact that the reason for modifying Article 87 of the new Regulation was precisely to eliminate that past procedure.

All the arguments for detaching the Kilia Branch from the E.C.D. jurisdiction remained fruitless. The majority vote of the other Delegates was in favor of piloting tolls on the brief sector of maritime vessel navigation on the Kilia being included in the general pilot tolls on the Maritime Danube.

At the 1883 Conference of London, Russia was to take up again the same problems, this time succeeding in removing the Kilia Branch from the jurisdiction of the European Commission of the Danube.

General Considerations.

It is evident that the failure to apply the Regulation for Navigation. Police and Supervision between the Iron Gates and Galatz (Brăila) was due to Bulgaria's and Romania's obstructions. Yet, it would not have been excluded had it been applied by the Supervisory Commission, as proposed by Romania, under the control of the E.C.D. The success of such a formula would probably have depended upon a position of unity between the three small riparian countries, a unity which was not attained.

In spite of his country's lack of independence, Bulgaria's Representative aligned himself in some matters with the point of view of Romania's Delegate while, in others, he opposed those of the Delegate of his suzerain, Turkey, Serbia, in turn, was aligned with Austro-Hungary's position. Between these three countries there existed some tacit animosity, also influenced by the new situation created by the Treaty of Berlin.

The fact that Romania became a member of the European Commission for the Danube, due to her sovereignty over the Mouths of the Danube, gave rise to Serbia and Bulgarian aspirations towards the same status. In another aspect, Romania considered herself a co-riparian on the Lower Danube only with Bulgaria, not with Serbia.

The latter, in Kogălniceanu's opinion, "was not a Danubian State... having only five kms of river bank,"[195] that is, only to the right of the Iron Gates. Relating the position of riparian to the length of the river bank became controversial, especially since Serbia was a co-riparian with Romania at the important point of the Iron Gates and the Cataracts.

From the manner in which the debates developed one can deduce the basis of Romania's position as the riparian state most opposed to Austro-Hungary's. A country barely out from under Turkish suzerainty and having perspectives of developing technical and economic possibilities, Romania, defending her rights on the Lower Danube, opposed the pressure of the Great Powers. Austro-Hungary, her powerful neighbour who could have taken any coercive measures against her, tried to convince the Romanian Government of her major interests. Austro-Hungary had assured herself of Serbia's submission, through her political and economic position and, by proposing the port of Roustchouk as the seat of the Mixed Commission, attempted to attract Bulgaria also to her point of view. England, France and Italy had concentrated their attention on Romania's obstructions to the Regulation. While the attitude of these three Great Powers towards the small Danubian states was more sympathetic and more considerate of their susceptibilities and their self respect, Austro-Hungary, in other circumstances, not only evaluated them otherwise, but some of her diplomats even displayed attitudes of complete disregard of the political dignity and even of the territorial sovereignty of these small states.

This attitude was evident also in a letter from Vienna's Ambassador to London to Granville, in which the former claimed that only a Mixed Commission would be entrusted to apply the Regulation, inasmuch "... l'impartialité des autorités territoriales ne nous inspirent qu'une confiance limitée."[196] "Les autorités territoriales," with the longest river banks were those of Bulgaria and Romania, who were opposing Vienna. Moreover, perhaps in error, perhaps deliberately, the Ambassador extended Vienna's interests also on the Lower Danube. "Il nous est impossible," he wrote, "d'admettre la façon de voir de la Roumanie qu'à partir de l'endroit où le Danube quitte notre territoire les Etats Riverains auraient seuls le droit de régler les intérêts de la navigation, qui même à cet endroit sont presque exclusivement Autrichiens." However, the Iron Gates and the Cataracts, situated between Serbian and Romanian river banks, were not part of Austro-Hungarian territory. When the Barrère proposal was presented, as well as during the debates on it, Paris and London were interceding with Bucharest in Vienna's favor.[197] Also, at this time, direct negotiations were being conducted to find a compromise between Bucharest and Vienna, with no success.

From the debates within the E.C.D. one can deduce the advantages of a Regulation which would have more rapidly modernized the entire navigation regime on a sector of the river over which chaos still reigned. Still, it must be noted that its rapid application would have produced anomalies and difficulties. Some navigation at the time was being carried out with outdated transportation methods and by personnel of long experience but no theoretical preparation and discipline in the exercise of navigation. The lack of discipline and, at times, the abusive interference with outmoded methods of navigation in the traffic of vessels of larger tonnage, especially Austro-Hungary's steam-operated ones, also created difficulties. It was also hard for illiterate personnel on tugboats or on barges to get work permits, which required even minimal ability to read and write. In modernizing the navigation methods as drawn up by Vienna, objections arose which had some basis.

Turkey's Delegate and Bulgaria's Representative in E.C.D objected that the provisions in the Regulation, regarding the granting of ships papers, of navigation licenses become, in their opinion, obstacles to freedom of navigation, in that they constituted a modification of the regime of navigation current until then.[198]

In his response, Austro-Hungary's Delegate argued that there was a need to replace the status quo with a regulation which he did not consider an obstacle to freedom of navigation, a point of view which Romania's Delegate supported.

The navigational difficulties existing before 1882 did not consist only in personnel, but also in natural obstacles in the watercourse. "Que de misères devait endurer le navigateur," noted an Austrian traveller concerning the difficulties that ships operators encountered because of the sand bars and other obstacles. He also estimated a three to four week duration for passage between Turnu-Severin and Brăila, "A cette époque," he added, "en Walachie, personne ne s'occupait du Danube et l'on ne faisait rien pour la navigation."[199]

In reference to the Bulgarian sector of the Lower Danube, the Austro-Hungarian Consul at Roustchouk wrote, on May 19, 1886, that no navigation police existed and that conditions were worse than during the Turkish presence there.[200] These obstacles could have been eliminated much sooner had the Mixed Commission been functioning and the Regulation applied in accordance with the riparians' views. The fact that it was not being applied did not signify the abandonment of any attempt to improve the old navigation conditions. For example, Romania with her own resources had already begun to take measures to organize the ports and to improve navigational conditions on her fluvial sectors. The existence of such navigational organization is proven by the documents of the Study Commission for drawing up the Draft Project of a Regulation for Navigation, by the inclusion also of a Regulation for Navigation and Police for the ports in the Romanian fluvial sector.

Twenty-five years after his noting the "misères" on the Lower Danube, that same previously mentioned Austrian traveller described in great detail the improvements in navigation conditions. "L'Etat roumain," he wrote, "qui progresse à pas de géant à tous les points de vue, s'est occupé depuis quelques années de la navigation et il s'efforce de devenir pour le Danube, en amont de Brăila, le même facteur que la Commission Européenne en aval de Brăila. Bien que les rives du Danube appartiennent à differents Etats, seule la Roumanie a organisé un service régulier des eaux denommé Service Hydraulique."

Among the many aspects of activity yet to be organized after Romania obtained her independence (1878), that of improving and equipping the national navigation system was given prime importance. The improvements were pushed along also, by the ever increasing rhythm of Danubian commerce, to an international level, developing mainly in the Romanian waters, ports and warehouses. "Do we want the Danube?," asked Iorga. "Let us work, economize, cover the great river with our vessels carrying the products of our national labor."[201] Through successive laws applied between 1863 and the First World War, measures were taken to carry out purely technical construction connected with improving navigation, as well as to equip the ports. Perhaps most of the achievements were not at the level of those which might have been reached by the Mixed Commission, but they gradually progressed. After 1921, Walker D. Hines, an expert sent by the League of Nations to check on navigation conditions on the Danube, reported the improvements made by Romania, Bulgaria and Serbia, in the field of navigational organization.[202]

Romania's stand and reaction to the way in which Vienna viewed the organization of the Mixed Commission and the application of the Regulation, had a negative effect on the activity of the Austro-Hungarian river fleet. To that effect there contributed, along with the rivalry of the Romanian fluvial fleet, the Bulgarian and Serbian ones, in growing numbers, and the effect of the 1876 "customs war" between Romania and Austro-Hungary. Of the effects of the "war" a director of the Austrian Society of Navigation (DDSG) reported the "complète ruine de la navigation autrichienne sur le Bas-Danube si l'on ne trouvait pas un accord avec la Roumanie."[203] The non-realization of Austro-Hungarian supremacy over the Lower Danube as Vienna envisioned it was the result also of sabotage by administrations in Romanian ports and even by private individuals.

Another cause, and probably the most important one for barring that supremacy, was the competition of the experienced and outmoded local river fleet on the Lower Danube, the greater part of it under Turkish and Greek ownership. The miserable conditions of the crews on these ships, the reduced daily rations, the excessive number of hours worked, as well as the experience of the crews in the specific traditional problems of that river navigation, all these factors reduced the operating cost and influenced the freight charges. Faced with this situation, the Austro-Hungarian fleet, with its higher administrative level, found the competition difficult. The fleet also ran up against the competition provided by the low-capacity transports of small local boats, wind driven, operated by small motors or drawn by tugboats in groups of three or four, their crews consisting of one or two persons. Transporting small quantities of grain, these boats along with their reduced costs also had the advantage of easy maneuverability in small ports lacking quays and other technical facilities. The Austro-Hungarian vessels, with their greater capacity, could not made use of these advantages.

The Austro-Hungarian fleet and its commercial activity also met a linguistic obstacle. Although all this had been reported as being current at the end of the 18th century, it had not yet lost its effect.

The Austrian Engineer Sultzer, sent to examine the economic conditions on the Lower Danube, reported the difficulties persented by the variety of languages used in the commercial and navigational circles, where Greek, Turkish, French and English were often encountered.[204]

These, briefly, were the conditions under which Austro-Hungary's commerce and navigation were unable to reap the expected benefits, even if the Regulation had been applied by the Mixed Commission. As mentioned in a previous chapter, Austro-Hungarian supremacy was maintained only by its passenger vessels, but even this traffic had lessened gradually up to the onset of World War I and was later replaced completely by the development of the national fleets of Bulgaria, Romania and Serbia.

Chapter 5

THE CONFERENCE AND TREATY OF LONDON, OF 1883

Introduction.

The 1883 Conference of London can also be evaluated as a bargaining stage between the Great Powers, each one of them getting its share. Since certain of the problems had not been resolved by the 1878 Congress of Berlin, the London Conference can be considered actually a continuation of the former. It had to resolve three principal problems respecting the international regime of navigation, namely: extension of the European Commission of the Danube's mandate, which was to expire in 1883; the extension of its jurisdiction as far as Brăila; the removal of the Kilia Branch from the authority of the E.C.D. and the approval of the Regulation for Navigation, Police and Supervision between the Iron Gates and Galatz (Brăila).

To resolve these problems favorably, England, France and Italy would have to yield again to pressure from Russia and Austro-Hungary. Russia obtained the removal of the Kilia Branch from the E.C.D.'s jurisdiction, while Austro-Hungary got the approval of the Regulation and the establishment of the Mixed Commission of the Danube. England and France won the extension of the E.C.D. mandate and the extension of its jurisdiction up to Brăila.

The negotiations, compensations and adjustments among the Great Powers were carried on during and immediately after the Berlin Conference, leaving it up to the London Conference to make them definite.

From these arrangements, the three small riparian states endeavoured to put forth their rights and complaints to a Conference in which their participation with deliberative vote was contested. While Serbia and Bulgaria's efforts were concentrated principally on their being admitted to the Conference with deliberative vote, Romania had two additional aims: rejection or amendment of the Regulation and opposition to the extension of the E.C.D.'s jurisdiction as far as Brăila. The debates and controversies over the first objective were carried on between Romania and Austro-Hungary, those over the second were between Romania and England. In both cases Romania was unsuccessful. As in 1878, the small riparian states of the Lower Danube did not form a common bloc in defense of their rights. An exception of sorts was a Bulgaria's part when in some cases she sided with Romania.

Convocation and Work of the Conference.

The convening of a new Danubian Conference was required inasmuch as a decision had to be made over carrying out Article 54 of the 1878 Treaty, regarding the prolongation of the European Commission's mandate, due to expire on April 23, 1883. France having declined the initiative of convening the Conference, England took it over.[205]

In accepting the initiative, England requested France's support for a favorable resolving of the following problems: extension of the E.C.D. mandate including the extension of its jurisdiction up to Brăila, and the approval of the Regulation for Navigation, Police and Supervision between the Iron Gates and Galatz (Brăila).

With regard to the Regulation, it was stated that it was approved by the Delegates of the E.C.D. "with the exception of those of Romania and Bulgaria." Romania was to send one delegate to the Conference, after the Conference had met. The French Government, by verbal accord on November 4, 1882, agreed with the English proposal. In that same agreement, the French Government suggested a prior understanding between the Great Powers over the proceeding to be followed if Romania were to create difficulties in the matter of the Regulation, if she were to be invited to the Conference, as well as in case Russia's attitude towards extending the mandate of the E.C.D. created difficulty.

The admission of the riparian states of the Lower Danube to the Conference — a subject to be developed in continuation — constituted a difficult problem in the negotiations between the Great Powers. This problem, interposed among others, was part of an exchange of seventy

CONFERENCE AND TREATY OF LONDON, OF 1883

letters and notes between the governments of England, Germany, Italy, Russia, Romania, Bulgaria, and Serbia.[206]

The work of the Conference took place from February 8 to March 10, under Grandville's presidency, England's foreign Minister, following which the 1883 Treaty was concluded, eight protocols being drawn up, plus an additional three after the signing of the Treaty.[207] The agenda of the Conference included problems brought up by England and France to be resolved. The debates were in the following order, as stated in the Preamble to the Protocols of the Conference: extension of the E.C.D.'s jurisdiction as far as Brăila; approval of the Regulation between the Iron Gates and Galatz (Brăila); as drawn up by the E.C.D.; and prolongation of the E.C.D.'s mandate.

The order of the agenda as mentioned above was not adhered to at the Conference debates on the problems were interspersed. To them was added the problem of the participation of the Lower Danube countries and that of removing the Kilia Branch from the E.C.D.'s jurisdiction. The debates will be taken up here in the following order:

- The participation of the riparian countries on the Lower Danube at the Conference;
- Approval of the Regulation for Navigation, Police and Supervision between the Iron Gates and Galatz (Brăila);
- Prolongation of the European Commission's mandate and extension of its jurisdiction up to Brăila;
- Removal of the Kilia Branch from the jurisdiction of the European Commission of the Danube.

The Problem of the Participation of the Riparian States of the Lower Danube: Bulgaria, Romania, Serbia.

Attention is given here to the participation of the Lower Danube countries in the Conference inasmuch as their grievances were not taken into consideration in the debates and the decisions made over certain problems related to their own fluvial sectors. It is to be noted that the question of their participation was debated by "ifs" and "buts."

Whether out of respect for the Principles of 1815, or out of considerations of justice, England and Austro-Hungary, with all their indifference, had initially taken positions favoring the participation of the small riparian states in the Conference. Later, they changed their stand on the premise that the 1883 Conference was evaluated as a continuation of that of 1878, to which these countries had not been convoked, not being independent nations then. The change in position taken by the two Great Powers did not consider the fact that in 1883 Romania and Serbia were independent and Bulgaria was an autonomous Principality. The problem of their participation at the Conference was considered differently by some jurists and researchers.

The evaluation of the principles of the Act of 1815 and the mode of application in the case of the riparian states was the object of study for "L'Institut de Droit International" at Heidelberg, pro and con points of view being expressed and presented even in some publications.

In a letter addressed to the Institute, M. Martens noted that "... les intérêts[208] ou aspirations politiques ont remplacé, en grande partie, les intérêts commerciaux qui avaient provoqué, dans le principe, les mesures internationales prises d'un commun accord par les puissances intéressées à la liberté de la navigation fluviale. Cette déviation des principes juridiques proclamés en 1815 comme faisant partie du droit public de l'Europe, a fait naître les conflits d'opinions et les malentendus qui ont éclatés, spécialement pendant la dernière Conférence de Londres entre les grandes Puissances européennes, d'une part, et la Roumanie de l'autre."

The points of view held by Martens and Engelhardt expressed in two separate motions favoring the rights of the riparian States, especially of Romania, were adopted in a motion of the Institut de Droit International.[209] When the motion was disregarded, Martens noted: "Presque toutes les conventions internationales concernant la navigation fluviale se rapportent expréssement aux stipulations de l'année 1815 et presque tous les appliquent différemment."[210]

Theodore Bunsen, Legation Counsellor, attributed to the caprices of certain Great Powers (leaving it to be understood England, France and Russia), the complete failure of Austro-Hungary's position in the problem of the Regulation. Referring to Romania's opposition - a reference that could be extended also to Serbia — he wrote: "Cette question ne constitue plus un litige entre l'Autriche-Hongrie et la Roumanie; c'est devenue un différent entre la Roumanie et les grandes Puissances."[211]

Referring to the disregard of the small riparian States, Holtzendorff wrote: "... le droit d'un petit état doit toujours peser plus dans la balance que l'intérêt d'une Grande Puissance."[212] This, however, was the opinion of a jurist, not also that of a politician.

ROMANIA

Romania's case can be considered different from that of Bulgaria and Serbia, inasmuch as the Treaty of Berlin had accorded her, along with her independence, the right to take part in the European Commission of the Danube on an equal basis with the other member states. In addition, the Maritime Danube had come under her sovereignty and she possessed the longest section of the Lower Danube, through which imports and exports were channeled to and from the Black Sea.

Romania's stand was the "Gordian knot" in the problem of the riparian states of the Lower Danube participating in the Conference with deliberative vote. The viewpoints of the Great Powers towards convoking Romania were ambiguous and oscillating. Aside from Considering the Conference of 1883 actually a continuation of that of 1878, their basic positions can be described in the words of Germany's Plenipotentiary Münster: "Si, tout en maintenant le principe de l'unanimité dans la Conférence on donnait une voix à la Roumanie, on lui créerait une position qui ne serait nullement désirable, celle de pouvoir, à sa volonté, imposer son veto. La Roumanie ne pourrait donc être admise qu'en qualité d'invitée et non comme maîtresse de maison."[213] According to Demorgny, the exclusion of Romania from the Conference, as predicated by Münster, had as its real aim "... pour imposer la volonté germanique au royaume danubien."[214]

England, on the other hand, with all her initial good will, worried about complications that could arise from an eventual Romanian opposition to the prolongation of the existence of the European Commission and to the extension of its jurisdiction as far as Brăila. The Plenipotentiary of Austro-Hungary had the same worry concerning the matter of approving the Regulation between the Iron Gates and Galatz (Brăila). The points of view of the Great Powers as expressed during the Conference with respect to Romania's participation contrasted with their earlier ones. In 1882, Granville, as England's Minister for Foreign Affairs, mentioning Romania's non-participation in the signing of the Treaty of 1878, was of the opinion that she could not request a place at the Conference in 1883. Yet, inasmuch as Romania had been admitted to the E.C.D. he added that it would be right that she be placed in the most favorable position to express her opinions...[215] by sending a representative when the Powers were to meet in Conference."

Italy's position was vacillatory. Considering the admitting Romania on an equal footing with the other Powers could create a precedent which could have inconveniences for future deliberations, the Italian Government felt that because Romania was part of the E.D.C. her admission would not present any inconvenience.²¹⁶

France and Russia were in favor of participation with consultative vote, while Kállay — Austro-Hungary's Minister for Foreign Affairs — wrote that he would second Romania's participation "... voulant lui donner une nouvelle preuve de nos bons sentiments...."²¹⁷

Aside from England's reasons for opposing Romania's participation, it seems that the former continued to regard Romania as a vassal of Turkey. In pointing out that Romania's non-signing of the 1878 Treaty did not give her the right to participate in the Conference of 1883, England's Ambassador to Constantinople asked the Sublime Porte's consent to accord Romania the right to send a representative "... qui assisterait aux seances sur le même pied que les Puissances signataires du Traité de Berlin."²¹⁸ This occurred before the closing of the Treaty of London of 1883.

Austro-Hungary's Károlyi was of the opinion that the discussions over the Regulation between the Iron Gates and Galatz would never end and no practical result would be reached in Romania participated with deliberative vote. The Regulation, which Romania would not accept, was considered by Károlyi as Vienna's most important objective.²¹⁹

Barrère, although subscribing to Münster's objections opposing Romania's participation on an equal footing with the Great Powers and thus avoiding an eventual veto, was disposed to admit Romania under the condition of majority decision, an opinion to which Russia's Mohrenheim and Italy's Nigra also adhered.²²⁰

The only one to have a more favorable position was Musurus Pasha, Plenipotentiary of Turkey, the former suzerain of Romania, who opted for convoking Romania, but without admitting her to the signing of the Protocols, a right reserved to the Great Powers.²²¹

The Conference decided to invite Romania and Serbia to attend the sessions as auditors and consultants; Bulgaria was to be informed of the developments by Turkey, her suzerain.²²² The Participation was to begin after the opening of the Conference work, not before. Ghika (Romania) and Marinovich (Serbia) refused to take part on those terms. Two days later (February 12), in a letter sent to Granville, Ghika protested against any decisions to be taken by the Conference without Romania's participation with deliberative vote, declaring those decisions "non obligatoires pour elle."²²³ Serbia later accepted participation with consultative vote. In Granville's opinion, Romania's not being admitted with deliberative vote was due to the fact that

"… la Conférence a cru devoir se considérer en quelque sorte comme la prolongation et la suite du Congrès de Berlin, auquel la Roumanie n'a pas participé comme signataire."

The strongest support received for Romania's request was the invitation of her Delegate in the European Commission of the Danube to take part in the 1881 signing of the Additional Act to the 1856 Public Act on an equal basis with the Delegates of the Great Powers. The only obstacle to this argument was that Romania had not been invited to the approval of that same Act, at which the Great Powers had been represented by their Plenipotentiaries, not by their Delegates, thus invoking again the lack of equal rights at the Congress of Berlin. In this matter, the German jurisconsult, Holtzendorff found no difference between the Delegates of the Powers in the European Commission and the Plenipotentiaries of those same Powers in a Conference at the highest level.[224]

The fact that the Additional Act had been signed also by Romania's Delegate in the European Commission and that, without this signature unanimity of votes could not have been attained meant that Romania's equality of position with the other Powers had been recongized. Furthermore, the Additional Act, signed also by Romania, was a result of the 1865 Act, requested at the 1878 Conference. Since Romania had not taken part in either the drawing up or the signing of the 1865 Act, she could not have participated in the signing of the Additional Act drawn up in continuation of the one of 1865.

Fitzmaurice of England was in favor of Romania, stating that "although she was not a Great Power," having now been accepted in the European Commission she could not be an obstacle at the Conference. Furthermore, he stated that, "of all the riparian states, she was one of the most concerned, being mistress of the two riverbanks in the greatest part of the watercourse over which the E.C.D. was functioning the having Galatz as the seat of the Commission itself."[225]

As mentioned earlier, Romania's right to participate in the Conference of London, as well as in other problems concerning navigation was upheld by personages of European renown. Although Holzendorff's opinion had been solicited by the Romanian Ministry for Foreign Affairs, he would not have compromised his reputation of European level jurist just for the honorarium accorded him. "A mon avis," he stated, "les questions déférées à mon examen appartiennent exclusivement au domaine du droit."[226]

Referring to a possible Romanian veto, which some of the Great Powers feared, Holtzendorff stated, "Il y aurait une contradiction directe du droit internationale positif et de la morale internationale à voir une Puissance quelconque méditer de réjeter à la Conférence de Londres, le droit de co-délibération de la Roumanie sous motif qu'on avait la pensée de suppléer au défaut d'unanimité dans l'oeuvre de la Commission Européenne, par une unanimité formelle des Puissances de la Conférence, à l' exclusion de la Roumanie."[227]

This was, in general, the case of Romania's participation in the 1883 Conference.

SERBIA

Certain differences of attitude are apparent between the position taken by Romania, in the matter of admission to the Conference of London, and that taken by Serbia, differences that were to the detriment of a united bloc of the smaller riparian states. While Romania, in her intercessions, invoked principles of law consecrated in the Danube regime and precedents of the same, Serbia pleaded her case in the light of comparisons between herself and Romania. In contrast to Romania's intercessions expressed in a more categoriec form, Serbia's had more of a petitioning tone, invoking the "sentiments de justice et bienveillance dont les Grandes Puissances son animées à l'égard de la Serbie."[228]

Just like Romania's, Serbia's intercessions antedated the opening of the Conference. In spite of the strong ties between Serbia and Austro-Hungary, Károlyi seemed to be less favorable than at first to admitting Serbia to the Conference.[229] He, too, conditioned her admittance to the majority decision. England, whose representative at Belgrade had discussed the matter with Pirotchanatz, Foreign Minister of Serbia, had the same opinion. Referring to the possible admission of Romania, on the basis that she had a greater fluvial extension, Serbia's Minister was of the opinion what the principle based on her position as a riparian was a prime importance. In his opinion, Serbia, as an independent nation, would have had greater rights than Bulgaria, whose political regime was that of vassal to Turkey.

On January 4, 1883, Marinovitch repeated the request for admission, addressing himself directly to Granville, in the latter's capacity as Foreign Minister.[230] Granville answered favorably, but left the final decision over the request to the signers of the Treaty of Berlin, inasmuch as the request came from a country which had not taken part in concluding that treaty.[231] Thus, Serbia's admission, like Romania's, was contingent upon prior participation at the signing of the Treaty

CONFERENCE AND TREATY OF LONDON, OF 1883   393

of Berlin and on the elimination of that condition with the approval of the members of the Conference of London. Even though later, in the matter of the Regulation and of the Mixed Commission, Austro-Hungary was successful in dividing the anemic bloc of small riparian states due to Belgrade's dissidence, she was unable to be of help in getting Serbia admitted since it would have implied the acceptance of the other riparians, especially of Romania, whose presence Vienna in no case wanted at the Conference.

As a riparian of the Lower Danube, Serbia, too had the right to participate with deliberative vote in the discussions of Danubian problems, even through her direct interests were limited especially to the Regulation for Navigation, Police, and Supervision of the Lower Danube, which was to be accepted or rejected by the Conference. The other two major problems on the agenda of the Conference, that of extending the mandate of the E.C.D. and its jurisdiction up to Brăila were of interest only to Romania, on whose territory the Commission functioned. Serbia's points of view were detailed in the Memorandum of February 11, 1883, presented to Granville, as President of the Conference.[232]

The Memorandum listed Serbia's navigation interest, her rights of territorial sovereignty, as well as those normally due her as riparian on a river of indivisible character. Referring to the collectivity of riparian states, she was included in the advantages the Great Powers accorded.

As to Serbia's interests down river from her frontier, the Memorandum stated "... car de même que la liberté de navigation sur toutes les parties du cours du Danube également est importante pour chaque Puissance, celle sur le Bas Danube est de même intérêt pour la Serbie que celle sur le Haut Danube pour la Roumanie."

By showing the equal positions of Serbia and Romania and by paraphrasing the proof of Serbia's rights, ideas were brought out in the Memorandum which indirectly supported the viewpoints of the Great Powers to not admit them to the Conference. In the matter of the European Commission of the Danube it was stated: "Ni la Serbie, ni la Roumanie n'ayant participé à la signature du Traité (de Berlin), aucune d'elles ne peut invoquer ce Traité pour demander le droit de siéger à la Conférence (1883) pour décider de la prolongation des pouvoirs de la Commission Européenne..." Article 54 of the Treaty of Berlin was invoked in support of this idea. That same statement showed the lack of solidarity among the riparian nations. Furthermore stating the Great Powers' possible favoring of Romania, on the basis of her longer extend of the Danubian water course and her many ports in that sector, the Serbian Government asked, "... pourquoi l'Article 54 du Traité de Berlin même n'a pas assuré à la Roumanie un siège au sein de la Conférence?" In continuation, it stressed, "... pourquoi la question des travaux de régularisation des Portes — de-Fer, quoiqu'ils se fassent sur la rive Serbe, a été réglée sans la participation de la Serbie?"

In bringing this up, attention can be called to the position taken not too long before, when the same Serbian Government not only accepted, but collaborated with the Power that had regulated the work at the Iron Gates through the "Convention provisoire entre la Serbie et l'Autriche-Hongrie, concernant les chemins de fer et la régulation des Portes de Fer" (1878). While Romania opposed the assignment of the works to Austro-Hungary, Serbia had accepted it in exchange for certain navigation advantages. After Serbia gained independence, she concluded a Treaty of Navigation with Austro-Hungary, on February 10, 1882. Article XI of this Treaty included certain norms regarding the Iron Gates.[233]

One cannot overlook the latent antagonism existing between these two neighbours, due also to the fact that, in the matter of the Regulation, Romania had contested Serbia's rights in consideration of the fact that she had riparian position for only a brief distance to the right of the Iron Gates.

In the February 20th session, Serbia Representative requested a permanent seat on the European Commission of the Danube, on an equal basis with Romania.[234] Observing that Serbia's request was based on the idea of parity between Serbia and Romania, President Granville expressed the opinion that actually, the two Kingdoms were in different situations.[235] The existence of the seat of the E.C.D. on Romanian territory and the avoidance of such requests from other countries were the reasons for Granville's decision in the comparison between Romania's and Serbia's status. This comparison is also reminiscent of Fitzmaurice's previously mentioned statement, on February 20.

Serbia's Representative claimed that "... en supposant même que l'intérêt de la Serbia se représentât par une distance géometrique moindre que celles des autres riverains... la Serbia aurait le droit, au même titre que la Roumanie, d'être représentée dans la Commission Europeenne..."[236]

Serbia's request for admission to the Conference with deliberative vote was rejected. Faced with this result, Serbia's Representative accepted participation as a consultant.

BULGARIA

Admitting Bulgaria to the workings of the Conference presented a somewhat different aspect from that of Romania and Serbia. While the two latter countries were independent, Bulgaria was still under Ottoman Empire suzerainty. Aside from this political status, Bulgaria's association with Romania and her contribution to hampering the drawing up of the Regulation and the establishment of the Mixed Commission, weighed against her.

In a note addressed to the representative of England at Sofia, on January 17, 1883. Voulcovitz — the Foreign Minister — expressed his fear that only Romania was invited from the riparian states. He asked the English Government that "... dans son esprit de justice et d'impartialité" to recognize Bulgaria's right just as those of the other Lower Danube riparian countries.[237]

The London Government's answer assured Bulgaria of its entire cooperation, stressing the fact that the decision depended upon the Conference.[238] As for the Vienna Government's opinion concerning admitting Bulgaria, it seems from a letter of Granville's that Government felt it was better not even to raise the question.[239]

On February 13, 1883, Voulcovitz and B. Schichmareff, respectively the first and second representative of Bulgaria, referring to the decisions of the February 10th session of the Conference in which the admission of the riparian countries was discussed again requested in a note addressed to the President, that the case of their country be considered.[240] They recalled Bulgaria's participation in the drawing up of the Regulation for Navigation, Police and Supervision, a right accorded by Article 55 of the Treaty of Berlin. As distinguished from Article 17 of the 1856 Treaty of Paris, which subordinated the admission of the vassals Principality Commissars to the approval of the Sublime Porte, the provisions of Article 55, they stated, completely modified and dispositions of Article 17.

Even before the Conference opened, Musurus, Turkey's Ambassador to Londre, communicated to the Foreign Minister of England that, inasmuch as Bulgaria was a vassal province, the right of this province's representation at the Conference belonged to Turkey's Plenipotentiary.[241]

At the second session of the Conference, when the entire problem of admitting the riparians was taken up, Granville as president took the Turkish point of view. Pointing out Bulgaria's regime of vassality, he concluded that the defense of Bulgaria's interests fell to the Turkish Plenipotentiary.[242]

The other members of the Conference subscribed to that opinion, with the exception of Russia's Plenipotentiary, who this time proposed that Bulgaria be given the right to consultative vote, the same as Romania and Serbia. In support of this proposal, he recalled Bulgaria's participation in drawing up the Regulation on the Lower Danube. He added that he would not insist if faced with the general opinion of the Conference. The Conference then adopted the Turkish objection in the sense of having the Sublime Porte's Plenipotentiary represent Bulgaria's interests.[243]

Although Russia's support of Bulgaria and Serbia's requests was circumstantial, one could ask whether she would have succeeded had she created of the incident a case of veto. It seems not. In the first place, she would have come up against the opposition of the entire Conference, which had not satisfied the requests made by Romania and Serbia. In the second place, Russia's persistence in this matter would have diminished the potential of the demand she was about to make, in that same Conference, that the Kilia Branch be removed from the jurisdiction of the European Commission. In the third place, rejecting the admission of the riparian countries was also a matter of arrangements among the Great Powers.

Faced with the rejections of her requests, Bulgaria's attitude was categoric and dignified. On February 19, 1883, in a note addressed to Granville, Voulcovitz and Schichmareff communicated that the Prince Governor of Bulgaria could not accept the status created to Bulgaria at the Conference. Furthermore, referring to Bulgaria's assistance in drawing up the E.C.D. Regulations for Navigation, Police and Supervision on the Lower Danube, they announced that Bulgaria did not consider herself bound by any decisions that might be taken by the Conference in the matter of the Regulation.[244]

At the penultimate session of the Conference, Turkey's Plenipotentiary raised also the question of the participation of the Principality of Bulgaria's representative in the Mixed Commission of the Danube, requesting that his appointment be conditional to the approval of the Sublime Porte.[245] Although Article 96 of the Regulation, by which the Mixed Commission was established, had not provided for this condition, the President admitted Turkey's reservation in this matter through a special protocol.

In conclusion, the debates over the admission on the three riparian countries with deliberative vote were futile. The Conference had preordained the decision by adopting the following amendment proposed

earlier by Plenipotentiary Münster of Prussia, just before the closing of the Conference:
"A la suite d'un échange de vues, et adoptant l'avis de la majorité, la Conférence décide qu'elle invitera la Roumanie et la Serbie à assister à ses séances, afin de les consulter et de les entendre. La Conférence décide également que les observations de la Bulgarie seront portées textuellement à la connaissance de la Conférence par l'entremise de l'Ambassadeur de Turquie."[246]

By this amendment the three riparian countries were admitted to the Conference, with consultative vote only. As shown previously, only Bulgaria and Romania refused to participate under those conditions.

Sanction of the Navigation, Police and Supervision Regulation between the Iron Gates and Galatz (Brăila).

The application of the new Regulation for the Iron Gates-Galatz section, addition to the objections of Romania and Bulgaria would have met also with the problem of executive power since it was drawn up by the members in the E.C.D. in their capacity of Delegates, rather that that of Plenipotentiaries of their respective governments. This lack had to be filled by the Conference of 1883.

The lack of executive power had been revealed earlier by the English Government. On December 11, 1882, in a circular distributed to London's representatives abroad, Granville noted the fact that the European Commission had not been able, up to that point, to reach a unanimous decision with respect either to the Regulation or to establishing the authority to be entrusted with carrying it out.[247]

While England, during the European Commission debates over the Regulation, had raised the problem of unanimity, Austria-Hungary neglected it, even refusing the opportunity of discussing it. In 1882 she suggested to Granville that the scope of the Conference be limited to the three principal themes initially set. The discussion over the Regulation would be eliminated since the debates on the matter had been carried on for years by the E.C.D. and its basis had been accepted by the Members, with the exception of Romania's Delegate.[248]

Károlyi also declared, in connection with the Regulation, that he would accept it as drawn up by the European Commission, its examination in detail being superfluous. He pointed out the Regulation's contribution to the benefit of navigation and the need for

Austro-Hungary's priority in the Mixed Commission. He rejected the doubts held by others concerning this priority, doubts he considered "chimérique."[249]

Prussia's and Italy's Plenipotentiaries adhered to this statement, while France's conditioned his adherence to the prolongation of the E.D.C.'s mandate. Turkey's Plenipotentiary also adhered, but under the condition that Bulgaria not be admitted to the Conference.

Giving up on the matter of examination, the Conference Plenary sanctioned the Regulation in the form and on the basis drawn up by the European Commission and annexed to Protocol No. 24 of June 2 and to the 1883 Treaty of London.[250] The Regulation also included the Barrère amendments which Romania had rejected in the European Commission. Immediately after the decision was read, Károlyi declared that "... desirous of exhausting all possible means of conciliation towards Romania, his Government would be disposed to add to the concessions already made during the previous negotiations a definite accord respecting: giving up the double voice in the Mixed Commission in reciprocity to Romania's double voice; admitting Romania's demand that the Lower Danube be sectioned off longitutinally in order to avoid conflicts of authority; and appointment of inspectors and assistant inspectors, for navigation by the riparian countries, not by the Mixed Commission.[251]

All the Conference members were in accord with the concessions made. In the next session, Serbia's representative declared that his country could not be other than happy at those concessions.[252]

This time, too, as in the European Commission, Romania protested and rejected the manner in which the Regulation had been drawn up as well as the preferential position granted to Austro-Hungary in the Mixed Commission.

In connection with Romania's opposition in the European Commission debates, an error on the part of her Delegate to the Commission provoked a lively discussion in the Romanian Parliament.[253] The error was that Romania's Delegate overlooked the fact that it was not necessary to establish a Mixed Commission, inasmuch as the application of any international Regulation was customarily carried out by the riparian states, in accordance with the general principles of International Public Law. From the reports of the debates on this matter it seems that Pencovici, Romania's Delegate, had opposed invoking general principles of International Public Law, as well as those of the Act of 1815 respecting the rights of riparian countries.[254] Furthermore, his refusal to sign the Regulation was also based on the lack of unanimity in the votes — a fact that had already been pointed out by Russia's Delegate as well as by the English Government, as has been mentioned.[255]

The only action Pencovici could have taken in the matter of the unanimity would have been to fall back upon the provisions of Article 12 of the Regulation for Administrative Works of the European Commission, of Nov. 10, 1879, which had made provision for the norms of voting, in respect to the importance of the questions.

Aside from the delay which would have resulted from prolonging the debates in the European Commission — which England and France would not have permitted — the problem of evaluating the Regulation would raise, either from an administrative aspect or as to its basis. Undoubtedly, drawing up the Regulation was a basic matter, but evaluating it at that level would have required a unanimous vote. This, if not impossible, would have demanded a long period of time. The difficulties of such an evaluation arose during the debates over the Mixed Commission, when the matters assigned to the E.C.D. were to be set, that is, to decide which were of administrative order, which were of principle, and which were basic.[256] The evaluation of the Regulation as a basic matter also came from the geographic modification in its application. Initially, the Regulation was to have been applied on the Lower Danube sector between the Iron Gates and Galatz. With the 1883 Conference, approval of the extension of the E.C.D. jurisdiction up to Brăila, the application of the Regulation also was extended to this port.

In spite of its being approved by the 1883 Conference, still "le Règlement est donc resté lettre morte...." This was the conclusion drawn over the juridical evolution of the Danubian problems, as stated by France's Delegates on the occasion of a temporary session of the nucleus of the E.C.D. in Exile, in 1956, in Rome.[257]

The Prolongation of the Existence of the European Commission for the Danube (E.C.D.) and the Extension of its Juridiction as far as Brăila.

The prolongation of the European Commission was the most important problem of the London Conference and the one in which England and France showed the greatest interest. Its favorable solution was the result of the compensations and compromises made among the Great Powers.

Article 4 of the 1871 Treaty of London was the basis for listing the prolongation of the European Commission's mandate on the agenda of the 1883 Conference. The debates were to be concentrated on the eventual modifications that might be found necessary as had been provided for by Article 54 of the 1878 Treaty.

The circumstances under which the prolongation was to be decided upon differed from those of the past. Between 1856, when the Commission had been established, and 1883 political events had developed which changed the territorial status of the Lower Danube valley and which had repercussions on the old navigation regime, as well as on the balance between the interests of the Great Powers.

On the other hand, the attributes given to the European Commission by Article 55 of the 1878 Treaty, signified the anticipation of the need to prolong the term of its mandate. The prolongation was directly tied in with satisfying Austria complaints concerning the Regulation and Russia's with respect to removing the Kilia Branch from E.C.D. jurisdiction.

Károlyi declared that, if the Conference encountered difficulties in resolving the problem of the prolongation, it would be self evident that it could not resolve any other questions.[258] Mohrenheim (Russia), in turn, stated that any consent he were to give for the prolongation could be only provisional and dependent upon the resolution of the "just complaints" he was to bring up:[259] this in reference to the case of the Kilia Branch. Through these complaints he was aiming at changing the order of the debates and adding to the initial agenda of the Conference.

Granville declared that the order of the debates had been adopted beforehand by the Plenipotentiaries, whom he had consulted, a statement upheld by all those present. In his response, Mohrenheim let it be understood that there was on the agenda of the Conference the matter of finding a solution for the provisions of Article 54 of the 1878 Treaty, which had stipulated the conclusion of an accord between the Powers for extending the mandate of the E.C.D. Through this accord, he intended to bring into discussion the jurisdiction of the European Commission on the Kilia Branch, as being within the framework of "... modifications qu'elles (les Puissances) jugeraient nécessaires d'y introduire," a condition foreseen by Article 54 of the 1878 Treaty of Berlin.

Turkey's Plenipotentiary presented a different interpretation. According to him, the prolongation of the Commission's mandate was a result of the principles of the 1878 Treaty. In response, Mohrenheim maintained that the question of the permanence of the E.C.D. as raised at the Congress of Berlin in 1878 had been abandoned.[260] His answer referred to a controversy, not to a decision to abandon the E.C.D. As has been shown, at the Congress of Berlin, point 3, of the Haymerlé (Austro-Hungary) proposal provided that "the European Commission of the Danube be maintained in its function...and its duration would be extended after 1883 up to the conclusion of a new accord."[261]

The whole text of Article 54 of the Treaty of 1878 had been the result of controversies; a text that was edited following the agreement between the Representatives of Austro-Hungary and Russia. Hence, at the Congress of Berlin, no steps had been taken for either the permanency of for the cessation of the Commission's mandate; simply the statement of an accord between Powers over its prolongation to be established at the Conference of London. In the end, the incident was closed by Mohrenheim who, though maintaining his opinion, stated that he did not wish to raise difficulties for the Conference.

Granville proposed a permanent prolongation of the mandate of the Commission.[262] The Plenipotententiaries of France and Italy adhered to this proposal; those of Austro-Hungary and Prussia suggested terms of eight or ten years. Finally, in a change of mind, Russia's Plenipotentiary praised the Commission's activity without eliminating the idea of diminishing its powers in the administration of the Kilia Branch. The fact that the problem of this branch was apart from the three topics on the agenda of the Conference surprised the other members. Granville, aware of the aims of Russia's Plenipotentiary, proposed and the other Plenipotentiaries approved the adjournment of the session and the postponement of the discussions in order that the grave questions presented to the Conference be carefully examined.[263]

The problem of the Kilia being settled at the next session, in Russia's favor, the last obstacle to the prolongation of the mandate of the European Commission for the Danube was removed. As in the case of the Regulation between the Iron Gates and Galatz, Barrère's proposal was the one which led not only to the liquidation of the controversy over the prolongation of the mandate, but also over the extension of its jurisdiction between Galatz and Brăila.

On the basis of the Barrère proposal — the complete text of which was part of Article 2 of the 1883 Treaty — the Commission's mandate was extended for a period of twenty-one years, beginning on April 24, 1883.[264] On the expiration of this period, the mandate was to be implicitly prolonged, under the same conditions, every three years, unless one of the contracting Great Powers announced the introduction of modifications in the composition or the attributes of the Commission one year before the expiration of the mandate.

The Plenipotentiaries of England, France and Italy subscribed to the prolongation; those of Austro-Hungary, Germany and Russia also accepted, but with the condition that the term be the same as for the term of the Regulation between the Iron Gates and Brăila, thus respecting the correlation between the European Commission and the Mixed Commission, as provided for in Article 97 of the Regulation. Turkey's Plenipotentiary also approved, although he would have preferred a permanent Commission. On this occasion, too, the one most damaged as a result of the 1878 Treaty — Turkey — was the most understanding one.

Still within the new political circumstances occuring after the 1878 Treaty, the 1883 Conference also debated the extension of the European Commission's jurisdiction between the ports of Galatz and Brăila. The matter was debated in staged, on February 10 and 13 and on March 7, its resolution entered into Article 1 of the 1883 Treaty of London.

The decision over the extension was to England's satisfaction, but was opposed by Romania, on the basis of her territorial sovereignty over the Galatz-Brăila sector. In arguing Romania's justification, D. Sturdza, her Minister for Foreign Affairs, invoked past respecting of Turkish suzerainty on the Galatz-Brăila sector. "In 1866 and 1871" he argued, "the Powers did not believe they had the right to extend the Commission's jurisdiction between Galatz and Brăila against the opposition of the suzerain Turkey. How could that very jurisdiction be extended today on that same sector, now under Romanian sovereignty, without Romania's participation in the Conference"?[265]

At the time of the 1878 Conference, when the decision to remove the European Commission from under the territorial authority of Romania, the latter was not yet independent; however, in 1883 she did exercise her prerogative. From this aspect the 1883 decision can be considered lacking in logic, justice and the respect for the most elementary principles of International Law. "Sui generis" was the qualification given by F. Holtzendorff to the extension of the European Commission's Jurisdiction over the Galatz-Brăila sector under Romania's sovereignty.[266]

Through this extension, a new consolidation of the European Commission was effectuated. De facto the extension was to the advantage of navigation; de jure, it lessened Romania's sovereignty over that sector.

The Detachment of the Kilia Branch from the Jurisdiction of the European Commission for the Danube.

The decision of the 1883 Conference to detach the Kilia Branch from the jurisdiction of the European Commission can be considered proof of the permanence of Russian policy to extend its presence and influence also along the banks of the Lower Danube River. In view of her reduced commercial interests, that presence has been, is, and will be exclusively political, justified by needs of strategic military order.

In 1812, by annexing Bessarabia, Russia became riparian to the Danube along the Kilia Branch and, in 1829, ruler over the Sulina Mouth and Branch. In 1856, Russia was expelled from the Danube, only to become a riparian again in 1878 and to succeed in 1883 in detaching the Kilia Branch from the jurisdiction of the European Commission.

At the 1883 Conference of London, Mohrenheim categorically demanded the detachment of the Kilia Branch. This time, the aim was reached without too much difficulty, thanks to the prearrangements among the Great Powers. Aside from the preconditions to Russia's acceptance of the prolongation of the European Commission mandate and other problems, she had informed the other Great Powers of her intentions concerning Kilia, before the opening of the Conference. In her note of January 26, 1883, she justified her exclusive jurisdiction over the Kilia, this time by the necessity for carrying out technical works," which could have been necessary for the economic interests of Bessarabia and the Russian ports in the South."[267] This note also included the idea of compensation, mention being made to the effect that "... the recognition of the legitimacy of this request might lead Russia to agree to the prolongation of the European Commission."

Although the order of the problems to be resolved at the Conference did not include that of the Kilia Branch, still Mohrenheim's request was debated. Its inclusion had become necessary inasmuch as Russia had, in the note of January 26, 1883, conditioned her participation in the debates on the prolongation of the European Commission mandate to her complaints over the Kilia being taken into consideration. Romanenko in 1881, as well as Mohrenheim in 1883, Russia's Representatives had based their arguments on concrete past decisions and actual situations, all partially favorable to them. In upholding his point of view, Mohrenheim cited Article 54 of the 1878 Treaty which stated that "... the Powers will agree on the prolongation of the mandate of the European Commission for the Danube and on the modifications they will find necessary to introduce."

Removing the Kilia Branch from the European Commission's jurisdiction was nothing other than a change which one of the Powers judged necessary to be introduced into the future jurisdictional structure of the Commission, if its mandate were to be extended. Mohrenheim also tried to prove that the Kilia Branch and Mouth were not to be included in the authority of the Commission inasmuch as the latter's attention was directed to the Sulina Mouth. In other words, as Romanenko had declared in 1881, the Kilia Branch had been abandoned by the European Commission and Mohrenheim added that, of the three branches of the river, the Sulina Branch had been selected in 1856. In reality, the Kilia Branch, and especially the Kilia Mouth, had not been abandoned. The technical works carried out by the European Commission were not permanent, but emergency ones, whenever the navigational depths at the Sulina Mouth were threatened by the alluvial deposits from the Kilia Branch. In 1881, Siborne, England's Delegate to the European Commission, called attention to Article 15 of the Treaty of 1856, which had assigned to the European Commission the execution of the technical works at "the mouths of the Danube," hence, at all the mouths including those of the Kilia Branch.

Acknowledging that "in the beginning, the European Commission had at its disposition all the mouths," Romanenko still invoked in 1881 the need for some modification. In his opinion, those who had drawn up the 1856 Treaty used the expression "embouchures du Danube," without knowing which of the three would be chosen by the European Commission and that, in the end, the Commission would decide upon one. This, according to him, was only the Sulina Mouth, whose technical works and organization encompassed also the branch of that name and were inscribed in the Public Act of 1865.[268] To this just interpretation the Delegates of France and England in 1881, and Granville in the 1883 Conference, responded in a single but well-founded argument resulting from the rationale itself for establishing the European Commission for the Danube; that "of clearing the mouths of the Danube of sands and other obstacles and impediments and the maintenance of navigation at the mouths of the Danube."[269] The choosing of a permanent exit to the sea being a very controversial problem after the European Commission was established in 1856, it was presented in 1858 to a technical Commission meeting in Paris. Of the three branches and mouths, the Sulina, the Kilia and the St. George, the latter two were reported as presenting the best hydrotechnical and hydrographic conditions.[270] However, under the

CONFERENCE AND TREATY OF LONDON, OF 1883   405

pressure of continually increasing traffic, the Sulina Branch and Mouth were chosen, "temporarily" since their working arrangments presenting bydrographic and financial conveniences.

After 1856, the problem of alluvia brought down by the Kilia branches was continually in the technical studies of the European Commission. In 1881, Siborne declared that Protocol No. 270, of May 2, 1872, made provision for credits for the study of the natural phenomena of the mouths and branches of the St. George and the Kilia.[271]

The report of Sir Charles Hartley, former Chief Engineer of the European Commission, concerning the studies made of the natural phenomena at the Danube Mouths included also the Stary-Stamboul, the sub-branch of the Kilia, these studies made between 1856 and 1881.[272]

Conversely, in Article 3 of the Draft Project for the Additional Act to the 1865 Public Act, presented to the Commission by the Delegate of Austro-Hungary, provision was made for "tous travaux qui seraient jugés nécessaires pour améliorer les bras et les embouchures de St. Georges et de Kilia."

These several measures and existing projects were indubitable proofs of the constant presence of the Kilia Branch and mouths in the European Commissions preoccupations which Russia's Representative contested. All these preoccupations were historic facts in the activity of the European Commission, just as were the "faits historiques" invoked by Mohrenheim in upholding the modifications of the Commission's functions.[273]

The seriousness of Mohrenheim's demande lay in the attacks against the political — juridical rationale for the establishment of the European Commission. He let it be understood that rejecting his demands would lead his Government to contest the activity of the European Commission in other navigation sectors, in which it operated by acknowledging "... the extension of Europe's jurisdiction only on the international Sulina Branch."[274] In other words he contested the entire international regime fixed by the 1856 Treaty also on the other navigation sectors, as for example that upriver from the Sulina Branch and the Kilia and the St. Geroge Branches. Mohrenheim's demand as formulated in the February 20th session of the Conference of London contained the following:[275] inclusion of the branch and sub-branches and mouth of the Kilia, along the entire length adjacent to Russia territory; transferring to exclusive Russian territorial authority of the mixed course of the Kilia whose thalweg formed the frontier between Russia and Romania; application of the Fluvial Regulation of Navigation on the Kilia Branch by Russia and Romania; the Regulation to be carried out using that of the European Commission as a basis; avoiding prejudicing navigation on the Sulina Branch by the technical work carried out by Russia on her water sectors; and, in case of conflicts between Russia and the European Commission, recourse to arbitration of the Contracting Powers; and finally, taking into consideration the counsel of the European Commission with respect to the Regulation for Navigation taxes and recourse to the arbitration by the Contracting Powers, in case of divergences.

The above formulations had the appearance of the modifications provided for in Article 54 of the 1878 Treaty concerning the prolongation of the European Commission mandate. Basically, through them an entirely new regime was being introduced, completely independent of the authority, control and especially the responsibility of the Commission, with respect to maintenance of navigation on the sectors assigned to it by the Treaty of 1856, as well as with respect to supervision of the methods of application of the international regime of navigation. For this reason, in spite of the cessions and compromises which England and France were disposed to make, they refused to accede completely to Mohrenheim's demands. They were determined to take away some minor attributes of the Commission's powers, but not also to diminish its general control over the method of applying the international regime of navigation at all the river mouths.

Diminuation of the European Commission's jurisdiction, as demanded by Russia, would have signified transforming this institution into a simple European enterprise for administration of navigation only at the Sulina Mouth and Branch, depriving it of its function of custodian of the navigation regime on the Danube and its mouths.

In the February 24th session, Granville made two declarations.[276] As president of the Conference, he regretfully announced the conditions Russia's Plenipotentiary attached to acceptance of the prolongation of the European Commission's mandate: that is, approval of the modifications he requested with regard to the Kilia Branch. He overlooked the fact that the Anglo-Russian accord concerning Kilia had been concluded in the pre-arrangements made before the Conference.[277] This might explain the fact that in this session he presented the compromise proposal in which some of the European Commission attributes over the Kilia were retained, in order to maintain to some degree the Commission's partial authority over the Kilia.[278]

Granville's misgivings were raised by the disadvantage to the European Commission in the eventuality that the Russians would create a second navigable exit to the sea out of the Kilia Branch. This explains the setting of the Commission's supervision, proposed by him, over the Regulation for Navigation Taxes on the Kilia.

This became the subject of a discussion between Granville and Russia's Plenipotentiary, the former's point of view being that the tolls to be set in such a way as to avoid any confict of interest between the Russian authorities on the Kilia and the European Commission. Only after an exchange of correspondence between the cabinets was it possible to reach a compromise, the text of which became part of Article 6 of the 1883 Treaty.

Removing the Kilia Branch from the actual control of Commission had effects also on the Russo-Romanian relations, creating even a diplomatic conflict caused by a change in the Russian point of view over the initial setting of the frontier and the erroneous interpretation of the clause of Article 45 of the 1878 Treaty of Berlin.

At the Conference of the signatories of the 1857 Treaty of Paris, for the new delimitation of the frontier between Bessarabia and the Danube Delta, Russia demanded — without its being approved — that the line of demarcation pass through the thalweg of the Belgarod waters, the northernmost sub-branch of the Kilia, but not through that of the Stary-Stamboul sub-branch at the southernmost extremity of the Kilia Delta. Russia maintained that some stand also in the European Commission session of May 20, 27, and of June 29, 1861, on the occasion of the debates over those same frontiers. In 1878, after the reannexation of Southern Bessarabia, when the problem of the new frontier between Russia and Romania was raised, Russia's representatives requested and obtained the agreement of the Conference of Berlin that the new line of delimitation be the Stary-Stamboul this time, that is, the Kilia sub-branch close to the Sulina Mouth.

Later, Grigore Antipa (Romania) took, as a basis, the on-site studies of Sir Charles Hartley, former chief engineer of the European Commission, Mucczinki, Spratt, etc, of the growth of the bars in front of the Kilia Mouths, and concluded that the Russians were meeting technical difficulties in opening the mouth of the Otchacov sub-branch to the north. The bar there was increasing continually, so the Russians concentrated their attentions on the Stary-Stamboul, which presented easier possibilities for being made navigable.[279]

The tendency of the Russians after 1878 was to include in their possession the entire course of the Stary-Stamboul, especially its mouth. Russian actions followed; small conflicts arose between Romanian frontier guards and Russian fishermen who crossed over on the Romanian banks, and the appearance of Russian military vessels.[280] Mohrenheim's declaration at the Conference of London, in the sense of referring to the signatory Powers of the 1883 Treaty any divergences arising between Russia, Romania and the European Commission remained theoretically valid, given the difficulties that might arise if Romania took recourse to the support of the Great Powers. In order to avoid any conflict with Russia, "the entire question was treated with so much discretion by the Romanian Government that nothing leaked out to the press," — wrote Antipa.[281]

Russia's note to the Romanian Government in 1884 requested the appointment of a Mixed Commission to examine the problem of Stary-Stamboul.[282] The Russian side argued the theory that the courses of the Stary-Stamboul water, including their thalweg, extended into the sea beyond the shore. In support of the Romanian contrary argument, there were invoked scientific definitions by celebrated foreign hydrographers, hydrologists and specialists in Danubian problems.[283] Grigore Antipa, one of the members of the Mixed Commission, revealed the fact that, in the framework of the negotiations, the Russians had invoked a different text of Article 45 of the 1878 Treaty of Berlin, in reference to the delimitation in the reannexation of Southern Bessarabia.[284]

The note of the Russian Government stated "le thalweg des bouches de Staro-Stamboulou," not "l'embouchure de Staro-Stamboulou" (sic), as the delimitation had been stipulated in Article 45. The Romanians considered the frontier line to be the thalweg of the Stary-Stamboul, up to its mouth, in accordance with Article 45, but the Russians maintained it to be up to the thalweg of the mouths of that sub-branch, a thalweg that extended into the sea, not just to the mouth of the sub-branch.

The conflict provoked by Russia seemed to be more political, to support a public reaffirmation of the exclusion of the Kilia from the jurisdiction of the European Commission, that it was a vital navigation problem. As to the technical work on the Kilia Branch and Mouth invoked by the Russians, Hajnal cited the opinion of the Austro-Hungarian Ambassador to St. Petersburg, in the sense that Russia intended to provoke a conflict analogous to the one Holland created in the matter of navigation at the mouths of the Rhine.[285]

After 1938, when Romania assumed some of the attributes of the European Commission, signs of reopening the Russo-Romanian conflict appeared. This time, Romania remained alone, without the international support of the European Commission.

Between June 1940 and June 1941, along with Russia's reannexation of all of Bessarabia, the Romanian administration's access to the

Stary-Stamboul Mouth was restricted to a single study session of a small group of Romanian and Russian hydrographers.

Between June 22, 1941 and August 23, 1944, i.e. during the period of the war against Soviet Russia, the hydrographic studies at that same mouth were resumed by the Romanian administration. On the basis of the 1948 Danubian Convention in Belgrad, the Russians included under their sovereignty the entire Kilia Branch, with all its sub-branches, they being completely detached from the international regime of navigation.

Clauses of the Treaty of London Concerning the Lower Danube. The Annexes and the Final Protocols.

The Treaty of London was signed on March 10, 1883, having as annexes the Regulation for Navigation, Police and Supervision applicable on the Lower Danube sector between the Iron Gates and Brăila, and three additional Protocols. It was ratified in London and August 21, 1883.[286]

Summing up, the contents of the nine Articles of the Treaty concerning the Lower Danube were as follows: extension of the jurisdiction of the European Commission for the Danube from Galatz to Brăila (Article 1); prolongation of the Commission's power for a term of twenty-one years, beginning April 24, 1883 (Article 2); removal of the Kilia Branch from the jurisdiction of the European Commission (Article 3); application of the Regulation in force on the Sulina Branch also on the Kilia Branch (Article 4); reporting to the European Commission the technical work being carried out on the Kilia Branch by Russia and Romania (Article 5); Russia's rights to apply customs taxes on the Kilia (Article 6); adoption of the approval of the Regulations for Navigation, Police and Supervision applicable between the Iron Gates and Brăila (Article 7); respecting all previous treaties, conventions and arrangements concerning the Danube and its mouth, the clauses of which had not been abrogated by the 1883 Treaty (Article 8); ratification of the Treaty within six months (Article 9).

After the signing of the Treaty in London, on August and October 1883, three separate Protocols were also concluded.

Protocol No. 1 (August 21) referred to the procedure for ratification of the Treaty. By Protocol No. 2 (August 24), the President took note of Russia's reserve over the dependence of the Delegate of the Principality of Bulgaria upon Turkey (its suzerain); and in Protocol

No. 3 Turkey maintained her reservation over her naming the delegate of that same Principality to the Mixed Commission. The Treaty was radically modified after World War I.

Conclusions.

The Treaty of 1883, as can be seen by the above, was the result of a series of disputes, contradictions and especially of yieldings and compromises.

The prolongation of the European Commission's mandate was in support of the international regime of navigation, as was the extension of the jurisdiction as far as Brăila. Not in its favor was the detaching of the Kilia Branch from that same jurisdiction, resulting as it did in the strengthening of Russia's position at the mouths of the Danube. Austro-Hungary succeeded in getting the approval for the Regulation between the Iron Gates and Brăila, as well as the Mixed Commission of the Danube, both not practically applicable due to Romania's objections.

The modifications made in 1871, 1878 and 1883, of the original 1856 international regime of navigation, were to be followed by those of the 1919 Peace Treaty of Versailles, of the Convention for the Definitive Statute of the Danube in 1921, and the Danubian Convention at Belgrade in 1948.

Notes

Chapter 1

1. Published November 15, 1870, in the "Journal of St. Petersburg."
2. Prokesch-Osten to Beust, Constantinople, January 3, 1871 and Beust to Prokesch-Osten, Vienna, January 21, 1871; in "La Question du Danube," M.A.E., op. cit., p. 402.
3. Protocols No. 3 of February 3 and No. 5, of March 13, 1871; D. Sturdza, "Recueil...," pp. 100-107; "La Question du Danube," M.A.E., op. cit., pp. 405-408.
4. Hajnal in "Le Droit...," p. 102, and note 3.
5. Idem, pp. 101-102.
6. Idem, p. 102.
7. V.T. Văcărescu "Serbia in 1871-1872"; in "Două Memorii," published by N. Iorga, Bucharest, 1916, p. 31.
8. M. Kogălniceanu, Foreign Minister of Romania to I. Strat, Diplomatic Agent at Paris; in "M. Kogălniceanu, documente diplomatice," p. 92.
9. Le Ministre des Affaires Etrangères de S.M. Britanique aux Représentants de l'Angleterre à l'Etranger, London, March 14, 1883; in D. Sturdza, "Recueil...," p. 400.
10. Beust to Prokesch-Osten, Vienna, January 21, 1871; op. cit.
11. Idem.
12. Idem.
13. Idem.
14. Protocol No. 3, February 1871.
15. Protocol No. 3, February 1871.
16. Ibid.
17. N. Iorga "Politica externă a Regelui Carol I," p. 107.
18. Beust to Prokesch-Osten, January 21, 1871, op. cit.
19. Hajnal, "Le Droit...," p. 92.
20. Idem, ibid., p. 93.
21. Idem, ibid., p. 93.
22. Ch. Stokes, "Projet d'un arrangement pour la future administration de la navigation du Danube"; quoted by Hajnal, in "Le Droit..."; p. 93.
23. Hajnal, "Le Droit...," p. 93.

24. Beust to the Austro-Hungarian Ambassador at Berlin, a letter published in Livre Rouge, quoted by Hajnal in "Le Droit...," p. 95, (translation from German text; "We which that the entire Commission of the Riparian States be reserved for the future")
25. Prokesch-Osten to Beust, January 3, 1871; Beust to Prokesch-Osten, January 21, 1871, op. cit.
26. Prokesch-Osten to Beust, January 3, 1871.
27. Beust to Prokesch-Osten, January 21, 1871.
28. Idem.
29. Protocol No. 3 of February 3, 1871.
30. Ibid.
31. Ibid.
32. Ibid.
33. Prokesch-Osten to Beust, op. cit.
34. Protocol No. 3 of February 3, 1871.
35. Protocol No. 5 of March 13, 1871.
36. Ibid.
37. Ibid.
38. Ibid.
39. Ibid.
40. Beust to Prokesch-Osten, January 21, 1871, op. cit.
41. Protocol No. 3, February 3, 1871.
42. Ibid., Annex.
43. Ibid.
44. Hajnal, "Le Droit...," p. 100.
45. Idem, ibid., p. 100, note 2.
46. Beust to Prokesch-Osten, January 21, 1871, op. cit.
47. Protocol No. 5, March 13, 1871.
48. Ibid.
49. Ibid.
50. England, Austro-Hungry, France, Italy, Prussia, Russia and Turkey.
51. "Traité portant modification du Traité de Paris du 30 Mars 1856," signé à Londres le 13 Mars 1871.
Four Articles 4 to 7, referring to the Lower Danube, see D. Sturdza, "Recueil..." p. 108.
"La Question du Danube" M.A.E., p. 412. For the entire Treaty, see Hertslert. "Map of Europe...," Vol. III, p. 109.

Chapter 2

52. W.N. Medlicott, "The Congress of Berlin and After," p. 2.
53. The United Romanian Principalities had adopted the name of România on January 24, 1862. This title was recognized by the Great Powers after 1878.

54. M. Kogălniceanu to General I. Ghica, Romania's Diplomatic Agent to Constantinople, Bucharest, June 18, 1876; In "Mihail Kogălniceanu, documente diplomatice," p. 128.
55. "Mihail Kogălniceanu, documente diplomatice," p. 162.
56. N. Iorga, "Politica externă...," op. cit., p. 209.
57. D. Berindei, "Reprezentantele diplomatice ale României," Vol. I, p. 129.
58. "Mihail Kogălniceanu, documente diplomatice," p. 89.
59. Ibid., pp. 98, 100.
60. Ibid., pp. 98, 101.
61. Ibid., p. 154.
62. Andrassy, Foreign Minister, to Vienna's Ambassador to St. Petersburg, Vienna, May 6, 1871; "La Question du Danube," M.A.E., p. 432.
63. "La Question du Danube," M.A.E., p. 433.
64. Hajnal, "Le Droit...," pp. 121, 122.
65. Idem, ibid., p. 119.
66. Idem, ibid., p. 121, note 2.
67. Idem, ibid., p. 121, note 2.
68. Iden, ibid., p. 122.
69. N. Iorga, "Politica externă...," pp. 212, 240.
70. Gh. Cazan "Petersburg," in "Representantele diplomatice ale României," Vol. 1, p. 209.
71. M. Kogălniceanu to N. Callimachi-Catargi, Romanian Diplomatic Agent to Paris, Bucharest, July 20, 1876; in "Mihai Kogălniceanu, documente diplomatice," op. cit. p. 134.
72. C.C. Giurescu, "Istoricul Orasului Brăila," p. 214.
73. "The History of Nations," Vol. XV. p. 332.
74. R.W. Seton-Watson, "A History of...," p. 336.

Chapter 3

75. Pozzi de Borgo, Capodistria, Nesselrode, Ribeaupierre, Brunow, etc.
76. "Russes et Turcs," op. cit., p. 991.
77. Emil Ludwig, "Bismarck," N.Y. 1932, p. 16.
78. D.C. Somervell, "Disraeli and Gladstone," p. 205.
79. André Maurois, "Disraeli," (trans. from the French by Hamish Milles), p. 328.
80. D.C. Somervell, p. 205.
81. Emil Ludwig, "Bismarck," op. cit., p. 515.
82. Protocols, No. 9, June 29; No. 11, July 2 and No. 12, July 4, 1878; in Sturdza "Recueil..."; "La Question du Danube," M.A.E., pp. 438-443.
83. W.N. Medlicott, "The Congress...," p. 33.

84. "Convention provisoire entre la Serbie et l'Autriche-Hongrie concernant les chemins de fer et la régularisation des Portes-de-Fer," Berlin, 8 Juillet, 1878; in D. Sturdza, "Recueil...," p. 125; also quoted by W.N. Medlicott, "The Congress...," p. 100, note 157.

85. W.N. Medlicott, "The Congress...," p. 28; and "Russes et Turcs," p. 1100, note 1.

86. N. Iorga, "Politica externă...," p. 293.

87. Protocol No. 9 June 29, 1878; "Russes et Turcs," pp. 1107-1108.

88. Medlicott, "The Congress...," p. 88.

89. From the August 15, 1877 report of Obedeanu, Romanian Diplomatic Agent at Rome; quoted by N. Iorga in "Politica externă...," p. 225.

90. Medlicott, op. cit., p. 31.

91. Idem, ibid., p. 358.

92. Viorica Moisuc, "Varsovia"; in "Reprezentantele diplomatice ale României," Vol. II, p. 141.

93. Concluded on February 19 (March 3) 1878; F. Israel, "Major Peace Treaties...," Vol. II, p. 959; Hertslet, "Map of...," Vol. IV, p. 2674, Martens, N.R.G.T., (s. II), Vol III, p. 246.

94. Protocol No. 9, June 29, 1878.

95. "Russes et Turcs, pp. 1047, 1052; Medlicott, "The Congress...," p. 15.

96. "Russes et Turcs," p. 1051.

97. Ibid., p. 1054.

98. Russes et Turcs," p. 1054.

99. Protocol No. 9, June 29, 1878.

100. Ibid.

101. Ibid.

102. Ibid.

103. Ibid.

104. Ibid.

105. "Russes et Turcs," pp. 472-474.

106. Ibid., pp. 472-474, 487, 686, 691.

107. Quoted by N. Iorga, "Politica externă...," p. 288, note 1.

108. Protocol No. 9, June 29, 1878.

109. He evaluated it at 3500 sq. kilometres from Dobruja, including the Danube Delta, with a population of 80,000.

110. Protocol No. 9, June 29, 1878.

NOTES 415

111. The cases to which he referred had been decided and approved by the signatories of the 1856 Treaty by the following acts: the Danube Delta, by the Treaty of 1857; the Union of the Romanian Principalities by Articles 1 and 3 of the Convention for the Definitive organization of the Principalities of Moldavia and Wallachia, Paris, August 19, 1858; the political union of the two Principalities had been approved by the Sultan in two firmans as well as by the Ambassadors of the signatory Powers of the 1856 Treaty, who concluded the Additional Act to the 1858 Convention, on June 28, 1864, at Constantinople; see T.W. Riker, "The Making of Roumania," p. 455. In 1867, the Sultan and the signatories of the 1856 Treaty acknowledged the election of Prince Carol Hohenzollern (the foreign prince) as sole ruler of Romania; Ibid., p. 565, note 4.

112. N. Iorga, "Politica externă...," report of Ghica, Romanian Envoy to St. Petersburg, January 26, 1878, p. 282, note 1.

113. Idem, ibid., p. 130.

114. "Russes et Turcs," p. 1025.

115. Report of Filipescu, Romania's Envoy to St. Petersburg, April 18, 1876; quoted by N. Iorga in "Politica externă...," p. 135, note 2.

116. Medlicott, "The Congress," pp. 2, 3; note 1.

117. Quoted by R.W. Seton-Watson, "A History...," p. 344.

118. Idem, ibid., p. 343.

119. Idem, ibid., p. 343.

120. Idem, ibid., p. 344.

121. "Russes et Turcs," pp. 1070, 1071, Point 11 of the Accord.

122. W.N. Medlicott, "The Congress...," p. 89.

123. See Bolgrad case.

124. Protocol No. 9, June 29, 1878.

125. Derby to Loftus, Foreign Office, January 29, 1878; letter published in British Blue Book; quoted in "Russes et Turcs," p. 1032.

126. R.W. Seton-Watson; "A History...," p. 258.

127. "Russes et Turcs," p. 754.

128. Somervell, op. cit., p. 263.

129. Idem, ibid., p. 198. According to another biographer this statement was expressed prior to the Congress of Berlin. Referring to his protection of British interests, Disraeli said: "Cosmopolitan critics, men who are the friends of every country save their own, have denounced this policy as a selfish policy: it is as selfish as patriotism"; Hesketh Pearson, "Disraeli: His Life."

130. Protocol No. 9, June 29, 1878.

131. Ibid.

132. Alex. Carathéodory, "Le Rapport Secret sur le Congrès de Berlin adressé à la Sublime Porte," p. 58.

133. "Russes et Turcs," p. 1023.

134. Quoted by Medlicott, "The Congress," p. 37.

135. "Germany has little interest in the Eastern Question and yet the Chancellor wished to direct everything; I am not at all disposed to follow in his wake"; Beaconfield to the French Ambassador; from Salisbury, quoted by Medlicott, op. cit., p. 159 and note 39.

136. A. Carathéodory, "Le Rapport Secret...," op. cit., p. 59.

137. Idem, ibid., p. 26.

138. Idem, ibid., p. 68.

139. "Russes et Turcs," p. 1023.

140. Protocol No. 12, July 4, 1878.

141. The traffic of steam vessels of the small German states within the German Empire will be taken into consideration, along with that of Prussia, in the statistical evaluation.

Between 1847 and 1856, the traffic of these vessels on the Maritime Danube, towards the Black Sea, was 1.30% in number, of a total of 19,498 vessels (repeated entrances); see Hajnal, "The Danube...," pp. 156, 157.

Between 1860 and 1890, the German flag registered 118 steamships through the Sulina Mouth; Hajnal, op. cit., p. 164.

142. "Russes et Turcs," p. 1110.

143. Quoted by N. Iorga, "Politica externă...," p. 236, note 2.

144. N. Iorga, "Politica externă...," p. 236, note 2.

145. See details in W.D. Medlicott, "The Congress," pp. 90, 184, 200-202.

146. Protocol No. 9, June 29, 1878.

147. R.W. Seton-Watson, "A History of...," p. 341.

148. Ghica report to his Government: "Empereur et Chancelier m'ont formellement fait connaître leur intention de reprendre partie de Bessarabie jusqu'à Kilia; en compensation Roumanie recevra Delta Danube, la Dobroudcha (sic) jusqu'a Kustenje." (sic) January 26, 1878; quoted by N. Iorga, in "Politica externă...," p. 282, note 1.

149. N. Iorga, "Politica externă...," pp. 331, 332.

150. Sturdza, "Recueil...," p. 110.

151. Instead of European Commission of the Danube, it was transcribed as the International Commission of the Danube.

152. Protocol No. 11 of July 2, 1878.

153. Hajnal, "Le Droit...," p. 129.

154. Idem, ibid., p. 134.

155. Protocol No. 11, July 2, 1878.

156. Ibid., No. 12, July 4, 1878.

157. Protocol No. 11, July 2, 1878.

158. Ibid.

159. For Articles 52 to 57, see D. Sturdza, "Recueil...," p. 123; "La Question du Danube," M.A.E., p. 445; For the entire Treaty, see: Martens, N.R.G.T. (S. II) Vol. III, p. 449; F. Israel, "Major...," Vol II, p. 997.

Chapter 4

160. D. Sturdza, "Recueil...," pp. 127-135; "La Question du Danube," M.A.E., pp. 451-455.

161. Idem., ibid., pp. 136-188.

162. The Protocols and Procès-Verbaux of the E.C.D. can be seen in "La Question du Danube," M.A.E., pp. 456, 522.

163. The French Delegate left Galatz; the English Delegate excused himself because of ill health; those of Russia and Germany were indisposed; Romania's had not yet received instructions from his Government; (Protocol of the E.C.D., No. 354, of January 3, 1880); Turkey's was temporarily absent from Galatz (E.C.D. Protocol 355 of January 3, 1880). The only one who was not ill was Austro-Hungary's; in "La Question du Danube," pp. 511-513.

164. "Projet d'un nouvel Acte Public relatif à la navigation des embouchures du Danube," annexe au Procès-Verbal de la Séance du Comité Executif, du 25 Février, 1879; in "La Question du Danube," pp. 461-465.

165. "Note du délégué de France à la Commission Européenne du Danube," Paris, Avril 2, 1879; "La Question du Danube," M.A.E., p. 466.

166. E.C.D., Protocol No. 318, Nov. 5, 1878; "La Question du Danube," M.A.E., p. 456.

167. Ibid., ibid., No. 318, November 5, 1878; "La Question du Danube," M.A.E., p. 456.

168. Ibid., ibid., No. 340, November 21, 1879; "La Question du Danube," M.A.E., p. 481.

169. E.C.D., Protocole No. 341. Novembre 24, 1879; "La Question du Danube," pp. 481-482.

170. "Acte Additionnel à l'Acte Public du 2 Novembre 1865," relatif à la navigation aux embouchures du Danube," Galatz, May 28, 1881; D. Sturdza, "Recueil...," pp. 189-193.

171. E.C.D., Protocol No. 384 of May 28, 1881; "La Question du Danube," p. 520.

172. Ibid., No. 380, May 17, 1881; ibid., p. 520.

173. "La Question du Danube," M.A.E., pp. 370-g, 570-h, 583-768.

174. E.C.D. Protocol No. 349 of Dember 17, 1870; "La Question du Danube," M.A.E., p. 570-g.

175. From the "Rapport des Délégués de la Commission Européenne du Danube," Galatz, May 12, 1880; "La Question du Danube," p. 570-h.

176. Hajnal, "Le Droit...," p. 148.

177. Idem., ibid., p. 133.

178. Idem., ibid., p. 133.

179. Idem., ibid., p. 149.

180. "In general, Austria is impelled by imperious necessity to not lose any occasion, offered her by carrying out the provisions of the Treaty of Berlin to strengthen her positions on the Danube down river from the Iron Gates"; quoted from "Der Berliner Vertrag und die Donau," an article published in the newspaper "Presse," Vienna, 29 December 1878; Hajnal, "Le Droit...," p. 149.

181. From the "Mihail Kogălniceanu, documente diplomatice," pp. 179, 349.

182. "Règlement de la Navigation, de Police Fluviale et de Surveillance de 1882 applicable à la parte du Danube située entre les Portes de Fer et Brăila, élaboré en exécution de l'article 55 du Traité de Berlin, du 13 Juillet 1878, par la Commission Européenne du Danube, avec l'assistance des Délégués des Etats Riverains"; Annexe au Traité de Londres, du 10 Mars 1883; Sturdza, "Recueil...," pp. 478-507; "La Question du Danube," M.A.E., pp. 741-767.

183. E.C.D., Protocol No. 5, Dec. 15, 1880; "La Question du Danube," M.A.E., p. 619.

184. Le Ministre des Affaires Etrangères de S.M. Britanique aux représentants de l'Angleterre à l'Etranger, Londres, 14 Mars, 1883; in D. Sturdza, "Recueil...," p. 404.

185. E.C.D., Protocole No. 5, December 15, 1880; in "La Question du Danube," M.A.E., p. 618.

186. Le Ministre des Affaires Etrangères de S.M. Britanique aux Représentants de l'Angleterre à l'Etranger; Londres, 14 Mars, 1883; D. Sturdza, "Recueil...," p. 404.

187. See Barrèrc's proposal versus the Romanian counter-proposal; in D. Sturdza, "Recueil...," p. 237; the European Commission for the Danube, Protocol No. 23 of May 27, 1882; in "La Question du Danube," M.A.E., p. 727.

188. Hajnal, "Le Droit...," p. 155.

189. E.C.D. Protocol No. 23, May 27, 1882.

190. P.S. Aurelian "Opere Economice," p. 367, note 1.

191. M. Kogălniceanu, "Chestiunea Dunării," from his speech of May 1 and 2, 1882, in the Romanian Parliament.

192. E.C.D., Protocol No. 345 of December 8, 1879; "La Question du Danube," M.A.E., p. 500.

193. The traffic of foreign maritime vessels participating in exports through the port of Ismail in 1831, recorded 97 vessels; Report of Sardinian Consul at Ismail, D. Bodin, op. cit., p. 77.

194. E.C.D, Protocol No. 345, of 8 December 1879.

195. M. Kogălniceanu, "Chestiunea Dunării," op. cit., pp. 1-55.

196. Pro-Memoria du Représentant de l'Autriche-Hongrie à Londres, au Comte Granville, 18 Jan., 1883; in D. Sturdza, "Recueil...," p. 344.

197. See Part of correspondence in D. Sturdza, "Recueil...," pp. 204, 213, 226.

198. E.C.D. Protocol No. 4, December 12, 1880; "La Question du Danube," M.A.E., p. 611.

199. Article in official newspaper "Österreichische Schifferzeitung," Vienna (no date) quoted by C. Băicoianu in "Le Danube apperçu...," p. 177.
200. Hajnal, "Le Droit...," p. 175.
201. N. Iorga, "A cui e Dunărea?" lecture given at Giurgiu, November 9, 1908, p. 15.
202. "Rapport relatif à la navigation sur le Danube, présenté à la Commission Consultative et du Travail de la Soc. des Nations," par Walker D. Hines, Genève, 20 Août, 1925.
203. Hajnal, "Le Droit...," p. 175.
204. N. Docan, "Memoriu despre lucrările cartografice privind răsboiul dintre 1787-1791," p. 16.

Chapter 5

205. Le Ministre des Affaires Etrangères de Grande-Bretagne au Vicomte Lyons, a Paris, 28 Octobre 1882; in D. Sturdza, "Recueil...," pp. 261, 263.
206. See D. Sturdza, "Recueil...," Table of Contents.
207. "Protocoles des Conférences tenues à Londres au sujet de la navigation du Danube, du 8 Février au 10 Mars 1883; Protocols No. 1, 2, 3, 4, 5, 6, 7, 8, respectively of February 8, 10, 13, 20, 24, and 1, 7, 10 March 1883; see D. Sturdza, "Recueil...," pp. 417-471; Martens N.R.G.T. (1876-1908) s. II, Vol. X. p. 346; "La Question du Danube," M.A.E., pp. 832-833, 841, 847, 856, 866.
208. Letter by M. Martens concerning navigation on international rivers, published in "Revue du Droit International et de Legislation Comparée." Vol. XV, 1883, pp. 626, 627.
209. L'Annuaire de "L'Institut de Droit International," Bruxelles, 1888, pp. 272-289; quoted by Hajnal, "Le Droit...," p. 178, note 1.
210. Hajnal, op. cit., p. 233, footnote 1.
211. The Bunsen, "La Question du Danube"; in "Revue de Droit International et de Legislation Comparée," Vol. XVI, Bruxelles (1884), pp. 551, 552.
212. F. Holtzendorf, "Les Droits riverains de la Roumanie sur le Danube," p. 100.
213. Protocol No. 2, February 10, 1883.
214. G. Demorgny, "Danube et Adriatique," p. 62.
215. Le Comte Granville au Ambassadeurs de S.M. Britanique, Londres, 11 December 1882; in D. Sturdza, "Recueil...," p. 284.
216. Sir A. Paget, England's Ambassador to Rome, to Count Granville, Rome, December 15, 1882, in D. Sturdza, op. cit., p. 288.
217. Le Ministre des Affaires Etrangères à Vienne au Chargé d'Affaires d'Autriche-Hongrie à Bucarest, 11 Avril, 1882; in D. Sturdza, "Recueil...," p. 202.

218. Note verbale de l'Ambassadeur d'Angleterre à Constantinople adressée à la Sublime Porte, 18 Décembre, 1882: in D. Sturdza, "Recueil...," p. 297.
219. L'Ambassadeur d'Angleterre à Vienne cu Comte Granville, 26 Dec. 1882 D. Sturza, p. 306. op. cit.
220. Protocol No. 2, February 10.
221. Ibid.
222. Ibid.
223. Le Ministre de Roumanie à Londres au Ministre des Affaires Etrangères à Bucharest, Londres, 20 Février 1883; D. Sturdza, op. cit., p. 368.
224. Franz von Holtzendorff, "Les Droits riverains de la Roumanie sur le Danube", op. cit., p. 107.
225. Protocol No. 4, February 20.
226. Franz von Holtzendorff, op. cit., p. V1.
227. Idem, p. 110.
228. D. Marinovitch, Ministre de Serbie, à Lord Grandville, Londres, February 2, 1882; D. Sturdza, "Recueil...," p. 429, Annexe B. au Protocole No. 1.
229. L'Ambassadeur d'Angleterre à Vienne, au Comte Granville, Décembre 26, 1882; D. Sturdza, "Recueil...," p. 308.
230. Représentant de Serbie à Londres, au Comte Granville, 4 Janvier 1883; D. Sturdza, "Recueil...," p. 324.
231. Le Ministre des Affaires Etrangères de la Grande Bretagne au Représentant de Serbie à Londres, 11 Janvier, 1883; D. Sturdza, "Recueil...," p. 339.
232. Memorandum du Gouvernment de Serbie, Février 11, 1883; in D. Sturdza, "Recueil...," p. 359.
233. "Traité de Navigation entre l'Autriche-Hongrie et la Serbie," signé à Belgrade, le 10 (22) Février 1882; D. Sturdza, "Recueil...," p. 843.
234. Protocol No. 4, February 20, 1883.
235. Ibid.
236. Ibid.
237. Le Ministre des Affaires Entrangères de Bulgarie au Représentant de la Grande Bretagne à Sofia, 5/17 Janvier 1883; D. Sturdza, "Recueil...," p. 343.
238. Le Ministre des Affaires Entragères de la Grande Bretagne au Représentant d'Angleterre à Sofia, 24 Janvier 1883; "Recueil...," p. 346.
239. Le Ministre des Affaires Etrangères de la Grande Bretagne au Representant d'Angleterre à Vienne; in D. Sturdza, "Recueil...," p. 345.
240. Les délégués de la Principauté de Bulgarie au Comte Granville, President de la Conference, 13 Février 1883, Annexe au Protocole No. 3, Fevrier 13; in D. Sturdza, Recueil...," p. 436.
241. L'Ambassadeur de Turquie à Londres, au Comte de Granville, Janvier 1883; in D. Sturdza "Recueil...," p. 354.
242. Protodol No. 2, February 10, 1883.
243. Ibid.

244. Les Délegués de la Principauté de Bulgarie au Comte Granville, Président de la Conférence; 19 Février 1883, Annexe au Protocole No. 4, 20 Février, 1883.
245. Protocol No. 7, March 7, 1883.
246. Protocol No. 2, February 10, 1883.
247. Le Ministre des Affaires Entrangères à Londres au représentants de la Grande Bretagne, 11 Décember 1882; in D. Sturdza, "Recueil...," p. 285.
248. "Pro Memoria de l'Ambassadeur de l'Autriche-Hongrie à Londres, au Comte Granville," 27 Décembre 1882; D. Sturdza, "Recueil...," p. 309.
249. Protocol No. 2, 10 February 1883.
250. Op., cit.
251. Protocol No. 3, 13 February 1883.
252. Protocol No. 4, February 20, 1883.
253. Dascovici, "Drept International Public"; lecture notes at the University of Jasi, p. 101.
254. E.C.D., Protocol No. 5, of Dec. 1880; No. 23 of 27 May, 1882; No. 24 of 2 June, 1882.
255. Ibid., No. 23, 27 May, 1882 and 24 June, 1882.
256. Protocol No. 6, Dec. 18, 1880; and No. 19, of June 18, 1881.
257. "Un siècle de cooperation internationale sur le Danube" (1856-1956), p. 38. Present were representatives of England, France, Italy and, very exceptionally, the Greece — all in the capacity of Delegates to the former European Commission of the Danube.
258. Protocol No. 2, 10 February 1883.
259. Ibid.
260. Ibid.
261. Ibid., No. 11, July 2, 1878.
262. Ibid., No. 4, February 20, 1883.
263. Ibid.
264. Ibid., No. 6, March 1, 1883.
265. Le Ministre des Affaires Etrangères à l'Envoyé de Roumanie à Londres, 24 Mai, 1883; in D. Sturdza, "Recueil...," p. 416.
266. F. von Holtzendorff, op. cit., p. 102.
267. Hajnal, "Le Droit...," p. 163, note 1.
268. E.C.D., Protocol No. 345, of December 8, 1881.
269. Treaty of Paris, 1856, Article 15.
270. Note sur les travaux de la C.E.D. de 1856 à 1902; D. Sturdza, "Recueil...," p. 876.
271. E.C.D. Protocol No. 345, 8 December 1881.
272. Rapport presenté à la C.E.D. par Sir. Charles Hartley, son ingenieur consultant, sur les changements constatés dans la configuration de la côte de Delta pendant les dix dernièrs années," 15 Mai 1882, Annexe No. 1 au Extrait du Protocole 393, continué le 20 Mai 1882; "La Question du Danube," M.A.E., pp. 768-771.
273. Protocol No. 4, February 20, 1883.
274. Ibid., No. 6, of March 1, 1883.

275. Ibid., No. 4, of February 20, 1883.
276. Ibid., No. 5, February 24, 1883.
277. "Accounts and Papers," 1883, Vol. LXXXII, dispatch to His Majesty's Representatives abroud respecting the Navigation of the Danube, p. 5.
278. Protocol No. 5, February 24, 1883.
279. Gr. Antipa, "Dunărea si...," p. 157.
280. Idem, ibid., p. 47.
281. Idem, ibid., p. 145.
282. Idem, ibid., p. 148.
283. George R. Credner, Karl Sonklar, Lapparent, Richthoffen, Hartley, Voisin Bey, John Stakes, Hoffner, Holtwendorff, Carathéodory, Engelhardt; quoted by Antipa in "Dunărea si...," p. 154-178.
284. Gr. Antipa, "Dunărea si...," p. 181-183.
285. Hajnal, "Le Droit...," p. 202, note 1.
286. "Treaty of London," 10 Mars 1883, concluded between England, Austro-Hungary, France, Germany, Italy, Russia, and Turkey; D. Sturdza, "Recueil...," p. 472-474; Martens, N.R.G.T. (s.II) Vol. 1X, p. 392; "La Question du Danube," M.A.E., p. 869.

PART SEVEN

THE FIRST WORLD WAR AND THE POST WAR PERIOD

"Absolute freedom of navigation upon the seas outside territorial waters alike in peace and war...."

From the Fourteen Points of President Wilson concerning the First World Peace.

THE FIRST WORLD WAR AND THE POST WAR PERIOD

Introduction.

The analysis of this period of time will be exclusively in reference to Romania's situation, due to three considerations. The first lies in the concentration of the attention of the Central Europe belligerent Powers towards the Lower Danube sector of Romania, and especially of the Maritime Danube. The second is due to the fact that the first acts of domination over navigation on the Lower Danube resulted from the 1918 Treaty of Bucharest, concluded after the capitulation of Romania. Of the three riparian countries, Serbia (for the name see note 1) had not concluded any separate treaty and Bulgaria had been an ally of the Central European Powers. The third consideration, after the end of the war, was due to the discords encountered between Romania, the Interallied Commission of the Danube and the European Commission of the Danube.

Between 1914 and 1920, navigation and the method of applying the regime of navigation on the Danube were carried out in four phases. In the first phase, between the onset of World War I on July 19, 1914, and Romania's entrance into this conflagration on August 15, 1916, there existed the neutrality of this country, under which the commercial traffic on the Danube registered increases toward Central Europe and decreases towards the Black Sea.

During the second phase, between Romania's entrance into the war alongside England, France and Russia, and the capitulation of Romania, all the activity on the Lower Danube was under the control of Austro-Hungary and Germany, a situation that lasted until 1918.

In the third phase, between the capitulation of the Central European Powers in 1918 and the Versailles Treaty (June 28, 1918), the traffic on the entire course of the Danube was subject to latest military needs of the victorious allies and the measures of reestablishment of order in navigation.

Finally, the fourth stage was that of the period between the Treaty of Versailles and the beginning of the Conference of Paris, 1920-1921, for the establishment of a new statute of the Danube.

Chapter 1

FROM THE BEGINNING OF THE WAR TO THE TREATY OF VERSAILLES

Prior the Romania's participation in the war (1914-1916).

Even before the outbreak of World War I, traffic along the Maritime Danube towards the Black Sea had begun to lessen because of the blocking of the Straits by Turkey, due to the belligerent atmosphere.[2]

During the time of her neutrality, Romania had attempted to oppose German and Austro-Hungary pressure with respect to monopolizing exports of cereal towards the Middle and Upper Danube. The English, in turn, organized commercial establishments in Romania, to acquire and block the available cereal, on the spot.

On the occasion of the Tsar's Nicholas I visit to Constanta, a collective Russo-Romanian communiqué was forwarded to Turkey, requesting freedom of passage through the Straits for Romanian cereal, on the basis of her neutrality.[3] With Turkey's negative response, all traffic through the Lower Danube towards the sea was paralyzed.

From the beginning of the war in 1914 and up to 1916, because of Romania's neutrality the European Commission for the Danube continued a reduced activity under the control of the Delegates of the belligerent states: Austro-Hungary, England, France, Germany, Italy, Russia and Turkey. The principal technical works were suspended because of the reduced income brought on by the reduced exports. From 2,430,883 gold francs, its budget of receipts for 1913, income fell to 1,926,043 gold francs in 1914.[4] To balance its budget for 1914, Romania had to accord the European Commission a credit of 540,000 Lei, and advance it 120,000 Lei monthly, also in 1915.[5]

In 1915, the Commission asked its component States for a collective advance of 3,200,000 gold francs, about 400,000 gold francs from each member.[6] The request receiving a favorable answer, the Commission was able to continue to carry out a minimum of the urgent work in 1915 and 1916.

From the Entrance of Romania in Action to the End of the War.

(1916 - 1918)
During the period between Romania's entering and ending its war activity, the entire Danube valley was included in the zone of military conflagration. Non-respecting of the Treaty of Berlin as to the limitation of naval forces on the Lower Danube offered the possibility of confrontation between the fluvial warships of Germany, Romania, Bulgaria and Austro-Hungary. The navigation situation at Sulina was aggravated in the meantime, as it became impossible because of insufficient revenues to maintain the navigable depths. At the beginning of 1917, Russia's and Romania's Delegates to the European Commission retreated to Odessa, leaving at Sulina one Romanian representative and a resident Danish engineer, both gerents of the European Commission. The Delegates at Odessa appealed to England and France, who sent 400,000 gold francs each, to maintain some minimum depths at the Sulina Mouth.[7] The enemy troops at that time were still far from the Mouths of the Danube.

The traffic of maritime vessels through the Sulina Mouth between the years 1916 and 1918 fell 60% in comparison with the traffic between 1911 and 1915 and 69% in tonnage: a situation that was reflected in the financial potential of the European Commission. Its income was 2,269,000 gold francs compared to expenditures of 6,095,729.[8]

The total loans and subventions accorded to the European Commission between 1914 and 1918 by all member States reached 2,000,000 gold francs.[9] The fact that, up to Romania's entrance into the war, Austro-Hungary, Germany and Turkey, all at war with the Allied Powers and Associates also participated in the financing of the European Commission and, in a way, made it possible for the Commission to keep its neutrality in some measure.[10]

The normal functioning of the Commission was disturbed also by another circumstance. On the eve of Romania's entering the war, some of the employes of the European Commission, of Austro-Hungarian,

German and Turkish citizenship,[11] being suspected of espionage were interned by Romanian military authorities in concentration camps, an action that aroused the protests of Magnusen, resident engineer of the European Commission, who invoked the right to immunity for the Commission's personnel. At Sulina, there appeared other signs of insecurity because of the nearness of the battlefronts. Local executive personnel of the Commission took refuge at Odessa, while others together with part of the populace were evacuated to ports upriver, Galatz and Brăila.

The measures taken by the Romanian authorities, against the Commission's foreign personnel from enemy countries, were approved by the European Commission. In a communiqué on September 8, 1916, from England's Delegate, Baldwin, the Commission recommended meeting the demands of the military authorities at the Sulina Mouth.[12] Furthermore, Baldwin also recommended certain measures by which the Commission and its reduced personnel still functioning could give their support to the Romanian military authorities, even to delivering to them material from the Commission's inventory.[13] Also, because of the chaotic conditions and the lack of other protection, he gave instructions that in case of alarms, citizens of the nonbelligerent countries of the Commission still on site, should submit to the orders of the Romanian military authorities and, if need be, the entire fleet of the Commission should be evacuated to the Kilia Branch, which was under Russian control.[14]

Other acts also occurred which were derogatory to the treaties concerned with the international regime on the Lower Danube, as well as derogatory to the authority of the European Commission.

Because of military necessity and with the aim of assuring navigation, the Russians sent warships to Sulina, installing there a military command and a civilian organization,[15] measures which infringed on the non-abrogated international regime of navigation. The collateral measures taken by the Russians were interpreted by Prof. Dascovici as having the purpose of eventually annexing the Danube Mouths, if the war was won. They drew up hydrographic maps of the Delta, established post offices, evacuated villages, planned projects of long duration, in Dascovici's opinion "all sorts of activities which had nothing in common with the war against the Central European Powers. Russia invoked pretexts to keep from freeing the Delta after the end of hostilities."[16] In order to keep the proper depths of the water at the Sulina and Kilia Mouths, the Russians requested the Commission's dredges.[17] The matter was solved by adopting a formula of leasing, for an annual fee of 2,060,000 gold francs.[18]

It seems that the leasing had the agreement of the European Commission, as the letter of response to the Russians (in which the conditions of the lease contract were outlined) was based on prior consultation of the Romanian and Russian Delegates in Odessa, who represented the European Commission. The letter also had the consent of the Romanian representative left in charge at Sulina, who signed "...pour la Commission Européenne du Danube."[19]

The closing contract signed on July 14, 1917, ended with the onset of the Russian Revolution in 1917; the dredges were returned, as only 300,000 francs had been paid.[20]

The explanation given by the European Commission concerning this leasing was "to assure, during the war, the maintenance in good shape of the canal, the port and the Sulina Mouth, Russians being substituted for the European Commission."[21] This explanation did not fit either into the neutrality status of the Commission, nor in its obligations concerning the method of applying the international regime. The down grading became even more accentuated by the fact that the Commission's flags over the ships and the fleet roadstead were replaced by Russian ones. The national symbol of Russia replace the international one of the European Commission of the Danube. All these derogations remained without consequences, their authors being aligned with the victors in World War I.

The Peace Treaty of Bucharest (1918)

After Romania's capitulation the peace preliminaries were concluded with Germany, Austro-Hungary, Bulgaria and Turkey[22] on March 5, 1918. The Peace Treaty of Bucharest was concluded on May 7, 1918.[23]

Before concluding the Treaty, the Central Powers obligated Romania to sign a Convention for the "underlayed" resumption of technical work on the Lower Danube and, in particular, on the Maritime Danube.[24] On the basis of the Convention, the "Zentral Transport Leitung" (Z.T.L.) was established, an Austro-Hungarian organ under whose orders were assigned all the technical and hydrographic services, port installations, cereal silos, etc., and at Sulina all technical services, dredges, service craft materials, buildings, etc. of the European Commission. The chief of the Romanian technical services, as well as Romania's Representative at the European Commission, opposed and protested against this Convention. In the protest to the Austro-Hungarian technical organization he said, "the material of the European was at the disposition of the technical works, in the interests of navigation and could not be put at the disposition of any other organ without the approval of the European Commission."[25] This protesting response referred to the neutrality of the technical inventory and of the fleet roadstead of the Commission, as established in previous treaties.

Count Demblin, Austro-Hungarian Minister to Bucharest, advised Romania's Minister of Foreign Affairs that "...the works which were to be carried out by the Z.T.L. organization could not be hampered either by the protests formulated nor by the ill will of any so-called Romanian authorities and organizations."[26] In this was, the Austrians requisitioned by force everything they could.

In general, the stipulations of the Treaty of Bucharest did not differ from any that are usually dictated to small nations conquered by some Great Powers, in accordance with the inexorable laws of warfare, with some exceptions. While in armed conflict between some Great Powers the dictates of the victors are conceived in the spirit of recovery and sometimes to subsidize the economic potential of the defeated with reparations in mind, in the case of Serbia and Romania, the procedure was different.

By the Treaty of Bucharest, Germany and Austro-Hungary understood to take over direct and indirect exploitation of all of Romania's economy, in view of including it in their own national economies. Included in this exploitation was all the navigation and its auxiliaries, from the smallest craft to the largest tugboat, from the largest shipyard to the most primitive, leaving only a small number of old vessels for the strict necessities of local transports.

Romania had to cede to Austro-Hungary the shipyard at Turnul-Severin for a period of ninety-nine years, at an annual rent of 1000 lei, and to Germany an area in the port of Giurgiu, for construction of a shipyard. The grain silos and the technical port installations were to be exploited by the Z.T.L.

The exploitation of the captured or ceded vessels, as well as the Romanian and Serbian cereal exports, were distributed to the following newly organized enterprises: E. Behles and Schiffahrts Abteilung Bergungsgruppe (S.A.B.), both of them German; Zentral Transport Leitung (Z.T.L.), Austro-Hungarian; and "Marine Bulgare" (M.B.)[27] Those same enterprises rented some small vessels at ridiculous rates. Romania was obligated also to retain the existing personnel to assure the usage of the port facilities, installations, silos, etc., as well as to support the activity of the four enterprises. Also on the basis of that same treaty, Berlin and Vienna proposed to change radically the existing regime of navigation on the Lower Danube. Actually, they had contemplated these changes even during the period of Romania's neutrality. In an "international" conference of the Danube, in which only Austro-Hungary, Germany and Romania were to participate to establish a new regime (without the other two riparian states Bulgaria and Serbia, and the non-riparian England, France and Italy). Romania delayed her participation until she reentered the war scene on the opposite front, along with the Allied and Associated Powers.

By Articles 24-28 the Bucharest Peace Treaty, Germany and Austro-Hungary had decided upon establishing a new regime along the entire course of the Danube River, to be administrated by a Commission for International Navigation. The new Commission was to be composed only of delegates from the riparian states: Austro-Hungary, Bulgaria, Germany, Romania, Serbia, and those states "riparian to the European shores of the Black Sea," that is, Turkey. A new organization to be called the Commission of the Mouths of the Danube was to replace the European Commission.

It was the first time in the history of the international regime of the Danube that the formula of "riparian to the European shore of the Black Sea" was used. It thus made room for Turkey, ally of the Central Powers, which had lost her riparian status on the Danube in 1908, when Bulgaria became independent. She had still remained a member of the European Commission on the basis of the older treaties. The new formula did not include Russia, which was also riparian to the European shore of the Black Sea. A work published by the European Commission of the Danube in Exile stated that Russia was to be included after the victory of the Allied and Associated Powers.[28]

The derogations flagrantly opposed the principles of the "Act of 1815, as well as the concept of the Central European Powers by which a regime of navigation under exclusive control of its riparians had been proposed, not also of those riparian to the European shore of the Black Sea.

All three branches of the river were to be under the jurisdiction of the new Commission of the Mouths of the Danube, with uniform application of Regulations drawn up by it. Unlike the past regime, Article 24 of the Bucharest Treaty of Peace accorded the States represented in the new Commission the right to sail warships on the river, under certain conditions, and one small warship at the mouth of the Danube by each country represented in the Commission.

By its new composition and by the elimination of the former non-riparian countries — England, France and Italy — the new

Commission would have been similar to the Riparian Commission initially proposed by the stipulations of Articles 17 and 18 of the 1856 Treaty and the 1857 Act of Navigation.

In accordance with the Treaty of Bucharest and the new principles conceived by Austro-Hungary and Germany, the entire navigable course of the Danube would be composed of three large sectors, as follows:

1.) The Upper and Middle Danube, between Ulm and the Iron Gates, to which the riparian countries, Germany (Bavaria and Württemberg) and Austro-Hungary would temporarily apply the 1857 Act of Navigation;

2.) The Lower Danube, between the Iron Gates and Brăila, to which the riparian countries — Serbia, Romania and Bulgaria — would apply, within the limits of their territorial waters, the Regulations for Navigation and Police, drawn up under Austro-Hungarian and German control;

3.) The Maritime Danube, between Brăila and Sulina, subjected to the supervision of the new Commission of the Mouths of the Danube, which was under the direct control of Germany and Austro-Hungary.

England, France and Italy protested on May 18, against the Bucharest Treaty, declaring null its stipulations respecting the new regime and demanding that the navigation problems be resolved with the participation and accord of all the interested countries.[29]

One could ask whether the realization of the formula "Freie eigene Verkehrs-strasse der Handels-Politischen Alliierten Donaustaaten" would have benefited both of the Great Powers in Central Europe or only one of them? In this hypothesis there might be revealed the economic and political ideas of German thinkers, headed by Frederick Nauman, concerning the vision of creating a "Mittel Europa,"[30] Germany extending her domination over lines of communication from the Baltic Sea to the Black Sea.

In the opinion of C. Băicoianu there was a tacit antagonism between Germany and Austro-Hungary over the priority in carrying out the technical works, as well as in the taking over of the materials and installations of the European Commission.[31] "For," states Băicoianu, "while the Austrians were seeking to monopolize the entire Danube, the Germans were not about to be left out. They quarreled over the loot."[32] The antagonism between the two Allies resulted in the fall of the entire Convention[33] conceived before the concluding of the Treaty of Bucharest, which had provided for the predominance of the Austro-Hungarian presence in the administration of the Mouths of the Danube. It was evident, however, that the antagonism existed only with respect to the new Commission at the Mouths of the Danube, not in the other navigation sectors or in the administration of the fluvial roadstead. There the booty was almost equally distributed as a result of the Treaty of Bucharest.

As to the use of the vessels captured by the Central European Powers and their Allies, a problem of international concern arose. Bearing in mind the international regime of navigation of the Lower Danube, was the seizure of the vessel and their use under other flags than those of the belligerents legitimate?

Inasmuch as the neutrality of the course and of the banks of the Danube had not been decided upon in any previous treaty, it meant that they were included in the military conflagration, a fact which suspended the application of the international regime. In the period of Romania's neutrality, vessels under French and English flags, i.e. those of the Allied Powers that were at war with the Central European Powers Bloc after 1914, could still be active without any restrictions. In this case, the neutrality regime of the Lower Danube was indirectly the result of Romania's neutrality.

After Romania entered the war, the situation changed. The vessels of the Western Allies and their Associates — England, France, Italy Serbia and Romania — found on the Danube were at the discretion of their adversaries.

Although Greece had joined in the war against the Central European Powers only by June 27, 1917, still the fluvial vessels under her flag also had been distributed to the new companies founded by Germany, Austro-Hungary and Bulgaria, after Romania's entrance in the war in 1916.

Chapter 2

FROM THE CAPITULATION OF THE CENTRAL EUROPEAN POWERS TO THE PEACE TREATY OF VERSAILLES

Divergences between Romania and the inter-Allied Commission of the Danube.

Between November 1918 and June 1919, after the capitulation of the Central European Powers, Allied Forces disembarked through the Southern Balkans to reach the Danube. Measures had to be taken to ensure the safety of the latest Allied military transports, as well as to reestablish normal navigation as quickly as possible. This created a very confused and complicated situation.

From the Iron Gates upriver, the entire navigation regime and its auxiliaries were under Austro-Hungarian administration. From this point downriver, confusion and disorder reigned after the retreat of the enemy armies. The Supreme Council of the Allied Powers and Associates in Paris established in 1918 and inter-Allied Commission of the Danube whose attributes were:[34] clearing the river of the ship wrecks left in the wake of military operations; the reorganization and putting in operation a new navigation administration at the Iron Gates and the Cataracts; identification and cataloguing of the war prizes; assurance of carrying out the minimum of technical work for maintenance of navigation and restoration of a normal commercial navigation. The Allied riparian countries — Romania and Serbia — had no other role than that of providing the vessels to be used by the inter-Allied Commission with fuel.[35]

Carrying out these attributes became a difficult problem to resolve under the chaotic postwar circumstances, especially since the inter-Allied Commission came up against some opposition from Romania and Serbia. In view of the small amount of military and commercial traffic, the Commission was obliged to keep in function some former enemy vessels, along with their crews; a circumstance that provoked Romania's and Serbia's protests since they were against the presence of these crews on the Danube. The measure was unjust also because of the disorganization and destruction of most of the Romanian and Serbian fleets by the former enemies. After the establishment of the inter-Allied Commission of the Danube, a divergence arose between it and Romania, due to a number of causes.

Romania, a country allied against the Central European Powers, requested the earliest possible reestablishment of her rights on the Lower Danube, in view of reconstructing her national economy destroyed during the war. Impediments to her realization of this aim were the chaotic situation created in navigation by the capitulation of Germany and Austro-Hungary and the retreat of their troops from the Lower Danube regions, as well as the fact that the Treaty of Versailles and the treaties with the other former enemy countries had not yet gone into effect. Faced with the military needs of the Allies, the General Command of the Allied Armies in the East, by order No. 100 of November 1918, established the Navigation Command of the Danube, under the command of Admiral Sir Ernest Troubridge, of the Royal British Navy, who installed his general staff at Belgrade.[36] The attributes of this Command were passed over to the inter-Allied Commission of the Danube, established May 22, 1919 and began functioning in October 1919, under the direction of that same Admiral.[37]

Within the framework of this Commission, the entire course of the river was divided into two sectors. The portion between Ulm and the Iron Gates inclusively, were under the administration of Admiral Troubridge, while from the latter point to the Black Sea under French Commander Belloy.[38] This temporary measure eliminated any interference from Romania and Serbia. Later, to the initial formation of the inter-Allied Commission were added Romania and Serbia a measure taken by the Allied Supreme Economic Council.[39]

In the autumn of 1919, the inter-Allied Commission informed Romania that it was taking over the administration and development of navigation at the Iron Gates.[40] Romania protested to the Allied Supreme Council, requesting that the administration be given to her, in view of the fact that the Iron Gates were situated on her territory.[41]

Later, in her Memoranda of September and October 1919, Romania requested the substitution of the International Commission of the Danube for the inter-Allied Commission, as provided for by Articles 347 and 348 of the Versailles Treaty and later by separate treaties with

Austria, Bulgaria, and Hungary. Romania's requests were without basis inasmuch as, between the clauses of the Treaty of Versailles regarding the establishment of the International Commission of the Danube and their entering in effect, certain intermediary situations occurred which prevented the transfer. Article 348 provided for the International Commission to meet "...as soon as possible after the present treaty goes into effect and shall take upon itself the temporary administration of the river..." Carrying out this Article there were other situations to be taken into consideration.

In the first place between the signing of the Versailles Treaty on June 28, 1919 and its entering into effect, there was a time gap of eight months and Romania ratified it after another eight months.[42] Hence, in 1919, when the inter-Allied Commission was still functioning, the International Commission of the Danube could not also be operative as the 1919 Treaty was not yet in effect.

In the second place, the Treaty of 1919 had merely set forth the establishment of the International Commission of the Danube; the establishment according to that same Treaty was to be effectuated by a Conference of the Definitive Statue of the Danube, which took place only between 1920 and 1921.

In the third place, the presence of an organization with military authority was absolutely essential in the postwar period during which there was an absence of any order in navigation along the entire course of the Danube River. At the beginning of the activity of the inter-Allied Commission freedom of navigation was divided between the measures taken by the Commission and the discretionary actions of the private shipowners, whether from the discretionary actions of the private shipowners, whether from the group of former enemies or from the victorious one.

In the fourth place, the International Commission of the Danube, in which one delegate from each riparian state would have taken part, could not be established before the conclusion of all the separate treaties with all the former enemy states. The dates of the concludings were September 10, 1919, with Austria; November 27, 1919, with Bulgaria; June 4, 1920, with Hungary; hence, after the establishment of the inter-Allied Commission.

Because of these four major points, the International Commission of the Danube could not take over the administration of the Iron Gates by replacing the inter-Allied Commission. During the period of the inter-Allied Commission's Administration the divergence between it and Romania became aggravated also because of the war seizures and the retaining of the former Hungarian technical and administrative personnel at the Iron Gates.

In the first of these causes, the tendency of the inter-Allied Commission to take over as many vessels as possible of the former enemy fleet was obvious, in contrast to Romania's move to reclaim her own vessels that had been captured during the war. The second was the temporary retention of the former Hungarian administration at the Iron Gates in order to facilitate navigation, was in opposition to Romania's and Serbia's position: demanding the removal of the personnel of an enemy state from that administration. The opposition of Romania and Serbia also came from considerations of a nationalistic order, in protest to the moving of the headquarters of the inter-Allied Commission from Belgrad to Budapest, the capital of a former enemy state with whom the Treaty of Peace was not concluded until 1920. At the same time, Romania protested against the increase in navigation taxes at the Iron Gates, a measure taken by Troubridge because of the depreciation of the currency of the neighbor states.

Between the resentment of the riparians — Romania and Serbia, the victims of the First World War — and the judgement of their distant Allies, drawing an objective conclusion became difficult. Replacing a personal familiar with the administration of the Iron Gates with a new and possibly untrained one would have been to the detriment of the traffic at the Iron Gates.

Because the opposition and divergences were such a controversial problem, recourse to the documentation in a later report by A. Baule, Secretary of the International Commission of the Danube, can be useful.[43] The objectivity and preciseness of the documentation stemmed from the author's official position. In his succinct statement Baule used, and quoted from the correspondence emanated from the Allied organs in Paris, along with his own considerations.

Baule considered the military administration inadequate, as did the Romanians and Serbs. "It is not a matter," he wrote, "of the role of the Commandant of the Danube as a military organ, but we must note that, under the pressure of circumstances, an administrative measure must be taken outside the military framework."

Taking into consideration the urgent need to reestablish a normal situation, he still felt that in resolving some specific problems "a simple military measure is not always apt at reaching results." To this complex situation was added the non-establishment of the new frontiers and the identification of the origin of the vessels captured during the war and now dispersed in different sectors of the river. In regard to this, he cited a resolution of the Allied Supreme Economic

THE PEACE TREATY OF VERSAILLES 439

Committee which stated: "...in spite of the uncertainty still reigning on the matter of frontiers, of the ownership of the river equipment and of the earliest possible resumption of normal conditions on the river, will decide to free the army of a problem which surpassed its competence, in order to assign it to an organ under the control of the chief Commandant."

In the meantime, the work of the Paris Peace Conference being near an end, the Conference of Ambassadors decided to invite the Allied and Associated Powers to a meeting on June 17, 1920, for the establishment of the International Commission of the Danube. The inter-Allied Commission of the Danube met, for the last time, from May 12 to May 20 in Paris where on June 17, 1920 after eight months of activity by military authorities, the task was passed to a civilian administration, that of the International Commission of the Danube.

Undoubtedly, the right of the riparian states in organizing navigation on their own fluvial sectors and, especially, in recuperating their fleets captured by the former enemies were justified. They became minor in the face of the major problems of general order which had to be met by the Allied Supreme Council in Paris.

On the other hand, the organization of Allied transports of military character and the measures for reorganizing navigation required on organization of neutral character to harmonize private interests, animosities and political views, in a region of former enemy countries — Czechoslovakia, Romania and Serbia.

Romania's opposition was justified and was counter to the tendency of some Great Powers to anticipate the organization of their own interests during the period of transition between the functioning of the inter-Allied Commission of the Danube and the beginning of that of the International Commission of the Danube.

In 1920, England founded the "Danube Navigation Company," with a capital of 1,200,000 pounds, for the purchase of some shares of former companies.[44] English investments in Germany, Austria and Hungary dated back to 1830, when the first steamoperated vessels were built. France, in turn, after 1920 obtained in her quota of reparations a considerable number of fluvial vessels, from the former enemy war prizes. To utilize these, she founded a society for navigation on the Danube.[45]

The disagreements ended only after the Convention for the Definitive Statute of the Danube entered in force; Romania, Czechoslovakia and Serbia having the freedom to reorganize and to reestablish their fluvial potential by means of the captured vessels and the war indemnities, in kind, as well as by new construction.

THE PEACE TREATY OF VERSAILLES

General Clauses.

The Peace Treaty concluded at Versailles in June 28, 1919, between the Allied and Associated Powers and Germany, also set the basis for the navigation and port regime on certain water communications lines of Europe, including the Danube.[46] In matters of communication concerning Germany, stipulations were provided by Articles 271-273 and 349. Article 350 cancelled the mandate given to Austro-Hungary by the 1878 Treaty of Berlin as to the exclusivity for the technical works at the Iron Gates and the Cataracts.

The bases of the new navigation regime on the entire course of the Danube were provided for in separate peace treaties with Austria, Bulgaria and Hungary, with some special additions.

Article 300 of the 1920 Peace Treaty with Austria provided for the operation, by the four Allied Great Powers, of the enemy vessels captured on the Danube, and Article 309 set the navigation regime for the waters in the Banat, passing through Romania and Serbia.[47] Among the additions included in the Treaty of Peace concluded with Hungary,[48] there was also the one in Article 289 of the same treaty, regarding navigation at the Iron Gates. The regime there was placed under the temporary jurisdiction of the International Commission of the Danube, which Articles 347 and 348 of the Treaty of Versailles had made provision for and which was to enter in force after the establishment of the Definitive Statue of the Danube (1921). As previously noted, Austro-Hungary had assigned the administration of navigation at the Iron Gates to Hungary.

Special Clauses Concerning the Danube River.

Along with the other water communication lines,[49] the Danube was declared international from Ulm to the Black Sea, including any navigable part of which naturally provided an exit to the sea for a number of states, with or without transshipment from one vessel to another (Article 331). The regulation of navigation on the Danube was prescribed also in Articles 346-352. The entire course of the river was divided into two conventional sectors. The one between Brăila and the Mouth of the Danube, i.e. the navigation sector of maritime vessels also, was put under the administration and supervision of the European Commission of the Danube, which retained its former jurisdictional authority, with the difference that its composition was limited temporarily to four states — England, France, Italy, and Romania. (Article 346). Not included were Austria-Hungary, Germany, Russia and Turkey.

The sector between Ulm and the point where the jurisdiction of the European Commission ceases, Brăila, was placed under the administration of the International Commission of the Danube, composed of two delegates from the German riparian states of Bavaria and Württemberg, a delegate from each riparian state — Austria, Bulgaria, Czechoslovakia, Romania, Serbia and, in addition, one delegate from the non-riparian states represented in the European Commission (Article 347). The International Commission of the Danube was to take over the administration of its sectors immediately after the Treaty of Versailles was to go into effect. (Article 348) until the establishment of a new Statue for the river.

By the basis stipulation of Article 349 of the Peace Treaty with Germany and the corresponding ones in the peace treaties with the other former enemy states, an International Conference of the Danube was programmed, with the participation of all the states represented in the two Commissions. This Conference was to establish, within one year, the Convention for the Definitive Statue of the Danube. Germany was obligated to restore to the European Commission all of the technical inventory and the roadstead which had been removed from the former's inventory, as well as to accord indemnities for the damages suffered by the Commission during the war. (Article 352).

Several remarks can be made concerning the new navigation regime for the Danube, as set by the Treaty of Versailles, both as to the new aspect as well as to certain omissions. Dividing the administration of the international regime into two sectors derogated from the principles of the Act of 1815 which had provided for a single sector and a single administration on international rivers. It also repeated the division proposed by the 1857 Act of Navigation, rejected by the 1858 Paris Conference, with the difference that the sector between Ulm and the Iron Gates was kept under the national administration of the riparian states, and that the internationalization of the Iron Gates-Mouth of the Danube sector, with certain restrictions, was provided for.

The authority of the European Commission over the Kilia Branch, removed from its control by Article III of the 1883 Treaty of London, vaguely resulted from the stipulation regarding the internationalization of the entire course of the Danube. The clarification was made later, by Article 7 of the Treaty for acknowledging the reunion of Bessarabia with Romania, concluded at Paris on October 28, 1920.[50]

In comparison with other treaties also with respect to setting the international regime of navigation on the Danube and to the past points of view of the representatives of certain non-riparian Great Powers, the Treaty of Versailles presented certain discrepancies, not to say ambiguities.

In contrast to the past, when certain principles and norms were set concerning the European Commission, the 1919 treaty fixed only the outlines for the new regime, assigning the task of developing the texts to a new International Conference, authorized by the new Statue for the Danube. Perhaps this procedure was due to the complications raised by a new regime which was to be established between the conquered and the victorious states, as well as in the presence of a new state, Czechoslovakia. This transfer of attributes, however, did not reach the results conceived by the Treaty of Versailles, inasmuch as at the level of the new Conference, many principles of that treaty and of the Act of 1815 were changed. Differing from previous treaties in which were mentioned the principles of the Act of 1815, or the fact that navigation was included in the "Public Law of Europe," or that this navigation was of "European interest" (1878), the Treaty of Versailles was silent on these points. Some defects of the Treaty were to become subjects disputed at the Conference for the Establishment of the new Statute for the Danube, at which some participants were to invoke the Act of 1815.

Either due to the consequences of a war not provoked by them, or to the intentions of reestablishing the political equilibrium on the Danube, the Allied and Associated Powers sought to eliminate the German and Austro-Hungarian preponderance in navigation, a measure to the advantage of small riparian states of the Lower Danube. In a very short time, however, Germany, Austria, and Hungary reestablished their naval potential. England and the United States of America contributed to their success by renouncing any acts of retribution, in the aim of again including the economic potentials of the Danubian countries in the European and world circuit. By the new frontiers set by the Treaty of Versailles, Russia was removed from the Lower Danube by the restitution of Bessarabia to the Kingdom of Romania.

To clarify this restitution and especially to respect the jurisdiction of the European Commission, a special treaty was concluded at Paris, in 1920, between the principal victorious states of World War I and

Romania.[51] Article 7 acknowledged the sovereignty of Romania over the territory of Bessarabia; Article 7 transferred the Mouth of the Kilia Branch to the jurisdiction of the European Commission.

The Situation on the Lower Danube and the Damages to the Fluvial Fleet.

Navigation and commerce on the Lower Danube were completely disorganized at the end of World War I. Although it was not known how navigation would develop, after the Treaty of Versailles, under the new international regime, it was hoped that a speedy return to normal would occur. The activity of the Companies organized by the former enemy countries for carrying out cereal commerce and navigation had ceased, causing the rise of uncertainty in the ranks of ship owners and local cereal merchants who had worked with those firms. E. Behles, a German enterprise, was to liquidate the contracts concluded with the local cereal merchants and the status of the captures or leased vessels also had to be liquidated. Local authorities were disoriented by the Activity and orders coming from the inter-Allied Commission of the Danube interfering with their activities.

Local transport needs were at the discretion of some improvised ships chandlers who constructed some rudimentary craft which they exploited at the black market, payment for the temporary transactions being exacted in English pounds. Many vessels were found moved to German and Austro-Hungarian fluvial sectors, their owners ignorant of their existence and awaiting the conclusion of the Peace Treaty in order to recuperate them and to fix their indemnities. The crews of the vessels exploited by the former enemies were demanding their pay from the former owners, who themselves were in failing financial situations. Credits were extremely tight, banks also waiting for the stabilization of the depreciated currencies put into circulation by the former occupants. The only source of financing was through private loans, with mortgages on real estate, interest rates being up to 20% to 40%, accorded by owners of gold currency or secret deposits of English pounds.

The general status of the fluvial fleet, regardless of the flag flown, registered in the Romanian ports had been reduced by 25%. Of the total of 899 vessels (barges, tugs, etc.) in existence in 1916, when Romania entered the war, by 1920 only 694 remained.[52]

The reduction was caused by sinking due to bombardments, by mines, storms on the Black Sea, evacuation of sale to Russia and Constantinople, and to capture by Germans, Austro-Hungarians or Bulgarians in military actions.[53]

The potential of the means of transport on the Romanian Danube after World War 1 was reduced by 179,600 tons for barges and 1588 HP for tugs. In comparison with other European ports, the reduction of this potential seems minor, but, in relation to the level of transportation on the Danube, it was important. Recuperation of these losses took place as follows: part of the vessels were returned or were indemnified by the German firm, E. Behles;[54] part of those found in the Lower Danube ports were taken over by their owners, and part were indemnified. The indemnification fund and part of the captured vessels were turned over to the Romanian Government, which in turn indemnified some ship owners by giving them the vessels from their own fleets to use without payment for a certain number of years, relative to their losses.

The operations of refloating some sunken vessels and of repairing the ones returned depended on the reestablishment of the technical potential of the old shipyards, as well as on the establishment of some new very rudimentary ones.

The First Postwar Meeting of the European Danube Commission in Paris and the Romanian Protest.

On the basis of Article 346 of the Versailles Peace Treaty of 1919, the European Danube Commission met at Paris in an extraordinary session, between October 15 and 17, 1919, in view of taking the first measures for reorganizing navigation after the end of the war. It is to be noted that this first meeting of the European Commission took place before the Treaty of Versailles, which had sustained it, had gone into effect.

Invited by the Allied Supreme Council and by Francis Rey, the General Secretary of the European Commission, Romania refused to participate, requesting that the first meeting take place at the Commission's headquarters in Galatz, so that its members could see, in person, the grave situation of navigation at the Sulina Mouth.[55]

Transportation difficulties were cited for holding the meeting in Paris, as well as the fact that some of the members were in Paris already, for the completion of the Conference of Paris. Also, meeting in Galatz would have been inappropriate, as the European Commission building had been destroyed.[56] A summary glance at the status of navigation at Sulina had taken place before the Paris meeting, when Francis Rey had come to Galatz to hold discussions with C. Contzesco, Romania's Delegate in the Commission.

The real aim of the Paris meeting was not to have the European Commission take up its activity immediately, but to procure the funds needed to carry out the urgently needed technical works. The financial situation being burdened with a debt of five million gold francs, the result of advances given by member Governments of the Commission before and during the war, it was necessary to review also the 1908 schedule of taxes with respect to raising them, in order to balance the budget in line with the cost of materials.[57] The inefficiency of this increase, because of the reduced postwar rates for navigation, determined the recourse to a loan of 3,750,000 French francs, contracted with great difficulty with the participation of some foreign banks and Bucharest, in addition to the amount advanced by the Romanian Government.[58]

Measures were also taken to reorganize the personnel of executive, administrative and technical cadres, thinned out by dispersal and by abandonment of posts during the war, as well as replacement of those holding citizenship in the former enemy countries. In this respect, it was decided to appoint persons of other than Romanian citizenship in order to keep the international character of the Commission. Only the position of Captain of the Port of Sulina was assigned to a Romanian citizen.[59]

Romania protested against the make-up of the personnel, invoking the contribution and the technical capacity of her nucleus of technicians who, during the war and in the absence of foreign personnel, had succeeded in maintaining the reduced navigation at the Sulina Mouth.[60] This contribution was officially acknowledged by the European Commission at the meeting in Paris.[61]

The lack of reliance on Romanian personnel or the retention of the international structure of the Commission were insulting for Romania. The protest was the most justified considering the sabotage activity against the European Commission during the war and, especially the bombing of the beacon at Serpents Island by the German vessel "Goeben,"[62] piloted by an Austro-Hungarian, a former Port Captain of Sulina.

In a Romanian source[63] it is stated that, following Romania's protest, implementation of the decisions taken at Paris in 1919 were postponed until after they were rediscussed at the first regular meeting, this time, held in Galatz on May 18, 1920.[64]

Notes

Chapter 1

1. We will use the name of Serbia instead of Kingdom of Serbs, Croats and Slovenes (1918-1929).
2. In 1911, War between Turkey and Italy in Tripolitania; the Greco-Turkish conflict, and the Balkan War of 1913.
3. Dascovici, "Dreptul International," p. 104.
4. La Commission Européenne et son...," p. 498.
5. Ibid., p. 128.
6. Ibid., p. 129.
7. Ibid., p. 129.
8. Statistics from "La Commission Européenne et son..," p. 439, 497.
9. "Un Siècle de cooperation...," p. 53.
10. "La Commission Européenne et son...," p. 39.
11. N. Dascovici, "Dreptul International...," p. 105.
12. C. Băicoianu, "Dunărea văzută prin...," p. 8.
13. Idem, ibid., p. 8.
14. Idem, ibid., p. 9.
15. Idem, ibid., p. 10.
16. N. Dascovici, "Conferință," printed by "Liga Navală Română," Bucharest, 1942, and N. Dascovici, "Dreptul International," p. 103.
17. C. Băicoianu, op. cit., p. 11.
18. "La Commission Européenne et son...," p. 129.
19. Letter No. 154 of the European Commission, of April 7, 1917, Odessa, sent to the Russians through the Romanian representative in charge at Sulina; reprinted in C. Băicoianu, "Dunărea văzută...," p. 12.
20. "La Commission Européenne et son...," p. 129.
21. C. Băicoianu, op. cit., p. 13, Note.
22. Peace preliminaries between Romania, Germany, Austro-Hungary, Bulgaria and Turkey; Buftea, March 5, 1918; Martens, N.R.G.T. (s.III), Vol. X, p. 855.
23. Treaty of Peace between Romania and Germany, Austro-Hungary, Bulgaria and Turkey, May 7, 1918, Idem, ibid., p. 856.

24. Convention (Proposal) respecting the immediate resumption of the technical, hydraulic and hydrographic work necessary for the reorganization of navigation between the maritime ports of the Danube below Brăila, on the Danube and on all the branches of the Delta. The Convention was concluded by the Romanian Delegates and the "Waffenstillstandskommission für das Schwarze Meer," at Bucharest, March 9/22, 1918; in "Condica tratatelor si a altor legăminte ale României (1354-1937)," Vol. II, Bucharest 1938; p. 425; edited by the Ministry for Foreign Affairs of Romania.

25. For this protest and for the complete correspondence exchanged between the Romanian and the Austro-Hungarian organizations, see the copies of the originals in C. Băicoianu, "Dunărea văzută...," p. 18-24.

26. Copy of Count Demblin's note to the Minister for Foreign Affairs of Romania, Bucharest, September 25, 1918; quoted by C. Băicoianu in "Dunărea văzută prin...," pp. 18, 19.

27. "Semaforul Dunării...," p. 7.

28. "Un Siècle de cooperation...," op. cit., p. 16.

29. Ibid., p. 39.

30. Fr. Nauman, "Mittel Europa," Berlin, 1916.

31. An opinion based upon the note of Count Demblin, Austro-Hungary's Minister to Bucharest, to the Minister for Foreign Affairs of Romania, Bucharest, 25 September, 1918; quoted by C. Băicoianu, "Dunărea văzută...," p. 18. Note.

32. C. Băicoianu, op. cit., p. 23.

33. Idem, ibid., p. 22

34. "Dix ans de régime international sur le Danube fluvial" (1920-1930), Chapter I, "L'Administration internationale du Danube fluvial de 1918 à 1920 "by A. Baule, Secretary General of the Commission Internationale du Danube; the brochure bears no place or date of publication.

35. V. Slăvescu," Curs de transporturi," p. 361.

36. "Dix and de régime...," p. 3.

37. Ibid., p. 3.

38. Ibid., p. 5.

39. V. Slăvescu, "Curs de...," p. 361.

40. Idem, ibid., p. 361 and "Dix ans de régime...."

41. Idem, ibid.,

42. The Treaty entered in effect on January 10, 1920. Romania ratified it on April 5, 1920, with the effective date of September 14, 1920; see "Condica tratatelor si a altor Conventii ale României" (1354-1937), Vol. II, p. 1938, pp. 427-428, drawn up under the auspieces of the M.A.E. of Romania.

43. "Dix ans...," pp. 4 and 7.

44. V. Brătianu, "Chestiunea Dunării"; a speech made in the Romanian Chamber of Deputies, May 5, 1920; published as a brochure in Bucharest, 1920, p. 18.

45. Société Française de Navigation Danubienne (S.F.N.D.) which, in 1930, had a fleet of 67 bárges of 57,588 tons, 4 oil tankers of 9301 tons, and 13 tugboats of 7878 HP, all under the French flag; see Alex, Vasilescu, "Anuarul Dunării pe anul 1930, Bucharest 1930.
46. Treaty of Versailles, June 28, 1919; F. Israel, "Major...," Vol. II, p. 1265; Martens, N.R.G.T. (s.III), Vol. XI, p. 323.
47. Treaty of Peace between the Allied and Associated Powers and Austria, Saint Germain en Laye, Sept. 10, 1920; Martens, op. cit., p. 691.
48. Treaty of Peace with Hungary, Trianon, June 4, 1920; ibid., p. 423.
49. The Elbe (Labe), from the Vlatva tributary (Moldau), beginning in Prague; the Oder, Niemen (Russtrom-Memel Niemen) from the Gronda.
50. Traité entre les Puissances Alliées et la Roumanie, reletif à la Bessarabie, Paris, 28 Octobre, 1920; Martens, N.R.G.T. (s.III), Vol. XII, p. 849; "La Commission Européenne et son...," p. 448.
51. Op. cit.
52. For 1916, see B.N. Youghaperian, "L'Annuaire du Danube," Brăila; for 1920, see "Semaforul Dunării si a Mării Negre."
53. 108 barges, of 103,000 tons capacity, sunk: 89 barges of 76,000 tons capacity evacuated or sold to Russia or Constantinople; and 8 tugs of 1558 HP sunk; see "Semaforul Dunării...," pp. 99, 103 and 124.
54. 80 Barges under the Romanian flag, of Romanian and German ownership, and 56 barges under Greek flag and ownership; see "Semaforul Dunării...," pp. 143-146.
55. N. Dascovici, "Dreptul international," p. 112.
56. "La Commission Européenne et son...," p. 50.
57. Ibid., p. 130.
58. Ibid., p. 131. Société Générale de Paris; Banca di Commercio Italiana of Milano; an English bank and Banca Marmorosh Blank of Bucharest.
59. Ibid., p. 314.
60. V. Brătianu, "Chestiunea Dunării," op. cit., pp. 14-16.
61. Protocol No. 1, October 15, 1919, of the European Commission Meeting in Paris.
62. According to an article in the Bucharest newspaper "Argus," of March 1928, written by C. Tonegaru, former captain in the Romanian navy and stationed at Sulina during the war, the German vessel "Goeben," piloted by a certain Viefan and Austro-Hungarian, former Port Captain at Sulina, bombed and destroyed the beacon at Serpent's Island across from Sulina"; quoted by N. Dascovici, in "Regimul Dunării si al Strâmtorilor in ultimele două decade," p. 31.
63. V. Brătianu, "Chestiunea Dunării"; pp. 16-17.
64. "La Commission Européenne et son...," pp. 4, 49.

PART EIGHT

BETWEEN THE TWO WORLD WARS

"Si nous y travaillons tous du même coeur et sans arrière-pensée... et nous apportons ici un véritable esprit de solidarité européenne, nous ferons une oeuvre durable... à la prospérité et à la paix du monde."

Albert Legrand, (France) President of the Conference for Establishment of the Definitive Statute on the Danube River, Paris, 1920-1921.

Chapter 1

THE CONFERENCE FOR THE ESTABLISHMENT OF A
CONVENTION OF THE DEFINITIVE STATUTE ON THE DANUBE
RIVER (PARIS, 1920-1921)

Introduction.

After the Conference of 1856, following which navigation on the Danube River was internationalized, the Conference to establish the Definitive Statute of the Danube (1920 - 1921), can be considered one more cornerstone in the history of the Danube Question. The way in which it unfolded presented various characteristics, namely: the high technical level of the Danubian problems brought out, due to the fact that Albert Legrand, the President, and Francis Rey, the Secretary, had both been active in the past in the European Commission; the repetition of the discussions around the same problems, in order to reach definite decisions, made it necessary to interrupt the 1920 Conference and to resume it in 1921; the participation of Greece and Belgium, two non-riparian states previously absent from any Danube conferences; the concluding of the Convention in the same chamber of the Ministry of Foreign Affairs of France where, in 1856, the Treaty of Peace had been signed which had established, for the first time, the international regime of navigation on the Danube River; the designation of "Convention," not of "Treaty," for the new Statue of the Danube; the international form of establishing navigation relations between riparians, as conceived in 1815 by Dalberg and Humboldt, within the framework of the Committee on International Rivers; the instituting of a new regime in a political atmosphere free of the influence of the three former riparian Great Powers, Austro-Hungary, Germany and Russia, and finally, the determined positions of England and France and the unity of the victorious riparian countries: Czechoslovakia, Romania and Kingdom of the Serbs, Croats and Slovens, which for the first time imposed their point of view (for the name of the latter riparian country see note)[1].

It can be maintained that, in general, the work of the Conference unfolded in an agitated atmosphere and with resentments between the victorious riparian states and those defeated in world War I. The debates, observations and divergences resulting from the text of the Convention's basis project, and the counterproposals and amendments were so dispersed and repetitious that following them chronologically became confusing and extremely difficult. Also, the upholding of their points of view by some of the participants were so weighed down with references to and quoting from international acts concerning the old navigation regulations that they became a repetition of the whole history of the Danube. The lengthy duration and the huge volume of works were similar to those of the Conference for the Riparian Commission for the 1857 Act of Navigation.

If, after the Crimean War, the political balance of the Danube was the result of the successive confrontations between England, Austro-Hungary, France, Germany, Italy and Russia, after World War I, it underwent modifications. The new balance was taken over by England, France and Italy, its unbalance being due to the opposition of the small Danube countries: Bulgaria, Romania and Yugoslavia, plus the new state of Czechoslovakia. Although the Convention for the new Statue of the Danube was entitled "Definitive," it underwent repeated changes up to its abrogation by Soviet Russia, in the Belgrade Danubian Conference of 1948.

The Opening of the Conference.

The work of the Conference[2] was opened by Paléologue, Secretary of the Ministry for Foreign Affairs of France, Albert Legrand, as President, Thomas Stelian, as Vice-president and Francis Rey, Secretary General appointed directly by the Allied Supreme Council.

The work of the Conference proceeded in two stages: the first between August 2 and November 16, 1920 and the second between April 5 and July 21, 1921, sixty-eight protocols being concluded.[3]

From the Allied and Associated Powers, England, Belgium, Czechoslovakia, France, Greece, Italy, Romania and Yugoslavia participated, while from the former enemy states Austria, Bulgaria,

Germany and Hungary, took part. The United States of America, although an Allied Power did not take part, saying that for the moment they could not send a representative to the Conference.[4]

The Conference was called on the basis of Article 349 of the 1919 Versailles Treaty concluded between the Allied and Associated Powers and Germany, and on the basis of the corresponding Articles in the Peace Treaties with Austria, Bulgaria and Hungary.

Without substantially moving away from the principles of the Versailles Treaty, the Conference had the latitude to adapt them to the specifics of navigation and to the new political situations created by World War I. In addition, the basic principles of the Barcelona Convention were to be the guide.

Also, in conformity with the decision of the Allied Supreme Council at Paris, the European Commission for the Danube had to be consulted by the Conference. This decision became unnecessary, inasmuch as Baldwin, England's Plenipotentiary who proposed it, was also the president of the Commission and the other three delegates of the same Commission were also present at the Conference. It was even more unnecessary since Baldwin, himself, stated that the Commission's decisions "...ne saurait engager la Conférence."[5]

In the midst of multiple contradictions, Legrand conducted the debates in conciliatory manner, understanding the contributions of all the participants as "une collaboration et non une servitude," recommending that the work be carried on "sans arrière pensée."[6] The Plenipotentiaries of the small riparian states in the Associated Powers: Czechoslovakia, Yugoslavia and Romania, took contrary attitudes.

The Basic Project of the Convention.

In the name of the eight Allied Powers and Associates, but not of the former enemy states, Legrand on August 2, 1920 presented the French Government's basic project relative to the Convention for the Definitive Statute of the Danube.[7]

After its adoption as a basis for discussion, the President stated, in the name of the French Government, that the project was not an untouchable text whose author would refuse to accept any modification thereof, but expressed the belief that this project would answer to the wishes and interests of the Conference.[8] In addition to the French project and then to the amended one, there were presented also the

Greek, Yugoslavian, Romanian and Czechoslovakian ones, as well as those of other participants.[9]

The basic project provided that, within the framework of the general administration along the entire course of the Danube from Ulm to the Black Sea, navigation be considered free and open to all flags, under conditions of complete equality. (Article 1)

The entire navigable course of the river was divided into two conventional geographic sectors placed under the control of two commissions (Article 2). The section between Ulm and Brăila, also called the "Fluvial Danube" was placed under the administration of an International Commission of the Danube — I.C.D. — (Article 3), made up of representatives of the riparian countries Austria, Germany (Bavaria and Württemberg), Bulgaria, Czechoslovakia, Romania, Yugoslavia and Hungary, and of one delegate from each nonriparian country in the European Commission of the Danube (Article 9).

The International Commission of the Danube was entrusted with drawing up the Regulation for Navigation and Police (Article 14) and with carrying out alone, or in collaboration with the riparian countries, all the technical work for the maintenance of navigation (Articles 12, 13, 21). A special body, composed of riparians, was created to maintain navigation at the difficult navigation points at the Iron Gates and Cataracts (Article 17). Any modification in the administration and composition of the International Commission of the Danube was subject to the approval of all the signatories to the Convention (Article 24).

The second sector, that between Brăila and the Black Sea, with all the mouths of the river and the Maritime Danube (Article 4), was placed — or rather, continued to be — under the administration of the European Commission of the Danube — E.C.D. — , temporarily composed of the delegates from the non-riparian powers: England, France, Italy and the riparian Romania (Article 5). All the rights, attributes and immunities accorded to the European Commission by previous treaties were retained. (Article 7).

In Article 8 discrimination was made between modification of the powers and the composition of the European Commission, a stipulation which would later allow for wide interpretations, with detrimental effects to the European Commission itself. While the modification of the European Commission's powers depended on the authority of all the signers to the Convention, modification of its composition depended exclusively on the unanimous and exclusive consent of its members.

Coordination between the two commissions was aimed at harmonizing the international regime of navigation along the entire course of the Danube (Article 24). Serious infractions to the dispositions of the Statute, or litigations between two riparians of such nature as to prejudice navigation, were assigned for solution the Council of the League of Nations (Article 15) which, in turn, could transfer them to the Permanent Court of International Justice.

Aside from some ambiguities and lack of clarity, the French project can be considered the most comprehensive act ever drawn up in the matter of Danube navigation. Due to the amendments and the observations made at the Conference, its 27 Articles increased to 44, plus 6 Additional Articles, which made up the final Convention for the Definitive Statute of the Danube.

The project for the Convention did not include the basic norms for cabotage navigation, for transshipment of goods and vessels, for navigation taxes, for the international regime in the national ports, etc. Aside from the fact that these norms were considered by the project's author as belonging to the future Regulation for Navigation, they were understood to issue from the concept of Article 1, in the sense that navigation was and should be free for all flags, under conditions of complete equality. By amendments and observations the omissions were filled in, new norms were added along with ample explanations.

In some of the projects tendered by other participants provision was made for division of the administration of the river, while in others the unification of the two sectors was considered. The general consideration in favor of division, was based on the idea a more efficient administration and application of the international regime of navigation, while the idea of unification was based on the principles of the Act of 1815.

In the projects of the representatives of Yugoslavia and Greece the division of the river, as provided for by the French Project, was adopted, but in those of Romania, Hungary, Austria and Germany a single section was proposed from Ulm to the Black Sea, under the control of a single administration.

The last four projects respected the principle of the geographic unity of a river whose navigation was internationalized. Actually, this unity had been initially conceived by the stipulations of Articles 17 and 18 of the 1856 Treaty of Paris, placing the entire course of the Danube River under a single administration: that of the Riparian Commission, which was not established.

Because of the victory of the non-riparian Great Allied Powers, the control and supervision of Europe and the method of applying the international regime were retained in continuation, by means of the European Commission on thc Danube. This also assured the continuity of the presence of England, France and Italy, as non-riparians, in the administration of navigation by the European Commission.

The presence of England and France was necessary also from the consideration of keeping up the new political balance, which could have been unbalanced on the one hand by the policies of the small riparian states and, on the other, by the pressures from other riparian countries seeking to be represented in that same Commission. During the debates, England and France, yielding on other problems strongly and assiduously sustained by the small riparian and victorious countries, including the new state of Czechoslovakia, obtained the conventional geographic division of the entire course of the river.

The discussions and controversies over the conventional geographic division of the Danube, placed under two commissions, would have been unnecessary, in view of this being provided for by Articles 346 and 347 of the Peace Treaty of Versailles.

The problem of the functions of those two commissions, together with their composition, aroused the most heated and controversial debates, the protagonists being the riparian countries, with Romania in the lead. To the pro and con points of view there were invoked considerations of national sovereignty, the effects of the new political situation resulting from the war, equality of treatment, commercial interests, etc. Not lacking, either, were antagonistic attitudes. Of the two international organs, the European Commission of the Danube was the focus of the debates.

As is known, the European Commission of the Danube was the creation of England and France. Its establishment in 1856 was justified by political considerations as well as commercial ones. After World War I, the situation changed.

In the aftermath of the Revolution in Russia, the peril of her expansion was eliminated. The results of World War I eliminated also the Austrian and German policies of supremacy of the Danube. Due to these two consequences, the small riparian countries, especially Romania, the victims in the past now basing themselves on more solid political situations, considered the continued presence of the European Commission on the Danube (until then a European body which was an indirect shield of their very independence) no longer necessary. In the light of national pride and prestige, their positions were very justifiable, but the practical results in time proved to be negative. Their new positions were not the result of ingratitude towards their former protectors, but of the flexibility of the policies of the Great Powers, leading to the abandonment of the small riparians in moments dictated by the interests of the powerful states. The past had proven it. "Out with the foreigners in the administration of our river; out with the non-riparians at the mouths of the Danube," seemed to be at the basis of the desiderata of the "little" victors; they conceived an administration of navigation conducted exclusively by themselves. Romania's stand concerning the presence of the European Commission varied in relation to her political situation as well as to the general situation in Europe and its Southeast. Romania's Plenipotentiary expressed the opinion that the Commission be abolished, retaining it would be "an anomaly from the point of view of the principles of the rights of nations," and its functioning would constitute."..a servitude exercised over Romania's territory and waters."[10]

Referring to the reason for the establishment of the European Commission in 1856, that same Plenipotentiary said that the political and other conditions which determined its creation had disappeared. As to reasons for which his country had not opposed the existence of the European Commission until then, he stressed that Romania "had tolerated it but had not accepted it."[11] This concept was to be kept up until the concluding of the Sinaia Arrangement of 1938.

With the text of Article 6 of the French Project coming up for discussion, concerning extending the jurisdiction of the European Commission as far as Brăila, the President presented an amendment encompassing the views of Romania's Plenipotentiary. Thus the Commission's jurisdiction was retained "up to Galatz"; only its technical competence was extended as far as Brăila.[12]

Through the 1883 Treaty of London, the European Commission's jurisdiction, fixed by the 1878 Treaty of Berlin as far as Galatz, was extended as far as Brăila. To the German Plenipotentiary's observation in reference to respecting the 1883 Treaty, Romania presented an argument of international juridic order and one of technical order. He stated that, because of the fact that Romania had not been invited to the Conference of London and had not signed the treaty concluded, the treaty was never recognized by Romania. Yet, he admitted only the technical authority, but not the juridic one. He said further that, aside from the technical works carried out between Galatz and Brăila, the European Commission had not exercised its juridic authority between the two ports.[13]

Following a change of attitudes during the debates of September 30, 1920 and April 20, 1921, a compromise was reached by adoption of an ambiguous formula at the second reading of the French Project. Eliminating the designation of the ports of Galatz and Brăila, the European Commission's competence was set to be "...from the mouths of the river to the point where the competence of the International Commission of the Danube begins." The fact that the jurisdiction of this Commission was as far as Brăila, in accordance with Article 3 of the French Project, indirectly meant maintenance of the technical as well as the juridic competence of the European Commission between Brăila and the Mouths of the Danube, an interpretation which remained definitive. Although Romania had accepted this formula, still in a very short time she took it up again, leading, as will be seen later, to the litigation between her and the European Commission in the matter of these jurisdictions.

The Problem of the Enlargement of the Composition of the European Commission of the Danube. (E.C.D.)

> "The basis of the argument was totally mistaken for it is not a matter of who is next to the water, but of who uses the water. Hence, the calculation must not be made geographically at the banks of the Danube, but economically along the course of the Danube."
>
> Nicolae Iorga[14]

Under the principle of the above statement can be followed one of the aspects of the development of ideas within the Conference of 1920-1921, concerning the composition of the European Commission. This question was very much disputed because of the requests of some countries to be admitted to this Commission; granting of which would have derogated the clause of Article 346 of the 1919 Versailles Treaty, which had established the Commission's provisional composition consisting of four states: England, France, Italy and Romania.

The requests were based on the Provisional States of the Commission's components. The countries requesting the change called for equality of treatment with the other members. To this basis was added the derogation from Article 356 as made by Article 5 of the French Project, by means of which Greece was proposed, in addition to the four states originally mentioned. The Gordian knot of the problem lay in the competence of the Conference to modify Article 346.

The debates over the enlargement the composition of the European Commission took place in an atmosphere of animosity and nationalistic tendencies, the principal opponent being Romania. The President, in an effort to calm the spirits in the session of September 30, 1920, by modifying Article 5 of the French Project, eliminated Greece, proposing in the new Article (4) a transitory formula: "Any European state which in the future can justify sufficient maritime and European interests at the mouths of the Danube, may on its request be admitted to be represented in the European Commission by decision of the governments themselves represented."[15]

These conditions did not include the one concerning "commercial interests," the term designated at Article 5 of the French Project. In order to take into consideration the requests of certain of the countries, Belgium among them, this condition was added to the final text of Article 5 — now become Article 4 — of the Convention for the Definitive Statute of the Danube.

Requests for admission to the European Commission were formulated by all the riparian countries and were rejected by the Conference. Those being considered by the Conference were Belgium and Greece, both non-riparians. Much agitated discussion developed around Greece's request, ending with a confrontation between the Plenipotentiaries of Romania and Greece.

In the second and the fifth sessions of the Conference, Belgium's Plenipotentiary expressed his surprise at the fact that his country was not included in the composition of the two Commissions proposed by the French Project.[16] In demonstrating his point of view, he recalled the substantial participation of his country in Danubian commerce, showing that in 1911, for example, 34% (1,832,000 tons) of Romania's total cereal export was directed towards Belgium.[17]

Some remarks must be made concerning this documentation. In the first place Romania's exports could have included all those through the Sulina Mouth as well as those by way of the maritime port of Constanta when the river was frozen, or even those upriver towards Central Europe. The average annual exports by way of the Sulina Mouth between 1911 and 1915 were of 2,180,000 tons for cereal and 2,440,000 tons for total exports.[18] Hence, the figure of 1,832,000 T. of cereal with the destination Belgium, being too large in relation to the average annual figure of 2,180,000 T. signifies that the exports were made also through other ports than the Sulina Mouth. Later, in 1939, exports of goods through the Sulina Mouth, destined for Belgium, were of 90,140 T. — 6% of the total exports of 1,371,490 T.[19] cereal and other goods.

Belgium's case fitted into the solving of the old problem of "freedom of navigation" or also of "freedom of commerce." It has been shown that through the Congress of 1815 and the Treaty of 1856 the basis was founded on the idea of the "navigation of vessels," not also of the goods being transported, that is, on the idea of commerce.

Not all the cereal exported remained in Belgium. It is well known that the ports of Anvers, in Belgium, just as those of Rotterdam, in Holland, are centers of transit to the regions of Northwestern and Northern Europe for goods, especially cereal, imported from various sources. One could ask what was more important in the navigation sector under the jurisdiction of the European Commission (Brăila-Sulina) the traffic of maritime vessels or the amount of goods transported? In the statistics presented to the Conference by Belgium's Plenipotentiary and in those of the European Commission there appeared a discrepancy between the evaluation of the idea of "navigation" and that of "commerce."

The entire concept for the establishment of the European Commission of the Danube was to facilitate the navigation of maritime vessels, from whose taxes were covered the maintenance expenses, whether they entered or exited from the Danube, loaded or empty. Naturally the taxes on the empty vessels were reduced, but the accent was on the effective capacity of the transport, not on the quantity of goods carried. Under this concept, the traffic flying the Belgian flag was much smaller, registering in 1911 only 35 vessels with a capacity of 44,914 T.R. against a total of 1532 vessels of 2,710,680 T.R. exiting from the Danube.[20] Hence if the figure of 34% of materials exported by means of the Danube with the destination Belgium is taken into consideration, as the Belgian Plenipotentiary stated, it meant that her flag represented only 2% of the total vessels going west.

As to supporting the maintenance costs of navigation, the Belgian flag was in a minority inasmuch as the maintenance taxes were levied on the load capacity of the vessel, not what could come from its being loaded. In 1914, the percent of navigation taxes for the Belgian flag was 3.5%.[21] Hence it would seem that the majority of exports of grain to Belgium were carried by flags other than the Belgian, especially by English and Greek.

The eventual resolution of Belgium's request was to be included in the solution provided in Article 4 of the Definitive Statute for the Danube, the condition of "future justification of sufficient maritime commercial and European interests at the Mouths of the Danube." Although, in general, these conditions were met, still Belgium's request, presented as a "suggestion," was not approval.[22]

Admitting Greece into the European Commission was provided for in the French Project, the proposal repeated and amended through the same project on September 15, 1920. In view of the complications raised by the many requests for membership in the Commission, Greece was not mentioned in the second reading of the Basic Project.

Greece's Plenipotentiary, upholding her inclusion in the European Commission, presented official proof to the Conference of the substantial participation of his country's flag and of Greek citizens in the Danube ports in the whole network of navigation on the Lower Danube. He did not omit any of the historic considerations concerning the presence of Greeks there since antiquity.

He showed that, in navigation of maritime vessels on the Danube, the Greek flag participated in number and in tonnage between 23% and 30%, and in fluvial navigation that same flag reached 35% to 42% of the total fluvial fleet registered in 1920 figures slightly larger than the official ones.[23] The participation of the Greek flag in the budget of navigation taxes levied by the European Commission he indicated to be 25%.

The substantial presence of the Greek ships and of the Greek element in the navigation of the Lower Danube was disclosed also by officials and knowledgeable persons in Romania.[24]

Romania's Plenipotentiary opposed the increase in the composition of the European Commission. His position was based on the historic succession of facts and circumstances springing from national and economic considerations and political sovereignty. Proof was the fact that the same Plenipotentiary had proposed Belgium and Greece in the composition of the International Commission of the Danube, but not for the European Commission.[25] The enlargement of the European Commission could have resulted in putting Romania's delegate in the minority, since Greece and Belgium were in the orbit of English policy. By the addition of new members, the European Commission would have been strengthened while Romania wished to have its existence terminated. On the other hand, the opposition of the Romanian Plenipotentiary was strongly influenced by the change of attitude of some of the Romanian politicians, especially of persons well versed in Danubian problems, among them Professor Grigore Antipa, who saw in the admission of new members the diminuation of Romania's role on the Lower Danube.[26]

In Romania's position, the past policies of Vienna on the Lower Danube must be taken into consideration, as well as those of former enemy states, especially Germany. In this connection, Take Ionescu's thinking on the enlargement of the European Commission is enlightening. "No matter how friendly the Danube riparians would be to us," he wrote, "if they were accepted, tomorrow, the day after tomorrow, the Bulgarians, the Hungarians, and what is more odious, the Germans would request the same."[27]

Aside from limiting the membership of the European Commission, Romania had no other objection to admitting Greece into the Commission. Besides the historical ties between the two countries, the friendship between Take Ionescu, Romania's Minister of Foreign Affairs and Elefterios Venizelos, Greece's Prime Minister, also influenced the support of Greece's request. From an exchange of correspondence between the two, it appears that an understanding of reciprocal collaboration existed between the two countries at the 1920-1921 Conference.

This collaboration could not be fruitful, partly because of Thomas Stelian's firm resistance against increasing the composition of the European Commission of the Danube, as well as because of the resentment of Koromilas, Greece's Plenipotentiary, a fact which later resulted in the resignation of the former[28] and the replacement of the latter.[29] The attitude of Stelian, who was a great jurist of perfect moral integrity and orthodox in his thinking, was the result of objective considerations, not of nationalistic resentments.

In his telegram of resignation to his Minister for Foreign Affairs, Thomas Stelian, Romania's representative, stated: "...your accord with Mr. Venizelos for Greece's entrance in the European Commission makes the situation impossible for me in the Conference." He also mentioned the strong ties with Yugoslavia and Czechoslovakia's Plenipotentiaries, of which he states: "... I have succeeded in removing the chain with which the French and British Delegates, seconded by the Greek one, intended to strangulate us from the very first day of the Conference."[30] In answer to Stelian's resignation, Take Ionescu referred to the personal animosities between Koromilas and Venizelos, as well as to the role of the former in the Macedo-Romanian disturbances during the war.[31]

In the end, Take Ionescu also had to adopt an ambiguous attitude, taking into consideration the Anglo-French influence over Greece's position and the opposition of other riparian states, invoking for the first time Article 346 of the Versailles Treaty, which limited the composition of the European Commission to four members.

Take Ionescu was a nationalist, but not a chauvinist. His concept was dominate by the European spirit which characterized him throughout his entire domestic and foreign policy. In meeting the difficulties in the problem of the European Commission, which he had foreseen, and to clarify the complaints of other states wishing to be part of the

Commission, he addressed himself to Millerand, the Minister for Foreign Affairs of France, suggesting the following solution:[32] the eventual addition to the representation in the European Commission to be decided upon through bilateral accord of the signatories of the Versailles Treaty. In such a case, clause 356 of the respective Treaty would have to be modified and the four states designated in that Article to be part of the European Commission be the ones to decide upon the opportuneness of admitting other states.

At the September 30, 1920 session, A. Andreadis, the new chief of the Greek Delegation, gave a long explanatory speech on the requests of his country.[33] Showing its economic character, he compared it with any incorporated company ("une autorité syndicale") which could operate by means of the financial contributions of its shareholders. According to him, Greece, whose flag contributed substantial navigation taxes, could not be excluded from the composition of the syndicate. He also showed that, at the Port Commission of the Conference of Barcelona, the Delegates of the United States of America, Italy, England and France admitted in principle the legitimacy of the admission of Greece.

Referring to the Romanian Plenipotentiary's invoking of the possibility of reducing his country's sovereignty by the existence of the European Commission on Romanian territory, Andreadis declared that such sovereignty in the framework of an international regime diminished its value. As an example, he cited Romania's presence in the Straits Commission, which operated on territory sovereign to Turkey. After a series of discussions, Andreadis declared that "to facilitate the work of the Conference...he would no longer insist on mention of the word Greece in the text of paragraph 1, Article 5 of the French Project." (Protocol No. 10, September 30, 1920).

Thus, an end was put to the long debates over the problem of increasing the membership of the European Commission, which by Article 7 of the Convention for the Definitive Statue of the Danube remained at its initial composition as provided by Article 346 of the Versailles Treaty__England, France, Italy and Romania.

The following remarks can be made with regard to Greece's request. According to the principles of the Act of 1815, Greece would not have been justified to participate in the administration of the international regime of navigation on a river to which she was not riparian. The derogation made by the Treaty of Paris in 1856 by admitting also some non-riparian countries in the European Commission, was the consequence of the modification of certain basic principles based upon the decisions of the 1856 Peace Conference. Including Greece in the

French Project was determined by the importance of the Greek flag participation in the maritime navigation on the Maritime Danube as well as on the fluvial one.

The only possibility lay with the clause of Article 4 of the Convention for the Definitive Statue of the Danube, which although derogative to the 1815 Act still could eventually have been applied.

With the exception of the possible effects of Greece's ties with England, her presence in the European Commission would not have been to Romania's detriment, inasmuch as Greece had never had any political or territorial interests in the Lower Danube, a fact that Andreadis stressed. "How could the economic character be shown more conclusively," he said, "than by the admission of states that, although they have economic interests, have no political interests in the Danube?" (Protocol No. 10, September 30, 1920).

Referring again to the point of view of the Romanian Plenipotentiary regarding the diminuation of Romanian sovereignty by the presence of non-riparian countries at the mouths of the Danube, Andreadis declared: "Greece will take care to uphold in the European Commission all the legitimate interests of Romania and will avoid anything which could offend the self-respect of the Romanian people." (Pr. 10, Sept. 20, 1920)

This declaration, of a sentimental nature, was not dissimilar to the political situation derived from the geographic setting of these two countries. Aside from the centuries-old ties between them, the fact that they were both neighbors to the Slav world, and had never had any conflicts of a territorial nature between themselves, always determined a common policy and reciprocal collaboration. This reciprocity was evident a year earlier, on the occasion of the incident between Brătianu, and Clemenceau, during the Conference at Versailles.[34]

The requests of other participants at the Conference for admittance were not accepted either. It must be noted that among their considerations, they did not invoke the lack of legitimacy of the present non-riparian countries in the European Commission, only the equality of their representation with Romania. Bulgaria's Plenipotentiary, referring to Articles 229 and 230 of the Peace Treaty of Neuilly, which had made the provision that the Maritime Danube be exclusively administrated by the European Commission, declared that in the name of the principle of equality his country ought to be represented since, after Romania, it was the one closest to the European Commission zone.[35]

The view of the Austrian Plenipotentiary, which could be valid also for the other riparian countries, was a logical one. Referring to the condition that future admittance of countries be based on their having maritime and commercial interests at the Danube Mouths, he pointed out the presence of Austrian fluvial vessels along with maritime vessels at those mouths. His remark was a just one, considering the transshipment operations, of goods transported by Austrian fluvial vessels to maritime ones, being carried out in the port of Brăila, as well as in the maritime roadstead of the port of Sulina. Austrian vessels, like all the fluvial vessels that came out to the Sulina roadstead, were subject to the taxation system for navigation. To solve his request, he asked for elimination of the word "maritime" from the text of Article 5 of the French Project, leaving only the phrase "sufficient interests at the mouths of the Danube."[36]

Germany Plenipotentiary expressed his fear that the provision designating only four Powers in the composition of the European Commission was a sanction directed against Germany had she been able to resume her place in the Commission. Had Greece been admitted, although he considered her request justified, in his opinion it would have meant a derogation of Article 346 of the Treaty of Versailles, a derogation which could have been applied also for Germany.[37]

Invoking the loss of an opening to the Adriatic Sea as a result of the Trianon Peace Treaty, Hungary's Plenipotentiary appealed to the goodwill of the Conference to replace the word "maritime," in the text of Article 5 of the French Project, with the words "commercial maritime," in view of an eventual including of Hungary in the composition of the European Commission.[38]

Requests for admission were presented also after 1926 to the countries in the European Commission, by Soviet Russia, Poland and Germany, the most insistent being the latter, A peculiarity in this matter was the fact that England and France had conditioned the solution of their requests upon the agreement of Romania, whose opposition to the enlargement of the composition of the European Commission was adamant. In an official note addressed to the Romanian Government on May 24, 1927, Germany requested the former's agreement to Germany's admittance, a request forwarded also to the governments of England, France, and Italy, the other members of the European Commission.[39]

In connection with this request, Contzescu, Romania's Delegate, reported later to the Romanian Government that "it is nonsense, in the moment in which the four Powers making up the European Commission are in conflict (author's note: litigation between the European Commission and Romania over the jurisdiction between Galatz and Brăila) to even conceive of the possibility of any modification in the composition of the Commission."[40]

Referring to Germany's request, Contzescu went on: "...today we are discussing with three allied and friendly countries (in the above mentioned litigation) and tomorrow we shall be discussing with a former enemy country and with one (Greece) which, in its politics, maybe even in its reminiscences of one which upheld her, would not bring us even a small dose of support against the tendencies of the others." The Romanian Government postponed giving a direct and complete answer to Germany and Germany's renewal of the request through two Aide-Mémoires (1929 and 1936) met the same refusal from Romania, this time with neutral positions on the part of England, France, and Italy.

A repetition of Soviet Russia's request in 1934, of Poland's in September 1935 and again in June 1936, met with the same Romanian position.[41] It is interesting to note that all the requests mentioned heretofore coincided with Romania's actions to abolish the European Commission, an action which was undertaken and strongly sustained by Titulescu, as shall be shown later in this work. Returning to the results of the debates in the Conference of 1920-1921 on the problem of enlargement the composition of the European Commission, in the end, the proposition in Article 5 of the French Project (which became Article 7 of the Convention of the Definitive Statute of the Danube) was adopted, the one in which were designated England, France, Italy and Romania in the provisional composition of the European Commission.

Poland's request could have been considered in the light of her collaboration after World War I with the Danubian agricultural countries that had been cut away from the former economic influence of Austro-Hungary and Germany. Although most of Poland's exports and imports were channeled through other European routes, still, according to Polish economist Jean Kostanecki, an eventual connection with the Danube was regarded in the light of a "Bloc Agraire" of the Danube countries, as well as a bloc of anti-revisionist nature against the former enemy states.[42]

Before the XVIII the century, Poland had economic ties by way of the Danube overland from Lemberg to Kilia-Galatz and on the Black Sea, by way of Cetatea Alba the port at the mouth of the Dniester River. As for Russia, her riparian status ended after World War I.

The Problem of the Composition and the Competence of the International Commission of the Danube (I.C.D.)

The juridical competence of the International Commission of the Danube, between Ulm and Brăila, having been established by Articles 332-337 and 347 of the Versailles Peace Treaty and the corresponding Articles in the Peace Treaties with Austria, Bulgaria and Hungary, the debates were neither long not very agitated as were those on the European Commission. As for the composition of this Commission, the French Project in Article 3 respected the stipulation of Article 347 of the Versailles Treaty and the articles of the separate treaties with the former enemy states, by including in its composition only the riparian states. Still by some projects and proposals attempts were made to increase the number of its components.

Romania, in her project, wished to include Belgium,[43] associated herself with the proposal that pleaded for the admittance of Greece.[44] The viewpoint of Romania's Plenipotentiary on the matter of admitting Belgium was based on "the navigational and commercial interests invoked by this Power on the consideration of an eventual juncture of the Rhine with the Danube." He also stated that the proposal concerning Belgium and Greece also was based upon "Romania's friendship (for them) and she would view with pleasure the entrance of these two countries in the International Commission of the Danube."[45] In upholding Belgium, the same Plenipotentiary in referring to the "provisional" composition of the C.I.D., expressed the opinion that the Conference "...was not obligated to (observe) Article 347 of the Versailles Treaty."[46]

The Plenipotentiaries of England, Austria, Bulgaria, Czechoslovakia and Hungary were of the opinion that composition set by Article 347 should be retained; Italy favored admitting Belgium, but later abandoned that position.

It is to be noted that the position of Romania's Plenipotentiary was oscillatory and contradictory in regard to changes or modifications of the clauses of the Versailles Treaty. While he admitted the composition of the European Commission as "provisional," he considered that of the International Commission as definitive.[47]

As for admitting Greece and Belgium, the opinion held by Prof. Grigore Andipa can be enlightening. Referring to the rejection of the admission of Greece into the European Commission, in spite of the great amount of the traffic of its flag in the Maritime Danube, he stated, "...on the Upper Danube under the administration of the

I.C.D. the Greek flag is not encountered at all. As for Belgium, even her representative was surprised by this proposal inasmuch as Belgium has no vessels on the Upper Danube."[48]

Also against admitting Greece to the I.C.D. was the statement of another member of the Romanian Delegation (Stănescu) who declared that as far as he knew, "not even a single barge flying the Greek flag had passed the Iron Gates towards the Middle and Upper Danube."[49]

The Romanian Plenipotentiary's proposal in favor of Belgium and Greece in the I.C.D. can be considered purely a courtesy, inasmuch as the fluvial traffic of flags of both countries was very little on Middle and Upper Danube.

The traffic depended upon the possibility of passing from the Lower Danube to the other sectors, through the difficult passage at the Iron Gates where, because of the natural obstacles and the low water levels, fluvial vessels of tonnage greater than circa 500-600 tons could not navigate. The capacity of the Belgian fluvial vessels was of an average of 800 T, and Greek flag traffic upriver from the Iron Gates from 1923 to 1929 was of only 0.22%.[50]

In the end, the Conference did not adopt the inclusion of Greece and Belgium into the International Commission of the Danube.

By establishing the I.C.D., the unification of the Regulation for Navigation and Police, as well as the framework of the formalities of administrating navigation between Ulm and Brăila were realized. The navigational relations between all the riparian countries under the aegis of the International Commission of the Danube proved to be peaceful for seventeen years. The beginning of the imbalance and of actions towards returning to the regime proposed in the past came after 1936, concurrent with German political interference and then with that of Russia in 1948.

Status of Former Enemy States.

According to international tradition, former enemy states are usually deprived of equal treatment with the victorious ones at the drawing up of treaties of peace or of conventions. Some minor exceptions are worth mentioning: those applied to France by the 1815 Congress of Vienna and to some extent, to Russia by the 1856 Peace Conference after the Crimean War.

THE DEFINITIVE STATUTE ON THE DANUBE RIVER 471

At the opening of the Conference, Legrand declared that its work had to be conducted without "arrière pensée" and framed in the spirit of European solidarity.[51] As to the role of the former enemy States, later the Commemorative publication of the European Commission (1856-1931) states, "...sans le concours desquelles on ne pourait espérer établir sur ce fleuve un statut durable."[52]

However, at the signing and the ratification of the Convention for the Statute of the Danube, Legrand faced the ex-enemy states with a fait accompli, declaring, "qu'ils le signent ou non, qu'ils le ratifient ou non, le résultat sera exactement le même, et la Convention voudra pour eux comme pour les autres."[53]

In the following session, he softened his statement, attempting to reestablish somewhat the prestige of the ex-enemy Plenipotentiaries. To the phrase in the Preamble "in the presence of," he added "with the participation of the Plenipotentiaries of Germany, Austria, Bulgaria and Hungary."[54] Hence, from a position of "observers," they became considered participants to the Conference, as was indicated also in the Convention for the Definitive Statute. The position of the ex-enemy riparians were made more difficult by the revisionist attitudes of the Plenipotentiaries of Czechoslovakia, Romania, and Yugoslavia, dominated by the phobia of the past navigational supremacy of Austro-Hungary and Germany.

The disadvantaging of the positions of the ex-enemy states was initially seen in Article 349 of the Versailles Peace Treaty, which provided that: "Germany is obliged to accept the regime to be established for the Danube by a Conference of Powers designated by the Allied Powers and Associates." It also stipulated that "...at this Conference Germany's representatives may be present." The sense of these phrases was included also in the Peace Treaties with other ex-enemy states (Bulgaria, Austria, and Hungary). From the expression "may be present" was indicated that the position of the representatives of the ex-enemy states was as spectatutors as those with consultative vote only.

Also, in the Preamble of the basic Project of the Convention for the Definitive Statue of the Danube it was stipulated that the decision for drawing it up was the attribute of the eight victorious states "in the presence of the representatives of Germany (Bavaria and Württemberg), Austria, Bulgaria and Hungary.

From the very beginning, the differentiation regarding the diplomatic hierarchy was apparent in the "title" of Plenipotentiary, applied to the representatives of the victorious states, and "representative" for those of the former enemy states. Later, this differentiation was changed, the title of Plenipotentiary being applied to all.[55]

The first protest to this change of title came from the Yugoslavian Plenipotentiary. He insisted that replacing the title of representative with that of Plenipotentiary would give the ex-enemy states a power he considered contrary to the Peace Treaty. The President was opposed to this point of view and invoked the necessity for applying the rules of diplomatic protocol. The Plenipotentiaries of England and France attempted, without positive results, to temper the rivalries. The position taken against the former enemy states were counter to the principles of the Act of 1815, which provided for equality of treatment for all riparians, in the establishment of the international regime of navigation.

Chapter 2

THE PROBLEM OF CABOTAGE NAVIGATION.

Cabotage navigation of fluvial and maritime vessels on the Danube was the most difficult problem of the debates at the 1920-1921 Conference. It developed in an atmosphere of rivalry, nationalism, political resentment, contradictions and flexibilities towards positions previously taken. At the bases of the debates two principal facts are apparent. The first was the tendency to set aside the Austro-Hungarian and the German superiority in the Lower Danube navigation and the second, to protect the development of the fluvial fleets of the victorious riparian states in that same fluvial sector.

England, France and Italy, non riparian countries, proposed the Regulation of cabotage navigation in the sense of complete freedom. Czechoslovakia, Romania and Yugoslavia, seconded by Bulgaria, were opposed to this. In support of the participation of their fleets to cabotage between the ports of the Lower Danube, Austria, Germany and Hungary sided with the positions of the three Great Powers. The initial French Project for the Convention for the Definitive Statute of the Danube did not mention the matter of cabotage navigation since it was understood to be included in the stipulations of Article I. That Article had established freedom of navigation under conditions of complete equality between Ulm and the Black Sea.

The opposition of the victorious riparian states was based on paragraph 2 of Article 332 of the Versailles Treaty, which provided for certain restrictions in the cabotage of German vessels, that being subject to the authorization of an Allied of Associated Powers. In opposition to the text of this Article was Article 378, which proposed restrictions for a period limited to five years.

The Plenipotentiaries of England, France, Italy and Greece supported this Article. Baldwin (England) declared that the reduction of the term of restrictions of five years to three, could not be considered of permanent order.[56]

In another session, Baldwin, still referring to cabotage, said that the text of paragraph 2 of Article 332 "was of derogatory form" and that "the principle of complete freedom stipulated in paragraph 1 of Article 332 is a rule and that this rule prevails."[57] The general points of view of the victorious riparians can be summarized up in the statements of the Romanian and the Yugoslavian Plenipotentiaries. Referring to the four ex-enemy states "which do not have the right to request freedom of cabotage "and to the fact that England, France and Italy, "never had in mind the establishment of a cabotage service," Thomas Stelian (Romania) mentioned the case of Greece, a non-riparian state "which insistently claims that such a service be assured her."[58]

M. G. Ristič, the Yugoslavia Plenipotentiary, was categoric in his opposition to including, in the Statute for the Danube, cabotage navigation between the ports, under the sovereignty or authority of that same riparian state. He requested the application of paragraph 2, of the Article 332 of the Versailles Treaty, stating that "freedom of navigation on the Danube yes, equality, yes, but it must be realized that no freedom exists without some restrictions nor equality without reciprocity."[59]

It was shown that the express omission of cabotage navigation in the French Project was exclusively due to its being included in the complete freedom of navigation. Nor were there mentioned the restrictions provided for in Paragraph 2 of Article 332, on the consideration of their provisional nature which was to end by the application of Article 378. Faced with the initial requests of the three riparian states, the President, admitting their point of view, added to Article 1 of the amended French Project that the according of freedom of navigation was to be "subject to the special dispositions for cabotage traffic, as provided for in Article 16 of the Project.[60]

This Article established that "traffic from one port to another, so-called fluvial cabotage, is free and open to all flags, riparian states not having the right to reserve for their national vessels or for authorized foreign vessels the operation of local transport of passengers, or of goods, with the condition that foreign vessels not provide services of continual and exclusive character." With some minor additions, this text finally took a definitive form accepted by the three victorious states.

The rationale for conditioning the cabotage can be considered in the light of the remarks made by Andreadis, Greece's Plenipotentiary. He stated that in the concept of the International Commission for Ports and Waterways and the Railway regime, as considered by the 1919 Peace Conference, the sense of the restrictions placed by Article 332 was "...to prevent the new states from being crushed by the competition, on the Danube, of the strong navigation companies of Germany and Austria, or of Hungary."[61] This point of view corresponded with those of Czechoslovakia, Romania and Yugoslavia.

Concerning limiting the application of restrictions on cabotage, as provided for by the Versailles Treaty, for the former enemy countries for so short a time, Andreadis stated that the idea came from the United States Delegation, "which refused to allow the Peace Treaty to hinder any competition."

The notion of competition was a just one, if applied within the framework of economic potential at the level of that of the U.S.A., but not at that of the small riparian states whose fluvial fleets had been almost annihilated during World War I. Such competition as had been current before the war by the fleets of the Central European States did not exist in the U.S.A. In the past, however, the United States had been opposed to the great maritime fleets of England and Spain.

Two or three decades before World War I, because of the lack of sufficient means and due to complete freedom of navigation, the transport of goods and passengers between the Bulgaria, Romanian and Serbian ports had been carried out mainly by Austrian and Hungarian vessels. The moment Czechoslovakia, Romania and Yugoslavia organized their own fleets, they started actions against competition. The chance to start this activity came with the losing of the war by the competing nations.

The Romanian Plenipotentiary's concept concerning the nationalization of cabotage between Romanian ports was not an exceptional measure. It was an integral part of the policy for the economic restoration of Romania after World War I. Far from being a xenophobe, Thomas Stelian was a thoughtful supporter of an evolving nationalization of Romanian economy, until then for the most part in foreign hands. With this in mind, it is difficult to reject the positions taken by the small victorious countries in defending cabotage between their own national ports.

Nor was the manner in which Thomas Stelian defended the national flag of Romania illogical. "And we ask this," he declared, "because if the other states can request the right to carry on commerce and to enrich themselves in Romanian ports, that is, on Romanian territory, Romania has that same right to exist, hence to defend the economic institutions which assure her existence and independence."[62]

Stelian's unexpected reaction can be attributed to the viewpoints of the Plenipotentiaries of England and Greece, who by proposing the complete freedom of cabotage indirectly supported the requests of the former enemy states. In his response, the Greek Plenipotentiary showed that the beneficiaries of the participation of foreign flags in the cabotage were also the riparian countries, not only the foreign shipowners.

Referring to the Greek and Italian shipowners, he stated that their own countries obtained only minimal benefits and that the shipowners and the crews of foreign fluvial vessels spent their benefits in Romanian ports, hence their activity fit into the Romanian economy.[63]

The Romanian Plenipotentiary's point of view had been influenced also by the development of economic nationalism, accentuated after World War I against the foreign elements, whose activity in commerce and navigation was due to certain specific circumstances.[64]

Objective research of the foreign element (Greek, Italian and Jewish) could prove that the profits realized from the exploitation of navigation and commerce on the Lower Danube were invested in other areas of the activity in Romania's economy, for example, in industry, banks, agricultural exploitation, construction of public facilities, etc., along with the contribution made by this element to the development of cereal export. The names of these foreigners who put down roots in their new country can be found in all Romanian statistics concerning the history of the Romanian economy.[65]

The problem of national cabotage was complicated also by the Romanian and Yugoslavian Plenipotentiaries calling attention to the exceptions in the Minorities Treaties they had concluded with some Allied and Associated Powers in 1919, in which some clauses concerning navigation had been written in.[66]

Article 14 of those treaties had specified the obligations of those two states to accord to vessels of all Allied and Associated countries the same treatment accorded other nationalities, on the basis of reciprocity. Paragraph 2 of that same Article, however, stated "...by exception to this decision, the right of Yugoslavia and of any other Associated State to restrict cabotage traffic to its national vessels is perfectly justified."

The introduction of certain norms for commerce and navigation on the Danube into the treaties concerning the treatment of the minority populations of the regions transferred to Romania and Yugoslavia, was the result of the omissions in the Versailles Peace Treaty and in those concluded with the other former enemy states. But, even with this rectification of the omissions, the new norms were confusing. Hence, in order to clarify the meaning of Article 14, it was necessary to have recourse to the texts of the articles preceding and following it. This lack of clarity occasioned long debates and broad interpretations among the members of the Conference and the Romanian and Yugoslavian Plenipotentiaries.

These two riparian countries interpreted the exceptions to paragraph 2 of Article 14 as applying to fluvial cabotage, in opposition to the view points of the nonriparians, who confused them with those of maritime cabotage.

In clarifying the problem, both sides invoked definitions from Larousse for the words "navire," "bateau," for the etymology of the expressions "fluvial cabotage" and "maritime cabotage," as well as the priority of the French text of Article 14 over the English text.

The Yugoslavian Plenipotentiary's insistence to taking into consideration the restriction of cabotage to national vessels, an exception provided for in paragraph 2 of Article 14, was based on fear of the consequences that might result from the expiration of the term of the restrictions imposed on the cabotage of the former enemy states by Article 332 of the Versailles Treaty. "Once the term expires," stated Ristič, "the respective state can claim the right to cabotage in full freedom, not according it to other states, including our Kingdom, except on the condition of reciprocity, carrying out its cabotage however it interprets it."[67]

Thomas Stelian, in turn, not insisting too much on the text of paragraph 2 of Article 14, considered applying the exceptions in maritime cabotage also on Danubian cabotage. He showed that all transports used loading or unloading maritime vessels, which could not navigate upriver from Brăila, were as free as in the past: "A maritime vessel which stopped in one of the Maritime Danube ports not only was free to unload cargo at each of these ports, but if it had goods destined for the ports in the fluvial Danube the cargo could be retransported in barges flying under any flag. We consider that in such cases these transports are an extension of the navigation of the respective vessel. If to such a vessel there could be applied the exception in maritime cabotage, all the more could it be applied to those on the Fluvial Danube, but under the condition of the approval of the riparian."[68]

Thomas Stelian was not opposed to the transports carried out by barges under foreign flags, between the ports of a single riparian state, with the condition that they be occasional, not regularly scheduled, and under the authority of the riparian state. He showed that, under the condition of approval of the cabotage of foreign flags by the riparian states, Romania could "...prevent competition in our own ports and diminish the activity of the railroad which makes the connection between these ports."

Referring to the stand of the Greek Plenipotentiary in support of freedom of cabotage between the ports of a riparian, Romania's Plenipotentiary declared, "...if the other non-riparian states adopted the same point of view as Greece, I request that this point of view be immediately recorded in a Proces Verbal, in the sense that these friendly states requested the Conference to establish this service in the ports of the riparian states for their exclusive benefit. The world must know of the claims made by these states against those riparian to the Danube, in a Conference which was considered to be under the aegis of principles of equality and freedom."

The clarification of Article 14 of the Minorities Treaty was assigned to M. Hostie, expert technician from the Belgian Delegation, who had taken part in the works of the Versailles Peace Conference, where the clauses relative to maritime as well as fluvial navigation in all the peace treaties were worked out and drawn up.[69]

In his explanation, Hostie cited the opening and closing texts of Article 14, showing that the phrase "up to the concluding of a general Convention," mentioned at the beginning of Article 14, was a reference to the text set by Article 13 in which was mentioned the equitable treatment in commerce, but not for navigation. Only in the final amended text of that article does there appear mention of "cabotage between the ports of the Adriatic Sea," hence, of maritime cabotage. "C'est dans l'article 14, au contraire," stated Hostie, "qu'il est question de la convention général (treaties of 1919) dont parle, dans sa partie XII, l'article 331 du Traité de Saint-Germain."

In Hostie's presentation of Article 14, not only do ambiguities appear, but also corrections in the text of that same article. In his opinion, it seems the "general convention" mentioned in Article 14 should be understood as that of Article 14, not that of Article 13 .

Inasmuch as neither Article 15 cleared up the problem, he invoked a collateral one (331) from the Peace Treaty with Austria to document his theory. Even more, in the explanation of the meaning of maritime cabotage in Article 14, Hostie cited similar examples in which the world maritime was mentioned.

The view points of the Romanian and Yugoslavian Plenipotentiaries were answered mainly by Baldwin, who cited Hostie's counsel, among others. Some of his remarks upset the spirits of those two riparian Plenipotentiaries even more. Referring to the authors of the quoted remarks, Baldwin declared, "...these ask for the right to apply to other riparian and non-riparian states the treatment imposed upon the former enemy states by the Versailles Treaty. "Add," he continued, "the word 'non-riparian' for the word 'German' at paragraph 2 of Article 332 of the Versailles Treaty and you will have the text itself of the decision which the riparian states wish to be inserted in the Convention for the Statute of the Danube."[70]

In elucidating the text of Article 14 of the Minorities Treaty, which the Plenipotentiaries of the two riparian states interpreted in support of fluvial cabotage of national vessels, that is, the lesser cabotage, long and futile debates ensued. Again, definitions of etymological order were quoted and even the validity of the article with regard to the language in which it was written.

In Baldwin's opinion, "...the English text of the Minorities Treaty was perfectly clear in that it referred to maritime cabotage not to fluvial."[71] To this assertion, the Yugoslavian Plenipotentiary cited an example in which it was stated that, in case of any divergence between the texts of any treaties drawn up in a number of languages, the French of the Minorities Treaty would be valid.[72]

The Romanian Plenipotentiary's point of view was also logical. Admitting, as a hypothesis, that the exception made by the text of Article 14 in favor of the maritime traffic of national vessels of a riparian, he asked "if it is a matter of maritime navigation, why can it not be also for fluvial navigation?"[73]

Later, on the resumption of the problem of Article 14, Greece's Plenipotentiary also cited the English text in which maritime cabotage was mentioned, saying that in this case there was no "divergence of interpretation" between the French and the English texts to which the Yugoslavian Plenipotentiary had referred.[74] It is to be noted that the basis of Hostie's documentation was the French text of Article 14, not the English one to which Baldwin and Andreadis had referred.

Regarded retrospectively, the elucidation of the meaning of maritime or fluvial cabotage, in the text of Article 14, brought on so many contradictions and interpretations of an etymological order that the debates over it seemed to be at the level of a seminar preparing for future jurists, rather than a meeting of dedicated jurists. A number of aspects can be considered in connection with this clarification. The first and most important was the lack of precision in the text of Article 14; it seemed to have been introduced hurriedly in a treaty totally apart from navigation, such as that of the Minorities.

The contradictions in the discrimination between maritime and fluvial cabotage seem flagrant, in comparison with past attitudes over the same problem. In 1858, the Conference of Paris rejected the 1857 Act of Navigation, drawn up by Austria on the consideration of restricting fluvial cabotage strictly to the riparian countries. In 1858, as well as at the 1920-1921 Conference, the problems connected with navigation on the Danube were debated, but not at all the problems referring also to maritime navigation. Under this aspect, invoking the maritime cabotage of Article 14 was totally inadequate for the discussions of a Conference which was to establish a new statute exclusively for the Danube River, not for the sea.

The Plenipotentiary of the same Austria, which in 1857 restricted fluvial cabotage exclusively for the riparian countries, in 1921 declared that "...the reservation of minor cabotage in favor of riparian countries was contrary, not only to the dispositions of the Peace Treaty, but also to those of a general convention which was to replace them."[75]

Interesting were also the evaluations of the idea of cabotage in view of documenting the meaning of maritime cabotage in Article 14. Italy's Plenipotentiary stated, "...in international law there never was employed the word 'cabotage' in navigation on rivers,"[76] while Greece's Plenipotentiary claimed that the word 'cabotage' was applied always and exclusively to maritime traffic.[77]

The Plenipotentiaries of England, Greece and Italy, were correct in invoking the definition of cabotage given in the Larousse dictionary, in the sense of commercial navigation on short distances between ports on a maritime coast of the same country. This definition corresponded with the meaning in the past, when cabotage navigation was known only between maritime ports and not the fluvial kind which was carried on exclusively by local feudal systems.

Only by 1815, with the occasion of the preparatory works for the Act of Vienna, was the problem of major cabotage and of the minor navigation or "petit cabotage," both exclusively concerning "les rivières," brought into discussion in connection with the Committee on International Rivers.

If the words "fluvial cabotage" were not found in international law, as Italy's Plenipotentiary mentioned, still in the work of the Committee in 1815 mention was made of "minor navigation" or "fluvial cabotage." The notion of fluvial cabotage, as well as that of restricting it to riparian countries was even more evident in the Act of Navigation on the Elbe River, in 1821. Article 1 of this Act provided for "cabotage or navigation of the riparian states on the entire course of a river will be reserved exclusively for the subjects of those

THE PROBLEM OF CABOTAGE NAVIGATION 481

states."[78] Hence, the words "fluvial cabotage" as well as its reference to navigation between riparian countries was in usage already in 1815.

If the viewpoints of the Plenipotentiaries of England, Greece and Italy were just, maritime navigation was inadequate in the case of Romania, whose sole port on the Black Sea coast equipped with technical installations is Constanta. But, between this port and the other maritime ports — Sulina, Cetatea-Albă and Mangalia — coastal maritime cabotage was carried out exclusively by small craft under the Romanian flag. Flags of the Allied and Associated States — England, France, Italy, etc. — mentioned in Article 14, never participated in its traffic, simply because it was considered economically inefficient. Thus, in Romania's case, the restriction of cabotage to its national vessels, as stipulated in Article 14, could have been in support of fluvial cabotage for riparian countries.

Only in Yugoslavia's case could the idea of maritime cabotage be of value, considering the existence of this country's ports on its Adriatic Sea coast. All the more so since paragraph 3 of Article 14 mentions the cabotage traffic "between ports on the Adriatic Sea."

Czechoslovakia had no maritime coasts, having only rivers, as Greece's Plenipotentiary pointed out; its only large river on which she borders being the Danube. In this respect, Czechoslovakia's Plenipotentiary took the same stand as his Romanian and Yugoslav colleagues, understanding that "the exercise of minor cabotage," that is, the fluvial one, to be in principle reserved to flags of the riparian states or to foreign vessels having special authorization.[79]

Greece's Plenipotentiary later supported the viewpoint of Romania in the exception to the meaning of maritime cabotage in the dispositions of Article 14. "If such dispositions are lacking from the Minorities Treaty with Czechoslovakia, it is because of the fact that this country has no maritime coast."[80] Austria's Plenipotentiary also supported this statement.[81]

The complicated debates over cabotage were interrupted in October 1920, in order to be resumed in the second session of the Conference, in its first session of April 1921. In the 1921 debates references are made also to some of the 1920 points of view.

At the session held May 28, 1921, the President presented another editing of Article 22 of the French Project, amended in reference to cabotage navigation. This time, paragraph 2 of the Article specifically mentions the countries whose cabotage navigation between their national ports was excepted from the application of the free navigation regime. The exception referred to Romania, Yugoslavia and the new state of Czechoslovakia. In conformity with this paragraph, the cabotage of foreign vessels between ports of the same riparian country was subject to the expressed approval of the respective country, under the conditions requested by Romania's Plenipotentiary. These conditions expressed the idea that the respective traffic have no character of regular local service or of fixed schedule.[82] The Romanian Plenipotentiary raised the question of the competition created by the Greek flag.[83]

Constantin Contzescu, the new head of the Romanian Delegation, remarked that the fleet park belonging to the Greek shipowners (in 1920-1921) "is incomparably larger than that of 1916."[84] He also mentioned the case of a single Greek shipowner in Brăila who had brought from Constantinople twelve tugs whose efficient utilization was "due to the many needs of Greater Romania, whose railroads could not keep up with the need." This last remark can mirror the efficient contribution of the foreign flag at a time of crisis in other means of transports of the riparians.

Regarding the increased fleet of Greek vessels in 1920 - 1921, compared with the situation in 1916, as remarked by Contzescu, existing statistics show the contrary. In 1920, the general fleet under Greek ownership, or under the Greek flag, registered a drop of 49% for barges and 62% for tugs. Furthermore, after 1920, some Greek shipowners replaced the Greek flag on barges with the Romanian one, because of the restrictions in cabotage.[85]

The Greco-Romanian incident seemed to be purely rhetorical, inasmuch as a 1920 statement by the President said, "... the Plenipotentiary of Romania stressed the fact that this Article (22) did not provide for any restriction in reference to navigation carried on until then by fluvial fleets under the Greek flag." In that same session, however, the pacifying intervention by the President was contradicted by the Romanian Plenipotentiary, who stated that it was "...not a question of setting down in the Definitive Statute everything that ever existed on the Danube in the past" and that "the dispositions of this Statute must be edited in such a way as to conciliate the principles of the Peace Treaty with the rights of the riparian states," an opinion shared by the Yugoslavian Plenipotentiary.

The "existing situation in the past," to which Contzescu referred, was due also because of the preponderance especially of Austrian and Hungarian passenger vessels, whose traffic between the ports of one and the same riparian was carried out regularly, on the basis of a timetable. In this regard, it must be remembered that the presence of that traffic was due to the lack of sufficient passenger vessels belonging to the Lower Danube riparians before World War I. This situation was changed later by the creation of their own means, the development of which had to be protected from the eventual Austrian and Hungarian competition. This was the principal consideration for the restrictions, demanded by Romania and Yugoslavia not to accord to vessels under other flags the right to carry on regularly scheduled traffic. As the discussions progressed, the two more intransigent countries modified somewhat their stands, Romania's Plenipotentiary declaring that he "understands giving the Greek Plenipotentiary all the satisfaction wished for" and the Greek Plenipotentiary answering that "...the position of the Greek Delegation was similar and in extremis would associate itself with a transactional text." As will be seen, because of this yielding, the two Plenipotentiaries were assigned to edit the text of the article respecting the restrictions in cabotage, for the final Protocol.

The Plenipotentiaries of Austria, Bulgaria, Germany and Hungary requested that the restrictions imposed upon the former enemy states not be included in the text of Article 22 of the Project for the Convention, a request granted in the end. Their viewpoint was based upon the interdependence between Article 332 and 378 of the Versailles Treaty, concerning the limitation of restrictions. The fact that Article 378 established the temporary character of the restrictions for a term of three years, as specified in paragraph 2 of Article 332, signified, according to these four Plenipotentiaries, that the restrictions were to become definitive if included in the text of Article 22. From their statements, it seemed that the Definitive Statute of the Danube had to contain the definitive regulations and dispositions, but not the ones limited to a period of time.

In the 1920 opinion of Seelinger, the German Plenipotentiary, the non-inclusion of certain restrictions of a temporary character in the definitive Article 22 would have to correspond with the cardinal line of the Conference in its work of creating "...a work of conciliation and pacification," the idea put forth by the Plenipotentiaries of England, Belgium and France.

Finally, the problem of fluvial cabotage was settled by the following text of Article 22, entered into the Convention for Establishment of the Statute: (translation in English from the French text).

> 'On the international waterway of the Danube, the transport of goods and passengers between the ports of separate riparian states as well as between the ports of the same state is unrestricted and open to all flags on a footing of perfect equality."

"Nevertheless, a regular local service for passengers or for nationalized goods between the ports of one and the same State may only be carried out by a vessel under a foreign flag in accordance with the national laws and in agreement with the authorities of the riparian State concerned."

At the May 28 and 29, 1921 sessions, Romania's and Greece's Plenipotentiaries accepted the task of preparing an Additional Article concerning the interpretation of paragraph 2 of Article 22. It had the following text:

"Ad. Art. 22, (a) "By the traffic referred to in the second paragraph of Article 22 shall be understood any public service for the transport of passengers and goods organized under a foreign flag between the ports of one and the same State, when that service is carried on sufficiently regularly, uninterruptedly and in volume sufficient to influence unfavorably, to the same extent as regular lines properly so called, the national interests of the State within which it is carried on";
(b) "It is understood that the provisions of Article 22 do not in any way modify the situation which exists by virtue of Article 332 of the Treaty of Versailles and the corresponding provisions of the other Treaties of Peace in respect of the relations between the Allied states on the one hand, and Germany, Austria, Bulgaria and Hungary on the other hand, or in respect of the relations of the latter States to each other, for the duration of the periods of time during which that situation shall be continued in execution of Article 378 of the Treaty of Versailles and of the corresponding Articles of the other Treaties of Peace."
"On the expiration of these periods of time, the provisions of Article 22 shall become applicable to all the States without exception."

The text of paragraph (b) of Additional Article 22 was the one proposed by Belgium's Plenipotentiary. The complaints of the former enemy States concerning the restrictions on cabotage navigation were satisfied by this text.

As to cabotage of maritime vessels in the navigation of the Sulina-Brăila sector, the respective regime was the one provided for by paragraph 1 of Article 22, that is, complete freedom with the reservation of the condition specified in paragraph 2 of the same Article.

The above articles resolved the thorny problem of cabotage navigation, debated in the final sessions of the 1920-1921 Conference.[86] Except for some minor differences, the Greek, Romanian and Belgian

THE PROBLEM OF CABOTAGE NAVIGATION 485

proposals for Article 22 and Additional Article 22 were not far apart from the English ones.

The texts of Articles 22 and Additional 22 were an integral part of the final Convention. The new cabotage regime was applied on the Pruth tributary, which had become a national river with the reannexation of Bessarabia to the Kingdom of Romania, on the basis of the Versailles Treaty.

By Article 16 of the Minorities Treaty in 1919, provision had been made that Romania was to continue the application of the former regime until the conclusion of the 1920-1921 Convention.[87] After July 23, 1921, at the same time as the signing of the Convention for the Statute of the Danube and after it entered in force following its ratification by Romania, on October 1, 1922, traffic on the Pruth was reserved for the Romanian flag. Because of this situation, some foreign shipowners, especially Greeks who were the majority of shipowners on this tributary, sold their vessels, while others adopted the Romanian flag.

The new cabotage regime on the Lower Danube and the Pruth had only a theoretic effect. Practically, because of their lack of vessels, the riparian states accorded temporary exceptions.

In conclusion by the new cabotage regime the small riparian States had imposed their point of view.

Chapter 3

OTHER REGULATIONS

The Danube Tributaries.

The debates over the Regulations of International Navigation on the Danube tributaries and lateral canals going through a number of states and serving as natural exits to the sea, were due to the lack of precision in the Peace Treaties, as well as to their non-inclusion in the French Project for the new Statute for the Danube. Through Article 331 of the Versailles Treaty, as well as through the corresponding Peace Treaties with the other former enemy states, the Regulations were stated only in general terms. These deficiencies were to be rectified by the 1920 - 1921 Conference.

To clarify the problem, the President proposed, and the Conference approved, that a Sub-Commission determine the tributaries which should be internationalized. The report of J. Hostie, President of the Sub-Commission, showed that the tributary problem presented the following three aspects over which the Conference was to take a decision: the inclusion or not of the tributaries in the jurisdiction of the International Commission of the Danube and what distinctions should be made in this matter; establishing which tributaries should be internationalized; and the regime to be applied to the canals.[88]

Divergences and opinions opposed to those of the Sub-Commission arose also in the matter of the tributaries. The Plenipotentiaries of Austria, Germany and Yugoslavia rejected the idea of internationalizing all the tributaries, a regime they had requested to be applied exclusively to the navigable ones only and not to the ones with possibilities for future navigation.

On the other hand, the Romanian Delegation Expert contested the capability of the Sub-Commission to determine the tributaries, since they had been predetermined by the Peace Treaties. The above points of view were also based on the absence of practical possibilities for navigation along the entire course of a tributary, a consideration based upon actual conditions. The arguments of the Sub-Commission's President can be enlightening. He explained that the possibility for navigation on the waters of a tributary is so uncertain that it would be impossible to determine precisely all its navigable sectors. He suggested the establishment of a mixed and transactional regime on the Tisa (Theiss) tributary and upriver from its confluence with the Somes (Szamus)[89] As to the Bega Canal, which made up the boundary between Romania and Yugoslavia, a temporary accord was proposed between the two countries, which later was concluded between their Plenipotentiaries.[90]

Finally, taking into consideration the harmonization of all the points of view, the Conference established the partial internationalization of the following affluents: Morava and Tisa, in the part of their course that constituted the border between Austria and Czechoslovakia; Drava, from the Somes, and the Mures (Muros) downriver from the city of Arad.

This distribution was part of Article 2 of the Convention for the Statute of the Danube, later operation of navigation on these tributaries being carried out under the best possible conditions, under the supervision of the international Commission of the Danube, despite the points of view of Romania's and Yugoslavia's Plenipotentiaries that such supervision infringed upon the sovereignty of the riparians.

Navigation in Transit.

In the matter of transit of goods, there are two well determined elements. The first is the navigation itself, of the vessels carrying the goods and the second is the goods transported in transit. In the first case, the navigation carried out under the international regime was subject to the navigation taxes, while in the second case goods in transit were excluded from taxes except for those unloaded and temporarily stored on the river banks.

Although transiting of goods on the Danube had been set by Article 334 of the Versailles Treaty, still England's Plenipotentiary proposed that it be regulated by the Conference of the new Statute. His opinion was based on the fact that the stipulation of the article was of a temporary nature.[91] Besides, this point of view was supported also by the stipulation in Article 338 of that same treaty, through which the regime formulated by Articles 332-337 was to be replaced by the one to be instituted by a general Convention, that of the Statute of the Danube. All the proposals respecting the regulation of transiting being of a very superficial and general nature, the President recommended the one proposed by the Plenipotentiary of Czechoslovakia, which established that "...the transit passage of sailboats, steamships, rafts and passenger ships were free on the Danube network. No customs duties or other duties are to be applied on transit passage."[92]

This solution could not be permanent because of opposition from the Plenipotentiaries of Romania, in whose ports the transit of cereal and other goods was chiefly carried out. The Plenipotentiary raised the question of using the port equipment in cases in which cargo had to be stored in warehouses, in the transit of prohibited material, of the formalities imposed in some cases in which goods had to be sealed, cases of sanitation protection, etc.

Opposing this point of view were those of the Plenipotentiaries of the riparian countries upriver, the ones most interested in exports in transit: Czechoslovakia, Germany, Austria, Hungary and Yugoslavia, as well as England and Greece, the last two invoking the principle of freedom of navigation.

As to the point of view of the Greek Plenipotentiary, the actual situation did not prove his affirmation that "Greek vessels on the Danube did not customarily practice the transit operation."[93] It could have been rare for maritime vessels but not for the Greek fluvial ones, which in 1920 carried out a proportion of 17% of the transit operations for tugboats and 20% for elevators.[94] To the operations of direct transport were added those of re-transporting and loading onto maritime vessels of goods stored on land (warehouses and silos), in which vessels under the Greek flag also participated.

The differences having been harmonized, the Conference adopted the definitive text of Article 23 of the Convention for the Statute of the Danube, in which attention had been given to the points of view expressed.

In connection with this article, two remarks can be made. The first is the right of the State transited to identify prohibited goods, the objection raised by the Plenipotentiary of Romania. This right was applied by all riparian states within the framework of the neutrality on the Danube, in the period preceding World War II.

The second remark refers to the assignment of the responsibility of respecting the transit regulations to the captains of the vessels, not to the owners of the cargo. This limitation avoided, to some extent, contraband goods.

The New Regime of the Iron Gates.

As could be noted from previous descriptions, navigation through the difficult sectors of the Iron Gates and the Cataracts was evaluated by Austria as the most important part of her economic expansion towards the Near East, via the Lower Danube towards the Black Sea. Within the framework of her interests, Vienna, even from 1856 on, sought to obtain exclusive carrying out of the technical works at these two sectors, a mandate accorded to Austro-Hungary by Article 57 of the 1878 Treaty of Berlin.

The cancellation of the 1878 mandate by Article 350 of the Versailles Treaty being of a general order, the details fixing the new regime of the Iron Gates were to be drawn up by the 1920 - 1921 Conference.

In Article 17 of the initial French Project for the Convention for the new Statute of the Danube, the regulation of the regime for the Iron Gates was incomplete and confusing. The International Commission for the Danube was to name a Sub-Commission to take over the administration and execution of the works. In the composition of the Sub-Commission there were not foreseen co-riparian States, that is, Romania and Yugoslavia, only "riparian ones"—a general term from which the participation of all the riparians could have resulted. This omission gave rise to divergences. In support of Article 17 were the Plenipotentiaries of other riparian States, in opposition to those of Romania and Yugoslavia. In conformity with their point of view, the Sub-Commission was to be composed exclusively of representatives from their countries, plus a non-riparian delegate from the International Commission of the Danube. (I.C.D.)

The definite solution of the problem met with difficulties at the moment in which the Yugoslavian Plenipotentiary proposed the extension of the regime at the Iron Gates also over other points of difficult navigation on Hungarian, Austrian and German fluvial sectors. In addition, he proposed, as did the Romanian Plenipotentiary, the establishment of a Technical Committee with powers over those of the Sub-Commission, to decide upon the nature of the technical works to be carried out.

The Plenipotentiaries of Austria, Germany and Hungary categorically opposed the establishment of a Technical Committee while Bulgaria's supported it with the condition that there be a delegate from one other riparian State in its composition. England's opposition to a Technical Committee, which could function independently of the International Commission, was founded on the dispossessing of the Committee of its international character.[95]

Renouncing the idea of a Sub-Commission, a formula was reached in which, by not mentioning a Technical Committee, "special technical and administrative services" were established, by common accord between the two riparian States, Romania and Yugoslavia, and the International Commission of the Danube, to maintain and improve navigation of those two passages. The activities of these special services were to be decided upon exclusively by the International Commission (Article 33 of the Definitive Statute).

The result, hence, was that the regime was limited exclusively to the Iron Gates and the Cataracts, not over the other sectors of the river, its application being under the control of an international organ, the International Commission of the Danube. The international character of these services consisted of the participation, along with the national Romanian and Yugoslav personnel, of the pilots who had to be chosen also from citizens of any other countries. According to existing documents, it seems that this method of operation was to the advantage of all the riparians. According to Article 288 of the Trianon Treaty of Peace with Hungary, all the floating inventory and all the technical installations were transferred to the new Romanian-Yugoslavian administration, its countervalue being distributed to the war-reparations account.

Ports and Free Zones.

Debates over the matter of ports and of free zones were brief, having been taken into consideration the prerogatives of the riparian states to establish the respective regimes, with the obligations of communicating to the International Commission of the Danube what measures were being taken.[96] The decision of the Conference was entered in Article 21 of the Convention for the Definitive Statute of the Danube. In fact, however, none of the riparian states established free zones and ports. The fact that Article 21 referred to the International Commission for the Danube and not to the European Commission signified that the free ports and zones could be established only on the Fluvial Danube (Ulm-Brăila), not on the Maritime Danube (Brăila-Danube Mouths). Only at Sulina was there a free port regime, under the European Commission, and exclusively for technical material and smaller quantities of household goods belonging to the foreign personnel. To some measure, material stored in silos or special warehouses in Brăila and Galatz, which were sold locally, could be considered to be under the free port regime, inasmuch as no duty had been imposed.

Chapter 4

CLOSING OF THE CONFERENCE

Signing of the Convention and its Most Important Clauses. Reservations on some Clauses.

The work of the Conference was effectively ended on June 25, 1921, when President Legrand presented to all the participants the Project for the Convention for establishment of the Definitive Statute of the Danube, in order to obtain the agreement of the participating governments. On this occasion, the Plenipotentiary of Yugoslavia, the Vice-President, thanked all for their collaboration, stressing that "if the Statute does not meet with all our hopes, we must console ourselves with the thought that we have learned to regulate totally new questions without the aid of necessary experience." (Protocol No. 67, June 25, 1921).

On July 23, 1921, the Convention for the establishment of the Definitive Statute of the Danube was signed by the Plenipotentiaries of the eight States: Belgium, Czechoslovakia, France, Greece, Italy, Great Britain, Romania and Yugoslavia.[97] The Plenipotentiaries of Austria, Bulgaria, Germany and Hungary did not sign; the Preamble to the Convention stated that the signing took place in their "presence" and with their "participation." The Convention entered in force on October 1, 1922. As an annex to it, there was a Final Protocol, containing seven additional articles to the basic ones of the Convention.

In the light of their importance for the new navigation regime and especially for future discussions concerning its validity, the principal regulations of the Convention of 1920 - 1921 could be the following: the composition of the European Commission, conditions for enlarging it in the future (Article 4) and for composition and ending its operations (Article 7); application of the Convention on two large sectors of the river, the Maritime Danube (Articles 3 to 7) and the Fluvial Danube (Article 9); regulation of cabotage navigation (Article 22 and Additional 22); establishment of conditions for revising the Convention or for eliminating the European Commission of the Danube (Article 42 and Additional 42).

Some of the participants expressed the following remarks: (Protocol 68) Yugoslavia, Article 4 (paragraph 2), concerning conditions for admitting new members into the European Commission and the ending of its mandate (Article 7, paragraph 1); to the navigation taxes on the Fluvial Danube (Article 18); to the regime at the Iron Gates (Article 32); to the entire Article 33.

Greece had reservations over the composition of the International Commission of the Danube (Article 8); Czechoslovakia, over the method for carrying out the technical works, for improving navigation by the riparian States (Article 15, paragraph 2) and to the decision of the International Commission for the execution of those same works in the Fluvial Danube (Article 33, Paragraph 1).

Romania's reservations concerned the customs rights (Article 19), paragraph 2) and the headquarters site of the International Commission (Article 36); Italy, the same reservation as to Article 36 and to the revision of the Definitive Statute of the Danube (Article 42). Belgium's reservations concerned Port installations (Article 20).

Conclusion:

The Convention for the establishment of the Definitive Statute of the Danube remained "definitive" until its annulment in 1948, by Soviet Russia, at the Belgrade Conference.

Chapter 5

THE LITIGATION BETWEEN ROMANIA AND THE EUROPEAN COMMISSION OF THE DANUBE REGARDING THE JURISDICTION BETWEEN GALATZ AND BRĂILA

Introduction.

The importance of this litigation in the evolution of the international regime for navigation exclusively on the Maritime Danube can be regarded under three aspects, namely: Romania's demands for the elimination of the juridic attributes of the European Commission between the ports of Galatz and Brăila; the opposition of England and France based upon the extension of the powers of the Commission as far as Brăila, as provided for by the 1883 Treaty of London, and the position of these two Great Powers with respect to avoiding the diminution of the powers of that Commission.

In general lines, the litigation developed among three states allied in World War I: England and France on the one side and Romania, on the other, In the end, the litigation was partially resolved by yieldings and compromises.

Brief History of the Litigation.

The litigation between the European Commission of the Danube and Romania over the Galatz-Brăila sector, arising after 1923, consisted of two opposing stands. The Commission invoked the exercise of its juridic and technical competence over this sector, on the basis of Article 1 of the 1883 Treaty of London, in opposition to Romania, which acknowledged only the Commission's Technical jurisdiction. The juridic authority included application of the European Commission's Regulation for Navigation and Police over this sector and the issuance of sentences for contraventions. The technical authority covered maintenance of navigation and carrying out the piloting service on that sector.

The actual origin of the litigation can be traced to 1878, when, by Article 53 of the Treaty of Berlin, the European Commission extended its powers to Galatz, in complete independence of the territorial authority of Romania, whose political sovereignty through that same treaty was applied over the entire course of the Maritime Danube, including also the Galatz-Brăila sector.

Aside from some insignificant incidents, and although Romania opposed and did not acknowledge Article I of the Treaty of London, she still tacitly tolerated the European Commission's exercise of both its attributes, out of a number of considerations.

In the first case, the presence of England and France in the composition of the European Commission represented an extra guarantee assuring Romania's independence, just acquired in 1878. In the second case, the presence of those two Great Powers held no threat of territorial acquisition, as was the case with Russia. In the third place, and probably the principal one, the role of that Commission in the maintenance of the navigability of the Sulina Mouth contributed in great measure also to the economic development of Romania.

The friendly relations that had existed between the European Commission and Romania up to World War I contributed to Romania's tolerance to the existence of the European Commission or more precisely said, to the suspension of any public action against it. In the past, public declarations made by King Carol I, by the Romanian Governments and by officials and private persons in technical circles acknowledged and praised the great contributions made by the European Commission to the improvement and development of navigation at the Sulina Mouth and on the Maritime Danube.[98] Also at the Versailles Peace Conference in 1919, the Romanian Delegation acknowledged that contribution of the European Commission to the development of Romanian commerce.[99]

Professor Grigore Antipa attributed to the European Commission "the role of buffer states between Romania and Russia and between all States whose interests found here a point of contention."[100]

M. Kogălniceanu, the most ardent opponent of the Commission, in referring to the European presence at the Mouth of the Danube, in 1880 said, "...under penalty of suicide, we are duty-bound to defend the freedom of the Danube as a matter of European interest, only thus will the Danube remain Romanian." As to the European Commission, his opinion was that "...it had made at the Mouths of the Danube work to be admired and it merited the good will of all the adjacent countries as well as the gratitude of worldwide commerce."[101] His position towards the European Commission was to change.

The European Commission of the Danube, in turn, spared Romania's sovereignty at the Mouths of the Danube, seeking to create an atmosphere and relationship of courtesy and good will. A favorable solution to a Romanian protest, formulated before World War I against the Commission's transgression of its competence, was based upon the consideration "...de continuer les bons rapports...pour éviter tout conflit."[102]

Aside from naming the European Commission's luxurious yacht the "Carolus Primus," the European Commission contributed financially to carrying out many public works in Sulina.[103] It is true that all these contributions served a population which directly and indirectly depended upon the activity of the Commission, without being part of its obligations. Romania, in turn, in 1880 accorded the Commission a loan of one million French francs to enable it to continue the work of eliminating the bends in the Sulina Branch.[104]

During the period of World War I, when the functioning of the European Commission was suspended, and in the absence of the other component states, Romania carried out the minimum technical work for maintaining navigation at the Sulina Mouth. Even during the time negotiations were being conducted for concluding the 1918 Treaty of Bucharest with the Central Powers, Romania supported maintaining the European Commission, which Germany and Austro-Hungary wanted to abolish. Even before World War I there were voices arguing against the existence of the European Commission. Among them was that of N. Iorga, who justified the need for its presence only for the immediate period needed to carry out the aims of the 1856 Treaty, but not also after Romania had gained her independence.[105]

After World War I, the relations between Romania and the European Commission began taking on critical forms, many factors contributing to them, among them also the political strengthening of Romania, a victor in the war. The most important factor which inflamed the dispute was the serious condition of navigation at the Sulina Mouth after the war, a condition which paralyzed Romania's exporting.

Between the Bucharest Treaty of 1918, when Romania had temporarily ceased hostilities, and the time of the Armistice to the European War, Germany and Austro-Hungary continued to work of maintaining the navigation, financing the purchases of necessary materials and fuel oil needed for the dredging operations. After the general Armistice was concluded, the work was continued under difficult financial conditions; Romania advanced the sum of 900,00 Lei and the English and French delivered the coal needed from the stocks in Constantinople.[106] In spite of all the urgent measures taken, it was still not possible to get the minimum depths (14-16 feet) needed for even restricted navigation. In 1919, C. Contzescu, Romania's Delegate in the European Commission, after a voyage on the Maritime Danube, stated that at Sulina and Galatz "almost everything was in a state of abandonment" and that the European Commission was "...a house without a master."[107] Not only the European Commission but also all Sulina corresponded with Contzescu's findings, activity was nonexistent. The Commission's entire service fleet: dredges, pilot ships, shops, the city power plant, etc., all were deteriorating, in need of much repair. With the use of loans contracted after 1920, the first measures of restoration were taken by the Commission and, in January 1921, a Consultant Committee of Engineers was created to establish a program of work.

Even with the intensification of dredging on the normal route of the navigable channel of the Danube Mouth it was not possible to obtain greater depths, the obstruction remained almost until the year 1924. The normal navigable channel was abandoned and deviated towards the north, creating an artificial one, which also did not serve to bring navigation back to normal. In order to get into the Danube, ships had to wait days on end in the Maritime roadstead of the port of Sulina, and those seeking to leave the river were anchored upriver of Sulina Port, causing strandings, thefts and accidents.

The grave technical situation at the Sulina Mouth coincided with the reduction in exports between 1921 and 1928, caused by the extremely unfavorable results of the agricultural production in the Lower Danube valley. At the same time, the traffic of maritime vessels fell in 1928 to the lowest level in forty years.

Government circles in Bucharest and the press blamed the European Commission for the state of navigation at Sulina; important persons even demanded that it be abolished because of incapability. Commercial circles expressed their opinion by "...our ports are dying."[108]

Aside from the variations in depth caused by natural phenomena, the concentration of attention on improving navigation by extending dikes ran up against the lack of funds. "The blame cast upon the European Commission," noted Professor Dascovici, "were exaggerated or even unjustified, if we take into consideration today (1943) the complexity of actual circumstances experienced by the Commission during the war."[109]

To the origin of the Galatz-Brăila litigation was added also the double juridical regime at Sulina. As mentioned previously, at Sulina there existed two sovereignties, that of the Romanian State exercised over the town and over a portion of the port, and that of the European Commission with the juridic status of "a state within a state." The latter's jurisdiction included the Commission's administrative and technical establishments, a portion of the port and the application of the Regulation for Navigation and Police independent of the authority of the Romanian State.

In support of the Romanian point of view in the matter of the litigation, the vague text of Article 1 of the 1883 Treaty can be cited. Its provision that "the jurisdiction of the European Commission is extended from Galatz to Brăila" did not make a distinction between the purely juridical jurisdiction and the technical one.

In the light of previous treaties and of navigation needs, the Commission's point of view can be justified. In the clauses of Articles 346 and 347, of the Versailles Treaty, and the Convention for the Definitive Statute of the Danube, the geographic limits of the Commission's jurisdiction were rather precise. Article 346 provided that "the European Commission reassumes the powers it possessed before the war...," that is, those immediately before, as provided by Article 53 of the 1878 Treaty and Article 1 of the Treaty of 1883. Article 347 provided that "...from the point where the competence of the European Commission ceases, the Danube regime referred to in Article 331 shall be placed under the administration of an International Commission composed as follows..." The lacuna in Article 347 consisted of omitting the indication of the point of the Commissions ended.

The Galatz-Brăila problem was taken up also at the Conference for the Establishment of the Convention for the Danube Statute in 1921, at which time the point of juncture of the two Commissions was specified. Article 6 of the French Project for the Convention stated, "...la jurisdiction de la Commission s'étend...sur toute la partie du fleuve accessible aux navires de haute mer, c'est à dire de Brăila à la Mer Noire." This clause also was confusing in that it did not mention "technical jurisdiction," leaving the general term "la jurisdiction" to imply both.

In Article 6 of the Convention, the text of the French Project was somewhat clearer, stating "la compétence s'étend, dans les mêmes conditions que par le passé et sans aucune modification à ses limites actuelles, sur le Danube Maritime, c'est à dire depuis les embouchures du fleuve jusqu'au point où commence la compétence de la Commission Internationale," that is, as far as Brăila, in conformity with Article 1 of the London Treaty of 1883. Neither did this Article mention the two jurisdictions.

Bearing in mind the fact that the jurisdiction of the International Commission of the Danube had been established between Ulm and Brăila (Article 9 of the Statute) and the 1883 Regulation for Navigation and Police of that same commission applied only between the Iron Gates and Brăila, there remained a gap in juridical and technical jurisdictional matters, between the Iron Gates and Brăila. This gap was presumed to have been covered by the text of Article 5 of the Convention, which stated "...la Commission Européenne exerce des pouvoirs qu'elle avait avant la guerre," which meant the powers resulting from the extension of its jurisdiction from Galatz to Brăila.

Resolving the gap was a matter of interpreting the new extension, whether it was "to Brăila" or "including" the port of Brăila. The fact that this port was the final point of the navigation of maritime vessels under the administration of the European Commission, signified that it was included in the extension of that Commission's jurisdiction between Galatz and Brăila. Elimination of the gap also came from the text of Article 6 of the French Project, in which the jurisdiction of the European Commission was extended over all the sections of the river accessible to maritime vessels; in other words, between Brăila and the Black Sea. This clarifying text did not appear in the final text of the 1921 convention. Only by 1924 did the League of Nations "Advisory and Technical Committee for Communications and Transit," called upon for advice in the litigation matter, indicate precisely that the limit of the European Commission's powers was "above Brăila," meaning "including" that port.

Referring to the clause of Article 346, of the Versailles Treaty, Contzescu in 1921 acknowledged the competence which the European Commission held, before the war, up to the point where the jurisdiction of the International Commission ended, that is, up to Brăila, but with the formal reservation of the de facto restrictions existing between Galatz and Brăila. By restrictions, he was referring to the juridical conception of the commission, not the technical one.

However, these restrictions had never been provided for in any previous treaties. In fact, up to World War I, because of the favorable navigation conditions, the jurisdictional competence of the Regulation for Navigation and Police had not been applied often between Galatz and Brăila.

In this connection, Popescu, Adjunct to the Romanian Delegation to the 1921 Conference for the Statute of the Danube, commented on the fact that before the war, the Commission had exercised only purely technical jurisdiction and piloting services. As for the technical matters, he noted the strong collaboration between the Commission and the Romanian technical organs, mentioning as an example, the case at Tiglina Point (Near Galatz), where a large sand bar had formed, bogging down maritime vessels. Since the remedial work undertaken by the European Commission did not bear results, it was continued and finished successfully by Romania's technical organs. In his opinion, the technical maintenance between Galatz and Brăila would be more efficiently carried out by collaboration between the Commission and Romania.

In the contradictory debates at the 1920-1921 Conference, the Romanian Delegation continued to maintain that the Commission's powers were applicable only in technical matters, the juridic ones pertaining to Romania. To this point of view, Baldwin (England's Plenipotentiary) seemed to agree, in remarking that the attributes actually exercised by the European Commission from Galatz to Brăila were those of dredging, marking out channels and pilotage.[110] Later, Baldwin also sustained the Commission's juridic competence as well. In order to clarify the contradictions between Articles 5 and 6 of the Project for the Convention, Romania's Plenipotentiary asked that the other members of the Commission (English, French and Italian) themselves specify the exact extent of the Commission's Powers, as exercised before the war, in a Special Protocol which would be an integral part of the Convention for the Definitive Statute of the Danube.

The Conference approved the request with the condition that the title of the Special Protocol be modified to Interpretative Protocol, rejecting its being an integral part of the Convention. The Interpretative Protocol was drawn up on May 6, 1921 and was signed only by the four members, in their capacity as Delegates in the European Commission.[111] The text of the protocol was very confused and ambiguous, avoiding the establishment of any firm decisions.

The Interpretative Protocol had no executive power, being signed only by the members of the Commission as Delegates, not as

Plenipotentiaries with specific mandates from their Governments. This protocol could not modify the 1883 London Treaty with respect to the European Commission's jurisdiction. They signed it only on the basis of Article 6 of the Project for the Danube Statute, adopted by the 1920-1921 Conference. The Interpretative Protocol resolved none of the problems in the way Romania wished. Its text contained that of Article 6 of the Statute, continuing with "...Article 6 of the Statute does not and shall not hereafter, entail any modification under which, or the limits within which this administrative regime has hitherto been applied" and "...it is clearly understood, therefore, that the powers of the Commission (E.C.D.) are not, in virtue of the provision either increased or diminished, and they should continue to be exercised on the river in the same way as in the past, in conformity with the treaties.

By "conformity with the treaties" was meant retaining the powers on the European Commission in the same way as in the past, extending the juridical and technical powers between Galatz and Brăila, in accordance with the 1883 Treaty of London. Furthermore, the same Protocol stated, "...it is also understood that between Galatz and Brăila the European Commission of the Danube will continue, as in the past, to maintain the navigable channel and its pilotage service." From this latter text, only the purely technical power, not the juridic one contested by Romania, is provided for. When the Galatz-Brăila problem was submitted for the advice of the Permanent Court of International Justice, the Interpretative Protocol was evaluated as a Cumulative Act of the juridic and technical powers of the European Commission. The confusion of the Interpretative Protocol brought about the presentation of the problem to the League of Nations and then to the Permanent Court of International Justice.

The Litigation at the League of Nations.

Shortly after the application of the Convention for the Definitive Statute of the Danube, in 1921, England's Delegate in the European Commission called repeatedly for the exercise of the Commission's juridic and technical competence over the Galatz-Brăila sector.[112]

On September 6, 1924, the British government — with which the French and Italian Governments soon associated themselves — had presented to the Secretary-General of the League of Nations a request which, in accordance with the relevant provisions of the international agreements in force, should be submitted to the Advisory and Technical Committee for Communications and Transit, of the League of Nations.[113]

After a series of meetings of the Advisory Committee with the parties concerned, an accord could not be reached. In order to identify the past practice in the exercise of jurisdiction by the European Commission between Galatz and Brăila, the Advisory Committee established a Special Committee of Enquiry, which went to the Danubian ports in the summer of 1925 to examine the problem. After an investigation conducted among the official organs and commercial circles of navigation, the Special Committee ascertained that between 1888 and 1911, the European Commission organs had issued about sixty sentences for infringements against the Commission's Regulation for Navigation and Police on the Galatz-Brăila sector. From this was deduced the Commission's juridic competence. The fact that the European Commission before the war did exercise over this sector not only purely administrative and technical attributes, but also those of juridic order was in the Special Committee's opinion, proof that its attributes were de facto and de jure.[114] The Special Committee concluded that, in conformity with the provision of the Definitive Statute of 1921, "the powers of the European Commission are to be exercised from Galatz to above Brăila, under the same de facto conditions as before the war." But it added, "...these conditions are not determined by the clause of the Treaty of London of 1883 extending the authority of the European Commission to Brăila, because the clause was not among those in force before 1914, but by usage having juridical force apply because it has grown up and been consistently applied with the unanimous consent of all States concerned."

In the end, the report of the Committee of Enquiry considered that "in the absence of any clearly proved practice to the contrary, the exercise of the power of regulation of that of punitive jurisdiction (that is to say of jurisdictional powers) merge. In absence of any texts in support, the Committee invoked the practice established on the Maritime Danube."

This last opinion corresponded with Romania's point of view in the sense of tacit toleration of the European Commission's exercise of its powers. "In this usage," the Committee stated, "the Romanian

Delegate to the European Commission tacitly but formally acquiesced in the sense that a modus vivendi was observed on both sides, according to which the sphere of action of the Commission in fact extended, in all respects as for as above Brăila."

Later, when the Galatz-Brăila case was being examined by the Permanent Court of International Justice, Deputy Judge Negulescu (Romania) was of a different opinion. He cited 433 cases which the Special Committee had omitted and in which the Romanian authorities in the port of Galatz had issued sentences for navigation offenses even through the European Commission's Regulation for Navigation and Police was applied on this sector. "If the Romanian Authorities had not the right of jurisdiction in the Galatz-Brăila sector" he asked, "how can the fact be explained that the European Commission never protested to the Romanian Government?"[115] Since the litigation was not resolved by the Advisory and Technical Committee, it was transferred to the Permanent Court of International Justice.

The Advisory Opinion of the Permanent Court of International Justice.

Faced with this new situation, the Delegates of England, France, Italy and Romania in the European Commission, empowered by their Governments drew up an Agreement, on September 18, 1926, accepting the submittal of the litigation to the Permanent Court of International Justice at the Hague, for resolution.[116]

In connection with this decision, it is interesting to note the caution expressed by Titulescu, Romania's representative to the League of Nations. He was not inclined to send the case to the Permanent Court since any decision of that Court would be of consultative value, not obligatory. "I am afraid of the fate of the suit in the Hague," he reported to Bucharest. "For that reason, I believe that direct negotiations should be activated in order to obtain a solution in conformity with national interests, which make judgment at the Hague useless."[117]

Titulescu also expressed his belief that Romania was forced by England, France and Italy's "invoking," he stressed, "our treaties of alliance as a weight to intervene against us."[118] To a statement made by Austen Chamberlain, England's representative in the League of Nations, to the effect that the paternity of the Commission's opposition was not exclusively England's but also France's and Italy's,

Titulescu answered "...if Sir Chamberlain does not wish that today's debates constitute an unfavorable precedent for Great Britain, I declare that neither do I wish these debates to constitute an unfavorable precedent for Romania, whose rights on the Danube are and remain complete."[119]

In order to assure the success of the Romanian point of view at the Permanent Court, Titulescue requested, and the Ministry for Foreign Affairs of Romania approved, the employment of three lawyers, one, a past president of the Republic of France, and two jurisconsults of European renown.[120] These three, together with C. Contzescu, Romania's Delegate to the European Commission, pleaded in favor of Romania's position, having as their opponents the representatives of the European Commission of the Danube.[121]

Between December 6 and 8, 1927, the Permanent Court in its 20th regular session studied the December 9, 1926 Resolution of the Council of the League of Nations, which had taken into consideration:[122] the letter dated September 25, 1926 of the chairman of the Advisory and Technical Committee of Communications and Transit and the Agreement made on September 18, 1926, between the governments of France, Great Britain, Italy and Romania. Also, all the treaties and Conventions relative to the navigational regime on the Danube were studied. The Council of the League of Nations asked the Permanent Court to give an Advisory Opinion on three questions formulated in the Agreement of September 18, 1926.[123]

The Opinions of the Permanent Court, all in favor of the European Commission, were 9 to 1 (Romania's Deputy Judge) recorded in the Advisory Opinion No. 24, of December 8, 1927.[124] The questions and opinions will be given here in resumé.

The first question: "If, under the law at present in force (author's note treaties and conventions), the European Commission of the Danube has the same powers on the maritime sector of the Danube between Galatz and Brăila as on the sector below Galatz; and if the answer is affirmative, how far upriver do these posers extend?"

Advisory opinion: "Under the law at present in force, the European Commission has the same powers on the maritime sector of the Danube from Galatz to Brăila as on the sector below Galatz and that these powers extend up to the port of Brăila, this port being included."

The second question: "Do the powers of the European Commission, between Galatz and Brăila, extend also over the territorial zones corresponding with those of navigation and those of the ports under the exclusive jurisdiction of Romanian authorities? If the answer is in the affirmative, to what criteria shall the line of demarcation be fixed, as between territorial zones under the competence of the European Commission and that of the Romanian authorities?"

Advisory opinion: "The powers of the European Commission are not excluded from zones territorially defined and corresponding to harbour zones. The dividing line between the respective competences of the European Commission and of the Romanian authorities in the ports of Galatz and Brăila is to be fixed according to the criteria of navigation in order to ensure freedom of navigation."

Third question: "If the European Commission does not have the same powers between Galatz and Brăila as on the sector down river from Galatz, then at what exact point shall the line of demarcation between the two regimes be fixed?"

Advisory Opinion: "It is not necessary to give an answer to this question, it being understood that the powers of the European Commission below Galatz extend also on the Galatz-Brăila sector, the latter port being included."

Judges N. G. Nyholm and J. B. Moore, while agreeing with the conclusion arrived at by the Court, added certain individual observations. Deputy Judge Negulescu (Romania), declared himself unable to concur in the Court's opinion and, availing himself of the right conferred upon him by Article 71 of the Rules of Court, delivered a Separate Opinion.

In conclusion, the clause of Article 1 of the 1883 Treaty of London and the convention for the Definitive Statute of the Danube were evaluated by the Advisory Council of the Permanent Court of International Justice, in 1921, i.e. maintaining the European Commission's juridical and technical competence between Galatz and Brăila.

Observations of Judges D. G. Nyholm and J. B. Moore of the Permanent Court of International Justice.

While agreeing with the conclusions arrived at by the Court, Nyholm still presented another point of view concerning the validity of the old treaties, on the basis of which the juridic and technical jurisdictions of the European Commission had been successively extended.[125] "What is the law in force for the Danube, which should have been taken into consideration?" he asked. "As regards treaties prior to the Treaty of Versailles, there seems to be no doubt that they have been abolished." He attributed the abrogation to the political and territorial changes in the Danube valley after World War I, as well as to the new composition of the European Commission as established by the above mentioned treaty.

It is difficult to agree with this point of view. In such a case, it would mean the invalidating of the very existence of the European Commission, established by the 1856 Treaty of Paris, "prior to the Treaty of Versailles." Such an annulment would have included the complete juridic and political framework covering the existence and activity of the European Commission.

By this annulment, Nyholm claimed the lack of validity of the extension of the European Commission's powers to — Galatz, as established by the 1878 Treaty of Berlin and of that to Brăila by the Treaty of London, in 1883. Taking into consideration only the Treaty of Versailles, he analysed the validity of Articles, 6, 5 and 9 of the 1921 Definitive Statute of the Danube. "The Court's opinion," he observed, "gives to Article 6 an interpretation which does not seem admissible... this interpretation overturns, in fact, all the principles of the Treaty, by declaring that Article 9, combined with Article 6, fixes Brăila as the terminus, whereas the Treaty, for all fixing of limits, refers to the past without any precise determination." He did not find the extension of the jurisdiction of the European Commission in clauses 5 and 6, but only in the factual exercise thereof, as seen from the examination made by the Special Committee of Enquiry, of the League of Nations.

From Nyholm's observations one concludes the absence of precisely named limitations of the European Commission powers, fixed and extended by Article 5 and 6 of the Statute for the Danube. He referred to the confusion resulting from this manner of setting the limits.

The observations of J.B. Moore referred to the problem of "whether under the law at present in force the European Commission has the same powers from Galatz to Brăila as it has below Galatz."[126] According to Moore, "this shrinks on legal analysis into a small compass and is essentially simple." In his opinion, the 1921 Definitive Statute of the Danube was the "undisputed law at present in force, Convention signed and notified by all the Parties to the present controversy." He also pointed out the lack of distinction in the powers of the Commission. "We look in vain in the Definitive Statute for any such distinction, nor is it to be found in any of the treaties and conventions which the Statute confirm." Nor did he find such distinction in the Interpretative Protocol.

Referring to Articles 5 and 6 of the Statute for the Danube, Moore ended his observation: "The supposition that the Contracting Parties implanted in the Statute, consciously or unconsciously, a disintegrant so subtle and extraordinary, is from the point of view of legal interpretation hardly conceivable."

Dissenting Opinion of the Romanian Deputy Judge of the Permanent Court.

In general, the dissenting opinion by Deputy Judge D. Negulescu, to the Advisory Opinion of the Permanent Court was based on a number of considerations.[127] He invoked Romania's nonrecognition of Article 1 of the 1883 Treaty of London, the lack of precision in Articles 5, 6 and 9 of the Convention for the Definitive Statute of the Danube and the Interpretative Protocol concluded by the European Commission Delegates. He also added certain decisions of the European Commission regarding the discontinuance by its organization of juridic activity in connection with transgressions of the Regulation for Navigation and Police on the Sulina - Galatz sector. In his opinion, the Treaty of 1883 "was concluded without the cooperation of Romania." Of the Statute for the Danube, he wrote "Articles 6 and 9, when taken together, lead to the inference that the jurisdiction of the European Commission extends from above Brăila down to the mouths of the river, but Articles 5, 6 and 41 of the Statute show that, in order to determine the limits of the jurisdiction of the European Commission between Galatz and Brăila, the de facto situation before the war must be considered..."

It must be noted that the "de facto situation before the war," mentioned by Negulescu was not the rule, which included as has been shown, the European Commission giving up the exercise of its juridic powers only in isolated cases, in order to satisfy certain Romanian protests and to reduce the number of law suits for infraction between Galatz and Brăila. The de jure situation was never set aside by any official act.

The idea expressed by some Powers, to the effect that recognition of the 1883 Treaty by Romania resulted from the fact that she has continually taken her seat in the European Commission, was a false one, Negulescu stressed. "Romania has never maintained that the 1883 Treaty of London is nonexistent. She has always maintained that the treaty exists between the other Powers, but cannot be set up as against herself."

He showed that the sentences for infractions, issued by the European Commission between Galatz and Brăila before the war, not being sanctioned by a unanimity of votes due to the protests of the Romanian Delegate, remained inoperative.

As an example of the protests of the Romanian Delegate in the European Commission against sentences pronounced by the European Commission Inspector of Navigation, Negulescu cited the order March 20, 1882, of the Executive Committee of the European Commission, prohibiting the exercise of juridical powers upriver from Galatz. With respect to Article 6 of the Statute for the Danube, he mentioned the opposition of the Plenipotentiary of Romania to the European Commission's juridic authority over the Galatz-Brăila sector. The Interpretative Protocol, at Article 6 of the Statute for the Danube, in which the Delegates of the European Commission had established the technical competence of the Commission between Galatz and Brăila, in his opinion was valid. Negulescu also noted "profound differences" between Article 346 of the Treaty of Versailles and Articles 5 and 6 of the Statute of the Danube, the differences being attributed to the words "powers" and "rights." The origin of the latter word he attributed to Article 1 of the 1881 Additional Act of Galatz, an act one year older. He believed that "the Statute of the Danube could not modify the provisions of the Treaty of Versailles." As to the difference between Articles 5 and 6 of the Statute of the Danube and Article 346 of the Treaty of Versailles, he showed that they did not come from their texts. He also noted another matter: "In applying the provisions of the Treaty of Versailles, it must be admitted that the point where the jurisdiction of the European Commission comes to an end, the Danube regime will be placed under the control of the International Commission. In conformity with Article 53 of the Treaty of Berlin, of 1878, it follows that the International Commission exercises its powers from Ulm to below Galatz."

It must be noted that the Statute, as fixed in 1878, had been modified in the meantime by Article 1 of the 1883 treaty, which extended the European Commission jurisdiction to Brăila, hence upriver from Galatz. This modification appeared also in the Regulation for Navigation and Police for the sector between the Iron Gates and Brăila. The initial application had been fixed over the Iron Gates-Galatz sector, but the Conference of London changed the limit to Brăila. Actually, the application of this Regulation, annexed to the Treaty of London, was entitled "Regulation...applied between the Iron Gates and Brăila." As for the leniency towards certain juridic authority exercised by the Commission between Galatz and Brăila up to the time of World War I, Negulescu attributed it to the "courtesy" of Romania.

In his dissenting opinion, Negulescu concluded: "that, in accordance with the law in force, the European Commission does not possess any powers over the Galatz-Brăila sector; that the powers of the European Commission extend on the Lower Danube as far as below Galatz, excluding that port; that the Galatz-Brăila sector and the navigable channel which crosses the ports of Galatz and Brăila come under the jurisdiction of the International Commission of the Danube; and that the line of demarcation between the powers of the European Commission and those of the International Commission must be fixed at the 71 1/2 milestone" (Author's note: below the port of Galatz).

This opinion excluded the technical authority, as well as the juridic one, of the European Commission between Galatz and Brăila. This would have eliminated also the effect of the Interpretative Protocol drawn up by the European Commission Delegates, including Romania's, establishing the technical jurisdiction.

Including the Galatz-Brăila sector under the jurisdiction of the International Commission of the Danube, as Negulescu maintained, and fixing the line of demarcation between the powers of the latter and those of the European Commission at the 71 1/2 milestone, would have signified modification of Articles 346 and 347 of the Versailles Treaty, as well as of Articles 5, 6 and 9 of the Convention for the Definitive Statute of the Danube. Such an action would have been impossible because of the international complications which would have resulted. In such a case, there would have been anticipated Germany's action in 1936 regarding the Treaty of Versailles and Russia's in 1948 modifying the Convention for the Definitive Statute of the Danube.

Any negotiations with regard to modification of the Convention would have had to obtain the approval of two-thirds of the signatories, in accordance with Article 42 of that Convention. Since the negotiations for solving the Galatz-Brăila litigation were being carried out exclusively among the representatives of England, France, Italy and Romania, they could not fulfill that condition.

Partial Agreements for Settlement of the Litigation.

Since Romania did not acknowledge the Advisory Opinion of the Permanent Court of Justice, resolution of the Galatz-Brăila litigation remained suspended. Negotiations between Romania's Delegate and the other Delegates of the countries represented in the European Commission were to continue under conditions of mutual understanding and compromises over the points of view of both parties. To this contributed the following developments: the strengthening of Romania's political position after World War I and the perspective of pressure from Germany, which impelled England and France to hasten as much as possible the solution of the litigation.

Obviously, Romania's position in this matter soured somewhat the rapport between her and her principal allies, England and France, a situation which added to others of the past was considered a mistake by Professor Dascovici. "The same error was made in the Galatz-Brăila matter. We could never find its usefulness for Romania, but we easily found the blame for being a country that never ends its law suits before international cours existing after the general peace."[128]

In an atmosphere of understanding displayed by both parties, the Galatz-Brăila litigation was taken up again, in 1928, by the Council of the League of Nations and by the Advisory and Technical Committee of Communications and Transit, in order to find a conciliatory formula.

After a series of meetings in which proposals and counterproposals were debated in the Advisory Committee, as well as between the four Delegates in the European Commission, it was possible to draw up a Project for convention which was concluded in Geneva in 1930 by the four Delegates of the European Commission.

The Project for Convention was taken into consideration by the Council of the League of Nations (August 13, 1930) and on March 16, 1931, the General Secretariat of the League sent the declaration of adherence (dated December 5, 1930) to the Project for Convention to the other members of the Convention for the Statute of the Danube, for signing.[129]

The two-thirds requirement of Article 42 of the 1921 Statute of the Danube was met by the signing of the Project for convention by the four member countries of the European commission (England, France, Italy and Romania), in addition to the adherence of Belgium, Bulgaria and Greece. Austria's representative adhered, with the reservation that the new Convention not be interpreted under any form contrary to Article 42 of the 1921 Definitive Statute of the Danube, "whose provisions are to remain in full and complete validity." This formality being completed, the Geneva Convention of 1930 was validated.

In summing up, the texts of the fifteen articles of the Convention were as follows:

The European Commission of the Danube exercises authority over police navigation for the Maritime Danube between the mouths of the river and Km. 174, the limit of Brăila Port. With the exception of the port of Sulina, which remains in continuation under the jurisdiction of the European Commission, navigation police in the other ports and their river banks remain under Romania's jurisdiction, it being exercised in such a way as not to prejudice the police regulations of the European Commission of the river (Art. I);

The Romanian government established Navigation Tribunals on the Maritime Danube (Art. 2), which had competence concerning all infractions of river police regulations and of the regulation for policing of the ports and river banks of the Maritime Danube;

Proceedings or sentences against any Agent of the European Commission or of the Romanian Government were pronounced by the European Commission or by the Romanian authorities (Art.3);

At Galatz, a Navigation Court was established, composed of the first president of the Court of Appeals at Galatz and of two other members nominated as follows: one, a national of a State represented on the European Commission and the other, a national of a State not represented on the Commission; their selection being made by the head of the Romanian State for a term of four years. The official languages of the Court were French and Romanian (Art. 4); Appeals from any Navigation Tribunal were to be made to the Navigation Court, whose decisions were final (Art. 5);

The authority of the European Commission Inspector of Navigation was limited to vessels in the course of navigation; that of the Captain of the Port of Sulina, to vessels stationed in that port. In the event of a conflict as to the limits of their authority, between judicial police officers of the European Commission, on the one hand, and the Romanian Government on the other, the matter was decided by the Navigation Tribunals subject to a right of appeal to the Navigation Court (Art. 6); Sentences pronounced by the Navigation Tribunals and the Navigation Court were given in the name of the ruler of the Romanian State (Art 7);

Expenditures and income resulting from the functioning of these two judiciary organs were divided equally between the Romanian government and the European Commission (Art. 8); The treatment of accused persons brought before these two bodies was equally indifferent of their nationality (Art. 9); The Regulations for the application of the Convention were annexed to the Convention (Art. 10); The Powers represented on the European Commission hereby renounced such rights as are conferred upon them by the treaties in force in connection with the guardships in the waters of the Maritime Danube (Art. 11); Any interested state could submit to the European Commission for its consideration any difficulties relating to the interpretation or application of any treaty provisions affecting the Maritime Danube (Art. 12); All treaty provisions and conventions applicable to the Maritime Danube remained in force on the date of this Convention (Art. 13); The Convention drawn up in French and in English was to be ratified, and the instruments of ratification transmitted to the Secretary General of the League of Nations (Art. 14); The date of the entry in force of the Convention was the twentieth day after its ratification (Art. 15).

The litigation did not end, even with this Convention, depending as it did on the concluding of an Accord over the drawing up of a Regulation for the method of its application. To this was added the fact that the appeals of the Navigation Tribunals could not be limited to the Navigation Court, as provided by Article 5 of the Convention. According to Romania's Constitution, they had recourse to the Court of Appeals, in Bucharest, the final Constitutional Court. For clarification, a new meeting of the Delegates of the European Commission was necessary, meeting in Paris on March 13, 1932.[130]

Because of political and economic circumstances in Europe at the moment, as well as because of the financial status of the European Commission and of Romania, the conclusion was reached to abandon any modification of the existing situation. A Modus Vivendi, signed by the European Commission Delegates, was decided upon and adopted on May 10, 1933, in accordance with which the European Commission would exercise its technical and juridical authority up to Brăila (Km 174).[131] This provision, however, was a theoretical one, for that same Commission obligated itself to abstain from exercising its juridical competence between Galatz and Brăila. At the request of the Romanian Delegate, the Modus Vivendi included a provision that, at the first vacancy, the European Commission Captain of the Port would be replaced by a Romanian one. Later, in order to avoid new complications because of the political situation in Europe brought about by the Hitler Government in Germany, those same European Commission Delegates met at Semmering, in Austria, where they concluded a new Modus Vivendi on June 25, 1933, on the basis of which Romania agreed to abstain from any contesting of the European Commission's jurisdiction between the Mouths of the Danube and Brăila (Km 174), and the European Commission would abstain from exercising its judiciary authority between Galatz and Brăila. As for the pilotage service, a sui-generis solution was agreed upon.

For vessels piloted by European Commission pilots, navigating to or from Brăila without stopping at Galatz, the juridic competence of the European Commission applied between Mile 79 (below Galatz) and Sulina. For vessels navigating with a stop at Galatz, the Commission's jurisdiction ceased the moment they docked for loading or unloading in that port. In such a case, the European Commission pilot was replaced by a Romanian pilot of the port of Galatz. From the moment the vessel left Galatz, the Romanian pilot was replaced by the European Commission's pilot at Mile 79, the point at which the juridic competence of the European Commission began towards Sulina.

* * *

The problem of the jurisdictions between Galatz and Brăila, as well as those of the European Commission over the entire Maritime Danube ended radically in 1938, by the concluding of the Arrangement of Sinaia, on the basis of which Romania took over al her sovereign rights, as well as some of the attributes of the European Commission.

Chapter 6

THE SINAIA ARRANGEMENT OF 1938 AND ITS IMMEDIATE CONSEQUENCES

Brief Historical Note.

As has been evident, Romania's complaint was to do away with the European Commission for the Danube, or at least to reduce its powers. The Sinaia Arrangement brought about the settlement of the latter. Romania's position in this matter had been dependent upon the political situation in Europe at the moment. It had taken acute aspects during the period when the political potential of England and France was weakening. Aside from that consideration, Romania's position towards the Commission had been encouraged also by Turkey's success in regaining its sovereignty over the Straits, through the Conference of Montreux in 1936.

Titulescu did not propose a unilateral disbanding of the European Commission; as he had stated in the Galatz-Brăila litigation case, in any force change in the status quo, "the risks for Romania would be great."[132] He was of the opinion that "this matter cannot be but the object of diplomatic exchanges, addressed to the interested chancelleries at the time the Royal government of Romania decided it would be opportune to raise it officially."[133]

After the conference of Montreux, his position was more categorical. "The new regime over the Straits," he stated, "brings after it the suppression of the European Commission of the Danube, for Romania no longer wishes to be subjugated to an international sovereignty."[134] The influence of the Montreux Conference over Titulescu developed during a time when Europa was divided, an atmosphere of revisionism prevailed, Italy was in conflict with almost everybody and Germany was tearing up a treaty a day.

Titulescu did not ask for the disbanding of the International Commission for the Danube, only for that of the European Commission, which, in his opinion, was "an unbelievable anachronism, a control by foreigners inadmissible on ancestral territory..."[135]

Not contesting the international character of the Danube, he tended towards extending the International Commission of the Danube to the Mouths of the Danube, excluding the attributes reserved for Romania's territorial authority.

Titulescu's attitude towards the European Commission was in contrast to those held in the past by prominent Romanians, in favor of that international body. Among the other points of view previously brought out in this work was that of D. Sturdza, former Prime Minister and author of the work "Recueil de documents relatifs à la liberté de navigation du Danube," an authoritative source material for researchers of the Danube question. Sturdza, after praising the Commission's activity, concluded a speech at Sulina, on May 13, 1902, with the following words, "J'exprime le sentiment de tout bon Roumain en addressant à la Commission Européenne du Danube le souhait sincère: Vivat, Crescat, Floreat!"[136] On another occasion, Sturdza, speaking of the same Commission, commented "...sa permanence est devenue une nécessité."[137]

Titulescu did not tie in the disbanding of the European Commission with territorial revisions of any of the treaties, but he stated, "I shall examine case by case, those provisions which do not affect territory and which will be drawn up in legal form."[138] In his opinion, an eventual disbanding of the European Commission would be a non-territorial revision, it being a matter of unifying the regime over the Danube.[139] This point of view had its reverse side.

By non-territorial revision, the entire international regime for navigation would have been disturbed. The case of the Galatz-Brăila litigation had its echo at the League of Nations, as well as in the ranks of some of the Great Powers. The litigation over some of the clauses of the Versailles Treaty and of the Convention for the Definitive Statute of the Danube was, perhaps, the spark which gave Germany the occasion to light the fire for the revisions on the Danube.

At a 1927 meeting of the European Commission in Rome, England, France and Italy called Romania's attention to the fact that any interference with the regime at the Mouths of the Danube could involve revision of the Versailles treaty. The Romanian Minister to Rome reported, in this connection, that "the Italian Government believes that disbanding the European Commission of the Danube raises problems of high politics and puts in question the principle of the inviolability of treaties."[140]

Although Titulescu rejected the revision of treaties under their territorial aspect, still, the disbanding of the European Commission would have been a revision of Article 346 of the Treaty of Versailles, which had maintained it, a treaty which included also territorial decisions. If the idea of revising the European Commission had been substituted for that of disbanding it, it would have had to be combined with the clauses of Articles 7 and 42 of the Convention for the Definitive Statute of the Danube.

Aside from the danger of an eventual revision of the Versailles Treaty and of the 1921 Convention for the Definitive Statute, Titulescu's opinion could have had other negative consequences, something which actually did happen after Germany started her denunciations of certain clauses of the Versailles Treaty, including those with respect to the internationalization of navigation on her rivers (1936).

While Yugoslavia upheld Titulescu's opinion,[141] the former enemy States Austria, Germany and Hungary, interpreted and exploited it as a definite territorial revision of the Versailles Treaty. Remarks to this effect appeared in the August 1936 newspapers of these countries.[142]

A Budapest newspaper described Titulescu as "the avantgardist of treaty revisions" and a Viennese one termed him the "new adversary of the dictate of Versailles." The German newspapers wrote: "Titulescu is the advocate of a cold revision" and "Titulescu demands the abolition of control over the Mouths of the Danube."

Titulescu had also been influenced by the ideas of C. Contzescu, longtime Romania's Delegate to the European Commission and an advocate of disbanding it. "In the century in which we are living," Contzescu declared, "after the treaties and conventions in which we have participated...an international commission with an archaic regime and with prerogatives of sovereignty, this European Commission can no longer exist, maintaining it being a scandalous defiance of the rights and sentiments of the country."[143]

Another influence was that of Professor Gr. Antipa. In 1921, after he had shown that the European Commission had identified itself with the interests of the country and was considered almost a national institution, "never provoking conflicts or seeking to indulge in politics of cheating or monopolizing to the detriment of the riparians.[144] Later he criticized that same Commission's position as a "State within a State."

Romania's position may have been set in motion by that of Ostrowski, the Soviet Russian Minister to Bucharest. In 1936, the latter asked G. Gafencu, who was soon to be Romania's Minister for Foreign Affairs, "How can you stand the European Commission?" But, in contradiction to what he had just said, Ostrowski continued by adding that he had just received orders from Moscow to request the admittance of Soviet Russia in that same Commission.[145] Professor N. Dascovici wrote of Ostrowski's advice, "...we must not allow ourselves to be pushed into error by suggestions which we were certain came from abroad, from a certain direction, poking at our natural feelings of national pride."[146]

In the end, England and France, caught in constrained relations with Germany, accepted the Sinaia Arrangement, of 1938, partially satisfying Romania's demands. The Arrangement, which could be considered actually a "Danubian Münich," later had consequences detrimental to Romania. It offered Germany, and later Russia, the justification for their policies of radically modifying the international regime of navigation, and the latter's setting it aside completely by the Danubian Conference of Belgrade, in 1948.

Political and Diplomatic Initiatives Prior to the Arrangement.

Initially, in two Aide-Mémoires addressed to Romania and to the other signatory States of the Convention for the Definitive Statute of the Danube, Germany demanded the revision of its provisions, in 1936, for the purpose of detaching the fluvial sector of the Danube in her territory (Bavaria and Württemberg) from the administration of the International Commission of the Danube.[147]

Aside from violating Article 347 of the Versailles Treaty and Articles 3, 4, 7 of the 1921 Convention for the Statute of the Danube, Germany's procedure was also contrary to Article 42 of that same Convention, which provided that requests for its revision were to be addressed to France, which in turn would have to convoke, within six months, two-thirds of the Convention's signatories in order to make a decision.

The Aide-Mémoires were followed in 1938 by the visits of Germany's special envoys (Martzius and Brauer)[148] to Bucharest, Belgrade, Sofia, Prague and Budapest, for the purpose of discussing the revision, in accordance with Berlin's view,[149] namely: putting the sector of fluvial navigation of the Danube under the administration of a technical organ composed of the representatives of all the riparian states; although disbanding of the International Commission of the Danube was not demanded, the new organization would be eliminating its role; putting the Iron Gates under the administration of a Special Committee within the framework of the new organization, this Committee to be composed of representatives of Romania and Yugoslavia, along with two representatives of other riparian States; retaining the European Commission with the condition of reducing its powers and its entering in function only after the revision of the Definitive Statute of the Danube. The results of the visit were negative at Bucharest, somewhat understood at Sofia, reticent at Prague, positive at Budapest and doubtful at Belgrade.[150]

In the meantime, England, France and Italy leaned towards satisfying Germany's demands. On May 4, 1938 France proposed to Romania the disbanding of the European Commission, leaving its attributes to be taken over by the International Commission of the Danube.[151]

This proposal brings to mind clauses 16 -17 of the 1856 Treaty, as well as Austria's position towards the unification of administration over the whole course of the river. Romania, finding herself alone in the face of German threats, was placed in the situation of a change of position, not only towards the European Commission, but also toward the presence of England, France and Italy in the Commission's framework. The problem was discussed in an urgent meeting on June 1, 1938 at the Romanian Ministry for Foreign Affairs in the presence of persons well informed in Danubian matters.[152] Faced with the possibility of Germany's domination over the Danube, some of those present changed their past stands towards the existence of the European Commission, as well as towards the presence of non-riparian Great Powers in its composition.

C. Contzescu, Romania's Delegate in the European Commission and the one most opposing it, declared that "...faced with a far-reaching German policy on the Danube, the presence of the three Great European Powers at the Danube assures an indispensable balance." As to the retention of the European Commission, he stated, "...it is a sort of international citadel which for us is a more serious shield than the International Commission on the Danube."[153] (the Riparian Commission).

G. Sofronie, Professor of International Law, stated: "The disbanding of the European Commission would please me, but I see that it is not at this moment a happy solution from the point of view of Romanian interests, Certain expansionist tendencies make the presence of the Great non-riparian Powers necessary at the Mouths of the Danube. Considerations of political expediency must be kept in mind."[154] As to the dilemma in which Romania found itself, Professor Sofronie wrote: "Who will bring us greater security? A European Commission or one of the Riparians? Which of these two offers us more assurance of being listened to and of seeing our interests best protected? A Riparian Commission or a European one?"[155] The preference for the European Commission over the Riparian one was due to the presence and domination Germany would have had in the Riparian one.

In general, the above opinions, to which other participants adhered, were reflected in Romania's position at the negotiations carried on in the Conference at Sinaia, from which was concluded the Sinaia Arrangement of 1938.

The Romanian Position.

Independent of Romania's past demands concerning the navigation regime on the Maritime Danube, and especially those concerning the European Commission, her position at the Conference of Sinaia was the one resulting from the debates that had taken place at the Ministry for Foreign Affairs at Bucharest on June 1, 1938, with respect to the following:[156] supporting the retention of England, France and Italy in the European Commission and the International Commission of the Danube, in order to keep the balance between the Danubian riparians and Germany, which was pursuing a policy of political and economic hegemony on the river; retaining the European Commission, but with the admittance of Germany; retaining the International Commission of the Danube as long as possible; rejecting the German project for regulating the Danubian regime on the basis of certain bilateral accords.

The solutions reached were communicated to the Governments of England, France and Italy, which empowered their Representatives to meet, together with Romania's, at Vienna, on June 15, 1938, where the following Fundamental Accord was reached:[157] cessation of application of the clause of Article 53 of the 1878 Treaty of Berlin with reference to the independence of the European Commission from the territorial authority of Romania; elimination of the international regime over the sector of the port of Sulina, where the European Commission functioned; the transfer to Romania of the execution of the technical works at the Mouths of the Danube, and of the maintenance of navigation between Sulina and Brăila by means of an autonomous organization under the supervision of a committee of technicians; complete transfer to Romania of the Navigation Health Services; transfer of the Kilia Branch to Romania's exclusive jurisdiction; placing under Romanian administration the lighthouses at the Mouths of the Sulina and St. George, including the one on Serpents Island; judicial procedures against infractions of the Regulation for Navigation and Police between the Mouths of the Danube and Brăila to be carried out by Romanian authorities; elimination of the international attributes of the Navigation Inspectorate, of the Port Captaincy and of their agents, all being transferred to Romania's authority; transfer of the stone quarry at Tulcea, the hospitals at Sulina and the buildings occupied by the European Commission to Romanian authority.

In connection with this Accord there are some observations to be made. The decision to end the application of the clause of Article 53 could not be taken by England, France and Italy alone, only together with all the signatories of the Berlin Treaty of 1878. Also, the yielding of certain European Commission attributes in favor of Romania required the consent of all the signatories of the former treaties, as well as those of the Convention for the Definitive Statute of the Danube (Article 42). These procedures had been established as principles when the previous Treaty and Convention had been concluded.

Significant is the fact that, at the basis of Romania's position, can be found the idea expressed by Antipa, as early as 1921, that the Mouths of the Danube be transferred to Romanian administration under international supervision and control.[158]

Faced with increasingly strong German pressure, Romania proposed hastening the meeting of the representatives of member countries in the European Commission in a Conference which took place at Sinaia, from 8 to 11 August 1938. Nine protocols and a final protocol were concluded at this conference.[159]

The procedures of the Conference took place under the presidency of C. Contzescu (Romania), with Douglas W. Keanne (England), and Jean du Saule (France) participating as Delegates in the European Commission, and Paul Charguerand, juridic counsellor for Foreign Affairs of France. Italy's Delegate did not take part. On August 18, 1938, they concluded the Sinaia Arrangement, drawn up in French, on the basis of which there were transferred to Romania part of the attributes of the European Commission, a body now left with only supervisory powers over the application of the international regime of navigation over the Maritime Danube.[160]

Certain remarks can be made with reference to the Arrangement, concerning the respecting of the norms for concluding it, as provided for by the 1921 Convention for the Definitive Statute of the Danube. By ceding to Romania some of the Commission's attributes, partial derogation of the clauses of Articles 4, 5 and 7 of the Convention was committed. Article 7 provided that: "The powers of the European Commission of the Danube cannot be ended except by an international arrangement concluded by all the States represented in the Commission" (England, France, Italy and Romania). Italy had not taken part in either the Conference at Sinaia or at the signing of the Arrangement. Although invited, she refused to participate, conditioning her attendance to the presence of her ally, Germany. She did adhere to the Arrangement in 1939, after Germany was included in the European Commission of the Danube.

The clause of Article 42 of that same Convention, to the effect that any modification or revision of the 1921 Convention be made in the presence of or with the approval of two-thirds of the signatories, was not fulfilled either. Not all the signers were present at Sinaia. The required two-thirds was arrived at later by written or tacit assents.

The problem raised after 1938 was whether the attributes of the European Commission were modified or revised by the Arrangement. The powers of the European Commission were not terminated by the Arrangement as had been provided for by Article 7 of the 1921 Convention; what was modified was the regime on the Maritime Danube. According to Article 9 of the Arrangement, the European Commission retained control over the methods of applying the international regime for navigation on the Maritime Danube as well as over certain other attributes of the Romanian Administration which replaced it. This problem was to be exploited by Soviet Russia at the Danube Conference at Belgrade in 1948.

The influence of the political moment which facilitated the concluding of the Arrangement cannot be disregarded. The question could be asked whether England and France would have agreed to cede certain of the attributes of the European Commission had they not been under the political pressure caused by Germany. The answer could be in the negative.

Still, the Sinaia Arrangement was a deliberate Act, two considerations influencing its being concluded. The one, of a subjective order, resulted from the sympathetic understanding accorded to Romania by England and France; the other derived from the complicated European political situation of the moment.

THE SINAIA ARRANGEMENT OF 1938 523

The concluding of the Arrangement was described by all the Romanian press as a really important Act of national satisfaction, revealing the positive role of England and France. The newspaper "Universul" wrote: "In the course of the debates in the framework of the Conference, one could note on the part of the French and English Delegates a perfect understanding of Romania's point of view. Romania in turn, through the voice of her Delegate responded with an equal goodwill."[161]

An Accord was concluded specifying the method of applying Article 19 of the Arrangement as to the privileges and immunities of the members of the European Commission of the Danube.[162]

Clauses of the Arrangement and the Final Protocol.

The Sinaia Arrangement consisted of twenty three Articles and a Final Protocol of three Additional Articles, signed on that date.

The provisions of Article 1 terminated the European Commission's exercise of the powers previously conferred upon it, regarding navigation, by Articles 8, 9 and 10, of the Public Act of November 2, 1865; Article 2 of the Additional Act of May 28, 1881, and Articles 1 and 119, of the Regulation for Navigation. The Commission also terminated its exercise of the special powers conferred upon it by Articles 4, 6, 8, 9, 10 and 21 of the Public Act; Article 2 of the Additional Act, and Articles 1, 4, and 112, of the Regulation for Navigation (Article 2).

The European Commission was to draw up the Regulation for Navigation and Police, applicable to the Maritime Danube and the Mouths of the Danube (Article 3).

The pilotage Corps was transferred to the Romanian authorities (Article 4) and the Romanian Government established the Maritime Danube Board, as special department changed with drawing up the work projects on the Maritime Danube and at its mouths, as well as with carrying them out, levying the new navigation taxes and administering them. (Article 5).

The same Maritime Danube Board also was to submit to the European Commission the projects for improvement and maintenance of navigation, as established in accord with the committee of Consulting Engineers, as constituted by the Commission (Article 6).

The Maritime Danube Board was to submit to the European Commission the tariff schedule, which had to be drawn up with a majority vote, provided the vote of the Romanian Delegate was included in that majority (Article 10). It also had to communicate to the European Commission the list of vessels entering and leaving the Danube (Article 11). The conditions for retaining or retiring pilots were to be established by the European Commission and the Romanian Government (Articles 13, 14, 15).

The European Commission was to place at the disposition of the Romanian authorities and of the Maritime Danube Board, all its liquid assets and properties (Article 17). The inspection yacht "Carolus Primus" was transferred to the Romanian government to be put at the disposition of the Delegates of the Commission for its plenary sessions and for the needs of the Committee of Consulting Engineers (Article 17). The Commission retained the Galatz and Sulina Administrative Palaces (Article 17).

The Romanian Government was to establish judiciary organs concerned with infractions to the Regulation for Navigation and Police (Article 18). Through an Accord, privileges and immunities were to be drawn up for the personnel of the European Commission (Article 19) and the Commission was to relinquish its tax, postal, telegraphic and telephonic exemptions (Article 20).

Procedural norms were set regarding and litigation concerning the interpretation and application of the Arrangement (Article 21); adhesion to the Arrangement was required of all states represented in the European Commission or which might be represented in the future (Article 22).

In 1939, the Romanian government established the Maritime Danube Board (Directiunea Dunării Maritime - D. D. M.).[163]

As can be seen, the Arrangement satisfied the positions of both sides. The European Commission remained as the supervisory international body and Romania gained her almost complete freedom and sovereignty over the Maritime Danube.

The Final Protocol.

The final Protocol of August 18, 1938, with three Additional Articles to Articles 5, 13 and 17 of the Arrangement, provided for the incorporation of the D. D. M. into the Commercial Administration of Ports and Water Communications (P. C. A.) and for Romania's obligation to take over a number of the former pilots of the European Commission and the administration of its assets.

As to the assets, they were left for Romania's use. The European Commission could not take them over without Romania's assent and the latter could not dispose of them without the approval of the former. The Final Protocol was signed by the Plenipotentiaries of the States which had signed the Arrangement.

The Accord of Bucharest Concerning the Admission of Germany in the European Commission of the Danube and the Adhering of Italy and Germany to the Arrangement.

In this Accord can be seen the weakness of England, France and Italy's detachment from her historic association, in the Danubian problems.

Since Italy did not participate, as the fourth member state of the European Commission, at the Conference of Sinaia as well as at the signing of the Arrangement, the Arrangement could not have any executive power, in accordance with the provisions of Article 7 of the 1921 Convention. To this was added the problem of Germany's demand to enter the European Commission. In Italy's case, as well as in Germany's, and without its having been expressly mentioned, Article 22 of the Arrangement provided that "the present Arrangement is open for the adherence of any state represented in the European Commission or which might be represented in the future."

In Italy's case, as a state already represented in the Commission, the formula of adherence was to be applied. Italy had conditioned her participation in the Conference of Sinaia, as well as at the signing of the Arrangement by the solution of Germany's acceptance into the Commission and the modification of certain articles in the Arrangement Romania's appeals to the Italian Government remained fruitless.

On November 25, 1938, Germany communicated to the Ministry for Foreign Affairs of Romania its rejection of the formulas of "adhesion," 'adherence" or of her "admission" into the European Commission, demanding the formula of being "invited," in view of her "entering" the European Commission, on the consideration that she would be resuming the position she had held before World War I. [164]

Germany also demanded that her entrance into the European Commission coincide with Italy's adherence to the Arrangement, and that in the procedure for entering the Commission no mention be made of the 1921 Convention for the Definitive Statute of the Danube, which had excluded her. By the formula of being "invited," Germany wanted to give value to the idea of the continuity of her presence in the European Commission.

The Romanian government made known to England and France all the measures and conditions of Germany and Italy, and the two Great Powers gave their consent. Thus, on March 1, 1939, the Accord for Germany's "entering" the European Commission of the Danube; for Germany and Italy's "adherence" to the Sinaia Arrangement and for the modification of Articles 4 and 23 of the Arrangement was concluded at Bucharest.[165]

The Accord was signed by the Plenipotentiaries of England, France, Germany, Italy and Romania, the ratification taking place at the same time as that of the Arrangement, at the first regular session of the European Commission, as Germany had demanded.[166]

The contents of the four Articles of the Accord, drawn up in French, were as follows: Germany's entrance into the European Commission "on a perfectly equal footing with the other States represented" (Article 1); "Italy's adherence to the Arrangement" (Article 2); modification of Article 4 of the Arrangement with reference to transfer of the Body of Pilots to Romanian Authorities, and as vacancies occurred in the ranks of the pilots, those of foreign nationality to be replaced by Romanian pilots; selection by the Romanian authorities of the chief pilot, from a list of three candidates, presented to the Commission, regardless of their nationality (Article 3); modification of paragraph 3 of Article 23 of the Arrangement, to the effect that it and the Accord be ratified and enter in effect at the first regular session of the European Commission (Article 4).

The modification of the regime for pilots and for the retention of their former salaries (Article 3) was requested by Italy, in view of protecting the Italian pilots who would continue to be in the service of the Commission. Actually, however, all the foreign pilots left the service, being accorded compensation.

The Arrangement and the Accord Coming into Operation. The Solemnities of the Transfer of some of the European Commission of the Danube Powers to Romania.

On May 13, 1939, the Delegates of England, France, Italy, Romania and for the first time, Germany met at the Galatz headquarters of the

THE SINAIA ARRANGEMENT OF 1938 527

European Commission in a plenary session presided over by C. Contzescu, Romania's Delegate.[167] He states that the transfer of some of the European Commissions attributes to Romania and "the raising of the Romanian flag on the vessels and the establishments of the Commission after 83 years, was an historic act for the Romanian Government."[168]

During the course of the evening of May 13, Contzescu communicated to all the services at Sulina and Tulcea the transfer of all the inventory and services of the European Commission of the Danube.[169]

On May 16, in the presence of the Romanian Government, of the Delegates and Alternates of the countries represented in the European Commission, and of the local authorities of Sulina, the concrete carrying out of the Arrangement took place. At 8 a.m., flags were raised on the two poles in front of the Commission's building, the Commission's flag on the pole to the West, Romania's on the pole to the East. At 10 a.m., the yacht "King Carol II," passed from the wharf on Romanian territory of the port of Sulina to anchor at the one on European Commission territory, where the Delegates received the Members of the Romanian Government. After a religious service was performed, the two flags were slowly lowered to the music of the national anthems of the countries represented in the Commission, following which only the Romanian flag was again raised. In this moment, Romania became de jure and de facto the country at the Mouths of the Danube.

On the occasion of the session at Galatz, Gafencu, Romania's Minister for Foreign Affairs, declared: "Romania and the friendly countries which make up the European Commission of the Danube, by common accord, on August 18, 1938, conciliated fully the rights and prerogatives of a sovereign State with the legal attributes necessary to an international institution to carry out its mission. This mission, actually, has not been changed. The European Commission will keep watch, just as before, over the respecting of freedom of navigation at the Mouths of the Danube and, as before, will do so in perfect understanding with the Romanian State. The Arrangement which lessens the prerogatives of the Commission and increases the responsibilities of the sovereign State, do not modify in any way the international importance which the States represented in the Commission, the riparian States as well as the other Powers, acknowledge as the Danube's."[170]

By this statement no incrimination was addressed to the European Commission; on the contrary, it emphasized the hyphen which was to be between the former and the future administration.

At the close of his statement, Gafencu stressed: "I do not believe I am mistaken in affirming that the European Commission, in all the different guises it has worn until today, has in its Actions and its existence always served the European cause of a strong and free Romania. Could the origins of the Commission not have been merged with the very origins of the modern Romanian State?"[171]

There existed also contrary voices. In a newspaper article, a rather negative accusation was made over the aims and activities of the commission.[172]

The Governments of England, France and Romania had previously and officially sent to the eight signers of the 1921 Definitive Statute of the Danube, the texts of the Sinaia Arrangement and of the Accord, explaining that these Acts did not contravene the respective Convention. The only signatory to express its concern was Yugoslavia. In its noted of April 12, 1939, addressed to the member states of the Commission, Yugoslavia raised the problem of the legality of the Arrangement and of the Accord of Bucharest, asking whether they were the result of a modification of the 1921 Convention or whether they had the value of new acts.

The question was justified if one took into consideration that, at the concluding of both Acts, the procedure of the clause of Article 42 of the Convention had not been applied. By concluding both Acts an actual revision of the 1921 Convention had been effectuated, hence it was necessary that a Conference be called, at which the agreement of two-thirds of the eight signatory states to the Convention would have to be attained.[173] Besides the presence of France, England and Romania at the Conference, then the later adherence of Italy, the conditions of Article 42 were met by tacit agreement of Belgium, Czechoslovakia and Greece.

Reorganization of the New Danube Maritime Board (D. D. M.)

It has been shown that, on the basis of Article 5 of the Sinaia Arrangement and in carrying out its new duties, Romania established the Danube Maritime Board (D. D. M.), an autonomous body which later, by Additional Article 5 of the Final Protocol, was put under the control of the Commercial Administration of Ports and Water Communications (P. C. A.). In connection with this and apart from any official documentation, the author has acquired certain information gathered while engaged in working in the framework of D. D. M.

THE SINAIA ARRANGEMENT OF 1938

In view of the great responsibility Romania had assumed towards Europe, as well as that of creating the new Romanian administration at the level of that of the European Commission, King Carol II, over the prerogatives of the Government, appointed his own Chief Adjutant as director, to supervise the continued application of the international regime for navigation.[174] "The eyes of Europe" — warned official circles — "will be directed at the way in which Romania will apply and respect the regime, as well as her ability to assure the maintenance of normal navigation."

In fulfilling this duty during a period in which the looming World War II raised financial problems and problems of supply of materials needed for maintaining navigation, it became imperative to strengthen and enlarge the possibilities of administration and to detach the Danube Maritime Board from the top-heavy mechanism of public state administration. This imperative was solved by the Romanian Government on June 7, 1941, by the reorganization of this Board, its new title being "The Special Autonomous Board of the Maritime Danube," under the supervision of the State Under-Secretariat of the Navy.[175]

In the law, concerning this modification, it is stated that "the complete autonomy is justified by the mandate given the Romanian State by the Sinaia Arrangement."[176] In justification of the complete autonomy of the Danube Maritime Board, there were invoked the difficulties encountered in prompt execution of technical and administrative works which had burdened the relations between the Board and the European Commission.

As to Romania's great responsibility towards Europe, it was stated that "only having a complete autonomy and freedom of action, as the organ carrying the direct responsibility, can the Danube Maritime Board be assured of the possibility of carrying out all the obligations of prestige and affirmation which would result from command of our sovereignty and establishment at the Mouths of the Danube, as well as those of international order, by guaranteeing the interests of navigation for all flags on the Maritime Danube."

In view of a large autonomy which would permit the execution of urgent work in the shortest time possible, the respective law provided that the budget of the Special Autonomous Board of the Maritime Danube figure separately in the General State Budget as an annex to the Budget of the Under-Secretariat of State of the Navy (Article IV). For the same reason, it was provided that, if the expenses of the works were to exceed the income of the Board, the Romanian State would accord subsidies (Article V).

Also in order to facilitate the Administration, the budget was detached from the heavy bureaucratic organization of the State Accounting Division (Article VI). Facilities were also provided for hiring technical personnel and for other financial exceptions to the State Laws.

All these facilities and exceptions were applied in order to strengthen Romania's mission. This was the intent of the qualifications of "special" and "autonomous" added to the initial title of Maritime Board of the Danube.

Despite the great difficulties in the supply of materials, especially during World War II, the Special Autonomous Board, with the subsidies accorded by the Romanian State, succeeded in maintaining navigable depths at the Mouth of the Sulina and normal navigation on the Maritime Danube route.

The existence of this Board ended when the Danubian Convention of Belgrade, in 1948, replaced it with a Russian-Romanian administration.

The New Navigation and Police Regulations on the Maritime Danube.

As a result of the Sinaia Arrangement, Romania had to revise and substitute, for the old Regulation of Navigation and Police abrogated by Articles 1 to 5 of the Arrangement, the former norms of the Public Act of 1865, the Additional Act of 1881 and the Regulation for Navigation and Police of the European Commission of the Danube.

To this end, the Romanian Government, on May 31, 1939, issued the Law for the exercise of navigation police and jurisdiction over the Maritime Danube, effective retroactively to May 13, 1939, the date of the official transfer of the European Commission powers to Romania.[177] The provision was made to transfer to the Romanian State the attributes of navigation, police and of the jurisdiction exercised in the past by the European Commission (Article 1), on the Maritime Danube and its branches, including the ports and roadsteads, up to Brăila (Article 2).

The European Commission's Regulation for Navigation and Police of November 11, 1911, with its later modifications, as well as notices to navigators issued by the same Commission, continued to be applied to the extent that they had not been modified by Article 1 of the Arrangement (Article 3).

THE SINAIA ARRANGEMENT OF 1938 531

The application of the Regulation for Navigation entered into the attributes of the Commercial Marine Board of Romania, by dint of its branches: the Regional Inspectorates and the Port Captaincies of the Maritime Danube Sector (Article 4). The Port Captaincies determined and judged infractions against the Regulation (Article 5), appeals being judged by the Galatz Court of Appeals (Article 6). The Body of Pilots and its remuneration were transferred to the administration of the commercial Marine Board (Article 9).

New Requests for Admission to the European Commission of the Danube.

At Sulina, on the occasion of the ceremonies for the transfer of power, Gafencu repeated the statement made in the Galatz session (May 13, 1939), stressing that "...other friendly States wish to participate in our common mission. We shall examine their requests in a spirit of the greatest goodwill."

Immediately after the signing of the Arrangement, Greece and Poland, in separate notes sent to Romania, again requested their admittance into the European Commission of the Danube. In reference to these requests, Gafencu had previously stated, "...there are still two States, friendly to Romania, which request admittance to the European Commission. These are Poland and Greece, whose requests meet with all our attention."[178]

In view of Romania's permanent position against enlarging the composition of the European Commission, the statement made by her Minister for Foreign Affairs, in favor of the repeated requests, seems to have been more on the order of political expediency and courtesy.

In the European Commission session at which Greece's request was discussed, the Delegates of England and France were in favor, Italy's retained its reserve, and Germany's although he was in accord — still refrained from expressing himself.

Poland's request was brought up on the occasion of the visit of Romania's Foreign Minister to Warsaw, in April 1939. Inasmuch as this request was tied to the plan of connecting the Baltic and Black Seas by the construction of sluice gates between the Pruth and the Dniester Rivers, decision on it was postponed. In the meantime, World War II intervened and the requests of Greece and Poland were left with only their written value.

Chapter 7

THE SITUATION PRIOR TO WAR AGAINST SOVIET RUSSIA

The Belgrade Agreement Concerning Neutralization of Navigation on the Lower Danube.

After the outbreak of World War II on September 1, 1939, the countries along the Lower Danube tried to take measures to protect the neutrality of navigation. Following some isolated acts, on the part of English aviation, of dropping magnetic mines at the Cataracts and the Iron Gates and on the Galatz-Tulcea sector (1940), Germany threatened neutral Romania with a take-over of the protection of navigation if the latter did not take the necessary steps. Although Romania had already taken some measures, as early as November 22, 1939, as for example forbidding access to her ports to armed commercial vessels of the belligerents,[179] she called for a meeting of the Executive Committee of the International Commission of the Danube, at Belgrade on April 17, 1940, and in the presence of the Delegates of Bulgaria, Romania, Hungary and Yugoslavia, to discuss the problem of neutralization of navigation during the Anglo-French-German War.

Neutralization of navigation had been a controversial problem also in the past. Article 52 of the 1878 Treaty of Berlin had established that no warships could navigate down river from the Iron Gates, with the exception of small armed vessels of the navigation police.

During the 1920-1921 Conference of Paris, for the establishment of the Definitive Statute of the Danube, the Anglo-French group upheld the idea of neutralization, with the exception of small military craft for the use of navigation police. Because of a Romanian

533

proposal, provision was made for the exclusive access of riparian's warships, excluding those of the former enemy states. Because no accord had been reached in 1921, the Executive Committee of the International Commission of the Danube had substituted neutralization by applying Article 10 of the Convention for the Definite Statute of the Danube, referring to the banning of any obstacles which could interfere with the normal course of navigation.

Through five articles of the Agreement concluded on April 17, 1940 by the Executive Committee of the International Commission of the Danube, was banned the traffic of materials which could be used for military purposes. Also, measures were taken for the avoidance of camouflaging military personnel as sailors.[180] Article 3 of the Agreement even referred to the transport of cement and gravel which could possibly cause blockage of the passage through the Iron Gates and the Cataracts.

The rationale for the Agreement can be attributed also to the new system of arming the commercial vessels belonging to the belligerents, an activity undertaken on the seas from the very beginning of the war. Along with the Agreement, the riparian States applied supplementary measures.

The Agreement was applied only on the strictly fluvial navigation between the Iron Gates and Brăila, which was under the jurisdiction of the International Commission, not on the Maritime Danube (Brăila Mouths of the Danube). Bearing in mind that, on the basis of the Sinaia Arrangement, navigation and Police order on the Maritime Danube were among Romania's attributes, Romania's Delegate in the European Commission on May 22, 1940, proposed the application of the Agreement also on this sector — a position approved in that same meeting.[181]

The adoption by the European Commission of the Agreement also had another significance. The fact that Germany, a belligerent state, was also in the composition of the European Commission indirectly involved her in respecting the measures taken by the International Commission, a commission she no longer recognized, having withdrawn her Delegate there two years before. From the neutralization of navigation on the Maritime Danube, there also resulted another situation. Neutralization also included elimination of acts of sabotage, a measure not respected by England, indirectly.

Although neutralization did not mean the abolition of the international regime for navigation, still "certain of the United Nations had chartered or secured ships of the Danube with the view of denying facilities to the enemy..." a fact confirmed also by the English

Delegation, on the occasion of the Peace Treaty with Romania in 1947.[182] For this purpose, England had formed the "Goeland" Shipping company, an enterprise without effective commercial activity, which leased fluvial vessels on the Lower Danube under foreign flags (especially Greek) which they kept inactive. France in turn sent navigation personnel to replace local personnel on ships under the French flag of the Société Française de Navigation Danubienne" (S.F.N.D.) already existing on the Danube.

Under this neutrality regime, there existed in the Danubian ports a most unusual situation. Because of the international regime of navigation, navigating personnel of the belligerent camps, French, English, German and Austrian, met on a friendly basis in restaurants, bars and tea shops. In the same way, the discussions in the European Commission were carried on between Delegates of the same belligerent camps. The atmosphere created by the benefits of the neutrality and of the international regime of navigation ended with Romania's entrance in the war against Russia, June 22, 1941.

Shortly, however, the Agreement lost its reason for being because of two actions on the part of Germany. The first was the transport of war materials and German troops, on the basis of the German-Romanian Accord regarding instructing the Romanian Army. The second was transport of war materials and troops through Romanian territory, as well as through the Bulgarian port of Ruse (Ruschuk), destined for the front to be opened against Greece.

With all the partial results of the Agreement, it must be noted that the lack of any clause referring to the neutralization of the navigation was remedied at Belgrade by the collaboration of the riparian States.

Return of Soviet Russia as a Riparian.

On the basis of the clauses in the Nazi-Soviet Non-Aggression Pact of August 23, 1939, referring to German-Russian interests in Southeastern Europe, Soviet Russia obtained the right to reannex Bessarabia, a province in which Germany claimed to have no interest. The reannexation was in contradiction with Molotov's earlier declaration that Russia was not interested in new annexations. In 1940, however, he demanded the return of Bessarabia on the consideration of non-recognition of its annexation by Romania after World War I[183] and, in addition to Bessarabia, he demanded Northern Bucovina in compensation for all the "sufferings" of the Bessarabian population under Romania.

By reannexing Bessarabia, Soviet Russia returned to the Lower Danube by means of the Kilia Branch, getting the port installations constructed by Romania at the ports of Reni and Ismail, together with all the fluvial vessels found under Romanian as well as foreign flags.

Germany's disinterest in the reannexation of Bessarabia was merely a formality, politically expedient for the moment; in reality, she could not accept Russia's presence at the Mouths of the Danube. If the reannexation of Bessarabia was motivated by Russia in consideration of its having been ceded to her by Turkey in the 1812 War, the annexation of Northern Bucovina was not founded on any justification, that province being under Romania's sovereignty. The sole justification lay in its forming a direct strategic line between the territory of Russia and Central Europe. Part of the Romanian population of both provinces was later transported to Siberia and replaced with Russians.

When the new Russo-Romanian frontier in the Danube Delta was being drawn up by the Russo-Romanian Commission established in 1940, the Russians demanded the extension of the limits initially set by the 1878 Treaty of Berlin and retained by the Versailles Treaty in 1919. They fixed the boundary line over the thalweg of the Kilia Branch, including the three small islands beside the Romanian bank, as well as the Musura Sub-branch and mouth.[184]

At the protest of the Romanian Minister to Molotov, Vishinsky responded, "the occupation of several islands was not an inimical act towards Romania, and while they had no great importance for Romania, for Russia they entered into her defensive system."[185]

At the same time, Russia undertook acts of espionage through the Lipovenes workers (of Russian origin) in the service of the Romanian administration at Sulina (D.D.M.), as well as small military incursions.[186] The Romanian authorities, in order to avoid any diplomatic conflict, withdrew their frontier guards from the points of Russian incursions, the Government and the press making no mention of them. In exchange, the Russian agency "TASS" denied any violations of Romanian territory.

Romania's First Restrictive Steps were Contrary to the International Regime of Navigation (January 1, 1940 - June 22, 1941).

The restrictions over the international regime for navigation on the Lower Danube were concentrated in two distinct periods: the first, on the outbreak of World War II, on September 1, 1939; the second, after the beginning of the war against Soviet Russia (June 22, 1941).

Although the restrictions applied also to Bulgaria and Yugoslavia, only Romania's will be studied, inasmuch as the Greatest Concentration of fluvial vessels occurs on her fluvial sector and the Maritime Danube is located there.

As early as September 1, 1939, at the time of Germany's attack against Poland and the worsening of the political situation in Europe, Romania was forced to take certain measures which impeded the freedom of action of the fluvial fleet in general, regardless of flag. The measures were increased in the autumn of 1940 and, after June 22, 1941, they were generalized and strictly applied. As for the navigation of maritime vessels under foreign flags, their reduced traffic was carried on until June 22, 1941, more or less in conformity with the international regime.

Military requisitions were applied to vessels flying the Romanian flag, regardless of the nationality of their owners. Regarding vessels under foreign flags, the formula for requisition "for economic purposes" was applied, interpreted as being in accord with the international regime for navigation, on the basis of individual "voluntary" contracts concluded with the respective owners.

The system of requisitions "for economic purposes" was introduced in December 1940 and applied in the same measure to Romanian ship owners as to foreign ones.[187] "Freedom" of contracting was relative inasmuch as German pressure was being imposed on the Danube. Among the ship owners of foreign citizenship, the majority were of the Greek element. In contrast with the military requisition system the vessels seized "for economic purposes" were distributed to national economic enterprises and to the Maritime Danube Board (D.D.M.) which were signing contracts with the owners.

Between the two systems of requisition there were certain differences as to rent charges and administration of vessels. While under military requisition the rent was very low and the administration of the vessels was, in general, carried out by military units, for those under requisition "for economic purposes" rents were somewhat higher, without reaching the level of those of supply and demand, the administration of the vessels being at time in the hands of their proprietors.

By requisitioning "for economic purposes," the Romanian State assured its economic needs by means of cheap and safe transportation, protected from the competition of the commercial market. The adoption of this method was, for the first time, applied on the navigation on the Romanian sector of the Danube, especially for foreign vessels under foreign flags. Its application was not general and neither on long term, contracts being signed even for one or two transports, proprietors of vessels under foreign flags being able at times to lease them with commercial freight charges, the most frequent applicants being private German organizations. Nevertheless, the regime was not particularly approved by foreign ship owners who felt that they had no assurance of their freedom of action. Furthermore, the vessels under foreign ownership, flying the Romanian flag, had to have navigating personnel of Romanian citizenship. The second period of restrictions will be studied with the outbreak of the war against Russia, when they were made more severe.

In general, navigation restrictions in the 1939 to June 22, 1941 period were flexible, Romanian authorities not going far afield from the international regime. In some cases, the deviation was due to pressure from Germany, in others, because of isolated abuses of local official organs. Not lacking, either, were cases of evasion either from under German or from English pressures. Two cases can serve as examples.

In 1940, shipowner George Portolo, a Greek citizen, asked the Romanian Government to approve the gradual expediting to Greece of twelve tugs, his property, flying the Greek flag. The approval was given on the basis of the international regime of navigation in force at that period. Under German pressure, only three tugs could leave the Danube, one of them (the Dionisia) under economic requisition, and the others were stopped at the Sulina Mouth at the last minute.[188]

The second case, also in 1940, was that of the emigration of a number of Austrian Jews, transported by Austrian river vessels as far as Sulina. In spite of England's interventions to the governments of Romania, Turkey and Greece, regarding the prohibiting of passage of emigrants through their territories, towards Palestine, still, by way of the Danube there were a number of exits, some transports being carried out under normal conditions, others under inhumane ones.

To the frustrations of English interventions and to ease these emigrations, the Romanian authorities applied illegal measures and deviations from the obligations written in Sinaia Arrangement.[189]

Chapter 8

GERMAN AND RUSSIAN ATTEMPTS TO MODIFY THE INTERNATIONAL REGIME OF NAVIGATION.

Introduction.

German and Russian attempts to modify the international regime for navigation on the entire course of the Danube were carried on during the period in which Europe began to feel Germany's powerful political pressure, followed by that of Russia. The principal objective of the attempts were along the Lower Danube sector, with its subsector the Maritime Danube, paths of communication supporting the political influence in the Balkans, disputed between Germany and Soviet Russia.

Faced with this dispute, what could be the situation of the countries of Central Europe and of the Lower Danube, especially that of Romania which, by means of the Sinaia Arrangement, had succeeded in obtaining the administration of navigation on the Maritime Danube. With no support on the part of France and England, themselves in difficult political situations, the answer could be that of Winston Churchill who, after the Munich Agreement, said the following: "The system of alliances in Central Europe upon which France has relied for her safety has been swept away, and I can see no means by which it can be reconstituted. The road down the Danube Valley to the Black Sea, the road which leads as far as Turkey, has been opened. In fact, if not in form, it seems to me that all these countries of Middle Europe, all those Danubian countries, will, one after another, be drawn into this vast system of power politics — not only power military politics but power economic politics — radiating from Berlin, and I believe this can be achieved quite smoothly and swiftly and will not necessarily entail the firing of a single shot."[190]

Along the road leading down the Danube valley there was Hitler, and on that going up there was Stalin. The final result of this meeting was among other matters, the Russo-German attempts to modify the international regime for navigation existing until then on the basis of the Treaty of Versailles and the 1921 Convention for the Definitive Statute of the Danube.

The origins of the modifications can be attributed to the unilateral rejection in 1936, by Germany, of the clauses of the Versailles Treaty concerning the internationalization and the restrictions drawn up for her navigable waters, which she had declared national.

Support of justification for modification of the Danube regime were the precedents created by the Convention for establishing the Definitive Statute of the Danube in 1921 and the method of resolving the litigation between Romania and the European Commission as to the competence of the Galatz-Brăila sector and the Sinaia Arrangement of 1938. By the modifications proposed by Germany, she was seeking to insure her economic interests on the entire course of the Danube by a political domination. Opposed to this policy was Soviet Russia's position which demanded her presence on the Danube for strategic-political reason, among others.

Aside from the fact that "tous les problèmes danubiens nous intéressent," as Vishinsky declared to Schulenberg, Germany's ambassador to Moscow, Molotov also invoked upon Russia by the Crimean War, when she was detached from her position of riparian to the Danube.[191]

According to the Versailles Treaty and the Statute for the Danube, the modification of the Danube regime as proposed by Germany would have been a non-territorial revision. Apparently this point of view had not been foreseen in Soviet Russia's policy.

In 1936, on the occasion of the Montreux Conference, respecting the revision of the regime over the Straits, as requested by Turkey, Litvinov, Soviet Russia's Minister for Foreign Affairs, declared that he "opposed not only territorial revisions, but also the non-territorial ones that do not serve the cause of peace."[192] In 1940, however, Soviet Russia applied territorial revision by annexing Bessarabia and, that same year, she sought also the non-territorial annexation by modification of the international regime for navigation on the Danube.

By the Russian and German modifications, the dismantling of the Danube Commissions was being pursued — the European Commission and the International Commission of the Danube — as well as their

ATTEMPTS TO MODIFY THE REGIME 541

replacement by new organs controlled by themselves and the exclusion of England and France from the control over the application of the international regime for navigation. Romania's position was to retain both commissions. By eliminating the political antagonism between them, Germany as well as Soviet Russia could have shielded and promoted their interests by retaining both commissions, in which they would also have been members, even without taking recourse to modification. For her economic interests, Germany could have used the entire course of the Danube to the Sulina Mouth, while Soviet Russia would have remained with sovereignty over the Kilia Branch, as had been stipulated in 1883, in the Treaty of London. The acts of modification were developed in four Conferences of the Danubian countries: that of Vienna in 1940, and those of Bucharest in 1941, 1942 and 1943.[193]

From the four Conferences certain characteristics can be extracted. The predominant voices were those of Germany and Soviet Russia. Germany, Italy, and particularly Romania, proposed a provisional modification of the international regime for navigation, the definitive one remaining to be made at the conclusion of the peace after World War II, in the case of a victory. Opposed to them was Soviet Russia, who demanded the immediate effectuation of the modification.

The main riparian of the Danube which was to be sacrificed by the German-Russian initiatives was Romania, possessor of the Mouths of the Danube River.[194] The weakening of Romania's position during the Conferences had been preceded by some of the actions of Soviet Russia and Germany. In 1940, Soviet Russia had reannexed Bessarabia; in August 1940, Germany and Italy forced Romania to conclude in the Craiova Accord, through which she ceded Southern Dobruja, called the "Quadrilateral," to Bulgaria. Also in August, the same two partners of the Berlin-Rome Axis, through the Vienna Arbitrage, forced Romania to cede to Hungary over half of the territory of Transylvania.

Concerning the English guarantee given to Romania as to protecting her against an eventual foreign attack, R.W. Seton-Watson declared, in 1942: "For better than two years, British policy has kept silent with regard to Romania. If this silence is due to avoiding conflicts with the Soviet Union it must not be criticized. We must admit, however, that our silence has increased the astonishment of the Romanians in their desperate position between the Devil and the Deep Sea."[195] The result was Romania's forced ceding under pressure from Berlin and her entrance into the war against Soviet Russia, beside Germany. Bulgaria, in turn, not finding satisfaction from England

and France, for her territorial complaints against Greece and Yugoslavia, also aligned herself with Germany.

The Conference of Vienna, September 1940.

In 1936 Germany's emissaries failed to convince the countries of the Lower Danube to establish a new regime for navigation on the Lower Danube by means of bilateral conventions. Her only success was to become a part of the European Commission of the Danube, after the Sinaia Arrangement was concluded. To realize the modification of the existing regime on the Danube, Germany together with Italy convoked on their own a Danubian Conference, which took place in Vienna between September 4 and 12, 1940.[196] Germany, Hungary, Italy, Romania, Slovakia and Yugoslavia participate. England and France had not been convoked, since they were at war with Germany. Along with the disbanding of the International Commission of the Danube, the Conference also took into consideration the European Commission and its replacement with another international body.

After long and controversial debates, a Provisional Arrangement (Accord) was concluded on September 12, 1940, providing for the following revisions on the 1921 Convention for the Definitive Statute of the Danube and its replacement with a Council of the Fluvial Danube, with jurisdiction between Bratislava and Brăila, under Germany's rule; inclusion of Germany in the Romanian-Yugoslavian Technical Commission for the Iron Gates; and according to Germany the exclusive jurisdiction of the Bratislava-Ulm fluvial sector.

In the Provisional Arrangement, Romania's representative succeeded in having the following texts included:[197] that the provisional state "did not in any way touch the actual regime in force on the Danube," with respect to freedom of navigation for all flags (Articles 1 and 2) and the provisional regime on the Fluvial Danube (Article 7).

Not being able to complete the Arrangement, the Conference was interrupted in order to open discussions for Soviet Russia's demands. Moscow could not allow Germany freedom of action for two principal reasons. The first, she had become a riparian on the Lower Danube by means of the Kilia Branch , acquired by her annexation of Bessarabia. The second, she considered Germany obliged to go along with her in changing the regime on the Danube, as one that was a partner of the German-Russian Non-aggression Pact. After the

ATTEMPTS TO MODIFY THE REGIME 543

close of the Conference of Vienna, Moscow immediately and categorically reacted, Vishinsky protesting to Schulenburg against the fact that Soviet Russia had not been convoked to the Vienna meeting.[198]

Through Schwartzev, Moscow's Ambassador to Berlin, Ribbentrop, Germany's Foreign Minister, assured Molotov on September 14, 1940, of the fact that at Vienna only matters concerning disbanding of the European Commission were discussed and that Germany acknowledged Soviet Russia's right to be part of the European Commission of the Danube.[199]

In a note sent to Germany on September 14, 1940, Molotov made it known that Russia was in agreement with the disbanding of the International Commission and the European Commission, proposing that they be replaced by a single Danubian Commission for the whole course of the river, from Bratislava to the Black Sea. Excluding England and France, the new Commission was to be made up exclusively of the riparians existing in 1940; that is, Bulgaria, Germany, Romania, Soviet Russia, Slovakia, Hungary and Yugoslavia.[200]

The disbanding of the European Commission demanded by Soviet Russia would have been in accordance with Germany's views also, since, as Gafencu noted, she would have realized three targets with one blow: the elimination of the English and French from one of the most important positions would have dug a trench between the USSR and Great Britain; and would have given the Soviet government proof of the goodwill and reconcile her to the policy of collaboration, still useful and profitable to German interests.[201] Soviet Russia's presence on the Danube, and especially at its Mouths, was regarded by Molotov in the light of remedying an "inferior status thrust upon her after the Crimean War."[202]

In 1940, England protested against the Conference of Vienna, but kept silent about the reannexation of Bessarabia by Soviet Russia, as well as about the latter's return to the banks of the Danube.

At the end of the Conference under German presidency, a communiqué was issued announcing the concluding of a "Provisional Accord" (Arrangement) on the basis of which a unanimous decision was taken to liquidate the International Commission of the Danube and to take measures to insure the continuation of navigation on the sector under that Commission.[203]

The Conference of Bucharest, (October - December 1940).

Representatives of Germany, Italy, Romania and Soviet Russia participated in the Conference of Bucharest. After the conclusion of the Conference of Vienna, the Moscow Government expressed to the Government of the Reich the interest it bore in contributing to the Regulation of the Danube Question, in particular to the liquidation of the European Commission.[204] The German Government hastened to accept the Moscow request, pro forma. In separate notes, the German government on October 18 and the Italian one, on October 21, 1940, without previous consultation with the Romanian government, announced the setting of a Conference at Bucharest that same month in which, along with Germany, Italy and Romania, Soviet Russia would also participate.[205] The Conference took place between October 28 and December 21, 1940. From the context of the two notes, it was obvious that the German and Italian governments were already agreed on the liquidation of the European Commission, a decision which could have only a provisional character.[206] In its answer agreeing to attend the Conference, the Romanian government conditioned it to consideration as a basis of the Provisional Arrangement for the Fluvial Danube concluded at Vienna in 1940, especially of Article I, which provided that this Act did not affect the principles actually in force on the Danube.[207]

When the Conference opened, the Representatives of Germany, Italy, and Romania presented a project referring to the problem of the Maritime Danube, which would have necessitated an immediate solution if the European Commission of the Danube were to be dissolved, leaving its definitive solution to take place after the peace was concluded.[208] The project provided for the establishment of a Provisional Council of the Maritime Danube, to be made up of representatives of Germany, Italy, Soviet Russia and Romania, and which would replace the European Commission, allowing for the possibility of an eventual basis for bilateral cooperation between Romania and Soviet Russia in some matters.[209]

On October 29, 1940, the Russian Government presented an Arrangement concerning the regime for the Maritime Danube, by means of which the modification of the German-Italo-Romanian project would have been the basis for discussion.

The Russian Arrangement[210] provided for: the dissolving of the European Commission (Article 1) and replacing it with a common Russo-Romanian Administration (Article 2); the Administration to carry on its activity of Romanian territory, Romania having exclusive authority over appointing personnel, over execution of the technical works, exercising sanitary control and assuring navigation police (Article 3); cessation of the activities of Romanian national authorities on Romanian territory where this Administration was to function, and the liquidation of the Special Autonomous Board of the Danube (Articles 3 and 4); subordination of German and Italian interests to a Unitary Commission of the Danube, to be established later (Article 4).

Differences appeared between the positions of Romania and those of Soviet Russia. Romania understood the Russo-Romanian Administration to be subordinate to the Council of the Maritime Danube, a body which would assume the attributes of the dissolved European Commission. Also, she understood that the international regime of navigation was to be applied on all the branches of the river, including the Kilia. Russia demanded that the Kilia Branch be detached, both from the proposed Administration and from the Council for the Maritime Danube. As to the personnel of the administration, heated discussions took place. The Russian Plenipotentiary demanded that the Russian personnel in this Administration be answerable only to the government at Moscow.[211]

Because common Administration was to be functioning on Romanian territory, Romania's Plenipotentiary demanded that the principal positions be held by Romanians. The discord between the Romanian and the Russian viewpoints concerning personnel caused the Russian Plenipotentiary to respond with a sort of threat. He stated that the refusal of the Romanian Delegation to adhere to the Russian Project "tends to violation of the rights of the sovereignty in the USSR's interests of State on the Danube."[212] The Russian Plenipotentiary's stand became paradoxical. By eliminating the Kilia Branch from the international regime, Soviet Russia, through the Russo-Romanian Administration at the Mouth of Sulina, would have become a Riparian to the maritime Danube in only a small portion of the river, between the mouth of the Prut River and Chatal Ismail. From the debates, it appears that Romania leaned towards partial retention of Romanian administration under the control of the council of the Maritime Danube, as set by the Sinaia Arrangement in place of the European Commission.

During the conference of Bucharest, the British government sent Molotov a note, through Sir Stafford Cripps, its Ambassador to Moscow, protesting against suppression of the European Commission, stating that England "reserves all her rights in the existing Accords and does not acknowledge the new ones."[213] In his answer,

Vishinsky recalled the injustice done to Russia by England's exclusion of her, through the Versailles Treaty, from all the Danubian Commissions after World War I, and contested England's interests on the Danube, ...she being distant from the river."[214]

In the end, Soviet Russia did not succeed in imposing her position, the principal obstacle being the opposition of Germany, Italy and Romania to the project setting Soviet Russia at the Mouths of the Danube by means of the common Russo-Romanian Administration.

The continuation of the debates of the Conference of Bucharest ended on December 21, 1940 to be taken up again at another Conference in the same place.

Conferences of Bucharest, February 1941 and November 1942.

Continuing the previous one, the Conference of Bucharest of 15 February 1941, with the participation of the Plenipotentiaries of Germany, Italy, Romania and Soviet Russia, resumed the discussions over the same unresolved items, to which were added other proposals especially those referring to the Maritime Danube. The principal theme of the debates was the continued persistence of Soviet Russia over her role in the administration of navigation on the Maritime Danube. In the first days of the Conference, Germany's Delegation succeeded in getting some modifications in the Russian Project, namely, the reconsideration of German and Italian participation in the Provisional Council of the Maritime Danube.

On February 15, 1941, V.V. Pella, Romania's Plenipotentiary, handed all the participants the "Memorandum of the Romanian government," in which the new regime of navigation did not differ much from the initial Italo-German views. In exchange, the Russian point of view was changed substantially. With regard to international cooperation on the Danube, the Romanian government insisted upon the establishment of a Provisional regime, under an international body composed of Germany, Italy, Romania and Soviet Russia.[215]

In opposition to Russia's idea concerning a common Russo-Romanian Administration, the Romanian Government preferred retaining Romanian administration over the Maritime Danube in accordance with the Sinaia Arrangement, under the supervision of the international body mentioned above, and the continuation of the activity of the Committee of Consulting Engineers. Proposing the retention of Romanian administration, as originated by the Sinaia

ATTEMPTS TO MODIFY THE REGIME

Arrangement, demonstrated the success of that administration's activity and of the projects for continuing the technical works of improvement of navigation.

In the end, this Conference, suspended in March, also took no definitive decisions, Germany intentionally dragging on the debates in expectation of the outbreak of her way against Soviet Russia, which took place three months later (June 22, 1941).

After her first successes on the Soviet Russian front, Germany called for a new Danubian Conference at Bucharest, in November 1942, to which the participants were herself, Italy and Romania. This time, Romania had to face the Italo-German position.

As of October 1942, the German Government presented to the Romanian one, along with the initial proposals of the Conference of Vienna, some similar to the Russian ones for the Maritime Danube. In addition, the idea of German hegemony on the entire course of the Danube River was proposed.

From the German proposals the following would result: cessation of the activity of the European Commission and the establishment, along with the present Romanian Administration, of a cooperative body made up of representatives of Germany, Italy and Romania; assigning a German technician to the Romanian administration, with effective attributes to carry out the technical works at the Mouths of the Danube; establishment of a "Unitary Commission" for the entire Danube, with two special sections: one at the Iron Gates and one at the Mouths of the Danube, the Commission to be composed of representatives of all the states riparian to the Danube and of Italy. This Commission was to take care itself with the problems presenting a common interest for the two sections of the river and, especially, for the problem of unifying the navigation and police regulations, as well as to set uniform rules for collecting taxes; revision of the Sinaia Arrangement and simplification of the attributes of the Maritime Board of the Danube (D.D.M.), which were "too complicated from an administrative and financial point of view," according to German opinion; reorganization of the pilotage service on the Maritime Danube and assignment of the number of pilots according to country (Germany, Italy and Romania); member states to pay the salaries of their citizens working as pilots, technicians or as office personnel in the new cooperative body to be attached to the D.D.M.; reservation by Germany of the right to make later proposals regarding financial questions, retaining the attributes of the D.D.M. to collect taxes.

As can be seen from Germany's proposals, Romania's situation at the Mouths of the Danube was becoming much worse and in no way was comparable to that established by the Sinaia Arrangement. While between 1938 and 1941, in accordance with the Arrangement, Romanian authority projected and carried out the technical works, which were submitted only pro forma to the control of the European Commission, in 1942, German technicians came, not only to verify and to supervise their application in their capacity as chiefs, but also to make decisions as to their suitability.

The head of the Romanian Delegation at the conference, Prof. V.V. Pella, and in particular, Prof. Gr. Antipa, tried to convince the Germans of the necessity of maintaining the European Commission, to which they belonged, as well as of the difficult situation in which Romania would be placed by violating certain obligations of international order. All these interventions not only were fruitless but attempts were made to have Minister Pella replaced, as he was considered an "anglophile."

In the "Memorandum of the Romanian government," V.V. Pella stressed that "any arrangement desired by Germany and Italy to be made in reference to the regime on the Maritime Danube do not contain any disposition incompatible with the sovereign rights of the riparian states, or with the fundamental participles of international law, as well as those of freedom and navigation and equality of treatment for all flags."

What is to be observed after the German-Russian attempts to modify the existing regime on the Danube is the disregard of certain decisions established in the past, in diplomatic Acts and Accords of international value. In the past, and after 1940, Germany as well as Soviet Russia demanded the dissolution of the European Commission on the grounds that certain Great Power Members did not have the qualification of "riparian" to the Danube (France, England and Italy). They also claimed that the administration and supervision of the freedom of navigation should be the attributes of riparian states.

When, by the Sinaia Arrangement, the Great Powers granted to Romania the administration of the Maritime Danube, apparently, no German voice was heard to oppose it or the retention of the European Commission. Germany adhered to that Arrangement in 1939, by means of a Special Accord, soliciting her own admittance in the European Commission along with England and Italy. After a year, however, at the 1940 Conference of Vienna, she demanded its abolition. In order that Germany's argument might have been valid and logical, it would have meant that Italy should not have participated at the Danubian Conferences of 1940, 1941 and 1942, for the simple reason that she, like England and France, is not riparian to the Danube. Italy's qualification as an ally of Germany could not constitute juridic justification for her presence. Germany and Soviet Russia accepted Italy, not only in all the institutions proposed by them for the administration of the Maritime Danube, they retained her also in the institution for the Upper Danube, where her navigation interests were non-existent. Furthermore, if in the administration of the Maritime Danube non-riparian States had no right to participate, it would mean that Germany could not take part in a conference which was to establish the regime for a navigation communication line over which — in accordance with the German and Russian points of view — only riparian states had a voice. Germany was riparian to the Danube only on its upper sector, not on the Lower Danube or on the Maritime Sector.

Faced with increasingly stronger pressure from Germany, the Romanian government was forced to accept, in principle, the modifications demanded at this Conference.

During the presence of the German Army in Romania, Germans were unable to carry out effectively the administration at the Mouths of the Danube. The Romanian Delegate in the European Commission and the Special Director of the Maritime Danube Board proceeded in such a way that the transfer of the application of the German proposals was delayed as much as possible, accepting all through the provisional period the formal assignment of a German observer whose function lasted only three months. Also contributing to the delay in setting in force the German initiatives was the beginning of defections along the front in Soviet Russia, a fact which took German attention away from the Danube.

By the loss of World War II, all the actions for modifying the international regime for navigation remained fruitless. From the Russo-German confrontation, Soviet Russia was able to realize her plans only in 1948, by the Danubian conference at Belgrade.

The Memorandum of Professor Gr. Antipa.

The importance of this Memoir lie in Romania's actual position towards the international regime on the Lower Danube, especially on her maritime navigation sector. Prof. Antipa's opinions are those which the Governments of Romania, Bulgaria and Yugoslavia could not express fully, publicly, under German-Russian pressure.

On the occasion of the 1942 conference of Bucharest, V.V. Pella sought the counsel of prof. Gr. Antipa, one of Romania's high-ranking authorities and scholar of Danubian matters. The latter answered him in the form of a Memorandum.[216] The object of this act was to defend Romania's rights on the Maritime Danube and at the Mouths of the Danube, rights acquired through the Sinaia Arrangement. In spite of his Philo-German sentiments, Antipa opposed Germany's pressures on Romania. For this reason, he renounced his previous stand against the European Commission, considering the Commission to be the European organization under which Romania's rights were better protected.

Besides showing the lack of an international juridic basis for Germany's position, Antipa reviewed briefly also the history of German pressure. Considering the magnitude of Antipa's position in a period during which Romania found itself practically a vassal to Germany, it is better to present some of his views in extenso.

Concerning German-Romanian collaboration on the Maritime Danube, as conceived by Berlin, he believed that "this led in fact to a restraint of Romanian national sovereignty and that the Romanian administration at the Mouths of the Danube and on the Maritime Sector were thus being placed under the patronage and complete control of the German and Italian Plenipotentiaries, who made all the decisions."

As to the break-up of the European Commission, as proposed by Germany, Antipa stressed that "...no mater how much we would wish to satisfy the requests of our Allies (Germany and Italy, author's note), the disintegration of the European Commission of the Danube, or even, as the German Delegate expresses it, the suspension of its activity and the liquidation of the assets pertaining to it, cannot be the object for discussion by only the Delegates of the three countries present today at this Conference (Germany, Italy and Romania). The political status of the European Commission, its future composition, organization and existence, as well as its rights and attributes, cannot be established except by the peace treaty or through the Congress for the organization of Europe that will follow it."

According to Antipa, the break-up of the European Commission would have been "a great step backwards in the organization of Europe. The explanation that it was able to resist other battles raged against it, especially by Russia, is due to the fact that the European Commission is a product of great European Congresses."

Indirectly, in referring to political procedures of the past, he noted "...the obstacles most difficult to set aside are the political ones, which come from the domineering tendencies of larger States and their violations of the natural rights of the smaller states. This being so, we believe that the path taken by Germany does not represent the shortest road to reach a hasty practical solution, even for her own needs."

Concerning the diminuation of the powers of the Romanian administration at the Mouths of the Danube as proposed by Germany, Antipa underlined the fact that "the aims of the German proposal, aside from (causing) a complete disorganization of all that has been accomplished until now, would also signify a great humiliation for us. I have tried to understand the real motives — those invoked by urgent necessity — which prompt the German Government to resort to such measures, which damage and humiliate its ally, the one whose blood is being shed in abundance on the field of battle in Russia. I have found no justification called for by the needs of the war; if there did exist such, it would be our duty to help our great ally in all possible ways. But there is no need for this, to start off on the path, mistakenly proposed, which would create so much injustice for Romania and would take us backwards more than half a century."

In supporting the maintenance of the European Commission, Antipa added "...ways could be found to take us to a sincere, brotherly collaboration, without striking out at an institution such as the European Commission, to which Romania owes so much, and from whose present organization still expects great services."

As to Russia's position, he mentioned "...her continual attempts since 1812 to get mastery over the Mouths of the Danube and to the adoption by Soviet Russia of the tsarist procedures, applied with much more brutal methods."

For the new regime for the Danube, Antipa counselled the following: stabilization of the European Commission at the concluding of the peace; respecting of the Sinaia Arrangement; maintenance of Romanian administration at the Mouths of the Danube, without foreign specialists; collaboration with Germany and Italy in technical and financial matters; reorganization of the Special Autonomous Board of the Danube, in view of a greater and an independent activity.

In the idea of regulation of the new regime for navigation through a "treaty of peace or by means of a Congress for the organization of Europe," as suggested by Antipa, there is reflected indirectly the hopes for a victory of the Western Powers.

By his attitude, Antipa broke off all personal contact with the German Legation in Bucharest, which previously he had frequented often. For him, Romania's rights at the Mouths of the Danube were a national postulate which he professed to the end of his life. In defense of these rights, he reversed his earlier attacks against the European Commission of the Danube.

Notes

Chapter 1

1. In order to avoid repetition of names of the component nations (Kingdom of Serbs, Croats and Slovens, 1918-1929), we will use the name of Yugoslavia which became a Federal Republic in 1945.
2. "Conférence internationale pour l'établissement du Statut Définitif du Danube," Vol. 1 and II, Paris 1921; hereafter abbreviated to the "Conference of 1920-1921."
3. Protocols No. 1-29, from 2 August to 16 November 1920 (Vol. I), and No. 30-68 from April 5 to July 21, 1921, (Vol. II).
4. Protocol No. 3, August 5, 1920.
5. Protocol No. 3, August 5, 1920.
6. Protocol No. 1, August 2, 1920.
7. Project of the Convention; in "Conference of 1920-1921," pp. 8-14, Annex, Protocol No. 1, August 2, 1920.
8. Protocol No. 1, of August 2, 1920.
9. For the amended French Project, see Protocol No. 6, of September 16, 1920; for the Greek, Yugoslavian and Romanian projects, see Protocol No. 4, Septembre 6; for Czechoslovakian, Protocol No. 7, of September 20.
10. Protocol No. 9, September 24, 1920.
11. Ibid.
12. Ibid., No. 10, September 30, 1920, annex III, project of the Convention.
13. Ibid.
14. N. Iorga, "Chestiunea Dunării..."; in "Analeye istoriei României," p. 256. This opinion does not refer directly to the 1920-1921 Conference, but to the general situation of navigation on the Lower Danube.
15. Protocol No. 10, September 30, 1920.
16. Ibid., No. 2, August 4; No. 5, August 8, 1920.
17. Ibid., No. 10, September 30, 1920.
18. "La Commission Européenne et son...," Annexe XXXV, p. 514.
19. "Un siècle de coopération...," p. 78.
20. Extracts from the European Commission's statistics, presented to the 1920-1921 Conference, p. 140.
21. "Conference of 1920-1921," p. 142; extracts from European Commission statistics. The total taxes of 1,881,136 gold francs, of which the Belgian flag paid 67,342 gold francs.

553

22. Ibid., p. 196, from the declaration of Belgium's Plenipotentiary, Protocol No. 32, 11 April 1921.
23. See "Semaforul Dunării si al Mării Negre."
24. Dascovici, "Drept international public," p. 113; G. Antipa, "Dunărea si problemele ei..." p. 136; Take Ionescu, Foreign Minister of Romania; "Documente privitoare la Dunăre si problemele ei internationale (1917-1920)," published by the "Superior Council for Transports and Tariffs." This council shall be referred to in continuation by the abbreviation "Documente C.S.T.T."
25. Protocol No. 11, October 1, 1920.
26. Gr. Antipa, "Dunărea si...," p. 136, 137.
27. "Documente C.S.T.T."
28. Telegram of resignation from Thomas Stelian to Take Ionescu, Romanian Minister of Foreign Affairs, Paris, September 1920; "Documente C.S.T.T.," pp. 209-215.
29. Protocol No. 22. October 29, 1920.
30. Thomas Stelian, Telegram of resignation.
31. From Take Ionescu's response to Stelian's resignation, Bucharest, September 12, 1920: "As for the attitude of Greece's representative, Mr. Koromilas's personality is not surprising and you must not believe that it corresponds with the position of the Greek Government. Mr. Koromilas took effective part in the Macedo-Romanian turbulent epoch. Furthermore, he is not a friend of Mr. Venizelos, who had given categorical orders for Greco-Romanian collaboration"; "Documente C.S.T.T.," p. 209.
32. "Documente C.S.T.T.," p. 206.
33. Protocol No. 10, September 30, 1920.
34. On the occasion of the concluding of the general peace, Clemenceau, the President of the Peace Conference, tried to oppose Romania's right of ally, on the consideration that she had signed the separate Peace Treaty of Bucharest with the Central Powers, a non-ratified treaty. Harold Nicolson, an official of the English Delegation, attributed to Elefterios Venizelos, head of the Greek Delegation, the deciding role in placating the incident, supporting the Romanian Delegation and Take Ionescu, who was substituting for Ionel Brătianu, the latter having had the conflict with Clemenceau; see Harold Nicolson, "Peace Making 1919," pp. 136-137.
35. Protocol No. 10, Septembre 30, 1920.
36. Ibid.
37. Ibid., No. 10, September 30, 1920.
38. Ibid.
39. "Dunărea in Istoria...," p. 273.
40. Ibid., p. 274; from report No. 834 of January 10, 1928, sent from Vienna by C. Contzescu to the Minister for Foreign Affairs, extract from the Archives of the Romanian Ministry for Foreign Affairs. The "friendly countries": England, France and Italy.
41. Ibid., p. 276.

NOTES

42. Jean Kostanecki, "La Pologne et le problème danubien," in "Affaires Danubiennes," No. 1, Bucharest 1938; translated into French from the original text in English.
43. Protocol No. 4, September 6, 1920, Annex V.
44. Ibid., No. 11, October 10, 1920.
45. Ibid., No. 35, April 18, 1921.
46. Ibid., No. 11, October 10, 1920.
47. Ibid., No. 10, September 30, 1920.
48. Grigore Antipa, "Dunărea si...," p. 136.
49. Protocol No. 33, April 13, 1921.
50. Commission Internationale du Danube: Dix ans de régime international sur le Danube Fluvial," p. 151.
51. Protocol No. 1, August 2, 1920.
52. "La Commission Européenne et son...," p. 43.
53. Protocol No. 63, June 17, 1921.
54. Ibid., No. 67, June 25, 1921.
55. Ibid., No. 62, June 12, 1921.

Chapter 2

56. Protocol No. 7, of September 20, 1920.
57. Ibid., No. 20 of October 25, 1920.
58. Ibid., No. 19, October 22, 1920.
59. Ibid.
60. Ibid., No. 6, September 15, 1920.
61. Ibid., No. 8, September 22, 1920.
62. Ibid., No. 19, October 22, 1920.
63. Ibid., No. 53 of May 28, 1921.
64. Four principal situations can be noted. First, was the great possibility for activity due to the international regime of navigation. The second was in Romania's agricultural activity, which was concentrated chiefly in the indigenous element, the cereal export being mainly in foreign hands. The third was the barring of access of the foreign element from activities other than that of commerce; and finally, the fourth, the great hospitality of the native element towards the foreign one.
65. To note a few: Greeks in industry: Flour mills in Brăila: Valerianos, Lychiardopol, Gheorghiadis, Milas, Serafides, Violatos, Ambatis;
Pasta factories in Brăila: Apostolos and Aristide Melissaratos;
Navy Yards, Brăila: Simatos, Manaras, etc;
Banks, Brăila: Chrisoveloni, Banca Elino-Română, Lazaris;
Agricultural exploitation: Chrisoveloni, Apostolos Melissaratos, Cavadia, Lychiardopol;

Large scale cereal exporters: Sekiaris, Valianos, Portolos, Podimatopol, Cotis, etc;

Italians: Verona, factory for cooking oil; large export company for cereal, insurances and marine exploitation, such as Pedemonte, Fanciotti, Gattorno, etc;

Jews: Large export firms for cereal and marine exploitation as were: Mendl, Dreyfus, Mocki, Loebl, etc.

66. Protocol No. 19, of October 22, 1920. Minorities Treaties concluded with Yugoslavia (Kingdom of Serbs, Croats, Slovens), on September 10, 1919 and Romania on December 9, 1919; see "Recueil des Traités de la Societé des Nations," Vol. V and XV.

67. Protocols No. 19 of October 22, 1920.
68. Ibid.
69. For Hostie's entire documentation, including the citing of texts of some articles, see Protocol No. 19, of October 22, 1920.
70. Protocol No. 20, October 25, 1920.
71. Ibid., No. 19, of October 22, 1920.
72. Ibid.
73. Ibid., No. 20, of October 25, 1920.
74. Ibid., No. 53, of May 28, 1921.
75. Ibid., No. 53, May 28, 1921. The "general convention" was to be the one concerning the new Statute of the Danube.
76. Ibid., No. 20, October 25, 1920.
77. Ibid., No. 53, May 28, 1921.
78. D. Sturdza, "Recueill...," Annexe III, p. 596.
79. Protocol No. 19, of October 20, 1920.
80. Ibid., No. 20, of October 25, 1920.
81. Ibid., No. 53, of May 28, 1921.
82. Ibid.
83. Ibid.
84. Ibid.
85. Status of the Greek Flag in 1916 compared with that in 1920; from Youghaperian, "L'Annuaire du Danube," 1916; and "Semaforul Dunării si a Mării Negre," op. cit.
86. See Protocols 53, 54, 55, respectively of May 28 and 30, and of June 1, 1921.
87. See "Minorities Treaties," op. cit.

Chapter 3

88. Protocol No. 2, of August 4 and No. 17 of October 18, 1920.
89. Ibid., No. 45, May 11, 1921.
90. Ibid., No. 66, June 23, 1921.

91. Ibid., No. 46, May 13, 1921.
92. Ibid., No. 48, May 19, 1921.
93. Ibid., No. 46, May 13, 1921.
94. See "Semaforul Dunării...," p. 48.
95. Protocol No. 25, November 8, 1920.
96. Protocol No. 53, May 28, 1921.

Chapter 4

97. "Convention établissant le Statut Définitif du Danube," Paris 23 Juillet 1921, Annexe I au Protocole 67, in the "Conférence of 1920-1921," pp. 1213, 1234; Martens, N.R.G.T. (S. III), Vol. XII, p. 606; Great Britain, F.O., Treaty Series, Vol. No. 16, 1922, Text in French and English. Signers: Jules Brunet, Belgium; Bohuslav Müller, Czechoslovakia; Albert Legrand, France; John Grey Baldwin, Great Britain; André Andréadis, Greece; Vannutelli Rey, Italy; Constantin Contzesco, Romania; Mihailo Ristič, Yugoslavia; In presence and participation of: Victor Ondraczek, Austria; Georges Lazaroff, Bulgaria; Arthur Seelinger, Germany and Edmont de Miklos de Miklosvar, Hungary. For Final Protocol see "Conference of 1920-1921," p. 1229.

Chapter 5

98. At the inauguration, in 1894, of the immense project that eliminated the three large bends in the Sulina Branch, King Carol I, on his visit to Sulina, congratulated the Commission's engineers "... de la conception et de la réussite d'une oeuvre aussi remarquable"; D. Sturdza, "Recueil...," VI, and "La Commission Européenne du Danube et son..." XXIV. The favorable influence of the improvement of navigation on Romania's economy was attributed by C. Băicoianu to the "... labeur providential accompli par la Commission Européenne aux Bouches du Danube"; in C. Băicoianu, "Le Danube, aperçu historique, économique, et politique," pp. 115-116.
99. In a brochure prepared by the Romanian Delegation to the Peace Conference of World War I, the following was stated: "... la Roumanie ne peut être aujourd'hui que reconnaissante à cette institution qui a rendu d'appreciables services au commerce européen, services dont le pays a profité aussi dans une large mesure," and went on to say that the works of the European Commission of the Danube were "une oeuvre grandiose, realisée au cours d'un demisiècle, qui mérite d'être admirée"; in "Le Danube et les interêts économiques de l'Europe," Paris, 1919, brochure, pp. 29-30, 54, 68; quoted in "La Commission Europeénne et son...," p. 398.

100. G. Antipa, Dunărea si...," p. 312.
101. M. Kogălniceanu, Romanian Minister to Paris, to V. Boerescu, Minister for Foreign Affairs of Romania, Paris, August 10, 1880; in "M. Kogălniceanu, documente diplomatice," pp. 339, 341.
102. From a European Commission communication to the Romanian Government: "La Commission Européenne, désireuse de continuer les bons rapports qui existent si heureusement entre elle et le gouvernement royal de Roumanie, s'engage à éviter tout conflit, en donnant les ordres nécessaires à l'Inspecteur de la navigation du Bas-Danube et à ses autres agents, de ne pas dresser d'actes de juridiction dans les localités situées en amont de Galatz;" quoted by Hajnal in "Le Droit...," p. 204, note 1.
103. A hospital for the crews of foreign vessels, to which the public also had free access; a hospital for epidemic diseases; an electric power plant and waterworks, sewer system; see D. Sturdza, "Recueil...," pp. 872-914. Subsidies for schools, construction up to 80% of a large church, establishment of cemeteries, a telegraph and telephone system between Sulina and Tulcea connected also with Galatz; and many other subsidies granted to schools and churches in Tulcea; "La Commission Européenne et son...," p. 342-349.
104. Hajnal, "Le Droit...," p. 206.
105. N. Iorga, "A cui e Dunărea?" from a lecture given at Giurgiu, Nov. 9, 1908; p. 14.
106. "La Commission Européenne et son...," p. 130.
107. "Dunărea în Istoria...," p. 144; from documentation in the archives of the Romanian Ministry for Foreign Affairs.
108. Popa Apostol, "Ne mor porturile," Galatz, 1925.
109. "Actual circumstances" included lack of funds, social and economic disorganization of Sulina, the dispersion of technical personnel during the war, etc.," in N. Dascovici, "Regimul Dunării si al Suâmtorilor în ultimele decade," op. cit.
110. Protocol No. 10, September 30, 1920.
111. Protocole Interprétatif de l'Article VI du Statut du Danube, arreté par la Commission Européenne du Danube," Annexe au Protocole 67, le 25 Juin, 1921.
112. European Commission of the Danube, Protocols 929, 940, 955, 964, 968, 977 of November 1921, October 1922 and May 1923.
113. "Publications of the Permanent Court of International Justice," Series B-14, Dec. 8, 1927 Collection of Advisory Opinions: Juridiction of the European Commission of the Danube between Galatz and Brăila, Leyde, 1927, pp. 14-16. In English and French text, the English text being authoritative.
114. Ibid., pp. 17-58.
115. Ibid., pp. 111, 112. Among these cases was also the infringement against the Regulation for Navigation and Police made by the European Commission's yacht, "Carolus Primus." (Sentences numbers 276, March 16, 1901 and 2537 of November 26, 1907, issued by the Romanian authorities).
116. Recueil des Traités de la Société des Nations, Vol. LIX, p. 237; Publication of the Permanent Court, p. 6.

117. N. Titulescu, to the Minister for Foreign Affairs, Geneva, December 10, 1926; in "N. Titulescu, documente diplomatice," p. 215.
118. Idem, ibid., p. 216.
119. Idem, ibid., p. 215.
120. E.A. Millerand, former President of France; N. Politis, Minister of Greece to France and Honorary Professor at the Paris Faculty of Law; and Professor Charles Vischer, from Belgium.
121. M. Basdevant (France); Sir Douglas Hog (England), Carlo Rossetti (Italy).
122. Publications of the Permanent Court, p. 6.
123. Ibid., pp. 7-9.
124. Ibid., p. 69.
125. Ibid., pp. 71-78.
126. Ibid., pp. 80-83.
127. Ibid., pp. 84-134.
128. N. Dascovici, "Interesele României," preface to a lecture published in "Insemnări Iesene," Nos. 13, 14, 1937; See also, N. Dascovici, "Regimul Dunării si al Strâmtorilor în ultimele două decade," p. 42-43.
129. Société des Nations, Journal Officiel, XII Année, Nr 4. Avril 1931.
130. "Un Siècle de Coopération Internationale sur le Danube"; La Commission Européenne du Danube (1856-1956).
131. Ibid., p. 42.

Chapter 6

132. Titulescu to the Ministry for Foreign Affairs of Romania, St. Moritz, August 19, 1927; in "N. Titulescu, documente diplomatice," p. 226.
133. From an interview granted to the newspaper "Le Temps," 24 July 1936; and "N. Titulescu Discursuri," p. 544.
134. Ibid.
135. "N. Titulescu: Discursuri," p. 544.
136. Extrait du Protocole Nr. 643 de la Séance de la Commission Européenne du Danube, du 13 Mai 1902; D. Sturdza, "Recueil...," XXXI.
137. "La Commission Européenne et son...," p. 394.
138. "N. Titulescu: Discursuri," p. 544.
139. Ibid., p. 544.
140. From the report of A. Lahovary, Minister to Rome, to the Ministry for Foreign Affairs of Romania, May 11, 1927; from the Ministry Archives quoted in "Dunărea în istoria poporului român," p. 242.
141. The Newspaper "Politica," Belgrad, August 5, 1936.
142. "Peste Lloyd," Budapest, August 6, 1936; Neuigkeits Weltblatt," Vienna, August 7, 1936; "Kölnische Zeitung," August 4, 1936; "Deutsche Allgemeine Zeitung," August 5, 1936. The statements from these newspapers were taken from "Dunărea în istoria poporului român," pp. 306, 307.

143. "Dunărea în istoria...," pp. 254-306.
144. Gr. Antipa, "Dunărea si...," p. 111.
145. Gr. Gafencu, "Dunărea Internaţională," an article appearing in the newspaper "Timpul," July, 16. Bucharest, 1938.
146. D. Dascovici, "Comisiunea Europeană a Dunării"; from an article in the newspaper "Argus," Bucharest 1936.
147. Aide-Mémoires of May 29 and June 12, 1936, sent by the German Legation at Bucharest to the Ministry for Foreign Affairs of Romania; quoted in "Dunărea în istoria poporului român," p. 286, footnotes 248, 249.
148. N. Dascovici "Regimul Dunării si al Strâmtorilor în ultimile decade," pp. 62, 64.
149. From the Proces-Verbal of the German-Romanian discussions at Bucharest, July 7, 8, 1938; information gathered from the Archives of the Romanian Ministry for Foreign Affairs, quoted in "Dunărea în istoria...," p. 320.
150. N. Dascovici, "Regimul Dunării si al Strâmtorilor," p. 64; and "Dunărea în istoria...," p. 321.
151. Note of May 4, 1938, of the Minister of France at Bucharest, to the Romanian Ministry for Foreign Affairs; quoted in "Dunărea în istoria...," p. 321.
152. "Dunărea în istoria...," p. 315.
153. "Dunărea în istoria...," pp. 315-316; from the Archives of the Romanian Ministry for Foreign Affairs.
154. Ibid., p. 316.
155. G. Sofronie, "Contributie la cunoasterea relatiilor dintre România si Comisiunea Europeană a Dunării," pp. 13, 14.
156. "Dunarea în istoria...," p. 316.
157. Ibid., p. 317; from the Archives of the Romanian Ministry for Foreign Affairs.
158. Gr. Antipa, "Dunărea si...," p. 124.
159. Protocols of the Conference of Sinaia of 1938, No. 1, August 8; No. 2, August 9; No. 7, August 15; No. 8, August 16; No. 9, August 17.
160. "Arrangement relatif à l'exercise des pouvoirs de la Commission Européenne du Danube"; Sinaia, 18 August 1938; in Great Britain, Foreign Office Treaty Series, No. 38, 1930; "Monitorul Oficial al României" No. 78, Aprilie 1, 1939 and "Affaires Danubiennes," No. 3, 1939.
161. "Universul," Bucharest, August 21, 1938.
162. "Accord between the European Commission of the Danube and the Romanian Government regarding the privileges and immunities of the European Commission of the Danube personnel," Sinaia, 18 August 1938; in "Condica tratatelor si a altor conventii ale României," published under the auspices of the Ministry for Foreign Affairs of Romania Vol. III, Bucharest, 1942, p. 73.
163. The Law establishing the D.D.M. was published in the "Monitorul Oficial al României," No. 110, of May 15, 1939.

NOTES 561

164. "Dunărea în istoria...," p. 330; from the Archives of the Romanian Ministry for Foreign Affairs.

165. "Monitorul Oficial" al României, 1939; "Recueil des Traités de la Société des Nations," Vol. CXCVI.

166. England, Sir Reginal Hoare; France, Adrian Thierry; Germany, Wilhelm Fabritzius; Italy, Pellagrino Ghighi; Romania, Grigore Gafencu, Minister for Foreign Affairs and C. Contzescu, Minister Plenipotentiary, Delegate in the European Commission of the Danube.

167. England: W. Douglas Keanne, Chief Delegate and Consul General McRey (to Galatz) as Alternate; France: Paul Morand, counsellor of the French Embassy, as chief Delegate, and Gaston Mouille, Consul General at Galatz, as Alternate; Italy: Publio Landucci, Minister Plenipotentiary and chief Delegate, Nardi, the Consul at Galatz as Alternate; Romania: C. Contzescu, Minister Plenipotentiary and Chief Delegate, and Ernest Rossi, Alternate; Germany: Dr. Martzius, Minister Plenipotentiary and Chief Delegate, and Bauer, as Alternate.

168. Newspaper "România," Bucharest 15 May, 1939.

169. Newspaper "Timpul," Bucharest, May 13, 1939.

170. Newspaper "România," May 18, 1939.

171. Ibid.

172. Newspaper "Universul," May 17, 1939, Bucharest; Article signed by R. Seisanu.

173. England, Belgium, Czechoslovakia, France, Greece, Italy, Romania and Yugoslavia.

174. Admiral Preda Fundăteanu, Dr. of International Maritime Law.

175. Law No. 1683, June 7, 1941; in "Monitorul Oficial al României," No. 134, June 10, 1941.

176. From the report of the Ministers of National Defense, Finance, and of the Under-Secretariat of State of the Navy, to Marshall I. Antonescu, Conductor of the State and President of the Council of Ministers, accompanying Law No. 1683.

177. Law 2248, May 31, 1939, published in "Monitorul Oficial al României,"Nr. 128, June 6, 1939.

178. The newspaper "Timpul," March 2, 1939, Bucharest.

Chapter 7

179. N.Dascovici, "Regimul Dunării si al Strâmtorilor...," p. 123.

180. "Affaires Danubiennes," No. 7 and 8, Bucharest, 1940.

181. European Commission, Protocol No. 1394, para. 9, May 22, 1940, and "Affaires Danubiennes," Nos. 7 and 8.

182. "Paris Conference," 1946, p. 794.

183. V. Molotov, "Foreign Policy of the Soviet Government" by the Chairman of the Council of Peoples' Commissars of the USSR and the People's Commissar of Foreign Affairs, at the Sixth Session of the Supreme Soviet of the USSR, March 29, 1940; p. 19; quoted by Stephan Goren in "Law and Politics of the Danube," p. 55, footnote 9.

184. Salangi Island, Greater Daler and Lesser Daler.

185. Gr. Gafencu, "Préliminaires de la guerre à l'Est," p. 98.

186. Romanian secret services had in 1939 discovered the espionage net, moving into the interior a number of suspected Lipovenes. Groups of Russian soldiers often raided the marshes and canals on the Romanian banks of the Kilia and, on the night of January 2, 1941, two Russian torpedo boats entered the Mouth of the Sulina, withdrawing only in the face of fire from the Romanian coastal batteries; Gafencu, "Préliminaires...," p. 99.

187. On the basis of Law No. 3983 of December 1940, published in "Monitorul Oficial" of Romania, No. 287 of 5 December, 1940.

188. "Paris Conference, Economic Commission for the Balkans and Finland," statement by the U.K. Delegation concerning the Romanian Treaty, 4, annex 4, section c., Shipping. p. 794 (32).

189. Fluvial vessels of Romania, Hungary and Austria, which carried immigrants, remained in front of the Sulina Mouth until the favorable moment for the immigrants to board a maritime vessel at anchor in the Maritime sector of the port. In case of storms at sea, the maritime vessel was brought into port during the night, when the transbordation was carried out. In both cases, the offices of the D.D.M. did not register the presence of either the fluvial vessels or of the maritime ones. In this way, the presence of both kinds of vessels did not appear in the official statistics, which, in accordance with Article 11 of the Sinaia Arrangment, had to be made known to the European Commission of the Danube. The above information is personally known to the author, who during that period was active in the D.D.M. and who had a relative participating as a sailor in these emigrations even after Romania was out of the war, effectuated then without restrictions and under humane conditions.

Chapter 8

190. Winston Churchill, "Into Battle," February 1941, p. 48.

191. Gr. Gafencu, "Préliminaires de la guerre...," pp. 88, 90.

192. From the analytical report of the "Convention for the regime on the Straits," sent to the Minister for Foreign Affairs of Romania by the Romanian Delegation at Montreu, Switzerland, July 21, 1936; the original is in the Archives of the Ministry for Foreign Affairs of Romania, a copy being in the possession of the author of this present work. See also, Titulescu, "Discursuri," p. 594.

193. The reference relative to this Conference were taken from the "Mémorandum du Gouvernement Roumain sur un regime provisoire du Danube Maritime," Bucarest, le 15 Fevrier, 1941; drawn up by Professor V.V. Pella, Minister Plenipotentiary and Delegate in the European Commission; a copy is in the possession of the author of this work.
194. See also the lecture given by Prof. R.W. Seton-Watson at Oxford, on December 31, 1942; quoted by Gr. Gafencu in "Préliminaires...," pp. 400-401.
195. Ibid., 401.
196. Gr. Gafencu, "Préliminaires...," Chapter III.
197. See "Mémorandum du Gouvernment Roumain...," p. 4.
198. Gr. Gafencu, "Préliminaires...," p. 88
199. Idem, ibid., p. 90.
200. Idem, ibid., p. 90. Slovakia, new state created by Germany,
201. Idem, ibid., p. 93.
202. Idem, ibid., p. 90.
203. "Affaires Danubiennes," 1-2, 1942.
204. From the "Mémorandum du Gouvernement Roumain...," p. 2; Gr. Gafencu, "Préliminaires...," p. 100
205. Ibid., pp. 3,4.
206. Ibid., p. 3.
207. Ibid., p. 4.
208. Ibid., p. 5
209. Ibid., p. 6.
210. Ibid., pp. 6, 7.
211. Ibid., p. 29.
212. Idem, ibid., p. 103.
213. Gr. Gafencu, "Préliminaires...," p. 103.
214. Idem, ibid., p. 103.
215. "Mémorandum du Gouvernement Roumain," p. 12.
216. Antipa "Memorandum" to V.V. Pella, November 29, 1942; a Document in the Archives of the Ministry for Foreign Affairs of Romania, a copy of which was published by the author in "Două Memorii...."

PART NINE

AFTER THE SECOND WORLD WAR

AFTER THE SECOND WORLD WAR

Introduction.

After the end of World War II, the Danube Question returned to the status that existed before 1699, with the sole difference that the domination of the Ottoman Empire was replaced by that of the Soviet Empire, which had taken on the old Tsarist policy.

This reversal in the situation was due also to Winston Churchill who, in his policy to reestablish the "reign of law and to protect the liberties of small countries" and in the name of "humanity rather than legality,"[1] conceded to Soviet Russia a 90% influence over Romania, in October 1944, as well as 50% over Yugoslavia, 50% over Hungary and 75% over Bulgaria; a decision Churchill considered "cynical" but which Stalin did not.[2]

The results of Soviet Russia's successes in the Danube region could be included, in a greater extension, within the concept of Churchill's book, "Triumph and Tragedy." The triumph was Stalin's, while the tragedy was that of the little Danubian countries.

Chapter 1

THE SITUATION ON THE LOWER DANUBE AFTER THE BEGINNING OF THE WAR AGAINST SOVIET RUSSIA (22 June, 1941)

The Worsening of the restrictive steps against the International regime of Navigation.

From the beginning of the war against Soviet Russia (June 22, 1941) navigation on the Lower Danube River, as well as on the entire course of the river, was restricted to supplying the German-Romanian Armies on the military front.

During the first month of this front's advance, the ports of Reni and Ismail, of the Kilia Branch, were overrun and Bassarabia was reannexed to Romania. This reannexation ended Soviet Russia's riparian status on the Lower Danube. From the port of Giurgiu (Romania) and from the oil region of Romania, petroleum products were sent to the German front in Western Europe, as well as to the one in Russia, Rustchiuk, the Bulgarian port, supplied the German occupation in Greece. Lumber products were shipped through the ports of Galatz and cereal through Brăila. Later on, when the armies had penetrated into the Soviet Russia interior, the ports of Constanta (Romania) and Varna (Bulgaria) served as communication lines on the Black Sea towards that front. The shipyards at Turnu Severin, Giurgiu, Brăila, Galatz and Rustchiuk were busy in support of military operations. Under the appearance of their independence, the national economies of Romania and Bulgaria were directed towards the needs of Germany.

In this new situation, the Belgrade Agreement concerning the neutrality of navigation, as well as of the International regime for navigation, became inoperable. The restrictive measure, taken in 1939 and after 1940, were tightened after June 22, 1941, being applied in Romania's case to the fluvial vessels of transportation under Romanian flag and ownership; to those under Romanian flag and foreign ownership; and those under foreign flag and foreign ownership.

The juridicat regime applied to these categories of vessels differed. Those under Romanian flag and ownership were covered by the exceptional war measures (military requisition, nationalization, and confiscation), their owners receiving ridiculous remuneration. These vessels owned by Jewish shipowners of Romanian citizenship were nationalized and placed under the administration of a special organization entitled "National Center for Romanization" (Centrul National de Românizare). The vessels under the Romanian flag, but of foreign ownership, were covered by the regime directly under the State Administration of its rights over its national flag. The vessels under foreign flag and ownership came under several categories: those belonging to citizens of countries not at war with Romania were faced with a harsher economic requisition system. In this category, were the vessels of Greek citizens and those of the French Navigation company, S.F.N.D. The vessels belonging to the English company "Goeland," were taken over by the Romanian state and registered separately in the 1942 list of vessels of the Commercial Marine Board of Romania, as vessels under the English flag operated by the Romanian Fluvial Navy, a State enterprise.[3] (N.F.R.).

The technical work for maintaining navigation at the Sulina Mouth was continued by Romanian State through the Special Autonomous Board of the Marine Danube, shielded by the small warships of Germany and Romania.

The Legitimacy of the new Restrictive Steps.

Undoubtedly, the restrictive measures caused great losses for all shipowners. The restrictions were justified with respect to those under the Romanian flag and national ownership, but the problem acquired other aspects with regard to the vessels under foreign flag and ownership.

If the international regime had not been suspended, but had remained under the benefit of neutrality, the vessels under foreign flags and ownership would have been free to participate in the commercial market of transports. In the absence of such a situation, the respective owners would have had the choice of evacuating their ships from the Danube. Because of the war and of the restrictive measures, both possibilities were excluded. This was the case of the English vessels of English ownership, their country being a belligerent. As mentioned before, a special category existed on the Lower Danube for vessels of Greek ownership since Greece was not at war with Romania. Still, vessels under the Greek flag were kept under the economic requisition regime. Those of Greek ownership but flying the Romanian flag continued to be under military requisition, under the principle of application of "the law of the land the respective flag represents."[4]

A typical case of illegal economic requisitioning, and then of tis legality, was that of the tugboat "Dionisia" of Brăila, under Greek ownership and flag (Gh. Portolo). By order No. 1269 of March 2, 1941 of the Ministry of the Romanian Navy, the tug was paced under the regime of economic requisitions and assigned for the use of the Special Autonomous Board of the Marine Danube. On April 20, 1945, at the end of the war, the shipowner requested the return of his tug or the increase of leasing charges to the market price. The settlement of this case by the Romanian authorities was in favor of the shipowner, due to the illegality of the requisitioning. After this settlement, the Romanian government paid the shipowner the difference in shipping charges from the date of the requisitioning, a new contract being drawn up approximately at current rates.[5] However, the contract was later cancelled by the Communist regime.

As to the exceptional measures taken by the Romanian Government, a remark made by a member of the U.K. Delegation could be cited. In the matter of preventing United Nations shipping from leaving the Danube, he remarked, "...no loss or damage could have been attributed to that Government with the result that on the occupation of the country much of this shipping fell into Axis hands.[6]"

The 1947 Peace Treaty with Romania and that with Bulgaria provided for reparations and for the return of vessels by the countries that had applied restrictive measures.

In general, the problem of requisitioning the vessels can be considered in the light of war needs, as well as that of the possibilities for according reparations. During World War II, the Western Powers, especially England, requisitioned national maritime vessels as well as some under Allied flags, later according reparations. In the case of the United States, partial repayment to its allies consisted of selling the former Liberty ships used during the war at very reduced prices.

A precedent, in Romania's case, was the according of reparations to foreign shipowners who had put their ships at her disposal during the 1877-1878 war against the Turks. Thus, also after World War II, vanquished Romania awarded idemnification within the limits of her financial possibilities, to foreign shipowners, among them Greeks, on the basis of the Romanian-Greek Convention in 1956.[7]

In general, the problem of the legality of the restrictive measures over the vessels of foreign flag and ownership operating under an international regime of navigation, remained to be resolved by competent jurists. A consequence of the exceptional measures applied on the Lower Danube before and after World War II was the disappearance of foreign shipowners. The only foreign fluvial vessels remaining were those under the Russian flag and the French; the latter being the property of the Société Française de Navigation Danubienne (S.F.N.D.)

Chapter 2

CONDITIONS OF NAVIGATION PRIOR TO AND AFTER THE ARMISTICE AGREEMENTS WITH SOME EX-ENEMY DANUBIAN STATES.

Conditions of Navigation.

Gradually, along with the Soviet troop advances into and occupation of the ex-enemy states — Romania, Bulgaria, Hungary, and Eastern Austria — the Danube became the principal path of communication, under the direct control of Soviet Russia, in continuing the war against Germany.

Without very much variance between the behavior of the German armies and their allies on Soviet Russian territory, during the war, and that of the Soviet armies in the countries they occupied, some difference can be pointed out.

With the advance of German troops into Soviet Russia, reorganization measures were taken in support of the military operation of the economics and the paths of communication of the occupied territories which had been deliberately disorganized by the retreating Soviet armies, in order to create vacuums to the detriment of the attackers. The conquests made by the Germans and their allies did not influence the organizational methods behind the front. The Russians had proceeded otherwise. Deliberately or not, instead of benefiting from the economics and almost intact means of communications of the countries they occupied, the Russians created voids in them. Included in the military operations was the disorganization of the normal economic structure of these countries, capturing and transporting to Soviet Russia the technical equipment of the industries and the shipyards, cereal and household goods considered by them to be spoils of war. No

573

exception was made with respect to fluvial transport means; the communications system on the Danube was left in chaos. A rather large number of barges, tugs, and other transport vessels in operative conditions anchored in the ports, were taken over and transported on the Kilia Branch and to Southern Russia. Because of the Lack of Experience with the specific problem of Danube navigation, on the part of the Russian sailors replacing the local ones, many vessels were wrecked on accidentally sunk.

Aside from this situation and inherent sentiments of revenge, the ineptness and organizational experience on the part of the Soviet Army commands contributed to the chaos on the Danube. This situation created great difficulties for the Commission applying the Armistices Agreements, in fulfillment of the conditions requiring the turning over of the vessels to the Soviet Army, in navigable condition. Neither the local State authorities, nor the private ship-owners had any information as to the whereabouts of their vessels. In the past, under other occupations, the operations of transferring vessels to the use of the Russian armies was much simpler, being taken care of directly by the local authorities.

Navigation through the Sulina Mouth, after the close of the war, was almost non-existent. Continuation of the technical works by Romanian organs were being hindered by the interference of inexperienced Russian technicians, during the first months of the Russian occupation of the Danubian countries. Under these conditions, all commercial navigation on the Lower Danube, up to Austria was as paralyzed.

The Armistice Agreements and their Navigation Clauses.

Regarding the Armistice Agreements concluded with the ex-enemy states, the Russian proceeded somewhat at variance with the norms of International Law. Instead of the agreements being signed at the same time as the military capitulation, they were concluded only after the complete occupation of the respective countries.[8]

This political measure anticipated the installation of communist regime by force, under the protection of the Soviet Armies, an act contrary to the 1945 Yalta Declaration, which had provided for democratic regimes freely elected.

Western acceptance of these forced "free elections" was gained by means of "Soviet camouflaging tactics," as Professor Stephen Gorove termed them.[9]

THE ARMISTICE AGREEMENTS 575

By postponing the signing of the Armistice Agreements and by the Soviet Armies advances into the territory of the ex-enemy states, many assets were captured, justified as soils of war.

Initially, the Armistice Agreements and supervision over their execution were to be established together with the Allied Control Commissions, composed of Moscow's representative, as chairman, and by one representative each from England and from United States. However, the formula of the Allied (Soviet) High Command was introduced in the Agreement with Bulgaria, Romania and Hungary the result being that the sole Allied Power was Soviet Russia. Any attempt on the part of the Western Powers for the respecting of the initial decision met with the obstacle of freedom of unilateral action, the result of Moscow's influence over these countries, granted her by these same Powers.

From the Armistice Agreements the clauses referring to navigation will be pointed out.[10] The Bulgarian, Romanian and Hungarian Governments had to give the Allied (Soviet) High Command "every possible assistance on land, on water and in the air," to assure "free movement" on their territories, "for use at its discretion during the armistice in complete good order and with the personnel required for their maintenance," and "...all military air and river fleet installations and buildings, ports, barracks, warehouses, air fields, means of communication and meteorological stations which might be required for military needs."

Aside from the spoils, the three countries had to surrender to that same Allied (Soviet) High Command the vessels owned by the States and the private ones under the national flag, as well as the German and satellite vessels found in the waters of those three countries. In this surrender were included also the United Nations national vessels found on the waters of those three countries, "...for use in the general interests of the Allies." All these vessels, with the exception of the war booty, were to be remanded to their owners at the end of the war.

The Allied (Soviet) High Command did not respect the clause, but continued to keep the vessels by obligating the governments of the three countries to requisition them and to support all the expenses of maintenance. The vessels of foreign ownership were supposed to be returned to their owners in good, navigable condition, with their complete initial inventory. The three countries were unable to respect the clauses, from financial causes as well as because the shipyards were unavailable for repairs, being at the disposition of the Russian Army for its use. Immediately after the Peace Treaties were concluded in 1947, a number of vessels in navigable condition were rented by the Russians, the rental being paid for by the Commission for the Application of the Armistice Agreements of Bulgaria, Romania, and Hungary. Futhermore, Romania — in order to supply Russia transport needs — was forced to apply requisition Law No. 3983, imposed by Germany in 1940.

The delay in returning the vessels owned by citizens of the Allied and Associated Powers was also due to three other main causes, namely; the disorientation of the communist regimes in Bulgaria, Romania, and Hungary, which unable to satisfy the Russian demands with their own national fleets, had to abusively requisition those of foreign ownership; the obligation of the three countries to contribute a quota of 50% of the fluvial inventory of the new Joint Companies established by the Russians, because of an insufficient number of national vessels, these countries had to requisition some foreign vessels in order to fulfill that quota; delays in resuming the diplomatic relations of these countries with the Allied and Associated powers, a situation which gave the communist regimes the opportunity to justify the delay in fulfilling the conditions of the 1947 Peace Treaty.

In turn, some of the Allied and Associated Powers conditioned the resumption of diplomatic ties to the fulfillment of the conditions of the Armistice Agreements and the peace treaties, the reimbursement for foreign shipowners having been assigned to the three conquered nations, Bulgaria, Romania, and Hungary.

In general, the method for carrying out the Armistice Agreements was confusing, since the Commissions for their application established in the three countries were disturbed by the frequent abusive interference from the Allied (Soviet) High Command.

Juridically, the Armistice Agreements ended with the signing of the Peace Treaties with Bulgaria, Romania and Hungary. Actually, however, the use by Soviet Russia of their fluvial fleets, naval shipyards and all the marine services continued in the framework of the Mixed (Joint) Companies.

The Joint (Mixed) Companies.

On the basis of the 1918 Treaty of Bucharest, Germany and Austro-Hungary were to exploit the Romanian fluvial fleet, shipyards, port installations, etc. by forced ceding and at symbolic rental fees. At the end of World War II, Soviet Russia applied the same method to the conquered Danube countries and, in an easier form on Yugoslavia, a friendly nation. To carry this out, mixed or joint companies were organized; Soviet-Bulgarian, Soviet-Romanian, Soviet-Hungarian, and Soviet-Yugoslavian.

The origin of the Joint Companies can be included in the much disputed problem of the German, Austrian, Bulgarian, Romanian, and Hungarian assets, a problem that was analyzed juridically, politically, and economically in a documented work by Professor Stephen Gorove, "The Law in Politics...."

Supposedly, the establishment of the Joint Companies was within the framework of the Agreements for economic collaboration with the countries that had been the former satellites of Germany, on an equal level. In reality, according to their juridic and economic structure, they were exclusively nuclei for exploitation. The agreements for their establishment seemed to have been concluded by the free will of the ex-enemy states to collaborate economically with Russia. This freedom was unilateral, Soviet Russia imposing her conditions on the method of collaboration.

Characteristic of the economic agreements between Soviet Russia, Bulgaria, Romania and Hungary, was the fact that they were concluded after the installation of the communist regimes in these three countries, by Soviet Russia. The Agreements were made up of three parts: the Central agreements for economic collaboration; the Protocol of the Agreement for economic collaboration; the Convention concerning the establishment of additional Joint Companies to exploit all economic sectors.

On the basis of the General Agreement, of the Protocol, and the Convention with Romania, a number of Joint Companies were successively established up to 1949, for the exploitation of the most important economic and commercial sectors. In Romania, they were call "Sovroms" (Sov for Soviet, Rom for Romanian), each bearing the suffix of the object exploited.

Establishment of the Sovromtransport (Soviet Romanian Navigation Company) took place by means of an Agreement signed at Bucharest on July 28, 1945.[11] The founders were the Soviet Union and Romania, the latter represented by the Romanian Fluvial Navigation (N.F.R.), the Commercial Administration of Ports and Water Communications, both of them State organizations, and the Romanian Danube Company (S.R.D.) a private corporation.

From the statutes of the Sovromtransport it appears that it functioned as a corporation under the jurisdiction of the Romanian Commercial Code. Its capital of three billion lei, represented by its inventory of liquid and fixed assets, was set at 600,000 shares, at

5,000 lei each; 50% being assigned to each part. Its attributes were administration, operation, construction, leasing and selling fluvial and maritime vessels, organization of fluvial and maritime transports of goods and passengers, with its own vessels as well as with vessels leased from private sources; operation and use of the maritime port of Constanta and of the fluvial ports of Galatz, Brăila and Giurgiu, with the right to lease or to operate their port installations; the establishment of leasing of holding in ownership enterprises for naval and dock construction, repair, etc.

Aside from its contribution of fluvial and maritime vessels, Romania put at its disposition: dock and silo installations in her fluvial and maritime ports; shipyards in the Danubian ports of Brăila, Galatz, Turnu Severin, Oltenita and the maritime port of Constanta: all the buildings, warehouses and establishments used previously by Romania.

Soviet Russia contributed not a single vessel or technical establishment of her own. Her contributions in vessels were only those captured during the war, vessels requisitioned by Romania during the war, and vessels leased by the Russians, the charged being paid by the Commission for Application of the Armistice. In the operations of Sovromtransport, the ports of Reni, Ismail and Kilia Veche, on the Kilia Branch, were not included inasmuch as they were considered to be under Russian sovereignty. The actual management by manager and vice-chairman was in Soviet hands, the Romanians holding only subordinate functions and Russian salaries were much higher than the Romanian ones.

Although the company operated under local regulations, it still benefited from a privileged fiscal treatment and from exemptions from customs taxes. Also regardless of the financial result of the operations, the Russian benefits were obligatory, the respective quota being transferred to Russia by deduction from the currency regulations of Romania. Soviet Russia also benefited from a quota share from the operations of the enterprises for supplying machinery and equipment for ports and hydraulic works, for construction and water communications and for distribution of electricity in cities. Through Sovromsantiere (shipyards) Russia received 50% of the net profit.

On the Lower Danube, there operated, aside from the vessels assigned to Sovromtransport, some small barges, wrecked during the war and repaired by their owners with primitive tools, in the hope of future return of normal navigation.

To suppress even this minor activity, the Communist regime took measures against the owners. The Mariners Syndicate imposed on the shipowners charges greater than their income and arrests for fictional acts of sabotage introduced terrorism. Because this small number of shipowners did not take under consideration the "invitation to participate in Sovromtransport," a condition required by the Protocol of the Russo-Romanian Agreement, the Ministry of Communications, under Communist leadership, issued on April 30, 1946 Decision No. 14802 on the basis of which any private activity was dissolved.[12] In accord with Article 4 of the Decision, private shipowners were obligated to surrender all the vessels they still possessed to the Sovromtransport company by May 15, 1946. The transfer was in the form of the economic requisitions established before the war by Decree No. 3983 of 1940, on the basis of leasing contracts concluded between Sovromtransport and the shipowners. In the case of refusal to comply, Sovromtransport was entitled to take immediate possession of the requisitioned vessels (Article 5).

Characteristic of these requisitions was the Sovromtransport company's privilege of drawing up the contracts with the proprietors of the vessels "by common accord." While the salaries of the crews and the maintenance of the vessels were the duty of the owner, their rights were set on the basis of "efficiency," Sovromtransport retaining the net profit to cover administration costs (Article 6). In other words, Sovromtransport benefited from the efficiency of leasing the vessels, regardless of whether their operation resulted in any profit for the owners. In this way, Russia's 50% quota of participation was assured.

Finally, by Romanian Law No. 119, of 11 June 1948 for nationalization of privately owned buildings, etc., were tranferred to State ownership and assigned to Sovromtransport without any compensation whatsoever. All the activity in the Romanian sector of the Lower Danube was carried on exclusively by Sovromtransport.

Joint companies similar to the Romanian ones were established also in Hungary, on the basis of the Hungarian-Soviet Agreement signed at Moscow on August 25, 1945. For navigation matters the Hungarian-Soviet Navigation Company (Meszhart) was established on the basis of a Special Agreement signed at Budapest on March 29, 1946.

In contrast to the port privileges acquired in Romania, Hungary ceded the port of Csepel, with the greatest number of modern installations serving all navigation, in the form of a thirty-year lease. Russian contributions to the Hungarian-Soviet Navigation Company were the Hungarian vessels found in Germany and Austria, returned to Hungary by the Allies.

In the framework of the same joint companies, one was established in Bulgaria on the basis of the Treaty for Commerce and Navigation, concluded at Moscow on April 1, 1948.[13]

In Yugoslavia, too, a Soviet-Yugoslav Shipping Company — Juspad — was established, on the basis of the Agreement of 4 February 1947. Aside from the absence of most of the privileges of the companies in Romania and Hungary, the Russians still held the leadership posts, retaining also the majority of financial benefits.

In a series of articles entitled "Thirty years after the Tito-Stalin Conflict" — a historical investigation with documents published for the first time, which appeared in Greece — certain data was given about de Soviet-Yugoslav economic Agreements, including the Soviet-Yugoslav Shipping Company, plus the company for operating certain economic sectors.[14] According to this source, the Soviet-Yugoslav Shipping Company had taken over the operation of the Yugoslav fluvial fleet on the Danube, composed of the best vessels, the administrative leadership being held by Russians.

As to leasing charges, it mentioned that while for transports of Soviet goods the freight charge was 0.19 dinars per KM Ton. For Yugoslavian ones it was 0.40 dinars.

At a meeting in March 1947, between Kardeli and Stalin, it was reported by the same newspaper that the former had rejected Russian conditions for establishing also other joint companies, because of "Economic as well as political considerations." Stalin's rely was "Very true. These joint companies are not for you; they are for the satellite countries..." Although Yugoslavia was not a satellite of Germany's, Joint Companies still were established, Yugoslavian opposition and the Tito-Stalin conflict terminated the Soviet-Yugoslav Joint Companies after only two years of existence (1949).

The opinions of certain researchers concerning the "economic collaboration" between Soviet Russia and her satellites in the joint companies can be conclusive. "The Soviet Union," noted Prof. Fischer-Galati, "established the bases for exclusive economic exploitation of Romania in May 6 1945."[15] In connection with the same "collaboration," Prof. Hugh Seton-Watson refers to Soviet Russian terminology: while economic collaboration between some Great Powers and smaller nations is described by Soviet Russia as "imperialism," that between her and her satellites in "socialist comradeship."[16]

As to that same exploitation, Milovan Djilas, formerly a great admirer of Stalin, later his critic, wrote that the wealth of the East European countries "was being extracted in various ways, most frequently through joint-stock companies in which the Russians barely invested anything except German capital, which they had simply declared a prize of war."[17]

"The creation of a series of joint Soviet-Romanian companies — the so-called Sovroms — for the 'exploitation and development of Romania's natural resources and industries,' " notes Prof. Stephen Fischer-Galati, "was tantamount to Russian control of the Romanian economy."[18]

Undoubtedly, Russia realized great financial profit from the joint companies she established in the Danubian countries. At the same time, through these companies she gained ample data concerning the economic systems of those countries. It is very possible that these companies might have acquired a permanent character, had they not been prematurely abolished by Yugoslavia; a precedent which the other satellite countries of Soviet Russia could not overlook.

In 1954, Soviet Russia decided to liquidate all the joint companies, concluding special Agreements with Bulgaria, Romania and Hungary, on the basis of which these three countries would pay the 50% quota of Russia's participation.[19]

Even after the liquidation of the joint companies, Russia benefited from other measures of "collaboration" with her satellites. Thus, the shipyards of Bulgaria, Romania, Hungary and even of Bratislava (Czechoslovakia) constructed vessels deliverable at ridiculously low prices, as indicated by Moscow, for the new socialist regime of Egypt, Syria, Yemen and some African states. Aside from the productions of the shipyards, the exploitation also extended to other economic sectors. As to the "efficient economic collaboration" between Soviet Russia and her satellite countries, in Romania there circulated the following saying: "The cow grazes in Romania and is milked in Russia."

Legitimacy of the Joint Companies?

The legitimacy of the establishment of the joint companies can be considered under the formula of a privilege created by a unilateral decision, that of Soviet Russia, without the opposition of the riparian countries, her satellites. The illegitimacy consists in its violation of a basis principle of internationalization of water communication lines, that of common interest, especially the principle of excluding any privilege and the application of a regime of equality of treatment for vessels of all nations. This was the principle of internationalization of navigation established by the Act of Vienna in 1815, the respecting of which was imposed by all treaties, conventions and Acts of navigation on the past. In this matter there can be cited the 1857 Act of Navigation, through which Austria and the riparian countries were to take over the administration of the international regime of navigation for the Danube, as fixed by the 1856 Treaty of Paris.

In view of incorporating the Act of Navigation within the principles of 1815, Austria had to withdraw privileges accorded until then to the most important navigation company (Erste Donau Dampfschiffahrtsgesellschaff, DDSG). In this same connection, the cancellation of the concession accorded to the French Magnan Company on the Siret and the Prut Rivers can also be mentioned.

By the 1921 Convention for the Definitive Statute of the Danube, instead of privileges, there were accorded vessels of other flags than the national one, generous port liberties, liberties which after 1945 were included in the monopoly and at the discretion of the joint companies. An exception to this Convention which could be considered actually a privilege, was the cabotage traffic of national vessels between ports of the same riparian state. The rest of the navigation on the international course of the Danube, (the thalweg) was not included in any restriction or in any privilege.

The privileges and exceptions to financial and national customs regulations of the Joint Companies were similar to those of the European Commission of the Danube, up to 1938, although Tsarist Russia had criticized them in the past, a position taken also by Soviet Russia.

By supposition, a correlation could be made between Russia's initial opposition to including the international regime of navigation in the Peace Treaties of 1947 and, for example, the establishment of the joint companies. Proposing the exclusivity of the riparians in establishing the regime and the method of organizing the navigation system, Russia could have imposed any measures she desired on the riparians.

In order to preclude any obstacle before the treaties were completed, Soviet Russia initiated the idea of economic collaborations in the framework of which were founded the joint companies, "legitimate" by free agreement, concluded with the "independent" satellite countries "liberated" by her. After the cancellation of the joint companies, the collaboration continued under the auspices of the "Comecon," another body established and conducted by Russia. Through the juridic and economic structure of this organization, existing today, any foreign presence (capitalist) in the economy of the satellite countries

THE ARMISTICE AGREEMENTS 583

is eliminated, Thus, regarding navigation, the proposal regarding the right of foreign commercial companies to establish headquarters in Danube ports, in the American Project for a new Danubian Convention, presented to the Belgrade Conference in 1948, was rejected although the idea had been provided in the past by the 1921 Convention for the Statute of the Danube.

The illegitimacy of the Joint Companies can be tied in with the "legitimacy" of Soviet Russia's political protectorate over the satellite Danubian States.

Chapter 3

NEGOTIATIONS REGARDING THE NEW REGIME OF NAVIGATION AND ITS INCLUSION IN THE PEACE TREATIES WITH SOME OF THE EX-ENEMY DANUBIAN STATES

Introduction.

The negotiations over the new regime, as well as their results, present certain discordances. While England, France and the United States proposed the application of the principles of the international regime established in 1856, that is, the participation in the new regime and control over its application also by non-riparians, Soviet Russia insisted and obtained the respecting of the 1815 Act of Vienna, exclusively for riparians.

Just as after World War I, the new regime was established exclusively by the Great victorious Powers, without the effective participation of all the riparian countries, Austria, Bulgaria, Germany, Romania and Hungary, these being obliged to accept the decisions made in their name by the Great Powers.

The predominant positions in these negotiations were held by Soviet Russia and the United States of America; England and France — the states which had proposed keeping the regime established — being more reserved.

With all its lack of commercial interest on the Danube, the position of the United States was the result of the intent to reestablish the European economy as quickly as possible by incorporating in it also the economies of the Danubian countries with the effective participation and collaboration of the Great Powers. In the spirit of this idea, the United States, England and France insisted upon including, in the peace treaties with the Lower Danube countries and Hungary, details of the provisions with respect to the complete freedom of navigation for all nations.

Initially Soviet Russia rejected the detailing of these provisions, but ultimately accepted a restricted listing. This was a repetition of Tsarist Russia's measure taken in the Treaty of San Stefano; a measure modified by the detailing of the navigation regime in the 1878 Treaty.

In the negotiations preceding the concluding of the Peace Treaties, as well as in those during the Paris Peace Conference, Soviet Russia succeeded in imposing her points of view by dint of controversial and lengthy discussion, far into the night, exhausting the participants of the Western Bloc Nations.

The First Initiative Regarding Freedom of Navigation on the Danube River.

The first initiatives, preliminary to establishment of the new international regime for navigation on the Danube, were those which referred primarily to the needs of the military occupations in Germany and secondarily to economic needs. For this purpose, an Agreement was concluded in London, in May 1945, for the establishment of a Provisional Organization for European Inland Transport. After the Potsdam Conference in 1945, and following a new Agreement, also of London, this organization took on the name of "European Central Inland Transport Organization" (ECITO).[20]

President Truman, in his report to the nation on August 9, 1945, declared: "One of the persistent causes for wars in the last two centuries has been the selfish control of the waterways of Europe, I mean the Danube, the Black Sea Straits, the Rhine, the Kiel Canal and all inland waterways of Europe which border on two or more states";

"The United States proposed at Berlin that there be free and unrestricted navigation of these inland waterways. We think this is important to the future peace and security of the world. We proposed that regulations for such navigation be provided by international authorities";

"The function of these agencies would be to develop the use of the waterways and assure equal treatment on them for all nations Membership in the agencies would include the United States, Great Britain, the Soviet Union and France, plus those states which border on the waterways";

"Our proposal was considered by the Conference and was referred to the Council of Foreign Ministers. There the United States intends to press for its adoption."[21]

Some remarks can be made concerning this report. By "the selfish control of the waterways," was Truman referring to the past policies of Austro-Hungary, England, Germany, France and Russia in setting the navigation regimes on the Danube?

As to establishing the regime on these waterways be the international authorities, which might have included the United States, Great Britain, the Soviet Union and France, plus those states "which border on the waterways...," Truman's idea ran counter to the principles of the 1815 Act of Vienna which, in the case of the Danube, left the establishment of the new regime exclusively to its riparians.

Indirectly, the new "agencies" referred to by Truman would have been similar to those established on the Danube after World War I, the European Commission of the Danube and the International Commission of the Danube. Soviet Russia could not agree with the establishment of any such agencies, a stand which she took even at the Conference of Vienna, in 1940, and that of Bucharest in 1940-1941. Under this aspect, Truman's declaration that "...our proposal was considered by the Conference (Potsdam) seems to have been futile," a fact later confirmed by Truman himself, noting that "Stalin did not want the internationalization of the principal waterways."[22]

As to Stalin's obstructions in this matter as well as in others discussed at Potsdam, even Truman, the peaceful, devout President, reached the conclusion known for centuries by Russia's neighbors that "force is the only thing the Russians understand."[23]

Faced with this opposition, the United States appealed also to the United Nations, where, on October 3, 1946, the Economic and Social Council adopted a resolution recommending the convoking of a Conference at Vienna, under the auspices of the United Nations and with the participation of all the allied riparian states and those citizens could prove having interests on the Danube, that is, non-riparians.[24] Besides the discussions over the new navigation regime, the Conference was also to resolve the problem of restitution of the vessels of the Allied and Associated countries found in the waters of the former enemy states.

On October 8, 1946, the Secretary General of the United Nations communicated the Resolution only to the following Allied States, which were being called to the Conference: England, Czechoslovakia, France, Greece, Soviet Russia and Yugoslavia. Although the Resolution had been adopted in the Plenary session of the United Nations, by a vote of 8 to 5,[25] Russia still rejected its application on the grounds that in a conference organized under the auspices of the United Nations, Russia's position would have been threatened by a majority of contrary votes. Yugoslavia and Czechoslovakia also subscribed to this rejection. Among Soviet Russia's objections was the lack of juridical basis on the part of the U.N. Economic and Social Council and on the part of the United States for being involved in Danubian problems, whose resolution was the attribute solely of the riparian states.

Flagrant deviations from the 1815 Act of Vienna appeared in the matter of establishing the new navigation regime. Attributing to riparian states exclusivity in establishing the new navigation regime, Soviet Russia did not understand also the participation of Germany and Hungary at the Conference proposed by the Economic and Social Council. From among the riparians she accepted only Yugoslavia and Czechoslovakia, allied countries and her concluding of the peace treaty with her, a decision which she herself kept postponing.

This stand against Germany was adopted, in part, also by the United States. The latter, on the basis of the proposals made by the Economic and Social Council, recommended the participation on the Danube of all vessels under their own national flag, with the exception of German ones.[26] By the fact that, due to that same recommendation, participation at the proposed Conference referred "all interested states," the result was that Austria, Germany and Hungary were not invited to the Conference, in spite of their riparian status: not being considered "interested" in Danubian traffic. As to discussing restitution of boats, the Soviet Russian Delegate in the Economic and Social Council rejected Greece's participation, on the grounds that he knew nothing of her interests on the Danube.[27] The fact that the Council also accepted the point of view that there was no proof of the existence of Greek vessels in the Lower Danube, seems curious.[28] Both positions were completely unfounded, in view of the fact that the Greek fluvial flag was present on 30 to 50% of the vessels on the Lower Danube River.

The Negotiations Regarding the Inclusion of the New Regime for Danube River Navigation in the Peace Treaties.

Resolving the establishment of the new navigation regime and its inclusion in the peace treaties with Bulgaria, Romania and Hungary became the responsibility of the Council of Foreign Ministers and of the Economic Commission for the Balkans and Finland, within the framework of the Paris Peace Conference of 1846.[29]

At the April 25 to May 6 16, 1946 meeting of the Council of Foreign Ministers in Paris, the United States Delegation proposed the following clause relating to the Danube, to be included in the Peace Treaty with Romania, as in the treaties with Bulgaria and Hungary "Freedom of navigation and commerce on terms of entire equality to the nationals, vessels of all states; sanitary, police and other laws and regulations applicable to the Danube River; non-discrimination tolls; and Romania shall enjoy a status equal to that of the other states."

The text which was to be applied to Bulgaria and Hungary was identical to the one proposed in common by the United States and England at the Peace Conference.[30]

England added to this proposal that, within a period of six months of the treaty's coming in force, a conference of all interested states establish the new permanent international regime for the Danube.[31]

In general, the Anglo-American proposal contained the navigation principles established by the Peace Conference of World War I, given concrete expression by the 1921 Convention for the Statute of the Danube, evaluated by the Western Powers as partially valid. The evaluation of the 1921 Convention is also evident in a statement made by Jebbe, a member of the British Delegation in the Economic Council for the Balkans and Finland. He stressed the fact that the Convention "...was still in force and would remain in force until modified by common consent."[32]

Soviet Russia disagreed with the Anglo-American proposal on the consideration that the question of the Danube could not be solved by the Peace Treaties with Romania, Bulgaria and Hungary, since it had to be settled with the participation of the Danubian states which included Allied States such as Czechoslovakia and Yugoslavia.[33]

Not reaching any accord either in the June 15 to July 12, 1946 meeting of the Council of Foreign Ministers, the problem was taken up again by the Economic Commission for the Balkans and Finland to which was sent also the common Anglo-American proposal and the Soviet Russian counter proposal. Put to a vote, the proposal of the Soviet Union received five votes for and 9 against.

In spite of the favorable result for the Anglo-American proposal, a decision was made to take into consideration the compromise proposal presented by the French Delegation in the Economic Commission for the Balkans and Finland.[34] This proposal contained the following: "freedom of navigation on terms of entire equality to the nationals, vessels of commerce and goods of all states, and the meeting of a Conference of the Four Powers and the Danubian States, with the object of establishing a new international regime for the Danube." Put to a vote, this proposal received 8 votes in favor and 5 against.[35]

The Economic Commission for the Balkans and Finland, being unable to submit a recommendation for the inclusion of Article 34 in the Draft Peace Treaty with Romania, referred this question to the plenary Conference for their decision.[36]

It must be observed that the proposal of the French Delegation did not have the character of a compromise formula, inasmuch as — with the addition of some supplementary words — it corresponded with the common Anglo-American proposal rejected by Soviet Russia. The French Delegation's proposal was the same, as regards Article 32 of the Treaty with Bulgaria and Article 33 of the Treaty with Hungary (Draft Peace Treaties).

Statements or reservations in connection with the Anglo-American proposal and that of the French Delegation were made by Belgium, Greece, Poland and Yugoslavia.[37]

Belgium and Greece associated themselves with the principles laid down in the Anglo-American proposal, which aimed at the establishment of a system of freedom and equality for navigation on the Danube. As to the Conference proposed by England, both states reserved their rights as signatories of the Paris Convention of 1921, establishing the Statute of the Danube. In other words, they agreed to participate at the Conference which would set the new regime. In addition, Greece pointed out the importance of Greek shipping in Danubian traffic.

Although the Polish Delegation was not a member of the Economic Commission for the Balkans and Finland, still in the Plenary Session of the Conference it made a declaration regarding Article 34 of the Peace Treaty with Romania, considering that Poland, situated near the Danube, made use of navigation for foreign trade. While agreeing that the navigation regime should be established exclusively by riparian states, the Polish Delegation still asked to participate in any international arrangements which might possibly affect a problem of such importance for the national economy of Poland.

The Yugoslav Delegation in the Economic Commission for the Balkans and Finland considered that the new Conference and the Commission were not competent to decide anything in connection with the regime of the Danube, and that not one of the delegations which voted in favor of the French proposal represented a riparian state and no decision could be binding on Yugoslavia.

The Price of the "bargain."

The debates, proposals and counterproposals over the establishment of the new regime of navigation and its inclusion in the Peace Treaties with Bulgaria, Romania and Hungary, passed through a maze which, omit to get out of, demanded recourse to a real "bargain," the price to be supported by the Western Powers and the three Danubian States.

In the past disputes between the Anglo-French-Austrian bloc and Tsarist Russia over the problems of the Danube, the pressures of the bloc were decisive; those after World War II between the Western Powers and Soviet Russia, are characterized by the United States, England and France yielding to the Soviet Pressure. By yielding, in apparent compromise, the Western Powers were aiming at getting Russia's agreement in the establishment of the new navigation regime and a conference for working out the details, in the hope of finding a solution corresponding with their points of view.

They yielded on the point to not invite to the negotiations for establishing the new regime: Belgium, Greece and Italy, the three states signatories to the 1921 Convention. Austria was admitted to the Conference, but only with consultative vote; Germany was excluded.

Initially, the Western Powers had understood that the new regime would take into consideration some principles of the Convention of 1921, but they ended up with rhetorical interpretations and protests. The causes for yielding were in matters of political and commercial interests of each of the Western Powers.

The principal position of the United States was to reach a reasonable understanding. Towards this aim the following factors concurred: lack of commercial interests on the Danube; the desire to establish in the Danube valley "an area of constructive cooperation," as Secretary of State George Marshall stated it.[38]

England and France, in yielding, hoped to be retained in the administration of the new regime, as ones that had been present there since 1856.

The "bargaining" seemed to develop on a scale whose gradations of measurements depended upon the weights put in by the opposing groups. When the weights of the Western Powers lowered the scale, those of soviet Russia were raised, benefiting from the yielding. Thus through oscillations of the scale was born the new regime for navigation, as conceived by Soviet Russia.

The Navigation Clause of the Peace Treaties of 1947.

Following new discussions, the four Powers of the Council of Foreign Ministers, through the Separate Declaration of December 12, 1946, reached the following formula with regard to the new regime of navigation and its inclusion in the Peace Treaties with Bulgaria, Romania and Hungary: "Navigation on the Danube shall be free and open for nationals, vessels of commerce, and goods of all States, on a footing of equality in regard to port and navigation charges and conditions for merchant shipping. The foregoing shall not apply to traffic between ports of the same State."[39]

A text identical with this formula was included in the Peace Treaties concluded with the three Danubian States, at Paris, on February 10, 1947, entering in force on September 15, 1947.[40] From this resulted the failure of the Western Powers to add any details to the new regime for navigation.

The same Declaration called for a new conference at which would participate England, France, Soviet Russia, the United States and the countries riparian to the Danube: Bulgaria, Czechoslovakia, Romania, Yugoslavia and the Ukraine.

The economic articles of these treaties referred to reparations, compensations and restoration of goods (referring to fluvial vessels), of United Nations national (individuals, corporations or associations) which, under the laws in force during the war, had been treated as enemies.

Getting Soviet Russia's agreement to the December 12, 1946 Declaration was considered a success by the Western Powers; one writer even wrote of the Agreement as one that came from "a new spirit of cooperation which seems to be reshaping Russian diplomacy."[41]

The same Agreement was described by Secretary of State Byrnes as "a reasonable compromise."[42] This description is not surprising considering its author's lack of knowledge of the essence of Moscow's policies and of the real situation in Eastern Europe. It is said that for his information he consulted books on international affairs and the advice of Cavendish Cannon, called urgently from Lisbon "to brief Byrnes on Eastern Europe."[43]

It seems that later Byrnes changed his views. In his book, "Speaking Frankly" (1947, pp. 281 - 282) he calls attention to the fact that it "...must be kept in mind in evaluating any Soviet action" that "...to Russians, the end justify the means."

THE ARMISTICE AGREEMENTS 593

Regarding traffic "between ports of the same state," respectively the cabotage navigation, mentioned at the end of the new clause for the navigation regime, certain contradictions can be seen from the former positions of England and France.

Among the principal reasons for England and France rejecting the 1857 Act of Navigation presented by Austria in the name of the Riparian Commission, was the reservation of cabotage to the riparian countries, a position subscribed to even by Tsarist Russia.

In 1921, at the establishment of the Convention for the Definitive Statute of the Danube, the same two Powers (Russia being absent) succeeded in obtaining certain freedoms in cabotage navigation which had been proposed by the riparians as exclusively their right.

The modifications later requested by the Western Powers at the 1948 Belgrade Conference, were rejected, being considered "imperialist" interference in the sovereignty of the riparians. According to the Convention concluded at Belgrade (Articles 23 and 24), freedom of cabotage depended on each riparian.

Chapter 4

THE 1948 BELGRADE CONFERENCE

"Les portes servent autant pour l'entrée que pour la sortie."
A. Vishinsky, addressing to the Western Powers at the Belgrade Conference of 1948.

"Nous ne sommes pas sortis; nous sommes restés, nous efforçant chaque jour de persuader la Conférence de faire quelques choses vue d'un véritable accord."
C. W. Cannon (U.S.A.) at the Conference of Belgrade.

Introduction.

The Conference of Belgrade in 1948, as well as the new Danube Convention established by it, can be considered a new principal turning point in the history of the Danube Question.

The Conference, besides its disregard of any diplomatic and traditional rules for international meetings, with respect to the participants rights of expression, was directed by a single leader, Soviet Russia. The Conference could be compared to a sporting match where the victory of one team — the satellite States, with prior instruction and discipline — is discretely decided by a single arbiter. The similar 1857 Conference of the Riparian Commission could be described in the same manner, under the aegis of Austria. The similarity between the two conference lies in their establishment of a navigation regime by riparians exclusively. The difference lies between the failure of that of 1857 and the success of that of 1948.

The results of the Conference were, if not known as least presumed; the dispute centering about the details of the proposed navigation regime established by the 1947 treaties was to be carried on between the minority bloc of the three Western Powers and the majority of seven, the Soviet bloc. In spite of the numerical discrepancy, the Western bloc hoped for some minimal concessions on the part of Soviet Russia.

As to those concessions, J.C. Campbell wrote "...on the surface, the Western Powers won a victory," but he added, "actually, the Soviet Union made only paper concessions" and "...nothing in past history or in recent Soviet diplomatic conduct led one to believe that the USSR was ready to agree to an effective regime guaranteeing freedom of navigation on the Danube."[44]

Faced with the hostile atmosphere in which the Western Powers tried to sustain their points of view, the question arises as to why they were present at Belgrade. They could not withdraw since they themselves had proposed meeting in a conference to establish a new navigation regime, with the participation of riparian and non-riparian states.

The presence of the United States at the negotiations for establishment of the navigation regime on the Danube and at the Conference of Belgrade was due to a number of considerations. In the first place, the U.S. sought application of the Truman Doctrine, for complete freedom of navigation on international waterways including the Danube, in view of the reestablishment of the European economy. In the second place, there was hope of an eventual diminuation of Moscow's obstructions and adoption of an attitude of negotiation more on the order of those generally used at conference of international character. In the third place, Washington had expected a stronger attitude on the part of the other Western Powers. J.C. Campbell mentioned three reasons for the decision that the U.S. participate in and continue to remain at the Conference, even after Vishinsky's threat to exclude the Western Powers.[45]

The first reason he attributed to the desire of the United States not to appear before world opinion in the position of "bad sports who would participate in international congresses only when in a majority." The second reason was that "...its proposals for a new Danube regime were based on the permanent interests of all nations, including the Danubian nations, in a maximum flow of trade on the river, proposals to get them on record... even if the assembled communists voted them down without a single thought." And finally, the third reason: "...the United States wished to give Vishinsky full opportunity to show the world how a Soviet Delegation conducted itself when it held the whip hand." J. C. Campbell also mentioned — still in connection with the U.S. participation—"...it was a decision which may have been taken without full consideration of all the political consequences."[46]

Despite all the obstacles, the American Delegation presented the Project for a new Danubian Convention on the stage of a Conference whose leader, instead of coordinating the ideas and counter ideas of the participants in order to obtain a synthesis, used the whip hand.[47]

The proposals of the American Project were not substantially different from the navigation regulations set by the 1921 Convention. They became futile in the face of the Project dictated by Moscow. "The Project of the American Delegation" — states Campbell — "overemphasized the technical side of its preparation at the expense of the political. Moscow did not send Vishinsky to Belgrade to negotiate on port charges and docking facilities."[48]

In exchange, the French and English Delegations, presented no project. They restricted themselves to bringing up principles from the past, with the aim of obtaining their previous positions on the basis of the 1921 Convention for the Definitive Statute of the Danube, which they considered still in force, or at least to obtain some advantages thereby.

As to the atmosphere at the Conference, it can be observed that the representatives of the Western Bloc, as well as those of the Moscow bloc, made use of un-protocol like expressions.[49]

The Opening of the Conference and the Problem of its Participants.

After many delays as to the date and location of the meeting for the Conference as proposed by the December 12, 1946 Declaration of the Council of Foreign Ministers, it finally took place at Belgrade between July 30th and August 18, 1948.[50] The significance of the site chosen could be attributed to its geographic location at the middle of the entire course of the river.

There were disagreements as to the official language to be used during the debates. The use of English, in Vishinsky's opinion, "...put some Delegations in a minority"; he proposed French and Russian as official languages, a proposal adopted by the Conference with a vote of 7 to 3.[51] The statements of some Delegates were in French or in their native language, others in Russian, the respective texts being translated into Russian and French by the Secretary of the Conference. The English texts of the Western Powers were translated into French and Russian.

The discourses of Vishinsky, chief of the Russian Delegation, were clear, comprehensive and detailed. Those of the French and English

Delegates contained frequent repetition of arguments in support of their past positions on the Danube. The points of view of the chief of the U.S. Delegation were expressed concisely, clearly and comprehensively. Aside from the statements of the chiefs of the Hungarian, Yugoslavian, Bulgarian and Czech Delegation, the statements of Anna Pauker, chief of the Romanian Delegation, were in Russian, mainly in criticism of former Romanian political figures; the essence of her statements being of a propagandistic nature in favor of Soviet Russia.

Vishinsky's discourses and those of the Delegates of the satellite countries were printed in entirety in the official presentation of the work of the Conference, by the Ministry for Foreign Affairs of Yugoslavia. Those of the Delegates of the Western Powers were printed in summary and some of the remarks of the head of the English Delegation were given under the mention "...d'après des sténogrammes non-officiels" of the General Secretariat of the Conference, made up of representatives of the satellite States. The presidency of the Conference had been held in rotation by each of the heads of delegations.

Vishinsky's behavior was totally un-protocol-like. He addressed Delegates of the Western Powers with expressions such as "les portes servent autant pour l'entrée que pour la sortie."[52] While at first England's and France's Delegates were ready "to take a walk," finally all three Western Powers "wished to maintain solidarity at least to the point of staying on or quitting together.[53] They participated in fact at all the Conference meetings.

On the Agenda of the Conference there were three principal themes, namely: establishment of the new regime for navigation, exclusively by riparians, by excluding non-riparians; defining the international principle of navigation; and validation or invalidation of the 1921 Convention for the Definitive Statute of the Danube.

Soviet Russia, through the voice of V. Clementis, Czechoslovakian Delegate, on August 11, 1948, stated the following: "There is a substantial difference between free navigation and an internationalized river. Internationalization means equal treatment for riparians and non-riparians and this is a principle we cannot accept. As far as we are concerned, there is no longer any internationalization of the Danube. There can be no equal treatment for riparians and non-riparians. When we speak of free navigation, we mean navigation under the control of the riparians. The internationalized system is a system of the past and we are replacing it with riparian control."[54]

This purely rhetorical statement was contrary to the general principle of freedom of navigation as provided for in the peace treaties with the three ex-enemy Danubian countries, treaties signed also by

Soviet Russia. The statement could also be considered a political strategem of Soviet Russia in her interpretation of the international principle of navigation.

The differentiation made by Clementis as to "free navigation and an internationalized river" can refer to rivers crossing a single territory where navigation is free exclusively for national flags, but when by the principle established by the treaties of 1947 provision was made for navigation for "all states," it signified that the river was internationalized.

The contradiction appears also in the assertion "there can be no equal treatment for riparians and non-riparians," when that very same principle of the treaties of 1947 provided for "...footing of equality in regard to port and navigation for merchant shipping." Furthermore, none of the treaties of the past, signed also by Tsarist Russia had made any distinction between free navigation and international navigation, both being in conjunction. Clementis' only just idea was that concerning the "riparian control" of navigation, which could have been justified through the principles of the Act of 1815 and the exclusivity of cabotage navigation.

Representatives of the riparian countries, Bulgaria, Czechoslovakia, Hungary, Romania, Soviet Russia and Yugoslavia, and the Ukraine, participated in the Conference work, as did the non-riparian ones, England, France and the United States. Of the riparian countries, Germany was not invited, Austria had a single consultative vote. By the absence of these two riparian states, the Russian concept that "the Danube belongs to the riparians" fell.

The participation of England and France, non-riparians to the Danube, but signatories of the 1921 Convention, and that of the United States was due to the December 12, 1946 Declaration of the Council of Foreign Ministers.

Aside from the obstructions of Soviet Russia, the nonparticipation of Belgium and Greece, signatories to the 1921 Convention, was the fault of the Western Powers which, in the Council of Foreign Ministers Declaration of December 12, 1946 did not press for their being convoked. As to the legality of the states attending the Conference of 1948, some observations can be made.

In conformity with the participles of the Project for the Convention of 1948, the theme can be sustained that Russia was being deprived of her capacity as riparian on an equal footing with the other riparian states. By applying the new Convention only "à la partie navigable du Danube d'Ulm à la Mer Noire, en suivant le bras de Soulina avec accès à la mer par le Canal Soulina" (Article 2), did not also mean its application on the Kilia Branch also, through which Russia was a riparian, that branch being excluded from the range of the discussions of the Conference. Although the Kilia Branch in its geographic location is between Soviet Russia and Romania, the former regarded it as belonging under her political sovereignty and therefore was excluded from the international regime.

The only international fluvial portion of Soviet Russia is that section between the Prut River and the beginning of the Kilia Branch (at the point named Chatal Ismail), on the main course of the Danube. With such a portion of about thirty miles, Soviet Russia could not be entitled to consider herself an initiator in establishing the new regime, from Ulm to the Black sea, in the name of the riparian holders of greater fluvial distances.

This disproportion may have determined Moscow to set down, in Article 44 of the Project for the Convention, precise specifications of the qualifications of the riparian states in the sense of "un état danubien" or "un pays danubian" must hold at least one bank "...du Danube tel qu'il est défini à l'article 2." This shore is none other than the portion mentioned before, on the Ulm-Black Sea sector, as defined by Article 2.

The Ukraine's participation at the signing of the 1947 Peace Treaties, as well as at the Belgrade Conference of 1948, cannot be justified, the Ukraine being neither a Danubian state nor a Danubian country. Her participation seems paradoxical and contrary to the position of Tsarist as well as Soviet Russia; in neither of which was she considered a riparian to the Lower Danube.

In the 1812 Treaty of Bucharest, when Russia annexed Bessarabia, no mention was made of the Ukraine. Nor was it mentioned in the 1878 Treaty of Berlin or that of London in 1883.

At the Fifth World Congress of the Comintern on the National Question in Central Europe and the Balkans, "the separation of Ukrainian lands from Poland, Czechoslovakia, and Romania" and their union with the Soviet Ukraine was decided, and through it with the USSR.[55]

At the fifth session of the 1948 Belgrade Conference (August 4) Vishinsky declared that in the composition of the new Commission of the Danube, there would participate exclusively "des représentants des Etats danubiens maîtres des territoires traversés par le Danube."[56] Although the territory of the Ukraine is not crossed by the Danube, he still included her in the Conference.

At the last meeting of the Conference, Vishinsky changed his stand, stating that Soviet Russia was giving up two votes in the new Commission of the Danube, in which she would be present with only one member. That member would represent "les autres Républiques Soviétiques y compris l'Ukraine."[57] The fact that this renunciation was inspired, in Vishinsky's opinion, by the "principe d'égalité en droits de tous les pays danubiens..."[58] signifies that the Ukraine was not considered to be a riparian. This could explain the Ukraine's absence from the composition of the Special River Administration between the Mouth of the Sulina Channel and Brăila inclusive a Russo-Romanian body provided for by Article 20 of the Convention of Belgrade, in which the presence of Soviet Russia was justified as "being an adjacent riparian state," yet not as a true riparian.

Baranovsky, the Ukrainian Delegate, tried to justify his country's participation at the Conference because of "...les intérêts fondamentaux d'Ukraine en tant que l'état riverain de la Mer Noire et du Danube." He also mentioned the commercial and economic relations of the Ukraine with the riparian countries of the Danube, "...au cours de plusieurs siècles" and that in the tenth and eleventh centuries "la Principauté Ukrainienne de Galicie-Volhynie, par ses villes situées sur le Danube, les ports de Belgorode (Akkerman), Renn (Reni) et Kivetz (Kilia) faisaient un commerce actif avec Byzance et les Etats du basin danubien."[59]

Bringing up, in 1948, certain possible rights of the past would mean a difficult solutioning of the successive politico-territorial sovereignties during the course of history. During the Greek colonization in the hinterlands inland of the Black Sea and the Danube, the port of Akkerman (Turkish name) was Asprocastro (Cetatea Alba), a name kept by the Romanians and which, under the Genoese, was Moncastro. Taking into consideration the historic dates propounded by Baranovsky would mean invoking the rights of the Greeks, the Genoese and the Turks, former occupants of Southern Bessarabia, where the Ukraine was evaluated as a riparian. The lack of a riparian position for the Ukraine appears evident even in the specific works by members of satellite Countries in which, as is well known, concepts contrary to the policy and doctrines of Moscow are forbidden. After showing the superiority of the 1948 Convention as shown by the participation in the new "Commission of the Danube of only riparian countries," a Romanian author listed only the eight states riparian to the Danube, excluding the Ukraine,[60] (Germany, Austria, Czechoslovakia, Yugoslavia, Bulgaria, Romania, Hungary and the Soviet Russia). From what has been shown so far, it appears that before, as well as after, the 1948 Conference, the Ukraine was not considered riparian to the Danube. furthermore, in no geographic-political map of either Tsarist or Soviet Russia is it included as a riparian.

Austria's participation at Belgrade became an unresolved problem. Rosenberg, Austria's delegate, opposed his country's participation with only consultative vote. Referring to the December 1946 Declaration of the Council of Foreign Ministers, which had conditioned Austria's effective participation to the establishment of the new regime of navigation only after the signing of the Peace Treaty with Austria, he considered it actually unjustified discrimination that Austria, though not responsible for the delay, be placed in a position of inferiority in comparison with other ex-enemy states, satellites to Moscow, that had been admitted to the Conference with deliberative vote.

Rosenberg also referred to Austria's importance as a riparian which had the greatest interest to maintain freedom of navigation on the course of the Danube to the Black Sea. In the face of the inequitable and unjust treatment to which his country was subjected, he declared that the Austrian Government "...se réserverait le droit de faire connaître ultérieurement sa position envers un accord auquel il n'aurait pas pu collaborer sur un pied d'égalité."[61]

Cavendish Cannon, chief of the U.S. Delegation, upheld Rosenberg's position, stating, "...non seulement le Danube est important pour l'Autriche, mais l'Autriche est importante pour le Danube." He stated that among the motives for the direct participation of the United States in the Conference was also the provisional situation with respect to the treaty with Austria and the American occupation of Germany's zone crossed by a navigable sector of the Danube.[62] The Peake, England's Chief Delegate, reminded the Conference of his government's previous intervention to the Government of Soviet Russia requesting that Austria be invited to the Conference "...avec pleins droits," a request denied by Soviet Russia.[63]

The U.S. proposal that Austria be accorded participation in the conference "avec pleins droits y compris le droit de vote deliberatif" was rejected by a vote of seven (Soviet Russia and her satellites) to two (England and France) and one abstention (the U.S.). Austria was invited with only consultative vote.[64] With this vote, too, Soviet Russia belied her position of defender of the rights of all riparian states.

Chapter 5

THE VALIDITY PROBLEM OF THE DANUBE CONVENTION OF 1921

The debates at the Belgrade Conference over the validity or nonvalidity of the 1921 Convention for the Definitive Statute of the Danube were lengthy and controversial. There were two positions, diametrically opposed: That of the Western Powers which evaluated some of the 1921 principles as having to be taken into consideration in the drawing up of the new Convention of 1948, a position opposed to that of Soviet Russia who, with her satellites, considered the 1921 Convention as completely abrogated. In this confrontation, the position of England and France, although they had been firm and categorical, also contained some wavering. The position of the United States was more conciliatory proposing the solving of the problem through negotiation.

Following the course of the debates reveals frequent repetitions and insertions by delegates of both sides. In order to be followed more easily, they will be compressed here.

Among the causes for which Vishinsky considered the 1921 Convention abrogated was the fact that Russia had not been invited to the drawing up of that Convention. He accused England and France of excluding Soviet Russia from the make-up of the European Commission although Tsarist Russia had been a member in the past.[65] The composition of the European Commission of the Danube had not been established by the 1921 Convention, but by the Treaty of Versailles. In any case, through this latter treaty, as well as through the 1921 Convention, the composition was considered "provisional." The aim of this was to accord the possibility to any state to request its representation on the European Commission, on the basis of sufficient interests on the Danube. (Articles 4 and 7 of the Convention). Concerning this Convention, Vishinsky stated that it was nothing more than "un veto, proprement dit, dirigé contre la Russie Soviétique."[66] Vishinsky's point of view was justified in 1948, but not at the end of World War I and immediately after, when Soviet Russia, a new state barely established, found itself in a difficult situation. On the other hand, Russia's not being invited to the 1921 Convention was in direct connection with the General Peace Conference and the Peace Treaty of Versailles, in which she did not participate and on the basis of which was decided the convoking of the Conference for the establishment of the new Definitive Statute of the Danube in 1921.

It is said that in 1919, at President Wilson's proposal, the Supreme War Council had proposed inviting the Russians to the Peace Conference at Paris, but "Russia had made it known that she considered the Treaty of Versailles null and void."[67]

In Peake's reply, he called attention to the fact that Soviet Russia did not consider herself bound by the treaties concluded by Tsarist Russia, the treaties of 1856, 1878, 1883, on which Vishinsky in 1948 supported his country's rights on the Danube. Peake also stated the conditions of Article 4 of the Convention.[68] (1921).

France's position, as shown before, was to regain the rights due her on the basis of the 1921 Convention. At the second session of the Conference, Thierry — France's Delegate — declared that his Government intended to validate all the rights attributed to France by all past documents concerning the Danube, and that France would not consider herself bound by any new convention which did not consider "les droits acquis" of France as well as of the other Powers not represented at the Conference. Acceptance of these requests he considered the conditions sine qua non of France's participation at Belgrade.[69] Nevertheless, in spite of the rejection of his point of view, France still took part.

As to the "droits acquis," Thierry added that a juridic statute could not be unilaterally replaced, but only with the consent of all interested parties.[70] The juridic statute was the one established through the 1921 Convention and the interested parties were all its signatories.

To A. Bebler's statement (Yugoslavia) that contested the right of France to put conditions, Vishinsky attributed "certains intérêts" before which "la morale se tait," leaving it to be understood the imperialist interests of the Western Powers.[71]

Although Peake's statement contained the same considerations expounded by Thierry, it was rather confused. He did not refer directly to the 1921 Convention, but to the rights of its participants, including Belgium and Greece, to free navigation on the Danube.

Cavendish Cannon (U.S.A.) later stated that the new Convention "... tend arbitrairement à annuler celle de 1921" and that its content was contrary not only "...aux droits de certains Etats qui participent à cette Conférence, mais encore à ceux d'autres signataires de la Convention de 1921, comme la Belgique, la Grèce, et l'Italie."[72]

In his long discourse, Vishinsky answered vehemently to Thierry's statement, especially to the assertion that the signing of the new Convention be conditioned to respecting the "droits acquis"—a condition he described as an "ultimatum." Concerning the condition, he said, "ce n'est pas un langage de cooperation et de travail entre camarades...mais un langage de diktat."[73] As to Vishinsky's expressions, Thierry declared, "...un pareil langage...est celui de l'hysterie," and that his government "...ne bondira pas à ses claquements de fouet."[74] Cannon, in turn, described the evolution of the Conference, under the pressures of the Soviet Delegation and its satellites actually as baiting.[75]

As to the language of the Delegates of the Western Powers, Vishinsky declared: "...en ce qui concerne la Délégation Soviétique, je répète qu'elle rejette énergiquement ce langage comme étant déplacé à une Conférence internationale et elle n'examinera aucune proposition sous menace de pression de la part des Délégues des Etats Unis, de la Grande Bretagne et de la France..."[76] The pressure continued; however, throughout the Conference, it was being exercised by Soviet Russia and the representatives of her satellite countries.

The primary conditions for respecting and reestablishing the "droits acquis" in drawing up the Convention, were taking into consideration the principles of the 1921 Convention. The Western Powers upheld its validity, and in the case of its abrogation, obtained the agreement of its signers present at the Belgrade Convention, and in addition of the other three states: Belgium, Greece, and Italy, these not invited.

The position of Soviet Russia and her satellite bloc was opposed. Among their arguments was the total lack of mention of the 1921 Convention in the treaties which led to concluding the 1946 Declaration through which the decision was made to call the Conference of Belgrade. As a matter of fact, in that Declaration, "nothing was said as to the continued validity of the 1921 Convention," according to J.C. Campbell.[77]

Precise identification of those responsible for not inviting the three states was confused. Vishinsky maintained that the proposal to limit the number of states participating in the Conference was made in the Council of Foreign Ministers by the delegates of the Western Powers, while Peake attributed it to Molotov, a member of the same Council.[78]

Indirectly in support of Vishinsky's position came the American revised proposal which, wrote Gorove, "eventually led to a recommendation by the Paris Conference, excluding some of the signatures to the 1921 Convention from participation in the proposed Conference."[79]

The error, or lack of coordination in the position of the Western Powers in the negotiations preparatory to the 1946 Declaration strengthened the position of Soviet Russia. "A further net loss for the Western Powers," wrote Gorove, "from their legal point of view, was their failure to secure participation in the Conference for all the signatories to the 1921 Convention."[80] The attempts to correct the mistakes of the Western Powers were too late.

One of the arguments of Soviet Russia and of the satellites concerning the nullity of the 1921 Convention was based also on the doctrine of "rebus sic stantibus." Concerning the application of this doctrine, one author expressed the opinion that "...treaties are concluded with the conditions that the situations will remain the same and that a treaty can cease to be obligatory when the conditions existing when they were concluded were later subjected to changes essentially important for the relations between the contracting parties." The same author, however, maintained that this doctrine was not applicable in the case of the unilateral abrogation of treaties, "without the accord of the contracting parties to verify the changes of circumstances."[81] In the case of the 1921 Convention, its elimination would have been the result only of the consent of all its signers.

As to the accord of all parties, two precedents can be mentioned namely, the unilateral measure taken by Russia regarding the abrogation in 1870, of naval restrictions on the Black Sea imposed by the 1856 Treaty and the 1878 San Stefano Treaty. Both cases being considered as violating the principles provided by the 1856 Treaty, it seemed necessary to get the accord of the signers of this Treaty.

In the first case, the accord was reached by means of the 1871 Treaty of London, on the basis of the Protocol of 17 January 1871, and in the second case, by the 1878 Treaty of Berlin.

Invoking the doctrine of "rebus sic stantibus," in reference to the caducity of the 1821 Convention, corresponded with changing the political and economic conditions developed in the period between the establishment of the Convention up to the Second World War, conditions influencing the navigation regime existing on the Danube.

In 1935, Germany, denouncing the international regime of navigation established by the Treaty of Versailles, nationalized her fluvial sectors and, on March 11, 1938, because of the Anschluss, Vienna was no longer an independent Riparian State. That same Germany proposed replacing the international regime by bilateral accords between riparian by excluding non-riparians and abolishing the two Commissions established by the Versailles Treaty and the 1921 Convention. The revisionist acts of the Treaty of Versailles resulted in certain territorial modifications for the German, Italian, Bulgarian, Hungarian group. Czechoslovakia's riparian position was practically annihilated, and Bulgaria extended her fluvial sector. Yet, in 1940, by her reannexation of Bessarabia by force, Soviet Russia again became a riparian.

The Arrangement of Sinaia of 1938 and its consequent acts modified certain clauses of the Versailles Treaty and the 1921 Convention. The juridic powers of the European Commission were transferred to Romania and, in 1939, Germany was admitted into the composition of the Commission.

Before and during World War II, Germany had obtained supremacy over the Lower Danube and its mouths by suspending the international regime of navigation and abolishing the two Commissions. These modifications of previous conditions could be in favor of invoking the doctrine of "rebus sic stantibus."

Vishinsky referred the changes of conditions in the past to the creation of a new Convention, found to be necessary by the Council of Minister's Declaration of 1946, as well as to the establishment of the new regime for navigation by the Peace Treaties of 1947. Referring to political conditions under which the 1921 Convention had been drawn up, in comparison with the new, Vishinsky declared that "during new times one did not have to sing old songs" and that the "past no longer counted."[82]

As to the past, Bebler (Yugoslavia) referred to the "economic penetration of Western Powers on the Danube and the inability of the riparian states invoked by those same powers to themselves organize the technical conditions for navigation." Cannon answered by calling attention to Soviet Russia's effective and direct economic penetration by the establishment of Joint companies.[83] If the relative technical inability for the organization of navigation existed on the Lower Danube exclusively, nevertheless on the Maritime Danube, the creative development of navigation conditions belonged to the European Commission.

Clementis (Czechoslovakia) also referring to the 1946 Conference, stated that drawing up of a new Convention was due to "...un nouvel état de choses et la situation politique actuelle..." As to the new situation, he pointed out Soviet Russia's presence, "which took after World War II a position belonging to her, on the Danube," and that "...she brought to international relations the respect, sovereignty and states' rights without taking into consideration their power."[84]

In fact, Soviet Russia's presence on the Danube was real, but its effects were negative if one takes into consideration the dependence of the sovereignty and rights of the riparians on Moscow. Actually, their "independence" was very obvious in the Conference of Belgrade.

The question arises as to whether, during a war and after, provisions of previous treaties remain in force; in the case of the Danube, the old navigation regime. Soviet Russia's position as to the inoperability of the 1921 Convention, after World War II, raises the problem of the effect of war on treaties. In this matter Sinclair gives the opinion of an American judge: "International Law today," wrote the judge, "does not preserve treaties or annul them, regardless of the effects produced. It deals with each problem pragmatically, preserving or annulling as the necessity of war exacts. It established standards, but it does not fetter itself with rules. When it attempts to do more, it finds that there is neither unanimity of opinions, nor uniformity of practice."[85]

"This empirical approach to the problem," added Sinclair "leaves unsettled the question whether it is possible to categorize treaties and say that certain treaties are terminated, or whether it is necessary to base the conclusion reached upon the intention, express or implied, of the parties at the time of the signature."[86]

Referring to the existence of the international regime for navigation on the Danube as far back as 1856, Sinclair pointed out, "...seeing that the international regime of the Danube has been in operation for more than 80 years and had survived two major wars prior to 1939, the presumption must be that the framers of the 1921 Convention, in default of any specific provisions to the contrary, intended the new regime to be permanent and to survive any fresh outbreak of hostilities."

The survival of the regime established in 1856 was due to the superiority of England and France, which despite some minor modifications were able to maintain the initial principles of 1815, with which even Tsarist Russia agreed. If these two Great Powers had not been victorious in World War I, Germany and Austria would have applied an international regime of regional character, a position taken by Soviet Russia in 1948. Aside from the influence given to her over

Eastern Europe by the Western Powers, Soviet Russia succeeded in asserting her own points of view in reference to the "default of any specific provisions to the contrary" of the Convention of 1921, mentioned by Sinclair.

Referring to the doctrine of "rebus sic stantibus," interpreted by Soviet Russia as the basis for the new conditions resulting from the meaning of the Declaration of 1946 and the Peace Treaties of 1947, Sinclair states, "...it would appear doubtful whether these instruments create a new state of things incompatible with the intentions of the parties or the purposes of the original Convention."[87]

In that same matter, Peake proposed to the Conference that the International Court of Justice, or a special court to be set up by the United Nations, investigate "what international agreements relating to navigation on the Danube are now in force, and which states are party to them." The proposal was rejected by the majority of the Conference.[88]

In the past, exercise of the "rebus sic stantibus" doctrine in navigation problems on the Danube depended largely on the interpretation by England, France and Austro-Hungary. In 1948, at Belgrade, it depended exclusively and categorically on Soviet Russia. The word of the small riparian states in that problem depended and will still depend on the will of the Great Powers no matter which one.

The abrogation of the 1921 Convention as invoked by Soviet Russia was attributed principally to the concluding of the Sinaia Agreement and the admittance of Germany in the European Commission. Both of these actions were considered by Vishinsky to be violations of Articles 7 and 42 of the 1921 Convention. In his opinion, there was a direct connection both juridical and in application between these two articles.

Article 7 established that "the powers of the European Commission of the Danube can only come to an end as the result of an international agreement, concluded by all the States represented in the Commission." Article 42 provided that "revision of the Convention could take place if two-thirds of the signatory states so requested and specified the stipulations considered to be in need of revision."

As to the meaning of these articles, Sinclair said, "...these two Articles of the Convention are hard to reconcile, and it is possible to argue, as did the Soviet Delegate, that the two articles read in conjunction." (Articles 7 and 42) He concluded that the Convention could be "voidable, not void."[89]

Vishinsky argued that the Sinaia Arrangement was concluded only between three states represented in the European Commission, not with the fourth, Italy. Also, aside from these states, it was necessary to get the agreement of two-thirds of all the twelve state's signatories to the Convention, in conformity with the provisions of Article 42,[90] that is, twelve states.

His argument did not correspond with the facts inasmuch as, at the concluding of the Arrangement, the two-thirds percentage had been attained, England, France and Romania signed it; Belgium, Greece, Italy, Czechoslovakia and Yugoslavia adhered tacitly, in other words, did not make any objection verbally or in writing.

The Western Powers upheld the lack of connection between the two articles also on the consideration of the extension of the powers of the four component members of the European Commission. Peake declared "...if the powers of the European Commission of the Danube could have been ended on the basis of the provisions of Article 7, those same powers could have been modified all the more by those same members."[91]

In Vishinsky's opinion, violation of the 1921 Convention applied also to the admittance of Germany into the components of the European Commission, as being contrary to the provisions of Article 7 and 42. He omitted the fact that through the Conference of Vienna and that of Bucharest (1940 and 1941) the Soviet and German Governments proposed a common division of the administration of Danube navigation.

Application of Article 7 together with Article 42 in the case of the Arrangement and of Germany, was explained by the Western Powers with the principle "in toto jure genus, per speciem derogatur," in the sense that the special rule (Article 7) prevailed over the general rule in the interpretation of the treaties.[92]

Acknowledging that Article 7 "...contient une règle spéciale," Vishinsky still upheld the obligation to respect Article 42. He believed that this special rule was none other than the right of veto by the four states, and the Article 7 guaranteed and insured the interests of Great Britain and France, the privileges of the four states members of the European Commission of the Danube, and permitted them to hold in their hands the principal positions of command and control over all the navigation on the Danube.[93] This statement calls for some remarks.

The European Commission by its componence in article 7 did not "control" or "command" anything but the navigation on the Maritime Danube and not over all Danube navigation. The fluvial sector between Brăila and Ulm being under the jurisdiction of the International Commission of the Danube, was composed exclusively of riparian states. Vishinsky omitted the fact that exclusive "control," "privilege" and "command role" had been assigned to a Special River Administration on the Maritime Danube, as provided for by Article 20 of the new Project for a new Convention presented by him to the Belgrade Conference, and that in the new Commission of the Danube provided for by that same Project for the administration of the entire fluvial navigation of the Danube, Soviet Russia held the right of veto. Furthermore, in the eventuality that Soviet Russia were to enter into the European Commission, as she requested in 1934 the decision would have been made by five states which would not have exercised the "veto."

As to the problem of the conjuncture between the provisions of article 7 and article 42, one could ask whether by concluding the Sinaia Arrangement and the admittance of Germany in the European Commission, a "revision" would have been made as foreseen in Article 42, or a "modification" of the 1921 Convention? Solving the problem contains both positive and negative elements.

Article 5 of the 1921 Convention stipulated the exercise of the powers held by the European Commission of the Danube before the war, not changing any of them. The Additional Article to Article 42 provided for the accord of all signatories of the Convention in case the "elimination of the European Commission of the Danube were decided upon before the expiration of the five-year term."

The Sinaia Arrangement was not eliminated this Commission; some of its powers were reduced by being transferred to Romania. The fact that the 1921 Convention did not mention any eventual reduction of the Commission's powers can be attributed to a broader interpretation of Article 4.

If the admission of another state within the componence of the European Commission, as foreseen by Article 4 of the 1921 Convention, depended on a "unanimous decision taken by the Governments which themselves are represented in the Commission," those same Governments could all the more modify its technical and juridical structure.

From a brief presentation by Romanian Professor Gh. Sofronie can be seen the modifying character of the Sinaia Arrangement. "L'Arrangement de Sinaia est particulièrement intéressant par les modifications qu'il apporte à l'exercice des pouvoirs de la Commission Européenne du Danube. Cet act juridique international vise à harmoniser l'exercice des attributions de l'organism danubien avec le droit de souveraineté de la Roumanie."[94]

In reference to the admittance of Germany into the European Commission, the action was based on Article 4, justified by the commercial interests, along with the political one, as well as that of Article 346 of the Versailles Treaty, both referring to the "provisional" componence of the European Commission, the provisional status being made complete with the admittance of Germany.

The negative aspect of the Arrangement can be attributed to the modification of the jurisdiction of the European Commission on the Maritime Danube, in the exercise of its juridic and technical powers, as well as those over navigation police. These attributes making up the principal basis of the international regime for navigation as far back as 1856, it can be maintained that any modification of its structure should have been made in the presence of all signers of the Convention of 1921. All the arguments of the Western Powers regarding the lack of foundation for abrogation of the convention were rejected by the Conference of Belgrade.

Chapter 6

VISHINSKY'S COMPARISON OF THE 1948 CONVENTION WITH THAT OF THE CONVENTION OF 1921

At the fifth session of the Conference, (August 4th) Vishinsky spoke at length, comparing the project for the new Convention, presented by Soviet Russia, with that of 1921.[95] The basis for his documentation was the navigation regime provided for in the Peace Treaties of 1947 and the Declaration of the Council of Foreign Ministers, of December 12, 1946. Among other things, he stressed the special attention given by the Conference to the riparian states, bringing out the fact that the new Convention would eliminate the privileges provided in the 1921 Convention for non-riparian states, as well as for the members of the European and the International Commissions of the Danube.

Absolutely no clause of the 1921 Convention made provision for privileges for non-riparian states or for their vessels. As for the two Commissions, their members had diplomatic immunity, but this exception was provided for also by Article 16 of the new Convention, for the members of the new Special River Administration of the Maritime Danube, as well as for the employees of Soviet citizenship.

Vishinsky invoked the absence of any difference between the establishment of the new regime by the treaties of 1947 and the Article 1 of the 1921 Convention, or by the project for the new Convention. By this, he was referring to the freedom of navigation provided for in the new Convention for all flags, "on a footing of equality in regard to port and navigation charges..."

With the exception of the phrase "on a footing of equality," the Western Powers did not contest the provision of Article 1 of the new Convention. Their objections were in reference to the side effects of

613

the Soviet Russian monopoly created by means of the Joint Companies which, as Cannon remarked, "non seulement dominent les flottes danubiennes de différents pays, mais, ce qui est plus important, ont obtenue le contrôle de la plupart des ports et installations portuaires utilisables."[96]

Cannon's remark was justified also in reference to the discrimination in Article 41 of the new Convention, which provided that port operations could be carried out "en vertue d'accords avec les services respectifs chargés du transport et de l'expédition." These services were none other than the Joint Companies, whose privileges violated freedom of navigation "on an equal footing."

An important remark of Vishinsky's was that concerning "la notion même du Danube," which in the fluvial Danube system of the 1921 Convention, included navigation on the tributaries along with that from Ulm to the Black Sea.

Vishinsky justified the absence of the tributaries in the new Convention by the introduction of a single regime on the Danube, as well as "political and economic circumstances" without, however, identifying them. This omission left in suspension the application of the international regime on the Prut tributary, a partially navigable water between two states, Soviet Russia and Romania.

In support of his point of view, Vishinsky invoked the fact that the 1856 Treaty "limitait au Danube seul le système fluvial danubien," without tributaries. He overlooked the fact that this limitation was due to the fact that the international regime of navigation was introduced in 1856, on only a short sector of the Danube, between Sulina and Isaktcha, not on the entire course of the river where there are more tributaries. Still in the matter of the tributaries, Vishinsky also brought out the difference between the method of organizing navigation between that of the 1921 Convention and the new one. In the place of two Commissions, the European Commission of the Danube and the International Commission of the Danube, he revealed the new Convention's establishment of "une seule et unique Commission danubienne, composée uniquement des représentants des états danubiens...maîtres des territoires traversés par le Danube."

Including the tributaries by the 1921 Convention (Article 2) was decided on the basis of Article 331 of the Treaty of Versailles, on the consideration that their inclusion in the navigable network of the Danube, which serves naturally, both the right of access to the sea, through a number of states and that of reuniting two naturally navigable sections of that same watercourse. Between the new navigation regime of the 1948 Convention, evaluated by Vishinsky as much more effective than the past one or the 1921 Convention, there were no great differences, aside from two exceptions, both Conventions having three separate regimes.

In 1921, there were the following systems: the one for fluvial navigation between Ulm and Brăila, under the administration of the International Commission of the Danube; the difficult navigation system on the sector of the Iron Gates, included in the administration of that same Commission, but administrated in common with the two states riparian to the respective sector — Romania and Yugoslavia; and the maritime navigation regime between Brăila and the Mouths of the Danube, including the three branches of the river put under the administration of the European Commission of the Danube.

In 1948, by the new Convention, the former International Commission was replaced by the new Commission of the Danube; the Iron Gates under the administration of the same two riparian states; and, in place of the European Commission, the new Romanian-Russian Special River Administration which Vishinsky did not mention in the comparison he made. The exceptions were in the Convention of 1948. The Special River Administration was to function outside the jurisdiction of the new Commission of the Danube, and navigation on the Kilia Branch, under Soviet Russian sovereignty, was excluded from the international regime.

Keeping the common administration at the Iron Gates was justified by Vishinsky by the geographical consideration that the sector was located between two riparian states. He did not apply that same consideration, however also on the Hungarian-Czechoslovak sector between Gabacikova and Gonyii, where navigation came up against the same physical obstacles as those at the Iron Gates. The Czechoslovak and the Hungarian Delegations proposed that there be added Annex III at Article 4 of the Project for Soviet convention (sic), in which the Commission for the Danube could "discuss" the establishment of a separate administration on that sector.[97] The proposal was rejected by the Russian Delegation and by those of the other satellite nations.

Vishinsky attacked the clauses of the previous treaties, as well as those of the 1921 Convention, regarding the placement of small warships of the states represented in the European Commission in order to supervise the application of the international regime of navigation. These clauses were only theoretical inasmuch as, after World War I, the presence of these vessels at Sulina was not a permanent one. They had no access upriver from Sulina, being only "en stationnement" as Vishinsky himself acknowledged.

Article 30 of the new Convention prohibited the navigation of actual warships, with the exceptions of those of the riparians on their own fluvial sectors, or beyond those limits with the approval of the other riparian states. Under this stipulation, the warships of Soviet Russia on the Kilia Branch could navigate also on other sectors, the approval depending on Soviet Russia's satellite states.

At the end of his comparison, Vishinsky stressed the fact that Soviet Russia had proposed "une Convention juste," based upon the "respect des droits souverains des Etats et des peuples danubiens, sur l'évincement de la position privilegiée dont jouissaient sur le Danube les Etats non danubiens..." Not rejecting the principle of freedom of navigation, he also stressed that "nous tendons à empêcher dans l'avenir tout abus de ce principe."

The statements of the satellite riparian delegations regarding the comparison, being simple paraphrasings of Vishinsky's points of view, do not merit repetition here, with the exception of that made by Anna Pauker, Foreign Minister of the Peoples Republic of Romania. She attacked the existence of the European Commission, which she termed a "Commission pretexte," with leanings towards domination of navigation.[98]

In connection with the attacks against the European Commission by Pauker (Romania), as well as by the Communist Government of Bucharest, an incongruous occurrence must be noted. In 1981, the Bucharest Government issued a series of postal stamps of different values, commemorating the 125 years of the presence of the very same Commission (1856-1981).[99] The same year, another series of stamps, also of various denominations, bearing the motto "European Navigation on the Danube"[100] was issued. Of some significance is the fact that, on the latter series, the Danube Delta is sketched, including the Kilia Branch of the river, considered by Soviet Russia as part of her territory.

Chapter 7

THE USA PROJECT REGARDING THE NEW CONVENTION

Of the Western Bloc Powers only the U.S.A. had Cannon present to the Conference the Project of a new Danubian Convention, which will be compared here with certain clauses of the 1921 Convention and with some of those of the Soviet Russian Project of 1948.[101] The English and French Delegations limited themselves to making amendments.

Before the presentation of the American Project and amendments, Vishinsky warned their authors that: "ceux qui ne seront pas d'accord (with the convention he proposed) seront obligés ou bien d'adhérer à la majorité, ou bien de se retirer. C'est leur affaire, c'est leur droit." ("Danube Conference of 1948," p.71).

As seen from Cannon's statement, the American Project was conceived in a spirit of negotiation and compromise. The Preamble of the Project took into consideration the navigation regime established by the 1947 Treaties with Bulgaria, Romania and Hungary; the December 12th Declaration of the Council of Foreign Ministers; and the encouragement of good economic and peaceful relations between nations, in accordance with the United Nations Charter. The objectives of the Project in developing the regime in the three treaties were: to activate the fluvial traffic and to attract the commerce of other countries to the Danubian ports; to eliminate any discrimination in the navigation and access of all flags in the fluvial ports; to establish a regime for navigation adapted to the fluvial system serving all states and coordinating the administration of the Danube with other international organizations through the United Nations. Between Article 1 of this project and that of the Soviet one relative to freedom of navigation and of the fluvial network, a discrepancy can be observed in its application. To the Soviet text referring to freedom of navigation, the American text added the expression "sans aucune discrimination" (sic), an expression which was not introduced in Article 1 of the 1948 Convention.

The American Project made provision for the access for all flags to the port installations, docks, quays and for operations for loading and unloading to be free in all ports (Article 3). This access was provided for in articles 10 and 20 of the 1921 Convention excepting for cases in which it was obvious that the necessities of the moment and the interests of the country demanded a derogation (Article 20).

In Article 41 of the 1948 Russian Project, access was conditioned "en vertu d'accords avec les services respectifs chargés du transport et de l'expédition." Hence, while in the 1921 Convention the eventual measure suspending these rights belonged to the State Powers, by the 1948 Convention the access depended on the approval of the Joint Companies which held the monopoly of all port installations. Navigation companies, regardless of their nationality, had the right to establish their own agents in all the Danubian ports, to carry out their activities (Article 4 of the American Project), a right that was a provision of the 1921 Convention (Article 20), but not of the Soviet Project.

By Articles 8 and 9 of the American Project, provision was made for the establishment of a Commission for the Danube, with jurisdiction over the entire navigable fluvial network. It was to be composed of the riparian states: Austria, Bulgaria, Czechoslovakia, Romania, the Ukraine, U.S.S.R. and Yugoslavia, in addition to the non-riparian ones: England, France and the United States. Each country was to have one representative. Germany was excluded from the riparian states; her acceptance in the Commission was to take place after the Treaty of Peace entered in force, or even before, by means of an accord with the parties of the new Convention.

The Cannon Project did not provide for the Special Fluvial Administration between Brăila and the Sulina Mouth, which in conformity with Article 20 of the 1948 Convention Project was to be composed exclusively of Romania and Soviet Russia. Hence, instead of the two provided for a single one for the entire Danube network.

By Article 20 of the American project, all contracting parties accorded the new Commission of the Danube the facilities for exercising its functions, and the right of free circulation for its personnel on the river and in all the ports.

The same contracting parties accorded the Commission the privileges and immunities which would be necessary for carrying out their duties (Article 24 of the Cannon Project). These rights were provided for also in Article 16 of the 1948 Russian Convention, with the difference that, in the Convention of 1921, diplomatic immunities were granted only to the Delegates to the two Commissions (the International and the European). In accordance with article 25 of the American Project, the Commission of the Danube would have to cooperate with the organs of the United Nations, to maintain an exchange of information with that organization; its representatives having the right to attend the sessions of the Commission as observers. This clause was not in the 1848 Convention; in the 1921 Convention only in cases of violations of the International regime or of conflicts between states in matter of navigation were appeals made to the League of Nations (Article 38). Article 31 provided for the right of riparian states to establish free zones and ports, accessible to all flags — a provision existing in the 1921 Convention, but not in the 1948 one.

In the matter of fluvial cabotage navigation, between ports of one and the same riparian state, the American Project understood it to be within the framework of freedoms of navigation. Through article 25 of the Russian project, cabotage navigation of a foreign flag was dependent on the national regulations of the riparian states.

In general, the objections of the American Delegation to the Russian Project were the following: discrimination in the method of applying freedom of navigation; not including the interests of the riparian states with those of the rest of the world; not including the non-riparian states in the supervision of the method of application of the international regime; elimination of the affluents and their canals from the international — navigable network; exclusion of Austria from the Conference of 1948 and complete disregard of her; arbitrary annulment of the Convention of 1921 and the rejection of the participation of its signatories to the Conference. Soviet Russia and her satellites rejected the American Project.

Chapter 8

THE NEW CONVENTION OF BELGRADE AND ITS MAIN CLAUSES

At the voting for the new Convention, the majority was represented by the Soviet Union's oneness, and the minority by the majority of her satellites.

The project presented by Vishinsky at Belgrade and the definitive Convention concluded in 1948 was not changed an iota, not even the "change of a comma."[102]

As calm, patient and tolerant as the Americans could be, still Cavendish W. Cannon could not refrain from declaring to the Conference that: "C'est un fait unique dans l'histoire des négociations internationales où la majorité des participants ait, avec une solidarité cynique, évité de proposer même de légères modifications au texte soumis à leur discussion.[103]"

As to Vishinsky's warning that "les portes servent pour l'entrée..." Cannon answered: "Nous ne sommes pas sortis; nous sommes restés, nous efforçant chaque jour de persuader la Conférence de faire quelque chose en vue d'un véritable accord."[104]

The "docile majority," as the Conference was described by the representative of France, rejected the observations and the 28 amendments of the Western Powers.[105]

And, in this way, for the first time since 1856, the navigation regime on the Danube passed from being disputed between England, France and Austria to the single control of Soviet Russia. The new Convention regarding the regime of Navigation on the Danube, was signed at Belgrade on 18 August 1948, by seven of the ten participating states and came into force on 11 May 1949, after having been ratified, step by step.[106] It contained 47 articles assigned to five chapters, namely:

621

Chapter I, General Dispositions (Articles 1 to 4); Chapter II, Dispositions referring to Organization (Articles 5 to 22); Chapter III, the Navigation Regime (Articles 23 to 33); Chapter IV, Method of covering the Expenditures for ensuring Navigation (Articles 34 to 43); Chapter V, Final Dispositions (Articles 44 to 47). A supplementary Protocol, with respect to the elimination of the European Commission of the Danube and the International Commission of the Danube, was added to the Convention. Following are English translations of the principal clauses of the Convention:

Article 1 . "Navigation on the Danube shall be free and open for the nationals, vessels of commerce and goods of all States, on a footing of equality in regard to port and navigation charges and conditions for merchant shipping. The foregoing shall not apply to traffic between ports of the same State."

In comparing this text with that of the Peace Treaties, it is obvious that the Western Powers failed to add the details of the navigation regime. The establishment of the two systems of navigation is also apparent, the general regime and the special one for cabotage.

Article 2. "The regime established by this Convention shall apply to the navigable part of the Danube River, between Ulm and the Black Sea through the Sulina Arm, with outlet to the sea through the Sulina Channel."

From this text it is evident that the only international part of navigation towards the Black Sea is the Sulina Arm, that of Kilia remaining under the sovereignty of Soviet Russia and the St. George's under that of Romania.

Article 5. "There shall be established a Danube Commission, hereinafter called "the Commission," to consist of one representative of each Danubian State."

This Article replaced the International Commission of the Danube, which had been established by the 1921 Convention.

De jure, the competence of the Commission was established between Ulm and the Mouth of the Sulina; de facto, it exists to Brăila, the port where the competence of the Special River Administration (Article 20) begins to the Mouth of the Sulina, a discrimination also noted by a Romanian researcher in 1973.

In detailing the limited jurisdiction of the new Commission, Prof. Glaser (Romania) mentions the Special Fluvial Administration in section II of the Convention, indicating "...especially the administration of the Iron Gates, organized in accordance with Article 2 of the Convention,"[107] omitting the Special River Administration, the new

THE NEW CONVENTION OF BELGRADE 623

common Russo-Romanian Administration, established through Article 20 whose jurisdiction is between Brăila and the Mouth of the Sulina.

Article 20. "There shall be established a Special River Administration in the Lower Danube (between the Mouth of the Sulina Channel and Brăila inclusive) for the execution of hydraulic engineering works and the regulation of navigation, such Administration to consist of the adjacent riparian states (Peoples Republic of Romania and the Union of Soviet Socialist Republics)." "The Administration shall act on the basis of an agreement between the governments of the country's members of the Administration." "The seat of the Administration shall be at Galatz."

Several observations can be made concerning this clause. By the expression "adjacent riparian states," the presence of Soviet Russia is justified, although she is not a riparian on the Sulina Channel and the Sulina Mouth. In replacing the European Commission with the new Administration, the European control at the Sulina Mouth passed to regional control. As to the "agreement" between Soviet Russia and Romania — mentioned in Article 20 — a conclusion can be drawn as to the relationship between the political potentials of these two countries which concluded it.

In a summary review, Vishinsky presented also the contents of a Supplementary Protocol to the Convention, composed of 5 points, among which was noted:[108] 1) that the former regime of navigation on the Danube and the instruments providing for the establishment of that regime, in particular the Convention of 1921 are no longer in force; 2) all property owned by the former European Danube Commission shall be transferred to the Special River Administration of the Lower Danube, established under Article 20 of the Convention; 3) all obligations of the former European Danube Commission to repay credits granted to it by Great Britain, France, Russia, or other States, shall be considered cancelled; 4) the same obligations of the former International Danube Commission shall be considered cancelled; 5) unliquidated property of the former International Danube Commission shall be transferred to the Danube Commission provided for in Article 5 of the Convention and the property of the former Administration of the Iron Gates and Cataracts, transferred to the new Special River Administration of the Iron Gates, established by Article 21 of the Convention.

The negative aspects of this Protocol will be examined in the next chapter.

Some of the eulogies to the Convention, expressed at the Conference, as well as in later commentaries, follow:

After thanking the Soviet Delegation, Ales. Bebler, chief of the Yugoslav Delegation, evaluated the Project for Convention as "a veritable defender of peace in the world and of international cooperation sovereign to the States...and saluted the project and approved it in its entirety...without reservations."[109]

This declaration on August 4, 1948 was the sequel to an earlier disagreement between Bebler, Molotov and Vishinsky, which was solved in favor of the Yugoslav Delegate.

Because of a retrospective presentation of Bebler's, a meeting was called on June 28, 1948, in Moscow, preliminary to the Belgrade meeting, with the aim of getting the anticipated accord of the representatives of the Danubian states over the Soviet Project for the Danubian Convention. While the other delegates accepted the Project without any objections, Bebler requested modification of the clause by means of which the new Commission of the Danube would have the right to undertake technical works facing the territory of each riparian, an act Bebler considered to be interference in Yugoslavian sovereignty.[110]

The next day, on June 29th Bebler noted that, because of the political breakdown between Moscow and Belgrade, "...everyone fell silent when I entered the room"; a gesture of disapproval, after which Vishinsky accused him of "Yugoslavian bourgeois nationalism."

The meeting was interrupted and Vishinsky later informed Bebler "..our disagreements were communicated personally to Comrade Stalin, who decided to present a different project with regard to the disputed Article, which is very intelligent and we can say that it is a truly Stalinist solution to the problem."[111]

Although his proposal that a separate Administration be created also on the Hungarian-Czechoslovak fluvial portion at Gabcikovo and Gonyii had not been taken into consideration, the Czechoslovakian Delegate declared that the Soviet Project and the Convention gave complete satisfaction in its structure, to the political claims of the Czechoslovakian Delegation."[112]

In speaking of the Danubian Commissions, Prof. Glaser, considered the new Commission of the Danube as "the most interesting from a juridical and political point of view," without mentioning again the Special River Administration (Brăila-Sulina), whose functions and powers negated the saying, "Romania, the land at the Mouths of the Danube."[113]

Practically, the Convention of 1948 entered in force on the occasion of the first meeting of the new Danube Commission, at Galatz, from November 11 to 17, 1949, at which the delegates of Soviet Russia, Bulgaria, Romania, Yugoslavia, Czechoslovakia, and Hungary participated.[114]

The Western Powers recognized neither the new Convention nor the Supplementary Protocol, and forwarded protests. Although the protests of France,[115] England,[116] and the United States[117] were similar, still there appear some differences in their objectives.

France put the accent on the validity of the 1921 Convention, which had included her in the European Commission of the Danube. England, by invoking the major commercial interests on the Danube, also included her own. The United States, not having any commercial interests, defended freedom of navigation and of commerce for all nations, Austria and Germany were excluded from the monopolistic frame of the 1948 Convention.

Belgium, Greece, Italy and Austria invoked the benefits of the 1921 Convention, which they had signed, and presented to the Secretariat of the Belgrade Conference separate notes, containing their reservations about the 1948 Convention.[118] Austria's representative, having only consultative vote, expressed reservations over the Convention, although he was not signing it.

Chapter 9

CADUCITY OR VALIDITY OF THE NEW CONVENTION?

De facto, it can be maintained that through the 1948 Convention certain principles of the Vienna Act of 1815 were applied. De jure, however some principal deviations, among others, can be invoked for its failures.

Not all the riparian states were convoked to the drafting and the signing of the Convention, a condition expressly provided for in Article 108 of the Act of 1815. Nor were the principles applied, of Articles 110 and 111 of the same Act, referring to the unification of the navigation regime, since it was divided into fluvial sectors under different jurisdictions. Complete freedom of navigation was restricted by according to the riparian states the right to impose discriminatory norms.

The caducity of the Convention can be attributed also to the non-respect of certain engagements drawn up between the Four Powers before the Conference of Belgrade. While these engagements were considered binding by England, France and the United States, Soviet Russia violated them by the majority of the votes of the satellite riparians. Another element of the caducity consisted of the abrogation of the principle of Article 15 of the 1856 Treaty of Paris, by means of which it had been established that "les Puissances contractantes stipulent entre elles qu'à l'avenir les principes de l'Acte du Congrès de Vienne seront également appliqués au Danube et à ses embouchures. Elles déclarent que cette disposition fait désormais partie du Droit Public de L'Europe et la prennent sous leur garantie." Tsarist Russia had adhered to this principle, a position maintained in all treaties following the year 1856.

Instead of European and international cooperation among the parties which established the Belgrade Conference, a regional regime was applied under the concept of the rights of the riparians, rights which actually were not respected.

Regarding the nonrecognition of the Convention of 1948 by the Western Powers, Ch. Rousseau presented an interesting comment. Comparing the Convention with that of 1921, he states "...nous nous trouvons en présence de deux traités multilateraux, successifs, contradictoires, ayant des signatures differentes."[119]

On the one hand there were Bulgaria, Czechoslovakia, Romania and Yugoslavia, which signed the 1948 Convention and rejected that of 1921. Austria, England and France, which had signed the 1921 Convention, did not acknowledge the Convention of 1948. Soviet Russia and the Ukraine, which had not been present at the Convention of 1921, signed that of 1948, rejecting the former one.

On this matter Rousseau noted "...on se trouve ainsi en présence d'un dualisme nominatif, dont le Droit International positif offre de nombreux examples."[120]

The caducity of the Convention of 1948 can also be regarded under the aspect of the measures taken by the Supplementary Protocol to the respective Convention and of the principles of International Public Law. By unilaterally transferring to the Special River Administration all the properties owned by the former European Danube Commission and by the cancellation of all its obligations, the treaties of the past, as well as the Sinaia Arrangement of 1938 were countermanded.

On the basis of Article 17 of the Arrangement, it was stipulated that the European Commission "...met à la disposition des autorités roumaines, selon le cas, pour être utilisés en pleine liberté" all its properties, "dans l'intérêt de la navigation," with the exception of administrative buildings at Galatz and Sulina, over which it reserved its right of disposition.

By Article 15, the Autonomous Board of the Danube, established by Romania on the basis of that same Arrangement, was obligated to repay to the European Commission the loans accorded by France, England and Italy, which in 1920 had reached two million gold francs and by 1930, 8,500,000 gold francs.[121]

At the Belgrade Conference, the Western Powers voted against the Supplementary Protocol, but they were in the minority.[122] In view of the measures taken through the supplementary Protocol, the problem of Romania's responsibility is raised, because of the obligations taken by her through the Sinaia Agreement.

CADUCITY OR VALIDITY OF THE NEW CONVENTION?

In financial matters, another situation arose, from which a partial compensation of the cancellations towards the European Commission could be derived. An examination of the financial status of the European Commission in 1939-1940, revealed assets in its accounts of 773,000 gold francs, the sum distributed among England, France, Italy and Switzerland. Of this sum, 117,000 gold francs were in Barclays Bank, blocked on the basis of dispositions over "trading with the enemy."[123] Through a resolution taken at the 1953 meeting of the European Commission of the Danube in exile, the debts towards the former personnel of the commission were acknowledged and paid and part of the loans were liquidated in 1955.[124] The remainder of the loans were left in suspension, a problem to be resolved by Romania or by the organization to be established in case of a new regime of the Danube.

From the documentation of the European Commission in Exile, it appears that, if not in reality at least symbolically, it does exist, with a difference in its new composition. Through the Peace Treaty of Versailles in 1919, as well as through the Convention for the Definitive Statute of the Danube in 1921, the Commission was composed provisionally of England, France, Italy and Romania (Article 4). After the 1948 Convention, when the European Commission was disbanded, Romania was no longer part of the European Commission in Exile. In exchange Greece was admitted.

From the contents of the work "Un siècle de cooperation internationale sur le Danube, 1856-1956," it appears that this organization has met in 1953 and 1956. In the 1956 edition from Rome, four studies are given concerning the evolution of Danubian problems and of the European Commission, signed by the representatives of the four governments.[125]

General Conclusions.

Taken in relation to the precedents set in the establishment of the international regime for navigation on the Danube, the preponderance of Soviet Russia in drawing up the new Convention cannot be considered unique and exceptional. From the distant beginning up to the Conference of Belgrade, the regime for freedom of navigation on the Danube evolved through a "tour de rôle," each Great Power intent on promoting its own political, strategic and economic interests.

Up to 1829, the navigation regime depended upon the Ottoman Empire; between 1829 and 1856, the mouths of the Lower Danube were under the domination of Tsarist Russia. In 1856, England and France introduced the international body of the European Commission of the Danube for the Maritime Danube, with powers of a "State within a State." In 1857, Austria tried, unsuccessfully, to apply her supremacy on the Lower Danube. After 1878, the small riparian states on the Lower Danube Bulgaria, Romania and Yugoslavia, obtained a partial respecting of their rights.

After the First World War, England and France resumed the leadership position over that same area by the elimination of Austro-Hungary, Germany and Soviet Russia. After the Second World War, Soviet Russia imposed her sole domination, eliminating England and France, subordinating also the independence of the small riparian states of the Lower Danube in the matter of establishing their own regimes.

For the time being, the future establishment of a real and complete freedom of navigation on the Lower Danube and its mouths remains uncertain. Among the opinions expressed concerning the future, J.C. Campbell has written "...the Danube can be free and open only when it unites Europe. A solution to the problem of the Danube can be found only when we are much nearer to a solution of the problem of Europe."[126]

Referring to the establishment of the new regime, of 1948, on the Danube by an accord of the nations of Eastern and Western Europe, Secretary of State George Marshall declared, "...until we reach agreement on a new Convention, this important sphere remains an unsettled area in international relations."[127] The agreement has been impossible to obtain.

Notes

Introduction

1. W.S. Churchill, "The Second World War: The Gathering Storm," p. 547.
2. Idem, "The Second World War: Triumph and Tragedy," pp. 227, 228. "After this there was a long silence. The pencilled paper lay in the centre of the table. At length I said, "Might it not be thought rather cynical if it seemed we had disposed of these issues, so fateful to millions of people, in such an offhand manner? Let us burn the paper." "No, you keep it," said Stalin.

Chapter 1

3. "Lista vaselor pe anul 1942," of the Directiunea Marinei Comerciale (D.M.C.), Bucharest 1942, pp. 48, 49 and 226.
4. Doctrine upheld by Ph. Potamianos in "Le nouveau droit maritim grec," p. 12.
5. Opinion No. 320 of June 26, 1945, of the Legal Department of the Ministry of Public Works and Communications: "... the requisitioning was abusive inasmuch as the tug was under the Greek flag and the owner was a citizen of a foreign country, on the basis of the Romanian-Greek Convention of 1931 it could not be requisitioned, hence, the contract drawn up for 1944-1945 must be drawn up with free understanding." Opinion No. 146 of 17 June 1945, of the Legal Department of the Ministry of the Navy" "... since the tug was under Greek flag and the property of Greek citizen, it should not have been requisitioned for economic reasons." (Copies of the entire correspondence connected with this case is in the possession of the author).
6. Statement of the U.K. Declaration at the Economic Commission for the Balkans and Finland concerning Roumanian Treaty, Annex 4, Section c. Shipping: in "Paris Conference, 1946," p. 794 (31)
7. Romanian-Greek Convention, August 25, 1956, Athens; Greek Government Publication, Vol. I, No. 206, October 12, 1957.

Chapter 2

8. After Romania's capitulation (the first) on August 23, 1944, the signing of the Armistice took place on September 12, 1944; (See text in U.S. Dept. of State Bulletin XI, Sept. 17, 1944, p. 286.
- The capitulation of Bulgaria took place Sept. 9, 1944, the signing of the Armistice on October 28, 1944; U.S. Dept. of State Bulletin XI, Oct. 29, 1944, p. 492; The capitulation of Hungary took place February 3, 1944; the Armistice was signed January 20, 1945; U.S. Dept. of State Bulletin XII, January 21, 1945, p. 83.
9. Stephen Gorove, "The Law and Politics...," p. 68.
10. Art. 3, of the Romanian, Bulgarian and Hungarian Armistice Agreements; Art. 7 of the Romanian and Hungarian Armistice Agreements. Art. 9 of the Hungarian and Romanian, and Article 12 of the Bulgarian Armistice Agreements; Article 9 of the Hungrian and Article 14, of the Bulgarian Armistice Agreement.
11. The Agreement was a part of Law No. 616, of July 28, 1945, published in "Monitorul Oficial al României," No. 172, of August 1, 1945.
12. Published in "Monitorul Oficial al României," No. 106, May 8, 1946.
13. For Hungary and Bulgaria, see St. Gorove, "The Law...," pp. 122, 123 and footnote 71.
14. "Ta Nea" (The News), September 7, 1978, Athens, Greece.
15. Stephen Fischer-Galati, "20th Century Romania," p. 98.
16. Hugh Seton-Watson, "The East European Revolution," p. 403.
17. Milovan Djilas, "Conversations with Stalin," p. 139.
18. Stephen Fischer-Galati, "20th Century Romania," p. 98, with subquote from Montias, "Economic Development," pp. 19 ff.
19. The liquidation: Hungary, November 6, 1954; Bulgaria, October 9, 1954; Romania, March 31, 1954.

Chapter 3

20. St. Gorove "The Law and...," p. 78, note 46. Also, U.S. Dept. of State, "Foreign Relations of the United States, Diplomatic Papers," The Conference of Berlin, 1945, II; Washington D.C., 1960, p. 199.
21. Dept. of State Bulletin XIII, August 12, 1945, p. 212.
22. Harry S. Truman, "Year of Decisions," Vol. II, p. 412.
23. Idem, ibid., p. 412.
24. U.N., the Economic and Social Council, doc. E/254, Jan. 28, 1947.
25. U.N. Bulletin I, October 14, 1946.
26. The United States Draft Resolution adopted and recommended by the Economic and Social Council; Dept. of State Bulletin, XV, Oct. 13, 1946, p. 658.

NOTES 633

27. U.N. Bulletin I, Oct. 7, 1946, pp. 5-7.
28. Ibid., Oct. 14, 1946, p. 4.
29. "Paris Conference to consider the Draft Treaties of Peace with Italy, Romania, Bulgaria, Hungary and Finland," selected documents, 1946, U.S. Dept. of State, Paris Peace Conference, publication No. 2868, series 103, 1946. Washington, D.C. 1947. (N.Y. Public Library under XBI). This source will be referred to as "Paris Peace Conference 1946," in further references.
30. U.S. Dept. of State Bul., Vol. XVIII, nos. 468, June 20, 1948 and Paris Peace Conf., 1946, p. 675.
31. Paris Peace Conference, 1946, p. 675.
32. Ibid., p. 790.
33. Ibid., p. 676.
34. Ibid., 1946, p. 174
35. Ibid., p. 754.
36. "Paris Peace Conference," 1946, p. 754.
37. Ibid., p. 754.
38. U.S., Dept. of State Bull., Vol. XVIII, No. 460, June 6, 1948, p. 736.
39. U.S. Dept. of State Bulletin, Vol. XVIII, No. 466; June 6, 1948; p. 736.
40. Peace Treaties of Paris, February 10, 1947; in Israel, op. cit., Vol. IV. Articles: 34 for Bulgaria; 36 for Romania and 38 for Hungary.
41. C.B. Rasmussen, "Freedom of the Danube," in "Current History," XII, January 1947, p. 27.
42. Statement of Secretary of State Byrnes before the Senate Committee on Foreign Relations, March 4, 1947; U.S. Senate, 8th Congress, first session, "Hearings," Washington D.C.; quoted by Stephen Gorove, "Law and Politics...," p. 92, note 85.
43. Ellis M. Zacharias in collaboration with Ladislas Farago, "Behind Closed Doors," the Secret History of the Cold War, pp. 66, 67. For the same information, see John C. Campbell, "The U.S. in World Affairs," (1945-1947), p. 157.

Chapter 4

44. J.C. Campbell, "Diplomacy on the Danube," in "Foreign Affairs," January 1949, pp. 319, 321.
45. Idem., ibid., pp. 322, 323.
46. Idem., ibid., p. 320.
47. Idem., ibid., p. 323.
48. Idem., ibid., p. 321.
49. "Hysteria," "ultimatum" "docile satellites," accusations of "dishonesty" "new frauds," "the golden wand of the dollar," "dictate," "deluded," "cynical solidarity," "imperialist schemes," etc. etc.

50. The principal documentation used in this work with respect to the Conference and Convention of Belgrade in "Conférence Danubiënne de Belgrade, recueil des documents," published in a Russian and French text by the Ministry for Foreign Affairs of Yugoslavia at Belgrade, 1948. In this present work the shortened title will be "Danube Conference of 1948" and "Belgrade Convention of 1948."
51. "Danube Conference of 1948," p. 51.
52. "Danube Conference of 1948," p. 65. This is the expression written into the official documentation. In the American documentation, the expression is given as "... the door was open to come in; the same door is open to go out of it that is what you wish"; U.S. Depart. of State Documents and State Papers, Vol. I, Nos. 8 and 9 (November and December 1948).
53. J.C. Campbell, op. cit., p. 322.
54. U.S. Dept. of State Documents and State Papers, Vol. I, Nos. 8 and 9, (November-December, 1948), p. 487.
55. S. Gorove, "Law and...," p. 50 and 50 note from "The Communist International," new series, No. 7, December, 1924, January, 1935, p. 93.
56. "Danube Conference of 1948," p. 121.
57. Ibid., p. 243.
58. Ibid., p. 243.
59. Ibid., p. 157.
60. E. Glaser, "Comisiile fluviale internationale," in "Drept international fluvial," pp. 219, 248.
61. "Danube Conference of 1948," pp. 55-59.
62. "Danube Conference of 1948," pp. 61, 143.
63. Ibid., p. 63.
64. Ibid., p. 77.

Chapter 5

65. "Danube Conference of 1948," p. 67.
66. Ibid., p. 103.
67. Herbert A. Gibbond, "Europe since 1918," 3rd edit., (1923), pp. 40-41, and 58, at the meeting of the Supreme War Council.
68. "Danube Conferece of 1948," pp. 103-104.
69. Ibid., pp. 36, 103-104.
70. Ibid., p. 61.
71. Ibid., pp. 59, 105.
72. Ibid., p. 255.
73. Ibid., pp. 63-77.
74. Ibid., p. 101.
75. Ibid., p. 251.
76. Ibid., p. 65.

77. J.C. Campbell, "Diplomacy...," p. 319.
78. "Danube Conference of 1948," pp. 69, 101.
79. S. Gorove, "The Law...," p. 89.
80. Idem., ibid., p. 94.
81. Ch. Rousseau: "Principles Généraux du Droit International Public," t. 1, No. 368.
82. "Danube Conference of 1948," pp. 103, 105.
83. Ibid., p. 145.
84. Ibid., p. 137.
85. Judge Cartozo, in Techt v. Hughes (1920), New York 222. cited by I.M. Sinclair, "The Danube Conference of 1948," in "The British Yearbook of International Law," XXV, 1948, pp. 400-401.
86. In Sinclair, op. cit., p. 401
87. I.M. Sinclair, p. 400.
88. "Danube Conference of 1948," p. 177.
89. I.M. Sinclair, p. 400.
90. England, Austria, Belgium, Bulgaria, Czechoslovakia, France, Germany, Greece, Italy, Yugoslavia, Romania and Hungary.
91. "Danube Conference of 1948," p. 103.
92. L. Imbert, "Le régime juridique actuel du Danube," in Revue Générale de Droit Internationale Public," January-March, 1951, p. 82 (10).
93. "Danube Conference of 1948," p. 113.
94. Gh. Sofronic, "Le Statut International du Danube Maritime et la position de la Roumanie à la lumière de l'Arrangement de Sinaia et de l'Accord de Bucharest, du l-er Mars 1939," in "Revue Générale de Droit International Public," Paris, Mars, 1945, p. 61.

Chapter 6

95. "Danube Conference of 1948," pp. 117-127.
96. Ibid., p. 145.
97. Ibid., p. 133.
98. Ibid., pp. 173, 249.
99. Postage stamps of .55 bani, (cents); 2.15, 3.40, 1, 1.50, 4.80 Lei.
100. Postage stamps of 3.00, 3.40, 4.80 Lei.

Chapter 7

101. "Danube Conference of 1948," pp. 337-351.

Chapter 8

102. J.C. Campbell, "Diplomacy...," p. 322.

103. "Danube Conference of 1948," p. 251.

104. Ibid., p. 253.

105. Ibid., pp. 243, 247, 253.

106. See the complete text of the Convention, in the Russian and the French language, in "Danube Conference of Belgrade, 1948," published by the Ministry for Foreign Affairs of Yugoslavia, pp. 373-385. For English text, see U.N. Treaty Series, Recueil des Traités, Vol. 32, pp. 197-222 and Great Britain, Foreign Office Treaty Series (1949). Ratification: Bulgaria, on 22 February 1949; Czechoslovakia and Yugoslavia, 23 February, 1949; Romania, March 5, 1949; Hungary, 14 March 1949; Union of Soviet Socialist Rebublics, 11 May 1949; Ukraine Soviet Socialist Republic 14 May 1949.

107. E. Glaser, "Drept International Fluvial," p. 247.

108. "Danube Conference of 1948," p. 395.

109. Ibid., p. 133.

110. Ales. Bebler, "Trois rencontres avec Molotov (Souvenirs)" in "Questions actuelles du Socialisme," January, February, 1953.

111. Ibid., pp 57, 58, Art. 8 and 4 of the Definitive Convention of 1948.

112. "Danube Conference of 1948," p. 133.

113. E. Glaser, op. cit., p. 247.

114. "La Navigation du Rhin," Revue, Décembre 1949, p. 529.

115. "Le Gouvernement français ne reconnait aucune validité internationale à la Convention de Belgrade et considere que le seul acte international définissant le Régime du Danube demeure la Convention établissant le Statut Définitif du Danube de 1921."

See: "Le communiqué de presse publié par la Direction des Accords Techniques du Ministère des Affaires Etrangères." U.S. Dept. of State, Doc. 8 State Papers, Vol. I, No. 8 and 9 (November December 1948, p. 507).

116. "His Majesty's Government must therefore state categorically that they cannot recognise any new Danube Convention which claims to place certain users of the Danube in a monopolistic position, nor any Convention which denies to non-riparian Powers, with major commercial interests in that waterway, any voice in the Commission which is to be responsible for its administration"; U.S. Dept. of State, Doc. and State Papers, Vol. I, Nos. 8 and 9 (November and December 1948), p. 506.

117. "It is obvious that the United States cannot accept the draft convention which the Soviet Union is imposing upon its satellites. In the view of the United States, this instrument does not guarantee freedom and equality of trade. It does not fulfill the mandate of the Council of Foreign Ministers. The United States will not, of course, recognise, either for itself or for those parts of Austria and Germany which are under its control, the authority of any commission set up in this manner to exercise any jurisdiction in those portions of Austria and Germany."; Dept. of State, Doc. and State Papers, Vol. I, No. 8 and 9, pp. 506, 507.
118. "La Navigation du Rhin," October 1948, p. 410; see also "Paris Conference," 1946, pp. 789, 790; U.S. Dept. of State, op cit., pp. 508 (Austria); 513 (Belgium) 509 (Greece) and 512 (Italy).

Chapter 9

119. Ch. Rousseau, "Principes généraux...," No. 456-2.
120. Idem., ibid.
121. "Un siècle de cooperation internationale sur le Danube," p. 54, 55. (European Commission of the Danube).
122. "Danube Conference of 1948," p. 367.
123. "Un siècle...," op. cit., p. 65.
124. Ibid., pp. 66-68.
125. Aperçu historique (Italy); Evolution Juridique (France); Histoire financière (England); Rapport économique (Greece).
126. John C. Campbell, "Diplomacy...," op. cit., p. 327.
127. Statement by Secretary of State George Marshall, Department of State Bull., Vol. XVIII, No. 466, June 6, 1948, p. 736.

PART TEN

THE TRAFFIC OF THE MARITIME DANUBE

THE TRAFFIC OF THE MARITIME DANUBE

Introduction.

The purpose of this study has been limited exclusively to the Maritime Danube — the section between the port of Brăila and the mouths of the river — because of the fact that a great part of the volume of exports and imports of all the Danubian countries is carried on through this subsector.

Special attention is given to Brăila and Galatz because these two port-cities serve not only the Romanian traffic of goods, but also the transit goods from and to the other Danubian countries, through the transshipment operations from the fluvial to the maritime vessels and vice-versa. The export of cereal, especially, is carried out through Brăila, while lumber products pass through Galatz.

In the past, along with political considerations, Western and Central European commercial interests also concentrated on the Maritime Danube. The principal objective sought by England and France through the international litigation on navigation, in 1856, was freedom of navigation on the Maritime Danube, not on the Middle and Upper sectors of the river. The Maritime Danube represented the Gordian knot of the Danube Question, the point at which the confrontations between the Great Powers developed. Actually, as mentioned before, the beginning of commercial navigation in antiquity took place on the Maritime Danube.

Chapter 1

FROM ANTIQUITY TO THE FIRST WORLD WAR

Until 1829.

Traffic on the Maritime Danube up to 1829 can be divided into a number of subdivisions. From antiquity to the onset of the Fourth Century A.D. the link with the Black Sea was the St. George Branch, presumably also the Sulina Branch. Between the XVth century and the Treaties of Passarowitz (1718) and Belgrade (1739), all traffic was at the discretion of the Ottoman Empire. After these two treaties, the presence of Austrian vessels was gradually limited. The Ottoman Empire, after the Treaty of Kütschuk-Kainardji (1774), accorded the Russians the right to navigate on the Black Sea and the Maritime Danube. After this year, the effective presence of Austrian vessels also became noted on the Maritime Danube and on the Black Sea, as a result of the right bestowed by the Ottoman Empire.

Naturally, there are no statistical data available for the period of antiquity, the traffic at that time being mentioned only by archaeologists and historians. In antiquity the load capacity of the maritime ships can be estimated at 50 to 100 tons, hence they could navigate also through lesser depths of the river. The wooden vessels, propelled by sails, and manned with small crews, were privately owned and there was practically no competition.

Between 1829 and 1856.

The period of long distance commercial traffic in the European framework can be considered a result of the Treaty of Adrianople.[1]

Traffic statistics up to 1856 are from sources, from which only a general conclusion can be drawn. Between 1829 and 1856, the traffic of maritime vessels through the Sulina Mouth and Branch was at Russia's discretion. Some characteristics of this period can be noted: the load capacity and the type of construction of local vessels were not very different from those of the immediately preceding period. The vessels under foreign flags, however, already bore signs of Western European improvement of means of transportation. After 1836, Austria's first steamships appeared on the Maritime Danube.

Among the difficulties encountered by the European vessels were the instability of the depths of the water at the Sulina Mouth and the character of the laborers available for navigation service.

The amount of traffic passing through the Sulina Mouth can be deduced from the traffic of maritime vessels in the ports of Brăila and Galatz, in 1839:[2]

Ships Flags.	Number of vessels.
Greek	202
Ionic	38
Samian 3)	11
Turkish	199
Sardinian	111
Austrian	94
Russian	75
Belgian	42
Wallachian	10
English	5
Others	7
	Total 794

Other Statistics also register the flags of Tuscany (Italy), Hamburg, Hannover, Prussia, Macklenburgh and Naples.[4]

Between 1847 and 1850 the frequency of the traffic of the vessels of the principal flags through the Sulina Mouth was the following:[5] (repeated entry)

Vessels.		Tons Capacity.
Greek	3008	514,021
Turkish	1393	191,522
Austrian	623	152,350
English	524	83,414
Russian	368	72,094
Italian	309	42,763
Roman	216	36,160
French	64	8,676
German	30	6,049
Others	85	2,594
Total	6,620	1,109,643 (T.R.)[6]

A comparison of the 1839 statistics with those of the 1847-1850 period shows the preponderance of the Greek flag and ownership, followed by the Turkish flag which included also Greek-owned vessels from those islands still under the Ottoman Empire.

During the 1847-1850, the average load capacity of the principal flags in Tons Registered was: Greek 170; Turkish, 140; Austrian, 241; English, 160; Russian, 196. Actually, the average capacity of vessels flying the English flag was greater, but the above reflects that of the smaller, Greek-owned ships from the Ionian Islands (under English protectorate) which were flying the English flag. In connection with this flag, the Anglo-Russian dispute, referred to earlier, and which had resulted from the navigational difficulties at the Sulina Branch and Mouth, must be taken into consideration.

As was shown in the subheading "Was Danube Commerce prejudiced between 1829 and 1857? (Part Three), commercial traffic on the Maritime Danube reported increases.

Regarding exports and imports through the Sulina Mouth, from and to the countries of the Lower Danube and of Central Europe, statistics of the period following 1829 can only be general, their accuracy being relative. The figures given will be those from the reports (some as to quantity, others as to value) made by the Sardinian Consuls, concerning the traffic at Galatz and Brăila.

Exports from Galatz, in 1838 76,999 Tons at 1000 Kgr.[7]
Export from Brăila, in 1845 28,694,423 Piastres[8]
Imports from Brăila, in 1845 17,114,491 Piastres.[9]
Imports from Galatz, in 1843 10,579,680 Piastres.[10]

From the above figures, it is obvious that the exports were greater than the imports. Principal articles exported were cereal and lumber; main imports were textiles, metals, citric products, sugar, spices, etc.

The 1829-1856 period showed an accentuation of European interests, especially — English interests in the economy of the Lower Danube. That participation would have been even greater but for the existence of navigational difficulties through the Sulina Mouth during the Russian occupation.

Between 1856 and the First World War.

After the internationalization of navigation, through the Treaty of Paris (1856) and the establishment of the European Commission of the Danube (E.C.D.), a new era was inaugurated in which the traffic on the Maritime Danube registered continuous growth, due to the technical improvement of navigation being carried out by the European Commission at the Sulina Mouth and Branch.

It must be pointed out that some statistical date, for the period immediately prior to 1856, and all the dates following that year are accurate, having recorded and published by the European Commission of the Danube, as well as by other official and semiofficial sources.

The general evolution of maritime vessel traffic through the Sulina Mouth between 1851 and 1910 were the following:[11] (repeated passage)

Period	Number of vessels	Register Tons
1851-1855	10,728	1,969,000
1866-1870	12,821	2,740,521
1891-1895	8,391	8,007,024
1906-1910	5,853	9,837,926

The increase in traffic presents a number of aspects. The discrepancy between the number of vessels and their load capacity was due to the increase in the average tonnage per vessel, which grew from 184 Register Tons between 1851-1855 to 1,672 tons between 1906-1910. The load capacity of the larger vessels grew from 1567 between 1866 and 1870 to 4047 Register Tons in the 1906-1910 period.

The participation of the different flags varied.[12] Up to 1867, the Greek flag was predominant with a 37% and 47% of the total number of the vessels and 27% of the total tonnage carried. After 1856, with few exceptions, the English flag held first place, followed by the Greek, Turkish, Austrian and Italian flags.

An important aspect after 1856 was the gradual replacement of sailing vessels by steamships, as shown by the following figures:[13]

Period	% of sailing ships		% of steamships.	
	Ships	Tonnage	Ships	Tonnage
1847-1850	97.77	95.50	2.23	4.50
1856-1860	94.11	88.57	5.89	11.43
1881-1885	47.83	12.59	52.17	87.41
1906-1910	9.89	1.38	90.11	98.62
1926-1930	-	-	100.00	100.00

Along with the maritime vessels from other regions which contributed to the decrease from 97.77, in the numerical sailing ship traffic between 1847-1850, to zero between 1926-1930, there were also the Austrian and Hungarian steamships, some of them although for fluvial use were of increased tonnage, allowing maritime navigation as well.

The chief competition in this traffic was between ships of the Greek and the English flags. The ownership of maritime vessels also contributed to the competition, reflecting as it did on the financial potential of the operations, Greek vessels were privately owned and operated, while the English, Austrian, Hungarian and Italian ones were run by corporations, some of them even being subsidized by the state. To the advantage of the Greek fleet was the reduced operational expenses, but to its disadvantage was the lack of coordinated competition caused by the individualistic tendencies of the owners.

Over all the new aspects of navigation were notable the gradual efforts of the European Commission to introduce a favorable condition by eliminating previous situations such as the piracies, the lack of moral responsibility of those working in navigational services, etc.

Also, the manner in which the traffic was carried out underwent many changes in the activity of the shipping agents, the rigorous control of the insurance of vessels and cargo, regulation of pilotage and modernization of Brăila and Galatz, the terminal and transit ports on the Maritime Danube gradually being equipped by Romania with technical machinery, mechanical silos for cereal, quays, docks anchorages, etc.

Along with the improvement in navigation, exports through the Sulina Mouth increased in the following quantitative value:[14] (in tons)

	Cereal	Lumber	Misc.	Total	Cereal %
1868-1870	2,718,509	41,583	26,284	2,786,376	97.00
1881-1885	5,725,392	227,453	68,194	6,021,039	95.00
1906-1910	13.434,673	1,962,784	409,475	15,806,932	85.00
1911-1915	10,911,438	910,154	416,391	12,237,983	89.00

As is evident from these statistics the main article of export was that of cereal from Bulgaria, Romania, Serbia and Hungary destined for England, the Near East, Greece, Italy, etc. The total of exports from 1911 to 1915 reflects especially the supplies of cereal stored up by the countries of Western Europe (especially England and France) and the Mediterranean ones, on the eve of World War I.

To Romania's exports through Brăila and Galatz were added those of the other Danubian countries, sent in transit through these ports. In the periods of low water at the Sulina Mouth, the vessels finished their loading in the roadstead of the port of Sulina by transshipment.

Following is an example of their transsshipments:[15]

	Vessels	T.R.	Quantities of Cereal
In 1887	1387	860,336	537,074 quarters
In 1902	1131	1,506,883	1,243,548 quarters

A general review of the servicing of the volume of the exports of cereal, of Romania and of that transited through Brăila and Galatz during the period prior to World War I, can be obtained from the growth in the means of transport in the Lower Danube; in 1916, 754 barges were registered, in comparison with the 502 registered in 1900.[16]

Exports through the Sulina Mouth, destined for Western Europe and the Near East, ceased upon Romania's entry into the war (1916) and the blockading of the Straits of Bosphorus by Turkey. From a total of 12,237,983 tons, exported from 1911 to 1915, they shrank to 982,937 tons between 1916 and 1920.[17] A large part of the cereal exports of Bulgaria, Romania and Serbia was directed towards Central Europe, and to supply the German and Austro-Hungarian Armies of occupation in Romania (1916-1918).

From 1880 to the eve of the First World War, the financial potential of the shipowners and of the cereal companies along the entire Danube route had been practically unlimited. For example, in Brăila, there were established industries turning to good effect that principal product. To facilitate the export of cereal-derived products through the Maritime Danube, these industries (flour mills and pasta products factories) were constructed within the port radius, the property of Greeks, some of whom were also shipowners on the Lower Danube.[18]

Chapter 2

BETWEEN THE TWO WORLD WARS

1920 to 1930.

Due to the new navigation regime established by the Peace Treaty of World War I, followed by that of the Definitive Statute of the Danube (1921), traffic on the Maritime Danube gradually resumed its prewar pace, without surpassing it.

The traffic of maritime vessels through the Sulina Mouth in the decade following World War I (1921 - 1930), in relation to the decade preceding the war, presented the following decreases:[19] (repeated passages)

1891-1900	15,004 vessels	14,998,870 Reg. Tons
1921-1930	7,625 vessels	13.998,316 Reg. Tons

While the loading capacity in (Register Tons) of the vessels varied little in the two periods, the difference in their number was due to the increase in the average tonnage per vessel. The traffic of the flags passing through the Sulina Mouth in 1930 was the following:[20] (repeated passages)

Countries	Vessels	Reg. Tons
Greece	221	466,057
Italy	156	434,255
England	140	369,351
Romania	57	125,875
France	45	67,344
Germany	33	86,496
Turkey	17	20,137
Other countries	182	430,274
Totals	851	1,999,789

The following factors can also be attributed to the gradual numerical decrease in the traffic during the 1921-1930 period: the instability of the navigable water depths at the Sulina Mouth; England's reduced interest in Danubian trade; disorganization of the fluvial potential because of the cabotage restrictions; the European Commission's disinterest in view of the divergences with Romania; reduction of exports, etc.

The volume of exports through the Sulina Mouth decreased gradually between 1921 and 1930 to 19,651,406 Tons, compared with 23,194,796 Tons between 1891 and 1900.[21]

The following factors contributed to the decrease in the export of cereal, the main product, after World War I: two consecutive years of drought in the Lower Danube region; supplying the new territories annexed by Romania; insufficient provision of equipment for the land apportioned to agriculture (especially in Romania); the agricultural potential unbalanced by the break-up of the Austro-Hungarian Empire; Bulgaria's losing the war; territorial transformations in Yugoslavia; increased domestic consumption; the economic depression in Europe following the financial crisis in New York (1929) which affected Danubian commerce; lack of local and international credits; intensification of exports through Constanta, the Romanian maritime ports, etc.

The reduction in cereal exports shows a temporary reversal in 1929 and 1930, brought about by the massive supply measures taken in Western Europe after the end of World War I and because of the rise in the prices of cereal on the Western markets. From the 54%

proportion of cereal as registered in 1928, by 1929 it had risen to 77% and to 75% in 1930.[22] This situation also affected the traffic through the Sulina Mouth, where it registered an increase from 474 vessels in 1928 to 648 vessels in 1929, and to 851 vessels in 1930.[23] The numeric average of the vessels of the major flags between 1928 and 1930 were as follows, in the order of their frequency: Greek, 32%; Italian, 17%; English, 16%; Romanian, 6%; French, 6%; other flags, 23%.[24]

Between 1931 and 1939.

After 1931, commercial activity along the entire route of the Maritime Danube was as though paralyzed. Even before 1931 there had been failures of banks and cereal exporting companies, unemployment in the ranks of seamen, and repatriation of foreign seamen, especially Greeks. To this crisis the absence of the credits that had come from Vienna also had contributed. As a note of social order, even the famous bars in the ports of Brăila and Galatz, formerly frequented by seamen of the foreign maritime vessels, had disappeared.

In comparison with the previous decade, the traffic of Maritime vessels registered through Brăila and Galatz showed the following decreases:[25]

	Vessels	Register Tons
1921-1930	7,625	13,998,316
1931-1939	4,639	10,596,531

The frequency of the various flags passing through the Sulina Mouth between 1931-1939 was as follows: (repeated passage)

Flags	Vessels	Reg. Tons
Totals of which:	4,637	10,596,531
Greek	1,560	3,000,000
Italian	890	2,500,000
Romanian	560	1,600,000
English	460	1,000,000
Other	1,167	2,496,531

The volume of cereal export between 1931 and 1939 was lower, the average being between 73% and 76%, followed by that of lumber. The destinations were: (approximate)[26]

Italy	554,000 Tons	Gibraltar	54,000
Greece	184,000	Holland	52,000
England	170,000	France	45,000
Egypt	99,000	Germany	21,000
Belgium	90,000	Other Countries	40,000
Syria	63,000		

The reduction in the traffic through the Sulina Mouth was also influenced by the continued economic and financial crisis in which Europe found itself after 1930. Romania's exports of cereal to other Danubian countries (Bulgaria, Slovakia, Germany, Yugoslavia, Hungary), increasing from 145,917 tons in 1938 to 269,528 Tons in eight months of 1939, also contributed to that reduction.[27]

Between 1940 and 1944.

In the period prior to and immediately after the beginning of the war with Russia (on June 22, 1941), the traffic through the Sulina Mouth registered variations. From 386 vessels and 1,037,000 T.R. in 1940 the traffic was recorded at 603 vessels and 351,000 T.R. in 1943, the lowest figures being in 1941 (102 vessels and 277,000 T.R.), the year the war broke out in Eastern Europe.[28]

The traffic of vessels as well as that of cargo was carried out on a regional rather than an international basis. The great majority of both ships and exports served the economic needs of Germany and of the coalition against Soviet Russia, the route of the coalition being the Danube Southern Ukraine, via the Black Sea.

The English, Greek, Turkish and other maritime flags did not appear in the statistics of traffic after 1941; most of the traffic included the barges passing from the Danube towards Southern Russia, to the military front.

Navigation through the Sulina Mouth, as well as that on the Maritime Danube was suspended for the maritime vessels of the coalition against Germany. This amounted to abrogation of the principles of previous treaties, of the 1921 Convention for the Definitive Statute of the Danube, as well as those of the 1938 Sinaia Arrangement.

After 1944, with the capitulation of Bulgaria and Romania, statistical research of the traffic becomes difficult due to the lack of statistical date of the actual situation.

Conclusion.

The problem of the maintenance of the present outlet to the Black Sea, through the Sulina Canal and Mouth, could be raised at an eventual modification of the 1948 Belgrade Convention, when the new Danube-Black Sea Canal on the Cernavoda - Midia route enters into operation.

The premises of this problem — as well as the technical and economic plans for the construction of the new canal — could well be the result of a Russian concept dating back to the beginning of the nineteenth century.

As shown in Part Four, Chapter II, the idea of creating a new exit to the sea, by means of a Cernavoda - Black Sea Canal, had been suggested by Tsar Nicolas I in 1836. In 1948 the idea of the canal, as well as the framework of the technical and economic plans, was suggested by Soviet Russia.

In 1949, the author of this present work, at that time in the service of the Romanian Administration charged with the construction of the new canal, was chosen to edit a brief history of the technical work carried out up to the end of that year. For this purpose he had at his disposition the confidential technical and economic plans of the projected canal. From these documents it was evident that the new canal was to shorten the economic ties of all Danubian countries with the economic potential of Southern Soviet Russia.

Among other provisions were the transfer of Romanian metallurgical industries from Western Romania to the East, along the route of the new canal, in order to be supplied with raw materials — metallurgic coal and iron — from the Donetz Basin in the Ukraine. The principal large former industries designated were Resita and Astra-Vagoane from the Banat and Transylvania, and Malaxa, from Bucharest.

Also, other industries were planned along the canal route, industries which after completion of the project would continue in operation their products to be exported. At present, the Central Power Plan at Ovidiu Point exports electric power to Northern Bulgaria. The cement factory in Medgidia (by the canal) exports cement in sacks bearing the inscription "Made in the U.S.S.R." The large crusher at Navodari exports limestone to the Middle East.

After Stalin's death and up to 1979, the digging of the canal was suspended. It was resumed in 1980 and partially completed by 1984.

The conclusions and results drawn up by the author in a brief report, for internal distribution within the canal administration, were eliminated by the political department of the administration.

Some speculation could be made over the replacement of the present outlet to the sea. The possibility exists for a repetition of the situation in 1829, when Tsarist Russia annexed almost all the Delta of the Danube and when commercial activity and navigation through the Sulina Mouth depended on that same Great Power.

The efficiency of the canal for Romania would be minimal, inasmuch as her foreign trade, up to the present time, is handled through the ports of Brăila and Galatz, ports of her traditional and natural economic ties. The diminuation of the activities of these two ports, as well as of the ports of Reni and Ismail on the Kilia Branch, could be a negative influence of the economy of the Maritime Danube region. The major advantage would be to the other Danubian countries, whose routes to the Black Sea would thus be shortened.

Navigation through the new canal would be possible only by means of barges of a maximum capacity of 1000 - 1500 tons. The transshipment operation would have to be carried out at the future port of Midia, which will need to be supplied by Romania with all the necessary technical equipment.

During periods of freezing, the usefulness of the canal would be limited, which is the case also on the entire course of the Danube and at the present outlet at Sulina.

The efficiency of the new Canal remains to be seen in the future.

Notes

Chapter 1

1. Due to release of the foreign trade of the Romanian and the Serbian Principalities from the Ottoman monopoly and to the freedom of navigation granted under the Russian occupation, indirectly derived from the freedom of navigation for all flags on the Black Sea, proclaimed by the 1829 Treaty of Adrianople.
2. March 1839, Report of the Sardinian Consul at Galatz; Bodin, "Documente Sarde," p. 50.
3. From the Island of Samos (Aegean Sea), under the Ottoman Empire.
4. July 24, 1851 Report of the Sardinian Consul at Galatz; in Bodin, op cit., p. 231.
5. From the statistics presented by the European Commission of the Danube.
6. Register Ton, or net tonnage, is the gross tonnage minus certain deductions for space occupied by engines, crews, etc.
7. The original figure was 153,999 Kile, one Kile being of 500 Kgr., hence the figure of 76,999 T of 1000 Kgr; the Report of the Sardinian Consul in Galatz, November 5, 1838; Bodin, "Documente Sarde," p. 53.
8. From the March 26, 1846 Report of the Sardinian Consul; Bodin, op. cit., p. 177.
9. Ibid.
10. From the 31 August 1843 Report of the Sardinian Consul at Galatz; Bodin, op. cit., pp. 153-157.
11. "La Commission Européenne et son...," p. 372.
12. Ibid., pp. 374, 510.
13. Ibid., p. 373.
14. Ibid., pp. 377 and 514. The first satistics were recorded starting in 1868.
15. D. Sturdza, "Recueil...," p. 901.
16. For 1900, see "L'Annuaire du Danube (1902-1903; for 1916," ibid (1916); both by Youghaperian.
17. "La Commission Européenne et son...," p. 514.
18. Mills; Valerianos and Lychiardopol; Violatos and Gheorghiadis; Pasta factories: the brothers Apostol and Aristide Melissaratos; Ambatis, Milas, etc., C.C. Giurgiu, "Istoricul Orasului Brăila," p. 225.
19. "La Commission Européenne et son...," p. 510.

657

20. Ibid., p. 374.
21. Ibid., 514.
22. Ibid., p. 377.
23. Ibid., pp. 510, 511.
24. Ibid., p. 511.
25. For the 1921-1930 period; see "La Commission Européenne...," p. 510; for 1931-1939, "Statistica Directiunii Speciale Autonome a Dunării Maritime" (D.D.M.).
26. "C.E.D., Un Siècle de cooperation...," p. 78.
27. "Annuarul Directiunii Speciale Autonome a Dunării Maritime," (D.D.M.) p. 3. (Yearbook of the Special Autonomous Division of the Maritime Danube).
28. From the Statistics of the "Special Autonomous Division of the Maritime Danube," 1944, quoted in "Traffic through the Sulina Canal in the period of the two World Wars," Sp. Focas, in "The Economic and Statistical Annals of Romania, No. 4-6," Bucharest 1945.

BIBLIOGRAPHY

BIBLIOGRAPHY

ALEXANDRI, K., "I anabiosis tis thalasinis mas dinameos kata tin tourkokratian"; in Greek, Athens, 1960. (The Revival of our Sea-Power during the Turkish rule).
"ANNALES DES PONTS ET CHAUSSEES," Vol. I. (1893), Paris, p.24.
ANDERSON, M.S., "The Eastern Question," Mac.Millan, St. Martin's Press, New York, 1966.
ANTIPA, Grigore, "Dunărea si problemele ei stiintifice, economice si politice," Bucuresti, 1921. (The Danube and its Scientific, Economic and Political Problems).
_____. "Câteva probleme stiintifice si economice relative la Delta Dunării," Bucuresti, 1914. (Some Scientific and Economic Problems concerning the Danube Delta).
_____. "Chestiunea Dunării în politica externă a României," Bucuresti, 1924. (The Danube Question in the Foreign Policy of Romania).
_____. "Memoriul din 29 Noembrie 1942 către V.V.Pella, reprezentantul României la Conferintele dunărene dintre 1940 si 1942"; în Spiridon G. Focas, "Două Memorii cu privire la încălcarea drepturilor României la Gurile Dunării." New York, 1976. (Memorandum of November 29, 1942, to V.V. Pella, Romania's Representative at the Vienna and Bucharest Danubian Conferences between 1940 and 1942). Published by Sp. G.Focas in "Two Memoirs concerning the infringement of Romania's rights at the Mouths of the Danube," New York, 1976.
_____. "Quelques observations sur la navigabilité aux embouchures du Danube"; in Bull. Sect. Scient., Acad. Roum., 10 Bucharest, 1926, pp. 83-93.
_____. "Rapport separé presenté à la Commission Européenne du Danube au sujet du bras de Stary-Stambul," Sulina, 1932-1933, pp. 3-32.
_____. "Quelques observations concernant les bases géophysiques des travaux destinés à assurer la navigabilité des bouches du Danube"; Bull. Sect., Scient., Académie Roumaine, pp. 19, 153-171, (1937-1938).
ANTONOPOULOU, K.N., "I istoria tou emporicou nafticou"; in Greek, "History of the Merchant Marine).

"ANUARUL INSTITUTULUI DE ISTORIE SI ARHEOLOGIE, A.D.XENOPOL," IX, Iasi, 1972. (Yearbook of the A.D.Xenopol Institute of History and Archaeology).
ARGYLL, Duke of, "The Eastern Question," (1856-1878). Strahan, London, 1879.
ARION, Dinu, "Chestia Dunării," Bucuresti, 1916. (The Danube Question).
ARS, G.L., see Ioanidou-Bitsiadou.
ASBURY, Herbert, "The Barbary Coast. An Informal History of the San Francisco Underworld," Alfred A. Knoff, New York, 1933.
ASTLEY, Joan Bright, "The Inner Circle. A view of War at the Top." An Atlantic Monthly Press Book. Little, Brown and Co., Boston-Toronto, 1971.
AURELIAN, P.S., "Opere economice," Bucuresti, 1867. (Economic Studies).
D'AVRIL, A., "Négociations relatives au traité de Berlin et aux arrangements qui suivis" (1875-1886), Paris, 1886.
BAICOIANU, C., "Le Danube aperçu historique, économique et politique," Paris, 1917.
_____. Dunărea, privire istorică, economică si politică," Bucuresti, 1918. (The Danube, an Historic, Economic and Political View).
_____. "Studii economice, politice si sociale," (1898-1940), Bucuresti, 1941. (Economic, Political and Social Studies).
_____. "Dunărea văzută prin prizma Tratatului dela Bucuresti din 1918," Bucuresti, 1938. (The Danube Viewed in the Light of 1918 Treaty of Bucharest).
BAKER, B.Granville, "The Danube with pen and pencil by Captain B. Granville, Baker with 99 illustrations." London, 1911.
BALCANICUS, (Stoian Pratic), "The Aspirations of Bulgaria," London, 1915.
BANESCU, N., "La domination byzantine sur les régions du bas Danube," Bucarest, 1927.
BARANY, George, "Stephen Szechenyi and the Awakening of Hungarian Nationalism," (1791-1841). Princeton University Press, New Jersey, 1968.
BART, Jean, (pen name), see Botez, Eugen.
BASH, Ant., "The Danube River and the German Economic Sphere," Columbia University Press, New York, 1943.
BEBLER, Ales., "Trois rencontres avec Molotov"; in Questions Actuelles du Socialism, Paris, Janvier-Février, 1953.
BELDICEANU, Nicoara, "La Moldavie Ottomane à la fin du XV-e Siècle et au début du XVI-e Siècle"; Extrait de la "Revue des études islamiques," Paris, 1969.
BERINDEI, D., "Roma"; în "Reprezentantele Diplomatice ale României," Vol.I, Bucuresti, 1967 ("Rome," in "Romania's Diplomatic Representations").
BERNARD, Paul, "Joseph II," Twayne Publishers, New York, 1968.
THE BLACK SEA PILOT, Published by the Hydrographic Department of the British Admirality, 9th ed., London, 1942.

BLANK, Louis, "La question du Danube"; in "Revue économique internationale," Année 21, Bruxelles, 1929.
BODIN, D., "Documente privitoare la legăturile economice dintre Principatele Române si Regatul Sardiniei," Bucuresti, 1941. (Documents Concerning the Economic Ties between the Romanian Principalities and the Kingdom of Sardinia) Abbreviation: "Documente Sarde," (Sardinian Documents).
_____. "Politica economică a Regatului Sardiniei în Marea Neagra si pe Dunăre în legătură cu Principatele Române," Bucuresti, 1944. (The Economic Policy of the Kingdom of Sardinia concerning the Black Sea and the Danube River in connection with the Romanian Principalities).
BOERESCU, B., "Discursuri politice," Vol. II, Bucuresti, 1920. (Political Discourses).
BOICU, L., "Austria si Principatele Române în vremea răsboiului Crimeei," (1853-1856), Bucuresti, 1972. (Austria and the Romanian Principalities at the time of the Crimean War).
_____. "Incercări franceze de pătrundere în economia Moldovei în epoca răsboiului Crimeei si a Unirii," (1853-1859); în "Revista Studii privind Unirea Principatelor," Bucuresti, 1960. (French Attempts to penetrate the Moldavian Economy at the Time of the Crimean War and the Union," (1853-1859); in "The Journal of Studies Concerning the Union of Principalities).
BOLSOVER, G.H., "David Urquhart and Eastern Question, (1833-1837). A Study in Publicity and Diplomacy"; in "Journal of Modern History," (U.S.A.), Vol. III, No.4, December, 1936, pp.444-467.
_____. "Lord Bonsoby and the Eastern Question" (1833-1839); in "Slavonic Review," Vol. XIII, pp. 98-118, (USA).
_____. "Great Britain, Russia and the Eastern Question," (1831-1841); in "Institute of Historical Research," Vol. XI, No. 32, p.131, (USA).
BOSSY, R.V., "Vechi năzuinte federaliste în Sud-Estul European," Bucuresti, 1939-1940. (Old Federalist Aspirations in Southeastern Europe).
_____. "L'Autriche et les Prinicipautés Unies," Bucarest, 1938.
BOTEZ, Eugen, (Jean Bart) "La Question du Danube et sa solution," Galatz, 1920.
_____. "Europolis," Bucarest, 1939.
BRATIANU, George, "La Mer Noire, des origines à la conquête ottomane"; Societa Academica Dacoromana, Act Historica, Tom IX, Monachii, Germany, 1969.
BRATIANU, Vintila, "Chestia Dunării," expozeu în Adunarea Deputatilor, 5 Martie 1920, Bucuresti, 1920 (The Danube Question, presentation in the Chamber of Deputies, March 5, 1920).
BRENER, Robert, "Excursion in the interior of Russia; including sketches of the Character and Policy of the Emperor Nicholas," Vol. I, London, 1840.
BREZEZINSKI, Zbigniew, "Peaceful Engagement in Europe's Future"; School of International Affairs, Columbia University, New York, 1965.

BUEL, J.W., "Metropolitan Life Unveiled or the Mysteries and Miseries of America's Great Cities," San Francisco, 1882.
BULGARIA, "La question bulgare et les états balcaniques." Sofia, 1919.
BUNSEN, Th., "La Question du Danube"; in "Revue de droit international et de législation comparée," Tome XVI, Bruxelles, 1884.
BURY, J.B.. "History of Greece," London 1931; see W. Durant: "Life in Greece."
BYRNES, Robert, (Editor) "The United States and Eastern Europe"; Published by the American Assembly, Columbia University, Prentice-Hall, Inc., Englewood Cliffs, New Jersey, 1967.
BYZANTIUS, Dionisius, in "Anaplus Bospori"; ed. R. Guengerich, Berlin, 1927.
CAMARIANO, Nestor, "Alexandre Mavrocordato, le Grand Dragoman: Son activité diplomatique," (1673-1709). Institute for Balkan Studies, Thessaloniki, Greece, 1971.
CAMPBELL, C. John, "Diplomacy on the Danube"; in "Foreign Affairs," January, 1949, New York.
_____. "America Policy toward communist Eastern Europe: The Choices Ahead." University of Minnesota Press, Minneapolis, 1965.
_____. "The United States in World Affairs," (1945-1947), New York, 1948.
CARPENTER, Rhys, "The Greek Penetration of the Black Sea"; in "American Journal of Archaeology," LII, (1948).
"CARTEA DE AUR," a semicentenarului firmei L. Mendl & Co. în navigatia si comertul dunărean," (1850-1900), Galati-Brăila; (Golden Anniversary of L. Mendl & Co. (1850-1900), in Danubian Navigation and Commerce).
CARTER, James, Cooldge, "Law: its Origin Growth and Function." G.P. Putnam's Sons, New York, 1907.
CARTANA, Iulian, and SEFTIUC, Ilie, "Dunărea în istoria poporului român." Bucuresti, 1972. (The Danube in the History of the Romanian People).
CHAMBERLAIN, Joseph, "The Regime of the International Rivers: Danube and Rhine." Faculty of Political Science, Columbia University, New York, 1923.
_____. "The Danube," Government Printing Office, Washington, D.C., 1918.
CHURCHILL, S.W., "Into Batle," Speeches, fifth ed., February 1941, Cassel and Co., Ltd., London, Toronto, Melbourne and Sydney.
_____. "The Second World War," Vol. I, "The Gathering Storm," Houghton Mifflin, Co., Boston. The Riverside Press Cambridge, Cambridge, Mass., 1948.
_____. "The Second World War, Vol. 6, "Triumph and Tragedy," Houghton Mifflin Co., Boston. The Riverside Press Cambridge, 1953.
CIORICEANU, G.D., "Les grands ports de Roumanie," Paris, 1928.
CIUREA, G., "Cauzele decăderii portului Brăila," Brăila, 1936. (Causes for the Decline of the Port of Brăila).

"COLECTIA DE DOCUMENTE HURMUZACHI," Vol. V, (Collection of Documents).
"LA COMMISSION EUROPÉENNE DU DANUBE ET SON OEUVRE, 1856 A 1931" (C.E.D.) or European Commission of the Danube (E.C.D.), Paris, 1931. Abbreviated: "La Commission Européenne et son...", (C.E.D., or E.C.D.).
──────. "Un siècle de cooperation internationale sur le Danube" (1856-1956), Rome, 1956.
──────. "Acte public relatif à la navigation des embouchures du Danube," Galatz le 2 Novembre 1865, in D. Sturdza, "Recueil...", op. cit., pp. 80-89.
──────. Règlement de navigation et de police applicable à la partie du Danube comprise entre Galatz et les embouchures," arrêté par la Commission Européenne du Danube le 19 Mai 1881.
"CONDICA TRATATELOR SI A ALTOR LEGAMINTE ALE ROMANIEI" (1354-1937), Vol. II edited by the Ministry for Foreign Affairs of Romania, Bucharest, 1938.
"CONSILIUL SUPERIOR AL TRANSPORTURILOR SI TARIFELOR" (C.S.T.T.), Bucuresti, 1940. (Executive Council of Transports and Tariffs). Abbreviation: "Documente C.S.T.T."; (C.S.T.T. Documents).
"CORRESPONDENCE BETWEEN GREAT BRITAIN AND RUSSIA, respecting Obstructions to the Navigation of the Sulina Channel of the Danube," in "State Papers" (1853-1854), see Vol. 44, at the Public Library, New York.
COSMIN, Edward, "Dossiers Secrets de la Triple Entente," Grèce, (1914-1922). Nouvelles Editions Latines, Paris, 1969.
"CRONICA LUI NESTOR," Traducere din limba rusă, comentată de G. Popa-Liseanu în "Izvoarele Istoriei Românilor," Vol. VII, Bucuresti, 1975. (The Chronicle of Nestor, translated from the Russian Language, commentary by G.Popa-Liseanu, in "Sources of Romanian History).
DALLIN, David, J., "Russia and Postwar Europe," 3rd ed., Yale University Press, New Haven, May, 1944.
──────. "The Real Soviet Russia," 3rd ed. New Haven, February, 1945.
──────. "The Big Three: United States, Great Britain and Russia." Yale University Press, New Haven. 1945.
DANUBIUS, "La poussée anglaise en Europe Centrale et Orientale"; in "Affaires Danubiennes," No.4, Juin, 1936, Bucarest.
"THE DANUBIAN PRINCIPALITIES: THE FRONTIER LANDS OF CHRISTIAN AND THE TURK." Edited by a British Resident of Twenty years in the East (anonymous), 2 Vol. Richard Bentley, Publisher, London, 1854.
DASCOVICI, Nicolae, "La Question du Bosphore et des Dardanelles," Genève, 1915.
──────. "Regimul Dunării si al Strâmtorilor în ultimele decade." Iasi, 1943. (The Regime of the Danube and the Straits in the latest Decades).

———. "Drept international public." Note de prelegeri la Universitatea din Iasi, 1931. (International Public Law, notes for Lectures at the University of Iasi).

———. "Interesele României"; în "Revista Insemnări iesene," No. 13-14, 1945. (Romania's interests: in the Review of Notes on Iasi).

———. "Comisiunea Europeana a Dunării," în ziarul "Argus," Iulie, 1936, Bucuresti. (The European Commission of the Danube; in the newspaper "Argus," Bucharest).

———. "Le Danube et les intérêts économiques de l'Europe," Paris, 1919.

———. "Le problème du Danube"; in "Affaires Danubiennes," No. 1, Bucarest. 1938.

———. "Politica rusească la gurile Dunării si în Marea Neagră"; Conferintă la "Liga Navală Română," publicatia 45, Bucuresti, 1942. (Russian Policy at the Mouths of the Danube and the Black Sea; lecture given at the Romanian Naval League).

———. "Dunărea noastră," Bucuresti, 1927. (Our Danube).

———. "Politica comercială a Dunării," Bucuresti, 1926. (Danubian Commercial Policy).

DEMORGNY, G., "La question du Danube." Paris, 1911.

———. "Danube et Adriatique." Les Editions Domat-Montchrestien, Paris 1934.

"DICTIONARUL LIMBEI ROMANE LITERARE CONTEMPORANE," Vol. I, Bucuresti, 1955. (Dictionary of Contemporary Romanian Literature).

"DICTIONAIRE ENCYCLOPEDIQUE DE SCIENCES MEDICALE," III, Serie 1, Paris.

DICULESCU, D., IANOVICI, C., DANIELOPOL, C., and POPA, N., "Relatiile comerciale ale Tărilor Românesti cu Peninsula Balcanică." (1829-1858), Bucuresti, 1970. (Commercial Ties of the Romanian Countries with the Balkan Peninsula).

DIEHL, CH., "Venetia"; traducere în limba română. Bucuresti, 1942. (Venice).

"DISPATCH," by Lieutenant-Colonel Sir. H. Trotter; see Trotter.

DJILAS, Milovan, "Conversation with Stalin"; translated from the Serbo-Croat by Michael B. Petrovich. Harcourt, Brace, and World, Inc., New York, 1962.

DJUVARA, T.G., "Raport asupra situatiunii comerciale al Bulgariei," Bucuresti. (Report on Bulgaria's Commercial Situation).

DOCAN, N., "Exploratiuni austriace pe Dunăre la sfârsitul veacului al XVIII," Bucuresti, 1914. (Austrian Exploitations of the Danube at the end of the XVIIIth Century).

———. "Memoriu despre lucrările cartografice privitoare la răsboiul dintre 1787-1791," Bucuresti, 1911. (Memorandum on Cartographic Studies Concerning the War of 1787-1791).

"DOCUMENTE SARDE" see D. Bodin.

"DOCUMENTE C.S.T.T." see "Consiliul Superior al Transporturilor si Tarifelor.
"DOCUMENTE DIPLOMATICE": Opera diplomatică a lui Kogălniceanu, by a Collective of Editors, Bucuresti, 1972. (Diplomatic Documents: Diplomatic works of Kogălniceanu).
"DIE DONAU": "Ihre Wirtschaftliche und Kulturelle Mission in Mittel und Osteuropa." Wien, October, 1932.
DRAGE, Geoffrei, "Austro-Hungary." London, 1909.
DUBOIS et BAUER, "Le Danube et les intérêts économiques de l'Europe." Paris, 1919.
DUMITRESCU, V., "Berna": Studiu publicat în "Reprezentantele diplomatice ale României, Vol. II, Bucuresti, 1971. ("Berne," study published in "Romanian Diplomatic Representations)."
"DUNAREA IN ISTORIA POPORULUI ROMAN." (The Danube in the History of the Romanian People); see Cartana and Septiuc.
DUPUIS, CH., "La Liberté des voies de communication"; in "Recueil de Cours de l'Académie du Droit International," Paris, 1924.
EAST, W.G., "The Union of Moldavia and Wallachia (1859): An Episode in Diplomatic History"; Cambridge University Press, Cambride, 1929.
"L'EMPEREUR NAPOLEON III ET LES PRINCIPAUTES ROUMAINES." Paris, 1858.
"THE ENCYCLOPEDIEC DICTIONARY," Vol. I, Philadelphia.
"ENCYCLOPAEDIA BRITANICA," 14th ed., London, 1929.
ENGELHARDT, E., "Etudes sur les embouchures du Danube." Galatz, 1862.
_____. "Du régime conventionnel des fleuves internationaux." Paris, 1879.
_____. "Les embouchures du Danube et la Commission instituée par le Congrès de Paris"; in "Revue des Deux Mondes," XL Année, seconde période, tome quatre-vingt-huitième, Paris, 1870.
_____. "L'Origine et la constitution des communautés fluviales conventionelles"; in "Revue d'histoire diplomatique," pp.497-512. Paris, 1888.
_____. "Histoire du droit fluvial conventionnel": précédée d'une étude sur le régime de la navigation interieure aux temps de Rome et au Moyen Age, Paris, 1889.
_____. "Discussion des derniers actes conventionnels relatifs au régime des fleuves internationaux"; in "Revue de Droit International et de Legislation Comparée," tome XIII, Bruxelles et Leipzig, 1881.
"EUROPEAN COMMISSION OF THE DANUBE," see "La Commission Européenne du Danube.
EVANS, A., "The Palace of Minos," Vol. III. London, 1921.
EYSINGA, W.J., "Evolution du Droit Fluvial International du Congrès de Vienne au traité de Versailles." (1815-1919). Leyda, 1920.
FILITI, Ion, "Domniile române sub Regulamentul Organic," (1834-1848). Bucuresti, 1915. (Romanian reigns under the Organic Regulation).

FILITI, Gr., "Securité européenne"; in "Aspects des relations Soviéto-Roumaines," Vol. II, (1967-1971), pp.71-153, Diffusion Minard, Paris 1971.
FINLEY, M.I., "The Ancient Greeks." London, 1963.
FISCHER-GALATI, Stephen, "Eastern Europe in the Sixties." Frederick A. Praeger, Publishers, New York, Washington, D.C., London, New York, 1963.
_____. "20th Century Rumania"; Columbia University Press, New York and London, 1970.
_____. "The New Rumania": From People's Democracy to Socialist Republic." Cambridge, Mass., the M.I.T. Press, 1967.
_____. "Rumania": A Bibliographic Guide. The Library of Congress, Washington, D.C., 1963.
FLORESCU, Radu, R.N., "Les incidents de Sulina"; in "Aspects des relations Russo-Roumaines, rétrospectives et orientations," pp.38-46. Diffusion Minard, Paris, 1967.
_____. "The Struggle against Russia in the Roumanian Principalities," (1821-1854); "Acta Historica," tomus II, Societas Academica Dacoromana, Monachii, 1962.
_____. British Reaction to the Russian Regime in the Danubian Principalities"; in "Journal of Central European Affairs" Vol. XXII, pp.27-42, April, 1962.
_____. "Lord Strangford and the Problem of the Danubian Principalities, 1821-1824"; in "Slavonic and East European Review, Vol XXXIX, pp. 472-488, June, 1961.
FOCAS, Spiridon G., "Traficul prin Canalul Suez," Bucuresti, 1944. (Traffic through the Suez Canal).
_____. "Traficul prin Canalul Sulina, in perioada celor două răsboaie mondiale"; in "Analele Economice si Statistice," No. 4-6, 1945. (Traffic through the Sulina Canal during the Period of the Two World Wars).
_____. "Grecii in massa româna," Bucuresti, 1946. (Greeks within the Romanian Population).
_____. "Două Memorii cu privire la încălcarea drepturilor României la Gurile Dunării" New York, 1967. (Memoirs concerning the infringement of Romania's rights at the Mouths of the Danube River).
_____. "Bessarabia in the Political Order of Southeast Europe in the 19th Century"; in "Acta Historica," tomus VIII, pp. 119-144, Romae, 1968. Also excerptum in booklet, Roman, 1968.
_____. "The Greeks in the Fluvial Navigation of the Lower Danube River." in Greek langauage. Institute for Balkan Studies, Thessaloniki, 1975. Awarded by the Academy of Athens.
FOURNIER, M., "Le nouveau Danube." in "Revue politique et parlamentaire," t.95, Paris, 1918.
FUNDATEANU, Preda, "Esirea la mare." Bucuresti, 1944. (Outlet to the Sea).

"Consideratiuni geofizice asupra fenomenului dela gurile Dunării si raportul lor cu problema desăvârsirii navigatiei pe Dunărea Maritimă" Academia Română, 14, pp.99-106. (Geophysical Considerations on the Pheonomenon at the Mouths of the Danube and their Relation to the Problem of Improving Navigation on the Maritime Danube).

GAFENCU, Grigore, "Dunărea internationala"; in Ziarul "Timpul," Bucuresti, 1938. (The International Danube," in the newspaper "Timpul" (The Times).

———. "Preliminaires de la guerre à l'Est." Egloff, Paris, 1944.

———. "Derniers jours de l'Europe: un voyage diplomatique en 1939." Egloff, Paris, 1946.

———. "Roumania at the Peace Conference" (1946-1947). Paris, 1946.

———. "Observations concerning the Draft Peace Treaty with Roumania" (1941-1947), Octobre, 1946, Paris.

———. "Eastern Countries and the European Order"; "International Affairs," No.2, April, Vol. XXIII, 1947, pp. 160-177.

GALCA, Th., "Navigatia fluvială si maritimă în România." Bucuresti, 1930. (Fluvial and Maritime Navigation in Romania).

GEFFCKEN, F.H., "La question du Danube." Berlin, 1883.

GENOV, Georgi, "Bulgaria and the Treaty of Neuilly," Sofia, 1935.

"GEOGRAFIA VAII DUNARII ROMANESTI." Institutul de Geografie si Geologie. Bucuresti, 1969. (The Geography of the Romanian Danube Vallay, by the Institute of Geography and Geology").

GEORGEVITCH, V., "La Serbie au Congrès de Berlin"; in "Revue d'Histoire Diplomatique," Paris, 1891.

GEORGAKOPOULOS, G.E., "To elinikon naftikon dia mesou ton aionon"; Athens, 1933. in Greek. (The Greek Navy through the Ages).

GIBBOND, Herbert, A., "Europe since 1918." third ed. New York and London, 1923.

GILBERT, Martin, "Russian History Atlas." The MacMillan, Co., New York, 1972.

GIRARDIN, Saint-Marc, "Souvenir de voyages et d'études." (2 Vol.), Vol.I, Paris, 1852.

GIURESCU, C.C., "Istoria pescuitului." Vol.I., Bucuresti, 1964 (History of Fishing)

———. "Istoricul orasului Brăila din cele mai vechi timpuri până astăzi," Bucuresti, 1968. (History of the city of Brăila from Ancient Times to the Present).

———. "Istoria Românilor," Bucuresti, 1938. (History of the Romanians).

GLASSER, E.,and others, "Drept International Fluvial," Bucuresti, 1973. (International Fluvial Law).

GOROVE, Stephen, "Law and Politics of the Danube: An interdisciplinary Study." Martinus Nijhoff, the Hague, 1964.

———. "Internationalization of the Danube": A Lesson in History"; in "Journal of Public Law," VIII, No.1, pp.124-154. Emory University Law School, Atlanta, Georgia.

GOSTAR, N., "Danubius," Bucuresti, 1967.
GRAHAM, Hutton, "Les nouveaux destins du Danube où va l'Europe." Paris, 1939.
GRAHAM, A.J., "The Date of the Greek Penetration of the Black Sea." in Bull. Inst., Class., Studies of University of London," London, 1958.
GREAT BRITAIN, Foreign Office, "Danube," 1882, No. 2. Correspondence respecting the execution of the provisions of the Treaty of Berlin regard to the navigation of the Danube, London, 1882.
_____ . "Conference on the navigation of the Danube," London, 1883. Protocoles of Conference.
GRECEANU, N., "Comisiunea Europeană a Dunării si Gurile Dunării," Bucuresti, 1938. (The European Commission of the Danube and the Mouths of the Danube).
_____ . "La barre de Soulina," Bucarest, 1934.
GYULAY, L., "Die Donau, Ungar und die anderen Donaustaaten"; see "Die Donau," Ihre wirtschaftliche...".
HAJNAL, Henry, "The Danube, its Historical, Political and Economic Importance." Martinus Nijhoff, the Hague, 1920.
_____ . "Le Droit du Danube International." Martinus Nijhoff, la Hague, 1929.
_____ . "La Commission Européenne du Danube et le dernier avis consultatif de la Cour Internationale de justice"; in "Revue de Droit International et de Législation Comparée," pp.588-645, IX, Paris, 1928.
HANCIU, D., "Evreii in Tările Românesti," Bucuresti, 1923. (The Jews in the Romanian Countries).
HANC, Joseph., "Eastern Europe and the United States," Boston, 1942.
HARTUCHE, N., and DRAGOMIR, I.T., "Săpăturile arheologice dela Brăilita în 1955"; în "Materiale si Cercetări Arheologice," III, Bucuresti, 1956. (Archaeological Explorations at Brăilita in 1935"; in Archaeological Materials and Researches).
_____ . "Pagini din istoria veche a orasului si raionului Brăila; în ziarul "Inainte," Brăila, 1966. (Pages from the Ancient History of the City and Raion of Brăila).
HARTLEY, A., "Description of the Danube and the works of recently executed at the Soulina Mouth"; in "Inst. Civ., Eng., pp. 277-308, London, 1862.
HAUSEN, W. Baldwin, "25 Years ago: Hitler Strikes"; in "New York Times Magazine," August 30, 1964.
HAYNOL, H., "Le Droit du Danube International." La Haye, 1929.
HERTSLET, Edward, "Map of Europe by Treaty," Vol. I., London, 1875.
HINES, Walker, "Rapport relatif à la navigation sur le Danube presenté à la Commission Consultative et du Transit de la Société des Nations." Société des Nations, Genève, 20 Août, 1921.

THE HISTORY OF NATIONS, Editor in Chief Henry Cabot Lodge; P.F. Collier & Son Co., Publishers, New York, 1928. "Turkey," Vol. 14; "Russia and Poland," Vol. 15; "England," Vol. 11; "Colonies," Vol. 20.
HOLTZENDORFF, Franz, "Les droits riveraines de la Roumanie sur le Danube"; Consultaion de Droit International, Leipzig, 1884.
HORN, Emil., "Etiene Szechenyi et la navigation du Danube"; in "Institut de France, Acad. de Sciences Morales et Politiques," Mars-Avril, Paris, 1931.
HOSTIE, J., "Examen de quelques règles du droit international dans le domain de communication et du travail"; in "Recueil des Cours de l'Académie du Droit International," Vol. II, Paris, 1932.
HURMUZACHI, see Colectia de documente.
IMBERT, L., "Le régime juridique actuel du Danube"; in "Revue Générale de Droit International Public," Janiver-Mars, Paris, 1951.
IONIDOU-MBITSIADOU: G.L. Ars of "O russkoj sistem pokrovitel' stva, i o nekotoryk ee social no-ekonomiceskih i politiceskin posledstvijah deja neselenije balcan-konec, XVII-nacalo, XIXVI, review in "Balkaniki Bibiographie," Tom. V, 1951, ed by K.A. Dimakis, published by the "Institute for Balkan Studies," Thessaloniki, 1967.
IORGA, N., "Le Danube d'Empire"; in "Mélanges offerts a M. Gustave Schlumberger à l'occasion du quatre-vingtième anniversaire de sa naissance," 17 Octobre 1924, Paris.
_____. "La révolution française et le Sud-Est de l'Europe"; Bucarest, 1934.
_____. "Roumains et Grecs au cours des siècles"; Bucarest, 1921.
_____. "Byzance après Byzance; continuation de l'histoire de la vie Byzantine"; Bucarest, 1971.
_____. "La révolution grecque sur le Danube"; Bucarest, 1916.
_____. "Les premières relations entre l'Angleterre et les Pays Roumains du Danube" (1477-1611); in "Mélange d'Historie," Paris, 1913.
_____. "Politica externă a Regelui Carol I"; Bucuresti, 1923. (The Foreign Policy of King Carol I).
_____. "Ce este Bizantul?," conferinta la "Universitatea Liberă"; Bucuresti, 1939. (What is Byznatium?, Lecture given at the Free University).
_____. "Istoria Comertului"; Bucuresti, 1937. (The History of Commerce).
_____. "Populatia Dobrogei la 1850"; in "Revista Dobrogei," Anul III, No.1, Constanta, 1922. (The Population of Dobruja).
_____. "Drumurile de comert creatoare ale statelor românesti; Bucuresti, 1928. (Routes of Commerce creators of the Romanian States).
_____. "Românii în cadrul vietii economice din Balcani"; Bucuresti, 1935. (The Romanians in the framework of Balkan Economic Life).
_____. "Poporul român si marea"; Vălenii de Munte (România), 1938. "The Romanian People and the Sea).
_____. "Istoria Românilor prin călători"; Vol. II, Bucuresti, 1925. (History of the Romanians see by Travellers).

"A cui e Dunărea?" Conferintă tinută la Giurgiu, 9 Noembrie 1908; Vălenii de Munte, 1908. "Whose is the Danube?."
──────. "Studii asupra Chiliei si Cetătii Albe"; Bucuresti, 1899.
──────. (Studies on Kilia and Cetatea Albă).
──────. "Din trecutul istoricului orasului Brăila"; Brăila, 1926. (From the Past History of the City of Brăila).
──────. "Din viata socială a Brăilei sub Turci"; Bucuresti, 1933. (From the Social Life of Brăila under the Turks).
──────. "Chestiunea Dunării"; in "Analele istoriei României" (The Danube Question).
──────. "Histoire des Etats Balcaniques jusqu'à 1924"; Paris, 1925.
──────. "Histoire des relations entre la France et les Roumains"; Paris, 1918.
──────. "Histoire des relations Russo-Roumain"; Paris, 1917.
──────. "The Problem of the Danube: A Roumanian View"; in "New Europe," 8, Vol.4, London, 1920.
──────. "Contributii la istoria modernă a portului Galati"; Bucuresti, 1932. (Contributions to the Modern History of the Port of Galatz).
──────. "Chestiunea Dunării"; în "Analele Istoriei României," Bucuresti, 1888. (The Danube Question).
──────. "Istoria comertului român, epoca veche"; Bucuresti, 1925. (History of Romanian Commerce, in Ancient times).
ISRAEL, Fred, "Major Peace Treaties of Modern History" (1648-1967) Vol. I, II; New York, 1967.
ISTORIA ORASULUI BUCURESTI," Bucuresti, 1965. (History of Bucharest).
JOMINI, A., "Etude diplomatique sur la guerre de Crimée," (1852-1856), Vol. II; St. Petersbourg, 1878.
JOURNAL DES DEBATS, "Souvenir de voyages et d'études," Vol. 1, Paris, 1852-1853.
KARATHEODORI, Alex, Pasha, "Le rapport secret sur le Congrès de Berlin adressé à la Sublime Porte"; (ed. B. Bareilles), Paris, 1919.
KENAN, George, T., "The Decision to Intervene: Soviet-American Relations"; (1917-1920), Vol. II, Atheneum, New York, 1967.
──────. "Memoirs" (1925-1950); An Atlantic Monthly Press Book, Little, Brown and Co., Boston, Toronto, 1967.
──────. "American Diplomacy:, (1900-1950); The University of Chicago Press, 1951.
──────. "Realities of American Foreign Policy"; The Norton Library, W.W. Norton and Co., Inc., New York, 1966.
KESSELING, A., "A Soldier's Record"; New York, 1954.
KOGALNICEANU, Mihail, "Chestiunea Dunării"; Bucuresti, 1883. (The Danube Question).
──────. "Kogălniceanu, Mihail, documente diplomatice," de un colectiv, Bucuresti, 1972. (Diplomatic Documents, by a collective of editors).

KORDATOU, Iani, "Istoria tis archaias Ellados"; In Greek, Athens, 1960. (History of ancient Greece).
KUHL, Charles, H.L. "The Sulina Branch of the Danube"; in "Inst. Civ. Eng, 91, London, 1891.
_____. "The Sulina Mouth of the Danube;" in "inst. Civ. Eng., 91, London, 1887.
KVASSAY, Jeno, "Le Danube international et la Hongrie"; in "Revue de Hongrie," August 15, 1913, Budapesta.
LABAREE, B.W., How the Greeks Sailed into the Black Sea"; in "American Journal of Archaeology," LXI, 1957.
LACROIX, "Les blasons des villes grecques"; in "Etudes d'archeologie classique," I (1955-11950), Paris.
LAHOVARI, Ch., "Mémoirs de l'amiral Paul Tchitchagof," Paris, 1909.
LAIMOU, Andrea, "To Naftikon tou Ghenous ton Hellinon," in Greek, Tom. A (1968; Tom B. (1969), Athens. (The Navy of the Greek Nation).
LALANE, M.L., "La Question du Danube"; in "Revue Nouvelle," Paris, 1880.
_____. "Rapport sur les travaux de la Commission Technique Européenne formés en vertue d'un accord intervenu entre les Puissances signataires du Traité de Berlin de 1878," Paris, 1879.
LAMBRINO, S., "Tomis, cité greco-gète chez Ovide: L'Ovidiana," Paris, 1958.
LEAHY, D.V., "I WAS THERE," New York, 1950.
LEMAN, John, "The meaning of the Danube"; in "Geographical Magazine," London, 1928.
LENGYEL, "The Danube," New York, 1939.
LEVI, Armand, "La Russie sur le Danube," Paris, 1854.
_____. "La Roumanie et la liberté du Danube," Paris, 1883.
"LEXICOGRAFUL SUIDAS," Tom.I, Bucuresti, 1896; see Papadopol-Calimachi, "Dunărea in literatura si traditiuni," Bucuresti, 1886.
"LONDON'S UNDERWORLD," see Quennel, Peter.
LOON, H.W., "Ships and how they sailed the Seven Seas"; translated in Greek, Athens, 1960.
LUDWIG, Emil, "Bismarck": The Story of a Fighter, translated from the German by Eden and Cedar Paul. Blue Ribbon Books, reprinted in February, New York, 1932.
MACARTENEY, C.A., "The Habsburg Empire," (1790-1918). The MacMillan Co., New York, 1969.
MACHRAY, Robert, "The Struggle for the Danube and the Little Entente," (1929-1938), London, 1929.
MAGHERU, C., "Memoriul în legătură cu Circulara otomana din 7 August 1856," Bucuresti, 26 Octombrie 1856; manuscris la Academia Română, vezi Sp. Focas, "Două Memorii cu privire la încălcarea drepturilor României la Gurile Dunării," New York, 1967. (Memorandum with reference to the Ottoman Circular of 7 August 1856; manuscript at the Romanian Academy, published by Sp. Focas in "Două memorii..." (Two Memoirs concerning..."

MALITA, Mircea, "Romanian Diplomacy: A Historical Survey," Bucharest, 1970.
MAMATEY, Victor, "The United States and East Central Europe" (1914-1918); in "Journal of Central European Affairs," Vol. 10, Boulder, Colorado, October, 1950.
MANCE, Osborne, "International River and Canal Transport," London, 1944.
MANCIU, V., "România si conferinta dela Constantinopol din Decembrie 1876-Januarie 1877"; în "Revista Universitătii C.A. Parhon," No.9, Bucuresti, 1957. (Romania and the December 1876-Jan. 1877 Conference of Constantinople).
MARCANTONATO, Leon, "L'Evolution du Statut International du Danube Maritime de 1938 à 1948"; in "Revue Hellenique de Droit International," No.1 et 2, Athens, 1948.
MARTIAN, Dionise, Pop, "Despre navigatia pe Dunăre"; în "Revista Analele Economice," Anul III, No. 9-12, Bucuresti, 1862. (Of Navigation on the Danube).
_____ . "Câteva roade ale monopolului austriac pe Dunăre"; in "Revista Analele Economice, Bucuresti, 1862. (Some advantages of the Austrian Monopoly on the Danube."
MARTIN, Gilbert, "Russian History Atlas." The MacMillan Co., New York, 1972.
MARX, Karl, "Insemnări despre România," Bucuresti, 1964. (Notes on romanians," manuscript discovered in an Amsterdam Library and first published by the Academy of the Republic of Romania)
_____ . "Marx, K., vs. Russia." Russia, A cure for Russophobia (pamphlet). edit. with an introduction by A. Doering; Ungar Paper Book, New York, 1962.
_____ . "People's Paper," December 17, 1853; in Marxism Nationality and War," part two: "National War," (1848-1871), edit. by Dona Torr, London, 1941.
MAUROIS, Andre, "Disraeli: A Picture of the Victorian Age," translated from French by Hamish Miles. D. Appleton and Co., New York, 1928.
_____ . "Lyanty," Paris, 1981.
MAY, Arthur, J., "The Hapsburg Monarchy," (1867-1914). The Norton Library, W.W. Norton and Co., New York, 1951.
McGREW and RODERICK, E., "Russia and Cholera," (1823-1832); University of Wisconsin, 1965; quoted by Hugh Seton-Watson in "The Russian Empire," p.213, note. 1.
McLAUGHLIN, Terence, M., "Dirt: A. Social History as Seen Through the Uses and Abuses of Dirt." Stein and Day, Publishers, New York, 1971.
MEDLICOTT, W.M., "The Congress of Berlin and After: A Diplomatic History of the Near Eastern Settlement," (1878-1880). Methuen and Co., Ltd., London, 1938.
_____ . "The Berlin Treaty: Fifty Years Afterwards"; in "Quarterly Review," July, 1928.

BIBLIOGRAPHY 675

"MEMORANDUM," du Gouvernement Roumain sur un régime provisoire du Danube Maritime, Bucarest, 15 Février, 1941, presented by V.V. Pella, Romania's representative at the 1941 Danubian Conference at Bucharest. The original in the Archives of the Ministry for Foreign Affairs of Romania, a copy being in author's possession.
"MEMOIRE SUR LA QUESTION DU DANUBE," par Porumbaru, Em., Brătianu, V., Băicoianu, C., et Stefănescu, N., Bucarest, 1915-1916.
"MEMOIRE SUR LA LIBERTE DU DANUBE ET SUR L'ACTE DE NAVIGATION DU 7 NOVEMBRE," Paris, 1858. (anonymous).
"MEMOIRES DE L'AMIRAL P. Tchitchagof"; see Lahovari.
"MEMOIRES DU PRINCE NICH.SOUTZO," see Soutzo P.
"MEMOIRE DU GOUVERNEMENT ROYAL DE PRUSSE SUR L'ACTE DE NAVIGATION DU DANUBE DU 7 NOVEMBRE 1857, BERLIN, MARS, 1858"; in "La Question du Danube," M.A.E. de Roumanie, p. 319.
"MEMOIRE DU GOUVERNEMENT IMPERIAL D'AUTRICHE SUR LES DROITS DES ETATS RIVERAINES DU DANUBE, DE CONCLURE, DE RATIFIER ET DE METTRE EN EXECUTION L'ACTE DE NAVIGATION DU 7 NOVEMBRE 1857"; in "La Question du Danube," M.A.E. de Roumanie, p. 310.
MENDL, L. et Co., see "Cartea de aur."
MIHANOVIC, "Rapport du 6 Juillet 1855"; see L. Boicu, "Austria and the Romanian Principalities," p. 417.
MOISUC, VIORICA, "Varsovia"; in Reprezentantele Diplomatice ale României" Bucuresti, 1971, Vol.II, p. 141.
MORUZI, A.D., "Progrès et liberté: Commerce, finances, agriculture."; Galatz, 1861, see V. Slăvescu in "Life and Work of the Economist A. Moruzi."
———. "Rapport sur les entrepots de la ville de Galatz," Galatz, 1874.
MOUSSOU, Basile, "The Danube and the Romanian Black Sea Ports," London, 1931.
———. "The Danube Handy Book for Captains and Shipowners"; London, 1937.
NASTASE, Gh.,"Peuce: contributii la cunoasterea geografică, fizică si omenească a Deltei Dunării în antichitate"; in "Buletinul Societătii de Geografie," Bucuresti, 1932. (Pence, contributions to the Geographic, Physical and Human geography of the Danube Delta in Antiquity).
NENITESCU, M., "La Question du Danube," Bucarest, 1903.
———. "Dunărea în dreptul international," Bucuresti, 1903. (The Danube in International Law).
NETTA, Gheron, "Istoria Comertului," Bucuresti, 1923. (The History of Commerce).
———. "Incercări de navigatie pe râul Olt," Bucuresti, 1930. (Attempts of Navigation on the Olt River).
NEWMAN, Bernard, "Balkan Background," The MacMillan Publishing Co., New York, 1945.
———. "Balkans, horizons d'hier et d'aujourd'hui," Paris, 1946.

———. "The Blue Danube and Ride to Russia"; London, 1935.

NICOLSON, Harold, "The Congress of Vienna: A Study in Allied Unity"; (1812-1822); in Viking Press, seventh printing, March, 1965. New York, 1965.

———. "Peace Making 1919," The Universal Library, Grosset and Dunlap, New York, 1965.

———. "Diplomacy"; see ed. 1950. Geoffrey Camberlege, Oxford University Press, London, reprinted in 1952.

NISTOR, Ion, "Bizantinii în lupta pentru recucerirea Daciei si Transdanubiei"; Bucuresti, 1943. (The Byzantines in the Struggle for the Reconquest of Dacia and Transdanubia).

———. "Corespondenta lui Coronini din Principate: Acte si rapoarte din Iunie 1854-Martie 1857." Cernăuti; 1938. (Coronini's Correspondence from the Principalities: Documents and Reports of June 1854-March 1857).

———. "Temeiurile româno-bizantine ale începuturilor organizatiei noastre de Stat"; Bucuresti, 1943. (Roman-Byzantine Foundations of the Beginnings of our Organization as a State).

"NOTE DU COMTE DE CAVOUR SUR LA QUESTION DU DANUBE." publiée dans la "Gazette Piemontaise," du 12 Janvier 1859; in "La Question de Danube," M.A.E. de Roumanie, pp. 359-361.

OBEDEANU, C., "Grecii in Tările Românesti"; Bucuresti, 1900. (Greeks in the Romanians Countries).

OBOLESNKY, D., "The Byzantine Commonwealth: Eastern Europe"; (500-1453) Praeger Publishing, New York, 1971.

OTETEA, Andrei, "Tudor Vladimirescu si miscarea eteristă în Tările Românesti"; (1821-1823), Bucuresti, 1945. (Tudor Vladimirescu and the Eterist Movement in the Romanian Countries).

PAPADOPOL-CALIMACHI, "Generalul Pavelu Kisselev în Moldova si Tara Românească după documente rusesti"; Bucuresti, 1887. (General Pavelu Kisselev in Moldavia and Romanian Country according to Russian Documents).

———. "Dunărea în literatura si traditiuni," Bucuresti, 1886. (The Danube in Literature and Traditions).

PAPACOSTEA, Serban, "Oltenia sub stăpânirea austriacă" (1718-1739); Bucuresti, 1971, (Oltenia (the Little Wallachia) under Austrian Domination).

PARVAN, Vasile, "Ulmetul" (Cetate); Bucuresti, 1923. (Ulmetum-Fortress).

———. "Histria" (10), "Inscriptii găsite în anii 1914 si 1915, Bucuresti, 1923. (Histria, (10), Inscriptions discovered in the years 1914 and 1915.

———. "Histria" (VII): "Inscriptii găsite în anii 1916, 1921 si 1922"; Bucuresti, 1923. (Histria (VII): Inscriptions discovered in the Years 1916, 1921 and 1922.

———. "Gânduri despre lumea si viata la Greco-Romani din Pontul Stâng"; Bucuresti, 1920. (Reflections on the People and the Social Life in the Left Pontus).

———. "Gerusia din Calatis"; Bucuresti, 1920. (Gerusia of Calatis).
———. "Getica," O preistorie a Daciei"; Bucuresti, 1926. (Getica: a Prehistory of Dacia).
———. "Die Nationalität der Kaufleute in römische Kaiserreiche," Berlin.
———. "La pénétration héllénique et héllénistique dans la vallée du Danube"; Bucarest, 1931.
PETRESCU. G., COLESCU-VARTIC, STOURDZA, D., and STOURDZA, D.C., (ed). "Actes et documents relatifs à l'histoire de la régéneration de la Roumanie" (Vol.9); Bucarest, 1888-1901.
"PETIT LAROUSSE ILLUSTRE," Paris 1910.
PEYSSONEL, Ch., "Traité sur le commerce de la mer noire"; Paris, 1787.
PIPPIDE, D.M., "I Greci nel Basso Danubio: Dall'eta arcaico alla conquista romana." Biblioteca Storica dell' Antichita, Milano, 1971
———. "Histria," I, Bucuresti, 1964.
PIPPIDE, D.M. and BERCIU, D., "Din istoria Dobrogei: Getii si Grecii la Dunărea de Jos din cele mai vechi timpuri până la cucerirea romană," Vol.I; Bucuresti, 1965. (From the History of Dobruja: the Getae and the Greeks at the Lower Danube from the Earliest Times to the Roman Conquest).
POPA, Apostol, "Ne mor porturile"; Galati, 1925. (Our Ports are Dying).
POPESCU, Gh., "La navigation et la politique commerciale"; Bucarest, 1927.
———. "La navigation sur le Danube"; Bucarest, 1917.
———. "Le régime du Danube"; Paris, 1921.
———. "La liberté de la navigation sur les fleuves internationaux"; Paris, 1920.
POTAMIANOS, F., "Le nouveau droit maritime Grec"; Athènes, 1958.
POTEMKIN, V.P. "Istoria diplomatiei," I (traducere) Bucuresti, 1902. (History of Diplomacy-translation).
PRIGRADA, Anthony, "International Agreements Concerning the Danube"; New York, 1953.
PSOMIADES, Harry, J., "The Eastern Question: The Last Phase: A study in Greek-Turkish Diplomacy"; Institute for Balkan Studies, Thessaloniki, 1968.
"PUBLICATIONS OF THE PERMANENT COURT OF INTERNATIONAL JUSTICE," Series B., No. 14, December 8th 1927. Collection of Advisory Opinions. Jurisdiction of the European Commission of the Danube Between Galatz and Brăila; Leyde, 1927.
PURYEAR, Vernon J., "England, Russia and the Straits Question"; (1844-1856). Archon Books, Hamden, Connecticut, 1965.
———. "Odessa,: its Rise and International Importance," (1815-1850); "Pacific Historical Review," Vol. III, 1934, pp.192-215.
———. "New Light of the Origine of the Crimean War"; in "Journal of Modern History," Vol. III, 1931, pp.219-234.
———. "International Economics and Diplomacy in the Near East: A Study of British Commercial Policy in the Levant," (1834-1853), Stranford, 1935.

QUENNEL, Peter, Editor of "London's Underworld"; selections from "Those that will not work," the fourth volume of "London Labour and the London Poor," by H. Myhew, London; no date of publication.
"LA QUESTION DU DANUBE," ed. par le Ministère des Affairs Etrangèrs de Roumanie (M.A.E.), Bucarest; 1883, Also in Romanian text.
QUIN, M.J., "Steam Jurney down the Danube" (2 Vol.); London, 1835.
"RAPPORTS DE LA COMMISSION TECHNIQUE INTERNATIONALE POUR L'EXAMENE DES QUESTIONS RELATIVES A L'AMELLIORATION DES BRANCHES DU DANUBE" Paris, 1858.
RASMUSSEN, C.B., "Freedom of Danube"; in "Current History," XII, January 1947, p.27 (U.S.A.).
RAVARD, Carlo, "Il Danubio, fiume internazionale"; Milano, 1937.
REGNAULT, Elias, "Mystères diplomatiques au bords du Danube"; Paris, 1858.
RELATIILE INTERNATIONALE ALE ROMANIEI IN DOCUMENTE" (1368-1900), de Ionescu, I., Bărbulescu, P., si Gheorghe, Gh.; Bucuresti, 1971. (Romania's International Relations in Documents," compeled by a collective.
REPREZENTANTELE DIPLOMATICE ALE ROMANIEI," Vol.I (1859-1917); Bucuresti, 1967 si Vol. II (1911-1939); Bucuresti, 1971, (Romania's Diplomatic Representations, Vol. I (1859-1917), 1967 and Vol. II (1911-1939); compeled by a collective.
REY, Williams, "Autriche, Hongrie et Turquie" (1839-1848); Paris, 1849.
RICKER, T.W., "The Making of Roumania: A Study of an International Problem, (1856-1866). Oxford University Press: Humphrey Millford, London, 1931.
ROBERT, Henry, "The Satellites in Eastern Europe"; in "The Annals," Vol. CCCXVII, May, 1968, (U.S.A.).
ROUSSEAU, Charles, "Principles generaux du Droit International Public," T.I, Paris, (see L. Imbert, op. cit., p.81).
RUSSES ET TURKS: "La guerre d'Orient," (1877-1878); Paris, 1878. (anonymous).
SAVEANU, Sauciuc, "Cultura cerealelor în Grecia antică si politica cerealistă a Atenienilor"; Bucuresti, 1925. (Cereal Culture in Ancient Greece and the Athenian Cereal Policy).
SCHLIEMANN, H., "Ilios," New York, 1881.
SCHROEDER, Paul, W., "Austria and the Danubian Principalities" (1853-1856); in "Central European History," Vol. III, No.3, September 1969.
SCATT, John, "Duel for Europe: Stalin versus Hitler"; Hughton Mifflin Co., Boston, the Riverside Press, Cambridge, Cambridge, 1942.
SEMAFORUL DUNARII SI AL MARII NEGRE, de Constantin Tonegaru, Gustav Eder si Jack Corbu; Brăila, 1920. (Semaphore of the Danube and Black Sea).
SETON-WATSON, R.W., "A History of the Roumanians: From Roman Times to the Completion of Unity"; Archon Books, 1963 (reprinted).

SETON-WATSON, Hugh, "The Russian Empire"; University Press, Oxford at the Clarendon Press, 1967.
_____. "The East European Revolution"; Frederick A. Praeger, Publishers, New York, Washington, 1966.
_____. "Eastern Europe Between the Wars 1918-1941." Harper Torch books, Harper and Publishers, New York, Evanston, and London, 1967.
SHANKLAND, P., and HUNTER, A., "Dardanelles Patrol"; New York, 1964.
SINCLAIR, I.M., "The Danube Conference of 1948"; in "The British Year Book of International Law," XXV, pp. 398-404, London, 1948.
SLAVESCU, Victor, "Viata si opera lui Petre Mavrogheni"; Bucuresti, 1939. (Life and Works of P. Mavrogheni).
_____. "Viata si opera economistului Nicolae Sutu" (1798-1871); Bucuresti, 1941. (Life and Works of the Economist Nicolae Sutu).
_____. "Viata si opera economistului Alexandru D. Moruzi "(1815-1878); Bucuresti, 1941. (Life and Works of the Economist Alexandru Moruzi).
_____. "Curs de transporturi"; Bucuresti, 1930. (Transportations Course).
SOCIETE DES NATIONS, "Journal Officiel," XII Année, No.4, Avril, 1931.
SOFRONIE, G., "Contributie la cunoasterea relatiilor dintre România si Comisiunea Europeană a Dunării"; Cluj (România), 1939. (Contributions to knowledge on Relations between Romania and the European Commission of the Danube).
_____. "Lupta diplomatică a României pentru Suveranitatea la Dunăre"; in "Revista economie teoretică, organizare politică si socială," Vol. I, Brasov, 1944. (Romania's Diplomatic Struggle for Sovereignty over the Danube).
SOLZHENITSYN, Aleks., "The Gulag Archipelago"; Harper and Row, New York, 1974 (paperback).
SOMERVELL, D.C., "Disraeli and Gladstone: A Due-Biographical Sketch," Garden City Publishing Co., Garden City, New York, 1936.
SOULANGE, Bodin, "Le Danube, fleuve international"; in "Revue hebdomadaire," Tome 8, Paris, 1921.
SOUTZO, Nicolas, "Mémoires du Prince Soutzo, publiés par Panaioti Rizos, Vienne, 1899; see Slăvescu V., "Viata si opera economistului Nicolae Sutu," p.17, note 1.
SPULBER, N., "The Economics of Communist Eastern Europe"; Willey, New York, 1957.
STEAD, Alfred, "Servia by the Servians"; London, 1909.
STEDMAN'S MEDICAL DICTIONARY, Baltimore, 1933.
STOIAN, Iorgu, "Tomitana: contributii epigrafice la istoria cetatii Tomis"; Ed. Institutul de Arheologie al Academiei Române, Bucuresti, 1962. (Tomitana, Epigraphic Contributions to the History of the Tomis Fortress).
STOKES, John, "Notes on the Lower Danube" (1860) Communicated by Capt. R. Collinson, May 9, 1859; in "Royal Geographical Soc. Journal," London 1860.

———. Conference at London, April 22, 1890, in "La Commission Européenne et son oeuvre" (1856-1931), p.4, op. cit.
STRABON, "Géographie de Strabon"; traduite du grec en français, tome III, Paris, 1812.
STRAITS, "Darea de seamă analitică asupra Conventiei privitoare la regimul Strâmtorilor" de către Delegatiunea României la Conferinta Strâmtorilor dela Montreux, 21 Iulie 1936; in Arhiva Ministerului Afacerilor Străine al României. Copie în posesia autorului prezentei lucrări. (Analytical Report of the Convention concerning the Regime of the Straits, by the Romanian Delegation to the Montreux Conference of the Straits, July 21, 1936. The original is in the Archives of the Romanian Ministry for Foreign Affairs; a copy is in the possession of the Author of the present work).
STURDZA, D., "Recueil de documents relatifs à la liberté de navigation au Danube"; Berlin, 1904.
———. "Insemnătatea lucrărilor Comisiunii Europene de la Gurile Dunării"; Bucuresti, 1913. (Significance of the Works of the European Commission at the Mouths of the Danube).
STURDZA, D.A., "Les travaux de la Commission Européenne des bouches du Danube," 1859 a 1911"; Vienne, 1913.
SUMNER, B.H. "Peter the Great and the Emergence of Russia"; Collier Books, New York, 1962.
———. "Russie and the Balkans"; (1870-1880), Oxford, 1937.
SUTU, Nicolae, "Exposé des procédés à employer pour assurer la navigation du Sereth" (1850-1851); in Slăvescu, Victor, "Viata si opera economistului N. Sutu," pp. 452-456.
TARLE, E.V., "Răsboiul Crimeei," Vol. I-11, Bucuresti, 1952. (The Crimean War," translated from the Russian).
TAYLOR, A.J.P., "The Habsburg Monarchy: A History of the Austrian Empire and Austria-Hungary" (1809-1918). Harper Torchbooks, the Academy Library, Harper and Row Publishers, New York and Evanton, 1965.
TEMPERLY, N.W., "A History of the Peace Conference of Paris," I; London, 1920-1924.
THOMAZI, A., "Istoria navigatiei," traducere de V. Cipu, Bucuresti, 1942. (History of Navigation," translation by V. Cipu).
THOOVENEL, L., "Trois années de la question d'Orient" (1856-1859). Paris, 1897.
TITULESCU, Nicolae, "Documente diplomatice"; Bucuresti, 1967. (Diplomatic Documents, by a collective).
———. "Discursuri," Bucuresti, 1967. (Discourses).
TROTTER, Henry "Dispatch," Reporting upon the Operations of the European Commission of the Danube during the years 1894-1906, presented to both Houses of Parliament, August 1907, with the reference to "Commercial," No.9 (1907), printed for his Majesty's Sationary Officel London, 1907.
TRUFASU, M., si EMILIAN, S., "Istoricul portului Brăila"; Brăila, 1930. (History of the Port of Brăila).

BIBLIOGRAPHY 681

TRUMAN, Harry, "Mémoirs" Vol.1, "Year of Decisions"; Doubleday and Company, Inc., Garden City; New York, 1955.
_____. "Mémoirs," Vol. II, "Years of Trial and Hope," Doubleday and Company, Inc., Garden City, New York, 1956.
_____. "Report to the Nation on the Potsdam Conference, on August 9, 1945; in Dep. State Bull., XIII, August 12, 1945.
TSOURKAS, Cleobule, "Les débuts de l'enseignement philosophique et la libre pensée dans les Balkans: la vie et l'oeuvre de Théophile Corydallée"; (1563-1646), Bucarest, 1948. Second edition published by the "Institute for Balkan Studies," Thessaloniki, 1967.
TURDEANU, Emil, "Două campanii rusesti în Moldova" (1711 si 1729); in "Revista Fiinta Românească," No.3, Paris, 1965. (Two Russian Campaigns in Moldavia).
UKASE, OF 1836 in "Petersburgerzeitung," Febr. 7, 1836; reproduced by D. Urquhart; in "The Mistery of the Danube"; see Urquhart.
URQUHART, David, "The Mystery of the Danube, showing how through secret diplomacy that River has been closed"; London, 1851.
_____. "Progress of Russia"; London, 1853.
UNITED STATES OF AMERICA, Dept. of State. Office of Strategic Services: "The Danube River and its Control since 1938," Washington, D.C., 1945.
_____. "Documents on German Foreign Policy" (1918-1945), II, Washington, D.C., 1953.
_____. "Depart. of State, "Toward the Peace"; Documents, publ., No. 2298, Washington, D.C., 1945.
THE UNITED STATES AND EASTERN EUROPE, ed. by Robert F. Byrnes, Published by the "American Assembly," Columbia University. Anglewood. Cliffs, New Jersey, 1967.
UNITED NATIONS: "Economic Commission for Europe"; in "Annual Bull., of Transport, Statistic for Europe," 1961; New York, 1962.
_____. "Bull I, October 7, 1946.
_____. "Bull I, October 14, 1946.
"UN SIECLE DE COOPERATION INTERNATIONALE SUR LE DANUBE: (1856-1956)," Rome, 1956. (Former European Commission of the Danube), Rome 1958.
VACARESCO, V.T., "Serbia in 1871-1872"; in "Două memorii," publicate de Nicolae Iorga; Bucuresti, 1916. (Serbia in 1871-1872; in "Two Memoranda," published by N. Iorga).
VALSAN, G., "Dunărea de Jos în viata poporului român"; Bucuresti, 1927; (The Lower Danube River in the Life of the Romanian People).
VALLOTON, James, "Le régime juridique du Danube Maritime devant la Cour Permanente de Justice Internationale," Lausanne, 1928.
VANDERBERG, Arthur, Jy. "Private papers of Senator Vanderberg"; Boston, 1952.
VARDALA, Ion, "Exposé de quelques solutions du problème concernant l'aménagement de la voie navigable du Danube à la Mer"; Galatz, 1932.

VASILESCU, Alex. "Anuarul Dunării pe anul 1930"; Bucuresti, 1930.
VASILESCO, Gr., "Inghetul Dunării si navigatia maritimă"; Bucuresti, 1928. (The Freezing of the Danube and its Maritime Navigation).
VIDRASCU, Ion, "La voie navigable maritime du Danube"; Bucuresti, 1924.
_____. "Bratul Chilia"; Bucuresti, 1924. (The Kilia Branch).
VILAS, Martins, "The Barbary Coast San Francisco"; San Francisco, 1915.
VOISIN, Bey, "Notices sur les travaux d'amélioration du Danube et du bras de Soulina (1857-1891); Paris, 1893.
VULPE, Radu "The Dobruja Through the Centuries, its Historical Evolution and Geopolitical Aspects"; Bucharest, 1939.
_____. "La Dobruja dans l'antiquité"; Bucarest, 1938.
VULPE, Radu si BARNEA, Ion, "Din istoria Dobrogei: Românii la Dunărea de Jos," Vol.II, Bucuresti, 1968. (From the History of Dobruja: Romans at the Lower Danube).
WALTZIG, J.P., "Etudes historiques sur les corporations professionnelles chez les Romains depuis les origines jusqu'à la chute de l'Empire d'Occident," Vol. III (1895-1909); Louvain, 1895-1900.
WILKINSON, William, "An Account of the Principalites of Wallachia and Moldavia with Various Political Observations relative to them"; London, 1820.
THE WONDERFUL STORY OF LONDON: General editor Harold Weeler, revised edition edited by Webster Smith. Odhams Press London, Long Acre, London (no date of publication).
WOODWARD, E.L., "The Congress of Berlin," London, 1920.
WOOLFF, Robert, Lee, "The Balkans in Our Times." The Norton Library, W.W. Norton and Co., New York, 1967.
WURM, C.T., "Vier Briefe," Leipzig, 1855.
YOST, Charles, The Conduct and Misconduct of Foreign Affairs"; Reflections on U.S. Foreign Policy since World War II; Random House, New York, 1972
YOUGHAPERIAN, B.M., "L'Annuaire du Danube," 1902-1903 and 1916, Brăila.
YOONG, Georges, "Constantinople, des origins à nos jours"; Payot, Paris, 1948.
XENOPOL, A.D., "Istoria Românilor din Dacia Traiana," traducere din limba franceză de N.S. Govora (4 Vol.), Madrid, 1953, 1953, 1954, 1957.(History of the Romanians of Dacia Traiana (Trajan); translation from the French, by N.S. Govora, (4 Vol.); Madrid. 1953, 1953, 1954, 1957.
ZACHARIAS, Ellis, in collaboration with Ladislas Farago, "Behind closed Doors: the Secret of the Cold War." G.P. Putnam's Sons, New York, 1950.

INDEX

INDEX

Aarif, Pasha, Turk, Stat., 348
Accord, of Bucharest (1939), 525
Achilles, Pontarchos, 22
Act of Navigation (1857), 254-255 (see also Riparian Commission)
Ackerman, Convention (1826), 104
Acropolis, 25
Adakaleh, small island on the Lower Danube, 342
Adrianopol, Peace Treaty (1829); clauses, 101; Quarantine, 105; England's position, 106
Adriatic Sea, 71
Aegean Sea, 12, 18, 70, (see also White Sea)
Aegean, islands, 18, 31
Allège, 115, 182
Alderman, Boydell, Mayor of London, 135
Alexander I, Tsar of Russia, 81, 85, 228
Alexander II, Tsar of Russia, 348
Allied Control Commission, (1944), 575
Allied and Associated Powers (W.W.I), 432
Allied (Soviet) High Command, (1944), 525
Allied and Associated Powers, 454, 473
Allied Suprem Council (W.W.I.), 444, 454
Aluvium, 112, 114
America of Balkans, 185
Anarcharis, 20

Anderson, J., 108, 155, 212
Andrassy, Gyula, Count, Austro-Hung. Stat., 272, 326, 336, 342, 353, 342, 358, 371.
Andreadis, A., Gr., dipl., 465-466, 475, 479
Anglo-Russian conflict, (see also Obstacles)
Antipa, Grig., 407, 408, 463, 469, 496, 517, 548; Memorandum of (1942), 549-552
Apoikiae, anc., Greek colonies, 23
Apoikismos, (mégas great ancient Greek colonization), 22
Apollonia, 35
Arendt, 374
Argani (Arganis), bend of the Sulina Canal, 117, 138
Arges, river, 28
Argo, 11, 21
Argonauts, 11, 19, 20
Aristotle, 25
Armenians, 43
Armistice Agreements (W.W.II, between the U.S.S.R., with Bulgaria, România and Hungary, 574-576
Asbury, H., Am., hist., 188
Asprocastro, ancient Greek name (today port Cetatea Albă), 38

683

Austria, Attempts for internationalization of the navigation, 1, 59; see the Peace Treaty of Karlowitz (1699), 59-61; Peace Treaty of Passarowitz (1718), 61; Peace Treaty of Belgrade (1739), 66, 71 and the 1815 Vienna Congress, 82, 88; and the 1829 Peace Treaty of Adrianople, 106; measures at the Sulina Mouth, 183; and a new outlet to the Black Sea, 191-194; at the 1856 Paris Treaty, 228; at the 1855 Vienna Conf., 232-235; at the 1856 Paris Conf., 237-244, at the Riparian Commission (1857), 253-261, 286, 288; at the 1920-1921 Danube Statute, 470, 483, 490; at the 1948 Conf., of Belgrade, reservations over the Convention, 625.

Austrian traveler, 381

Austrian Danube Steam Navigation Co., (Erste Ostereichische Donau Dampfschiffarts - Gesellschaft - D.D.S.G.), 116, 192, 240, 242

Austrian East Indian Co., 71

Austrian-Russian Convention of Navigation, (1840), 201-204

Austria-Hungary; at the 1871 London Conf., and Treaty, 321-331; neutralization of the Danube (1877-1878), 335; at the 1878 Berlin Congress, 342, 344, 355-359; on the reorganization of E.C.D., 364, 365, 370-375; at the 1883 Treaty of London, 385, 382, 397, 400; at the 1918 Peace Treaty of Bucarest, 430-433; at the 1919 Peace Treaty of Versailles, 440

Avril, Count, 325

Axeinos Pontos (Black Sea), the inhospitable sea, 19, 20

Axiopolis, Greek colony, (today Hinog), 30

Axiopolis (today Hinog), ancient Greek colony, 30

Azof, sea of, 64

Azof, port, 59

Babadag, town, 33, in Dobruja
Băicoianu, Const., 433
Balcic, town, Dobruja, 23
Bălăceanu, C., 353
Baldwin, J.C., 455, 474, 478, 479
Baldwin, England's delegate at E.C.D., 429
Balkan, Southern, 67, 68
Baltic, Sea, 68
Balta Liman, Conv., (1849), 208
Banat, 62, 65
Bar of Sulina, 113 (see also Obstacles)
Bărăgan, the granary field of România, 29, 75
Baranovsky, (1948), 601
Barbary, Coast, 187
Barbarians, 6, 26
Barrère, 369, 371, 376, 380, 390, 401
Barrocyn, Baron, 209
Bart, Jean, (pen name of Eugen Botez)
Baule, Secretary of the International Commission, (I.C.D.), 438
Baumrucker, 183
Beauvale, Lord, 148
Bebler, Al., 604, 507, 624
Becke, 115, 294
Behles, (1918), 431, 443-444
Belgium, at the 1920-1921 Paris Conf., 461, 462, 470
Belloy, Commander, 436
Bell, G., 108, 155, 212
Belgrade, port, 62
Belgrade Agreement for neutralization of the Lower Danube (1940), 534
Belgrade Peace Treaty (1739), 66-67
Berlin Congress and Treaty (1878), 339-361; the problem of participation of the small riparian countries, 341-343; return of Russia as a riparian country, 345-355; débats on the San Stefano Treaty, 355, the extension of E.C.D. to Galatz, 357; the entrusting of Austro-Hungary with the removal of the Obstacles of the Cataracts and Iron Gates 359, clauses and inclusion of România in E.C.D., 360
Bessarabia, 74, passim.
Beust, Count, 323-325, 327-329, 371

INDEX 685

Bismarck, E.L. Prince, at 1878 Berlin Congress; 340-344, 349, 351-354, 356
Blackhouse, I., 127
Bleichroder, C., 340
Bloomfield, 116, 119
Blutte, E.L., 107, 108, 146, 153, 157, 208
Bodin, D., Rom., hist., author of "Documente Sarde" (Sardinian Documents), reference, passim.
Boicu, Ion, Rom., hist., 122, 285
Bolgrad, Case (1856-1857), 248-251
Bosnia, 67
Bosphorus, Strait, 69, 350, passim.
Botez, Eugen, (see also Jean Bart).
Bourdonnaye, (1814-1815), 77, 79, 233
Bourquency, Baron, 79
Brăila, port, 62, passim.
Brăila-Odessa, competition, 205-210, (see also Odessa)
Brașov, Road, 40
Brâcoveanu, Const., Prince of Wallachia, 60
Brătianu, Ion, 343, 466
Brauer, 518
British, Protégés (Ionians).
Bruck, 240
Bucharest Peace Treaty (1812), 72-76
Bucharest, Accord (1939), for admission of Germany in the E.C.D. (1939), 525
Buchanan, A., Sir, 116, 120, 123, 336
Budapest, 66, 242
Bulgaria, and the neutralization of the Lower Danube, 333-337; at the 1883 London Conf., 386, 395-397; and the W.W.I, 431; at the 1948 Belgrade Conf., 598-599, 618
Buol-Shauestein, Count, 6, 231, 239, 240, 241, 257, 286, 288
Bursen, Th., 388
Byrnes, James, 592
Bizantius, Dionisius, 16
Byzantines, 37, 39
Byzantium, 25, 41
Byzantine Empire, 38-41

Cabotage, navigation of, (1858), 273, 281, 473-485
Caffa, 40
Calafat, port (ancient Kalafatis), 33
California, see Little California, 179
Camariano, Nestor, 52n
Campbell, John, Am., hist., 596, 597, 605, 633n, 634n, 635n, 636n, 637n
Camberi, bar in Sulina, 187
Campo Formi Treaty, 78
Câmpineanu, Ioan, 209
Cantacuzino, 337
Canal Danube-Black Sea, 198
Canal navigable, at the Sulina Mouth, 168n, 124
Cannon, Cavendish, Am., dipl., 592, 595, 605, 607, 614, 617-619, 621
Cape of Kaliacra (Caliakra) at the Black Sea, 21
Cape of Good Hope, 21
Cape of Storms, 21
Caracalla, Rom., Emp., 34
Caraffa, 60
Carasu, Hypotetical branch of the Danube, 198
Caratheodory, Pasha, 352
Carians, ancient Greeks, 23
Carolus Primus, yacht of the European Danube Commission, 497, 524
Carol, Prince of România, 335, 347, 354
Carol I, King of România, 496
Carol II, King of România, 529
Carpenter, Rhys, Am., hist., 15, 16
Cataracts (Kataracts), water fall, 32, 62, passim
Catherine I, Empress of Russia (1782), 56
Catherine II, Empress, 56, 66, 68, 70, 71
Cavour, Camilo, Count., It., stat., 257, 280, 375
Chamberlain, Austen., 504, 505
Chamberlain, Joseph, 349
Central European Powers, capitulation, 435
Cernavodă-Constanța Canal (1839), 150, 193
Cernavodă-Black Sea Canal (1948), 198-200

Charles VI, of Austria, 68
Charles II of England, 64
Charles II of Sweden, 66
Charles V of Austria, 66
Chestiunea Dunării (see also La Question du Danube), reference, passim.
Chașinău, town in Bessarabia, 245
Cholera, epidemy of, 156, (see also Quarantine).
Charlotte, Princess of England, 135
Chlumetzky, 370, 371
Churchill, W., 539, 567
Clancarty, Lord, 82, 86, 271
Clarendon, Lord, 115, 239, 240, 241, 242
Clemenceau, G., 466
Clementis, V., Czech., dipl., 598, 599, 607
Cold War, see Anglo-Russian conflict on Obstacles to navigation (1836-1856).
Colecția de Documente Hurmuzachi, reference, passim.
Colonies of ancient Greeks at Euxeinos Pontos, 22-27
Conquhoun, Rob., Engl., consul, 155
Comecon, 582
Commission Européenne du Danube (C.E.D.) (see European Commission of the Danube)
Commission Internationale du Danube (C.I.D.) (see Internation Commission of the Danube)
Commission of the Mouths of the Danube (1918), 432
Commission of the Danube by the 1948 Belgrade Convention, 622
Committee on International Rivers (1815), 82-84.
Commercial Administration of Ports and Water Communications of România (P.C.A.), 324
Constanța, port, 21, 23, passim.
Constantin the Great, 34, 38
Constantin Grand Duke, 146
Council of Foreign Ministers, 587, 589, 592, 597, 599, 606, 613
Constantinopol, 37, passim.

Conférence for the establishment of a Convention of the Definitive Statute of the Danube, Paris, 1920-1921, 454-492 (see also Definitive Statute of the Danube, or Statue of 1921
Constantin the Great, 34
Contzescu, C., 467, 468, 482, 498, 505, 517, 519, 521, 527
Convention of Navigation Austrian-Russian (1840), 201-205
Convention of 1921 (see Definitive Statute of the Danube)
Corsicon, Greek colony, (today Harșova), 30
Coronini, 183
Cowley, H., Lord, 107, 109, 207, 275, 276, 283, 285, 291
Cracov, Engl., vessel, 148
Cristič, (1851), 258
Crimea, penins., 40
Crimea War, 43, 206, 243
Cripps, Stafford, Sir, 545
Cromwell, 64
Crusade, 39
Cunningham, John, Engl., vice-consul, 108, 116-119, 121, 127, 136, 143, 179-181, 183, 185, 187-189, 193, 195-197, 211-214
Cuza, Alex., Rom., Prince, 299
Cyprus, island, 340, 351
Czechoslovakia, 456, 469, 473, 475, 481, 489, 598, 610, 620

Dacia, 24, 27, 56
Dalberg, Duke, 81-86, 88, 271, 453
Dallin, D.J., Prof., 156
Danăvăt, natural canal, 31
Danube Delta case, (1856-1857), 245-247
Danube Question, 3, 55, 56, 75, 106, passim.
Danube commerce was prejudiced between 1829-1856, 2, 210-214
Danubian Múnich, 518
Danubian, Limes, 34
Danube Lower, damages of fleet after W.W.I., 443

ID# INDEX

Danube Navigation, English Navigation Co., on the Lower Danube, (1920), 439
Danube Mouths under Russia, 99
Dardanelles, Strait (ancient Hellespont), 18, 25, 37, 69
D.D.S.G.-Donau-Dampfschiffahrtsgesellschaft, Austrian Navigation Co., 192
Dascovici, Prof., 420, 499, 511, 518, Davoud, G.A., 258
Declaration of the Council of Foreign Ministers (1946), 597, 599, 613
Definitive Statute of the Danube (Convention) Paris, 1920-1921; Conference 454-460; participants, 454-455; project for Convention, 455; Problems: the enlargement of the E.C.D., 460-468; composition of I.C.D., 469-470; Status of former enemy States, 470; the cabotage problem, 473-455; Danube Tributaries, 487; navigation on transit, 488; regime of Iron Gates, 490; ports and free zones, 49. Caluses of the Convention, 493; some modification by the Arrangement of Sinai (1938) and Accord of Bucharest, 515, 525; abolished, 623
Delta of the Danube; controversy over its appuntenance (1856-1857), 245-248; România's and Turkey's point of view, 245-248
Demblin, 431
Demosthenes, 25
Demorgny, 389
Depuis, Ch., 82
Diaspora, Greek, 22
Diebitsch, Marshal, 146
Dionisopolis, Greek colony, 23
D.D.M. Direcțiunea Danării Maritime (Romanian Administration of the Maritime Danube, see also Maritime Danube Board).
Disraeli, Earl of Beaconsfield, 156, 340, 349, 350, 351
Djilas, Milovan, 580
Dniester, river, 38, 40, 73
Dobruja, (Dobrogea), passim.

Documente Sarde (see Bodin), reference, passim.
Două Memorii cu privire la incălcarea drepturilor României la gurile Dunării (two Mémoires concerning the infringement of Romanian's rights at the Mouths of the Danube), by Spiridon G. Focas, reference, passim.
Dredging at the Sulina Mouth, 115-122 (see also Obstacles)
Dunăvătz, natural Canal, 31, 193, 194
Durham, Lord, 141
Dudley, Stuart, 126, 128, 152

Eastern Question, 55, 61, 81, 106, 333
East, W.G., 155
East and Levant, Co., 143
East Indian, Co., of Austria, 71
Emporium, 23
Enactment of the Principles of Internationalization of navigation (1815) (see Congress of Vienna).
England, and 1829 Adrianople Peace Treaty, 106-110; English-Russian conflict, 111-131; reaction to the Quarantine and to the 1836 Russian Ukase, 141-152; and the troubles made by the Greeks-Ionians on navigation, 180-189; the improuvement of navigation, and Russia's pozition, 195-197; English commerce and navigation after 1829, 211-213; at the 1815 Congress of Vienna, 82; Conf. of Vienna (1855-1856) and Paris (1856), 231, 236, 239-241; and the Navigation Act (1857), 270; and the E.C.D., 290, 357, 399; and the Danube Statue (1920-1921), 453, 479, 480; the litigation between Romania and E.C.D., 495, 502-505; the Sinaia Arrangement (1938), 519-522, 526; the modification of the old regime of navigation, 545; restrictions on the England's vessels, 570; navigations for a new regime, 586, 589; at the Belgrade Conference (1948), 589, 604, 609-610, 625; on the Danube traffic, 647, 652

Engelhardt, Ed., 112, 115, 117, 119
English, traveler, 136, 142, 143, 202
Epidemics, at the Danube regions, (see Quarantine)
Escaut, river, 80
Eumenides, goddesses, 20
Euominos Pontos, 22
Europolis, pen name of Sulina, 180, 190
European Commission of the Danube (E.C.D.); proposal, 234; established, 244; consolidation of the, 293-297; the 1865 Public Act of the 293-295; other Regulations 295-296; reorganization (1878-1879), 363-368; the Regulation for Navigation, Police and Supervision between Iron Gates and Galatz, 369-372; the Mixed Commission of the Lower Danube, 372-376; the juridiction on the Kilia Branch, 377-378; retreated to Odessa (1916), 428; limited to four Powers, 460-468; litigation with România, 529; attempts to abolished it, 539-549; abolished (1948), 623
European Central Island Transport Organization (E.C.I.T.O.), 586
Euxeinos Pontos, (Black Sea) hospitable sea, 19, 20, 25

Fadeoeff, R.A., 340
Feodoroff, 119, 122
Fischer-Galati, Stephen, Prof., 581, 632n
Fitzmaurice, 391, 394
Florescu, R.R.N., Prof., 100, 101, 107, 109, 154-155, 164n, 167n, 169n, 172n, 173n, 174n, 175n, 215n, 216n, 219n, 221n, 223n, 307n
Focas G. Spiridon, auth, 306n
Forerunners of the Lower Danube Navigation: Greeks; Graeco-Roman epoch; Byzantines; Italians; Turks

France and origin of internationalization of navigation, 77-79; and the 1815 Congress of Vienna, 80-83; internationalization of the navigation (1856), Crimea War, 232; 233, 238, 243, 246, 250; at the Paris Conf. (1858), 266; and the Magnan Case, 288; and the London Conf. (1871), 321, 326; neutralization of the Lower Danube (1877-1878), 335; protest against the Bucharest Treaty of 1918, 433; reparations after W.W.I., 439; and the Conf. for the Statute of the Danube (1920-1921), 453, 455, 466, 469, 471; the problem of Cabotage (1920), 473; and the 1948 Belgrade Conf., 604, 605, 625
Francis, J., of Austria, 228, 239, 246
Frederick II, of Prussia, 68

Gafencu, Grig., 463, 518, 527, 528, 531, 543
Galatz, (Galați) port, passim.
Gagarin, Russ., navig. Co., 209
Gardner, 207
Gentz, 229
Geffcken, 227
Genova, 39
Germany (Prussia), principles on the navigable rivers, 82, 84, 85, 88; on the 1857 Act of Navigation, 280; and the Congress of Berlin, 340, 343, 349, 352, 353, 358; at the London Conf., 389, 390, 397; the Treaty of Bucharest (1918), 431-433; prior and after the 1938 Arrangement of Sinaia, 518, 525; attempts to modify the old regime of navigation, 539, 542, 544, 546; Antipa's Memorandum, 549-552
Gettae, 35
Geto-Hellenic, Road, 32
Geymet, Bartolomeo, Sardinia's Consul, (1838), 99, 101
Ghica, Ion, 354, 390
Ghica, Grig., Prince of Moldavia, 285, 286
Giurescu, C.C., 32
Giurgiu, port, 33 (San Giorgio), 40

INDEX 689

Gladstone, 349
Glasser, E., 622, 624
Goa, 24
Goben, Germ. Warship, 445
Godel, Lauray, 262, 286
Goeland, Engl., navigation Co., in România (1940), 535
Golden Grain Fields, 21
Golden Fleece, 19, 20, 21
Gorchacow, M.D. Prince, 228, 232, 233, 321, 340, 345-348
Gordon, R., Sir, 109
Gorove, Stephen, Prof., 574, 632n., 577, 606, 576, 632n., 633n., 634n., 606, 635n
Graham, A., 15, 16
Granville, Earl, 321, 324, 374, 380, 387, 389, 390, 394, 395-397, 400, 401, 404, 406
Greaco-Roman epoch, 33
Greek Lake (Black Sea), 19
Greeks, ancient: date of penetration into Euxeinos Pontos, 15-19, navigation conditions, 19; colonies on Euxeinos Pontos, 22: penetration on the Lower Danube, 27; their successors, 37; warehouses on the Danube, 30
Greeks after 1829 and 1856; Russian flag on their vessels, 70; creating obstacles to navigation (see Sulina a Little California); reduction of their activity after W.W.I, 437, 431; and after W.W.II, 536, 569; and after their presence in navigtion, 576
Greece at the 1920 Paris for the Statute of the Danube, 460-466, 465-466, 475, 479, 482, 483; Maritime traffic, 643, 644, 653, 654; at the 1948 Belgrade Conf., 625

Haan, 374
Hague, Treaty (1795), 78

Hajnal, Henry, Hung., hist., 93n, 82n, 86, 94n, 95n, 115n, 164n, 165n, 167n, 215n, 216n, 217n, 218n, 219n, 205n, 220n, 222n, 223n, 260, 276, 278n, 305n, 309n, 330, 312n, 313n, 314n, 315n, 323, 330, 356, 370, 371, 412n, 413n, 416n, 419n, 408, 421n, 422n
Hârșova, former (Corsicon), 30
Hartley, Ch., Sir., 112, 114, 325, 405, 407
Haymerlé, H., Von, 344, 355, 356, 357, 358, 364, 366, 370, 373, 374
Hecateus, of Miletus, 30, 57
Hellespont, ancient Greek name of Dardanelles Streit, 18, 25
Hersepolis, Greek colony, (today Vârciorova), 30
Hertsler, reference, passim.
Hessiod, 17, 22
Hines, Walter, 382
Histria, Gr., colony, 18, 23
Histrians, 28
Hitler, 513, 540
Holland, 83, King of, 88
Holy Alliance (1699), 59
Holy Alliance (1815), 106
Holtzendorff, 388, 391, 402
Homer, 21
Hong Kong, 24
Horace, 22
Hostie, M., 478-479
Hübner, Fr., 185, 276, 281
Hübner, J.A., Count., 267, 271, 272, 276, 281, 283
Humbold, Baron, 82, 84, 85, 271, 453
Hungary, 360, 438, 469, 471, 475, 589

Ialomița, river, 28
Iași, Peace Treaty (1793), 71-72
Ignatief, Count, 340
Institute de Droit International (1883), 388
Inter-Allied Commission of the Danube, (1919-1920), diverg. with România, 435-439
International Commission of the Danube, (I.C.D.); established and composition (1921), 469

Internationalization of the Danube, Austria and Russian attempts, 59
Internationalization of the Danube River, Paris (1856), 227-252, (see also E.C.D.); first Conf. of Vienna, (1855), 231-235; second Conf. of Vienna, (1856), 235; Conference and Treaty (1856), 236; the geografic division, 237-242; exclusion of Russia from the Danube, 243-244; clauses, 244; divergencies, controversies and rectification after 1856, (see also Delta case Serpents island case, Bolgrad case); Versailles Treaty (1919), Def. Statute of the Danube); attempts for modification of the 539-549, 587-593; modified by the 1948 Conv. of Belgrade, 622-623
Ionian, island, 183
Ionians, 183, British protégés, 184; (see also the Little California)
Ionescu, Take, 463, 464
Iorga, Nic., Prof., 3, 26, 27, 29, 35, 38, 41-44, 51n, 52n, 143, 216n, 343, 382, 460, 497
Iron Gates, gorge of the Danube, 29, 30, 62, passim.
Isaktcha (Isaccea) small port, 63, 67, 244
Israel, F., reference, passim.
Ismail, Chatal of, 74, 103, 137
Ismail, port, 74, 137, 139, passim.
Istros (Ister), ancient name of the Danube, 27
Italy, 42; at the 1883 London Conf., 390; after the Sinaia Arragement (1938), 525, 547; Belgrade Conf., (1948), 625
Italians, 37

Jean de Saule, 521
Jasson, argonaut, 21
Jassy, see Iasi
Jew, nationalization of the fleet, 570
Jew, emigration through the Danube, 538
Joint (Mixed) Co., 576
Joltuchin, F., 133, 146

Jomini, A., 121, 167n
Joseph II of Austria, 68, 77
Joseph, Franz of Austria, 228
Juspad, Soviet-Yug. shipping co., 580, (see also Joint Co)

Kallatis (today Mangalia) Greek colony, 23, 30
Kaliacra, (today Caliacra) Greek colony, 21
Kalafatis (today Calafat) Greek colony, 30
Kallay, B., 390
Karavi, Greek colony (today Corabia), 30
Karlowitz Peace Treaty (1699), 55, 59
Karolyi, A., Count, 390, 392, 397, 398, 400
Kardeli, Ed., 580
Kataracts, (Cataracts) waterfall of the Danube, 621, passim.
Keanne, Douglas, 521
Kell, phys., 155
Kennan, G., Prof., 229
Kerson, port, 119
Kilia New, port, passim.
Kilia, Branch, 74; passim.
Kisselev, Paul, 106, 146, 154, 156, 157, 209
Koch, Rob., phys., 133
Kogalniceanu, Mihail, 360, 334, 335, 343, 344, 347, 371, 377, 380, 496
Kongurlui, lake, (see Bolgrad case)
Koromilas, 464
Kostanacki, Jean, 468
Kremer, 121, 122
Kutusov, M., 133
Kütschük-Kainardji, Peace Treaty (1774), 68-71

Labaree, R.V., 15
Latin, Citadel, 75, 251
Latin, Empire, 39
Launay, Godel, 262
Law Officers of the Crown, 126, 127, 141, 148, 269
Legrand, Albert, 453-455, 471, 493
Lemberg, 40
League of Nations, 502-504

INDEX 691

Leopold I. Albert, Emp. of Austria, 59, 60
Lete (Ieti), island of the Danube Delta, 73, 101, 137, passim.
Leuke (Serpents island), 22
Licostomo (Mouth of Wolf) (today Vâlcov) Greek colony, 30
Ligney, Ch., 303n
Limbo (limbare), 115, 165n (see also Obstacles)
Litigation, Romania-E.C.D., 495-502; at the League of Nations, 502-504; at the Permanent Court of International Justice, 504-510; partial agreement, 510-514
Little California (the Sulina), 179-190
Little Wallachia (Oltenia) annexed by Austria (1718) and lost in 1739, 62, 65, 67
Livorno, 212
Lloyd, Vincent, 108, 123, 181
Lloyd, Aust, navig., Co., 116, 193
Londonderry, Marquis, 154
London Underworld, 189
London Conf., and Treaty (1871), 319-332; the problem of the Riparian Commission 322-327; prolongation of the E.C.D., 327-329; problem of extension of E.C.D. competence as far as Brăila, 329-331, clauses 331-332.
London Conf. and Treaty (1883), the problem of participation of România, Serbia and Bulgaria, 387-397; sanction of the Navigation Regulation, 397-399; prolongation and entension of E.C.D., to Braila, 399-400; detachement of the Kilia Branch from E.C.D., 403-409; clauses, 409
Loon, H.W. Von, 17
Ludwig, Emil, 340

Macedonia, commerce traffic, 66
Magnan, André Françios, 285
Magheru, G., General, 245-247
Magnusen, eng. of E.C.D., 429
Maglavitis, (now Maglavit), Greek colony, 30
Mc. Laughlin, Am., hist., 135, 157

Malta, isl., 174
Malmesbury, Lord, 114
Maria, Theresa, Austr, Emp., 68, 71
Marinovich, Serb. dipl., 390, 392
Marine Bulgare (M.B.) Co., during W.W.I., 431
Maritime Danube, 37
Maritime Danube Board (see also Direcţiunea Danării Maritime D.D.M.); established, 523; reorganization, 528-530
Marday, Trevor, 194
Marmara, Sea (Hellespont), 18
Marshal, G., 591, 630
Marseille, 212
Martens, M., 82, 93n, 368, 388
Marzius, 518
Marx, Karlig, 133
Mavrocordato, Alex., Prince of Wallachia, 60
Mavros, Nich., and the Quarantine, 155
Mavri Thalassa, Greek name of Black Sea.
Mayflower, vessel, 11
Medina, Engl., vessel, 144, 214
Medlicott, W.N., 342, 343, 350, 415
Megas apoikismos, (Great Greek colonization), 22
Maritime Danube, new Navigation Regulations, after the Sinaia Arrangement, 530
Melbourne, W., Lord, 108
Melissaratos, Apostol, shipowner and industr., 555n
Melissaratos, Aristidis, shipowner and industr., 555n
Mémorandum of the Romanian Gov, (1941-1942), 546
Mémorandum of Prof. Gr. Antipa (1943), 549-552
Meszhart, Soviet-Hung., navig., Co., 579
Metropolis, 23
Metternich, Kl., Von, 88
Midia, cap of, 198
Mihanovici, 193
Milesian Limni (Lake), 23
Milesians, 19, 23
Mitterand, E.A., 465, 559
Minorities Treaty (1919), 476

Mixed Commission of the Danube, 372-376
Mohrenheim, 400, 406
Moldavia, Road, 40
Moldavia, 40, 56, 60, and passim.
Molotov, V., 535, 536, 543, 545, 606, 624
Montreux, Conf., (1936), 515, 540
Moore, J.B., jurist, 506, 507
Morava, river 62
Mucczinski, 407
Múchangratz, Russian-Austrian Agreement (1833), 201
Münster, G.H., 389, 390, 397
Müller, A., (1857), 261
Mureş (Maros), river, 59
Mustafa, II, Sultan, 60
Musurus, Pasha, 390, 396

Napoleon, Bonapart I, 72, 78
Napoleon III, 75, 228, 248, 251, 352
Naparis, river (today Ialomiţa), 30
Nassau, 83
Nauman, Fr., 433
Navigation Act, (1857), 290, (see also Riparian Commission)
Navigation, tolls, (Obstacles)
Navigation, Russo-Austr., Conv. (1840), 201-204
Navigation conditions prior and after the W.W.II, 573
N.F.R., Navigaţiunea Fluvială Română (Romanian State River Shipping Co.), 577
Neale, 116, 117
Negotations for the new regime for navig. after W.W.II, 585
Negulescu, D., 508-510
Neigebaur, Consul, 212
Nesselrode, K.V., Count, 82, 83, 117, 119, 120-123
Neutralization of the Danube (1877-1878), 333-338
Nicobar, islands, 71
Nicholas I, Tsar of Russia, 81, 192, 197, 349, 437
Nicholas, Russian Grand Duke, 349
Nicholson, 107, 228, 229
Nigra, E., 390

Nobiling, eng., 114
Nyholm, N.G. jurist, 506, 507

Ottoman Empire, 55, and passim.
Obstacles at the Kataracts and Iron Gates, 322-326
Obstacles to navigation at the Sulina Mouth (1829-1856); a different point of view, 111; the Sulina Bar, 113; the dredging, 115; the pilots, 123; the tolls, 125; Quarantine, 131-160
Odessa, competition with Brăila, 205-210
Odessus, ancient Greek colony, 23
Odessa, port, 119
Olt, river, 28, 61
Oltenia (see Little Wallachia)
Organic Regulations of Wallachia and Moldavia (Regulamente Organice), 105, 143, 208
Orloff, A.T., 236, 250
Osler, 133
Oriental, or Greek Projet, 56
Osborne, 156, 228
Orşova, port, 71
Ostrowsky, 518
Osten, Co., 71
Ostrovs, of the Kilia Branch, 73
Otchacov, sub-branch of Kilia, 74, 194
Oubril, P.P., 356, 374
Outlet, to the Black Sea, 192-194
Ovid, 35

Paddy, Goos, English brothel, 189
Paget, Lord, 60
Paleologue, 454
Palmerston, H., Lord, 107, 108, 116, 165n, 126-128, 141, 144-146, 148-151, 156, 157, 197, 211, 213, 250, 283
Panonia, 26
Panslavism, 75
Parker, Admiral, 183
Paris Conf. and Treaty (1814), 79
Paris Conf. and Treaty (1856), see Internationalization of the Danube River

INDEX 693

Paris Conference of 1858, regarding navigation 265-292., the problem of Cabotage navigation, 273-280; Cabotage and territorial sovereignty 281-284; the tributaries, 285-287; prolongation of the mandate of the E.C.D., 290; additional articles to the 1857 Act of Navigation, 290
Paris Conf., of 1866, regarding navigation; sanction of the 1865 Public Act of E.C.D.; extension the juridiction of the E.C.D. to Brăila, and the function of the Riparian Commission, 299-302
Paris Conf. for the Statute of the Danube (1920-1921), (see Definitive Statute of the Danube).
Pârvan, Vasile, 24, 27-29, 31, 32, 35
Passarowitz, Peace Treaty (1718), 61, 65
Passarowitz, Treaty of Commerce and Navig., 62, 65
Pasteur, L., 133
Patriarchate of Constantinople, 40
Pauker, Ana, 616
Pax Romana, 34
Peake, 604, 609, 610
Pella, V.V., 546, 548, 550
Pentapolis, Confederation, 23
Penteconter, ancient Greek vessel, 16
Permanent Court of Internat., Justice, 504-510
Peter the Great, 60, 68, 145
Peter the Greek, famous bar in Sulina, 189
Peuce, ancient Greek name of today St. George Mouth, 28, 31
Peyssonel, Ch., 44
Phanariots, (Fanar), 41, 43, 44
Philip II, King of Macedonia, 25
Pilgrims, 11, 23
Pilots, at the Sulina Mouth, 123-125
Pippidi, D.M., Rom., archaeol., 19
Piraeus, port, 25
Pirotchanatz, 392
Plevna, town in Bulgaria, 347
Poland, (Poles), 40
Ponsonby, 107, 109, 206
Popescu, N., 301
Portolo, G., 538, 571

Portița, natural passage to Black Sea, 31, 193
P.C.A. Administrația Comercială a Porturilor și Căilor de Comunicație pe Ape. (Romanian State Commercial Administration for Ports and Ways of Communications).
Price of Bargain, 591
Prokesch-Osten, Austr. dipl, 122, 232-235, 237-238, 243, 249, 268-269, 281, 289, 305, 321, 334, 335n, 328-331, 304n,
Prussia and the 1857 Act of Navigation, 280
Provisional Organization for European Inland Transport, (1945), 586
Prut, tributary of the Danube, 32, 73, 286 and passim.
Posdam, Conference, (1945), 587
Public Act of the European Commission (1865), 293-296, (see also E.C.D.).
Punktation, Austria (1856).
Purgachon, Russ, revolutionar, 70
Puryer, Vernon, Prof., 164n, 206, 207, 212, 223n, 303n

Quarantine, 106, 131, 132, 135, 136, 141, 148, 153, in England 154, 157, (see also Obstacles)
Question du Danube, (Chestiunea Dunarii), reference, passim.

Radstadt, Congress of (1798), 78, 79
Radestsky, Austr., vessel, 335
Razelm, lake, 31, 193
Regulamente Organice (see Organic Regulations)
Restrictions to navigation (1940-1941), 536-538
Rey, Francis, 444, 445, 453
Rhin, (Rhine), river, 60, 78, 80, 227
Riparian Commission of the Danube established (1856), 244; Conf. of the 253-263; Act of Navigation of 1857, 254-255
Ribbentrop, J., 543
Ricker, T.W., 249, 306, 352, 314
Richelieu, Fr., archit., in Russia, 209
Ristič, (1857), 323, 342, 474, 477

Romanenko, 404

Romanian Principalities (Moldavia and Wallachia), 55, 56, 68, 104; and after 1856 Peace Treaty 245-248; and the Riparian Commission, (1857), 256, 258, 260, 261; at the 1858 Paris Conf., 265; neutralization of the Lower Danube, (1877-1878), 333; at the 1878 Berlin Conf., 341, 344

România, Kingdom of at the 1883 London Conf., 386, 387, 390, 391; neutrality (1914-1916), 427; entrance in W.W.I., 428; Peace Treaty of Bucharest (1918), 430; divergences with inter-Allied Commission, 435; at the 1920-1921 Conf. for the Statute of the Danube, 454, 463, 464, 475-477; litigation with E.C.D., 495; the Sinaia Arrangement (1938) and after, 516-531; restrictions to the navigations, 536, 569; Conferences of Vienna (1940), 542, of Bucharest (1940), 544, of Bucharest (1941-1942), 546; Mémorandum of Prof. Antipa, 549; War against Soviet Russia, 569; the Armistice Agreement, 575; Joint Co., 577-581; Paris Conf. of 1946 relating to Danube, 589; the 1947 Peace Treaty clauses on navigation, 592; and at the Belgrade Convention (1948), 616, 622-623

Roman, lines, 38, 251

Romioi, citizens of Rome, 34

Rosetti, N., 109, 258

Rousseau, Ch., 628

Rothschild, bancher, 192, 199

Royal Palace, of England, 135

Russia, (Tsarist), attempts for internationalization, 59; at the 1815 Congress of Vienna, 82, 83; the Peace Treaty of Adrianopole, 99, 101-106; the Russian-English Conflict regarding the Obstacles to navigation, 111-129; the Quarantine and the 1836 Ukase, 131-140; the 1840 Austrian-Russian Convention, 201-205; the Brăila-Odessa Competition, 205-210; the internationalization of the Danube (1856); 227-228, 231-232, 235; exclusion from the Lower Danube, 243; the Bolgrad Case, 248-251; at the 1871 Treaty of London, 319; at the 1878 Congress of Berlin: 340 returns as riparian, 345-354; debates on the San Stefano Treaty, 356; neutralization of the Lower Danube, 358; against the E.C.D., jurisdiction on the Kilia Branch, 377-379; at the 1883 Treaty of London: detachment of the Kilia Branch from the E.C.D., 403-409; and the W.W.I., 427, 429-430

Russia, Soviet (U.S.S.R.), non participant at the 1921 Conf. for the Danube Statute, 604; modification of the international regime, (1940-1942), 539-546; Armistice Agreements, 573-576; the Joint Co., 576-581; negotiations for a new regime of navigation (1945), 586-588 and the inclusion of it in the Peace Treaties, 586-591; clauses of the Peace Treaties (1947), 592-593; at the Belgrade Conf. (1948), 536, 546, 595-598, 600-601, 609-610, 613-617, 621-624

"Russes et Turks, La guerre d'Orient," Paris, (1877-1878), reference, passim.

Russel, John, Lord, 109, 243, 343

Ruschuk (Ruse), port, 63

Saint-Germain en Laye, Peace Treaty with Austria, 440, (1920)

Saint Vallier, 357

INDEX 695

Saint-Marc, Giraldin, 133
Salonica (Thessaloniki), 66
Salisbury, R., Marquis of, 272, 343, 345, 346, 347, 353, 356, 358
Sambuy, Count, 196
San Stefano Peace Treaty, (1877), 339, 340, 342, 345, 355, 356
San Francisco, 188
Sardinias, 183
Sardinian, Kingdom of, 280, 231
Sardinian Consuls, reference, passim. (see Bodin, Documente Sarde)
Sava, river, 62, 65
Săveanu, Săuciuc, 48n
Schickmareff, B., 395, 396
Schliemann, H., 17
Schiffarts-Abteilung Bergungsgruppe (S.A.B.), Germ., navig. Co. (1918), 431
Schwartzev, 543
Sebastiani, 72
Seelinger, 483
Sened (1784), 103, 286
Separate Treaty, Russo-Turk regarding Romanian Principalites (1829), 105, 208
Serbia (Servia) (see also Yugoslavia), 67, 104, 254, 258, 322, 323, 334, 341, 342, 388, 392, 394, 435
Sevastopol, 119, 225, fall of, 235
Serpants, Island, 22, 248
Serpants Island, Case, 248
Seton-Watson, R.W., 54, 61, 133, 146, 337, 349, 354, 454
Seton-Watson, Hug., 146, 580
Shouvalov, Peter, 346, 347, 348, 356, 358
Shanghai-ing, 188
S.F.N.D., Societé Française de Navigation sur le Danube, 535
S.R.D., Societate Română Danubiană (Romanian Danubian Co.)
Siborne, 375, 405
Sinclair, 608, 609
Sinoe, Lagoon, 19
Sina, 192, 199
Siret, river 75, 287

Sinaia Arrangement (1938), 515-531; Istoric, 515-518; political initiatives prior, 518-519; Germany position, 518; England's, France's and Italy's position, 519; Romania's position, 520-523; clauses and final Protocol, 523; transfer the European Commission powers to Romania, 526; new requests for admission to E.C.D., 531; abolished, 628
Siret, river, 32
Sisters, Engl., vessel, 124
Sistov Peace Treaty (1711), 71
Sitophory, granary, 20
Slăvescu, Victor, Prof., 448
Sofronie, Prof., 519, 520, 611
Solomonoff, sub-branch of Kilia
Somervell, D.C., 340
Soutzo (suțu), 211, 286
Sovromtransport, Soviet-Romanian Navig. Co., 577; (see also Joint Co.)
Sovrom, Santier (Shipyard), 578
Stratt, Engl., captain, 114, 144, 214, 407
Stamati, Café in Sulina, 187
Stalin, 567, 580, 587, 624
Stamboulou, 337
Starhemberg, Count, 60
Stary-Stamboul, sub-branch of Kilia, 74, 114, 364, passim.
Statute of the Danube (see Definitive Statute)
St. George, branch of the Danube, passim.
St. George, big island of the Danube Delta, 101, passim.
Stelian, Thomas, 454, 464, 475-477
Steege, (1857), 258, 261
Stokes, John, 115, 124, 181, 182, 183, 206, 336
Strabo, 30
Straford, Canning, Lord, 109, 116, 117, 211, 289
Strouberg, 344
Sturdza, D., Rom., stat., and author of "Recueil de documents relatifs à la liberté de navigation du Danube," reference, passim.
Sturdza, D., as dipl., 402, 516
Sublime Porte, 63, passim.

Successors of the Greeks and Romans, 37
Suez Canal, 112, 230
Sulina, Mouth, project for improvement, 195, Russia's position, 196
Sulina, port, as a Little California, 179-190
Sunderland, port, in England, 154, 157
Suprem Council of the Allied Powers, (1918), 435

Tabak, 249 (see Bolgrad Case)
Taggenburg, (1857), 254
Talleyrand-Perigord, 6, 80-82
Tarlé, E., 121, 122
Tatars, 40
Thames, river, 156, 189
Tchitchagof, Paul, 133
Tchernaieff, 340
Thalassa, (Sea), 20
Thalassakratores (Masters of the Sea), 23
Thalweg, 73
Theophrastus, 18, 20
Theogony, 17
Thierry, Adrien, 604, 605
Thovenel, Ed., 288
Tisa (Tisza), river, 59, 61, 62
Timoc, river, 62, 65
Tito, Iosef, Marshal, 580
Titulescu, N., 468, 504, 505, 515-517
Tomis, (Constanța), 21, 23
Tolls of navigation, 125-129, (see also Obstacles)
Towing, 16
Trajan's column, 35
Traffic, on Maritime Danube (1829-1944), 643-656
Transhipment, 63
Transylvania, 40, 59
Trieste, port, 71
Trotter, 112 (see also Dispatch)
Troubridge, E., Admiral, 436, 438
Truman, President of the U.S.A., 586, 587, 596
Tulcea, port, 116, 137, passim.
Tunis, 69

Turks, Turkey, (Ottoman Empire), successors of the Byzantines, 42-45; Karlowitz, 59-61; Passarowitz Treaty (1718), 61; Belgrade Treaty (1739), 66; Kütschük-Kainardji, Treaty, 68; Bucharest Treaty (1812), 72-76; Adrianopole Treaty (1829), 101-106; the dreging at the Sulina Mouth, 116, 618; the Crimean War, 231; the Danube Delta Case, 245-247; the Bolgrad Case, 248-250; the Riparian Commission, 254, 261; Cabotage and territorial sovereignty, 282; limit of the E.C.D., 295, Bulgaria at the 1883 London Conf., 396; Ally to Central European Powers, 427; Turkish flag on the Danube traffic, 645-649
Turkish, Lake, 64
Turkish, method of dreging, 118
Turis, Greek colony, (now Turnu Severin); 30
Turnu-Severin, (Turis), 30, 62
Tyras (now Cetatea Albă), 38

Ukase, on Quarantine (1836), 136
Ukraine, 67
Ukraine, Southern, 75
Ulmet, 29
Ulm, 433
Unkair-Skelessi Treaty (1833), 107, 191, 201
United States of America; Truman's Report, (1945), 586; 591; at the Belgrade Conf. (1948), 592, 595, 605, 607, 614, 617-619, 691
United Nations, Economic and Social Council, 588; Economic Commission for Balkans and Finland, 589, 590
Urquhart, David, 6, 107, 125, 148, 155n, 167n, 121, 125, 141, 144, 146, 154-156, 193, 198, 199, 207

Vâlcov, port, 30
Vârciorova, port, 323
Varna, port in Bulgaria, 23, 116
Vasco da Gama, 21

INDEX

Vassilevoussa, Kapital of King (Bizantium), 36
Venetian, 36
Venice, 39
Venizelos, Elefterie, 464
Versailles Peace Treaty of 1919, clauses concerning the Danube, 440-442
Victoria, Queen of England, 156, 228
Villeneuve, 67
Vienna Congress (1815), 77, 80-89
Vienna Conf., (1855), 231-235; (1856); 235-236
Vienna Conf., (Sept. 1940), 542
Vikings, 23
Vishinsky, Andrei, 536, 546; at Belgrade Conf. (1948), 595-598, 600-607, 609-610, 613-616, 617, 621, 623, 624
Voulcovich, 395, 396
Vogoride, 262
Vorontzov, M.S., Prince, 122, 143, 144, 146, 207
Vissier, Ch., 51n

Wachter, Baron, 276
Waddingtron, W.H., 343, 357
Wallewsky, Alex., 236, 238, 243, 246, 250, 261, 266, 276, 291
Wallachia, the Little, 62, 65, 67

Wallachia, Rom., Principality, 67, passim.
Wellington, Duke of, 101, 107
Westmorland, Count, 304n
Wessenberg, Baron, (1815), 82, 281
White Sea, (Aegean), 69
Widin, (Vidin), port, 63
Wilson, W., Pres., of U.S.A., 604
Wolkenstein, W., 371-396
Works and Days, (Hesiod), 17
World War I, 424-426

Xenopol, D. Al., 133, 154, 208
Xenophon, 25
Xerxes, 19

Yalpouk, Lake, 249
Young, C., 43
Yugoslavia, (Kingdom of Serbs, Croats and Slovenes until 1945); 456, 471; at the Belgrade Conf., (1948), 599, 604, 607, 624

Z.T.L. - Zentral Transport Leitung, (1918), 431
Zuguldak, Turkish port, 120

LIST OF ILLUSTRATIONS

1. The Lower Danube River.
2. Greek and Roman settlements, in the Lower Danube regions.
3. Mouth of Sulina (about 1840).
4. Sulina port (1828).
5. Local freight flat-boat, Galatz, XVII cent.
6. Brăila. The lazaretto (1840).
7. Mouth of Sulina before 1856.
8. Mouth of Sulina. Towing ships before 1856.
9. Turkish vessels on the lower Danube (about 1880).
10. Sulina. The lighthouse.
11. The Maritime Danube.
12. Sulina Canal. The entrance towards the Black Sea.
13. Sulina. The Administration Building.
14. The delegates of the European Commission (1859).
15. Views of the Sulina until 1948.
16. Greek barges on the Danube and the Prut tributary (before 1921).
17. Sulina. Section of the quay (1925).
18. Brăila. Plan of the city and port (1834).
19. The Black Sea in front of Sulina. Painting of Artemis Melissarato.
20. Ice-breaker on the Lower Danube.
21. Galatz. Dock and warehouse.
22. Brăila. Partial view of the port. Warehouses of cereals (1936).
23. Brăila. Steam factory for pasta products near bank of Danube (1887).
24. Lower Danube in winter.
25. Postage stamps of the Socialist Republic of Romania issued to mark the 125th Anniversary of the former European Commission of the Danube (1856-1981).

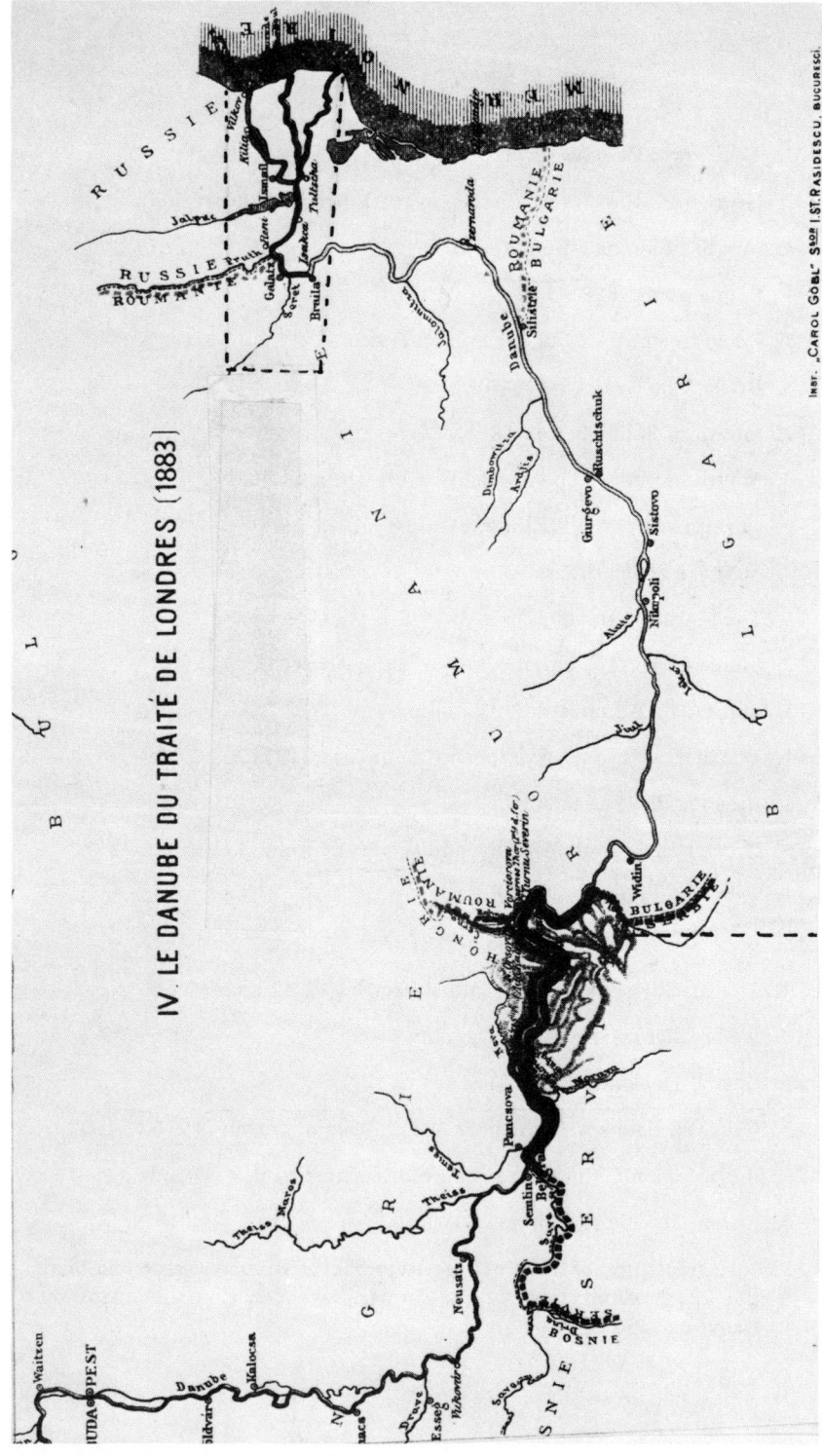

1. The Lower Danube River.

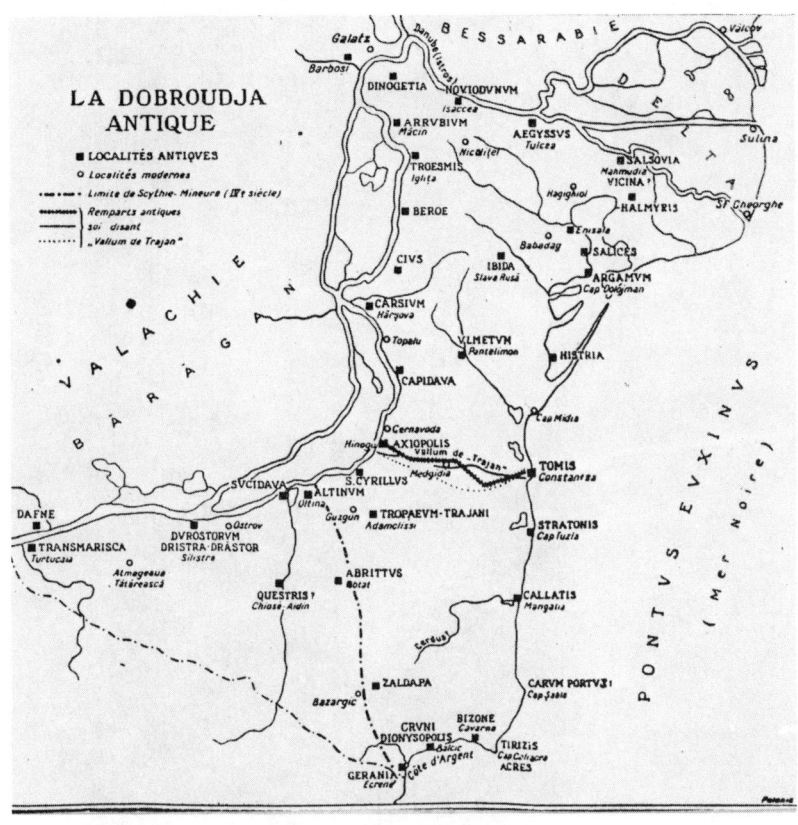

2. Greek and Roman settlements, in the Lower Danube regions.

3. Mouth of Sulina (about 1840).

5. Local freight flat-boat, Galatz, XVII cent.

4. Sulina port (1828).

LOCAL FREIGHT FLAT-BOAT

6. Brăila. The lazaretto (1840).

7. Mouth of Sulina before 1856. On the right, the lighthouse erected by the Russians after 1840; in the center, the ship "Lloyd" (Austrian), the first steamship to exit from the Danube.

8. Mouth of Sulina. Towing sailing ships before 1856.

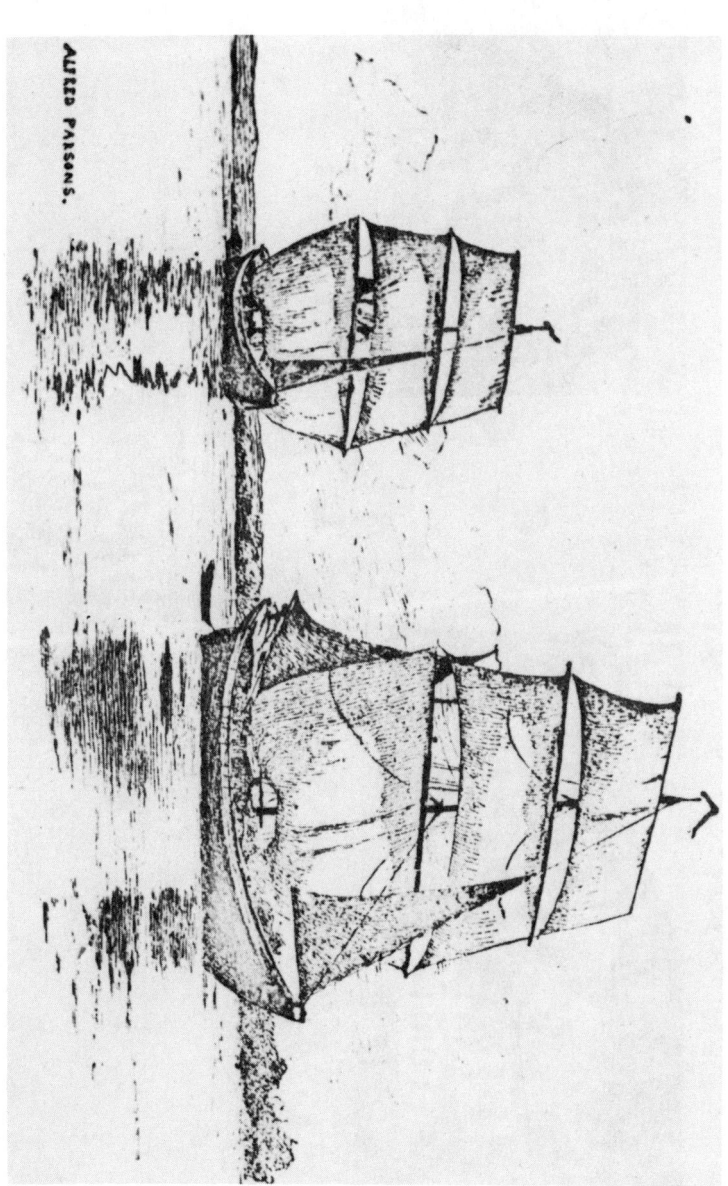

9. Turkish vessels on the lower Danube (about 1880).

10. Sulina. The lighthouse with the indication (24), in feet, of the depth at the Sulina Mouth.

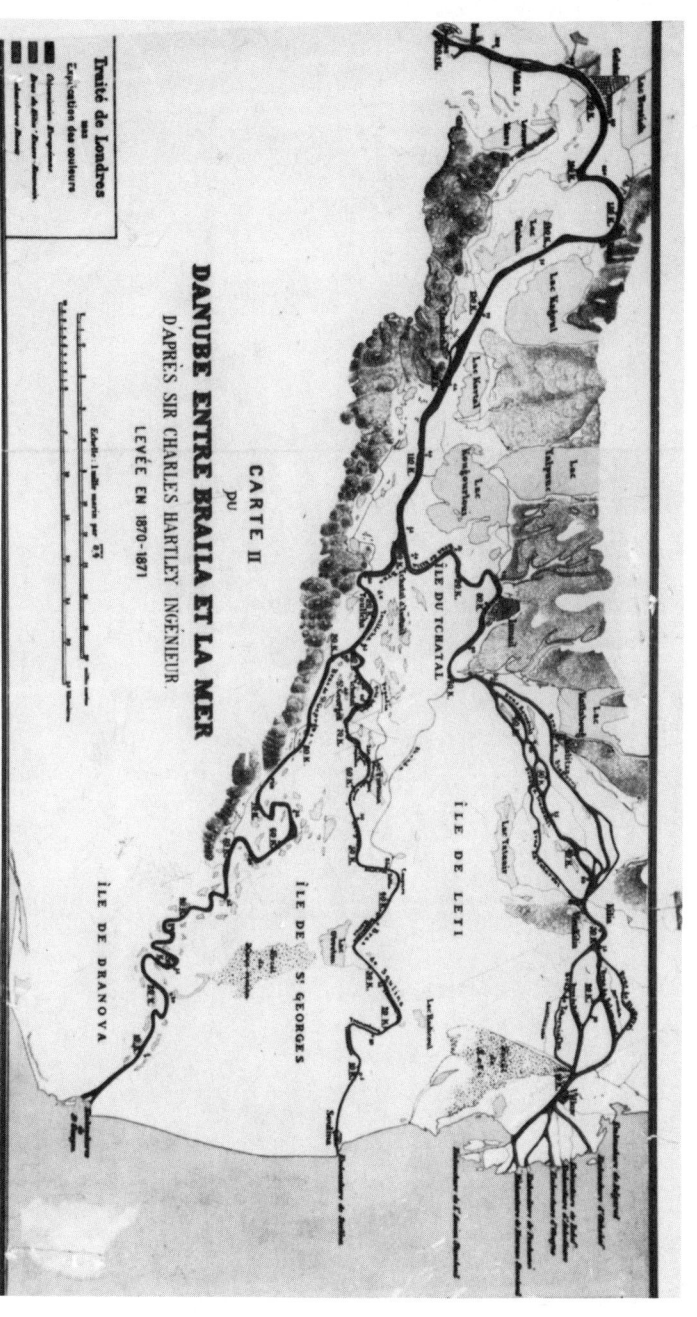

11. The Maritime Danube.

12. Sulina Canal. The entrance through the Sulina Canal towards the Black Sea; on the right, the beginning of the St. George's Branch.

13. Sulina. The Administration Building of the European Commission of the Danube (until 1848); today, that of the Soviet-Romanian Administration.

14. The delegates of the European Commission on a street of Galatz, near the Danube (1859).

15. Views of the Sulina as it was up to 1948.

16. Greek barges on the international section of the Prut tributary of the Danube (before 1921).

17. Sulina. Section of the quay (1921).

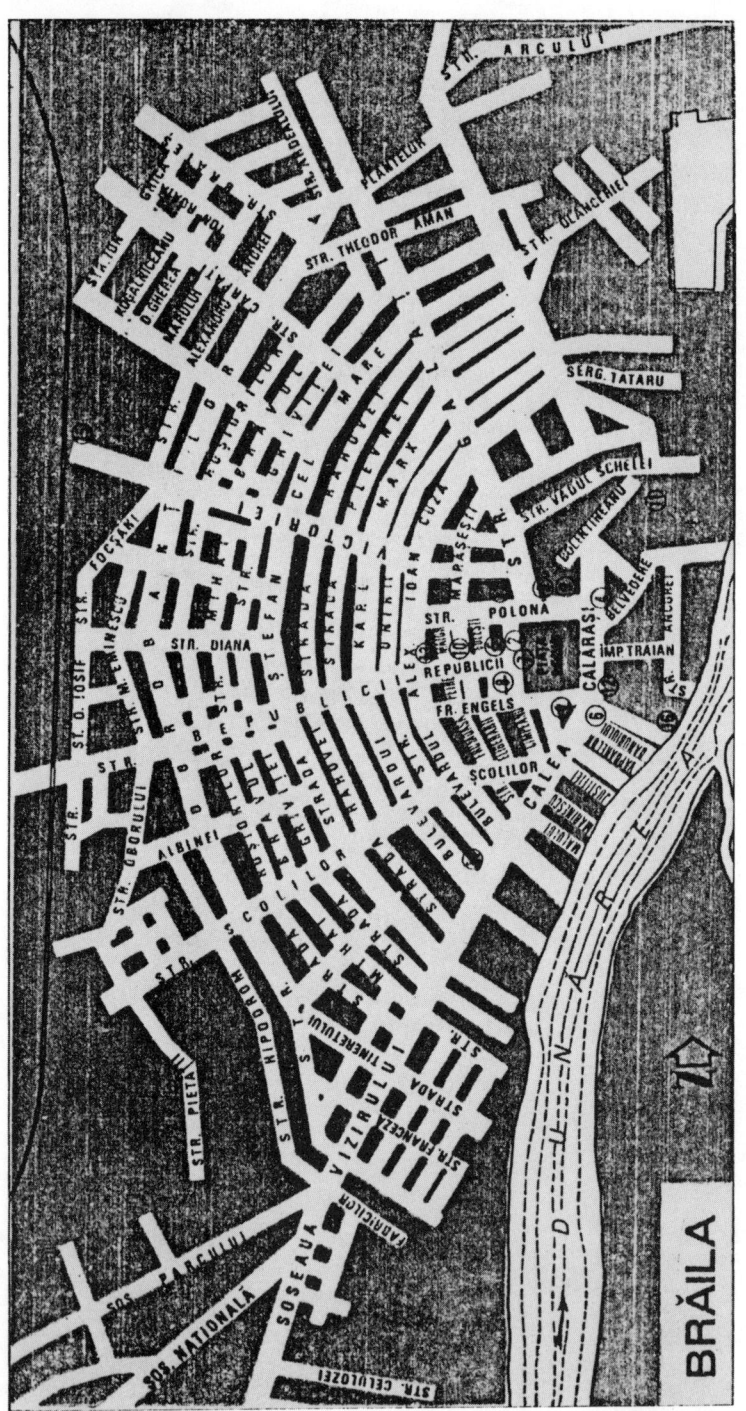

18. Brăila. Map of the city and port (1834). (Street names of 1940).

19. The Black Sea in front of Sulina. Painting of Artemis Melissarato.

20. Ice-breaker on the Lower Danube.

21. Galatz. Dock and warehouse.

22. Brăila. Partial view of port. Warehouses of cereals (1936).

23. Brăila. Steam factory for pasta products near the bank of the Danube (1887).

24. The Lower Danube in Winter.

25. Postage stamps of the Socialist Republic of Romania issued to mark the 125th anniversary (1856-1981) of the former European Commission of the Danube, illustrating European navigation on the Maritime Danube.